THE PETERSON REFERENCE GUIDE SERIES

GULLS

OF THE AMERICAS

THE PETERSON REFERENCE GUIDE SERIES

A REFERENCE GUIDE TO

GULLS

OF THE AMERICAS

STEVE N. G. HOWELL

AND

JON DUNN

SPONSORED BY

THE ROGER TORY PETERSON INSTITUTE AND

THE NATIONAL WILDLIFE FEDERATION

 HOUGHTON MIFFLIN COMPANY

BOSTON   NEW YORK   2007

For information about permission to reproduce selections from
this book, write to Permissions, Houghton Mifflin Company,
215 Park Avenue South, New York, New York 10003.

Visit our Web site: www.houghtonmifflinbooks.com.

PETERSON FIELD GUIDES and PETERSON FIELD GUIDE
Series are registered trademarks of Houghton Mifflin Company.

Library of Congress Cataloging-in-Publication Data

Howell, Steve N. G.
Gulls of the Americas / Steve N. G. Howell and Jon L. Dunn;
sponsored by the National Wildlife Federation
and the Roger Tory Peterson Institute.
p. cm. — (The Peterson reference guide series)
Includes bibliographical references.
ISBN-13: 978-0-618-72641-7
ISBN-10: 0-618-72641-1
1. Gulls — America.   I. Dunn, Jon, date.   II. Title.
QL696.C46H675   2007
598.3'38097 — dc22   2006024132

Maps by Mapping Specialists, Ltd.

Paintings on pages 71, 73, 79, and 81 by Martin T. Elliott

Photographs on pages ii and 47 by Steve N. G. Howell

Photograph on page 299 by Bruce Mactavish

Book design by Anne Chalmers

Typeface: LH Fairfield
Printed in Singapore

TWP 10 9 8 7 6 5 4 3 2 1

DEDICATED
TO THE MEMORY OF JONATHAN DWIGHT
AND PETER J. GRANT,
WHO HELPED SET THE STAGE
FOR MODERN FIELD IDENTIFICATION OF GULLS

AND TO LARRY B. SPEAR (1945–2006),
A LAROPHILE AND SCIENTIST EXTRAORDINAIRE,
WHO IS GREATLY MISSED

Contents

LIST OF SPECIES

PREFACE

Gulls—a word of inherent paradox. Almost anyone can recognize a gull—or "seagull"—as such, but to identify certain gulls to species can vex the most experienced observers. Gull identification offers something for everyone—from studying the different plumages of Laughing Gulls at a beach parking lot to puzzling over winter flocks of large gulls at a river mouth or reservoir. You can take identification to any level you choose, and still there's an unknown, a new frontier, another question to be answered. That's what makes gulls so much fun—and they're easy to watch, as well.

Some 22 species of gulls (out of about 50 species worldwide) breed in North America, and another 10 in South America. In addition, 4 species have occurred in the Americas as visitors from the Old World. This guide brings together identification criteria for these 36 species, including a few well-marked taxa sometimes treated as separate species. The area covered by this guide is the Americas, including Greenland, the Galápagos, Falkland, and Scotia Arc islands, South Georgia, and the Antarctic Peninsula. For the purposes of this guide we mostly follow the taxonomy of the AOU (American Ornithologists' Union) *Check-list of North American Birds*[1] (and subsequent supplements), although we describe some taxa in separate accounts and comment on alternative taxonomic treatments.

Modern identification studies of gulls began in 1925 with Jonathan Dwight's seminal work, *The Gulls (Laridae) of the World: Their Plumages, Moults, Variations, Relationships and Distribution.*[2] That ambitious work treats the plumages and molts of all species and subspecies of gulls then described, based on museum specimens. Black-and-white plates illustrate the patterns of the outer 5 primaries and tails of most ages of all species, and a few pages of color plates show the bill and foot colors of several North American species. Not until 1982 did another specialist gull book arrive on the scene: Peter Grant's classic, *Gulls: A Guide to Identification,*[3] the first edition of which covered 23 species recorded in the western Palearctic; the second edition, published in 1986,[4] added 8 North American species. Grant's work set a high standard and has been the starting point for serious subsequent identification papers on this challenging group of birds. In recent years gull identification criteria have become increasingly refined. Numerous papers are now documenting variation within taxa while allowing that much remains to be learned.

We acknowledge our debts to Dwight, Grant, and many others who have contributed important information to this dynamic field. Although we have field experience with all species and subspecies covered here, we recognize that there is still much to be learned. This book attempts to synthesize present knowledge but is simply another stepping stone through the seeming quicksand of gull identification. Inevitably, some of what we propose here will be modified as collective knowledge about gulls continues to grow, and we encourage observers to publish new, peer-reviewed information where it is available for all to use.

Notes

1. AOU 1998; 2. Dwight 1925; 3. Grant 1982; 4. Grant 1986

THE PETERSON REFERENCE GUIDE SERIES

GULLS

OF THE AMERICAS

How to Use This Book

When opening up any new bird book, one is almost overwhelmingly tempted to flip straight to the pictures or to check the species accounts to answer a specific question. Ultimately, however, you will get more out of a book by familiarizing yourself with the contents and by reading the introductory material, starting with this section on how the book is laid out.

PLATES

Immediately following the introduction, photographs of all species covered are arranged on plates with captions that highlight identification criteria for each species and plumage cycle. Photos were selected to show a representative range of plumages, with an emphasis on birds of typical appearance. Nonbreeding and breeding adults are shown first; then come juvenile through subsequent immature ages, typically arranged in chronological sequence; birds at rest are shown first, followed by birds in flight (including those with wings stretched to show wingtip patterns). Note that photos 1.0, 2.0, 3.0, 4.0, 5.0, etc. are grouped at the start of relevant chapters (e.g., the first group = Masked Gulls).

SPECIES ACCOUNTS

The accounts of each subgroup of gulls (see Taxonomy and an Identification Framework, p. 10) are prefaced with a summary of the subgroup's characters. Individual species accounts then follow. The English and scientific names of each species are given, followed by length in inches (and centimeters). These standardized lengths are taken from museum specimens laid on their backs and represent the full length of each species from tip of bill to tip of tail. Thus, they do not equate strictly with "size" (or bulk), but they do provide a rough guide to the average dimensions of each species. Other measurements, such as bill length and depth, tarsus length, and wing

chord, are not given for all species because these also span ranges and overlap broadly among species, particularly among similar-looking species (see table 1).

Photos of each species are listed, including references to photos elsewhere in the book (such as in the introduction); note that photo numbers with a zero suffix, such as 18.0, refer to photos grouped together for comparison. The Identification Summary, Taxonomy, and Status and Distribution sections then provide background information for each species, followed by characters, that relate directly to field identification; last is a list of references cited in each account.

IDENTIFICATION SUMMARY

This section summarizes background information on a species, such as geographic range, structural characters, diagnostic features, and other points relevant to identification. Because gull identification can be complex, you are often referred to the similar species section for more-detailed information.

TAXONOMY

This section includes a brief notation about subspecies (if any), taxonomic relationships, and alternative common names. If no subspecies are recognized for a species, then it is termed monotypic.

STATUS AND DISTRIBUTION

The world range of each species is summarized first for reference and context. Then follows more detailed information for the Americas on breeding and nonbreeding ranges, migration routes and timing, vagrant occurrences, etc. Information on status and distribution was gathered from published and unpublished sources (see Acknowledgments); references are cited mainly for specific records or for information not included in, or subsequent to, the main references consulted (see pp. 509–12). Acceptance criteria for records vary among sources. Our aim has been to provide an overview of distribution and patterns of occurrence, not a comprehensive treatise listing (or evaluating) every known record. Seasonal ranges given for "breeding" (from egg laying to fledging), migration, and nonbreeding occurrence are broad-brush and should be viewed as such; more-detailed information can be found in regional and species-specific sources. We have tried to use widely understood terms of abundance, including *rare*: occurs annually but in small numbers; *casual*: on average, less than annual in occurrence but fitting a pattern of known occurrence; *exceptional* or *accidental*: of extremely rare occurrence, including records that do not conform to presently understood patterns of vagrancy. See pp. 498–499 for an explanation of how geographic terms (such as Atlantic Canada, Midwest, and Northeast) are defined; our subdivisions of Alaska follow Kessel and Gibson.[1]

MAPS

Maps are included for all taxa except those very rare or local in the region (namely, Ross's, Lava, Black-tailed, Common, Kamchatka, Yellow-legged, European Herring, Vega, and Slaty-backed Gulls). Specific breeding sites are not mapped except in a few cases, mainly for highly local species (such as Red-legged

TABLE 1. Typical ranges of standard measurements (in mm) for adults of selected taxa of white-headed gulls recorded in the Americas (from Pyle and Howell, unpublished data). Sexes are combined, and sample sizes (n) vary for each character (for example, fewer tail lengths were measured than other characters); wing = unflattened wing chord; bill-exposed culmen. Measurements of first-cycle birds average 1–5 percent smaller (especially in wing and bill dimensions). BDB: bill depth at base; BDG: bill depth at point of gonydeal expansion. Note the overlap (often extensive) in most characters among similar species.

	WING	TAIL	BILL	BDB	BDG	TARSUS
Mew Gull[a] (n = 60–206)	325–365	128–144	29.4–38.5	9.1–11.6	8.7–11.1	43–54
Ring-billed Gull (n = 46–355)	333–391	132–157	33.6–46.3	11.3–15.9	11.7–15.2	50–62
California Gull[b] (n = 42–491)	353–426	137–162	38.5–57.4	12.7–18.0	13.1–19.2	49–69
American Herring Gull (n = 55–181)	396–458	149–190	46.1–61.5	16.0–21.8	16.2–22.1	56–73
Lesser Black-backed Gull[c] (n = 73–560)	380–446	140–171	45.0–57.9	15.0–20.4	13.9–19.3	54–69
Kelp Gull[d] (n = 16–62)	387–456	152–185	45.8–57.4	16.4–21.5	18.1–23.5	55–72
Great Black-backed Gull (n = 118–393)	442–511	168–208	54.0–71.7	20.6–27.6	21.0–27.6	67–84
Slaty-backed Gull (n = 42–82)	402–465	165–197	49.4–61.3	17.4–22.8	17.7–22.8	60–75
Western Gull[b] (n = 60–256)	368–434	143–177	47.0–61.3	16.1–22.5	17.4–23.8	59–74
Yellow-footed Gull (n = 45–108)	390–450	147–170	49.7–60.5	16.9–23.9	18.6–24.0	60–75
Glaucous-winged Gull (n = 45–141)	390–455	159–187	48.7–63.8	17.0–22.1	17.4–22.7	60–75
Glaucous Gull[b] (n = 78–395)	417–494	170–210	48.6–70.0	17.2–25.4	17.9–23.7	61–80
Iceland Gull (n = 34–140)	379–435	153–175	36.7–49.6	13.3–17.7	13.3–17.5	50–65
Kumlien's Gull (n = 26–104)	382–431	154–175	38.5–50.1	13.5–17.2	14.0–17.4	51–65
Thayer's Gull (n = 56–139)	380–439	146–175	42.6–55.2	14.3–19.4	14.4–19.0	53–68

[a] *L. c. brachyrhynchus* only; [b] all subspecies combined; [c] *L. f. graellsii* and *L. f. intermedius* only; [d] *L. d. dominicanus* only.

Kittiwake). Migration routes are not generally mapped, but arrows indicate primary migration routes for some species. Maps do not generally show areas where a species is rare or casual (for example, Thayer's Gull along the Atlantic and Gulf of Mexico coasts of North America); such information may be summarized by a sentence or two accompanying the map, and details of rare occurrences are summarized in the status and distribution sections.

FIELD IDENTIFICATION

The following four sections cover aspects relating more directly to field identification.

SIMILAR SPECIES AND RARER SPECIES

There are two kinds of similar species: those that often occur together or might reasonably be expected in the same geographic range (for example, Bonaparte's and Black-headed Gulls) and those species whose geographic ranges do not normally overlap, so that separating them is not usually a consideration (such as Black-headed and Brown-hooded Gulls). But because gulls have such a great propensity for vagrancy, in some cases we have divided the similar species section into two parts: one for Similar Species (those likely to occur in the same range) and one for Rarer Species (those unlikely to occur in the same range but which might be considered when

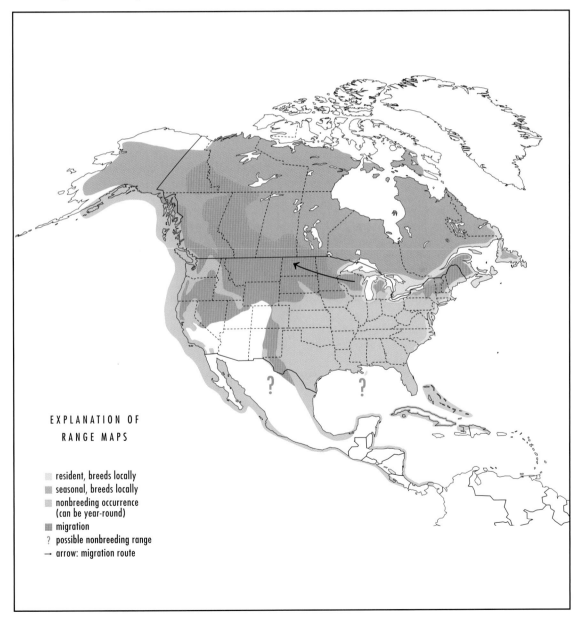

EXPLANATION OF
RANGE MAPS

resident, breeds locally
seasonal, breeds locally
nonbreeding occurrence
(can be year-round)
migration
? possible nonbreeding range
→ arrow: migration route

extralimital records are involved). For Similar Species we treat distinguishing features in each species account, making comparisons relative to the species being discussed. To save space, for Rarer Species we usually treat distinguishing features only once, under the species where differences are first noted. Capsulized ranges are given in parentheses at the first mention of a similar species.

Distinguishing features are given for species and for hybrids (other than hybrids involving the species in question, for which you should check the separate accounts for hybrids). These lists of characters, usually arranged by plumage cycle and then species, are not exhaustive but are the main characters (structure, wingtip pattern, leg color, etc.) that should allow you to distinguish most birds. Remember that many features useful for identification are relative (such as bill size and shape) and require some experience to use in the field. Structural features are noted at the first mention of a similar species and are repeated only under subsequent plumage cycles for species in which structure is one of the most important identification criteria. Additional identification features can be found in the detailed descriptions and photo captions (photos are often better than long-winded text for conveying structural differences).

Species are listed in a subjective order from most similar and most likely to overlap to least similar and least likely to occur together. We acknowledge that some users may not consider some species we list as "similar" to be very similar; but we have tried to err on the inclusive rather than the exclusive side of similarity.

HABITAT AND BEHAVIOR
An overview of habitat and behavioral characters emphasizes features relevant to identification.

DESCRIPTION AND MOLT
Descriptions are based on our own examination of museum specimens and photos and on field observations. Because periods of gull molt can span up to six or more months, it is not realistic to pigeonhole plumages into discrete basic and alternate plumages—gulls are in transition from one plumage to another for much of their lives. We thus integrate molts and plumages, and we use plumage cycles, which allow direct comparisons among all species (see Molts and Plumages, p. 30). In photo captions, however, we also use the more familiar terms "breeding" and "non-

breeding" for adult or near-adult plumages (for example, "breeding" usually refers to the white-headed aspect of adult large white-headed gulls or the dark-hooded aspect of many small gulls). Descriptions start with the adult cycle, followed by the first cycle (from juvenal plumage to initiation of the second prebasic molt, which can be equated to the normal loss of the innermost primary), and then second and third cycles, when relevant. Note that cycles start with the prebasic primary molt, so a "first summer" bird that has started primary molt is in its second plumage cycle.

Because of the myriad appearances exhibited by gulls, descriptions are synthetic rather than exhaustive. Almost all sentences could be prefaced by "typically" and followed by "but exceptions occur." When relevant to problematic identifications, the descriptions should be interpreted in relation to the Similar Species accounts. Periods given for juvenal plumage (Juvenile) indicate approximate timings when birds in full juvenal plumage can be seen. Timings given for molts are approximate and, in many cases, provisional (*provisional dates are given in italics*). There may also be marked interannual variation in molt timing depending on environmental conditions: in good food years Heermann's Gulls complete prebasic molt up to a month earlier than in poor food years, such as during El Niño events.[2] Thus, a period of prebasic molt given as June–Dec. might extend from mid-May to mid-January, although most birds typically molt between June and December. In particular, the timing of prealternate molts is in need of review for most species: for example, for most if not all large white-headed gulls, the start of prealternate molt probably overlaps in timing with the end of prebasic molt. In cases when data exist, approximate start and end ranges of a molt are indicated: thus, a prebasic molt period noted as mid-May/mid-July–Sept./Oct. indicates that the molt can start between mid-May and mid-July (varying with latitude, breeding status of the bird, etc.) and it can complete between early September and late October.

HYBRIDS
Known or presumed hybrids are listed, including mixed-species pairings for which eggs were laid. Hybridism is frequent in certain of the large white-headed gulls (mainly among Western, Glaucous-winged, American Herring, and Glaucous Gulls) but among most other species it occurs rarely or not at all.

NOTES

References (to published and unpublished data) are noted by superscripts in the text and are listed at the end of each account by author and date. Citations are provided only for some specific distributional information (see under Status and Distribution, p. 3) and for specific statements and information that we consider not to be general knowledge. Full citations for published works can be found in the bibliography.

Notes

1. Kessel and Gibson 1978; 2. Howell unpubl. data

INTRODUCTION

WHAT ARE GULLS?

Put simply, gulls comprise a widespread group of frequently gregarious, web-footed birds characteristically found near water. Taxonomically, gulls, together with shorebirds, skuas, terns, skimmers, and auks, constitute the order Charadriiformes of traditional classifications, such as that of the AOU,[1] which we follow here. Based on DNA studies, Sibley and Monroe[2] treated this assemblage as a suborder (Charadrii) of the greatly expanded order Ciconiiformes, which they considered to include such diverse groups as penguins, albatrosses, and hawks. The traditional Charadriiformes comprise four suborders: the Charadrii (plovers, oystercatchers, and allies); Scolopaci (sandpipers and allies); Lari (skuas, gulls, terns, and skimmers); and Alcae (auks and allies).

Within the Lari, relationships among gulls, terns, skimmers, and skuas are debated: these four groups are variably treated as comprising from one family[3] to four families.[4] Regardless of this uncertainty, gulls are a distinctive group, although defining them is not easy. Overall, gulls are medium to large in size with fairly long wings and fairly short, usually squared tails. The bill shape of smaller species tends to be relatively straight, slender, and pointed, whereas large gulls have notably stout bills with a decurved culmen, hooked tip to the maxilla, and distinct gonydeal expansion. Thus, the bills of small gulls are good for picking small food items from or near the water surface, whereas the bills of large gulls enable them to rip open larger prey and scavenge a variety of items. Gull legs are generally medium length—with the three front toes connected by webbing—and are good for walking, swimming, and gripping wet surfaces.

The plumage of adult gulls tends to be a handsome combination of gray, white, and black. Immatures tend to be brown and gray, less boldly patterned than adults. Many of the smaller species attain dark hoods for the breeding season, and some have a variable pink flush to their underparts. Bills, legs, and orbital rings are often brightly colored, especially on breeding birds. Sexes appear alike in plumage, although males, mainly of the larger species, average larger than females in bulk and in bill size.

Molt in gulls is relatively little studied. Recent observations have brought into question some time-honored beliefs about gull molts and plumages. Still, most species have two molts during their adult cycle: a complete prebasic molt and a partial prealternate molt. From one to four cycles are required for plumage to attain adult (or definitive) appearance. A species in which most individuals attain the adult plumage aspect in their fourth cycle, via their fourth prebasic molt, is known as a "four-cycle gull."

The voices of gulls are mostly crowing, wailing, screeching, and mewing cries, generally lower-pitched in larger species; adults of a given species usually have lower-pitched calls than immatures. Calls, in conjunction with ritualized display postures, serve important social functions during courtship, territorial disputes, and arguments over food.

Gulls are omnivorous, eating mainly fish and other aquatic animals, bird eggs, young and even adult birds, garbage, and offal. They associate with feeding flocks of other bird species over schooling marine fish, over power station outflows that spew out stunned fish, and over water being pumped up at sewage-treatment ponds, swooping and dipping down to pick their prey from near the surface; they gather and scavenge around fishing boats and at garbage dumps; they soar on thermals to catch flying insects; they eat eggs and young of other birds; they wade or swim, picking daintily at small invertebrates; they gather in swirling blizzards following plows that turn up earthworms; they steal food from pelicans; they bloody themselves at whale carcasses along the ice edge; they take bread at duck ponds; and flying birds can even pluck berries from trees!

Most gulls breed colonially, often on predator-free islands. Nests may be on level ground or on cliffs, in trees, or anchored to floating vegetation. Some nests are simply scrapes in the ground; others are fairly bulky platforms of grass and water weeds. Clutches number 1 to 4 eggs (2 to 3 in most species), varying among and within species. The ground color of eggs ranges from pale buff to dark olive and is patterned with dark spots, scrawls, and blotches. Incubation averages 3 to 4 weeks in most species, with fledging in 4 to 8 weeks after hatching. Like young of other Charadriiformes, such as *Calidris* sandpipers and jaegers, the immature plumages of gulls exhibit almost innumerable variations in pattern, which make it difficult to find consistent criteria for species identification.

TAXONOMY AND AN IDENTIFICATION FRAMEWORK

Taxonomy is the science of classification. It allows us to place birds within a frame of reference. In field identification we constantly make taxonomic decisions, although we may not realize it: for example, in recognizing a gull as such, we rule out ducks, sparrows, and everything else. Hence, a basic understanding of taxonomy is an asset to field identification.

Birds, like all living organisms, are classified by a hierarchial system. The category most familar to birders is the species. An important category just above the species level is the genus; a subgenus is a grouping between the levels of genus and species. Each known organism on Earth has a scientific name, which is italicized and comprises its genus name (capitalized) and species name (lower case). Variation within a species, if noticeable and correlated with geographic populations, may be expressed by means of *subspecies* (also called races); species with recognized subspecies are termed polytypic; a species is monotypic if no subspecies are recognized. A subspecies name is the third and last part (also termed the trinomial) of the scientific name. With few exceptions, the first described population has the same trinomial as the specific epithet and is known as the nominate subspecies. For example, the nominate subspecies of Western Gull is *Larus occidentalis occidentalis* (often written *Larus o. occidentalis*), which breeds along the North American Pacific Coast from Washington to central California. The subspecies *Larus occidentalis wymani*

breeds from southern California to Baja California and can be classified as:

> Class: Aves
> Order: Charadriiformes
> Suborder: Charadrii
> Family: Laridae
> Genus: *Larus*
> Species: *occidentalis*
> Subspecies: *wymani*

Each genus has certain characteristics, an appreciation of which can be helpful for the purpose of identification. Gulls, however, are such a uniform group that generic distinctions in most current lists do not provide much help in narrowing choices for an identification. The number of genera recognized recently among gulls varies from simply a single genus, *Larus*,[5] to seven genera (as discussed by Burger and Gochfeld[6]), all of which occur in the Americas. Given this diversity of opinion, we have broken down the species into a number of groups based upon studies by Moynihan,[7] Chu,[8] and Crochet et al.[9]

Basically, gulls can be divided into two well-marked groups (table 2). One group is the generally smaller, more slender-billed species with screechy and chippering vocalizations, called the ternlike, or sternine, gulls;[10] these include species such as Bonaparte's, Little, Sabine's, Ivory, and kittiwakes. The other group is the generally larger, stouter-billed species with laughing and crowing vocalizations, called the "typical," or larine, gulls;[11] these include species such as Laughing, Heermann's, Mew, and Herring. We have further divided species into five subgroups of ternlike gulls and four of typical gulls (table 2). These subgroups are a convenience for field identification and do not necessarily reflect taxonomic groupings.

FIELD IDENTIFICATION OF GULLS

Although what follows may seem an almost overwhelming amount of information to digest, there is no rush. Time and the associated experience gained are key parts of watching and identifying gulls. Remember that synthesis of characters should be applied to the identification process—don't rely on single field marks. For example, a Herring Gull with yellow legs isn't necessarily a Yellow-legged Gull. Check the bill shape and pattern, wingtip pattern, and other characters to see whether they support such a conclusion. A large dark-backed gull with an extensive pattern of white tongues on the outer primaries

TABLE 2. Gulls can be divided into two well-marked groups: the ternlike gulls and the typical gulls; we further subdivide the former into five subgroups and the latter into four subgroups.

TERNLIKE GULLS	TYPICAL GULLS
MASKED GULLS	**HOODED GULLS**
Bonaparte's Gull	Laughing Gull
Black-headed Gull	Franklin's Gull
Gray-hooded Gull	Lava Gull
Brown-hooded Gull	**PRIMITIVE WHITE-HEADED GULLS**
Andean Gull	Heermann's Gull
SMALL GULLS	Gray Gull
Little Gull	Dolphin Gull
Ross's Gull	Belcher's Gull
KITTIWAKES	Olrog's Gull
Black-legged Kittiwake	Black-tailed Gull
Red-legged Kittiwake	**SMALL WHITE-HEADED GULLS**
FORK-TAILED GULLS	Mew Gull
Swallow-tailed Gull	Ring-billed Gull
Sabine's Gull	**LARGE WHITE-HEADED GULLS**
IVORY GULL	California Gull
Ivory Gull	Herring Gull
	Yellow-legged Gull
	Lesser Black-backed Gull
	Kelp Gull
	Great Black-backed Gull
	Slaty-backed Gull
	Western Gull
	Yellow-footed Gull
	Glaucous-winged Gull
	Glaucous Gull
	Iceland Gull
	Thayer's Gull

isn't necessarily a Slaty-backed Gull—hybrids such as Western × Glaucous-winged Gulls also exhibit this feature. Check the bird's overall structure, its bill shape and color pattern, extent and pattern of head streaking, gray tone of the upperparts, exact pattern of black and white on the wingtips, etc.

The following discussions simply provide background that should put your observations into context. Armed with this information, you are in a position not only to identify most gulls you see but also to contribute to knowledge about gull identification.

APPRECIATING INDIVIDUAL VARIATION

"Variable" sums up the appearance of most gull species. Largely for this reason, gulls are an equalizing force among bird watchers in field identification—they can readily humble each and any one of us by defying specific identification. Both patterns of broad similarity and points of small difference can be important for identifying gulls, and knowing when to focus on which is a matter of experience—the name we give to our mistakes. Gull identification involves a perpetual learning curve: The proportion of unidentifiable gulls never reaches zero. Once you accept this limitation, gull watching should become easier.

As with any identification challenge, finding a needle is difficult if you're not familiar with the haystack. Rather than looking to pick out the odd gull from a flock of 100 birds, first learn what the other 99 birds are. The key to distinguishing gulls lies with time spent watching and studying the common species. Don't take them for granted; pay critical attention to their plumage pattern variations, bill size variations, bill patterns, eye colors, leg colors, molts, behavior, and so on. And don't rely on your memory—write things down or make sketches in a notebook. Be prepared to see birds you can't identify. At first it may be best to ignore these. Start with adult gulls and learn their variations in size and structure, winter head and neck streaking, wingtip pattern, eye color, bill size and pattern, and so on. After you feel comfortable with adults, work into immatures.

After a while, you'll begin to recognize the normal range of variation in some of the more common species, such as Ring-billed Gull or, in the West, California Gull. For example, the tail of second-cycle Ring-billeds varies from all-white, like an adult, to having a solid black distal band. Eye color in second-cycle Ring-billeds varies from dark to pale. First-winter California Gulls seen on the same day can be extremely variable in plumage (photos I.1–I.4),[12] because of the extent of molt, bleaching, and wear, in combination with individual variation in plumage pattern. Post-juvenal scapulars, for example, can vary from dark brown with pale edgings to pale gray with dark anchor marks to plain grayish. But note that overall structure and—in this case—bill pattern are not as variable. If you look carefully at any species, you can find aspects of variation (such as in tail pattern or eye color) that will fall outside the descriptions and illustrations in any guide, including this one.

Still, despite the potential for great individual variation, most gulls can be identified to species fairly readily. Some species are even unmistakable—but others are mistakable.

I.1. *First-cycle California Gull. Photos I.1–I.4 were taken at the same site in late Dec. of the same year to illustrate individual variation in appearance. Specific identification points for all birds are the long wing projections and the sharply bicolored, relatively parallel-sided bills. This individual is still in fairly fresh juvenal plumage, with only very limited molt (one shorter scapular has been replaced). Steve N. G. Howell. Petaluma, California, 26 Dec. 2001.*

I.2. *First-cycle California Gull (compare with I.1). This individual has replaced many of its head and body feathers and scapulars but no wing coverts or tertials. The scapulars have dark centers and broad grayish edgings, suggesting a Western Gull in pattern. Steve N. G. Howell. Petaluma, California, 27 Dec. 2001.*

I.3. *First-cycle California Gull (compare with I.1). This individual has replaced many of its head and body feathers and scapulars, plus an inner tertial, but no wing coverts. The scapulars have variable dark bars and anchor patterns typical of California Gull but quite different from I.2. Steve N. G. Howell. Petaluma, California, 26 Dec. 2001.*

I.4. *First-cycle California Gull (compare with I.1). This individual has replaced many of its head and body feathers and scapulars, upperwing coverts, and inner tertials, while the head and chest have already bleached to whitish. Steve N. G. Howell. Petaluma, California, 26 Dec. 2001.*

Most identification difficulties lie among the large white-headed gulls. But until variation within each age class of each species and hybrid combination is well defined, the chances of identifying atypical birds are unlikely to improve. Thus, although it is possible to describe the characters of a population (with its inherent variability), identifying any individual (which shows "typical" characters of its population to varying degrees) can be difficult—and sometimes not possible, such as with a vagrant. It should be accepted that the magnitude of individual variation in many large white-headed gulls—compounded in some cases by hybridization—means that a proportion of large gulls cannot be identified to species (or parentage) in the field.

Fortunately, gulls show no appreciable sex-related variation in plumage or bare part colors. But males usually are larger bodied, thicker necked, broader winged, and stouter billed than females, on average, especially among the large white-headed gulls (photo I.32). All species, however, have distinct—and often variable—immature plumages. In general, adult gulls tend to be cleanly gray and white whereas immatures have some brownish plumage markings. A flock of gulls frequently shows much more variation in appearance because of age differences within a species than because of differences among species. Smaller species generally attain adult plumage in their second or third plumage cycle; most large species attain adult plumage in their fourth or fifth plumage cycle. Details of plumage cycles and changing appearance with age are covered in the section on molts and plumages.

GEOGRAPHIC VARIATION

Some species of gulls exhibit geographic variation that may be consistent enough for subspecies to be distinguished, such as by differences in bill measurements or in gray tone of the upperparts. In order to define subspecific characters, birds of known breeding provenance are needed—but adequate numbers of such specimens are often lacking. Consequently, the study of geographic variation is dynamic, and specimen analyses continue to identify new subspecies or redefine and validate subspecies described by earlier authors, such as for California Gull[13] and Glaucous Gull.[14]

For the 36 species we deal with, subspecific variation is recognized within 4 or 5 ternlike gulls and 9 or 10 typical gulls. Certain of these subspecies are considered full species by some authors: for example, Herring Gull populations from Siberia and the Bering Sea region (*L. [a.] vegae,* or Vega Gull) are increasingly being treated as a species distinct from the widespread American Herring Gull (*L. [a.] smithsonianus*), and both are distinct from the European Herring Gull (*L. [a.] argentatus*).[15]

Subspecific variation in the ternlike gulls usually does not pose any identification problems, but in white-headed gulls it can. For example, individuals of a small subspecies of Glaucous Gull (*L. h. barrovianus*) might be mistaken for Iceland Gull. And the European subspecies of Mew Gull (*L. c. canus*)—also known as Common Gull—can resemble Ring-billed Gull as much as the American subspecies of Mew Gull (*L. c. brachyrhynchus*).

HYBRIDS

Hybrid gulls—derived from two species interbreeding—can cause serious identification problems, but you should recognize that, with a few notable exceptions, hybrid gulls are generally very rare and infrequently seen (photo I.5). The exceptions lie among some large white-headed gulls, and nowhere else in the world is the presence of hybrid gulls more prevalent than along the Pacific Coast of North America (photos I.6–I.7).

The best-studied example of hybridization is that of Western and Glaucous-winged Gulls interbreeding along the coasts of Washington and Oregon, where hybrids and their progeny comprise up to 75 percent or more of some colonies.[16] Glaucous-winged Gulls also hybridize with Herring Gulls in southern Alaska and with Glaucous Gulls in western Alaska, and Herring Gulls also hybridize with Glaucous Gulls! Hybrids can show almost any combination of parental characters, and they often look intermediate between the parent species. Sometimes they can closely resemble another species—for example, Western Gull × Glaucous-winged Gull hybrids can resemble Slaty-backed Gulls, and Herring Gull × Glaucous Gull hybrids can resemble Thayer's and Kumlien's Gulls.

An acceptance of hybridization should be enough for most birders, although tentative identifications of presumed hybrids allow one to form an idea about the geographic distribution and relative abundance of each type. For example, in central California (Sonoma to Monterey Counties), hybrid Western × Glaucous-winged Gulls are numerous in winter along the coast, less so offshore and inland; presumed hybrid Glaucous-winged × Herring Gulls are locally numerous inland and offshore, less so along the immediate coast; presumed Herring × Glaucous hybrids are slightly more common than pure Glaucous Gulls; and presumed Glaucous-winged × Glaucous hybrids are about as rare as pure Glaucous Gulls.[17,18]

ENVIRONMENTAL FACTORS

In addition to inherent variation and hybrids, observers contend with the effects of a variety of environmental conditions when watching and identifying gulls. Environmental factors may operate directly on the gull or may be indirect but affect an observer's perception.

I.5. *Adult presumed hybrid Laughing Gull × Ring-billed Gull (left) with adult Ring-billed Gull (right). Hybrids among the small and medium-sized gulls are rare enough that most observers will never encounter one. Although such birds can be puzzling and striking, they are unlikely to be mistaken for some other species. This individual's upperpart tone, wingtip pattern, and bill and leg color are intermediate between the parent species. KOCI Inc. Two Rivers, Wisconsin, 16 Mar. 2003.*

I.6. *A mated adult pair of female American Herring Gull or Herring-like hybrid (left) and male Glaucous Gull (right). Larry B. Spear. MacKenzie Delta, Yukon, Aug. 1984.*

I.7. *First-cycle presumed hybrid Glaucous-winged × Western Gull (left) and Glaucous-winged × Herring Gull (right) with Glaucous-winged Gull at rear. The former looks like a dark Glaucous-winged Gull. The latter suggests a Herring Gull in structure (for example, bill shape), but its plumage is too pale. Such birds can be mistaken for Thayer's Gull, which is best separated from hybrids by its size and structure. Steve N. G. Howell. Petaluma, California, 15 Dec. 2001.*

I.8. *Second-cycle California Gull in early stages of PB2 molt. Inner primaries shed, not visible here, with very bleached and worn juvenal upperwing coverts, tertials, and wingtip (compare with fresh first-winter birds, I.1–I.4). Identification points are the bill shape and pattern, medium gray upperparts, and bluish joints on the legs. Steve N. G. Howell. Stinson Beach, California, 24 June 2002.*

Bleaching and wear are two processes that work together to cause the deterioration of feathers.[19] The most extreme cases are usually seen on birds in their second plumage cycle (mainly June to August in Northern Hemisphere species) while some juvenal feathers remain. Bleaching tends to be most pronounced on exposed portions of the plumage, such as the head, wingtips, and exposed upperwing coverts. For example, the whitish heads and chests of many first-cycle large gulls are caused by bleaching—not by molt of incoming whiter feathers, as is often believed. The white tips to new outer primaries of many species often abrade within a few months so that a wingtip can change from black, boldly

I.9. *Leucistic Great Black-backed Gull (presumed third cycle by bill pattern). This bird could be mistaken for a Glaucous Gull, but note the brownish outer primaries, plus the head and bill structure typical of Great Black-backed. Michael D. Stubble-field. Cape May, New Jersey, Oct. 2000.*

I.10. *Leucistic large gull; species and age uncertain. Size and structure (for example, bill) most like Glaucous-winged Gull or hybrid Glaucous-winged × Western Gull. Dark marks on the tail and scattered dark bars on the tail coverts may indicate a first-cycle bird, but the bill pattern is more adultlike. Note the heavy wear of the unpigmented tertials and wingtip. Steve N. G. Howell. Stinson Beach, California, 19 May 2002.*

I.11. *Unhealthy juvenile Thayer's Gull. The slim shape, with strongly projecting chest and sloping stance, is typical of weak individuals, which are often quite tame and reluctant to fly (compare with I.12). Steve N. G. Howell. Petaluma, California, 24 Dec. 1998.*

marked with white, to uniformly blackish. Black wingtips can also fade to dark brown. The neatly patterned brown and white upper-wing coverts of juvenile gulls can bleach and wear to a messy whitish panel on which no pattern can be discerned (photo I.8).

Several species of hooded gulls can show a pink flush to their underparts—most pronounced and extensive on Ross's Gull but also common on Franklin's and Sabine's Gulls, among others. This pink color is apparently diet related and is manifested to varying degrees by different species and populations.[20] The pink flush can occur in breeding and non-breeding birds and in adults as well as imma-

tures. It is best seen in indirect light, such as on cloudy days, because it tends to be washed out by bright sunlight.

Leucistic gulls can be puzzling. In particular, some can be mistaken for white-winged gulls such as Glaucous Gull (photos I.9–I.10). Usually, the white areas on leucistic gulls do not correspond exactly to the white areas on whiter species, and they also lack the patterning shown by most first-cycle white-headed gulls. Albinos (all-white birds with pink bills) are rare, and they look odd enough to stand out as abnormal. In cases of leucism, check structural clues to resolve an identification.

Dark discoloration due to oiling is not infrequent, and blackish to reddish brown oil patches can appear almost anywhere on a bird, although most commonly on the underparts. Observers should always bear in mind such factors when viewing what appears to be an unusual plumage.

Another problem can be caused by sick individuals, which occur quite frequently in some species, perhaps owing to their scavenging habits. Sick and weak birds lack the upright stance of healthy birds and tend to have a hunched-forward, horizontal posture with the chest projecting; such birds can confuse an observer simply because they look atypical of their species (photos I.11–I.12). Other oddballs occur from time to time, some of which can be puzzling (photos I.13–I.15).

Distance and lighting are two environmen-

I.12. *Normal, healthy juvenile Thayer's Gull. Compare stance and shape with I.11. Identification points for both birds are bill size and shape, short legs, neatly checkered upperparts, and dark brown primaries with neat whitish fringes. Steve N. G. Howell. Petaluma, California, 27 Dec. 2001.*

I.13. *First-cycle Western Gull. Aberrant individuals with mostly pale flesh bills are occasionally seen. Identification points are bill size and shape, short wing projection relative to California Gull (compare with I.1), secondary skirt, and overall dark brown plumage with blackish primaries. Michael D. Stubblefield. Morro Bay, California, Nov. 1999.*

I.14–I.15. *First-cycle unidentified gull. Although this bird's plumage is similar to Ring-billed Gull, its dark bill and (apparently) legs, and perhaps also its overall shape, look atypical of that species and suggest a first-cycle Relict Gull L. relictus (of eastern Asia). John Sorensen. Monterey, California, May 2000.*

tal factors that affect the observer. If a bird is simply too far away to distinguish features clearly, there is little to be gained by watching it. Remember, distance is the great deceiver and imagination the great receiver; more can usually be learned by studying closer birds.

An appreciation of the effects of lighting on your perception is important. Tonal differences in grays are often very useful for specific identification of adult gulls, but bright light can wash out grays and make them appear paler, whereas shadows or overcast conditions usually make grays appear darker (photo I.16). Bright light reflecting off pale sand, snow, or ice often causes gray upperparts to appear darker than they are, even though it is sunny (photos I.17–I.18), and people looking for Slaty-backed Gulls in Alaska can be fooled by how dark the backs of Vega Gulls look when birds are standing on ice (photo I.19). Also, be aware that the angle of light—such as backlighting—can affect apparent leg color: yellow legs can sometimes look pinkish and vice versa. Immature gulls seen on sunny days can look warmer toned (photo I.11), whereas birds in shade often look colder toned (photo I.12).

Days with high clouds that filter sunlight are best for assessing gray tones. Even then, be aware that apparent gray tones can change noticeably depending on the angle of light and the position of a bird (photo I.20). Thus, the apparently darker- or paler-backed gull in a flock may simply be standing at a different angle. Photographs can be particularly misleading when attempting to evaluate gray tones, because variation in the intensity of

I.16. *Adult Great Black-backed Gull. Note how different lighting affects the apparent gray tone of the upperwings, and thus the contrast of the black wingtip. Identification points are the slaty blackish upperparts and wingtip pattern. Bruce Hallett. Cape Cod, Massachussetts, Mar. 1994.*

I.17. *Adult Herring Gull on snow. This photo was taken with the exposure reading from the snow, which underexposes the image so that the bird's upperparts look unusually dark gray; compare with I.18 (of the same bird) and I.19. Identification points are the pale gray upperparts, black primaries, staring pale yellow eye, and bill size and shape. Steve N. G. Howell. St. John's, Newfoundland, 4 Feb. 2002.*

I.18. *Adult Herring Gull on snow. This photo was taken with a compensation of +1 stop (that is, slightly overexposed) and more accurately represents the gray tone of the upperparts; compare with I.17 of the same bird. Steve N. G. Howell. St. John's, Newfoundland, 4 Feb. 2002.*

I.19. *Adult Vega Gull on ice. Reflection from pale surfaces heightens contrast and often makes gray tones look darker than they are. Identification points are bill size and shape, and distinct contrast between the black wingtip and gray upperparts. Larry Sansone. Gambell, Alaska, 13 June 1999.*

I.20. *Pair of adult Glaucous Gulls. Note the apparent differences in gray tone of the upperparts, due largely if not entirely to the angles the birds are standing relative to the light and to the observer. Identification points are bill size and shape and pale gray upperparts with white wingtips. Kevin T. Karlson. Prudhoe Bay, Alaska, July 1992.*

lighting and angle of light can be compounded by different films and developing processes.

"Jizz"

The term "jizz" is often used by more experienced birders to describe the overall impression created by a bird—a combination of its structure, plumage, behavior, and an observer's cumulative experience. But treatment of jizz in identification guides is not particularly helpful. For example, saying that Leach's Storm-Petrel (*Oceanodroma leucorhoa*) differs in jizz from Wilson's Storm-Petrel (*Oceanites oceanicus*) is true, but it doesn't help if you haven't seen either species. Some birders have also pointed out that the term is lazy; it circumvents the need to pay critical attention and to describe features that, for the most part, have a structural or behavioral basis.

Because gulls are such a uniform group of birds overall, and because identification problems occur among closely similar species, the use of jizz for gull identification is helpful only in a limited way. Experienced birders often agree that an individual is of a certain species or hybrid combination: some gulls have a "feel" to them that defies the most eloquent attempts at articulation or quantification. An anthropomorphic "gentle expression" or "star-ing face" can help convey the feel of a bird, and we use such terms occasionally. Photos can often convey structure and posture better than long-winded text, and we designate some photos as showing typical postures or shapes that can be helpful in identification.

GULL TOPOGRAPHY AND APPEARANCE

An understanding of gull topography is important for being able to describe accurately what you see. Gulls have the same general structure as most birds, but some of the proportions differ. The general features of gull topography are shown in photos I.21–I.27.

Overall Size and Structure

Determining the overall size and structure of a gull is a fundamental first step that many birders take for granted. These determinations are most easily achieved when other species are present for comparison. For example, a lone first-cycle Ring-billed Gull (a small white-headed gull) might be confused with a second-cycle Herring Gull (a large white-headed gull), but the size difference would be obvious if the species were together. Structural features that lend gulls distinctive

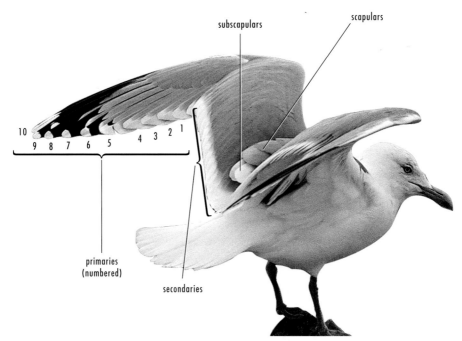

I.21. *Adult American Herring Gull. Identification points are the pink legs, pale gray upperparts, wingtip pattern, and staring pale eye. Bruce Mactavish. St. John's, Newfoundland, 25 Feb. 2001.*

I.22. *Adult Slaty-backed Gull. Compare the hunched posture with I.23 (and also note individual variation in the amount of dusky brown head and neck markings). Identification points are bill shape, pale eyes, pinkish orbital ring, broad white tertial crescent, bright pink legs, and pattern on the underside of P10 on the far wing—note that the area basal to ("inside") the white mirror is gray (not blackish). Brian E. Small. Honshu, Japan, Feb. 1998.*

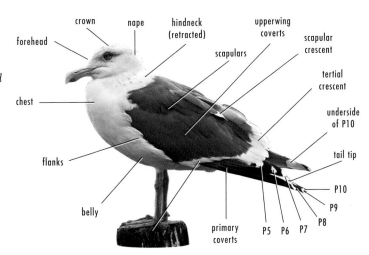

I.23. *Adult Slaty-backed Gull. Compare the stretched neck with I.22. Identification points are similar to I.22, although this bird has darker eyes and the underside of the far wingtip is in shadow. Brian E. Small. Honshu, Japan, Feb. 1998.*

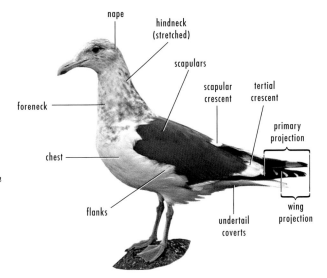

I.24. *First-cycle Thayer's Gull. Compare the slightly spread wing with I.25. Steve N. G. Howell. Petaluma, California, 26 Dec. 2001.*

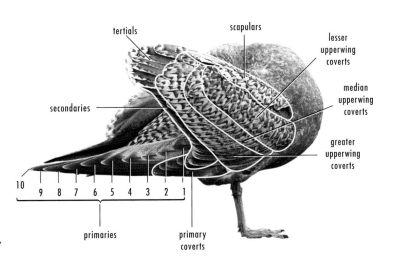

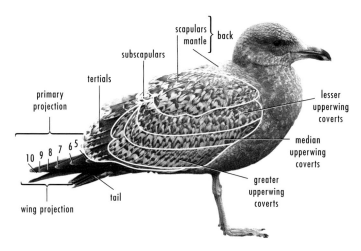

I.25. *First-cycle Thayer's Gull. Compare the closed wing with I.24. Identification points are bill size and shape (but with atypically extensive pinkish basally), dark brown (not black) wingtips and tail. This bird was with other Thayer's Gulls and also seen in flight, which confirmed its identity. Steve N. G. Howell. Petaluma, California, 26 Dec. 2001.*

scapulars
mantle
back
subscapulars
tertials
primary projection
lesser upperwing coverts
median upperwing coverts
greater upperwing coverts
10 9 8 7 6 5
tail
wing projection

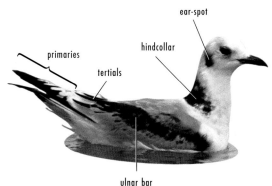

I.26. *First-cycle Black-legged Kittiwake. Identification points are the black hindcollar, medium gray upperparts, and medium-length, tapered bill. Jon Dunn. Boca Chica, Texas, 6 Jan. 1992.*

ear-spot
hindcollar
primaries
tertials
ulnar bar

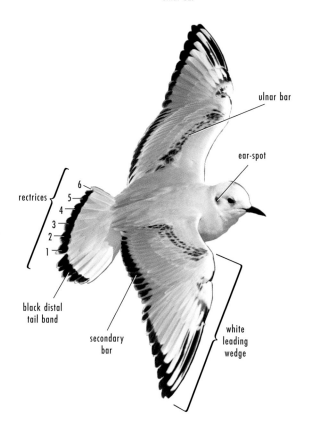

ulnar bar
ear-spot
rectrices
6
5
4
3
2
1
black distal tail band
secondary bar
white leading wedge

I.27. *First-cycle Bonaparte's Gull. Identification points are the slender black bill and upperwing pattern (notably, dark marks on outer primary coverts, reducing the prominence of the white leading wedge). Michael D. Stubblefield. Long Island, New York, Apr. 2002.*

shapes are leg length, wing width, and wing projection (the projection of the wingtips beyond the tail tip on standing birds). For example, Western and Glaucous Gulls have a relatively short wing projection; California and Kumlien's Gulls have a longer wing projection (photos I.28–I.29). Keep in mind that shape can vary greatly with a bird's posture, such as whether the neck is retracted or extended (photos I.22–I.23). Also, males—particularly among the large white-headed gulls—average larger, thicker necked, flatter crowned, broader winged, and stouter billed than females (photo I.32).

BILL SIZE AND SHAPE (PHOTOS I.30–I.35)

The bill comprises upper and lower halves: the maxilla (often called the upper mandible) and the mandible (or lower mandible). The culmen is the dorsal ridge of the maxilla, which curves down distally and may project over the tip of the mandible as a hook. The mandible comprises two lateral plates that meet near the tip (at the gonydeal expansion) and fuse into the gonys, which is the ventral ridge of the mandible tip. The ventral edges of the mandible plates often expand slightly at the gonys and accentuate the gonydeal expansion (photo I.30).

Bill size and shape are important in gull identification, but be aware that males of larger species have stouter and bigger bills than females and that immatures can have noticeably more slender and smaller bills than adults. For example, small immature female Glaucous-winged Gulls have relatively small bills that could suggest male Thayer's Gull. Comparing the bill size and shape of one bird

I.28. *Adult Glaucous Gull. Relative to Kumlien's Gull (compare with I.29), note the larger bulk and more massive bill of Glaucous, plus the longer secondaries (reflecting broader wings) and longer tail—hence, a relatively short wing projection. The tail tip falls close to the tip of P8. Steve N. G. Howell. St. John's, Newfoundland, 5 Feb. 2002.*

I.29. *Adult Kumlien's Gull. Relative to Glaucous Gull (compare with I.28), note the slighter bulk and smaller bill of Kumlien's, plus the shorter secondaries (reflecting narrower wings) and shorter tail—hence, a relatively long wing projection. The tail tip falls at less than or equal to the tip of P7. Steve N. G. Howell. St. John's, Newfoundland, 5 Feb. 2002.*

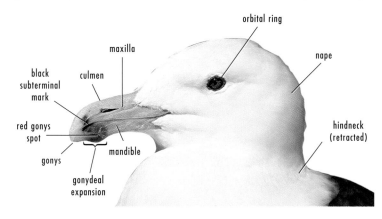

I.30. *Adult Great Black-backed Gull. Note the slaty blackish back, bulging gonydeal expansion, and deep orange orbital ring. Michael D. Stubblefield. Monmouth, New Jersey, Feb. 2000.*

I.31. *Adult Swallow-tailed Gull. Unmistakable; note the large eye, which reflects this species' nocturnal feeding habits. Steve N. G. Howell. Seymour Norte, Galápagos Islands, 20 July 2001.*

red orbital ring

black hood

loral spot

I.32. *Pair of Glaucous-winged Gulls. The male (at right) is noticeably bulkier with a stouter bill than the female. Identification points are pink legs, pale gray upperparts, and gray wingtips. Steve N. G. Howell. Seward, Alaska, 15 June 1999.*

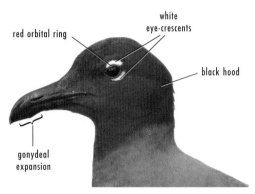

white
eye-crescents

red orbital ring

black hood

gonydeal
expansion

I.33. *Adult or near-adult Lava Gull. Atypical of hooded gulls, this distinctive species has a dark hood year-round. Steve N. G. Howell. Santa Cruz, Galápagos Islands, 21 July 2001.*

I.34. *Adult Heermann's Gull in basic plumage. Besides the mottled head, note that the orbital ring is dark grayish and the bill, while bright, is paler than I.35. John Sorensen. Pacific Grove, California, Sept. 1998.*

I.35. *Adult Heermann's Gull in alternate plumage. Note the bright red orbital ring and bill (compare with I.34). John Sorensen. Monterey, California, Mar. 1998.*

to others of known species can be useful, but note the ages and the (presumed) sexes of the species used for comparison.

Noting how steeply the culmen curves down can be useful—whether it rises slightly before doing so, accentuating a bulbous-tipped effect (as on many adult Yellow-footed Gulls), or simply curves down evenly (as on a typical adult Kelp Gull). Comparing bill depth at the base with depth at the gonydeal expansion can be helpful; greater depth at the base creates a tapered bill (see Swallow-tailed Gull, photo I.31) whereas greater depth at the gonydeal expansion creates a bulbous-tipped bill (see Great Black-backed Gull, photo I.30); similar depth at both points creates a relatively parallel-edged bill (see California Gull, photos I.1–I.4).

BILL COLOR AND PATTERN (PHOTOS I.30–I.35)
Bill color and pattern can vary greatly among and within species and age classes, but should always be noted when describing an unfamiliar gull. Things to note include overall bill color, along with the presence or absence of red and black subterminal marks. Size and shape of the reddish spot on the mandible around the gonydeal expansion (the gonydeal spot) can be useful in some species: for example, it tends to be smaller on adult Western Gulls, larger on adult Yellow-footed Gulls. Be aware that bills often change in color and sometimes pattern depending on a bird's hormonal state and diet. Colors are often brightest as the breeding season approaches and palest after breeding, when adults of many white-headed gulls also attain dark subterminal marks on their bills.

HEAD SHAPE
The head shape of gulls, in conjunction with eye color, bill size, and bill structure, often creates a distinctive appearance, but one that can be difficult to describe. Remember that in large white-headed gulls, males have larger heads with shallower, more sloping foreheads than females. Also, head shape should be used for purposes of identification only with due regard to other factors, such as posture and varying weather conditions. For example, a Thayer's Gull standing around on a nice day can show the "textbook" domed head shape with a fairly steep forehead, a break in angle at the forecrown, and a rounded nape (photo I.12). If, however, the bird becomes alarmed, its head feathers sleek down to create a less domed shape; as it swims off, the forehead looks flatter; and when the bird faces into the wind, its forehead flattens down and its nape angle squares off, thus making it look more like a "textbook" Herring Gull.

HEAD PATTERN, EYE COLOR, AND ORBITAL RING COLOR (PHOTOS I.30–I.35)
As with almost all characters, head pattern varies among and within species and age classes. Breeding adults of most smaller gulls have a dark hood (photo I.33), which may extend down the nape. Many of these hooded gulls have white eye-crescents (photo I.33), which may be narrow or thick or joined at the rear of the eye. Be aware of how hoods can look different in extent depending on a bird's posture: with the neck hunched, a hood often appears less extensive than with the neck fully stretched. Immatures and nonbreeding birds have hoods reduced in extent or replaced by a dark ear-spot (photos I.26–I.27), but specific patterns can vary: note the half-hood typical of nonbreeding Franklin's Gull versus the dusky smudge through the eye typical of nonbreeding Laughing Gull. Immatures of some species have a dark hindcollar (photo I.26).

In white-headed gulls nonbreeding adults tend to have dusky markings on their heads and necks (photos I.23, I.34). These vary from relatively indistinct fine streaks to heavy, blurry smudges; they can be concentrated on the crown, around the eyes, or on the hindneck, and on some species they extend down to the chest or flanks.

Eye color (the color of the iris) can vary greatly among and within adults of the same species, as well as between immatures and adults, but should always be checked. Close-range views may be needed to determine exact patterns. Note that pupils expand in dull conditions (possibly making eyes look darker) and contract in bright conditions (increasing the prominence of pale eyes). In general, relatively large brown eyes create a "gentle" expression (photo I.31), whereas small pale eyes create a "staring" look (photo I.28).

The orbital ring is the naked ring of skin around the eye—unlike an eye-ring, which is a ring of feathers around the eye. Many gulls, especially breeding adults, show brightly colored orbital rings (photos I.30–I.31, I.33, I.35), mainly variations on red and yellow. Orbital-ring color appears consistent in some species, but in others it is more variable; it can also vary seasonally, being shrunken and dull in the nonbreeding season, then swollen and bright during the breeding season (photos I.34–I.35).

The mantle (the interscapular area) and *scapulars* together form the back. The scapulars are a group of feathers that originate from a point at the base of the humerus bone. They fan out to protect the base of the wings at rest and form a seamless joint between the wings and body in flight. Because scapulars grow from a single point, it is not strictly accurate to speak of upper and lower rows; for gulls it is more useful to speak of shorter and longer scapulars. The 3 to 4 longest, underlying scapulars—the subscapulars—are tipped boldly with white on adults and older immatures of many species, forming a scapular crescent on resting birds (photos I.21–I.23). The relative width and contrast of the scapular crescent can be worth noting: for example, it is poorly contrasting on adult Ring-billed Gulls but relatively distinct on adult Mew and California Gulls. In flight, the scapular crescent aligns with the trailing edge of the inner secondaries.

On first-cycle gulls the scapulars can exhibit seemingly endless variations in pattern, even within a single species: For example, no two first-winter Herring Gulls look quite the same. Average differences in patterns exist, but few absolutes. If one looks at enough birds it becomes difficult, if not impossible, to find patterns that consistently separate some species. An appreciation of molt is also helpful when evaluating scapular patterns: For example, many first-cycle large gulls retain most or all juvenal plumage into mid- or late winter.[21,22] Differences in appearance between two birds of the same species and same age can be due to the timing and extent of molt in combination with individual variation (photo I.1–I.4).

The greater secondary upperwing coverts (often just called the greater coverts) mostly or completely conceal the secondaries on resting birds (photos I.24–I.25). The coverts immediately above the greater coverts are usually termed median coverts. (For simplicity we follow this convention here, but note that so-called median coverts are not homologous feather groups across species: On gulls they are ostensibly a second row of greater coverts, whereas on passerines they are simply the largest lesser coverts.) On first-cycle white-headed gulls the greater coverts are often patterned differently from other wing coverts, and they can show helpful differences between species, such as pale grayish overall on Ring-billed Gull or dark brown and marked with whitish on California Gull.

The tertials are the elongated inner secondaries, which act as coverts for the closed wing. On adults of many species the tertials are tipped white, forming a tertial crescent at rest (photos I.22–I.23). On immatures of many species the tertials are dark centered with variably patterned pale tips. Tertial patterns on first-cycle white-headed gulls are almost as variable as scapular patterns, and—because the white areas are prone to wear away—the patterns are best evaluated on fresh plumage. Particularly on broad-winged species, the secondary tips often show as a skirt on resting birds: for example, adult Western and Slaty-backed Gulls typically show a white skirt that borders the lower edge of the closed wing and joins the tertial crescent (photo I.22).

On gulls of all ages, the contrast between folded wingtips and the rest of the upperparts can be helpful for identification. For example, the primaries and upperparts of first-cycle Glaucous-winged Gulls are similar in tone or the primaries are only slightly darker or paler. First-cycle Thayer's Gulls typically have the primaries contrastingly darker than the upperparts.

All adult gulls—except Ivory Gull—are some shade of gray on their upperparts. The gray shade of the upperparts is often the most immediately obvious feature to distinguish species that otherwise look quite similar: Ring-billed Gulls, for example, are noticeably paler above than California Gulls (photo I.36).

A standard reference for describing and comparing gray tones with some degree of

I.36. *Five adult and near-adult California Gulls (left) and three adult Ring-billed Gulls (right). The medium gray upperparts of the California Gulls are noticeably darker than the pale gray upperparts of the Ring-billeds; also note the brighter yellow legs of the latter. Steve N. G. Howell. Point Reyes, California, 15 Sept. 2003.*

consistency, and one that has been used in gull identification articles, is the Kodak Gray Scale. Its full title is the Kodak Color Separation Guide and Gray Scale (catalog numbers 152–7654 [small] and 152–7662 [large]). It presents 19 equal-step neutral gray values ranging from 1 (very pale gray) to 19 (black); white can be considered zero but is not numbered as such. (A neutral gray is simply a measure of lightness or darkness and does not include a spectral hue—no bluish or brownish, for example.) These values (and halftones that observers can estimate between them) allow a start to be made in comparing different gull taxa. But always be aware of potential difficulties in assessing gray tones in the field (see above, under Environmental Factors).

Table 3 lists typical Kodak scores for the back (the mantle and scapulars) of taxa covered by this guide. Some of these ranges differ slightly from those given elsewhere;[23] this is because of the larger number of samples examined for this guide. As a rough guide, Kodak 3–6 is pale gray, Kodak 6–8 medium gray, Kodak 8–10 pale slaty gray, Kodak 10–12 slaty gray, Kodak 12–14 dark slaty gray, and Kodak 14–17 slaty black. Note how almost all taxa are fairly consistent in the gray shade of their upperparts; most vary by only 1 to 1.5 Kodak values and, within these ranges, most individuals of most taxa do not vary by more than half a Kodak value. Larger series of specimens are sure to reveal occasional birds slightly darker or paler than indicated, and other observers might judge Kodak values slightly differently. Even with a single observer in controlled museum conditions, it can be difficult to score and reproduce values accurately—because of factors such as the reflective quality of feathers, bluer or browner hues that differ from neutral gray, and feather bleaching.

In the field, gray tones are even more difficult to assess; nonetheless, these scores should help you gauge relative tones. Note that bluer hues tend to make grays look slightly paler, whereas browner hues can create darker tones. Thus, Heermann's and Slaty-backed Gulls have almost the same Kodak values, but the former looks darker because of its browner, duskier upperparts relative to the cleaner, bluer upperparts of the latter. In many species the upperwings are similar in shade to the back, but in some they can be slightly paler (as in Black-legged Kittiwake) or slightly darker (as in Gray-hooded Gull).

The best lighting conditions for evaluating gray tones are under high overcast or partly cloudy skies. Direct sunlight tends to wash out grays so that subtle differences are hard to detect, and direct shading, such as occurs late in the day, can exaggerate blue hues. Under some conditions, such as against pale surfaces like sand or ice, reflected sunlight can backlight birds so that grays look darker than they are (photos I.17–I.19). Also remember when making comparisons that the angle at which a bird is standing relative to you and to the light can cause differences in apparent gray tones (photo I.20). Hence, it is best to compare gulls standing at the same angle and preferably not on sunny days.

Among large white-headed gulls, most species start to attain adultlike gray coloration on their backs during the second cycle. Gray tones on second- and third-cycle birds may not be as consistent as adult gray tones and should be used with caution when an identification rests on such subtle differences. Because of different film types or processing procedures (and printing in books and magazines), photos can be unreliable for judging shades of gray; field observations are better for a range of evaluations.

The pigment melanin, which helps create dark gray or black plumage, is relatively resistant to bleaching but is also relatively costly to produce. Thus, many mid-latitude gulls have black restricted to the wingtips; note how the extent of black wingtips corresponds closely to the exposed portions of P5 to P10 on the closed wing. Gulls of high latitudes with low-angle sunlight lack black wingtips (such as Ivory and Glaucous Gulls), whereas those of hot tropical zones with strong sunlight have extensively dark plumages (such as Heermann's and Lava Gulls). Or note the north-south cline in upperpart darkness from Glaucous-winged Gull through northern Western Gull to southern Western Gull and Yellow-footed Gull: The upperparts increase in darkness at lower latitudes with stronger sunlight. Upperpart and primary pigmentation may also reflect nonbreeding ranges—as with the dark backs of northern-breeding Lesser Black-backed Gulls (subspecies *fuscus*) that winter in tropical Africa[24] and the blacker wingtips of Thayer's Gull, which averages a more southerly winter distribution than the paler-winged Kumlien's Gull.

WING TOPOGRAPHY AND PATTERN (PHOTOS I.21–I.25, I.27, I.37–I.39)

Wing pattern, particularly of the outer primaries, is often one of the most important characters for distinguishing different species of

TABLE 3. Kodak Gray Scale values for the upperparts of adult gulls recorded in the Americas, judged from museum specimens (approximate breeding ranges for subspecies in parentheses).

0	Ivory Gull *Pagophila eburnea*
3–4	Glaucous Gull *Larus hyperboreus pallidissimus* (Siberia)
3–4	Glaucous Gull *Larus h. hyperboreus* (Canada)
3–4	Iceland Gull *Larus g. glaucoides* (Greenland)
3.5–4.5	Ross's Gull *Rhodostethia rosea*
3.5–4.5	Brown-hooded Gull *Larus maculipennis*
3.5–4.5	Andean Gull *Larus serranus*
4–5	Glaucous Gull *Larus hyperboreus barrovianus* (Alaska)
4–5	Kumlien's Gull *Larus [glaucoides] kumlieni* (Canada)
4–5	Black-headed Gull *Larus r. ridibundus* (W. Asia)
4–5	Black-headed Gull *Larus ridibundus sibiricus* (E. Asia)
4–5	Ring-billed Gull *Larus delawarensis*
4–5	American Herring Gull *Larus argentatus smithsonianus* (N. America)
4–5	European Herring Gull *Larus argentatus argenteus* (W. Europe)
4.5–5.5	Little Gull *Larus minutus*
5–6	Bonaparte's Gull *Larus philadelphia*
5–6	Gray-hooded Gull *Larus c. cirrocephalus* (S. America)
5–6	California Gull *Larus californicus albertaensis* (n. interior N. America)
5–6	Thayer's Gull *Larus thayeri*
5–6	Glaucous-winged Gull *Larus glaucescens*
5–6.5	Common Gull *Larus c. canus* (Europe)
5.5–7	Common Gull *Larus canus heinei* (cen. Asia)
5.5–7	European Herring Gull *Larus a. argentatus* (N. Europe)
6–7	Yellow-legged Gull *Larus m. michahellis* (Mediterranean)
6–7.5	California Gull *Larus c. californicus* (s. interior N. America)
6–7.5	Mew Gull *Larus canus brachyrhynchus* (N. America)
6–8	Glaucous-winged Gull × Western Gull
6.5–8	Kamchatka Gull *Larus canus kamtschatschensis* (E. Asia)
6.5–7.5	Black-legged Kittiwake *Rissa t. tridactyla* (N. Atlantic)
7	European Herring Gull × Lesser Black-backed Gull (Britain)
7–8	Black-legged Kittiwake *Rissa tridactyla pollicaris* (N. Pacific)
7–8	Swallow-tailed Gull *Creagrus furcatus*
7–8	Vega Gull *Larus [argentatus] vegae* (E. Asia)
7–8.5	Yellow-legged Gull *Larus michahellis atlantis* (Azores)
7–9	Sabine's Gull *Xema sabini*
8–9	Laughing Gull *Larus atricilla*
8–9	Franklin's Gull *Larus pipixcan*
8–9.5	Western Gull *Larus o. occidentalis* (nw. U.S.)
8–9.5	Black-tailed Gull *Larus crassirostris*
8.5–9.5	Red-legged Kittiwake *Rissa brevirostris*
8.5–9.5	Gray Gull *Larus modestus*
9–10.5	Yellow-footed Gull *Larus livens*
9–11	Lesser Black-backed Gull *Larus fuscus graellsii* (W. Europe)
9.5–10.5	Lava Gull *Larus fuliginosus*
9.5–11	Western Gull *Larus occidentalis wymani* (sw. U.S.)
9.5–11.5	Slaty-backed Gull *Larus schistisagus*
10–11.5	Heermann's Gull *Larus heermanni*
11–13	Lesser Black-backed Gull *Larus fuscus intermedius* (N. Europe)
12.5–13.5	Dolphin Gull *Larus scoresbii*
12.5–14	Kelp Gull *Larus dominicanus austrinus* (Antarctic region)
13–15	Great Black-backed Gull *Larus marinus*
14–15.5	Kelp Gull *Larus d. dominicanus* (S. America)
14–16	Belcher's Gull *Larus belcheri*
15–17	Olrog's Gull *Larus atlanticus*

gulls—such as adult Western and Slaty-backed Gulls, or first-cycle Glaucous-winged, Thayer's, and Herring Gulls (photo I.37). Evaluating and describing such patterns is aided by an understanding of how the wing is put together, discussed briefly below.

Gulls have ten primary flight feathers, or primaries (P). These are attached to the hand bones and are numbered outward. Thus, P1 is the short innermost primary and P10 the long outermost primary (photos I.21, I.24). As the wing closes, the bases of outer primaries slide under the inner primaries, and the primaries overall slide under the secondaries and tertials (photos I.24–I.25). Mostly what you see of the primaries on a closed wing is the tips

of the outer primaries. The primary projection is the projection of the primaries beyond the tertials on resting birds (as a rule, the tertial tips lie about equal with the tip of P5), whereas the wing projection is the projection of the wingtip beyond the tail tip (photos I.23, I.25). Males of large white-headed gull species tend to be broader winged than females (that is, they have longer secondaries), so that males on average have a shorter primary projection than females. First-cycle birds (especially those with worn tertials) often show a longer primary projection than adults. The primary projection typically comprises three well-spaced primary tips, then a shorter space between the tips of P8 and P9; the P10 tip

I.37. *Upperwings of first-cycle Glaucous-winged Gull (left), Thayer's Gull (middle), and American Herring Gull (right). Glaucous-winged has a relatively muted pattern overall with little contrast between the outer and inner webs of the outer primaries. On Thayer's, the outer webs of the outer primaries are contrastingly darker (with strong contrast near the shaft) and create a two-tone pattern on the outer wing. On Herring, the blackish outer webs of the secondaries create a dark secondary bar, and the dark inner webs of the outer primaries (dark near the shaft) create a more solidly dark outer wing, such that the pale inner primary panel is more contrasting. The more aerial-feeding Thayer's and Herring have narrower and more-pointed wings with noticeably narrower secondaries than the broad-winged, more terrestrial-feeding Glaucous-winged. All birds found freshly dead at Petaluma, California, Dec. 1997 (now specimens at California Academy of Sciences, San Francisco). Steve N. G. Howell. Jan. 1998.*

can be slightly longer than or slightly shorter than (and cloaked by) the tip of P9 (see photos I.25 and I.22–I.23). How far the wingtips project beyond the tail on standing birds may be useful for identification: for example, the tail tip falls about equal with the tip of P7 on a typical Kumlien's Gull but closer to the tip of P8 on a typical Glaucous Gull (photos I.28–I.29).

Each primary has a wide inner web and narrow outer web (photos I.38–I.39). Because inner primaries lay over outer primaries, most of the inner webs are covered in a typical view of the upperwing (photos I.21, I.38). Conversely, on the underside of a spread wing only the inner webs of the primaries are visible, plus the outer web of P10 and the tips of the outer webs of the other primaries (photo I.39). Therefore, if the inner webs and outer webs are patterned and colored differently, the upperside and underside of a spread wing can look quite different—as on many first-

cycle large white-headed gulls, which have dark upperwing tips but overall pale underwing tips. The degree and point of contrast between outer and inner primary webs can be important for distinguishing some first-cycle gulls (photo I.37), as can the number of primaries with contrast. Contrasting pale inner webs extend out through the outer primaries on first-cycle Thayer's and Slaty-backed Gulls but only to the middle primaries on first-cycle Herring Gulls. Beyond species identification, the overall pattern of the primaries, especially the inner and middle ones (P1–P5/P6), can be helpful in determining a bird's age or plumage cycle. In most large white-headed gulls the second-cycle primaries tend to resemble those of the first cycle, but the third-cycle primaries (especially P1–P6) are more adultlike (with clean and fairly broad white tips; see photos 31.17–31.18 vs. 31.20–31.21). Rarely, one or more second-cycle inner primaries appear adultlike (photo 25a.48).

The dark outer primaries often have white tips (also called apical spots), which become abraded through bleaching and wear. In addition to white tips, the outer primaries of many adult white-headed gulls have white subterminal spots, known as mirrors, and some species have white tongue-tips separating the dark tips from the gray tongues of the primary bases (photos I.38–I.39). Adults of the masked gulls have the leading edge of the outer primaries mostly white, forming a bold white leading wedge (see photo I.27).

The patterns of black, white, and gray in the wingtips of adult gulls can be helpful in identification. But patterns can be difficult to see clearly in the field and are often best evaluated from photographs. One trick is to note the pattern on the *underside* of the wingtip farthest from you: This can help to establish the pattern of P10 (photo I.22). As with other characters, there is generally intraspecific variation in wingtip pattern.

When evaluating wingtip pattern or structure, beware of pitfalls provided by molting birds (photo I.40). Molt can affect evaluation of wing/tail projection and make flying birds look shorter winged and blunter winged. More subtly, it can affect the apparent pattern of the wingtip. For example, if an old P10 has been recently shed and the new P10 is not yet visible, you might think the pattern on P9 is that of P10.

The secondary flight feathers, or secondaries, are attached to the ulna bone of the forearm. Secondaries vary in number among species (from 16 in Little and Ross's Gulls to 23

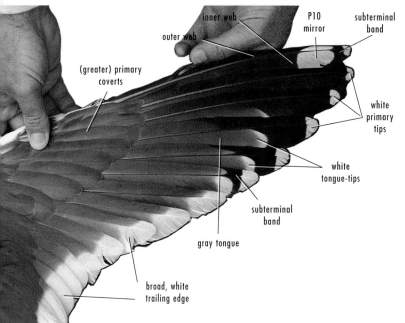

inner web
outer web
(greater) primary coverts
P10 mirror
subterminal band
white primary tips
white tongue-tips
subterminal band
gray tongue
broad, white trailing edge

I.38–I.39. *Upperwing and underwing patterns of adult Slaty-backed Gull. Identification points are the dark slaty gray upper surface with white tongue-tips out to P8, and the steely gray underside to the primaries with a blended blackish wingtip. Steve N. G. Howell. St. Paul, Pribilof Islands, Alaska, 10 June 1999 (now specimen at University of Alaska, Fairbanks).*

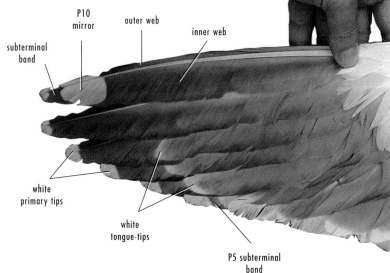

P10 mirror
outer web
inner web
subterminal band
white primary tips
white tongue-tips
P5 subterminal band

I.40. *Adult Slaty-backed Gull. Note the limited amount of black in the wingtip (compare with I.38) due to molt of the outer primaries; also note the ragged-looking secondaries, which are in heavy molt. Identification points are the dark slaty gray upperparts with a broad white trailing edge to the inner primaries, bill shape, and the pale eye with pinkish orbital ring. Mike Danzenbaker. Aomori, Japan, 19 Oct. 1997.*

in many of the large white-headed gulls) and are numbered inward; thus, secondary number 1 is the outermost, adjacent to P1, and the innermost secondaries are the so-called tertials. When dark secondary bases contrast strongly with their coverts, as on many immature gulls, they form a secondary bar (photos I.24, I.27). On adult gulls the secondaries are often tipped white. The width of these white tips varies among species, so, for example, it averages broader on Slaty-backed Gull than on Western Gull.

Immatures of several species of ternlike gulls have a dark ulnar bar (also called a carpal bar) that cuts diagonally across the upperwing coverts, more or less following the path of the underlying ulna (photo I.27). This bar corresponds to the most exposed upperwing coverts on aerial-feeding species, and the dark pigment helps protect these feathers.

Patterns—or at least overall darkness—of the underwing coverts can be helpful in determining a bird's age and identity. The underwing coverts of second-cycle Western Gulls are dark brown overall whereas those of third-cycle birds are pale overall (whitish with variable brown markings). The underwings of a first-cycle California Gull are dark brown overall, strikingly different from the mostly whitish underwings of a first-cycle Ring-billed Gull. The medium gray upperpart tone of an adult California Gull shows through on the backlit underwing as a dusky gray band across the secondary bases, an effect not shown, or much more muted, on adult Ring-billed and American Herring Gulls, which have paler gray upperparts.

TAIL TOPOGRAPHY AND PATTERN (PHOTOS I.27, I.41–I.43)

The tails of gulls consist of 12 rectrices (the singular of which is rectrix), six on each side of the midpoint. Rectrices are numbered outward from the central rectrix (R1) to the outermost rectrix (R6) (photo I.27). Tail shape is rarely of use in gull identification, although exceptions include the diagnostic long and graduated tail of Ross's Gull and the distinctly forked tail of Sabine's Gull. Most species of adult gulls have unmarked white tails, but among immatures, mainly first-cycle birds, tail patterns vary among species and can aid in identification. It is important, though, to be aware of how a tail can look different if spread rather than closed, or if seen from above rather than from below (photos I.41–I.43). As with the primaries, from above you see mostly

I.41. *Dorsal surfaces of tails of first-cycle Glaucous-winged Gull (left), presumed Glaucous-winged × Western Gull hybrid (center), and Western Gull (right), with left R6 pulled out to reveal the inner web pattern (usually concealed from above). From above the tail looks almost solidly dark with limited whitish ribbing on the outer web of R6; but note how the inner webs could create a different pattern from below if the tail were spread (and compare with photos I.42–I.43). All birds found freshly dead at Petaluma, California, Dec. 1997 (now specimens at California Academy of Sciences). Steve N. G. Howell. Feb. 1998.*

the outer webs of the rectrices (which are often extensively dark) but from below or on a widely fanned tail you see more of the inner webs of the outer rectrices (which can be differently patterned). Hence, a tail can look solidly dark from above, but from below or when widely fanned it can appear pale based with a broad dark distal band (photos I.42–I.43).

Many first-cycle gulls have a black tail tip or distal tail band, the extent of which can be a useful character, as, for example, in separating first-cycle Laughing and Franklin's Gulls. In the former, the black tail band is broader and extends to the sides of the tail—that is, to the outer web of R6. In the latter, the tail band is narrower and does not extend to the edge of R6.

Tail patterns of first-cycle large white-headed gulls vary among species from almost solidly dark, to white with a blackish distal band, to whitish with fine dusky barring. They also show intraspecific variation but can still help in identification, such as between Great Black-backed Gull and American Herring Gull. Second-cycle and especially third-cycle tail patterns of large white-headed gulls are highly variable and appear to be of limited use

I.42–I.43. *First-cycle American Herring Gull. From above the tail looks almost solidly blackish with limited white ribbing on the outer rectrices. From below, because of pale on the inner webs, the tail looks extensively pale-based with a broad dark distal band; also note the long undertail coverts (typical of gulls) extending almost to the tail tip. Identification points are bill shape and pattern, tail pattern, and the pale panel on the upper surface of the inner primaries. Bruce Hallett. Patuxent River, Maryland, 15 Mar. 1999.*

for species identification. In general, second-cycle tails resemble first-cycle tails, whereas third-cycle tails range from mostly dark (similar to second cycle) to entirely white (like an adult).

LEG LENGTH AND COLOR

All gulls have "medium-long" legs, although those of cliff-nesting species, such as kittiwakes, are relatively short, and those of a few species, such as Belcher's Gull, are relatively long. Leg color can be important in identification and should always be noted. Most tern-

like gulls have red or blackish legs. Immatures of red-legged species generally have pink legs that change to red late in the first cycle or in the second cycle. Legs of hooded and primitive white-headed gulls range from black to red and yellow. Most adult white-headed gulls have yellow or pink legs; immatures of both yellow-legged and pink-legged adults have pinkish legs. Yellow-legged species usually attain adult leg color in their second or third cycle.

Leg color often changes in intensity and sometimes in color depending on the hormonal state of a bird. Legs are often brighter at the start of the breeding season, duller at the end: Compare, for example, the bright orange-yellow legs of a prebreeding spring adult California Gull with the grayish green legs of a postbreeding fall adult. Alternatively, some adults of pink-legged species (such as Western and Herring Gulls) can attain yellowish legs for brief periods, especially in the spring.[25]

MOLTS AND PLUMAGES

Feathers are not permanent—they wear out and need to be replaced. Molt is simply the normal and regular growth of feathers, by which plumages are attained. When identifying gulls, it is often important to establish their age and to understand how the appearance of their plumage changes with age; hence, an understanding of molt is helpful. The principles of gull molt are relatively simple (see below), but the reality is more complex. This is because in many species, especially large white-headed gulls, molt may be an almost continuous process for the first two or three years of life; and even in adults there is often overlap in timing between different molts. In addition, plumage patterns and bill colors can vary greatly among individuals of the same age[26,27] although some general patterns of development can usually be discerned.

AGE TERMINOLOGY AND PLUMAGE CYCLES

In this book we use the Humphrey-Parkes (H-P) system of naming molts and plumages, which is based upon plumage cycles and the concept of homology.[28,29,30] In the H-P system a bird can have no more, and no fewer, plumages than it has molts. For two molts to occur, some feathers must be replaced twice in a plumage cycle. A plumage cycle (often shortened simply to cycle) runs from a given plumage or molt to the next occurrence of the same plumage or molt.

One departure we make from the H-P system is to use the more readily understood term "adult" for what the H-P system more precisely calls "definitive plumage," that is, a plumage that does not continue to change in appearance (or aspect). Small gulls generally attain adult plumage aspect in their second or third cycle. Most medium-sized to large gulls attain adult plumage aspect in their third or fourth cycle. The definition of "adult" plumage aspect is somewhat fuzzy, however, because maturation occurs at different individual rates. Fourth-cycle birds of several large gulls (such as Herring Gull) often show immature plumage aspect characters on their wings and tail,[31] and some much older birds can also show dark marks on the primary coverts, alula, and tail.[32,33] Thus, aging any bird after the second cycle is problematic; such birds are best termed third-cycle type, fourth-cycle type, and so on. The pattern of the wingtips can also continue to change through the sixth or seventh cycle;[34] in general, more white and less black develops on the wingtips of older birds. For simplicity (and because of a general lack of information from known-age birds) we subsume such variation under the heading of "adult."

How do plumage cycles relate to conventional terminology? In the Northern Hemisphere we can speak of first-winter gulls, or even a second-calendar-year gull, and have no difficulty being understood. This is because of well-marked seasons with breeding in the middle of the calendar year. When dealing with Northern and Southern Hemispheres, however, a "winter" Sabine's Gull off Mexico in November would be a "summer" Sabine's Gull off Chile in November. One could still use the calendar-year system with respect to the bird's hatching date, but this approach can cause confusion in the Southern Hemisphere. For example, some South American gulls hatch during December and January, so a second-calendar-year bird could be just one day older than a first-calendar-year bird, if they hatched on 31 December and 1 January, respectively. The use of plumage cycles is a neutral system that avoids such difficulties. This system works in any part of the world: A second-cycle Kelp Gull is a second-cycle Kelp Gull whether it was hatched in January in Tierra del Fuego, July in Louisiana, or September in Brazil, and all are comparable to a second-cycle Lesser Black-backed Gull. This system also works in cases when the cycle is less than a year. In most birds the plumage cycle is an annual cycle, but in some species—such as gulls breeding on the Galápagos Islands—the cycle can be 9 to 11 months, and, over the course of three years, some birds could undergo four cycles of breeding and molt.

We use the basic plumage cycle (the period between prebasic molts) as a convenient system for describing molts independent of seasons and breeding status. The first (basic) plumage cycle starts with juvenal plumage, the second with the initiation of the second prebasic molt (which often corresponds to the start of primary molt), the third with the initiation of the third prebasic molt, and so on. However, because molts can overlap in timing, using the H-P system in the field is often not practical. Therefore, in photo captions (mainly for white-headed gulls) we often use the terms "breeding" and "nonbreeding" to describe a bird's aspect (that is, its overall appearance regardless of what plumage it may be wearing). Aspect often relates largely to a bird's head and neck: For example, a cleanly white-headed Herring Gull in July still has a breeding aspect (and is simply termed "breeding" in photo captions), even though it has started prebasic primary molt. A December California Gull with extensive dusky head and neck markings has a nonbreeding aspect ("nonbreeding" in photo captions) even though its back may be largely in alternate plumage.

BASIC, ALTERNATE, AND FORMATIVE PLUMAGES

As adults, all birds follow a fundamentally similar pattern of plumage succession and have a presumed homologous molt by which most or all of their feathers are replaced. This is the prebasic molt, which produces basic plumage. In most temperate-breeding gulls the basic plumage cycle is about 12 months; that is, an annual cycle. The prebasic molt typically starts just after breeding, although in larger gulls it often starts during incubation; and in the Ivory Gull it is mostly completed *before* breeding. In migratory species the prebasic molt may be: 1) on the breeding grounds before migration; 2) on the nonbreeding grounds after migration; 3) interrupted, or suspended (started before migration, finished afterward); or 4) partly or entirely at staging areas between breeding and nonbreeding areas.

Some species (including most gulls) have a

second plumage added into their basic cycle. This added plumage is called an alternate plumage: It alternates with the basic plumage, and it is attained by a prealternate molt. Alternate plumages often equate to what are familiarly called "breeding" or "summer" plumages, but an alternate plumage is any second plumage inserted into the basic cycle, regardless of when it is attained. In general, prealternate molts tend to be less extensive than prebasic molts and in most gulls involve only head and body feathers (including much of the back and often some upperwing coverts). An exception is Franklin's Gull, adults of which typically have a complete prealternate molt. In gulls with cycles compressed to less than a year (for example, Swallow-tailed Gull and Lava Gull on the Galápagos Islands) the prealternate head and body molt occurs during the end of the prebasic molt of the outer primaries, as also happens in Sabine's Gull. And even in many large white-headed gulls, the prealternate molt starts before prebasic molt of the remiges is completed.

In their first cycle, gulls have molts that are more variable in terms of timing, extent, and even number than the relatively stereotyped molts of adults (figure 1). After the first cycle, molts follow a pattern like that of the adult. The simplest molt strategy is that of the Ivory Gull, which molts directly from juvenal to adult plumage and apparently lacks an alternate plumage (figure 1). Juveniles fledge in September, retain juvenal plumage through the winter, and then undergo a complete molt into all-white adult plumage from April to August of their second calendar year. In subsequent cycles there is a complete molt between March and September, suspended during mid-June to early August in breeding birds.[35]

In large white-headed gulls, the protracted molting periods and changing aspect of incoming plumage make it difficult to infer how many molts really occur in the first cycle. The ancestral pattern may have been two molts (as in most ternlike gulls), but recent observations suggest that this has been reduced to a single molt in most white-headed gulls[36] (figure 1). This post-juvenal molt is highly variable in extent, but it appears most similar in timing and extent to a prealternate molt; hence, it is called the first prealternate molt.[37,38] A limited second molt may (still) occur in some white-headed gulls but requires verification.

Most of the ternlike gulls have two molts added into their first cycle (figure 1): Between fledging and winter there is a fairly extensive molt of head and body feathers, and then in late winter and spring there is a second molt of head and body feathers. The latter molt appears homologous to the adult prealternate molt. But the former lacks a counterpart in the adult cycle and is termed a preformative molt, producing formative plumage. The preformative molt used to be called the first prebasic molt, but, although formative plumage often looks like adult basic plumage, the molts producing these plumages are not homologous.[39,40]

Translating the relatively straightforward strategies of figure 1 into what you see in the field can be difficult for a number of reasons: 1) molts are often protracted and can overlap

Figure 1. Diagrammatic representation (using Northern Hemisphere gulls, which have an annual cycle) to show molt strategies of increasing complexity. Ivory Gull simply has prebasic molts (Howell 2001c), Western Gull has a single added first-cycle molt (Howell and Corben 2000a), Bonaparte's Gull has two added first-cycle molts. Each cycle includes a complete molt, starting with the prejuvenal (= equivalent to first prebasic) molt. PJ = prejuvenal molt; PB = prebasic molt; pa = prealternate molt; pf = preformative molt; dashed line indicates suspended (interrupted) molt. Note how prebasic and prealternate molts can overlap in timing, such as in Western Gull.

MONTHS	JFMAMJJASOND	JFMAMJJASOND	JFMAMJJASOND	JFMAMJJASOND
	First Cycle	Second Cycle	Third Cycle	Fourth Cycle
Ivory Gull	P J	P B P B	P B P B ------P B	P B P B ------P B
Western Gull	P J	P B P B P B	P B P B P B	P B P B P B P B
	papapa----------papa	papapa-------------papa	papa-------papa	pa--
Bonaparte's Gull	P J	P B P B	P B P B	P B P B
	pfpfpf	pa	pa	pa

in timing; 2) plumage can change continually in aspect over the first cycle due both to the effect of changing hormones on the pattern of feathers grown in a protracted molt, and to feather bleaching—yet only a single molt is under way; and 3) the inertial mindset that insists fall molts have to be prebasic and spring molts have to be prealternate.

MOLT AND CHANGING APPEARANCE

The best way to appreciate molt in gulls, along with the associated changes in appearance, is to follow a species through its first few plumage cycles—from juvenal plumage to adult basic plumage. Here we'll review the Western Gull, which should reinforce an understanding of the timing and sequence of molts. Note that considerable variation occurs within age classes; that bill color and pattern exhibit much individual variation; and that immature Western Gulls of the southern subspecies *wymani* differ slightly in overall appearance and molt timing. Also note that molt timing and duration can vary within a species or population by up to about a month between different years, probably as a result of variation in food supply and food quality. When viewing birds in the field and using species accounts in this guide, consider that all white-headed gulls exhibit such variation—but space is not available to cover each species in this kind of detail.

In discussions of molts and plumages it is convenient to talk in terms of cycles (rather than years) and to think of the preformative molt as PF, the first prealternate molt as PA1, first alternate plumage as A1, the second prebasic molt as PB2, second basic plumage as B2, and so on. This jargon can be assimilated quickly and is useful for describing birds in the field. The time required to replace a complete set of primaries (whose molt typically spans the duration of a PB molt) is about 2 to 3 months in a small gull and up to 6 months in a large gull. The first and second plumage cycles of large gulls are only about 2 months ahead of those of adults, and molts align with the adult cycle over the 3 to 4 years it takes to reach adult plumage (see figure 1).

Before looking at molt in the field, an observer should appreciate two factors in terms of a gull's appearance. First, the contrasting white heads and chests seen on many gull species (such as Herring Gulls) molting from juvenal to A1 are mostly due to bleaching, not to incoming whiter feathers as is often believed. Second, *the appearance of feathers in the same generation can change depending on the hormonal state of the bird*—for example, during the first cycle concomitant with ongoing hormonal development, or perhaps in adults because of varying levels of hormones related to the breeding season. Thus, A1 scapulars of a Western Gull grown in September are often dark brownish with broad pale edgings, whereas A1 scapulars attained later can be darker and more uniformly grayish overall (see photos I.48, I.51–I.52). Some gulls breed in areas prone to food crashes and experience breeding failure or molt stress, such as Heermann's Gull, Gray Gull, and Pacific populations of Black-legged Kittiwakes (all potentially affected by El Niño events). If conditions for breeding are unsuitable, or if a bird's preceding molt was compromised by food shortages such that it is not fit enough to breed, then a fully white-headed alternate plumage may not be attained; instead, an alternate head plumage intermediate in aspect between typical alternate and basic may be grown (for example, white with variable dusky mottling).[41]

Now we'll follow a Western Gull (of the nominate, northern subspecies *occidentalis*) from fledging to its adult plumage cycle (see figure 1), based on a study by Howell and Corben.[42]

First Cycle. The juvenile (juv, or B1) Western Gull (photos I.44–I.46) is dark brownish overall, with pale edgings to the upperparts creating variable patterning. The tail is brownish black, often with limited white notching on the outer web of R6 and slight pale mottling and barring on the bases on the outer rectrices. The subscapulars often look contrastingly dark and fresh and, together with the longest primaries, appear to be the last juvenal feathers to become fully grown. The bill is black, the legs dusky flesh, and the eyes dark brown. PA1 molt typically starts between late August and late October. The first signs of the PA1 molt out of juvenal plumage are usually new mantle and scapular feathers that often have very broad pale tips, such that some birds show leucistic-looking patches in their back; the tips soon abrade to reveal dark feather centers. Molt progresses through the mantle and scapulars as well as the head, neck, chest, and flanks. By late October, 0 to 80 percent of the visible scapular area has been molted (50 to 60 percent molted on 75 percent of birds), together with much of the head, foreneck, chest, and flanks (photos I.47–I.48). Molt continues slowly into November and perhaps December, by which time 10 to 90

I.44. *First-cycle Western Gull in fresh juvenal (= B1) plumage, probably female (note small bill and compare with I.45). Plumage fairly typical. Note bulbous-tipped black bill, overall dark brown aspect with fairly narrow pale edgings to upperparts, and solidly dark tail. Steve N. G. Howell. Bodega Bay, California, 24 Aug. 1998.*

I.45. *First-cycle Western Gull in fresh juvenal (= B1) plumage, probably male (note large bill and compare with I.44). Upperparts have relatively broad and bright patterning (notably on the greater coverts) and belly feathers are marked with broad white tips forming a slight cutoff at the border with the chest. Steve N. G. Howell. Bodega Bay, California, 24 Aug. 1998.*

I.46. *First-cycle Western Gull in fresh juvenal (= B1) plumage. Some individuals, like this bird, have a contrastingly white and mostly unmarked belly. Steve N. G. Howell. Bodega Bay, California, 12 Aug. 2000.*

I.47. *First-cycle Western Gull. PA1 molt retarded (compare with I.48). Note single A1 mid-scapular and contrastingly fresh-looking juvenal subscapulars. Steve N. G. Howell. Bodega Bay, California, 13 Oct. 1998.*

I.48. *First-cycle Western Gull. PA1 molt fairly advanced (compare with I.47). Most juvenal scapulars have been replaced—note difference in pattern between shorter and longer scapulars. Also note grayer A1 feathers appearing on neck, chest, and sides, compared to faded and browner juvenal feathers. Steve N. G. Howell. Bodega Bay, California, 13 Oct. 1998.*

percent of the visible scapular area has been molted (70 to 80 percent molted on 80 percent of birds), plus most to all of the mantle and much of the head, neck, chest, and flanks (photos I.49–I.50). Some birds suspend or greatly slow molt over midwinter. The longest underlying scapulars, including the subscapulars, are still juvenal feathers, as is the belly and often much of the hindneck. Worn and faded juvenal feathers often appear brown or gingery in contrast to new and grayer A1 feathers. By the end of the year, bills often have some pinkish at the base but are dark overall, with the distal third subtly blacker than the base. The legs become dull flesh pink to pink.

PA1 molt may progress slowly through the same areas during January and February (or it may be suspended at this time); it then increases in intensity from March to April or May, with juvenal feathers continuing to be replaced. Some of the earliest-replaced mantle feathers can bleach to pale grayish, while a few fresh gray feathers appear on some birds from late January onward. Presumed PA1 molt continues through the scapulars into April and May (but distinguishing this molt from the succeeding PB2 molt is virtually impossible), and some birds replace most of their remaining juvenal scapulars during this period. By spring some birds have developed a pinkish basal two-thirds to the bill, although most still have largely dark bills; the legs are flesh pink.

The last juvenal scapulars to be replaced are generally the largest underlying feathers and the subscapulars. These late-grown scapulars are often relatively dark, grayish or mostly gray, and fairly uniform—in contrast to the browner, faded, and more strongly patterned scapulars attained months earlier (photos I.51–I.52). A1 head and neck feathers attained the previous fall can wear and bleach to whitish, as can retained juvenal feathers, whereas late-molting birds appear relatively dark and dusky on the head and body; how much this reflects the start of the overlapping PB2 molt is difficult to ascertain (photos I.51–I.52), and some birds might have a limited second molt added into their first cycle. One or two subscapulars can be replaced by March, but mostly these are molted later. The appearance of new subscapulars may correspond to the end of PA1 molt, which, in the Western Gull, involves replacement of most or all juvenal scapular, mantle, head, neck, chest, and flank feathers. PA1 molt does not usually include the belly, rump,

I.49. First-cycle Western Gull. PA1 molt retarded (compare with I.50). About 40 percent of scapular area is A1 (fresher, dark-centered, gray-edged feathers), as are some feathers of mantle, head, and chest. Steve N. G. Howell. Petaluma, California, 27 Dec. 2001.

I.50. First-cycle Western Gull. PA1 molt fairly advanced (compare with I.49). Almost all scapulars are A1 (note contrasting, worn brown subscapulars), as is most of the mantle, head, neck, chest, and flanks. Steve N. G. Howell. Petaluma, California, 27 Dec. 2001.

wing coverts, tail coverts, or flight feathers, including tertials.

Second Cycle. PB2 molt of inner primaries and median coverts starts in early April to late May (photos I.53–I.55), with the median coverts often shed almost synchronously. Molt of scapulars and of head, neck, and mantle feathers during April may involve overlapping PA1 and PB2 molts. In May to June PB2 molt progresses quite rapidly and extensively: Most to all of the median coverts, most greater coverts, many lesser coverts, some tertials, and many of the mantle and scapular feathers are

I.51. *First-cycle Western Gull. In A1 plumage or possibly starting PB2 molt. Note differences in scapular patterns, with the longer and dark-slaty scapulars presumably attained later in the PA1 molt. Steve N. G. Howell. Bolinas, California, 21 Apr. 2003.*

I.52. *First-cycle Western Gull. In A1 plumage or possibly starting PB2 molt. Note differences in scapular patterns, with the longer and plainer gray scapulars presumably attained later in the PA1 molt. Bleached whitish head and chest (compare with I.51) may be a mixture of juvenal and A1 feathers. Steve N. G. Howell. Bolinas, California, 21 Apr. 2003.*

I.53. *Second-cycle Western Gull starting PB2 molt with median and some lesser coverts dropped, exposing formerly protected bases of greater coverts (compare with I.52, I.54–I.55). Dark-sooty head and body plumage may represent mixture of A1 and B2 feathers. Steve N. G. Howell. Bolinas, California, 21 Apr. 2003.*

I.54. *Second-cycle Western Gull starting PB2 molt. Dropped median coverts expose a plain, paler area on the bases of the greater coverts (compare with I.52– I.53, I.55). Steve N. G. Howell. Bolinas, California, 13 May 2003.*

I.55. *Second-cycle Western Gull starting PB2 molt. Note fresh, incoming B2 median coverts, which contrast with the bleached lesser coverts above them (compare with I.53–I.54). Steve N. G. Howell. Bolinas, California, 13 May 2003.*

replaced by late June. Also by late June, most to all juvenal belly feathers are replaced. Most birds in June have many B2 feathers in the chest, neck, and head, although some "retarded" birds still have a few worn juvenal feathers in the neck, which will be replaced in July and August. The bill brightens overall in summer; the eyes become paler brown. Some bills become flesh pink with a black distal third and fine pale tip, but others remain largely blackish.

Molt of rectrices starts in early July, about when P7–P8 are growing in. Anything from the central pair to all but the outermost pair are shed almost synchronously—but with an overall inner to outer sequence—and a few birds appear to drop all rectrices at once. Growth of rectrices is fairly rapid: By mid- to late August most birds have new, apparently full-grown B2 tails, which are largely blackish with a whitish tip and a white outer edge to R6. Molt of the secondaries starts in early to mid-July (typically just after the initiation of rectrix molt), and groups of feathers may be shed almost synchronously. By late August a few birds have completed growth of new secondaries, but generally this occurs in September; the inner secondaries adjacent to the tertials are the last to be replaced. The outermost primaries become fully grown between early September and late October, marking the end of the complete PB2 molt.

Note that most nominate Western Gulls in fresh B2 plumage are brownish overall, as is true of many large white-headed gulls; the traditional "second-winter" large gulls of many field guides (with neat gray backs) are in fact in A2 plumage, at least on their backs. In northern Western Gulls, though, there is slight dimorphism at this stage: Most birds are brown overall (brown types; photo I.56), but others are whiter on the head and neck, grayer on the back (gray types; photo I.57). Bills of brown types often become blacker again in fall and winter, approaching the most "advanced" first-cycle pattern, whereas gray types more often retain pinkish, black-tipped bills like those of the most "retarded" third-cycle pattern. (Gray types are more common in *L. o. wymani*.)

Before PB2 molt is finished, up to a third of birds in mid- to late August start to molt median coverts again, signaling the start of PA2 molt. Thus PB2 and PA2 molts overlap in timing (photos I.58–I.59). The incoming A2 median coverts vary from patterned brownish (much like the surrounding B2 coverts) in early-molting or hormonally retarded birds to

I.56. *Second-cycle Western Gull. Brown type in PB2 molt (compare with I.57). Most of upperparts are B2. P10 is still juvenal, with P6 new, P7–P8 probably growing (but not yet projecting beyond tip of P6), and P9 shed. Steve N. G. Howell. Bodega Bay, California, 19 July 1998.*

I.57. *Second-cycle Western Gull. Gray type in PB2 molt (compare with I.56). Note heavily worn juvenal lesser coverts and P10 not yet replaced. Steve N. G. Howell. Bodega Bay, California, 19 July 1998.*

unmarked gray (in strong contrast to surrounding B2 coverts) in late-molting or hormonally advanced birds. The replaced feathers range from one to most median coverts; scattered lesser coverts and even a few greater coverts can also be replaced in September and October. PA2 molt of the head and body may not start until October or later, when new gray feathers appear in the face, mantle, and shorter scapulars (photos I.60–I.62).

PA2 molt in the scapulars, mantle, head, neck, chest, and sides continues at variable rates over the winter (often with a midwinter suspension) through April and possibly into May, by which time all birds appear to have replaced most feathers in these areas (photos

I.58. *Second-cycle Western Gull. A fairly typical dusky and mottled individual largely in fresh B2 plumage (outer primaries still growing, so wing projection looks short; lower rows of lesser coverts also growing—hence, median-covert bases are exposed). Steve N. G. Howell. Bolinas, California, 21 Aug. 2003.*

I.59. *Second-cycle Western Gull, starting PA2 molt but B2 outer primaries not quite fully grown. Note contrasting, new and growing A2 gray median coverts (which, on other individuals, can be patterned brownish, similar to B2 feathers); some scapulars are also likely A2 feathers. Steve N. G. Howell. Bolinas, California, 17 Oct. 2003.*

I.60. *Second-cycle Western Gull, a fairly typical second-winter individual. Gray median coverts—and probably some scapulars—are A2 feathers. Steve N. G. Howell. Bodega Bay, California, 24 Nov. 1998.*

I.61. *Second-cycle Western Gull. An extreme gray type with an atypically black bill. Gray scapulars may include A2 feathers or simply represent variation in appearance of late-molted B2 feathers; most median coverts are B2. Steve N. G. Howell. Bodega Bay, California, 24 Nov. 1998.*

I.62. *Second-cycle Western Gull with relatively retarded appearance (compare with photos I.60–I.61). Steve N. G. Howell. Petaluma, California, 11 Dec. 2003.*

I.63–I.65). A few B2 scapulars may be retained, and subscapulars are not usually replaced in this molt. As in the PA1 molt, no feathers of the belly, rump, or tail coverts appear to be replaced. Thus, the extent of this protracted PA molt is similar to that of first-cycle birds but also often includes some upperwing coverts. Incoming A2 plumage typically has variable dusky clouding on the head, neck, and chest, such that the white-headed "second-summer" plumage comes about largely through bleaching and wear of these feathers. The gray back typical of "second-summer" birds comes about through a combination of molt and wear: Brownish edgings to B2 and early molted A2 scapulars wear off to expose gray bases, and new all-gray A2 feathers are attained. Bill colors change quite strikingly from December and January through March, with most birds developing pink and then yellow on at least the basal two-thirds of the bill. By May many birds have bright yellow bills with a black subterminal band or ring, and up to 50 percent show a small orange-red gonys spot. Some attain bills barely distinguishable from those of adults, while others retain mostly blackish bills, similar to some first-cycle birds. The eyes often become paler during this period (photos I.63–I.64), and some birds have pale greenish eyes, as pale as on any adult. Thus, second-summer birds are highly variable in appearance, which is typical of large white-headed gulls.

Third Cycle. PB3 molt starts in late April to May, when the inner primaries are shed, along with median coverts and tertial coverts. Molt continues through the summer, much as in second-cycle birds although averaging slightly later in timing (photos I.66–I.67). Tail molt starts in July, and by mid-September almost all birds have fully grown B3 tails, which vary from being all-white to having a broad black distal band that usually does not extend to the outer web of R6. In some cases rectrices can alternate black and white; these "piano-key" or piebald tails can all be of the same feather generation, and they epitomize the variation possible in immature gull plumages

I.65. *Second-cycle Western Gull. Somewhat worn A2 plumage with mostly clean white head and neck and bright bill (compare with I.63–I.64). Median coverts look similar in pattern and wear to adjacent coverts; that is, PA2 molt presumably did not include any upperwing coverts (unlike I.64). Steve N. G. Howell. Bolinas, California, 15 Apr. 2003.*

I.63. *Second-cycle Western Gull mostly in A2 plumage with heavy dusky head and neck markings, which can abrade to produce the white-headed second-summer aspect (compare with I.64–I.66). Steve N. G. Howell. Bolinas, California, 15 Apr. 2003.*

I.64. *Second-cycle Western Gull in slightly worn A2 plumage; dusky mottling on head and neck usually abrades to reveal white-headed "second-summer" plumage (compare with I.65–I.66). Note new gray A2 median coverts, unlike I.65. Steve N. G. Howell. Bolinas, California, 15 Apr. 2003.*

I.66. *Third-cycle Western Gull in PB3 molt. Note bright bill (compare with I.63–I.65), new B3 upperwing coverts, and shed P6 — the black area on P7 indicates where P6 had covered and protected P7, in contrast to its faded, exposed tip. The white tip of the newly incoming P4 is just visible beyond the tips of the secondaries. Mid- to late-summer manifestation of adultlike bill colors often corresponds to the growth of middle primaries, which also tend to be adultlike in appearance. Steve N. G. Howell. Bodega Bay, California, 19 June 1998.*

I.67. *Third-cycle Western Gull in PB3 molt. P1–P6 are new (and are typical third-cycle feathers with adultlike pattern), P7–P8 are growing, P9 has been shed, and P10 is an old B2 feather. Also, outer secondaries are shed, as are R1–R5 (exposing white tail coverts), with the old black R6 visible. Compare advanced molt stage of this and I.66 with fourth cycle (I.73). The white band on this bird's left leg indicates it was a chick on Southeast Farallon Island in summer 1996. Steve N. G. Howell. Bodega Bay, California, 6 July 1998.*

(photo I.68). Secondary molt starts in mid- to late July and largely completes by late September. The belly is mostly replaced by mid-June, although a few birds retain brownish B2 belly feathers into early July. Traces of new dusky markings on the head and neck first appear in mid-June (about when P7 is shed). PB3 molt finishes with full growth of the outermost primaries in October to early November. Some B3 birds are much like adults but are distinguishable by "retarded" bill patterns, smaller white primary tips and mirrors, and blackish marks on the alula and primary coverts. A few B3 birds appear not very different from "advanced" B2 birds, although tail pattern, inner primary pattern, and whiter wing-linings are usually good indicators of age. Note also that there is typically some regression in appearance: The head and neck become duskier than in worn, white-headed summer birds, and bills become duller yellow and pinkish in fall, usually with extensive black markings (compare photos I.68–I.69 with I.66).

PA3 molt starts with renewed replacement of median coverts in late August and September, although PA molt in tracts other than upperwing coverts may not start much before November or later (photo I.69). Bills start to brighten again: By December a common pattern is a yellow bill with a black subterminal ring and often a small orange-red gonys blush (photo I.70). The eyes range from dark (olive

I.68. *Third-cycle Western Gull. Fresh B3 plumage. Note piebald tail pattern, regressing bill pattern (compare with I.65–I.66), and uniformly adultlike gray upperparts (unlike I.69, I.71–I.72). Steve N. G. Howell. Bodega Bay, California, 13 Oct. 1998.*

brown) to pale (greenish white), as on adults. Through at least February or March, PA3 molt continues on the mantle, scapulars, head, and neck, so that there is a partial molt much like second-cycle birds (and often with a midwinter suspension). Molt is harder to detect than in younger age classes because old and new feathers look more alike and are relatively less worn from a shorter period between molts. Bills brighten further in late winter: By March any black is usually reduced to a small subterminal mark, and a distinct orange-red gonys

I.69. *Third-cycle Western Gull in PA3 molt (which may suspend over winter). Note dusky head and neck clouding, regressing bill pattern (compare with I.65–I.66), and relatively brown B3 wing coverts (unlike I.68, I.70) with contrasting band of fresher A3 median coverts. Steve N. G. Howell. Bodega Bay, California, 24 Nov. 1998.*

I.70. *Third-cycle Western Gull. Brightening of head and clean gray of upperparts probably due to combination of wear and PA3 molt. The yellow "ring-bill" pattern is often shown at this time. Steve N. G. Howell. Bolinas, California, 3 Jan. 2002.*

I.71. *Third-cycle Western Gull. Similar to some second-cycle birds, but note plainer and more-uniform upperwing coverts, broad white skirt, white tail with reduced black (all much like I.69). In flight this bird showed adultlike inner primaries and mostly white underwing coverts. Steve N. G. Howell. Bodega Bay, California, 21 Apr. 1999.*

I.72. *Third-cycle type Western Gull. Adultlike bill and upperparts more advanced than I.71 (but similar to I.68, I.70). Aged by black on tail and primary coverts (not visible here but obvious in flight) and lack of white tips to outer primaries (compare with I.74–I.75). Some third-cycle birds have all-white tails. Steve N. G. Howell. Bolinas, California, 21 Apr. 2003.*

spot appears. The most "retarded" birds with black subterminal bill rings overlap some "advanced" second-cycle birds in bill pattern, while many birds have adultlike bills (photos I.71–I.72).

Fourth Cycle. PB4 molt (into adult, or definitive, basic plumage) starts from mid-May to mid-June with the dropping of inner primaries and median coverts, and continues in much the same sequence as PB molts during second and third cycles—although averaging later in timing (photo I.73). Tail molt and secondary molt start from late July to mid-August,

and the first traces of new dusky markings on the head and neck appear in late July (about when P7–P8 are shed). PB4 molt finishes with full growth of outermost primaries in mid-October through mid-November, about a month earlier than on most adults.

Gray scalloping attained on the head from late July through September is often so fine that it is difficult to see—and presumably it can abrade quickly, leaving the head and neck white. Consequently, determining the timing and extent of PA molt on the head and underparts is almost impossible without in-hand ex-

I.73. *Fourth-cycle Western Gull in PB4 molt. P5 has been shed, P6–P10 are old and faded B3 feathers (compare later molt timing with second-cycle birds, I.66–I.67), and bill base is tinged pinkish. Steve N. G. Howell. Bodega Bay, California, 6 July 1998.*

I.74. *Fourth-cycle Western Gull completing PB4 molt (outer primaries not fully grown) and starting PA4 molt in median coverts. Note regression of bill colors, with pinkish mandible base and dusky subterminal band, and dusky clouding on head (compare with I.72–I.73). Primary molt averages earlier than on adults (see I.76), and white primary tips are bolder than B3 (compare with I.68–I.72). Steve N. G. Howell. Bolinas, California, 17 Oct. 2003.*

I.75. *Adult-cycle Western Gull. Clean white head appears from Dec. onward and bright bill from Nov. onward. Eye color varies from pale to dark. Steve N. G. Howell. San Francisco, California, 3 Feb. 2004.*

amination. Bills become duller in fall: They often develop flesh pink areas at the base and show dark subterminal marks more often than do adult bills (photo I.74), but by early winter most birds have bright bills again.

PA4 molt starts with median coverts in late September. After the molt of diagnostic third-cycle feathers by October, birds cannot be aged confidently to distinguish fourth-cycle individuals from adults. The percentage of cleanly white-headed "adult" birds increases from around 50 percent in early January to 95 percent or more by early March (photo I.75), presumably because of a combination of wear and molt. At least some molt of scapulars, median coverts, and tertial coverts occurs over the winter, much as in the case of third-cycle birds.

Adult Cycle. Definitive prebasic molts (DPB) start between mid-May and early July, a wide date span that presumably reflects the wide potential age range and different breeding status of birds involved (Western Gulls first breed at 3 to 10 years of age).[43] Limited data on known breeding adults indicate that their primary molt starts between early June and early July (after eggs hatch). The most obvious signs of DPB molt starting are the shedding of median coverts, tertial coverts, and inner primaries. Molt then progresses much as in other age classes, but distinguishing generations of white body feathers is not possible in the field. Tail molt and secondary molt start in mid-August to September. Dusky markings appear on the head and neck of some birds in mid- to late August (about when

P7–P8 are shed), but others at the same molt stage have apparently fresh, almost glossy-looking, white head feathers with no trace of dusky. In September up to 75 percent of birds show dusky markings on their heads and necks. In October at least 90 percent of birds have such markings, which vary from light scaling (hard to see at other than close range) to moderately heavy dusky mottling and streaking (photos I.76–I.77). DPB molt ends with full growth of the outermost primaries in early November to late December, although most

I.76. *Adult-cycle Western Gull in PB molt (outer primaries growing and shed). Note slight dusky clouding on head and pinkish suffusion at mandible base (compare with I.75, I.77). Limited dusky markings on head and neck may be lost through a combination of wear and molt so that by early winter some adults have clean white heads (compare with I.75). Steve N. G. Howell. Bolinas, California, 17 Oct. 2003.*

I.77. *Adult-cycle Western Gull. Relatively extensive dusky mottling on head and neck may indicate a fourth-cycle bird or perhaps introgression with Glaucous-winged Gull—but all other characters typical of adult Western Gull. This may represent maximum midwinter dusky head and neck markings of pure birds. Steve N. G. Howell. Petaluma, California, 27 Dec. 2001.*

birds have fully grown outer primaries by early December. Bill and leg colors fade in late summer and fall, and in September the mandible base of most adults is suffused pinkish (photo I.76); by November, many birds again have bright yellow bills.

The first signs of definitive prealternate molt (DPA) are dropped median coverts in early October. Molt then probably progresses much as in other age classes, although detecting molt is difficult because the change in aspect is largely from gray to gray and from white to white feathers, almost all of which are relatively fresh at this time. Whitening of the head occurs through December (perhaps because of wear and molt), and by January up to 50 percent of adult-plumaged birds are white headed (see above under PA4 molt). Adult Western Gulls in winter have relatively bright bills, but colors often intensify in late winter to rich orange-yellow with an expanded red gonys spot.

From this point on DPB and DPA molts are repeated in a cyclic manner, as described above. Having read the foregoing, take a close look at any white-headed gull you see regularly. It won't take long to appreciate the range of individual variation in appearance, especially within second- and third-cycle birds. After a while the use of cycles should make sense—they liberate you from preconceptions derived from terms such as "first-winter plumage," "prebreeding molt," and so on.

Here's a summary of the Western Gull molts and age characters for quick reference: Juveniles fledge in July and August and are dark brown overall with a blackish bill, strongly barred tail coverts, solidly dark tail, and dark underwings (photos I.44–I.46). A protracted PA1 molt starts between late August and October. This molt involves feathers on the head, neck, sides, mantle, and scapulars, and the molt suspends or slows down in midwinter (photos I.47–I.50). In late winter and early spring molt picks up again as old juvenal scapulars continue to be replaced, while at the same time A1 head and neck feathers and juvenile upperwing coverts and inner primaries are replaced at the start of the complete PB2 molt, which extends from about April to September (photos I.50–I.59). Before the PB2 molt finishes, the PA2 molt starts from mid-August through September with the replacement of median upperwing coverts, scapulars, and probably other feathers (photos I.58–I.59). This PA2 molt continues through to spring, like PA1 molt, and may suspend in midwinter. Characters of B2 plumage are mostly white tail coverts without extensive dark barring, a solidly dark tail, dark underwings, and distinct pinkish on the bill base. In general, B2 birds resemble juveniles overall, whereas A2 birds develop more gray on their upperparts, their heads and underparts can wear and bleach to whitish, and their bill bases can become yellow (photos I.60–I.65).

PB3 molt starts in late April to May (possibly overlapping with the end of PA2) and completes by about October (overlapping with the start of PA3 molt of scapulars and wing coverts in late August to September). B3 birds look much more adultlike than do B2 birds, but their bill patterns and plumages often regress from the brighter and more adultlike A2 colors (photos I.66–I.69). In general, B3 birds resemble adults overall: Their tail coverts and tails are white, the tails often with some blackish (but not solidly black like B2), their underwings whitish with variable dusky markings, and their bills mostly yellowish or pinkish with variable blackish and red subterminal marks. PA3 molt extends from late August or September through winter, but the duration and extent of this molt are difficult to ascertain (photos I.70–I.72). PB4 molt starts in mid-May to June and ends around November, overlapping with PA4 molt, which starts in late September to October (photos I.73–I.74). From this point on, molts are adultlike in timing (PB mainly June to December, overlapping PA from October to February or later) and vary in timing because of factors such as breeding or nonbreeding status, successful or failed breeding, and food supply and quality.

Note that there are relatively few times when gulls are not molting. For large birds, which have numerous and often large feathers to replace, *molt is a default, ongoing activity* that is only interrupted during the energy-demanding phases of breeding, migration, or during periods of cold winter weather. That is, molt doesn't necessarily occur after and before breeding; instead, breeding appears to be fitted into the molt cycle. Long-lived birds such as gulls can miss a year of breeding (and immatures don't breed for a few years), but they need to molt every year or their feathers will be inadequate for insulation and flight.

MOLT STRATEGIES OF AMERICAN GULLS

The molt strategies of a bird reflect a finely honed balance with other aspects of its life cycle—mainly, breeding and migration—in combination with food availability, environmental conditions, foraging experience, fitness, and the overall size of an individual bird. American gulls can be divided into four groups depending on their first-cycle molt strategy (table 4).[44]

Group A. These species have an extensive PF molt *and* a variable PA1 molt, so that two molts are added into the first cycle. PA1 molts produce head patterns variably intermediate in aspect between adult breeding and non-breeding, the differences likely due to individual hormone levels. Group A species are all relatively small gulls, and individuals of some species attempt to breed in their first year. Franklin's and Sabine's Gulls are long-distance migrants that can—and presumably need to—undergo complete or near-complete first-cycle molts because both species travel to food-rich pelagic waters in equatorial and southern latitudes with strong sunlight. Franklin's undergoes a partial PF molt on or near the breeding grounds and a complete or near-complete PA1 molt on the nonbreeding grounds. Sabine's Gull molts almost entirely on the nonbreeding grounds, where its complete PF and partial PA1 molts overlap in timing. As adults, most species in this group have complete PB molts and partial PA molts, with the exception of Franklin's Gull, which has a complete or near-complete PA molt as well as a complete PB molt.

Group B. A single, typically extensive, and often protracted PA1 molt occurs in the first cycle (including upperwing coverts and tertials in several species); a limited second molt may occur in some species or individuals, but this remains to be determined. Most Group B species or populations are largely sedentary or short-distance migrants of mid- and low latitudes with strong sunlight. Differences in the extent of PA1 molt between Group B and Group C may be bridged by species whose breeding range has a wide latitudinal span.[45] Adults of species in this group have complete PB molts and partial PA molts, the latter typically involving at least the head, neck, chest, mantle, and scapulars.

Group C. A single, typically limited (possibly even absent in some individuals), and often delayed PA1 molt occurs in the first cycle. Group C species or populations breed at high latitudes, where long days and abundant rich food presumably enable birds to grow relatively strong juvenal plumage that does not need to be replaced quickly—particularly when birds do not winter at low latitudes with strong sunlight. Adults of species in this group have complete PB molts and partial PA molts.

Group D. This "group" consists exclusively of the Ivory Gull, whose molting reflects an adaptation to its high Arctic environment; the short summer means that molting and breeding overlap extensively. Juveniles lack an added molt in their first cycle. The adult has a complete PB molt and apparently lacks a PA molt.

HABITAT AND BEHAVIOR

Gulls can occur just about anywhere, although they are found mainly in fairly open

TABLE 4. First-cycle Molt Strategies of American Gulls

GROUP A. PREFORMATIVE MOLT EXTENSIVE (COMPLETE IN SABINE'S GULL), FIRST PREALTERNATE MOLT VARIABLE	GROUP B. FIRST PREALTERNATE MOLT MODERATE TO EXTENSIVE; NO PREFORMATIVE MOLT	GROUP C. FIRST PREALTERNATE MOLT LIMITED (OCCASIONALLY ABSENT?); NO PREFORMATIVE MOLT	GROUP D. PREALTERNATE AND PREFORMATIVE MOLTS ABSENT
Bonaparte's Gull	Heermann's Gull	Black-legged Kittiwake	Ivory Gull
Black-headed Gull	Gray Gull	Red-legged Kittiwake	
Gray-hooded Gull	Dolphin Gull	Herring Gull complex (some)	**GROUP E. INSUFFICIENT DATA**
Brown-hooded Gull	Belcher's Gull	Lesser Black-backed Gull (some)	Swallow-tailed Gull
Andean Gull	Olrog's Gull	Slaty-backed Gull (some)	
Little Gull	Black-tailed Gull	Glaucous-winged Gull (some)	
Ross's Gull	Mew Gull complex	Great Black-backed Gull (some)	
Sabine's Gull	Ring-billed Gull	Glaucous Gull	
Laughing Gull	California Gull	Iceland Gull	
Franklin's Gull	Herring Gull complex (some)	Thayer's Gull	
Lava Gull	Yellow-legged Gull		
	Lesser Black-backed Gull (some)		
	Kelp Gull		
	Slaty-backed Gull (some?)		
	Glaucous-winged Gull (some)		
	Western Gull		
	Yellow-footed Gull		
	Great Black-backed Gull (some?)		

environments and usually near water. Broad habitat preferences and behavioral characters can be useful for identification, however. For example, an all-white gull in Florida is more likely to be a leucistic or albino individual of some common species than the ice-loving Ivory Gull. Ring-billed Gull is rare offshore along the U.S. Pacific Coast, whereas California Gull is common. An apparent Thayer's Gull dominating Western and Glaucous-winged Gulls at a fish carcass on a beach is likely to be a hybrid Glaucous-winged × Western Gull rather than the smaller and less aggressive Thayer's Gull.

Voice is not used much for gull identification—there are so many visual characters that observers tend to ignore calls. Most gulls have a wide variety of vocalizations that vary in pitch with age and are of limited use unless you are familiar with the context of a given call and the range of vocal variation in a species. Still, we have noted a few cases for which calls are helpful in distinguishing similar species.

A distinctive call, especially among the large white-headed gulls, is the long-call given in conjunction with ritualistic posturing of the head, neck, and bill. In general, this is a hostile display, given by immatures as well as by adults at any time of year, such as when fighting over food. Attention to the long-call, particularly its pitch and quality and the way it is given, may help in field identification. For example, the higher-pitched long-call of an adult Western Gull can reveal its presence in a group of Yellow-footed Gulls. California Gulls give the main part of their long-call with the head and bill pointing up at about a 90° angle to the ground. Herring Gulls long-call with the head and neck stretched out at about a 45° angle. Note, though, that immatures have higher-pitched voices than adults and that the range of variation in long-call postures is not fully known for most species.

Notes

1. AOU 1998; 2. Sibley and Monroe 1990; 3. AOU 1998; 4. del Hoyo et al. 1996; 5. Moynihan 1959; 6. Burger and Gochfeld 1996; 7. Moynihan 1959; 8. Chu 1998; 9. Crochet et al. 2000; 10. Chu 1998; 11. Ibid.; 12. Howell 2002; 13. Jehl 1987; 14. Banks 1986; 15. Yésou 2002; 16. Bell 1996; 17. Howell unpubl. data; 18. Howell and Corben 2000c; 19. Howell 2001b; 20. Hardy 2003; 21. Howell 2001a; 22. Howell et al. 1999; 23. Howell 2003a; 24. Bergman 1982; 25. Howell unpubl. data; 26. Howell

2002; 27. Monaghan and Duncan 1979;
28. Howell et al. 2003; 29. Humphrey and
Parkes 1959; 30. Humphrey and Parkes 1963;
31. Monaghan and Duncan 1979; 32. M. T.
Elliott unpubl. data for European Herring
Gull and Lesser Black-backed Gull; 33. P.
Pyle unpubl. data for Western Gull; 34. M. T.
Elliott unpubl. data for European Herring
Gull and Lesser Black-backed Gull; 35. Howell
2001c; 36. Howell 2001a; 37. Howell and
Corben 2000a; 38. Howell and Corben
2000b; 39. Howell 2003b; 40. Howell et al.
2004; 41. Howell unpubl. data; 42. Howell
and Corben 2000a; 43. Spear et al. 1995;
44. Howell 2001a; 45. Howell et al. 1999

PLATES

1.0 ADULT BREEDING BONAPARTE'S GULL. Note slaty blackish hood with white eye-crescents, slender black bill, pinkish orange legs. Kevin T. Karlson. Churchill, Manitoba, June 1996. **PP. 49, 302**

2.0 ADULT BREEDING BLACK-HEADED GULL. Note chocolate brown hues of hood in sunlight (compare with photo 2.4), relatively stout red bill, and red legs. Steve Young. Seaforth, England, Mar. 1999. **PP. 53, 306**

3.0 ADULT BREEDING GRAY-HOODED GULL WITH NONBREED-ING FRANKLIN'S GULLS (BEHIND) AND BELCHER'S GULL (LEFT). Note smoky gray hood (in fresh plumage, compare with photo 3.2), pale eye, and wingtip pattern; hindneck looks clean white in sun (compare with photo 3.2). R. L. Pitman. Paracas, Peru, Mar. 1982. **PP. 56, 309**

4.0 ADULT BREEDING BROWN-HOODED GULLS *(L. M. GLAUCODES).* Note mostly white wingtips diagnostic of this subspecies, and dark chocolate brown hood. Steve N. G. Howell. Porvenir, Magallanes, Chile, 27 Oct. 2002. **PP. 59, 312**

5.0 ADULT BREEDING ANDEAN GULL. Note blackish hood, relatively small and dark red bill, and wingtip pattern. Steve N. G. Howell. Lago Chungará, Tarapacá, Chile, 27 Oct. 1999. **PP. 64, 316**

1.1 ADULT NONBREEDING BONAPARTE'S GULL. Note slender black bill, pink legs (compare with photos 2.1–2.2). Larry Sansone. Santa Barbara, California, 12 Dec. 1992.

1.2 ADULT NONBREEDING BONAPARTE'S GULL. Slender black bill can show dull reddish at base; note smoky gray hindneck. Brian E. Small. Ventura, California, Dec. 1996.

1.3 ADULT BONAPARTE'S GULL, BREEDING ASPECT. Very rarely, some midwinter birds have a slaty blackish hood, perhaps the result of hormonal asynchrony that produced a dark hood in basic plumage rather than an early prealternate molt. This bird also shows atypically extensive white on the closed primaries (compare with photos 1.1–1.2, 1.4); note also the bright legs, typical of breeding adults. Larry Sansone. Santa Barbara, California, 17 Dec. 1995.

1.4 ADULT BREEDING BONAPARTE'S GULL. Note the slaty blackish hood, white eye-crescents, and mostly white underside to wingtip. Unlike most gulls, Bonaparte's typically nests in trees. Brian E. Small. Churchill, Manitoba, July 1988.

1.5 JUVENILE BONAPARTE'S GULL (AND JUVENILE LAUGHING GULL, RIGHT). Note small size, dark cap and hindcollar, strong ulnar bar. Distinguished from first-cycle Little Gull by longer bill, longer wingtip, and extensive pale gray on tertials; in flight, upperwing pattern is diagnostic. Michael D. Stubblefield. Jamaica Bay, New York, Sept. 2000.

1.6 JUVENILE BONAPARTE'S GULL. Paler and more faded than fresh-plumaged birds but still with brownish centered juvenal scapulars (see photo 1.5); note slender blackish bill. Marshall J. Iliff. Bideford Pool, Maine, 10 Sept. 1995.

1.7 FIRST-CYCLE BONAPARTE'S GULL, FORMATIVE PLUMAGE. Note slender black bill (compare with photos 2.6–2.7), flesh pink legs. Mike Danzenbaker. Princeton Harbor, California, 8 Nov. 1987.

1.8 FIRST-CYCLE BONAPARTE'S GULL, ALTERNATE PLUMAGE. Some first-summer birds attain a basiclike head pattern; others, like this individual, attain a partial, slaty blackish hood. Note worn juvenal tertials, flesh pink legs. Steve N. G. Howell. Anchorage, Alaska, 29 May 1999.

1.9 SECOND-CYCLE BONAPARTE'S GULL, BASIC PLUMAGE.
Much like basic adult but PB molt finishes earlier;
note dark tertial and tail marks, reduced white tips
to outer primaries, and paler legs than typical of
adult (photos 1.1–1.2). Mike Danzenbaker.
Princeton Harbor, California, 26 Aug. 1988.

**1.10 SECOND-CYCLE BONAPARTE'S GULL, COMPLETING PB2
MOLT (P10 NOT FULLY GROWN).** The diminutive size of
Bonaparte's can be readily appreciated alongside
Ring-billed Gulls. Much like basic adult but PB
molt finishes earlier; note paler legs than typical of
adult (second-cycle upperwing pattern was
apparent in flight; see photo 1.16). Steve N. G.
Howell. Point Reyes, California, 15 Sept. 2003.

1.11 ADULT NONBREEDING BONAPARTE'S GULL. Note white
leading wedge to wings, pale gray underside to
middle and inner primaries (photos 2.8–2.9), and
slender black bill. Michael D. Stubblefield. Point
Lookout, New York, Mar. 2001.

1.12 ADULT BREEDING BONAPARTE'S GULL. Note same
features as photo 1.11, plus the slaty blackish
hood. Michael D. Stubblefield. Point Lookout,
New York, Apr. 2000.

1.13 FIRST-CYCLE BONAPARTE'S GULL, FORMATIVE PLUMAGE. A darkly pigmented individual (compare with photo 1.14). Note mostly dark outer primary coverts, extensive white tongue-tips on P8–P10 (compare with photos 2.11–2.12). Bruce Hallett. Coastal Maine, 23 Sept. 1998.

1.14 FIRST-CYCLE BONAPARTE'S GULL. An average or lightly pigmented individual (compare with photo 1.13). Note dark on outer primary coverts, extensive white tongue-tips on P8–P10 (compare with photos 2.11–2.12), and slender black bill; the white post-juvenal inner rectrix may have been replaced in PA1 molt. Michael D. Stubblefield. Point Lookout, New York, Apr. 2002.

1.15 FIRST-CYCLE BONAPARTE'S GULL. Note slightly translucent white underside to primaries (compare with photo 2.11), slender black bill; the "broken" black tail band is caused by overlapping long white undertail coverts. Michael D. Stubblefield. Point Lookout, New York, Mar. 2002.

1.16 SECOND-CYCLE BONAPARTE'S GULL, BASIC PLUMAGE. Distinguished from adult (photos 1.1–1.12) by black on primary coverts and outer web of P9. Eric Preston. Monterey Bay, California, 27 Oct. 2001.

2.1 ADULT NONBREEDING BLACK-HEADED GULL. Note relatively stout, black-tipped red bill, red legs (compare with photos 1.1–1.2). Bruce Mactavish. St. John's, Newfoundland, 28 Oct. 2001.

2.2 NONBREEDING ADULT BLACK-HEADED GULL AND BONAPARTE'S GULLS. Note Black-headed's larger size, stouter bill, and paler gray hindneck. Jon Dunn. Santa Barbara, California, Jan. 1994.

2.3 ADULT BLACK-HEADED GULL (SAME BIRD AS PHOTO 2.9; IN PA MOLT WITH HOOD COMING IN) AND BONAPARTE'S GULLS. Note larger size, stouter bill, appreciably longer red legs, and earlier PA molt timing of Black-headed. Michael D. Stubblefield. Point Lookout, New York, Mar. 2002.

2.4 ADULT-TYPE BREEDING BLACK-HEADED GULL (*L. R. SIBIRICUS*) which averages larger and longer billed than nominate birds (see photo 2.0); hood looks more blackish in overcast conditions (see photo 2.0). Yoshiaki Watanabe. Choshi Chiba, Japan, 21 Apr. 2001.

2.5 JUVENILE BLACK-HEADED GULL. A typical bird in fairly fresh plumage; brown areas on many birds bleach to paler and more cinnamon hues. Note relatively stout, extensively dull-pinkish bill (compare with photos 1.5–1.6). Henry Lehto. Topinoja, Finland, 28 July 1999.

2.6 FIRST-CYCLE BLACK-HEADED GULL, FORMATIVE PLUMAGE.
Note relatively stout, black-tipped, orange-pink
bill and legs (compare with photo 1.7). Michael D.
Stubblefield. Slimbridge, England, Oct. 2002.

2.7 FIRST-CYCLE BLACK-HEADED GULL, FORMATIVE PLUMAGE.
Note same features as photo 2.6 (and compare
with photo 1.7). Bruce Hallett. Riviera Beach,
Florida, Feb. 1993.

**2.8 ADULT NONBREEDING BLACK-HEADED GULL (*L. R.
SIBIRICUS*).** Note narrow white leading wedge
contrasting with blackish middle primaries
(compare with photos 1.11–1.12). East Asian
birds average later molts than North Atlantic birds
(compare with photos 2.3, 2.9). Mike Danzenbaker. Aomori Prefecture, Japan, 21 Mar. 1999.

2.9 ADULT BLACK-HEADED GULL (SAME BIRD AS PHOTO 2.3).
Note narrow white leading wedge contrasting with
blackish middle primaries (compare with photos
1.11–1.12) and stout red bill. North Atlantic birds
average earlier molts than East Asian birds
(compare with photo 2.8). Michael D. Stubblefield. Point Lookout, New York, Mar. 2002.

2.10 ADULT-TYPE BREEDING BLACK-HEADED GULL. Note stout bill and broad wings relative to Bonaparte's Gull. Black streaks on outer webs of outer primaries (other adults are pure white here) may indicate second-cycle plumage or simply adult variation. Steve N. G. Howell. Chew Valley Lake, England, 5 May 2003.

2.11 FIRST-CYCLE BLACK-HEADED GULLS, FORMATIVE PLUMAGE. Note narrow white leading wedge and dark underside to middle primaries, orangey bill base and legs (compare with photo 1.15). Bruce Mactavish. St. John's, Newfoundland, 28 Oct. 2001.

2.12 FIRST-CYCLE BLACK-HEADED GULL, FORMATIVE PLUMAGE. Note more-prominent white leading wedge than first-cycle Bonaparte's, with less dark on outer primary coverts and primary bases; also weaker ulnar bar and stouter, pinkish based bill (compare with photos 1.13–1.14). Geoff Carey. Choshi, Japan, 11 Nov. 1999.

2.13 FIRST-CYCLE BLACK-HEADED GULL, ALTERNATE PLUMAGE. Note more-prominent white leading wedge than first-cycle Bonaparte's, with less dark on outer primary coverts and primary bases; also bigger bill and solidly dark, chocolate brown hood; some first-summer birds attain a nonbreeding head pattern (compare with photos 1.13–1.14). Steve Young. Seaforth, England, June 2000.

3.1 ADULT NONBREEDING GRAY-HOODED GULL. Note pale eye, wingtip pattern, medium gray upperparts, and indistinct dusky ear-spot. R. L. Pitman. Paracas, Peru, Nov. 1981.

3.2 ADULT BREEDING GRAY-HOODED GULL. Note pale gray hood (in worn and bleached plumage, compare with photo 3.0), pale eye, and wingtip pattern; smoky gray clouding to lower hindneck apparent in overcast conditions (compare with photo 3.0). Steve N. G. Howell. Salinas, Ecuador, 31 July 1998.

3.3 ADULT BREEDING AND FIRST-CYCLE GRAY-HOODED GULLS. On adult, note smoky gray hood (in fresh plumage, compare with photo 3.2), pale eye, wingtip pattern. First cycle from Brown-hooded Gull (for example, photo 4.7) by medium gray upperparts and all-black wingtip, including underside to P10. Jorge Veiga. Mar del Plata, Buenos Aires, Argentina, Oct.

3.4 JUVENILE GRAY-HOODED GULL (PRIMARIES NOT FULLY GROWN). Note relatively cold and dark brown hue of head markings and upperparts, relatively stout bill (compare with photos 4.4–4.5, 5.4–5.5). Dan Lane. Villa, Peru, May 2001.

3.5 FIRST-CYCLE GRAY-HOODED GULL. Note indistinct dusky ear-spot, relatively long and stout bill, and all-black underside to wingtip. Steve N. G. Howell. Salinas, Ecuador, 1 Aug. 1998.

3.6 SECOND-CYCLE GRAY-HOODED GULL, COMPLETING PB2 MOLT (P9–P10 STILL GROWING, THUS NO WHITE MIRROR VISIBLE ON UNDERSIDE OF WINGTIP). Note indistinct, smudgy ear-spot, relatively long and stout bill, medium gray upperparts (compare with Brown-hooded Gull); aged by dark eyes. Steve N. G. Howell. Salinas, Ecuador, 31 July 1998.

3.7 SECOND-CYCLE BREEDING GRAY-HOODED GULL. Distinguished from adult by dark eyes and relatively extensive black bill tip. Steve N. G. Howell. Salinas, Ecuador, 1 Aug. 1998.

3.8 ADULT NONBREEDING GRAY-HOODED GULL, COMPLETING PB PRIMARY MOLT (P8–P10 OLD). Note extensive black wingtip with white mirror-band on P9–P10, dusky underwings, indistinct ear-spot, and long bill. R. L. Pitman. Paracas, Peru, Nov. 1981.

3.9 ADULT BREEDING GRAY-HOODED GULL. Note distinctive upperwing pattern, smoky gray hood. Dan Lane. Lima, Peru, late Aug. 2003.

3.10 ADULT BREEDING GRAY-HOODED GULL. Note broad wings, dark underwings with white mirror-band on P9–P10, smoky gray hood, and pale eyes. Steve N. G. Howell. Salinas, Ecuador, 31 July 1998.

3.11 FIRST-CYCLE GRAY-HOODED GULL. Note extensive black wingtip without subterminal white marks, indistinct ear-spot, and relatively long bill (compare with photo 4.16). Steve N. G. Howell. Salinas, Ecuador, 31 July 1998.

3.12 FIRST-CYCLE GRAY-HOODED GULL. Although this photo is of the nominate African subspecies *cirrocephalus*, no appreciable differences are known between the two subspecies in this plumage. Note the lack of a white mirror-band in the black wingtip; some birds, like this individual, lack black tips to primary coverts (compare with photo 3.11). Arnoud B. van den Berg. Lambert's Bay, Southwest Cape, South Africa, 13 Mar. 1999.

4.1 ADULT NONBREEDING BROWN-HOODED GULL *(L. M. GLAUCODES)*, COMPLETING PB MOLT (P7–P10 OLD). Note mostly white wingtip diagnostic of this subspecies; also note later molt timing than second-cycle (photo 4.10) and paler gray upperparts than Gray-hooded Gull. Steve N. G. Howell. Valdés Peninsula, Chubut, Argentina, 27 Jan. 1999.

4.2 ADULT BREEDING BROWN-HOODED GULL *(L. M. GLAUCODES)*. Note mostly white wingtips diagnostic of this subspecies (compare with photo 4.3) and dark chocolate brown hood. Steve N. G. Howell. Porvenir, Magallanes, Chile, 27 Oct. 2002.

4.3 ADULT BREEDING BROWN-HOODED GULL *(L. M. MACULIPENNIS)*, AND FIRST-SUMMER BIRD IN FOREGROUND. Note extensively black dorsal wingtips of this subspecies (compare with photo 4.2), and dark chocolate brown hood. Judy Davis. Punta Rasa, Buenos Aires, Argentina, 25 Nov. 2003.

4.4 JUVENILE BROWN-HOODED GULL *(L. M. GLAUCODES)*. Note relatively warm and medium brown tone of head markings and upperparts, relatively slender bill (compare with photo 3.4), and wingtip pattern: distinct white tips to outer primaries, large white mirror on underside of P10; northern subspecies *maculipennis* has smaller white primary tips and mirror (photo 4.7). Enrique Couve. Torres del Paine, Magallanes, Chile, Jan. 2003.

4.5 FIRST-CYCLE BROWN-HOODED GULL (PRESUMED *L. M. GLAUCODES*). Note same features as photo 4.4 (upperparts mixed with pale gray F1 scapulars). Steve N. G. Howell. Valdés Peninsula, Chubut, Argentina, 27 Jan. 1999.

4.6 FIRST-CYCLE BROWN-HOODED GULL (*L. M. GLAUCODES*). A very lightly pigmented individual (compare with photos 4.4–4.5), mostly or entirely in juvenal plumage and with an unmarked, all-white tail. Note wingtip pattern. Steve N. G. Howell. Río Grande, Tierra del Fuego, Argentina, 8 Feb. 1999.

4.7 FIRST-CYCLE BROWN-HOODED GULLS (*L. M. MACULIPENNIS*). Note reduced white primary tips and smaller mirror on underside of P10 (compare with photos 3.3, 4.4–4.6). Roberto Guller. Miramar, Buenos Aires, Argentina, late Feb. 2002.

4.8 FIRST-CYCLE BROWN-HOODED GULL (*L. M. MACULIPENNIS*). Note extensive molt of upperparts and that small white primary tips have worn away to leave mostly black wingtip (compare with photo 4.9). Roberto Guller. Costanera Sur, Buenos Aires, Argentina, 1 Oct. 2003.

4.9 FIRST-CYCLE BROWN-HOODED GULL (*L. M. GLAUCODES*). Note wingtip pattern, with relatively bold white primary tips, and no molt of upperwing coverts (compare with photo 4.8); also bright red bill and legs shown by some first-summer birds. Steve N. G. Howell. Punta Arenas, Magallanes, Chile, 3 Nov. 1994.

4.10 SECOND-CYCLE BROWN-HOODED GULL (PRESUMED *L. M. GLAUCODES*), COMPLETING PB2 MOLT (P10 NOT FULLY GROWN). Bold white primary tips and relatively long, bicolored bill rule out Gray-hooded and Andean Gulls, respectively. Aged by molt timing, bill color and pattern (compare with photos 4.1, 4.11). Outer primaries show a common pattern of second-cycle *glaucodes* (and similar to adult *maculipennis*; compare with photos 4.3, 4.15). Steve N. G. Howell. Valdés Peninsula, Chubut, Argentina, 27 Jan. 1999.

4.11 SECOND-CYCLE AND ADULT NONBREEDING BROWN-HOODED GULLS *(L. M. GLAUCODES)* WITH BLACKISH OYSTER-CATCHER *(HAEMATOPUS ATER)*. On second-cycle birds (for example, back right and front left of oyster-catcher) note bold black-and-white wingtip pattern (suggesting adult nominate *maculipennis*, which averages smaller white primary tips) and advanced molt timing; on adults (for example, back left and front right of oystercatcher) note all-white wingtips, with P10 still old on at least front bird. Gonzalo González Cifuentes. Chiloé, 18 Mar. 2003.

4.12 THIRD-CYCLE NONBREEDING BROWN-HOODED GULL (PRE-SUMED *L. M. GLAUCODES*) IN PB3 MOLT (P8–P10 OLD AND WITH B2 PATTERN). The possibility of extralimital *maculipennis* is difficult to rule out. Steve N. G. Howell. Río Grande, Tierra del Fuego, Argentina, 9 Feb. 1999.

4.13 ADULT BREEDING BROWN-HOODED GULLS *(L. M. GLAUCODES)*. Distinctive; note extensive white wingtips (compare with photo 4.15). Steve N. G. Howell. Porvenir, Magallanes, Chile, 27 Oct. 2002.

4.14 ADULT BREEDING BROWN-HOODED GULL *(L. M. GLAUCODES)*. Note same features as photo 4.13. Steve N. G. Howell. Porvenir, Magallanes, Chile, 27 Oct. 2002.

4.15 ADULT OR SECOND-CYCLE BROWN-HOODED GULL *(L. M. MACULIPENNIS)*. Compare extensive subterminal black on outer primaries with *glaucodes* (photos 4.13–4.14, 4.19). Alvaro Jaramillo. San Clemente del Tuyú, Buenos Aires, Argentina, 26 Nov. 1991.

4.17 FIRST-CYCLE BROWN-HOODED GULL *(L. M. GLAUCODES)*, ALTERNATE PLUMAGE. Note same features as photo 4.16. Steve N. G. Howell. Puerto Montt, Llanqui-hue, Chile, 31 Oct. 2002.

4.16 FIRST-CYCLE BROWN-HOODED GULL *(L. M. GLAUCODES)*, MOSTLY IN JUVENAL PLUMAGE. Distinguished from Gray-hooded Gull by white mirror-band, from Andean Gull by relatively long, bicolored bill and narrower black medial and subterminal bands on outer primaries. R. L. Pitman. Puerto Montt, Llanquihue, Chile, 7 Mar. 1994.

4.18 FIRST-CYCLE BROWN-HOODED GULL *(L. M. GLAUCODES)*, **ALTERNATE PLUMAGE.** Note relatively extensive black in wingtip (see photo 4.17; possibly overlapping with Andean Gull, although subterminal black on outer primaries is relatively narrow). Distinguished from Gray-hooded Gull by white mirror-band and dark hood, from Andean Gull by relatively long bill. Steve N. G. Howell. Puerto Montt, Llanquihue, Chile, 31 Oct. 2002.

4.19 FIRST-CYCLE BROWN-HOODED GULL *(L. M. GLAUCODES)*, **PRESUMABLY ALTERNATE PLUMAGE.** Distinguished from Gray-hooded Gull by wingtip pattern, from Andean Gull by reddish bill and legs and relatively narrow black subterminal band on outer primaries; note basiclike head pattern; compare with photos 4.17–4.18. Steve N. G. Howell. Porvenir, Magallanes, Chile, 26 Oct. 2004.

4.20 SECOND-CYCLE BROWN-HOODED GULL *(L. M. GLAU-CODES).* Aged by advanced molt timing (adults here at this time had old outer primaries yet to molt) and wingtip pattern (compare with photos 4.11, 4.13–4.14): black subterminal bands on outer primaries suggest adult *maculipennis*, but note bolder white tips to P6–P10 (compare with photo 4.15). R. L. Pitman. Puerto Montt, Llanquihue, Chile, 7 Mar. 1994.

4.21 SECOND-CYCLE BREEDING BROWN-HOODED GULL *(L. M. GLAUCODES).* Distinguished from adult *glaucodes* by black on tips of outer primaries (compare with photos 4.13–4.14), from adult Andean Gull by narrower subterminal black on outer primaries. Steve N. G. Howell. Laguna El Peral, Santiago, Chile, 5 Nov. 2003.

5.1 ADULT NONBREEDING ANDEAN GULLS. Note ample-chested profile that often accentuates relatively small head, which has a small dark ear-spot and relatively small dark bill. Dan Lane. Lago Titicaca, Bolivia, early Sept. 2000.

5.2 ADULT-TYPE NONBREEDING ANDEAN GULL WITH FIRST-CYCLE BELCHER'S GULL. Note large overall size, relatively small blackish bill, and wingtip pattern. Adult nonbreeding plumage similar but whiter headed with a distinct dark ear-spot (compare with photo 5.6). Most adults at this season and latitude are breeding (see photos 5.0, 5.3), so this may be a second-cycle bird in alternate plumage. Steve N. G. Howell. Lluta river mouth, Tarapacá, Chile, 24 Oct. 1999.

5.3 ADULT BREEDING ANDEAN GULL IN WORN ALTERNATE PLUMAGE (WHITE PRIMARY TIPS ABRADED). Note blackish hood, relatively small and dark-reddish bill, and wingtip pattern. This bird was feeding large young. Steve N. G. Howell. Lago Chungará, Tarapacá, Chile, 10 Nov. 2003.

5.4 JUVENILE ANDEAN GULLS. Note relatively small dark bills and variation in brown dappling on upper-parts. Steve N. G. Howell. Lago Chungará, Tarapacá, Chile, 10 Nov. 2003.

5.5 FIRST-CYCLE ANDEAN GULL, MOSTLY IN JUVENAL PLUMAGE (SOME SCAPULARS APPARENTLY SHED; SAME BIRD AS PHOTO 5.11). Note relatively small and blackish bill, fine white primary tips. Still being fed by parents. Steve N. G. Howell. Lago Chungará, Tarapacá, Chile, 10 Nov. 2003.

5.6 FIRST-CYCLE ANDEAN GULL, FORMATIVE PLUMAGE. Note clean white head with small but distinct dark ear-spot, relatively small and blackish bill, and wingtip pattern; aged by brownish ulnar bar and tertial centers (difficult to see at this angle). Steve N. G. Howell. Laguna del Laja, Bío-Bío, Chile, 24 Aug. 1997.

5.7 FIRST-CYCLE ANDEAN GULL, ALTERNATE PLUMAGE. Note relatively small dark bill, blackish speckled half-hood, and wingtip pattern. Steve N. G. Howell. Near Icalma, Malleco, Chile, 10 Nov. 1999.

5.8 ADULT BREEDING ANDEAN GULL. Note blackish hood and diagnostic wingtip pattern with black medial stripes and large white mirror-band. Steve N. G. Howell. Lago Chungará, Tarapacá, Chile, 27 Oct. 1999.

5.9 ADULT BREEDING ANDEAN GULL. Note diagnostic upperwing-tip pattern with black medial stripes and large white mirror-band. Steve N. G. Howell. Lago Chungará, Tarapacá, Chile, 27 Oct. 1999.

5.10 ADULT BREEDING ANDEAN GULLS. Note diagnostic underwing-tip pattern with large white mirror-band bordered black. Steve N. G. Howell. Lago Chungará, Tarapacá, Chile, 10 Nov. 2003.

5.11 FIRST-CYCLE ANDEAN GULL, MOSTLY IN JUVENAL PLUMAGE (SAME BIRD AS PHOTO 5.5). Note relatively broad black medial and subterminal bands on outer primaries, and blackish bill. Steve N. G. Howell. Lago Chungará, Tarapacá, Chile, 10 Nov. 2003.

5.12 FIRST-CYCLE ANDEAN GULL. Note small dark ear-spot, relatively small dark bill, broad black medial and subterminal bands on outer primaries, and adultlike white mirror-band. Steve N. G. Howell. Salar de Surire, Tarapacá, Chile, 30 Oct. 1999.

5.13 FIRST-CYCLE ANDEAN GULL. Underwing pattern suggests adult (photo 5.10) but some Brown-hooded Gulls similar (for example, photo 4.18); best separated by larger size but relatively smaller dark bill; note also smaller dark ear-spot and relatively broad black subterminal band on outer primaries. Alvaro Jaramillo. Lago Chungará, Tarapacá, Chile, 30 July 2001.

6.0 ADULT BREEDING LITTLE GULL. Note lack of white eye-crescents on extensive black hood, and relatively blunt whitish wingtips. Steve Young. Seaforth, England, May 2001. **PP. 68, 320**

7.0 ADULT BREEDING ROSS'S GULL. Unmistakable: note black neck ring, small bill, and long smoky gray wingtips. Kevin T. Karlson. Churchill, Manitoba, June 1996. **PP. 71, 323**

6.1 ADULT NONBREEDING LITTLE GULL. Note dark cap, slender black bill, solid whitish wingtip on near wing, and broad white tip on underside of far wing. Brian E. Small. Salton Sea, California, early Feb. 1994.

6.2 JUVENILE LITTLE GULL. Note bold, blackish-brown cap, hindcollar, and extensive dark upperpart markings, including tertials. Steve Young. Crosby, England, Sept. 1994.

6.3 FIRST-CYCLE LITTLE GULL. Note dark cap, slender black bill, and very dark ulnar bar and tertials. Mike Danzenbaker. Europe, Dec. 2001.

6.4 FIRST-CYCLE LITTLE GULL, ALTERNATE PLUMAGE. Note smoky gray cap and hindneck (some birds attain blackish hoods, rarely solid) and slender black bill; tertials have apparently been shed. Steve Young. Seaforth, England, May 2002.

6.5 SECOND-CYCLE LITTLE GULL (WITH SANDERLING, *CALIDRIS ALBA*); IN PB2 MOLT (P9–P10 OLD). Note small size, dark cap, and slender black bill; broad white tips to incoming middle primaries rule out Bonaparte's Gull (see photo 6.6). Greg W. Lasley. Port Mahon, Delaware, 24 July 1996.

6.6 SECOND-CYCLE LITTLE GULL (RIGHT) WITH BONAPARTE'S GULL (LEFT); BOTH IN PB2 MOLT (P9–P10 OLD). Note Little's small size, shorter bill and legs, and pattern of incoming middle and outer primaries: pale gray with broad white tips, as opposed to mostly black with fine white tips on Bonaparte's. Jon Dunn. Crowley Lake, California, 6 Aug. 1987.

6.7 SECOND-CYCLE BREEDING LITTLE GULL. Note lack of white eye-crescents; blackish wingtip markings indicate second cycle (compare with photo 6.15). Steve Young. Seaforth, England, May 1999.

6.8 ADULT NONBREEDING LITTLE GULL. Note white trailing edge and tip to pale gray upperwings; also dark cap and small, slender bill. Bruce Hallett. West Point, Georgia, 13 Feb. 1998.

6.9 ADULT BREEDING LITTLE GULL. Note white trailing edge and tip to pale gray upperwings and dusky underwings; also lack of white eye-crescents. Steve Young. Seaforth, England, May 1995.

6.10 JUVENILE LITTLE GULL. Note bold blackish M pattern on upperparts, dark cap and hindcollar/ mantle, and dark secondary bar. Greg W. Lasley. Lake Benbrook, Texas, 17 Nov. 1999 (late in the season to be in this plumage).

6.11 FIRST-CYCLE LITTLE GULL, FORMATIVE PLUMAGE. Note bold blackish M pattern on upperwings, dark cap, dark secondary bar, and slender bill. Mike Danzenbaker. Europe, Dec. 2001.

6.12 FIRST-CYCLE LITTLE GULL (SECOND FROM RIGHT) WITH BONAPARTE'S GULLS. Relative to Bonaparte's, note smaller size, much bolder blackish M pattern on upperwings, and lack of black trailing edge to inner primaries. S. LaFrance/VIREO. Cape May, New Jersey, May 1994.

6.13 FIRST-CYCLE LITTLE GULL. Occasional, aberrant individuals have a dark wash to the whole upperwing (compare with photo 6.11). Note underlying blackish M pattern and dark cap. Steve Young. Seaforth, England, May 2002.

6.14 FIRST-CYCLE LITTLE GULL, ALTERNATE PLUMAGE. Note bold blackish M pattern on upperwings, dark cap, and dark secondary bar. Steve Young. Seaforth, England, May 1998.

6.15 SECOND-CYCLE BREEDING LITTLE GULL. Distinguished from adult by blackish subterminal marks on outer primaries (compare with photo 6.7); relatively pale wing-linings also more typical of second cycle than adult. Steve Young. Seaforth, England, May 1998.

7.1 ADULT BREEDING ROSS'S GULL AT NEST. Unmistakable: note same features as photo 7.0. PB molt of inner primaries had started by this date (P5 shed). Igor Chupin. Taimyr, Russia, July 1991.

7.2 JUVENILE ROSS'S GULL (SAME BIRD AS PHOTO 7.9). Distinctive but rarely seen; note small bill, dark-brown upperparts with scaly pattern, white lores, and flared white postocular patch. George Higgins. Herschel Island, Yukon, late July 1991.

7.3 JUVENILE ROSS'S GULL. Distinctive but rarely seen; note same features as photo 7.2. Painting by Martin T. Elliott.

7.4 FIRST-CYCLE ROSS'S GULL, FORMATIVE PLUMAGE. Note long, pointed wingtip and tail (black tail tip raised slightly above wingtips), small and fairly stubby black bill, and bold upperwing pattern. This individual has fairly extensive smoky gray and dark markings on head and neck (compare with photos 7.5–7.6). Yasuhiro Kawasaki. Hokkaido, Japan, 4 Dec. 1995.

7.5 FIRST-CYCLE ROSS'S GULL, FORMATIVE PLUMAGE (LONGEST SCAPULARS STILL JUVENAL). Note long, pointed wingtip and tail (black tail tip visible under far wingtip), small and fairly stubby black bill, whitish crown, and bold upperwing pattern. Relatively weak head markings of this individual (compare with photo 7.4) accentuated by bright lighting. J. Fuhrman/VIREO. Honshu, Japan, Jan. 2000.

7.6 FIRST-CYCLE ROSS'S GULL, FORMATIVE PLUMAGE (SAME BIRD AS PHOTO 7.12). Note long, pointed, and boldly patterned wingtips, petite black bill, and whitish crown. Killian Mullarney. Galway, Ireland, Jan. 2000.

7.7 SECOND-CYCLE ROSS'S GULL (LEFT) WITH BLACK-HEADED GULL (RIGHT). Note long, pale gray wingtip, white crown, and petite black bill. Aged in field by dark marks on some lesser upperwing coverts; also note dull legs. Arnoud B. van den Berg. Ijmuiden, Netherlands, 23 Nov. 1992.

7.8 ADULT NONBREEDING ROSS'S GULL (SAME BIRD AS PHOTO 7.9). Unmistakable: note pale gray upperwings with broad white trailing edge out to inner primaries, graduated tail, and white head set off from gray neck and mantle. Steve Young. Fraserburgh Scotland, Jan. 1993.

7.9 ADULT NONBREEDING ROSS'S GULL (SAME BIRD AS PHOTO 7.8). Unmistakable: note dusky gray underwings with broad white trailing edge out to inner primaries, long, graduated tail, and smoky gray collar. Steve Young. Fraserburgh, Scotland, Jan. 1993.

7.10 JUVENILE ROSS'S GULL (SAME BIRD AS PHOTO 7.2).
Distinctive but rarely seen; note bright white
trailing triangle on upperwings, dark brown
median coverts, graduated tail with black-tipped
central rectrices, and face pattern. George
Higgins. Herschel Island, Yukon, late July 1991.

7.11 JUVENILE ROSS'S GULL. Distinctive but rarely
seen; note striking upperwing pattern and graduated tail with black tip to longest feathers.
Painting by Martin T. Elliott.

**7.12 FIRST-CYCLE ROSS'S GULL, FORMATIVE PLUMAGE (SAME
BIRD AS PHOTO 7.6).** Note long, pointed wings with
bold black M pattern and white secondaries, long,
black-tipped tail, contrasting white head, and
petite bill. Killian Mullarney. Galway, Ireland, Jan.
2000.

7.13 FIRST-CYCLE ROSS'S GULL, ALTERNATE PLUMAGE. Note
long, pointed wings with bold black M pattern and
white secondaries, long and graduated tail
(replaced in PA1 molt), and black neck ring. Pink
flush from head to tail shows most strongly in
overcast conditions like this. Marshall J. Iliff.
St. Lawrence Island, Alaska, 31 May 2001.

7.14 FIRST-CYCLE ROSS'S GULL, ALTERNATE PLUMAGE.
Unmistakable: note same features as photo 7.13.
Marshall J. Iliff. St. Lawrence Island, Alaska,
31 May 2001.

8.0 ADULT BLACK-LEGGED KITTIWAKE, ALTERNATE PLUMAGE *(R. T. POLLICARIS).* Note plain yellow bill and medium gray upperwings with clean-cut black wingtips. Distinguished from Red-legged Kittiwake (photo 9.0) by paler gray upperwings with less-contrasting white trailing edge (especially on inner primaries) and longer bill. Bruce Hallett. St. Paul Island, Alaska, June 1993. **PP. 75, 327**

9.0 ADULT BREEDING RED-LEGGED KITTIWAKE. Note evenly slaty gray upperparts with clean-cut white trailing edge out to inner primaries, relatively short, stubby bill (compare with photo 8.0). Martin Hale. Near Hall Island, Alaska, 12 June 2003. **PP. 79, 328**

8.1 ADULT NONBREEDING BLACK-LEGGED KITTIWAKE *(R. T. TRIDACTYLA)*. Note plain yellow bill, head pattern, and wingtip pattern (P6 shows black spot framed in white). PB molt complete or nearly so (P10 may not be fully grown; compare with photo 8.2). Bruce Hallett. Off Gloucester, Massachusetts, Oct. 1992.

8.2 ADULT NONBREEDING BLACK-LEGGED KITTIWAKE *(R. T. POLLICARIS)*, IN PB MOLT (WITH P7–P10 OLD). Note short black legs, all-black wingtips, and head pattern. Relatively long bill and later PB molt timing (compare with photo 8.1) are typical of North Pacific populations. Mike Danzenbaker. Aomori Prefecture, Japan, 11 Nov. 1998.

8.3 ADULT BREEDING BLACK-LEGGED KITTIWAKE *(R. T. TRIDACTYLA)*. Note plain yellow bill (relatively short; compare with photo 8.2), wingtip pattern. Steve Young. Seaforth, England, May 1994.

8.4 ADULT BREEDING BLACK-LEGGED KITTIWAKE *(R. T. POLLICARIS)*. Occasional indivduals have orangey legs; distinguished from Red-legged Kittiwake by relatively long and slender bill, and also paler gray upperparts (not visible here). Steve N. G. Howell. St. Paul Island, Alaska, 11 June 1998.

8.5 ADULT BREEDING AND JUVENILE BLACK-LEGGED KITTI-WAKE *(R. T. TRIDACTYLA).* Note short black legs and wingtip pattern of adult; plain gray back and black hindcollar of juvenile. Steve Young. Farne Islands, England, July 2000.

8.6 RECENTLY FLEDGED (WINGTIPS NOT FULLY GROWN) JUVENILE BLACK-LEGGED KITTIWAKE *(R. T. TRIDACTYLA).* Note medium-length black bill and black hindcollar. Steve Young. Crosby, England, July 2001.

8.7 FIRST-CYCLE BLACK-LEGGED KITTIWAKE (SUBSPECIES UNCERTAIN), MOSTLY OR ENTIRELY IN JUVENAL PLUMAGE. Note short dusky legs, black hindcollar, and medium-length black bill. Jon Dunn. Sandis Lake, Mississippi, 26 Dec. 1992.

8.8 FIRST-CYCLE BLACK-LEGGED KITTIWAKE *(R. T. POLLICA-RIS),* MOSTLY OR ENTIRELY IN JUVENAL PLUMAGE. Note short dusky legs and black hindcollar. Bill typically develops variable amounts of pale at base by mid- to late winter. Chris L. Wood. San Blas, Nayarit, Mexico, 9 Jan. 2004.

8.9 FIRST-CYCLE BLACK-LEGGED KITTIWAKE *(R. T. POLLICA-RIS).* By summer bill is mostly yellow (compare with photos 8.7–8.8), and dark collar reduced or absent. Gary H. Rosenberg. St. Paul Island, Alaska, June 1989.

8.10 ADULT NONBREEDING BLACK-LEGGED KITTIWAKE *(R. T. TRIDACTYLA).* Relative to Pacific birds (see photo 8.0), Atlantic kittiwakes average a smaller black wingtip and paler primary bases (see photo 8.17) but with contrast often washed out in sunlight, as on this bird. Steve N. G. Howell. St. John's, Newfoundland, 3 Feb. 2002.

8.11 ADULT BREEDING BLACK-LEGGED KITTIWAKE *(R. T. POLLICARIS)* **IN PB MOLT (P1 GROWING, P2 SHED).** Note plain yellow bill and medium gray upperwings with clean-cut black wingtips. Pacific populations average larger black wingtip than Atlantic birds (compare with photo 8.10). Steve N. G. Howell. Seward, Alaska, 2 July 2003.

8.12 ADULT NONBREEDING BLACK-LEGGED KITTIWAKE, BASIC PLUMAGE *(R. T. TRIDACTYLA).* Note pale underwings with clean-cut black wingtips, head pattern, and plain yellow bill. Steve N. G. Howell. St. John's, Newfoundland, 3 Feb. 2002.

8.13 ADULT NONBREEDING BLACK-LEGGED KITTIWAKE *(R. T. POLLICARIS)* **IN PB MOLT.** Note whitish underwings with clean-cut black wingtips, plain yellow bill. In years of poor food supply, PB molt of some Pacific birds can be protracted over the winter; in this Mar. individual P10 and most of the secondaries are still old, and the dark spot near the base of P10 is the black tip of the incoming P9. Larry Sansone. Ventura, California, 11 Mar. 1990.

8.14 FIRST-CYCLE BLACK-LEGGED KITTIWAKE *(R. T. POLLICA-RIS).* Note black M pattern on upperwing with bold whitish trailing triangle, black "double hindcollar." Mike Danzenbaker. Cordell Bank, California, 7 Dec. 1986.

8.15 FIRST-CYCLE BLACK-LEGGED KITTIWAKE *(R. T. POLLICA-RIS).* Note black "double hindcollar," and translucent white secondaries. R. L. Pitman. Oceanside, California, 1 Jan. 1979.

8.16 FIRST-CYCLE BLACK-LEGGED KITTIWAKE *(R. T. POLLICA-RIS).* Note black M pattern on upperwing with bold whitish trailing triangle, and black "double hindcollar." R. L. Pitman. Channel Islands, California, June 1976.

8.17 SECOND-CYCLE BREEDING BLACK-LEGGED KITTIWAKE *(R. T. TRIDACTYLA).* Resembles adult (compare with photo 8.10) but with slightly more extensive black wingtip and variable black on primary coverts and alula. Harry J. Lehto. Krýsuvíkurberg, Iceland, 31 May 1999.

9.1 NONBREEDING ADULT-TYPE RED-LEGGED KITTIWAKE.
Note short bill, slaty gray upperparts, and red legs.
Some nonbreeding summer birds (probably both
second-cycle and adult) attain basiclike head
patterns in alternate plumage, as on this individual. A. Morris/VIREO. St. Paul Island, Alaska,
July 1998.

**9.2 BREEDING ADULT RED-LEGGED KITTIWAKE (RIGHT) AND
BLACK-LEGGED KITTIWAKE (LEFT).** Red-legged is smaller
and stockier with a shorter bill, larger eye, and
darker gray upperparts with less-contrasting black
wingtips. Steve N. G. Howell. St. Paul Island,
Alaska, 11 June 1998.

**9.4 JUVENILE/FIRST-CYCLE RED-LEGGED KITTIWAKE IN EARLY
WINTER.** Note short bill and legs, weaker dark collar
than Black-legged Kittiwake. Painting by Martin T.
Elliott.

9.3 ADULT BREEDING RED-LEGGED KITTIWAKE. Besides the
short and bright red legs, note the relatively short
bill and slaty gray upperparts. Mike Danzenbaker.
St. Paul Island, Alaska, 1 June 1990.

9.5 SECOND-CYCLE RED-LEGGED KITTIWAKE (RIGHT) IN PB2 MOLT (COMPARE WITH PHOTO 9.6) AND BLACK-LEGGED KITTIWAKE (LEFT). Red-legged is smaller and stockier with a shorter bill and darker gray upperparts; legs orange-red by first summer. Jon Dunn. St. Paul Island, Alaska, 10 June 1988.

9.6 SECOND-CYCLE RED-LEGGED KITTIWAKE IN PB2 MOLT (P6–P10 OLD) AND BLACK-LEGGED KITTIWAKE (BEHIND). Note relatively short, stubby bill, slaty gray upperparts, and bright orange-red legs. Jon Dunn. St. Paul Island, Alaska, 10 June 1988.

9.7 ADULT BREEDING RED-LEGGED KITTIWAKE. Note relatively short bill and evenly slaty gray upperparts with clean-cut white trailing edge out to inner primaries; extensive black on outer web of P9 may indicate a second-cycle bird. Mike Danzenbaker. St. Paul Island, Alaska, 4 June 1990.

9.8 ADULT BREEDING RED-LEGGED KITTIWAKE. Besides red legs, note dusky gray bases to underside of remiges (compare with photos 8.12–8.13) and relatively short, stubby bill. Martin Hale. Near Hall Island, Alaska, 12 June 2003.

9.9 ADULT BREEDING RED-LEGGED KITTIWAKE. Besides bright red legs, note slaty gray upperparts with clean-cut white trailing edge out to inner primaries and dusky gray bases to underside of primaries (compare with photos 8.12–8.13). Steve N. G. Howell. St. Paul Island, Alaska, 11 June 1998.

9.10 JUVENILE/FIRST-CYCLE RED-LEGGED KITTIWAKE IN EARLY WINTER. Note extensive white trailing triangle on upperwings and all-white tail. Painting by Martin T. Elliott.

9.11 SECOND-CYCLE RED-LEGGED KITTIWAKE IN PB2 MOLT (P5–P10 OLD). Note broad white trailing edge to upperwings and all-white tail. Jon Dunn. St. Paul Island, Alaska, 10 June 1988.

9.12 SECOND-CYCLE RED-LEGGED KITTIWAKE IN PB2 MOLT (P7–P10 OLD). Note slaty gray upperwings with broad white trailing edge (uneven due to molt of greater coverts) and all-white tail; also bill size and shape, reddish feet. Martin Hale. Near Pribilof Islands, Alaska, 10 June 2003.

9.13 SECOND-CYCLE RED-LEGGED KITTIWAKE IN PB2 MOLT (P7–P10 OLD). Note dusky bases to primaries; also bill size and shape, reddish feet. Martin Hale. Near Pribilof Islands, Alaska, 10 June 2003.

9.14 SECOND-CYCLE RED-LEGGED KITTIWAKE (UPPER BIRD) IN PB2 MOLT (P8–P10 OLD) WITH BLACK-LEGGED KITTIWAKES. Note slaty gray upperwings with broad white trailing edge (uneven due to molt of greater coverts). W. Edward Harper. St. Paul Island, Alaska, 14 June 1993.

10.0 ADULT BREEDING SABINE'S GULL. Unmistakable: note dark slaty hood with red orbital ring and black neck ring (no white eye-crescents) and yellow-tipped bill; compare bold white tips to outermost primaries with photo 10.2. Brian E. Small. Nome, Alaska, June 1998. **PP. 83, 335**

11.0 ADULT BREEDING SWALLOW-TAILED GULL. Unmistakable: note how lighting and subtle posture differences affect appearance (compare with photo 11.2). Bruce Hallett. Galápagos, Ecuador, May 1997. **PP. 86, 339**

10.1 ADULT NONBREEDING SABINE'S GULL IN PB MOLT (SAME BIRD AS PHOTO. 10.8). Note blackish mottled hindcollar, slaty gray upperparts, and slender, yellow-tipped bill; the bold white primary tips typical of summer birds (for example, photo 10.0) are reduced by wear. Steve N. G. Howell. Celestún, Yucatán, Mexico, 18 Feb. 1989.

10.2 ADULT-TYPE BREEDING SABINE'S GULL. Unmistakable: note lack of bold white tips to P9–P10 (compare with photo 10.0), perhaps indicating a second-cycle bird. Kevin T. Karlson. Milne Point, Alaska, July 1994.

10.4 JUVENILE SABINE'S GULL. Distinctive: note same features as photo 10.3. Jon Dunn. Lake Mead, Nevada, 5 Oct. 1993.

10.3 JUVENILE SABINE'S GULL. Distinctive; note slaty brownish gray hindneck and scaly upperparts, elegant structure. Mike Danzenbaker. Palo Alto, California, 3 Oct. 1987.

10.5 PRESUMED FIRST-CYCLE (POSSIBLY RETARDED SECOND-CYCLE) SABINE'S GULL WITH ADULT LAUGHING GULL (BEHIND). Distinctive: note small size, dusky mottled head and hindneck (first-summer head and neck pattern variable; compare with photo 10.6), and yellow bill tip (absent on some first-summer birds). Kevin T. Karlson. Stone Harbor, New Jersey, May 2001.

10.6 SABINE'S GULLS. A fall group at sea: juvenile at front center, presumed adult at rear, first-summer bird at right, and perhaps another first-summer bird at left (note dusky smudge on hindneck, relatively pale bill tip). Steve N. G. Howell. Cordell Bank, California, 18 Aug. 2003.

10.7 ADULT NONBREEDING SABINE'S GULL. Note ghosting of boldly tricolored upperwing pattern, black hindcollar, and yellow bill tip. Head has molted to basic plumage but PB primary molt has yet to start. Göran Altstedt/Windrush Photos. Off South Africa, Nov.

10.8 ADULT NONBREEDING SABINE'S GULL IN PB MOLT (SAME BIRD AS PHOTO 10.1). Note blackish hindcollar, yellow bill tip, and forked tail. Primary molt on this bird had reached P6 being shed (gap in wing visible here reflects molt of outer secondaries). Steve N. G. Howell. Celestún, Yucatán, Mexico, 18 Feb. 1989.

10.9 ADULT BREEDING SABINE'S GULL. Unmistakable: note boldly tricolored upperwings, forked tail, dark slaty hood, and yellow bill tip. Mike Danzenbaker. Sunnyvale, California, 10 Sept. 1990.

10.10 SABINE'S GULL. Unmistakable but age uncertain: possibly an adult in PB head molt or perhaps a variation of first-alternate plumage (note dusky mottling on hindneck and more-extensive black on primaries than photo 10.9). Mike Danzenbaker. Off Monterey, California, 18 Aug. 1990.

10.11 SABINE'S GULLS WITH SOOTY SHEARWATERS _(PUFFINUS GRISEUS)._ A typical fall group at sea, perhaps mostly first-cycle birds, but aging of birds with more-solid hoods is problematic. Steve N. G. Howell. Cordell Bank, California, 13 Sept. 2002.

10.12 SABINE'S GULLS. Left-hand bird is either an adult starting PB head molt or an advanced first summer. Right-hand bird is a juvenile, with extensive brown on sides of head and neck and all-black bill. Steve N. G. Howell. Cordell Bank, California, 18 Aug. 2003.

10.13 JUVENILE SABINE'S GULL. Unmistakable, with boldly tricolored upperwings and forked tail. Eric Preston. Cordell Bank, California, 2 Sept. 2002.

10.14 JUVENILE SABINE'S GULL. From below, note ghosting of upperwing pattern, with dark band across secondary bases, dark neck sides, and forked tail. Mike Danzenbaker. Shoreline Park, California, 17 Sept. 1989.

11.1 ADULT NONBREEDING AND PRESUMED FIRST-CYCLE SWALLOW-TAILED GULLS. Unmistakable. Black eye-ring accentuates large black "goggle eyes" on white head. First-cycle birds aged by dark brown upperwing coverts and tertial centers, all-black bill. Arnoud B. van den Berg. Off Paracas, Peru, June 1980.

11.2 ADULT BREEDING SWALLOW-TAILED GULL. Unmistakable. Note how lighting and subtle posture differences affect appearance (compare with photo 11.0). Steve N. G. Howell. Isla Española, Galápagos, Ecuador, 18 July 2001.

11.3 FIRST-CYCLE SWALLOW-TAILED GULL, MOSTLY IN JUVENAL PLUMAGE (NOTE 1–2 GRAY, PRESUMED POST-JUVENAL SCAPULARS). Unmistakable. Kimball L. Garrett. Isla Genovesa, Galápagos, Ecuador, 13 May 1984.

11.4 FIRST-CYCLE SWALLOW-TAILED GULLS, THE LEFT-HAND BIRD STILL MOSTLY IN JUVENAL PLUMAGE. Note long, slightly droop-tipped black bills and black "goggle eyes" on white heads. Steve N. G. Howell. Off Arica, Tarapacá, Chile, 11 Nov. 2004.

11.5 ADULT BREEDING SWALLOW-TAILED GULL. Unmistakable. Bruce Hallett. Galápagos, Ecuador, May 1997.

11.6 ADULT BREEDING SWALLOW-TAILED GULL. Unmistakable. This bird was courting and carrying nest material, yet its prebasic primary molt had not finished; note how P9–P10 are still growing. Thus, two molts of head and body feathers occur during a single molt of primaries, and all are fitted into as short a period as possible between (or overlapping with) breeding. Steve N. G. Howell. Isla Española, Galápagos, Ecuador, 20 July 2001.

11.7 ADULT BREEDING SWALLOW-TAILED GULL. Unmistakable; from below note ghosting of upperwing pattern, forked tail. Steve N. G. Howell. Isla Española, Galápagos Islands, Ecuador, 18 July 2001.

11.9 FIRST-CYCLE SWALLOW-TAILED GULL (SAME BIRD AS PHOTO 11.8). Unmistakable: note start of post-juvenal molt on upperparts. R. L. Pitman. Eastern Tropical Pacific Ocean (3°22′S 85°16′W), 27 Oct. 1988.

11.8 FIRST-CYCLE SWALLOW-TAILED GULL (SAME BIRD AS PHOTO 11.9). Unmistakable; from below note ghosting of upperwing pattern, forked tail, and black eye-patch. R. L. Pitman. Eastern Tropical Pacific Ocean (3°22′S 85°16′W), 27 Oct. 1988.

11.10 SWALLOW-TAILED GULL. Unmistakable but age uncertain, possibly completing first PA or second PB/PA molt (depending on first-cycle molt strategy, which remains undescribed): P10 on far wing looks to be not fully grown, but adults at this molt stage usually have full hoods (see photo 11.6) and also have less-extensive black on primary coverts. R. L. Pitman. Near Malpelo Island, Colombia, Mar. 1993.

12.0 ADULT (LEFT) AND FIRST-CYCLE (RIGHT) IVORY GULLS AT CARCASS WITH FIRST-CYCLE GLAUCOUS GULL (AT REAR). Unmistakable. Bruce Mactavish. L'Anse-aux Meadows, Newfoundland, 13 Jan. 1998. **PP. 88, 343**

12.1 ADULT IVORY GULL. Unmistakable: note relatively well-developed claws, which help standing on ice. Bruce Mactavish. L'Anse-aux Meadows, Newfoundland, 15 Jan. 2002.

12.2 JUVENILE IVORY GULL. Unmistakable: a lightly marked individual (compare with photo 12.3). Bruce Mactavish. L'Anse-aux Meadows, Newfoundland, 15 Jan. 2002.

12.3 JUVENILE IVORY GULL. Unmistakable: a heavily marked individual (compare with photo 12.2). Bruce Mactavish. L'Anse-aux Meadows, Newfoundland, 15 Jan. 2002.

12.4 SECOND-CYCLE IVORY GULL IN PB2 MOLT (P6 HAS BEEN SHED AND P7–P10 ARE OLD, BLACK-TIPPED JUVENAL FEATHERS). Unmistakable: this molt stage is typical of first-summer birds in June. Bruce Hallett. Nome, Alaska, early June 2001.

12.5 IVORY GULL, ADULT OR SECOND-CYCLE. Unmistakable: note bill pattern and black feet. Some otherwise adult-plumaged birds have dusky flecking on the head (like this individual), which may indicate a second-cycle plumage. Bruce Mactavish. L'Anse-aux Meadows, Newfoundland, 15 Jan. 2002.

12.6 ADULT IVORY GULL. Unmistakable: note bill pattern and black feet. Steve N. G. Howell. St. John's, Newfoundland, 4 Feb. 2002.

12.7 JUVENILE IVORY GULL. Unmistakable. Bruce Mactavish. L'Anse-aux Meadows, Newfoundland, 13 Jan. 1998.

14.0 BREEDING ADULT FRANKLIN'S GULL (BEHIND) AND LAUGHING GULL. Note smaller size and more compact build of Franklin's, with smaller bill, bold white primary tips, and thicker white eye-crescents. Greg W. Lasley. Jefferson County, Texas, 16 Apr. 1993. **PP. 95, 350; 91, 346**

15.0 ADULT BREEDING LAVA GULLS IN ALTERNATE HEAD PLUMAGE BUT COMPLETING PB PRIMARY MOLT (PALE TIP TO INCOMING P9 VISIBLE NEAR PRIMARY BASES; P10 OLD). Note clean-cut black hood, bold white eye-crescents, slaty gray plumage; also bright bare parts relative to photo 15.1. Two molts of head and body feathers occur during a single molt of primaries, and all are fitted into as short a period as possible between (or overlapping with) breeding. W. Edward Harper. Isla Española, Galápagos, 27 July 2001. **PP. 98, 354**

13.1 ADULT NONBREEDING LAUGHING GULL. Distinguished from Franklin's Gull by longer and stouter bill, longer wing projection, head pattern (dusky mask rather than blackish half-hood), and small white primary tips (compare with photos 14.1–14.2). Brian E. Small. Sabine, Florida, Jan. 1997.

13.2 ADULT (RIGHT, NON-BREEDING) AND FIRST-CYCLE (LEFT, FORMATIVE PLUMAGE) LAUGHING GULLS. Distinguished from Franklin's Gull by lankier build, longer and stouter bill, and head pattern; also note dusky hindneck and chest of immature (see photos 14.1–14.2, 14.5). Kevin T. Karlson. New Smyrna, Florida, Nov. 2001.

13.3 ADULT BREEDING LAUGHING GULL. Distinguished from Franklin's Gull by lankier build, longer and stouter bill, narrower white eye-crescents, and small white primary tips (compare with photos 14.0, 14.3). Brian E. Small. Texas Gulf Coast, May 2002.

13.4 JUVENILE LAUGHING GULL. Distinctive: note overall brown aspect, scaly upperparts, and whitish belly. Kevin T. Karlson. Cape May, New Jersey, Aug. 1991.

13.5 FIRST-CYCLE LAUGHING GULL WITH RELATIVELY LIMITED PF MOLT OF SCAPULARS (COMPARE WITH PHOTO 13.6). Distinctive: note overall shape, bill shape, and head pattern. Greg W. Lasley. Surfside, Texas, 10 Sept. 1999.

13.6 FIRST-CYCLE LAUGHING GULL AFTER EXTENSIVE PF MOLT INCLUDING TERTIALS AND MANY OF THE VISIBLE UPPERWING COVERTS (COMPARE WITH PHOTO 13.5). Note same features as photo 13.5. Distinguished from second cycle by pointed primaries and dark brown secondaries (obvious in flight). Steve N. G. Howell. Puerto Vallarta, Jalisco, Mexico, 5 Jan. 2003.

13.7 FIRST-CYCLE LAUGHING GULL, ALTERNATE PLUMAGE. An "advanced" individual (most birds do not acquire so extensive a hood as this, and many have head patterns like nonbreeding adults; compare with photo 13.16). Note overall shape, bill size and shape, dusky neck, chest, and sides (compare with photo 14.6). Bruce Hallett. Nassau, Bahamas, May 2000.

13.8 SECOND-CYCLE NONBREEDING LAUGHING GULL IN PB2 MOLT (P8–P10 OLD AND FADED). Distinctive: note same features as photo 13.7. Steve N. G. Howell. Stinson Beach, California, 20 Aug. 1998.

13.9 SECOND-CYCLE NONBREEDING LAUGHING GULL.
Distinctive: note overall shape, bill size and shape, head pattern. Distinguished from adult (photos 13.1–13.2) by dusky neck sides and chest and lack of distinct white primary tips. Kevin T. Karlson. New Smyrna, Florida, Nov. 2001.

13.10 SECOND-CYCLE BREEDING LAUGHING GULL. Distinguished from adult by mottled hood (some individuals have complete, adultlike hoods; others have a half-hood suggesting Franklin's Gull), wing and tail patterns (best seen in flight, see photo 13.17). Brian E. Small. Dry Tortugas, Florida, Apr. 1994.

13.12 ADULT BREEDING LAUGHING GULL. Distinctive: note extensive black on outer primaries and long bill; P1–P2 look relatively fresh, perhaps indicating suspended PB molt. Bruce Hallett. Exumas, Bahamas, June 2000.

13.11 ADULT NONBREEDING LAUGHING GULL. Distinctive: note extensive black on outer primaries, long bill, and head pattern. Steve N. G. Howell. San Blas, Nayarit, Mexico, 9 Jan. 2002.

13.13 ADULT BREEDING LAUGHING GULL. Distinctive: note long pointed wings with extensive black underside to outer primaries (compare with photo 14.9). Larry Sansone. Galveston, Texas, 21 Apr. 2001.

13.14 JUVENILE LAUGHING GULL. Distinctive: note overall dusky brown aspect with white belly, black tail band extending to outer web of R6 (compare with photo 14.12). Michael D. Stubblefield. Jamaica Bay, New York, Aug. 2000.

13.15 FIRST-CYCLE LAUGHING GULLS WITH HEERMANN'S GULL (ON WATER). Note black tail band extending to outer web of R6, head pattern, and dusky neck and chest (compare with photo 14.13). Steve N. G. Howell. Manzanillo, Colima, 21 Feb. 2003.

13.16 FIRST-CYCLE LAUGHING GULL. Note nonbreeding aspect to alternate plumage, bill size and shape, and all-white tail replaced in PA molt. Steve N. G. Howell. Cape Hatteras, North Carolina, 28 May 2004.

13.17 SECOND-CYCLE BREEDING LAUGHING GULL. Distinguished from adult by more-extensive black on outer wing and black tail markings (compare with photos 13.11–13.12). Larry Sansone. Galveston, Texas, 24 Apr. 1996.

14.1 ADULT NONBREEDING FRANKLIN'S GULLS (GRAY GULL IN BACKGROUND). Distinguished from Laughing Gull by smaller bill, blackish half-hood with thick white eye-crescents, and bold white primary tips. Steve N. G. Howell. Arica, Tarapacá, Chile, 3 Nov. 1999.

14.2 ADULT NONBREEDING FRANKLIN'S GULL. Near the extreme in extensive blackish half-hood and very large white primary tips (compare with photo 14.1). Steve N. G. Howell. Arica, Tarapacá, Chile, 3 Nov. 1999.

14.3 ADULT BREEDING FRANKLIN'S GULL. White primary tips often reduced by wear in summer, but note bill size and shape and thick white eye-crescents relative to Laughing Gull (see photos 13.3, 14.0). Brian E. Small. Des Lacs, North Dakota, June 1994.

14.4 JUVENILE FRANKLIN'S GULL. Distinctive, with dark half-hood and thick white eye-crescents, overall whitish neck and chest (compare with photo 13.4). Chris Wood. Prewitt Reservoir, Colorado, 30 July 2003.

14.5 FIRST-CYCLE FRANKLIN'S GULL, FORMATIVE PLUMAGE. Typical appearance of a first-winter bird. Note blackish half-hood with thick white eye-crescents, relatively small bill, and gray back contrasting with mostly brownish upperwings. Brian E. Small. Ventura, California, Oct. 1998.

14.6 FIRST-CYCLE FRANKLIN'S GULL. This bird's PA1 molt was incomplete, with juvenal P8–P10 retained. Some birds replace all primaries in PA1 (see photo 14.15) and others none. Note typical half-hood with thick white eye-crescents, bill size, and bold white primary tips on new P6–P7. Marshall J. Iliff. Rockport, Texas, 20 Apr. 1999.

14.7 ADULT NONBREEDING FRANKLIN'S GULLS. Note neatly demarcated but relatively restricted black-and-white wingtip pattern and black half-hoods (compare with photo 13.11). White in basic wingtip averages less than in alternate plumage (see photo 14.9). Steve N. G. Howell. Arica, Tarapacá, Chile, 10 Nov. 2004.

14.8 ADULT NONBREEDING FRANKLIN'S GULLS (WITH BREEDING GRAY GULLS). Note bold black-and-white wingtip pattern (compare with photo 13.12), black half-hoods. Steve N. G. Howell. Arica, Tarapacá, Chile, 3 Nov. 1999.

14.9 ADULT BREEDING FRANKLIN'S GULL STARTING PB MOLT (P1–P2 SHED). Distinguished from Laughing Gull (see photo 13.13) by shorter and less-pointed wings with bold black-and-white tips (with much less black); also note smaller bill, thicker white eye-crescents. Brian E. Small. Benton Lake, Montana, June 2001.

14.10 ADULT-TYPE BREEDING FRANKLIN'S GULL STARTING PB MOLT (P1–P3 SHED). Relatively extensive black in wingtip, with white medial band all but absent, may indicate a second-cycle bird (see photo 14.9). Distinguished from Laughing Gull by clean-cut and restricted black wingtip area (see photo 13.13). Greg W. Lasley. Bowden, Montana, 19 June 2001.

14.11 JUVENILE FRANKLIN'S GULL. Note dark brown, scaly-edged scapulars, distinct white trailing edge to wings and white tips to outer primaries, and relatively narrow black tail band not reaching outer web of R6. Tony Leukering. Walden Reservoir, Colorado, 22 July 1995.

14.12 FIRST-CYCLE FRANKLIN'S GULL. Note blackish half-hood, mostly pale underwings, and white outer web to R6 (compare with photo 13.14). R. L. Pitman. Callao, Peru, 14 Nov. 1981.

14.13 FIRST-CYCLE FRANKLIN'S GULLS. Note black tail band not reaching outer web of R6, head pattern, and white hindneck and chest (compare with photo 13.15). Martin Reid. Arica, Tarapacá, Chile, Dec. 1993.

14.14 FIRST-CYCLE (UPPER) AND "RETARDED" SECOND-CYCLE (LOWER) FRANKLIN'S GULLS (THE LATTER PERHAPS A BIRD THAT MOLTED NO PRIMARIES IN PA1 MOLT?). On first-cycle note blackish half-hood, tail pattern, and relatively broad white trailing edge to wings. Second-cycle distinguished from adult by extensively blackish outer primaries and black marks on primary coverts and tail (most second-winter birds show more advanced, adultlike plumage). Martin Reid. Arica, Tarapacá, Chile, Dec. 1993.

14.15 SECOND-CYCLE (FIRST-SUMMER) FRANKLIN'S GULL, STARTING PB2 MOLT (P1–P4 SHED). All primaries on this individual were replaced in PA1 molt (compare with photo 14.6). Distinguished from Laughing Gull by relatively limited and clean-cut black on underwing tip (compare with photo 13.11); also note structure (including bill shape) and thicker white eye-crescents. Alvaro Jaramillo. Beaverhill Lake, Alberta, 28 June 1997.

15.1 ADULT NONBREEDING LAVA GULL IN PB MOLT (P7–P10 OLD). Note dull bare parts relative to photo 15.0. Steve N. G. Howell. Isla Santa Cruz, Galápagos, 21 July 2001.

15.2 FIRST-CYCLE LAVA GULL, MOSTLY IN JUVENAL PLUMAGE (SOME GRAY F1 SCAPULARS APPEARING). Distinctive in its limited range; note fairly heavy black bill and overall dark brown plumage. R. L. Pitman. Isla Santa Cruz, Galápagos, 8 Dec. 1984.

15.3 FIRST-CYCLE LAVA GULL. Slaty F1 plumage contrasts with bleached brown juvenal feathers. Steve N. G. Howell. Isla Santa Cruz, Galápagos, 21 July 2001.

15.4 FIRST-CYCLE LAVA GULL. Extensive PF molt produces overall grayish plumage (compare with photo 15.2); note pale gray uppertail coverts typical of all ages. Steve N. G. Howell. Isla Santa Cruz, Galápagos, 16 July 2001.

15.5 FIRST-CYCLE LAVA GULL IN F1 OR A1 PLUMAGE. R. L. Pitman. Isla Santa Cruz, Galápagos, 8 Dec. 1984.

15.6 FIRST-CYCLE LAVA GULL, ALTERNATE PLUMAGE.
Extensive PA1 molt can produce fairly uniform gray body with dark hood and whitish eye-crescents; note slightly contrasting and bleached browner F1 tertials, worn and pointed juvenal primaries (compare with photo 15.7). Steve N. G. Howell. Isla Santa Cruz, Galápagos, 21 July 2001.

15.7 SECOND-CYCLE LAVA GULL, BASIC PLUMAGE. Distinguished from first cycle by relatively fresh, broad, and blackish primaries and by tertials concolor with rest of upperparts (compare with photo 15.6). Steve N. G. Howell. Isla Santa Cruz, Galápagos, 21 July 2001.

15.8 PRESUMED SECOND-CYCLE LAVA GULL, ALTERNATE PLUMAGE. Blacker hood and whiter eye-crescents relative to B2 plumage (compare with photo 15.7). Hood demarcation messier and plumage with a brownish cast relative to adult (see photos 15.0–15.1). Steve N. G. Howell. Isla Santa Cruz, Galápagos, 21 July 2001.

15.9 ADULT LAVA GULL. Pale gray lateral uppertail coverts and outer rectrices are conspicuous in flight. Steve N. G. Howell. Isla Santa Cruz, Galápagos, 21 July 2001.

16.0 ADULT BREEDING HEERMANN'S GULL. Unmistakable: note bright red bill, black legs, and white head. Steve N. G. Howell. Puerto Peñasco, Sonora, Mexico, 22 Jan. 2003. **PP. 102, 357**

17.0 ADULT BREEDING GRAY GULL. Unmistakable: note slender black bill and black legs, white head, and uniform gray body. Steve N. G. Howell. Arica, Tarapacá, Chile, 21 Oct. 1999. **PP. 107, 360**

18.0 ADULT BREEDING DOLPHIN GULL. Unmistakable: note thick red bill, red legs, and smoky gray head and underparts. Steve N. G. Howell. Punta Arenas, Magallanes, Chile, 30 Oct. 2002. **PP. 110, 363**

19.0 ADULT BREEDING BELCHER'S GULL. Note blackish upperparts and long yellow bill with black-and-red tip; yellow orbital ring does not show well in this photo, and smoky clouding on neck and chest is washed out by sunny conditions (compare with photo 19.3). Steve N. G. Howell. Arica, Tarapacá, Chile, 22 Oct. 1999. **PP. 114, 366**

20.0 ADULT BREEDING OLROG'S GULL WITH CHICKS. Note blackish upperparts, stout bill with black-and-red tip, and red orbital ring. Pablo F. Petracci. Bahía Blanca, Buenos Aires, Argentina, late Oct. 2003. **PP. 118, 369**

21.0 ADULT BREEDING BLACK-TAILED GULL. Distinctive: note slaty gray upperparts, pale eye, and bill shape and pattern; legs brighter than winter birds (see photos 21.1–21.2). Mike Danzenbaker. Aomori Prefecture, Japan, 29 Mar. 1998. **PP. 121, 372**

16.1 ADULT NONBREEDING HEERMANN'S GULL, COMPLETING PB MOLT (P9–P10 OLD). Distinguished from third cycle by average later molt timing and, typically, finer and grayer head markings (compare with photo 16.12). Steve N. G. Howell. Stinson Beach, California, 23 Aug. 1998.

16.2 ADULT BREEDING HEERMANN'S GULL. Unmistakable. Larry B. Spear. Isla Raza, Baja California, Mexico, May 1977.

16.3 JUVENILE (FLEDGLING) HEERMANN'S GULL IN VERY FRESH PLUMAGE (PRIMARIES NOT FULLY GROWN). Note dull-pinkish bill base, apparent even at this age, and that broad buff edgings to upperparts quickly abrade (compare with photo 16.4). R. A. Behrstock/Naturewide Images. Isla Raza, Baja California, Mexico, mid-June 1988.

16.4 FIRST-CYCLE HEERMANN'S GULL. Note abraded, narrow pale edgings to scapulars relative to fresh juvenile (see photo 16.3), and a few grayer, post-juvenal scapulars. Steve N. G. Howell. Bodega Bay, California, 24 Aug. 1998.

16.5 FIRST-CYCLE HEERMANN'S GULL. Note contrast between worn and bleached juvenal upperwing coverts and tertials and fresher, grayer, post-juvenal head and body plumage (compare with photo 16.6). Steve N. G. Howell. Bolinas, California, 31 Dec. 2001.

16.6 FIRST-CYCLE HEERMANN'S GULL. This individual has replaced some upperwing coverts and tertials in its post-juvenal molt; compare with photo 16.5. Steve N. G. Howell. Puerto Peñasco, Sonora, Mexico, 21 Jan. 2003.

16.7 SOME FIRST-CYCLE HEERMANN'S GULLS WINTERING IN TROPICAL LATITUDES MOLT OUTER PRIMARIES IN THEIR FIRST WINTER. This bird has P1–P5 old (note contrast between faded and worn P5 and fresh blackish P6), P6–P7 new, and P8–P10 growing (and not visible beyond tip of P6; hence, the short wing projection). Steve N. G. Howell. San Blas, Nayarit, Mexico, 11 Jan. 2003.

16.8 SECOND-CYCLE HEERMANN'S GULL. Largely in fresh B2 plumage but PA2 molt has already started (for example, note some shed median coverts; and see photo 16.9). Suggests first cycle but upperparts grayer and more uniform, lacking scaly edgings (compare with photos 16.4–16.5). Steve N. G. Howell. Stinson Beach, California, 20 Aug. 1998.

16.9 SECOND-CYCLE HEERMANN'S GULL. PA2 molt has included much of upperparts (including some upperwing coverts and tertials) and underparts, but the head is usually last to molt and may still be mostly B2 (compare with photo 16.8). Steve N. G. Howell. Bodega Bay, California, 17 Dec. 1998.

16.10 SECOND-CYCLE HEERMANN'S GULL. An individual in relatively "retarded" A2 plumage, although head may yet attain some white feathers (compare with photo 16.11). Steve N. G. Howell. Puerto Peãsco, Sonora, Mexico, 21 Jan. 2003.

16.11 SECOND-CYCLE HEERMANN'S GULL IN A2 PLUMAGE. Note more "advanced" head and back plumage than photo 16.10. Some advanced birds resemble third cycle in head and body plumage (for example, photo 16.13), but note reduced white tips to secondaries and tail (compare photo 16.19 with photo 16.20). Steve N. G. Howell. San Felipe, Baja California, Mexico, 16 Apr. 2004.

16.12 THIRD-CYCLE NONBREEDING HEERMANN'S GULL, COMPLETING PB3 MOLT (OUTER PRIMARIES NOT FULLY GROWN). Rather variable at this age. Some birds suggest second cycle but with bold white tips to tail and secondaries; others are rather adultlike. In general averages browner overall than adult; also note earlier molt timing (compare with photo 16.1). Steve N. G. Howell. Stinson Beach, California, 20 Aug. 1998.

16.13 THIRD-CYCLE HEERMANN'S GULL, ALTERNATE PLUMAGE.
Some A3 birds are perhaps not distinguishable
from adults but others (and perhaps some nonbreeding adults) have mottled hoods that suggest
basic plumage or some second-cycle birds (compare with photo 16.11); distinguished from A2 by
wing and tail patterns (for example, bold white tips
to secondaries; compare photo 16.19 with photo
16.20). Steve N. G. Howell. Bodega Bay, California, 11 Mar. 1999.

16.14 ADULT NONBREEDING HEERMANN'S GULL. Note
broad white trailing edge to wings and tail, with
white tips out to P7 (compare with photos 16.20–
16.21). John Sorensen. Monterey Bay, California,
Oct. 1995.

16.16 ADULT BREEDING HEERMANN'S GULL. Unmistakable. Note wing and tail patterns relative to third
cycle (photos 16.20–16.21); also note that white
tips to outer primaries have abraded (compare
with photo 16.14). Larry Sansone. Near Newport,
California, 11 Jan. 2003.

16.15 ADULT NONBREEDING HEERMANN'S GULL. A few
adults (<1 percent) have some white upperpri-
mary coverts that create a striking white patch.
John Sorensen. Monterey Bay, California, Oct.
2000.

16.17 FIRST-CYCLE HEERMANN'S GULL. All-dark appearance and black legs distinctive; also note bicolored
bill, scaly upperwing coverts. Steve N. G. Howell.
Bodega Bay, California, 7 Sept. 2001.

16.18 FIRST-CYCLE (UPPER) AND SECOND-CYCLE (LOWER) HEERMANN'S GULLS. Note browner overall aspect of first cycle, which has pale tips to greater upper-wing coverts. Second cycle is grayer (for example, on uppertail coverts), with white tips to tertials, but lacks distinct white trailing edge to tail and secondaries of third cycle (photos 16.20–16.21). Larry Sansone. Near Newport, California, 11 Jan. 2003.

16.19 SECOND-CYCLE HEERMANN'S GULLS. Note grayer and more uniform appearance than first cycle (for example, uppertail coverts) and lack of distinct white trailing edge to tail and secondaries of third cycle (photos 16.20–16.21). Larry Sansone. Monterey, California, 17 Sept. 2003.

16.20 PRESUMED THIRD-CYCLE HEERMANN'S GULLS. A more "retarded" individual (compare with photo 16.21). Distinguished from second cycle by distinct white trailing edge to wings and tail (see photos 16.18–16.19). Larry Sansone. Near Newport, California, 11 Jan. 2003.

16.21 THIRD-CYCLE HEERMANN'S GULLS. A more "advanced" individual (compare with photo 16.20). Distinguished from second cycle by distinct white trailing edge to wings and tail (compare with photos 16.18–16.19), which averages narrower than adult (and extends only to inner primaries); most adults have fully white heads by this date (see photo 16.16). Larry Sansone. Near Newport, California, 11 Jan. 2003.

17.1 ADULT NONBREEDING GRAY GULL. Distinctive, especially in its range. Note neat brown hood (compare with alternate plumage, photo 17.2) and bold white trailing edge to secondaries. Gonzalo González Cifuentes. Quintero, Valparaíso, Chile, July 1998.

17.2 PAIR OF ADULT BREEDING GRAY GULLS. Unmistakable: note more-slender bill of female (on left) and how angle of light affects apparent shades of gray, although male was noticeably whiter headed even when viewed at the same angle. Steve N. G. Howell. Arica, Tarapacá, Chile, 22 Oct. 1999.

17.3 ADULT BREEDING GRAY GULL. Unmistakable: note very broad white secondary tips and mostly gray closed tail. Steve N. G. Howell. Arica, Tarapacá, Chile, 11 Nov. 2003.

17.4 JUVENILE GRAY GULL. Distinctive: note all-black bill. Alvaro Jaramillo. Arica, Tarapacá, Chile, 15 Feb. 2002.

17.5 FIRST-CYCLE GRAY GULL. Apparently largely in bleached juvenal plumage but with some post-juvenal scapulars (compare with photo 17.6). Steve N. G. Howell. Arica, Tarapacá, Chile, 12 Nov. 2002.

17.6 FIRST-CYCLE GRAY GULL WITH EXTENSIVE POST-JUVENAL MOLT OF UPPERPARTS, INCLUDING WING COVERTS AND TERTIALS (COMPARE WITH PHOTO 17.5). Steve N. G. Howell. Arica, Tarapacá, Chile, 12 Nov. 2002.

17.7 SECOND-CYCLE GRAY GULLS IN PB2 MOLT (NOTE BLACKISH AREA ON P7 EXPOSED BY SHED P6). R. L. Pitman. Paracas, Peru, 27 Nov. 1985.

17.8 NONBREEDING GRAY GULL (SAME BIRD AS PHOTO 17.14; AGE UNCERTAIN). Possibly second cycle with relatively broad white secondary tips (compare with photo 17.15) or perhaps third cycle. Distinguished from adult by messier brown hood extending down to chest; also note dark tertial center. Steve N. G. Howell. Salinas, Ecuador, 31 July 1998.

17.9 SECOND-CYCLE GRAY GULL. A relatively "retarded" individual (compare with photo 17.10); note messy head, brownish upperwing coverts, narrow whitish secondary tips, and extensively black tail. Steve N. G. Howell. Arica, Tarapacá, Chile, 11 Nov. 2003.

17.10 SECOND-CYCLE GRAY GULL, ALTERNATE PLUMAGE. A relatively "advanced" individual (compare with photo 17.9); distinguished from adult by brownish upperwing coverts and narrow whitish secondary tips. Steve N. G. Howell. Arica, Tarapacá, Chile, 11 Nov. 2003.

17.11 ADULT BREEDING GRAY GULL. Unmistakable. Note broad white trailing edge to secondaries and gray tail with incomplete black subterminal band. Some breeding adults have all-gray central rectrices, perhaps attained in PA molt (for example, photo 17.3). Steve N. G. Howell. Arica, Tarapacá, Chile, 9 Nov. 2005.

17.12 ADULT-TYPE BREEDING GRAY GULL. Unmistakable: broad black distal tail band may be adult variation or perhaps indicates a third-cycle bird (study needed; compare with photo 17.11). Steve N. G. Howell. Arica, Tarapacá, Chile, 9 Nov. 2005.

17.13 SECOND-CYCLE GRAY GULL, STARTING PB2 MOLT (P1– P2 SHED). Readily aged by overall brown plumage, all-black tail, and retained juvenal upperwing coverts. Steve N. G. Howell. Arica, Tarapacá, Chile, 12 Nov. 2002.

17.14 NONBREEDING GRAY GULL (SAME BIRD AS PHOTO 17.9; AGE UNCERTAIN). Second cycle, with relatively broad white secondary tips, or third cycle. Steve N. G. Howell. Salinas, Ecuador, 31 July 1998.

17.15 SECOND-CYCLE GRAY GULL. A relatively "advanced" individual; distinguished from adult by brownish cast to upperwings and mostly blackish tail without distinct whitish tip; white trailing edge to secondaries relatively bold (compare with photos 17.9–17.10) but still narrower than on adult. Steve N. G. Howell. Arica, Tarapacá, Chile, 12 Nov. 2002.

18.1 ADULT NONBREEDING DOLPHIN GULL IN PB MOLT. Note molt timing (P7–P10 old) and pattern on old outer primaries (compare with photo 18.14). Steve N. G. Howell. Ushuaia, Tierra del Fuego, Argentina, 15 Mar. 2002.

18.2 ADULT NONBREEDING DOLPHIN GULL. Unmistakable. Enrique Couve. Punta Arenas, Magallanes, Chile, July 2002.

18.3 ADULT BREEDING DOLPHIN GULL. Unmistakable. Steve N. G. Howell. Punta Arenas, Magallanes, Chile, 30 Oct. 2002.

18.4 JUVENILE DOLPHIN GULL. Distinctive. Unusual among larger gulls in lacking pale, scaly edgings to upperparts. Steve N. G. Howell. Ushuaia, Tierra del Fuego, Argentina, 7 Feb. 1999.

18.5 FIRST-CYCLE DOLPHIN GULL. As with many far northern gulls, much juvenal plumage is retained into winter. Enrique Couve. Fuerte Bulness, Magallanes, Chile, Aug. 2002.

18.6 FIRST-CYCLE DOLPHIN GULL. A relatively "retarded" first-summer individual (compare with photos 18.7–18.8). Steve N. G. Howell. Punta Arenas, Magallanes, Chile, 30 Oct. 2002.

18.7 FIRST-CYCLE DOLPHIN GULL. An average first-summer individual (compare with photos 18.6, 18.8). Steve N. G. Howell. Punta Arenas, Magallanes, Chile, 30 Oct. 2002.

18.8 FIRST-CYCLE DOLPHIN GULL. A relatively "advanced" first-summer individual (compare with photos 18.6–18.7). Steve N. G. Howell. Punta Arenas, Magallanes, Chile, 30 Oct. 2002.

18.9 SECOND-CYCLE DOLPHIN GULL, COMPLETING PB2 MOLT (P9–P10 OLD). Steve N. G. Howell. Ushuaia, Tierra del Fuego, Argentina, 7 Feb. 1999.

18.10 SECOND-CYCLE DOLPHIN GULL. A relatively "retarded" second-summer individual (compare with photos 18.11–18.12). Steve N. G. Howell. Punta Arenas, Magallanes, Chile, 30 Oct. 2002.

18.11 SECOND-CYCLE DOLPHIN GULL. An average second-summer individual (compare with photos 18.10, 18.12). Steve N. G. Howell. Punta Arenas, Magallanes, Chile, 30 Oct. 2002.

18.12 SECOND-CYCLE DOLPHIN GULL. A relatively "advanced" individual (compare with photos 18.10–18.11); note reduced white wingtips relative to adult. Steve N. G. Howell. Punta Arenas, Magallanes, Chile, 30 Oct. 2002.

18.13 DOLPHIN GULL, ALTERNATE PLUMAGE. Probably an "advanced" second-cycle bird (compare with photos 18.10–18.12) but perhaps a "retarded" third cycle (wingtip pattern typical of B2 plumage). Steve N. G. Howell. Punta Arenas, Magallanes, Chile, 30 Oct. 2002.

18.14 THIRD-CYCLE NONBREEDING DOLPHIN GULL IN PB3 MOLT. Note relatively advanced molt timing, with P7–P10 old (compare with photo 18.1), and pattern of old B2 outer primaries. Steve N. G. Howell. Ushuaia, Tierra del Fuego, Argentina, 7 Feb. 1999.

18.15 DOLPHIN GULLS: BREEDING ADULTS (FAR LEFT AND RIGHT), SECOND-CYCLE (CENTER-LEFT), AND FIRST-CYCLE (CENTER-RIGHT). Note bold white trailing edge to secondaries and inner primaries. Steve N. G. Howell. Punta Arenas, Magallanes, Chile, 30 Oct. 2002.

18.16 JUVENILE DOLPHIN GULL. Distinctive: note thick bill and broad white trailing edge to wings. Enrique Couve. Port Stanley, Falkland Islands, Mar. 1998.

19.1 ADULT NONBREEDING BELCHER'S GULL. Distinctive: dark hood variable (compare with photo 19.2) but always much more solid than Olrog's Gull (photo 20.1). Dan Lane. Lima, Peru, June 1996.

19.2 ADULT NONBREEDING BELCHER'S GULL; PRESUMED BASIC PLUMAGE BUT PERHAPS A THIRD-CYCLE OR ADULT BIRD IN NONBREEDING ALTERNATE PLUMAGE. Distinctive: dark hood variable (compare with photo 19.1) but always much more solid than Olrog's Gull (photo 20.1). Steve N. G. Howell. Arica, Tarapacá, Chile, 22 Oct. 1999.

19.3 ADULT BREEDING BELCHER'S GULL. Distinguished from Olrog's and Kelp Gulls by contrast between white "hood" and smoky clouding on neck and chest (but this can be washed out in sunny conditions; see photo 19.0); compare with adult Kelp Gull; also note all-black wingtips and black bill band. R. L. Pitman. Paracas, Peru, Nov. 1981.

19.4 JUVENILE BELCHER'S GULL IN FRESH PLUMAGE. Distinctive in range; dark brown head and chest hood heavily veiled whitish on this individual. Martin Reid. Arica, Tarapacá, Chile, Feb. 1990.

19.5 FIRST-CYCLE BELCHER'S GULL. Distinctive in range; Olrog's Gull has stouter bill and paler forehead. Upperparts suggest juvenile but may be juvenal-like A1 plumage (compare with photo 19.4, which has fresh primaries and less-advanced bill colors). Steve N. G. Howell. Arica, Tarapacá, Chile, 22 Oct. 1999.

19.6 FIRST-CYCLE BELCHER'S GULL. Distinctive in range; Olrog's Gull has stouter bill, paler forehead, and more-extensively brown underparts. Mostly in worn juvenal plumage (with no upperwing coverts replaced, unlike photos 19.5, 19.7). Steve N. G. Howell. Arica, Tarapacá, Chile, 22 Oct. 1999.

19.7 FIRST-CYCLE BELCHER'S GULL. Distinctive in range; Olrog's Gull has stouter bill, paler forehead, and darker underbody. PA1 molt of this individual has included some dark slaty feathers on upperparts (compare with photos 19.5–19.6). Steve N. G. Howell. Arica, Tarapacá, Chile, 22 Oct. 1999.

19.8 SECOND-CYCLE NONBREEDING BELCHER'S GULL, COMPLETING PB2 MOLT (P10 AND POSSIBLY P9 OLD). Distinctive in range; suggests some first-cycle birds but upperparts more uniform. Distinguished from Olrog's Gull by less stout bill, smoky gray (not white) hindcollar (compare with photos 20.7–20.8). Gonzalo González Cifuentes. Tarapacá, Chile, Feb. 1996.

19.9 SECOND-CYCLE BREEDING BELCHER'S GULL. Distinctive in range; Olrog's Gull has stouter bill, averages blacker upperparts. Extent of dusky head markings variable (compare with photo 19.10) and brown in upperwings variable (compare with photo 19.19); bill has more black than adult (see photo 19.0). Steve N. G. Howell. Arica, Tarapacá, Chile, 22 Oct. 1999.

19.10 SECOND-CYCLE BREEDING BELCHER'S GULL. Distinctive in range; Olrog's Gull averages blacker upperparts with more sharply defined white hindneck collar, has less-solid dark hood. Steve N. G. Howell. Arica, Tarapacá, Chile, 12 Nov. 2004.

19.11 THIRD-CYCLE OR ADULT NONBREEDING BELCHER'S GULL, COMPLETING PB MOLT (P10 OLD). Relatively extensive dark hood, including mottling on upper chest, may indicate B3 plumage. Larry Sansone. San Diego, California, 10 Aug. 1997.

19.12 ADULT NONBREEDING BELCHER'S GULL. Distinctive: distinguished from Olrog's Gull by solid dark hood, smoky gray underwing coverts, and dusky bases to secondaries (compare with photo 20.10). Alvaro Jaramillo. Taltal, Antofagasta, Chile, 24 July 2001.

19.13 ADULT BREEDING BELCHER'S GULL. Distinctive in range; Olrog's Gull has stouter bill, white secondaries (without dusky bases), and lacks smoky gray neck wash. Steve N. G. Howell. Arica, Tarapacá, Chile, 11 Nov. 2003.

19.14 ADULT BREEDING BELCHER'S GULL, STARTING PB MOLT. Distinctive: distinguished from Olrog's Gull by narrower white trailing edge to secondaries (see photos 20.10–20.12). Martin Reid. Arica, Tarapacá, Chile, Feb. 1990.

19.15 ADULT (AND ONE SECOND-CYCLE) BELCHER'S GULLS. Distinctive: distinguished from Olrog's Gull by narrower white trailing edge to secondaries. R. L. Pitman. Paracas, Peru, Nov. 1981.

19.16 FIRST-CYCLE BELCHER'S GULL. Distinctive: distinguished from Olrog's Gull by solid dark hood and more-extensive dark marks on uppertail coverts. Alvaro Jaramillo. Taltal, Antofagasta, Chile, 24 July 2001.

19.17 BELCHER'S GULL STARTING PB2 MOLT (P1–P2 SHED). Steve N. G. Howell. Arica, Tarapacá, Chile, 22 Oct. 1999.

19.18 SECOND-CYCLE NONBREEDING BELCHER'S GULL. Distinctive: distinguished from Olrog's Gull by smoky gray hindcollar, narrower white trailing edge to secondaries and inner primaries (compare with photo 20.13). Dan Lane. Lima, Peru, May 2001.

19.19 SECOND-CYCLE BREEDING BELCHER'S GULL. Distinctive in range; Olrog's Gull has stouter bill, averages blacker upperparts with wider white trailing edge to secondaries, and lacks smoky gray hindneck wash. Extent of dusky head markings and brown in upperwings variable (some birds have extensive dark hoods). Steve N. G. Howell. Arica, Tarapacá, Chile, 11 Nov. 2003.

20.1 ADULT NONBREEDING OLROG'S GULL IN PB MOLT (SAME BIRD AS PHOTO 20.10; PARENT OF BIRD IN PHOTO 20.4). Distinctive: dusky speckled hood (at about its heaviest on this individual) is distinct from solid dark hood of adult basic Belcher's Gull (see photos 19.1–19.2). Steve N. G. Howell. Bahía Blanca, Buenos Aires, Argentina, 23 Jan. 1999.

20.2 ADULT BREEDING OLROG'S GULLS (MALE AT LEFT WITH STOUTER BILL). Note bill shape and pattern, slaty blackish upperparts, white neck and underparts, and red orbital ring. Pablo F. Petracci. Bahía Blanca, Buenos Aires, Argentina, 28 Sept. 2002.

20.3 JUVENILE OLROG'S GULLS (PRE-FLEDGING). Note sooty brown head and neck starting to show whitish forehead on some birds. Bill base and legs quickly become much paler after fledging (see photo 20.4). Pablo F. Petracci. Bahía Blanca, Buenos Aires, Argentina, early Dec. 2003.

20.4 JUVENILE OLROG'S GULL. Distinctive in range; distinguished from Belcher's Gull (see photos 19.4–19.7) by stouter bill and paler brown head and chest with whitish forehead and lores. Steve N. G. Howell. Bahía Blanca, Buenos Aires, Argentina, 23 Jan. 1999.

20.5 FIRST-CYCLE AND ADULT BREEDING OLROG'S GULLS WITH PALE-FACED SHEATHBILL *(CHIONIS ALBA).* Molt and wear create darker appearance of first-cycle birds relative to juvenile; note whitish face and extensive dark brown on underparts; compare with Belcher's Gull (photos 19.5–19.7). Jorge Veiga. Necochea, Buenos Aires, Argentina, 12 June 1988.

20.6 SECOND-CYCLE OLROG'S GULL, MOLTING TO B2 PLUMAGE (OUTER PRIMARIES OLD). Distinctive: distinguished from Belcher's Gull by stouter bill, paler brown hood, and whitish face. Alvaro Jaramillo. Punta Rasa, Buenos Aires, Argentina, 26 Nov. 1991.

20.7 SECOND-CYCLE NONBREEDING OLROG'S GULL, COMPLETING PB2 MOLT (OUTER PRIMARIES GROWING). Distinctive: distinguished from Belcher's Gull by stouter bill, white hindcollar, and paler brown hood (compare with photo 19.8). Debra L. Shearwater. Punta Rasa, Buenos Aires, Argentina, 23 Jan. 2003.

20.8 SECOND-CYCLE NONBREEDING OLROG'S GULLS, COMPLETING PB2 MOLT. Distinguished from Belcher's Gull by same features as photo 20.7. Shed median coverts on left-hand bird indicate start of PA2 molt. Debra L. Shearwater. Punta Rasa, Buenos Aires, Argentina, 23 Jan. 2003.

20.9 THIRD-CYCLE OLROG'S GULL, MOLTING TO B3 PLUMAGE (P7–P10 OLD). Distinguished from adult by browner upperparts and more-extensive dusky markings on head and chest. Pablo F. Petracci. Punta, Rasa, Buenos Aires, Argentina, Jan. 2003.

20.10 ADULT NONBREEDING OLROG'S GULL (SAME BIRD AS PHOTO 20.1) IN PB MOLT (P8–P10 OLD). Distinctive: distinguished from Belcher's Gull by dusky speckled hood and broader white trailing edge to secondaries (compare with photos 19.13–19.14). Steve N. G. Howell. Bahía Blanca, Buenos Aires, Argentina, 23 Jan. 1999.

20.11 ADULT BREEDING OLROG'S GULL. Distinctive in range; distinguished from Belcher's Gull by stouter bill and slaty black upperparts with broader white trailing edge to wings. Pablo F. Petracci. Bahía Blanca, Buenos Aires, Argentina, early Dec. 2003.

20.12 ADULT BREEDING OLROG'S GULL. Distinctive in range; distinguished from Belcher's Gull by stouter bill, white underwing coverts, and all-white secondaries. Pablo F. Petracci. Bahía Blanca, Buenos Aires, Argentina, early Dec. 2003.

20.13 SECOND-CYCLE NONBREEDING OLROG'S GULL, COMPLETING PB2 MOLT (P10 NOT FULLY GROWN). Distinctive: distinguished from Belcher's Gull by blacker upperparts, white hindcollar, white underwing coverts, and bolder white trailing edge to upperwings (compare with photos 19.18–19.19). Debra L. Shearwater. Punta Rasa, Buenos Aires, Argentina, 23 Jan. 2003.

20.14 SECOND-CYCLE OLROG'S GULL. Distinctive: distinguished from Belcher's Gull by white hindcollar and bolder white trailing edge to upperwings (compare with photos 19.18–19.19). Some second-alternate birds may attain mostly white heads, as in Belcher's Gull. Jorge Veiga. Mar del Plata, Buenos Aires, Argentina, 12 July 1995.

21.1 ADULT NONBREEDING BLACK-TAILED GULL. Distinctive: note bill shape and pattern, pale eye, long wing projection, black tail band (largely concealed), yellow legs, and dusky nape markings. Yoshiaki Watanabe. Choshi Chiba, Japan, 17 Dec. 2000.

21.2 ADULT NONBREEDING BLACK-TAILED GULL. Distinctive: note same features as photo 21.1, but P10 not yet fully grown. Geoff Carey. Choshi, Japan, 13 Nov. 1999.

21.3 ADULT BREEDING BLACK-TAILED GULL WITH TWO ADULT RING-BILLED GULLS. Distinctive: note slaty gray upperparts, bill shape and pattern. Marshall J. Iliff. Chesapeake Bay Bridge-Tunnel, Virginia, Mar. 1998.

21.4 JUVENILE BLACK-TAILED GULL. Distinctive: note overall dark brown aspect, pale face, long bicolored bill, and pinkish legs. Harry J. Lehto. Chiba-ken, Choshi, Japan, 17 Aug. 1997.

21.5 FIRST-CYCLE BLACK-TAILED GULL. Distinctive: note bill shape and pattern, overall dark appearance, whitish face, white eye-crescents, and mostly white vent and undertail coverts. Some upperwing coverts have been replaced (compare with photo 21.6). Geoff Carey. Choshi, Japan, 16 Nov. 1999.

21.6 FIRST-CYCLE BLACK-TAILED GULL. Distinctive: note same features as photo 21.5, but no wing coverts have been replaced. Geoff Carey. Choshi, Japan, 12 Feb. 1999.

21.7 FIRST-CYCLE BLACK-TAILED GULL. Distinctive: note same features as photo 21.5, but face and chest have bleached to whitish. Mike Danzenbaker. Aomori Prefecture, Japan, 23 May 1998.

21.8 SECOND-CYCLE BLACK-TAILED GULL, COMPLETING PB2 MOLT (OUTER PRIMARIES GROWING). Distinctive: note same features as photo 21.5, but compare blacker and more-rounded primaries. Yoshiaki Watanabe. Choshi Chiba, Japan, 28 July 2001.

21.9 SECOND-CYCLE BLACK-TAILED GULL. Distinctive: note bill shape and pattern, overall gray-brown appearance, whitish face, white eye-crescents, and mostly white vent and undertail coverts; eye can be pale or dark (compare with photo 21.10). Geoff Carey. Choshi, Japan, 16 Nov. 1999.

21.10 SECOND-CYCLE BLACK-TAILED GULL. Distinctive: note same features as photo 21.9, but eye is still dark, bill and legs are turning greenish, and some upperparts (for example, median coverts) are new A2 feathers. Geoff Carey. Choshi, Japan, 13 Nov. 1999.

21.11 SECOND-CYCLE BLACK-TAILED GULL. Distinctive: note same features as photo 21.9, but underparts are much whiter and upperparts include many A2 feathers. Yoshiaki Watanabe. Choshi Chiba, Japan, 17 Dec. 2000.

21.12 THIRD-CYCLE BLACK-TAILED GULL IN PB3 MOLT (P9–P10 OLD). Distinctive: note bill shape and pattern, pale eye, and slaty gray back. Yoshiaki Watanabe. Choshi Chiba, Japan, 28 July 2001.

21.13 THIRD-CYCLE NONBREEDING BLACK-TAILED GULL, COMPLETING PB3 MOLT (OUTER PRIMARIES NOT FULLY GROWN). Distinguished from adult (see photos 21.1–21.2) by greener bill and legs, reduced white tips to outer primaries, and heavier dusky head markings. Steve Heinl. Ketchikan, Alaska, 8 Oct. 1992.

21.14 THIRD-CYCLE NONBREEDING BLACK-TAILED GULL. Distinguished from adult (see photos 21.1–21.2) by greener bill and legs, brownish on upperwing coverts, and reduced white tips to outer primaries. Yoshiaki Watanabe. Choshi Chiba, Japan, 17 Dec. 2000.

21.15 ADULT NONBREEDING BLACK-TAILED GULL, COMPLETING PB MOLT (OUTER PRIMARIES NOT FULLY GROWN). Distinctive: note black tail band, slaty gray upperparts, and lack of outer primary mirrors. Mike Danzenbaker. Aomori Prefecture, Japan, Oct. 1998.

21.16 ADULT NONBREEDING BLACK-TAILED GULL. Distinctive: note same features as photo 21.15; also bill shape and pattern. Marshall J. Iliff. Chesapeake Bay Bridge-Tunnel, Virginia, 27 Dec. 1998.

21.17 ADULT BLACK-TAILED GULL. Distinctive: note same features as photo 21.15. Brian E. Small. Honshu, Japan, Feb. 1998.

21.18 JUVENILE BLACK-TAILED GULL. Distinctive: note overall dark brown aspect with contrasting white uppertail coverts and long, bicolored bill. Harry J. Lehto. Chiba-ken, Choshi, Japan, 15 Aug. 1997.

21.19 FIRST-CYCLE BLACK-TAILED GULL. Distinctive: note overall dark aspect with whitish face, white eye-crescents, contrasting white uppertail coverts, and long, bicolored bill. Annika Forsten. Pohang, South Korea, 16 Feb. 2002.

21.20 SECOND-CYCLE BLACK-TAILED GULL. Distinctive: note face and bill pattern, slaty gray upperparts, and contrasting white tail coverts. Geoff Carey. Choshi, Japan, 16 Nov. 1999.

21.21 POSSIBLE THIRD-CYCLE NONBREEDING BLACK-TAILED GULL. Distinguished from adult by reduced white tips to outer primaries and bill pattern. Geoff Carey. Choshi, Japan, 13 Nov. 1999.

22A.0 ADULT NONBREEDING MEW GULL. Distinctive in range; note plain yellowish bill, dark eye, yellowish legs, smudgy dusky marks on head and chest, rounded head, relatively large and well-defined white tertial crescent, and large P9–P10 mirrors. Steve N. G. Howell. San Francisco, California, 3 Feb. 2004. **PP. 127, 376**

22B.0 ADULT NONBREEDING COMMON GULL. Relative to Mew Gull, note dusky subterminal bill ring and finer, more-spotted head markings; also note extensive white on underside of P10; compare with Ring-billed Gull. Steve Young. Crosby, England, Jan. 1999. **PP. 133, 381**

22C.0 ADULT NONBREEDING KAMCHATKA GULL. Relative to Mew Gull, note stouter bill, coarser and more-distinct dark markings on head and neck. Yoshiaki Watanabe. Niigata, Japan, 6 Jan. 2001. **PP. 136, 385**

23.0 ADULT NONBREEDING RING-BILLED GULL. Distinctive: note yellow bill with black ring, staring pale eye, yellow legs, pale gray upperparts (so tertial crescent contrasts less than Mew Gull), small P10 mirror, and relatively limited, fine dusky flecking on head. Steve N. G. Howell. Petaluma, California, 27 Dec. 2001. **PP. 139, 388**

22A.1 ADULT NONBREEDING MEW GULL. Distinctive in range; note plain yellowish bill (sometimes with dusky subterminal marks; see photos 22a.2, 22a.4), dark eye, yellowish legs, dusky smudging on head and chest, and rounded head. Steve N. G. Howell. San Francisco, California, 3 Feb. 2004.

22A.2 ADULT NONBREEDING MEW GULL. Note same features as photo 22a.1, although many individuals have more greenish bill base and legs, like this one. Steve N. G. Howell. San Francisco, California, 3 Feb. 2004.

22A.3 ADULT NONBREEDING MEW GULL. Note same features as photo 22a.1, although some individuals like this one have fairly pale eyes. Steve N. G. Howell. San Francisco, California, 25 Jan. 2004.

22A.4 ADULT NONBREEDING MEW GULL. This relatively large-billed individual (presumably a male) has an atypically low-sloping forehead and distinct dark subterminal bill band. Steve N. G. Howell. San Francisco, California, 17 Dec. 2002.

22A.5 ADULT BREEDING MEW GULL. Distinctive in range; note plain yellow bill, dark eyes, and yellow legs. Bruce Hallett. Anchorage, Alaska, 13 June 2001.

22A.6 JUVENILE MEW GULL. Distinctive in range; note small, slender bill and fairly uniform brownish gray appearance with scaly, dull-buff edgings to upperparts. Bruce Mactavish. Inuvik, Northwest Territories, 7 Aug. 2002.

22A.7 FIRST-CYCLE MEW GULL. Distinctive in range; note overall dusky appearance, small bill, and fine whitish edging to primaries; this individual's primaries look blacker than usual (perhaps accentuated by shadow), and it has undergone a fairly extensive post-juvenal molt and attained a mostly gray back (compare with photos 22a.8–22a.9). Brian E. Small. Santa Barbara, California, Dec. 1995.

22A.8 FIRST-CYCLE MEW GULL. A fairly typical midwinter individual with some gray on the back. Note same features as photo 22a.7 but primaries blackish brown. Steve N. G. Howell. San Francisco, California, 3 Feb. 2004.

22A.9 FIRST-CYCLE MEW GULL. A fairly dusky and brownish individual with limited gray on the back. Steve N. G. Howell. San Francisco, California, 25 Jan. 2004.

22A.10 FIRST-CYCLE MEW GULL. A fairly pale individual (same bird as photo 22a.23) with atypically whitish head and underparts (especially for midwinter). Steve N. G. Howell. San Francisco, California, 3 Feb. 2004.

22A.11 FIRST-CYCLE MEW GULL. Some individuals, like this bird, retain most juvenal plumage (compare with photo 22a.6) into midwinter; the head has bleached to whitish. Steve N. G. Howell. San Francisco, California, 3 Feb. 2004.

22A.12 FIRST-CYCLE MEW GULL (SAME BIRD AS PHOTOS 22A.21, 22A.25). Distinctive in range; note medium gray upperparts and small bill; head, foreneck, upperwing coverts, and wingtips have bleached over the winter. Steve N. G. Howell. Bolinas, California, 21 Apr. 2003.

22A.13 FIRST-CYCLE MEW GULL. Note same features as photo 22a.12. Head, neck, upperwing coverts, and wingtips have bleached over the winter and spring. Steve Heinl. Ketchikan, Alaska, 14 June 1993.

22A.14 SECOND-CYCLE NONBREEDING MEW GULL. Distinctive in range; note medium gray upperparts (often with more immature-looking feathers, compare with photo 22a.15) and small bill. Distinguished from adult by blackish bill tip, greenish bill base, flesh to greenish flesh legs, and lack of distinct white tips on outer primaries. Steve N. G. Howell. Tomales Bay, California, 18 Nov. 1999.

22A.15 SECOND-CYCLE NONBREEDING MEW GULL. Note same features as photo 22a.14, plus blackish on tertials and tail. Steve N. G. Howell. San Francisco, California, 3 Feb. 2004.

22A.16 THIRD-CYCLE TYPE NONBREEDING MEW GULL. Distinguished from adult by lack of distinct white tips on P8–P10, reduced white tips on P5–P7, and smaller P9–P10 mirrors (compare with photos 22a.0–22a.4). Steve N. G. Howell. San Francisco, California, 3 Feb. 2004.

22A.17 ADULT NONBREEDING MEW GULL. Distinctive in range; note bold white tongue-tips out to P8, medium gray upperparts, and small, plain yellowish bill. Steve N. G. Howell. Petaluma, California, 2 Jan. 2003.

22A.18 ADULT NONBREEDING MEW GULL. Distinctive in range; note same features as photo 22a.17; P8 has small white tongue-tip but still has a long gray tongue. Eric Preston. San Francisco, California, 4 Nov. 2002.

22A.19 ADULT NONBREEDING MEW GULL. Distinctive in range; note same features as photo 22a.17; P8 has very reduced white tongue-tip but still has a long gray tongue. Mike Danzenbaker. California, 6 Jan. 1997.

22A.20 ADULT NONBREEDING MEW GULL. Distinctive in range; note same features as photo 22a.17. Larry Sansone. Monterey, California, 8 Feb. 2003.

22A.21 FIRST-CYCLE MEW GULL (SAME BIRD AS PHOTOS 22A.12, 22A.25). Note fairly uniform, milky brown appearance with gray on back, paler greater coverts and inner primaries, and heavily marked uppertail coverts. Tail varies from almost solidly dark (like this typical "textbook" individual) to having a broad blackish distal band with variable pale basally (see photos 22a.22–22a.23). Steve N. G. Howell. Bolinas, California, 21 Apr. 2003.

22A.22 FIRST-CYCLE MEW GULL. Note same features as photo 22a.21 but with effect of broad, dark distal tail band and variable pale basal mottling. This tail pattern is fairly common, and bleaching can accentuate the banded effect by summer. Steve N. G. Howell. San Francisco, California, 3 Feb. 2004.

22A.23 FIRST-CYCLE MEW GULL (SAME BIRD AS PHOTO 22A.10). This lightly pigmented individual shows an extreme banded tail pattern much like Kamchatka Gull, from which it is best separated by smaller size, lighter build, and small bill; also note relatively diffuse dusky smudging on neck and underparts (see photo 22a.10). Steve N. G. Howell. San Francisco, California, 3 Feb. 2004.

22A.24 FIRST-CYCLE MEW GULL. Distinctive in range; note dusky brown underwings, heavily barred undertail coverts, and small bill. Louis R. Bevier. Santa Barbara, California, 10 Jan. 1985.

22A.25 FIRST-CYCLE MEW GULL (SAME BIRD AS PHOTOS 22A.12, 22A.21). Note same features as photo 22a.24 but plumage is more bleached. Steve N. G. Howell. Bolinas, California, 21 Apr. 2003.

22A.26 SECOND-CYCLE NONBREEDING MEW GULL. Distinctive in range; note small bill, medium gray upperparts; wing and tail patterns highly variable at this age (compare with photo 22a.27). Mike Danzenbaker. San Francisco, California, Mar. 2000.

22A.27 SECOND-CYCLE BREEDING MEW GULL. Distinctive in range; note small bill, medium gray upperparts; wing and tail patterns highly variable at this age (see photo 22a.26). Gary H. Rosenberg. Safety Lagoon, Alaska, 7 June 1995.

22A.28 THIRD-CYCLE TYPE NONBREEDING MEW GULL. Distinguished from adult by black on primary coverts and alula, extensive black on P8, and lack of white tips to P8–P10 (compare with photos 22a.17–22a.19). Steve N. G. Howell. Tomales Bay, California, 31 Dec. 1999.

22B.1 ADULT NONBREEDING COMMON GULL. Note same features as photo 22b.0. Killian Mullarney. Galway, Ireland, 16 Jan. 2003.

22B.2 JUVENILE COMMON GULL. Relative to Mew Gull, note whiter head and underparts, especially undertail coverts with only sparse dark marks. Steve N. G. Howell. Tampere, Finland, 9 Aug. 2002.

22B.3 FIRST-CYCLE COMMON GULL. Relative to Mew Gull (see photos 22a.6–22a.11) note whiter head and underparts with more-distinct dark markings. Bruce Mactavish. St. John's, Newfoundland, 1 Dec. 1990.

22B.4 FIRST-CYCLE COMMON GULL. Relative to Mew Gull (see photos 22a.6–22a.11) note whiter head and underparts with more-distinct dark markings, cleaner undertail coverts with sparse dark marks. Steve Young. Ainsdale, England, Nov. 2001.

22B.5 FIRST-CYCLE COMMON GULL. Relative to Mew Gull (see photos 22a.6–22a.11) note clean-cut black tail band. Steve Young. Seaforth, England, June 1993.

22B.6 SECOND-CYCLE COMMON GULL. Identification criteria relative to Mew Gull not well known but plumage averages more adultlike (see text). Steve Young. Crosby, England, Jan. 1999.

22B.7 ADULT NONBREEDING COMMON GULL. Relative to Mew Gull note dusky subterminal bill ring, finer and more-spotted head markings, and mostly black P8 (which can have a mirror; see photo 22b.8). Bruce Mactavish. St. John's, Newfoundland, 20 Dec. 1999.

22B.8 ADULT BREEDING COMMON GULL. Relative to Mew Gull (see photos 22a.17–22a.20) note more-extensive black on P8 (which can have a white mirror, as on this individual) and narrow white trailing edge to inner primaries. Harry J. Lehto. Salo, Halikonlahti, Finland, 15 May 1999.

22B.9 ADULT BREEDING COMMON GULL. Note same features as photo 22b.8. Harry J. Lehto. Porkkala, Finland, May 1998.

22B.10 FIRST-CYCLE COMMON GULL. Relative to Mew Gull (see photos 22a.21–22a.23) note striking white uppertail coverts and tail with clean-cut black distal band fading out on R6, lack of dark distal marks on inner webs of inner primaries. Bruce Mactavish. St. John's, Newfoundland, 1 Dec. 1990.

22B.11 FIRST-CYCLE COMMON GULL. Note same features as photo 22b.10. Steve N. G. Howell. Chew Valley Lake, England, 5 May 2003.

22B.12 FIRST-CYCLE COMMON GULL. Relative to Mew Gull (see photos 22a.24–22a.25) note white undertail coverts and tail with clean-cut black distal band, whitish underwing coverts with dark distal markings. Harry J. Lehto. Hanko, Finland, 3 Mar. 1997.

22B.13 SECOND-CYCLE NONBREEDING COMMON GULL. Identification criteria relative to Mew Gull not well known but tail typically all-white (see text). Bruce Mactavish. St. John's, Newfoundland, 20 Oct. 2000.

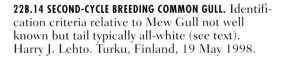

22B.14 SECOND-CYCLE BREEDING COMMON GULL. Identification criteria relative to Mew Gull not well known but tail typically all-white (see text). Harry J. Lehto. Turku, Finland, 19 May 1998.

22C.1 ADULT NONBREEDING KAMCHATKA GULL. Relative to Mew Gull (see photos 22a.0–22a.4) note stouter bill and coarser, more-distinct dark markings on head and neck. Geoff Carey. Chumunjin, South Korea, 30 Nov. 2000.

22C.2 ADULT PRESUMED KAMCHATKA GULL. Identification (relative to Mew Gull and Common Gull) based on range; *heinei* race of Common Gull probably cannot be eliminated based on this photo. Mike Danzenbaker. Aomori Prefecture, Japan, Apr. 1999.

22C.3 FIRST-CYCLE KAMCHATKA GULL, LARGELY IN JUVENAL PLUMAGE. Relative to Mew Gull (see photos 22a.7–22a.9) note coarser, more-distinct dark markings on head and underparts, stouter bill. Distinguished from Common Gull by more-extensive dark markings on underparts, especially undertail coverts. Yoshiaki Watanabe. Hokkaido, Japan, 9 Dec. 2000.

22C.4 FIRST-CYCLE KAMCHATKA GULL. Relative to Mew Gull (see photos 22a.7–22a.11) note coarser, more-distinct dark markings on head and underparts, stouter bill. Distinguished from Common Gull by more-extensive dark markings on underparts. Geoff Carey. Choshi, Japan, 11 Feb. 1999.

22C.5 FIRST-CYCLE KAMCHATKA GULL. Note same features as photo 22c.4. Geoff Carey. Choshi, Japan, 11 Feb. 1999.

22C.6 FIRST-CYCLE PRESUMED KAMCHATKA GULL. Identification (relative to Mew Gull) based on range and distinct dark marks on chest; *heinei* race of Common Gull probably cannot be eliminated based on this photo. Mike Danzenbaker. Aomori Prefecture, Japan, Apr. 1999.

22C.7 ADULT NONBREEDING KAMCHATKA GULL. Relative to Mew Gull (see photos 22a.17–22a.20) note stouter bill, more-defined dark markings on head and neck, narrower white trailing edge to inner primaries, and extensive black on P8. Distinguished from Common Gull by larger bill, coarser dark markings on head and neck, and darker upperparts. Mike Danzenbaker. Aomori Prefecture, Japan, 8 Nov. 1998.

22C.8 ADULT NONBREEDING KAMCHATKA GULL. Note same features as photo 22c.7; also small white mirrors and tongue-tips, pale eye. Geoff Carey. Choshi, Japan, 11 Feb. 1999.

22C.9 FIRST-CYCLE KAMCHATKA GULL. Relative to Mew Gull (see photos 22a.21–22a.23) note clean-cut blackish distal tail band, lack of dark distal marks on inner webs of inner primaries, more-distinct dark markings on head and underparts, and mottled underwings. Distinguished from Common Gull by darker underwings and tail base and relatively heavy dark barring on uppertail coverts. Geoff Carey. Choshi, Japan, 13 Nov. 1999.

22C.10 FIRST-CYCLE KAMCHATKA GULL. Note same features as photo 22c.9 but underwings not visible. Annika Forsten. Kanghwa, South Korea, 24 Feb. 2002.

22C.12 SECOND-CYCLE NONBREEDING KAMCHATKA GULL. Identification criteria relative to Mew Gull and Common Gull not well known (see text) but bill stouter and more often pinkish into second winter. Distinguished from Ring-billed Gull by coarser dark spotting on chest, larger white P10 mirror, presence of P9 mirror, and distinct black on P4. Geoff Carey. Choshi, Japan, 13 Feb. 1999.

22C.11 FIRST-CYCLE KAMCHATKA GULL. Relative to Mew Gull (see photos 22a.24–22a.25) note more-distinct dark markings on underparts and clean-cut blackish distal tail band. Distinguished from Common Gull and Ring-billed Gull by dusky underwings and heavier dark bars on undertail coverts. Geoff Carey. Choshi, Japan, 10 Feb. 1999.

22C.13 SECOND-CYCLE NONBREEDING KAMCHATKA GULL. Note same features as photo 22c.12; also medium gray upperparts relative to Ring-billed Gull. Yoshiaki Watanabe. Choshi Chiba, Japan, 20 Jan. 2001.

23.2 ADULT NONBREEDING RING-BILLED GULL. Distinctive: note same features as photo 23.0; heaviness of dusky head streaking varies in extent (this bird is heavily marked) but streaks typically fine and not smudged. Steve N. G. Howell. Puerto Peñasco, Sonora, Mexico, 23 Jan. 2003.

23.1 ADULT NONBREEDING RING-BILLED GULL. Distinctive and familiar throughout most of North America; note yellow bill with black ring and no red gonydeal spot, staring pale eye, and limited dusky flecking on head. Orbital ring can be dark gray in winter, brightening to orange-red by spring (see photos 23.0, 23.3). Michael D. Stubblefield. Long Island, New York, Nov. 2000.

23.3 ADULT BREEDING RING-BILLED GULL. Distinctive: note yellow bill with black ring, staring pale eye with orange-red orbital ring, yellow legs, and pale gray upperparts. Brian E. Small. Playa del Rey, California, Mar. 1998.

23.4 JUVENILE RING-BILLED GULL. Distinctive: note boldly spotted and checkered, overall brownish appearance with white ground color to head, neck, and underparts. Relative to Mew Gull, also note stout, pink-based bill and dark bars on greater coverts. Kevin T. Karlson. Narragansett, Rhode Island, July 1997.

23.5 FIRST-CYCLE RING-BILLED GULL (SAME BIRD AS PHOTO 23.23), MOSTLY IN JUVENAL PLUMAGE (SCAPULAR MOLT APPEARS TO HAVE STARTED). Note white ground color to underparts; bill can be mostly dark into fall (see photo 23.4). Steve N. G. Howell. Point Reyes, California, 10 Aug. 2005.

23.6 FIRST-CYCLE RING-BILLED GULL. Distinctive and still mostly in worn juvenal plumage (compare with photos 23.7–23.8). Distinguished from Mew Gull by coarsely marked and relatively whitish underparts, checkered upperparts, and blacker primaries; and from California Gull by relatively tapered bill, paler overall appearance, and shorter wing projection. Michael D. Stubblefield. New York City, New York, Dec. 1998.

23.7 FIRST-CYCLE RING-BILLED GULL. Distinctive: post-juvenal molt has included some upperwing coverts (compare with photos 23.6, 23.8). Distinguished from Mew Gull by distinctly marked, relatively whitish head and underparts, stouter, pink-based bill, and blacker primaries; and from first-cycle California Gull by relatively tapered bill, whiter overall appearance, pale gray upperparts, and shorter wing projection; see photo 23.10 for separation from second-cycle California Gull. Steve N. G. Howell. Petaluma, California, 24 Dec. 1998.

23.8 FIRST-CYCLE RING-BILLED GULL. A typical first-winter bird; post-juvenal molt has not included upperwing coverts (compare with photos 23.6–23.7). Note same features as photo 23.7. Steve N. G. Howell. Petaluma, California, 2 Jan. 2003.

23.9 FIRST-CYCLE RING-BILLED GULL. Distinctive: note same features as photo 23.7. By late winter bill can develop pale tip and eye can become paler. Steve N. G. Howell. Petaluma, California, 23 Mar. 2003.

23.10 FIRST-CYCLE RING-BILLED GULL AND SECOND-CYCLE CALIFORNIA GULL (BEHIND). Ring-billed has paler gray upperparts, finer dusky markings on head and neck, bleached whitish (not brown) greater coverts, and its smaller bill is often brighter pink. Steve N. G. Howell. Petaluma, California, 23 Mar. 2003.

23.11 SECOND-CYCLE RING-BILLED GULL, MOLTING TO B2 PLUMAGE (P6–P10 OLD). Bill often brightens to yellowish in first summer, although eye can remain dark. Note pale gray upperparts, bill shape and pattern. Steve N. G. Howell. Salisbury Beach, Massachusetts, 28 June 1998.

23.12 SECOND-CYCLE NONBREEDING RING-BILLED GULL. Distinguished from adult by reduced to absent white tips to outer primaries; also note pinkish bill base, greenish legs. Steve N. G. Howell. Petaluma, California, 27 Dec. 2001.

23.13 SECOND-CYCLE NONBREEDING RING-BILLED GULL. Distinguished from adult by reduced to absent white tips to outer primaries; also note duller eye, bill, and legs and black on tail. Steve N. G. Howell. Petaluma, California, 2 Jan. 2003.

23.14 SECOND-CYCLE NONBREEDING RING-BILLED GULL. Wings and dark eye relatively "retarded" but bill and legs average or "advanced" in color. Steve N. G. Howell. Puerto Peñasco, Sonora, Mexico, 23 Jan. 2003.

23.15 SECOND-CYCLE RING-BILLED GULL. Distinguished from adult (see photo 23.4) by reduced to absent white tips to outer primaries, bill and legs average duller with broader black bill ring; adults usually lack dusky head streaking by this date. Steve N. G. Howell. Petaluma, California, 23 Mar. 2003.

23.16 THIRD-CYCLE RING-BILLED GULL IN PB3 MOLT. Distinguished from adult by retained B2 wingtip pattern, dark on tertials and tail. Steve N. G. Howell. Salisbury Beach, Massachusetts, 28 June 1998.

23.17 ADULT BREEDING RING-BILLED GULL. Distinctive: note yellow bill with black ring and no red gonydeal spot, staring pale eye; some birds lack white mirror on P9. Bruce Mactavish. St. John's, Newfoundland, 18 May 2000.

23.19 JUVENILE RING-BILLED GULL. Distinctive: note brightly contrasting pattern with pale gray greater coverts, sparsely marked tail coverts, and tail pattern (compare with Mew Gull, photos 22a.21–22a.23). Eric Preston. Monterey Bay, California, 2 Sept. 2001.

23.18 ADULT RING-BILLED GULL. Distinctive: note same features as photo 23.17. From below, black wingtip contrasts with overall white underwing, lacking California Gull's dusky gray band along bases of remiges (see photo 24.32). Kevin T. Karlson. Fort Myers Beach, Florida, Mar. 1995.

23.21 FIRST-CYCLE RING-BILLED GULL. Some birds, like this individual, have less contrast on their upperwings, with relatively brown outer primaries and a reduced pale panel on the inner primaries. Steve N. G. Howell. Puerto Peñasco, Sonora, Mexico, 23 Jan. 2003.

23.20 FIRST-CYCLE RING-BILLED GULL. Distinctive: note same features as photo 23.19 (and compare with Mew Gull, photos 22a.21–22a.23). Steve N. G. Howell. Petaluma, California, 26 Mar. 2004.

23.22 FIRST-CYCLE RING-BILLED GULL WITH UPPERWING-COVERT PANEL BLEACHED TO WHITE, CLEAN-CUT BLACK TAIL BAND. Bruce Hallett. Tybee Island, Georgia, 14 Apr. 2000.

23.23 FIRST-CYCLE RING-BILLED GULL (SAME BIRD AS PHOTO 23.5). Distinctive: note overall whitish underwings and clean-cut black tail band (compare with Mew Gull, photos 22a.24–22a.25). Steve N. G. Howell. Point Reyes, California, 10 Aug. 2005.

23.24 SECOND-CYCLE NONBREEDING RING-BILLED GULL. Distinguished from adult by extensive black in wingtip, small P10 mirror; tail varies from a solid black band (like this) to unmarked, and eyes can be dark (see photo 23.25). Tony Leukering. Puerto Peñasco, Sonora, Mexico, 5 Feb. 2000.

23.25 SECOND-CYCLE BREEDING RING-BILLED GULL. Distinguished from adult by extensive black in outer portion of wing, dark eye; tail varies from all-white (like this) to having a solid black band (see photo 23.24). Bruce Mactavish. St. John's, Newfoundland, 18 May 2000.

23.26 ADULT PRESUMED RING-BILLED GULL × CALIFORNIA GULL HYBRID. Structurally similar to Ring-billed Gull but note dark eye, greenish bill and legs, and slightly darker upperparts. Distinguished from California Gull by structure (especially evident in direct comparison with both putative parent species) and lack of red on bill. Jon Dunn. Reno, Nevada, 6 Mar. 2002.

**23.27 FIRST-CYCLE PRESUMED RING-BILLED GULL ×
CALIFORNIA GULL HYBRID (SECOND-CYCLE CALIFORNIA GULL
BEHIND, ADULT RING-BILLED GULL TO RIGHT).** Same bird as
photo 23.28. Aged as first cycle by relatively
tapered primaries, juvenal tertials and upperwing
coverts. Initially mistaken for Ring-billed Gull but
intermediate between parent species in structure
and plumage. Distinguished from Ring-billed Gull
by structure (for example, long wing projection),
heavy dark head streaking with thick dark postocular line, and dusky belly smudging; also
mostly black tail and relatively heavy barring on
tail coverts (see photo 23.28). Distinguished
from (second-cycle) California Gull by juvenal
primaries, tertial pattern, and mostly black tail.
Steve N. G. Howell. Petaluma, California,
26 Mar. 2004.

**23.28 FIRST-CYCLE PRESUMED RING-BILLED GULL ×
CALIFORNIA GULL HYBRID (FIRST-CYCLE RING-BILLED GULL TO
RIGHT).** See caption for photo 23.27 of same bird.
Distinguished from Ring-billed Gull by heavy dark
head streaking with thick dark postocular line,
dusky belly smudging, mostly black tail, and
relatively heavy barring on tail coverts. Steve N. G.
Howell. Petaluma, California, 26 Mar. 2004.

**23.29 ADULT PRESUMED RING-BILLED GULL × MEW/COMMON
GULL HYBRID (SAME BIRD AS PHOTO 23.30) WITH ADULT
RING-BILLED GULL BEHIND.** Distinguished from Mew
Gull by stouter bill with black bill ring; from Ring-
billed Gull by overall structure, dark eye, and
slightly darker gray upperparts. Michael O'Brien.
Assateague Island, Maryland, 18 July 1992.

**23.30 ADULT PRESUMED RING-BILLED GULL × MEW/
COMMON GULL HYBRID (SAME BIRD AS PHOTO 23.29).**
Wingtip pattern intermediate between parent
species, for example, less white in P8–P10 than
typical of Mew/Common Gull. Michael O'Brien.
Assateague Island, Maryland, 18 July 1992.

24.0 ADULT NONBREEDING CALIFORNIA GULL (PRESUMED *L. C. CALIFORNICUS*). Distinctive: note medium gray upperparts, dark eye, black bill ring, red gonydeal spot, coarse dusky markings on head and neck, yellowish legs, and relatively long wing projection. Stockier build, relatively flat head and stout bill point to a male (compare with photo 24.1). Steve N. G. Howell. Petaluma, California, 27 Dec. 2001. **PP. 150, 395**

25A.0 ADULT NONBREEDING AMERICAN HERRING GULL. Note pale gray upperparts, bill size and shape, black wingtips, staring pale eye, orange-yellow orbital ring, and flesh pink legs. Bruce Mactavish. St. John's, Newfoundland, 25 Feb. 2001. **PP. 159, 401**

25B.0 ADULT NONBREEDING EUROPEAN HERRING GULLS. *L. a. argentatus* (behind) averages larger, bigger billed, darker above, and with more white in the wingtip than *argenteus* (front). Rudy Offereins. Wijster, Netherlands, 19 Dec. 1999. **PP. 170, 410**

25C.0 ADULT NONBREEDING VEGA GULL. Note medium gray upperparts, bill size and shape, dark eye with reddish orbital ring, and rich pink legs. Geoff Carey. Choshi, Japan, 9 Feb. 1999. **PP. 175, 412**

26.0 ADULT NONBREEDING YELLOW-LEGGED GULLS, PRE-SUMED MALE (BEHIND) AND FEMALE. Note medium gray upperparts, yellow legs, bill size and shape, orange-red orbital ring, and limited dusky head streaking. Theo Bakker. Sao Miguel, Azores, 12 Nov. 2001. **PP. 180, 417**

27.0 ADULT NONBREEDING LESSER BLACK-BACKED GULL *(L. F. GRAELLSII).* Note slaty gray upperparts, yellowish legs, distinct head and neck streaking, and bill size and shape. Killian Mullarney. Wexford, Ireland, 27 Jan. 1999. **PP. 187, 422**

28.0 ADULT BREEDING KELP GULL *(L. D. DOMINICANUS).* Note slaty blackish upperparts, yellowish legs, bill size and shape, and orange orbital ring. Nonbreeding birds look white headed but have faint dusky clouding and spotting mainly on lores and hindneck. Steve N. G. Howell. Concon, Valparaíso, Chile, 26 Oct. 2002. **PP. 196, 428**

29.0 ADULT NONBREEDING GREAT BLACK-BACKED GULL. Distinctive: note slaty blackish upperparts, bill size and shape, short wing projection, pale flesh pink legs, and typically reduced dusky streaking on head and hindneck. Yellow staining on face is from food. Kenneth Z. Kurland. Winthrop, Massachusetts, 27 Nov. 2001. **PP. 205, 434**

30.0 ADULT NONBREEDING SLATY-BACKED GULL. Note slaty gray upperparts, flesh pink legs, extensive dusky head and neck streaking, stout bill, and rich pink orbital ring. Geoff Carey. Hokkaido, Japan, 4 Feb. 1999. **PP. 213, 438**

31.0 ADULT NONBREEDING WESTERN GULL. Note slaty gray upperparts, flesh pink legs, white-headed aspect (typical of midwinter), stout, somewhat bulbous-tipped, and bright bill and yellow orbital ring. Steve N. G. Howell. Monterey, California, 24 Jan. 2004. **PP. 221, 442**

32.0 ADULT YELLOW-FOOTED GULL. Note slaty gray upperparts, yellowish legs, white-headed aspect, stout and bulbous-tipped bill with large red gonydeal spot, and yellow orbital ring. White primary tips of fresh plumage (compare with photo 32.1) are typically much reduced by midwinter. Steve N. G. Howell. Puerto Peñasco, Sonora, Mexico, 21 Jan. 2003. **PP. 226, 448**

33.0 ADULT NONBREEDING GLAUCOUS-WINGED GULL. Note gray wingtips, short wing projection, smudgy head and neck markings, and stout bill. Steve N. G. Howell. Petaluma, California, 27 Dec. 2001. **PP. 235, 453**

34.0 ADULT NONBREEDING GLAUCOUS GULL (*L. H. LEUCERETES* BY RANGE). Note white wingtips, stout bill (often deepest at base, as on this bird), and short wing projection. Bruce Mactavish. St. John's, Newfoundland, 1 Dec. 2000. **PP. 244, 458**

35A.0 ADULT NONBREEDING KUMLIEN'S GULL. A typical individual with slaty gray wingtips (stage 4 primary pattern; Howell and Mactavish 2003). Steve N. G. Howell. St. John's, Newfoundland, 4 Feb. 2002. **PP. 251, 463**

35B.0 ADULT NONBREEDING ICELAND GULL. Distinguished from Glaucous Gull by more petite build, smaller bill, and relatively longer wing projection; orbital ring in winter can be pinkish. Steve Young. Fraserburgh, Scotland, Jan. 1993. **PP. 260, 468**

36.0 ADULT NONBREEDING THAYER'S GULL. Note bill size and shape, blackish wingtips with large white primary tips and extensively whitish underside to P10, dark eye, raspberry pink orbital ring, and rich pink legs. Steve Heinl. Ketchikan, Alaska, 29 Dec. 1994. **PP. 263, 471**

24.1 ADULT NONBREEDING CALIFORNIA GULL (PRESUMED *L. C. CALIFORNICUS*). Distinctive: note same features as photo 24.0. Lighter build, relatively rounded head, and slender bill point to a female (compare with photo 24.0). Steve N. G. Howell. Petaluma, California, 27 Dec. 2001.

24.2 ADULT BREEDING CALIFORNIA GULLS *(L. C. CALIFORNICUS)*. Distinctive: note medium gray upperparts, dark eye, broken black bill ring, red gonydeal spot, and yellow legs. Differences in bill size and head shape between male (upper) and female can be striking in direct comparison, and note brighter bare parts relative to winter (photos 24.0–24.1). Marshall J. Iliff. Pyramid Lake, Nevada, late May 1998.

24.3 ADULT BREEDING CALIFORNIA GULL *(L. C. CALIFORNI-CUS)*. Distinctive: note same features as photo 24.2 (black bill ring is greatly reduced, and can even be absent, on breeding birds) and how plumage can be heavily worn by midsummer. Larry Sansone. Mono Lake, California, 6 July 2002.

24.4 ADULT BREEDING CALIFORNIA GULL *(L. C. ALBER-TAENSIS)*. Distinctive; note same features as photo 24.3. Bruce Mactavish. Red Deer, Alberta, 13 June 2002.

24.5 ADULT BREEDING CALIFORNIA GULL *(L. C. ALBERTAENSIS)* IN PB MOLT (P7–P10 OLD; BASE OF P7 EXPOSED BY SHED P6). Distinctive: note same features as photo 24.3. Some presumed male *albertaensis* (like this bird) are notably large and bulky with a stout bill and can suggest Herring Gull in structure. Note dark eyes, slightly darker gray upperparts than Herring, yellow legs, dark subterminal bill mark, and relatively long wing projection. Bruce Hallett. Madison River, Montana, July 1993.

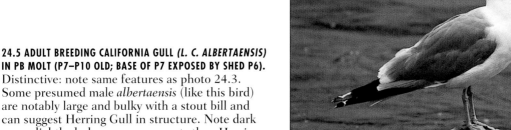

24.6 ADULT CALIFORNIA GULLS: *L. C. CALIFORNICUS* **(UPPER) AND** *L. C. ALBERTAENSIS* **(LOWER).** The northern-breeding subspecies *albertaensis* averages larger (especially in bill, compare with photo 24.5) and paler gray dorsally than *californicus,* although differences in gray tone can be difficult to evaluate in the field, especially in sunny conditions (for example, photos 24.2 versus 24.4). Steve N. G. Howell. University of Alaska Museum, Fairbanks, June 2000.

24.7 JUVENILE CALIFORNIA GULL. A relatively dark individual, and juvenile western gull (right). Note California's slender bill, long wing projection, and pale forehead. Steve N. G. Howell. Point Reyes, California, 22 Aug. 2003.

24.9 JUVENILE CALIFORNIA GULL. A typical cinnamon individual. Note same features as photo 24.7; also, bill is starting to show two-tone pattern. Steve N. G. Howell. Point Reyes, California, 22 Aug. 2003.

24.8 JUVENILE CALIFORNIA GULL. A typical brown individual. Note same features as photo 24.7. Steve N. G. Howell. Point Reyes, California, 25 Aug. 2003.

24.10 FIRST-CYCLE CALIFORNIA GULL. A fairly bleached individual (some birds bleach much paler overall; compare with photo 24.35). Note same features as photo 24.7; bill shows dull two-tone pattern, and post-juvenal molt (of darker and grayer feathers) is apparent on head and upperparts. Steve N. G. Howell. Point Reyes, California, 25 Aug. 2003.

24.11 FIRST-CYCLE CALIFORNIA GULL. By Oct. bill is usually brightly bicolored (compare with photos 24.7–24.10); note post-juvenal molt (incoming darker and grayer feathers) on face, chest, sides, and back. Steve N. G. Howell. Point Reyes, California, 15 Oct. 2003.

24.12 FIRST-CYCLE CALIFORNIA GULL, A TYPICAL FIRST-WINTER INDIVIDUAL. Distinctive: note bill shape and pattern, overall dark aspect, and dark anchor patterns on scapulars; upperwing coverts are also often replaced (see photos I.1–I.4). Steve N. G. Howell. Petaluma, California, 15 Dec. 2001.

24.13 FIRST-CYCLE CALIFORNIA GULL. Distinctive: note bill shape and pattern, long wing projection, overall dark aspect (face and chest have bleached whitish), and variegated scapular patterns. Steve N. G. Howell. Puerto Vallarta, Jalisco, Mexico, 5 Jan. 2003.

24.14 FIRST-CYCLE CALIFORNIA GULL. Distinctive: note same features as photo 24.13. Steve N. G. Howell. Petaluma, California, 23 Mar. 2003.

24.15 SECOND-CYCLE CALIFORNIA GULL (PRESUMABLY *L. C. ALBERTAENSIS*) STARTING PB2 MOLT (NOTE INCOMING MEDIAN COVERTS). Distinctive: note bill shape and pattern, long wing projection, and bluish cast to tibia. Gray back feathers may be mixture of A1 and B2 feathers. Bruce Mactavish. Red Deer, Alberta, 13 June 2002.

24.16 SECOND-CYCLE CALIFORNIA GULL COMPLETING PB2 MOLT (P9–P10 OLD). Distinctive: note bill shape and pattern and blue-gray cast to tibia. B2 plumage is highly variable: some "retarded" individuals, like this, have variegated upperparts (compare with photos 24.17–24.18). Larry Sansone. Monterey, California, 17 Aug. 2003.

24.17 SECOND-CYCLE CALIFORNIA GULL COMPLETING PB2 MOLT (P10 OLD). Distinctive: note bill shape and pattern and blue-gray cast to tibia. B2 plumage is highly variable: some individuals, like this bird, are overall dusky gray-brown (compare with photos 24.16, 24.18). Steve N. G. Howell. Point Reyes, California, 22 Aug. 2003.

24.18 SECOND-CYCLE CALIFORNIA GULL COMPLETING PB2 MOLT (P9–P10 OLD). Distinctive: note bill shape and pattern and blue-gray cast to tibia. B2 plumage is highly variable: some "advanced" individuals, like this, have a mostly gray back (compare with photos 24.17–24.18). Larry Sansone. Monterey, California, 17 Aug. 2003.

24.19 SECOND-CYCLE NONBREEDING CALIFORNIA GULL. Distinctive: note bill shape, color, and pattern, blue-gray cast to tibia, long wing projection, medium gray back feathers, and dark eye. This is a relatively "retarded" bird with reduced gray on the back. Steve N. G. Howell. Petaluma, California, 11 Dec. 2003.

24.20 SECOND-CYCLE NONBREEDING CALIFORNIA GULL.
Distinctive: note same features as photo 24.19,
but this individual is much more advanced in
appearance. Most second-winter birds have a gray
back (and often some gray upperwing coverts), the
PA2 molt having started in fall, before PB2 molt
completed. Steve N. G. Howell. Petaluma,
California, 26 Dec. 2001.

**24.21 SECOND-CYCLE NONBREEDING CALIFORNIA GULL (BACK
RIGHT) AND SECOND-CYCLE AMERICAN HERRING GULL (FRONT
LEFT).** Note same features as photo 24.19 (other
individuals by this date have a more advanced,
yellowish bill). Also note stockier build, stouter
and pinker-based bill, pink legs, and paler eye of
Herring Gull. Steve N. G. Howell. Petaluma,
California, 23 Mar. 2003.

**24.22 SECOND-CYCLE BREEDING CALIFORNIA GULL (PRESUM-
ABLY *L. C. CALIFORNICUS*).** Distinctive: note whiter head
and underparts and brighter bill and orbital ring
relative to birds two months earlier (photo 24.21).
Marshall J. Iliff. Pyramid Lake, Nevada, late May
1998.

**24.23 SECOND-CYCLE BREEDING CALIFORNIA GULL (PRESUM-
ABLY *L. C. ALBERTAENSIS*); PB3 MOLT MAY HAVE STARTED.**
Distinctive: note bill shape and pattern, dark eye
with pinkish red orbital ring, medium gray
upperparts, and yellowish-flesh legs. Bruce
Mactavish. Red Deer, Alberta, 13 June 2002.

24.24 THIRD-CYCLE NONBREEDING CALIFORNIA GULL. Note
how bill colors regress from second summer;
(compare with photos 24.22–24.23). Distinguished from adult by duller, more greenish bill
and legs, reduced white tips to outer primaries,
black on tail (which can be all-white), and variable brownish on upperwing coverts and tertials.
Steve N. G. Howell. Petaluma, California,
27 Dec. 2001.

24.25 THIRD-CYCLE NONBREEDING CALIFORNIA GULL. Note same features as photo 24.24 (other differences apparent in flight; for example photo 24.41). Steve N. G. Howell. Petaluma, California, 26 Dec. 2001.

24.26 THIRD-CYCLE NONBREEDING CALIFORNIA GULL. Some adults and third-cycle birds (<1 percent) can have pale eyes; adults at this date typically have much brighter bill and legs. Steve N. G. Howell. Petaluma, California, 23 Mar. 2003.

24.27 THIRD-CYCLE BREEDING CALIFORNIA GULL (PRESUMED *L. C. ALBERTAENSIS*). Distinguished from adult by reduced white tips to outer primaries and dark on primary coverts and tail. Bruce Mactavish. Red Deer, Alberta, 13 June 2002.

24.28 ADULT NONBREEDING CALIFORNIA GULL. Distinctive: note bill shape and pattern, dark eye, and medium gray upperparts with fairly contrasting white trailing edge to upperwings. Eric Preston. Monterey Bay, California, 6 Oct. 2002.

24.29 ADULT BREEDING CALIFORNIA GULL (*L. C. ALBERTAENSIS*). Note same features as photo 24.28 (subterminal black on bill absent). Relative to nominate *californicus* (photo 24.30), typically has longer and whiter-tipped gray tongue on P7. Brad Bolduan. Last Mountain Lake, Saskatchewan, 13 May 1995.

24.30 ADULT BREEDING CALIFORNIA GULL *(L. C. CALIFORNI-CUS)*, **IN PB MOLT (P6–P10 OLD).** Note same features as photo 24.28 (subterminal black on bill almost absent). Larry Sansone. Mono Lake, California, 6 July 2002.

24.31 ADULT NONBREEDING CALIFORNIA GULLS. Distinctive: note medium gray upperparts with fairly contrasting white trailing edge to upperwings, bill shape and pattern. Wingtip patterns (see text) suggest *L. c. californicus* (upper bird) and *L. c. albertaensis* (lower bird), supported by overall bulk, bill size, and relative gray tones of upperparts. Steve N. G. Howell. Point Reyes, California, 30 Jan. 2003.

24.32 ADULT NONBREEDING CALIFORNIA GULL. Distinctive: note bill shape and pattern, yellow feet, and relatively contrasting, smoky gray bases of remiges (compare with photo 23.18). Steve N. G. Howell. Bolinas Lagoon, California, 3 Feb. 2003.

24.33 JUVENILE CALIFORNIA GULL. Distinctive: separated from other large gulls by slender bill (not yet brightly bicolored; compare with photo 24.35), overall brightly checkered and mottled aspect, lack of a strongly contrasting pale panel on inner primaries, dark bases to outer greater coverts, and mostly black tail with bright white tips and subterminal marks. Eric Preston. Marin County, California, 20 July 2003.

24.34 FIRST-CYCLE CALIFORNIA GULL. Some individuals, like this bird, show a relatively contrasting paler panel on the inner 4 primaries; note slender, bicolored bill, plain bases to outer greater coverts, and relatively narrow pointed wings. Steve N. G. Howell. Point Reyes, California, 15 Sept. 2003.

24.35 FIRST-CYCLE CALIFORNIA GULL. Some fall birds have a very bleached-out creamy head (here with some darker post-juvenal feathers) and body, which can be puzzling, but this distinctive California trait is not regularly shown by any other North American gull (compare with photo 24.10). Note bill pattern and shape and the relatively narrow and pointed wings. Steve N. G. Howell. Off Fort Bragg, California, 27 Aug. 2005.

24.36 FIRST-CYCLE CALIFORNIA GULL. Note long, narrow, and pointed wings and slender, bicolored bill. Forehead often bleaches whitish, and some birds (like this individual) have pale cinnamon under-parts (compare with photo 24.35). Steve N. G. Howell. Off Fort Bragg, California, 16 Aug. 2003.

24.37 SECOND-CYCLE NONBREEDING CALIFORNIA GULL. Distinguished from other large gulls by structure, slender bicolored bill, and small pale inner primary panel (typically on 4 primaries), which, on this individual, is atypically advanced and adult-like in pattern (compare with photos 24.38–24.39, which are typical); many birds have a small P10 mirror (compare with photos 24.38–24.39). Eric Preston. Cordell Bank, California, 29 Sept. 2002.

24.38 SECOND-CYCLE BREEDING CALIFORNIA GULL. From other large gulls by structure, medium gray upperparts, and relatively small pale inner primary panel (dull brownish on this individual; compare with photos 24.37, 24.39). Steve N. G. Howell. Petaluma, California, 28 Dec. 2003.

24.39 SECOND-CYCLE BREEDING CALIFORNIA GULL. Note structure, bill shape and pattern, relatively small pale inner primary panel. Steve N. G. Howell. Off Fort Bragg, California, 11 May 2003.

24.40 SECOND-CYCLE CALIFORNIA GULL, COMPLETING PB2 MOLT (P10 NOT FULLY GROWN). Distinctive: distinguished from other large gulls by relatively narrow and pointed wings with limited brown markings on underwing coverts (solidly dark on B2 Western Gull), slender bicolored bill. Larry Sansone. Monterey Bay, California, 17 Sept. 2002.

24.41 THIRD-CYCLE NONBREEDING CALIFORNIA GULL. Distinguished from adult by black marks on primary coverts, alula, and tail (which can be all white), smaller white mirrors on outer primaries, and duller bill and legs. Steve N. G. Howell. Cordell Bank, California, 29 Sept. 2002.

25A.1 NONBREEDING AMERICAN HERRING GULLS. On adults note pale gray upperparts, staring pale eyes, bill size and shape, black wingtips, and variation in bill pattern and extent of dusky head and neck streaking. Steve N. G. Howell. St. John's, Newfoundland, 4 Feb. 2002.

25A.2 ADULT NONBREEDING AMERICAN HERRING GULL. Note pale gray upperparts, pink legs, staring pale eye, bill size and shape, and black wingtips; orbital ring in winter can look dark, as on this bird. Small-billed birds like this (probably a female; compare with photo 25a.6) can be confused with Thayer's Gull; note relatively small white primary tips and extensive black on underside of P10. Steve N. G. Howell. Tomales Bay, California, 29 Dec. 2002.

25A.3 ADULT NONBREEDING AMERICAN HERRING GULL. Note pale gray upperparts, bill size and shape, and black wingtips; orbital ring in winter can be suffused pinkish, as on this bird. Some adults, especially in the West, have fine dusky flecking in their eyes. Steve N. G. Howell. Puerto Peñasco, Sonora, Mexico, 23 Jan. 2003.

25A.4 ADULT NONBREEDING AMERICAN HERRING GULL. Note same features as photo 25a.3; small-billed adults with dusky speckling in their eyes, like this, can suggest Thayer's Gull; note relatively small white primary tips and wingtip pattern (best seen on spread wings); also note pinkish bill base and blackish gonys mark, both atypical of winter adult Thayer's. Steve N. G. Howell. Puerto Peñasco, Sonora, Mexico, 23 Jan. 2003.

**25A.5 ADULT BREEDING AMERICAN HERRING GULL, ALTER-
NATE PLUMAGE.** Note pale gray upperparts, bill size
and shape, staring pale eye with orange orbital
ring, and black wingtips. Bruce Mactavish.
St. John's, Newfoundland, 29 Apr. 2002.

**25A.6 ADULT BREEDING AMERICAN HERRING GULL, ALTER-
NATE PLUMAGE.** Note pale gray upperparts, bill size
(large, pointing to a male; compare with photo
25a.2) and shape, staring pale eye with orange-
yellow orbital ring, and black wingtips (white
primary tips reduced by wear). Kevin T. Karlson.
Reeds Beach, New Jersey, 1 June 2000.

25A.7 JUVENILE AMERICAN HERRING GULL. A fresh-
plumaged and dark individual. Note overall dark
brown aspect, blackish wingtips, bill size and
shape, and dull pinkish on bill base. Kevin T.
Karlson. Narragansett, Rhode Island, July 1996.

25A.8 JUVENILE AMERICAN HERRING GULL. Note overall
brown aspect (upperpart edgings have bleached to
whitish; compare with photo 25a.7), bill size and
shape, and dull pinkish on bill base; some birds,
like this individual, have narrow whitish fringes to
primary tips. Larry Sansone. Cape May, New
Jersey, 13 Sept. 1999.

**25A.9 FIRST-CYCLE AMERICAN HERRING GULL WITH LIMITED
POST-JUVENAL SCAPULAR MOLT.** Note overall brown
aspect, bill size and shape. Distinguished from
Thayer's Gull by blacker primaries and tertial
centers, stouter bill, and less-frosty upperparts.
Steve N. G. Howell. Petaluma, California, 31 Oct.
1997.

25A.10 FIRST-CYCLE AMERICAN HERRING GULL STILL MOSTLY OR ENTIRELY IN JUVENAL PLUMAGE. Note same features as photo 25a.8; also blackish underside to P10. Steve N. G. Howell. Petaluma, California, 12 Dec. 1998.

25A.11 FIRST-CYCLE AMERICAN HERRING GULL WITH MODERATE POST-JUVENAL SCAPULAR MOLT. Note same features as photo 25a.8. Steve N. G. Howell. Petaluma, California, 2 Jan. 2003.

25A.12 FIRST-CYCLE AMERICAN HERRING GULL WITH LIMITED POST-JUVENAL SCAPULAR MOLT. A darker and browner individual (head has bleached paler). Note same features as photo 25a.8 (low angle sunlight accentuates warm plumage tones). Steve N. G. Howell. Puerto Peñasco, Sonora, Mexico, 22 Jan. 2003.

25A.13 FIRST-CYCLE AMERICAN HERRING GULL WITH LIMITED POST-JUVENAL SCAPULAR MOLT. A paler and grayer individual with sparser dark barring on undertail coverts. Note overall gray-brown aspect, bill size and shape, and pink bill base. Steve N. G. Howell. Puerto Peñasco, Sonora, Mexico, 23 Jan. 2003.

25A.14 FIRST-CYCLE AMERICAN HERRING GULL WITH MODERATE POST-JUVENAL SCAPULAR MOLT. A paler and grayer individual. Note overall gray-brown aspect (head and chest have bleached to whitish; post-juvenal scapulars have fine dusky anchor patterns), bill size and shape, and pink bill base. Steve N. G. Howell. Puerto Peñasco, Sonora, Mexico, 23 Jan. 2003.

25A.15 FIRST-CYCLE AMERICAN HERRING GULL WITH MODERATE POST-JUVENAL SCAPULAR MOLT. A darker and browner individual. Note overall gray-brown aspect (head has bleached to whitish; post-juvenal scapulars have large blackish marks), bill size and shape, and pinkish on bill base. Steve N. G. Howell. Puerto Peñasco, Sonora, Mexico, 22 Jan. 2003.

25A.16 FIRST-CYCLE AMERICAN HERRING GULL WITH LIMITED POST-JUVENAL SCAPULAR MOLT. A darker and browner individual with scapulars and tertials less worn than birds wintering in sunny latitudes (for example photo 25a.15). Note overall gray-brown aspect, bill size and shape, and dull pinkish on bill base. Steve N. G. Howell. St. John's, Newfoundland, 4 Feb. 2002.

25A.17 FIRST-CYCLE AMERICAN HERRING GULL WITH EXTENSIVE POST-JUVENAL SCAPULAR MOLT. Plumage has bleached strikingly over the winter. Note bill size and shape, barred scapulars, and blackish wing-tips. Steve N. G. Howell. Petaluma, California, 8 Apr. 1997.

25A.18 SECOND-CYCLE AMERICAN HERRING GULL IN PB2 MOLT (P8–10 OLD). Note overall gray-brown aspect, bill size and shape. Steve N. G. Howell. Salisbury Beach, Massachusetts, 28 June 1998.

25A.19 SECOND-CYCLE AMERICAN HERRING GULL COMPLETING PB2 MOLT (OUTER PRIMARIES NOT FULLY GROWN). Note overall gray-brown aspect, bill size and shape. Michael D. Stubblefield. Jamaica Bay, New York, Oct. 1999.

25A.20 SECOND-CYCLE AMERICAN HERRING GULL. Distinguished from first cycle by more-rounded primaries, finer speckling on greater coverts, brightly bicolored bill, and pale eye (eye can be dark through second winter). Bruce Mactavish. St. John's, Newfoundland, 23 Oct. 2001.

25A.21 SECOND-CYCLE AMERICAN HERRING GULL. A relatively "retarded" individual. Distinguished from first cycle by finely patterned greater coverts and pale eye; also more-rounded primaries (not visible here). Steve N. G. Howell. Puerto Peñasco, Sonora, Mexico, 21 Jan. 2003.

25A.22 SECOND-CYCLE AMERICAN HERRING GULL. Distinguished from first cycle by more-rounded primaries, finely pattened greater coverts and tertials, and paler eye; head and foreneck have bleached to whitish. Steve N. G. Howell. Puerto Peñasco, Sonora, Mexico, 22 Jan. 2003.

25A.23 SECOND-CYCLE AMERICAN HERRING GULL. A relatively "advanced" individual. Distinguished from third cycle by inner primary pattern (seen in flight). Steve N. G. Howell. Puerto Peñasco, Sonora, Mexico, 22 Jan. 2003.

25A.24 SECOND-CYCLE AMERICAN HERRING GULL. A relatively "advanced" individual. Distinguished from third cycle by inner primary pattern (seen in flight). Steve N. G. Howell. Puerto Peñasco, Sonora, Mexico, 22 Jan. 2003.

25A.25 SECOND-CYCLE AMERICAN HERRING GULL. Distinguished from first cycle by more-rounded primaries, finely patterned greater coverts and tertials, paler eye, and incoming clear gray on scapulars. Steve N. G. Howell. St. John's, Newfoundland, 4 Feb. 2002.

25A.26 THIRD-CYCLE AMERICAN HERRING GULL IN PB3 MOLT. An "advanced" individual (compare with photo 25a.27). Distinguished from fourth cycle in PB4 molt by inner primary pattern (not visible here); also note brownish primaries, solidly dark tail, and dull eye (compare with photo 25a.34). Steve N. G. Howell. Salisbury Beach, Massachusetts, 28 June 1998.

25A.27 THIRD-CYCLE AMERICAN HERRING GULL IN PB3 MOLT. A more "retarded" individual (compare with photo 25a.26). Note pale gray upperparts, bill size and shape; most birds pale eyed by this date. Steve N. G. Howell. Salisbury Beach, Massachusetts, 30 June 1998.

25A.28 THIRD-CYCLE AMERICAN HERRING GULL. Distinguished from second cycle by black primaries with bold white tips, large white P10 mirror, and extensive white on tail. Bruce Mactavish. St. John's, Newfoundland, 10 Nov. 1998.

25A.29 THIRD-CYCLE TYPE AMERICAN HERRING GULL. A more "retarded" individual (compare with photos 25a.31–25A.32). Distinguished from second cycle by inner primary pattern (visible in flight). Steve N. G. Howell. Puerto Peñasco, Sonora, Mexico, 22 Jan. 2003.

25A.30 THIRD-CYCLE AMERICAN HERRING GULL. A more "retarded" individual (compare with photos 25a.31–25A.32). Distinguished from second cycle by inner primary pattern (visible in flight). Steve N. G. Howell. Puerto Peñasco, Sonora, Mexico, 22 Jan. 2003.

25A.31 THIRD-CYCLE TYPE AMERICAN HERRING GULL (SAME BIRD AS 25A.51). A more "advanced" individual (compare with photos 25a.29–25A.30). Distinguished from adult by brownish upperwing coverts and tertial bases, reduced white in wingtip; also note bill pattern. Steve N. G. Howell. Puerto Peñasco, Sonora, Mexico, 22 Jan. 2003.

25A.32 THIRD-CYCLE TYPE AMERICAN HERRING GULL. A more "advanced" individual (compare with photos 25a.29–25A.30). Distinguished from adult by brownish on greater coverts and tail; also note bill pattern. Steve N. G. Howell. Puerto Peñasco, Sonora, Mexico, 23 Jan. 2003.

25A.33 THIRD-CYCLE AMERICAN HERRING GULL. Distinguished from second cycle by inner primary pattern (visible in flight), black wingtips with distinct white primary tips, and obvious white in tail; also, this individual's bill color would be very advanced for a second cycle on this date. Bruce Mactavish. St. John's, Newfoundland, 15 Apr. 1997.

25A.34 FOURTH-CYCLE AMERICAN HERRING GULL IN PB4 MOLT. Distinguished from third cycle in PB3 molt (compare with photo 25a.26) by inner primary pattern (not visible here); also note blackish primaries, white in tail, and bold white secondary tips. Steve N. G. Howell. Salisbury Beach, Massachusetts, 30 June 1998.

25A.35 ADULT NONBREEDING AMERICAN HERRING GULL.
Note pale gray upperparts, and black wingtips with
relatively little white. Steve N. G. Howell. Puerto
Peñasco, Sonora, Mexico, 23 Jan. 2003.

25A.36 ADULT NONBREEDING AMERICAN HERRING GULL.
Note pale gray upperparts with neatly demarcated
black wingtips above and below; also staring pale
yellow eye. Michael D. Stubblefield. Long Island,
New York, Feb. 2001.

25A.37 ADULT BREEDING AMERICAN HERRING GULL. Note
same features as photo 25a.36; some birds, like
this one, have only a partial subterminal black
band on P5. Michael D. Stubblefield. Long Island,
New York, May 2000.

25A.38 ADULT AMERICAN HERRING GULL. Note pale gray
underside to primaries, with neatly demarcated
black wingtips. This type, with limited white
(mirror only on P10), is typical of adults wintering
in western North America. Tony Leukering. Puerto
Peñasco, Sonora, Mexico, 5 Feb. 2000.

25A.39 ADULT AMERICAN HERRING GULL. Note pale gray
underside to primaries, with neatly demarcated
blackish wingtips. This type, with limited and
washed-out black (large mirrors on P9–P10), is
found mainly in northeastern North America.
Bruce Mactavish. St. John's, Newfoundland,
25 Mar. 1996.

25A.40 FIRST-CYCLE AMERICAN HERRING GULL. Note paler panel on inner primaries, poor contrast between outer and inner webs on blackish outer primaries, mostly blackish tail, and bill size and shape. Steve N. G. Howell. Puerto Peñasco, Sonora, Mexico, 21 Jan. 2003.

25A.41 FIRST-CYCLE AMERICAN HERRING GULL. Note same features as photo 25a.40. Michael D. Stubblefield. Long Island, New York, Apr. 2002.

25A.42 FIRST-CYCLE AMERICAN HERRING GULL. Some darkly pigmented birds, like this individual, have a poorly contrasting paler panel on inner primaries. Steve N. G. Howell. Petaluma, California, 2 Jan. 2003.

25A.43 UPPERWINGS OF FIRST-CYCLE AMERICAN HERRING GULL (LEFT) AND THAYER'S GULL (RIGHT). Note blacker secondaries and more solidly dark outer primaries of Herring, which offset pale inner primary panel. Note two-tone outer primaries of Thayer's such that pale inner primary panel bleeds out into spread outer primaries. Steve N. G. Howell. Birds found freshly dead Dec. 1997, Petaluma, California (now specimens at California Academy of Sciences).

25A.44 FIRST-CYCLE AMERICAN HERRING GULL. Some birds, like this individual, have extensively pale bases to the outer rectrices so that the spread tail (especially from below) shows a broad blackish distal band (compare with solid blackish tail of photo 25a.40); note brownish underbody and whitish head, slightly translucent inner primaries. Steve N. G. Howell. Off Bodega, California, 11 Oct. 1998.

25A.45 FIRST-CYCLE AMERICAN HERRING GULL. Note brownish underbody and whitish head, slightly translucent inner primaries, and fairly extensive blackish tips to outer primaries. Tony Leukering. Cape May, New Jersey, 15 Dec. 1993.

25A.47 SECOND-CYCLE AMERICAN HERRING GULL. Note same features as photo 25a.46. Steve N. G. Howell. Puerto Peñasco, Sonora, Mexico, 23 Jan. 2003.

25A.46 SECOND-CYCLE AMERICAN HERRING GULL. Note contrasting pale panel on inner primaries, and solidly dark outer primaries, mostly black tail. Steve N. G. Howell. Puerto Peñasco, Sonora, Mexico, 21 Jan. 2003.

25A.48 SECOND-CYCLE AMERICAN HERRING GULL. Note same features as photo 25a.46; advanced pattern of P1–P2 on left wing may reflect asynchronous molt timing or adventitiously replaced feathers. Arnoud B. van den Berg. Cape May, New Jersey, 5 May 2001.

25A.49 SECOND-CYCLE AMERICAN HERRING GULL. Distinguished from first cycle by extensive dark tips to longest undertail coverts and diffuse pale bases (not distinctly barred) to outer rectrices; also note bill pattern. Kevin T. Karlson. Cape May, New Jersey, Dec. 2002.

25A.50 THIRD-CYCLE AMERICAN HERRING GULL, A RELATIVELY "RETARDED" INDIVIDUAL. Distinguished from second cycle (for example, photos 25a.46–25a.47) by primary pattern, especially adultlike inner primaries. Michael D. Stubblefield. Long Island, New York, Dec. 1999.

25A.51 THIRD-CYCLE AMERICAN HERRING GULL (SAME BIRD AS PHOTO 25A.31). Note same features as photo 25a.50. Steve N. G. Howell. Puerto Peñasco, Sonora, Mexico, 22 Jan. 2003.

25A.52 THIRD-CYCLE TYPE AMERICAN HERRING GULL, A RELATIVELY "ADVANCED" INDIVIDUAL. Distinguished from adult by brownish on greater coverts and black tail band; also note bill pattern. Steve N. G. Howell. Puerto Peñasco, Sonora, Mexico, 23 Jan. 2003.

25A.53 THIRD-CYCLE AMERICAN HERRING GULL. Distinguished from second cycle by primary pattern and tail pattern. Tony Leukering. Puerto Peñasco, Sonora, Mexico, 16 Nov. 1997.

25B.1 ADULT NONBREEDING EUROPEAN HERRING GULL *(L. A. ARGENTEUS).* Probably not safely separable from American Herring Gull. Killian Mullarney. Wexford, Ireland, 25 Dec. 2001.

25B.2 NONBREEDING ADULT EUROPEAN HERRING GULL *(L. A. ARGENTATUS;* **LEFT) AND AMERICAN HERRING GULL (RIGHT).** Note darker upperparts of *argentatus* and wingtip patterns. Bruce Mactavish. St. John's, Newfoundland, 31 Dec. 1995.

25B.3 ADULT NONBREEDING EUROPEAN HERRING GULL (PRESUMED *L. A. ARGENTATUS).* Much like American Herring Gull but upperparts average slightly darker (compare with photo 25b.2). Rik Winters. Wijster, Netherlands, 24 Feb. 2002.

25B.4 JUVENILE EUROPEAN HERRING GULL *(L. A. ARGENTEUS).* Paler overall than American Herring Gull with whiter ground color and more-streaky aspect to underparts; averages bolder white notching on tertial edges. Steve Young. Anglesey, Wales, Aug. 2001.

25B.5 JUVENILE EUROPEAN HERRING GULL *(L. A. ARGENTATUS).* Paler overall than American Herring Gull with whiter ground color and more-streaky aspect to underparts; also note sparse dark barring on vent and undertail coverts and extensive white at tail base. Nominate *argentatus* more often has distinct white primary tips than *argenteus* (compare with photo 25b.4). Steve N. G. Howell. Tampere, Finland, 8 Aug. 2002.

25B.6 FIRST-CYCLE EUROPEAN HERRING GULL *(L. A. ARGENTA-TUS)* WITH MODERATE POST-JUVENAL SCAPULAR MOLT. Typically paler overall than American Herring Gull with whiter ground color to underparts, relatively sparse dark bars on undertail coverts, and averages bolder pale checkering on greater coverts. Henry Lehto. Turku, Finland, 28 Dec. 1997.

25B.7 FIRST-CYCLE EUROPEAN HERRING GULL *(L. A. ARGENTA-TUS)* WITH LIMITED POST-JUVENAL SCAPULAR MOLT. Some birds, like this individual, are darker and browner overall, suggesting American Herring Gull. Note whitish mottling below, whitish ground color to barred flanks (compare with photos 25a.9–25a.16), extensive white at tail base. Henry Lehto. Turku, Finland, 28 Dec. 1997.

25B.8 FIRST-CYCLE EUROPEAN HERRING GULL *(L. A. ARGEN-TEUS)*. A typical individual with extensive post-juvenal scapular molt. Paler overall than American Herring Gull with whiter ground color to underparts. Steve Young. Ainsdale, England, Feb. 1999.

25B.9 FIRST-CYCLE (FRONT) AND SECOND-CYCLE (BACK) EUROPEAN HERRING GULLS (PRESUMED *L. A. ARGENTEUS*). Note overall paler aspect and more petite build than American Herring Gull; first cycle has whitish ground color to underparts, second cycle has extensively pale-patterned greater coverts. First cycle aged by barred post-juvenal scapulars and pointed primaries; second cycle aged by incoming plain pale gray on back; also note bill pattern. Philippe J. Dubois. Pas-de-Calais, France, Feb. 1998.

25B.10 SECOND-CYCLE EUROPEAN HERRING GULL (GRAY MEDIAN COVERTS — AND PROBABLY SCAPULARS — REFLECT PA2 MOLT). Some, like this individual, recall American Herring Gull; note bold patterning on greater coverts and that tail usually has more white (compare with photos 25b.20–25b.21). Rik Winters. Wijster, Netherlands, 24 Feb. 2002.

25B.11 THIRD-CYCLE EUROPEAN HERRING GULL. Distinguished from adult by brown on wing coverts and tertials and reduced white in wingtip; also note bill pattern. Tail averages more white than American Herring Gull. Rik Winters. Wijster, Netherlands, 24 Feb. 2002.

25B.12 ADULT EUROPEAN HERRING GULL (L. A. ARGENTEUS). Perhaps not safely separable from American Herring Gull (see text), although bill (at least of more-sedentary birds) may average brighter in winter. Steve Young. Caernarfon, Wales, 4 Jan. 2004.

25B.13 ADULT NONBREEDING EUROPEAN HERRING GULLS. Perhaps not safely separable from American Herring Gull (see text). Rik Winters. Wijster, Netherlands, 8 Dec. 2001.

25B.14 ADULT EUROPEAN HERRING GULL (L. A. ARGENTATUS). Similar to American Herring Gull but nominate *argentatus* typically has large white P10 tip, large P9 mirror, and typically lacks a subterminal black band on P5. Annika Forsten. Tallinn, Estonia, 1 Apr. 2002.

25B.16 FIRST-CYCLE PRESUMED EUROPEAN HERRING GULL.
Distinguished from American Herring Gull by
uppertail covert and tail pattern; typically lacks
dark distal marks on inner webs of inner primaries. Marshall J. Iliff. Buelah Landfill, Maryland,
25 Jan. 2002.

**25B.15 JUVENILE EUROPEAN HERRING GULL (*L. A. ARGENTA-
TUS*).** Distinguished from American Herring Gull
by mostly white uppertail coverts and tail with
relatively narrow black distal band; also typically
lacks dark distal marks on inner webs of inner
primaries. Nominate *argentatus* averages more-
distinct paler inner webs to outer primaries than
American Herring Gull or than *L. a. argenteus*, so
spread wingtip more often shows a two-tone
pattern, as on this individual (compare with
photos 25a.43, 25b.17). Harry J. Lehto. Marien-
hamm, Finland, 23 Aug. 1996.

**25B.17 FIRST-CYCLE EUROPEAN HERRING GULL, LARGELY IN
JUVENAL PLUMAGE.** Distinguished from American
Herring Gull by uppertail covert pattern (heavily
marked on this individual but spotted rather than
barred) and tail pattern; also note lack of dark
distal marks on inner webs of inner primaries,
two-tone outer primaries (atypical of American
Herring Gull; compare with photo 25b.15), and
boldly checkered greater coverts. Bruce Mactavish. St. John's, Newfoundland, 2 Feb. 1995.

**25B.18 FIRST-CYCLE EUROPEAN HERRING GULL (PRESUMED *L.
A. ARGENTEUS*), STILL LARGELY IN JUVENAL PLUMAGE.**
Distinguished from American Herring Gull by
uppertail covert and tail pattern; typically lacks
dark distal marks on inner webs of inner primaries. Killian Mullarney. Iceland, mid-Mar. 2003.

25B.19 FIRST-CYCLE EUROPEAN HERRING GULL *(L. A. ARGENTEUS).* Distinguished from American Herring Gull by extensively whitish ground color to underparts, relatively sparse dark bars on undertail coverts, and tail pattern. Great Black-backed Gull more massive and long winged, whiter head and underparts typically contrast more with underwings. Killian Mullarney. Wexford, Ireland, Apr. 2000.

25B.21 SECOND-CYCLE EUROPEAN HERRING GULL *(L. A. ARGENTATUS).* Note same features as photo 25b.20 (second-cycle American Herring Gull not known to show this much white on tail; third cycle has adultlike inner and middle primaries); also note more two-tone outer primaries. Killian Mullarney. Vadso, Norway, 28 Mar. 2002.

25B.23 THIRD-CYCLE EUROPEAN HERRING GULL *(L. A. ARGENTEUS).* Distinguished from second cycle by primary pattern; also averages less black on tail (often all white). Killian Mullarney. Rogerstown, Ireland, 2 Feb. 2001.

25B.20 SECOND-CYCLE EUROPEAN HERRING GULL *(L. A. ARGENTEUS).* Relative to American Herring Gull averages more white on tail (note whitish basal corners on this bird) and overall paler, more-coarsely patterned greater coverts, but identification criteria need elucidation. Killian Mullarney. Rogerstown, Ireland, 2 Feb. 2001.

25B.22 THIRD-CYCLE EUROPEAN HERRING GULL. Relative to American Herring Gull averages more white on tail and whiter underwings, but identification criteria need elucidation. Rik Winters. Wijster, Netherlands, 8 Jan. 2000.

25C.1 ADULT NONBREEDING VEGA GULL COMPLETING PB MOLT (OUTER PRIMARIES NOT FULLY GROWN). Note medium gray upperparts, rich pink legs, bill size and shape, and reddish orbital ring (eye varies from pale to dark; compare with photo 25c.0). Geoff Carey. Choshi, Japan, 12 Nov. 1999.

25C.2 NONBREEDING ADULT VEGA GULL AND ADULT SLATY-BACKED GULL (LEFT). Note Vega's medium gray upperparts (with broad and contrasting white scapular and tertial crescents), bill size and shape. Mike Danzenbaker. Aomori Prefecture, Japan, 7 Feb. 1998.

25C.3 ADULT BREEDING VEGA GULLS (FIRST-SUMMER VEGA BEHIND). Note same features as photo 25c.2; relatively late PB molt often means that white primary tips are not overly abraded through midsummer. On first cycle note typical summer contrast between fresher A1 back and bleached juvenal upperwing coverts. Bruce Hallett. Nome, Alaska, early June 2001.

25C.4 FIRST-CYCLE VEGA GULL WITH LIMITED POST-JUVENAL SCAPULAR MOLT. Paler overall than American Herring Gull with brighter, frosty checkering on upperparts, whitish ground color to underparts, extensive white tail base, and richer pink legs; perhaps not safely told from European Herring Gull. Distinguished from Slaty-backed Gull by less stout bill, coarser and frostier checkering on upperparts, for example, greater coverts; also note typical barred pattern of post-juvenal scapulars. Geoff Carey. Choshi, Japan, 12 Nov. 1999.

25C.5 FIRST-CYCLE VEGA GULL WITH MODERATE POST-JUVENAL SCAPULAR MOLT. Some birds, like this individual, are browner overall (compare with photo 25c.4); distinguished from American Herring Gull by brighter, frosty checkering on upperparts, tail pattern (not visible here); perhaps not safely told from European Herring Gull, but this individual is relatively brownish below. Separated from Slaty-backed Gull by less stout bill with more-distinct pink basally, coarser and frostier checkering on upperparts, for example, greater coverts; also note typical barred pattern of post-juvenal scapulars. Mike Danzenbaker. Aomori Prefecture, Japan, 26 Dec. 1998.

25C.6 FIRST-CYCLE VEGA GULL WITH EXTENSIVE POST-JUVENAL SCAPULAR MOLT. Paler overall than American Herring Gull with whitish ground color to underparts and rich pink legs; perhaps not safely told from European Herring Gull. Distinguished from Slaty-backed Gull by same features as photo 25c.5. Geoff Carey. Choshi, Japan, 11 Feb. 1999.

25C.8 SECOND-CYCLE PRESUMED VEGA GULL COMPLETING PB2 MOLT (OUTER PRIMARIES NOT FULLY GROWN). Plumage variation parallels American Herring Gull; some birds (like this individual) perhaps not safely identifiable, although upperwing coverts average more boldly barred, tail averages more white (not visible here), and any plain gray on back (not yet attained by this bird) is slightly darker (see photos 25c.9–25c.10). Kimball L. Garrett. Nome, Alaska, 14 Sept. 2002.

25C.7 FIRST-CYCLE VEGA GULL WITH GLAUCOUS-WINGED GULLS (SAME BIRD AS PHOTO 25C.17). Distinguished from Slaty-backed Gull by more slender bill, blacker wingtip and tail, from American Herring Gull by whiter head and underparts—especially note sparse dark bars on undertail coverts. Gary H. Rosenberg. St. Paul Island, Alaska, 6 June 2005.

25C.9 SECOND-CYCLE VEGA GULL COMPLETING PB2 MOLT (OUTER PRIMARIES NOT FULLY GROWN). Distinguished from American Herring Gull by medium gray back; also note boldly barred upperwing coverts, late molt timing. Geoff Carey. Choshi, Japan, 11 Nov. 1999.

25C.10 SECOND-CYCLE VEGA GULL. Distinguished from American Herring Gull by medium gray on upperparts, including A2 median coverts; also note brightly patterned greater coverts. Geoff Carey. Choshi, Japan, 12 Feb. 1999.

25C.11 THIRD-CYCLE VEGA GULL COMPLETING PB3 MOLT (OUTER PRIMARIES NOT FULLY GROWN). Distinguished from American Herring Gull by medium gray upperparts; also note late molt timing and dark eye. Geoff Carey. Choshi, Japan, 13 Nov. 1999.

25C.12 ADULT NONBREEDING VEGA GULL. Note medium gray upperparts (hence, contrasting white trailing edge to wings) and white tongue-tips on P6–P8. Geoff Carey. Choshi, Japan, 8 Feb. 1999.

25C.13 ADULT NONBREEDING VEGA GULL. Note medium gray upperparts, white tongue-tips on P6–P7, smoky gray underside to primaries. Mike Danzenbaker. Aomori Prefecture, Japan, 21 Feb. 1999.

25C.14 ADULT BREEDING VEGA GULL. Note medium gray upperparts, white tongue-tips on P6–P8, and smoky gray underside to inner primaries and secondaries. Bruce Mactavish. Barrow, Alaska, 30 May 2003.

25C.15 FIRST-CYCLE VEGA GULL. Note contrasting pale inner primary panel, dark outer primaries, brightly checkered upperparts, extensive white tail base, clean-cut black distal tail band, and dusky spotted effect on whitish underparts. Geoff Carey. Choshi, Japan, 14 Nov. 1999.

25C.16 FIRST-CYCLE PRESUMED VEGA GULL. Note pale inner primary panel (relatively weak on this individual), dark outer primaries, mostly white uppertail coverts and tail base with clean-cut blackish distal tail band. Mike Danzenbaker. Aomori Prefecture, Japan, 26 Dec. 1998.

25C.17 FIRST-CYCLE VEGA GULL. Distinguished from Slaty-backed Gull by more solidly blackish outer primaries and more-even (less irregular) white barring at tail base; also note blackish secondary bar and tail band. Relative to American Herring Gull, note contrasting white uppertail coverts (also see photo 25c.7 of same bird). Gary H. Rosenberg. St. Paul Island, Alaska, 6 June 2005.

25C.18 SECOND-CYCLE VEGA GULL. Note contrasting pale inner primary panel, dark outer primaries, medium gray back, and limited black on tail. Geoff Carey. Choshi, Japan, 13 Nov. 1999.

25C.19 SECOND-CYCLE VEGA GULL. Note same features as photo 25c.18. Mike Danzenbaker. Aomori Prefecture, Japan, 26 Dec. 1998.

25C.20 THIRD-CYCLE TYPE VEGA GULL. Distinguished from adult by brownish wash to upperwing coverts, black in tail, and reduced white in outer primaries; also note bill pattern. Geoff Carey. Choshi, Japan, 11 Nov. 1999.

26.1 ADULT NONBREEDING YELLOW-LEGGED GULL *(L. M. ATLANTIS),* IN PB MOLT (P9–P10 OLD). Note medium gray upperparts and yellowish legs (often dullest, like this, at height of PB molt; compare with photo 26.0), bill size and shape, and orange-red orbital ring; basic head streaking averages more extensive than nominate *michahellis* but still much less than American Herring Gull. Philippe J. Dubois. Pico, Azores, mid-Aug. 2000.

26.2 ADULT YELLOW-LEGGED GULL (ADULT AMERICAN HERRING GULL BEHIND). Note medium gray upperparts, yellowish legs, bill size and shape (relatively small bill suggests a female), and white-headed aspect. Bruce Mactavish. St. John's, Newfoundland, 10 Jan. 1995.

26.3 ADULT BREEDING YELLOW-LEGGED GULL. Note pale slaty gray upperparts (darkness accentuated by cloud; compare with photo 26.5), yellow legs, and bill size and shape. Harry J. Lehto. Tenerife, Canary Islands, 17 Feb. 1998.

26.4 ADULT BREEDING YELLOW-LEGGED GULL. Note bill size and shape (with red bleeding on to maxilla), deep orange orbital ring, pale slaty gray upperparts, and yellow legs. Theo Bakker. Essaouira, Morocco, 2 Mar. 1999.

26.5 ADULT BREEDING YELLOW-LEGGED GULL *(L. M. ATLAN-TIS)*. Note medium gray upperparts (bleached out by sunlight; compare with photo 26.3), yellow legs, bill size and shape, and reddish orbital ring. Steve N. G. Howell. San Miguel, Azores, 27 Apr. 2002.

26.6 ADULT BREEDING YELLOW-LEGGED GULL *(L. M. MICHA-HELLIS)*. Note medium gray upperparts, yellow legs, bill size and shape, and deep orange orbital ring. Antero Topp. Lesvos, Greece, Apr. 1999.

26.7 JUVENILE YELLOW-LEGGED GULL *(L. M. ATLANTIS)*. Overall dark aspect recalls a dark Lesser Black-backed Gull (see photo 27.6) rather than nominate *michahellis* (photo 26.9). Difficult to distinguish from Lesser Black-backed but averages broader winged, and white bases of outer rectrices have little or no dark barring (see photos 26.23–26.25). Philippe J. Dubois. Pico, Azores, mid-Aug. 2000.

26.8 JUVENILE YELLOW-LEGGED GULL. Perhaps not distinguishable from Lesser Black-backed Gull in this photo; averages bulkier and bigger billed with cleaner white tail base (see photos 26.23–26.25). Theo Bakker. Madeira, 3 Aug. 1993.

26.9 FIRST-CYCLE YELLOW-LEGGED GULL *(L. M. MICHAHELLIS).*
Perhaps not always separable from Lesser Black-backed Gull but averages bulkier and bigger billed: note relatively bleached, warm brown aspect to upperparts and post-juvenal scapular molt, both atypical of Lesser Black-backed Gull at this date. In flight check tail pattern (see photos 26.23–26.25). Rik Winters. Wijster, Netherlands, 18 Aug. 2001.

26.10 FIRST-CYCLE YELLOW-LEGGED GULL *(L. M. ATLANTIS).*
Note bill size and shape, relatively dusky aspect of freshly molted head, back, and underparts; some birds also replace upperwing coverts. Theo Bakker. Pico, Azores, 11 Nov. 2001.

26.11 FIRST-CYCLE YELLOW-LEGGED GULL (PRESUMED *L. M. MICHAHELLIS;* RIGHT) AND FIRST-CYCLE LESSER BLACK-BACKED GULL OR YELLOW-LEGGED GULL (LEFT). Right-hand bird is a fairly typical first-winter *michahellis,* with plumage suggesting much larger and stouter-billed Great Black-backed Gull. Note white head and underparts, pale silvery scapulars with fine anchor patterns, some post-juvenal upperwing coverts. Annika Forsten. Figuera da Foz, Portugal, 28 Mar. 2001.

26.12 FIRST-CYCLE YELLOW-LEGGED GULL; BANDED AS A CHICK ON ATLANTIC (CANTABRICAN) COAST OF NORTHWEST-ERN SPAIN. Note white head and underparts, pale gray scapulars with dark bars, and bill size and shape. Unlike nominate *michahellis* of the Mediterranean, Cantabrican birds (like this individual) often retain all juvenal upperwing coverts through the first cycle. From European Herring Gull best told by upperwing and tail patterns; also bill shape and pattern. Killian Mullarney. Porto, Portugal, 1 Apr. 2001.

26.13 SECOND-CYCLE YELLOW-LEGGED GULL *(L. M. ATLANTIS)*, A TYPICAL INDIVIDUAL STARTING PB2 MOLT (INNER PRIMARIES HAD BEEN SHED). Note darker overall aspect than *L. m. michahellis* (see photo 26.11). Distinguished from Lesser Black-backed Gull with difficulty but typically broader winged and with more white on bases of outer rectrices (see photos 26.23–26.25). Steve N. G. Howell. San Miguel, Azores, 27 Apr. 2002.

26.14 SECOND-CYCLE YELLOW-LEGGED GULL *(L. M. ATLANTIS)*; OUTER PRIMARIES NOT FULLY GROWN BUT STARTING PA2 MOLT (NOTE SHED MEDIAN COVERTS). Overall dark aspect recalls Lesser Black-backed Gull rather than nominate *michahellis*; Lesser Black-backed typically has whiter head and underparts, legs lack dusky leading edge. Philippe J. Dubois. Pico, Azores, mid-Aug. 2000.

26.15 SECOND-CYCLE YELLOW-LEGGED GULL. Perhaps not distinguishable from Lesser Black-backed Gull in this photo; averages bulkier and stouter billed; also note dusky leading edge to legs. Theo Bakker. Madeira, 3 Aug. 1993.

26.16 SECOND-CYCLE YELLOW-LEGGED GULL (PROBABLY CANTABRICAN TYPE); A RELATIVELY "RETARDED" INDIVIDUAL (COMPARE WITH PHOTO 26.17). Note medium gray back feathers, bill size and shape; in flight check dorsal pattern of primaries to rule out European Herring Gull. Killian Mullarney. Porto, Portugal, 1 Apr. 2001.

26.17 SECOND-CYCLE YELLOW-LEGGED GULL (*L. M. ATLANTIS*). A relatively "advanced" individual (compare with photo 26.16). From Lesser Black-backed Gull by slightly paler gray upperparts. Steve N. G. Howell. San Miguel, Azores, 27 Apr. 2002.

26.18 THIRD-CYCLE YELLOW-LEGGED GULL (*L. M. ATLANTIS*) AT LEFT WITH ADULT-TYPE BIRDS TO RIGHT (WITH BRIGHTER BILLS AND LEGS, LESS-EXTENSIVE DUSKY HEAD MARKINGS). Note medium gray upperparts, heavily streaked half-hood, and dark bill marks (compare with photo 26.17). Theo Bakker. Pico, Azores, 3 Oct. 1997.

26.19 THIRD-CYCLE YELLOW-LEGGED GULL (PROBABLY CANTABRICAN TYPE). Distinguished from Herring Gull by medium gray upperparts and yellowish legs; also note bill size and shape and dull eye. Killian Mullarney. Porto, Portugal, 1 Apr. 2001.

26.20 ADULT NONBREEDING YELLOW-LEGGED GULL, COMPLETING PB MOLT (P10 NOT FULLY GROWN). Note medium gray upperparts with contrasting white trailing edge to wings and dusky streaking limited to head. Black wingtip area more extensive than Lesser Black-backed Gull. Antero Topp. Tenerife, Canary Islands, Oct. 1998.

26.21 ADULT BREEDING YELLOW-LEGGED GULL. Distinguished from Lesser Black-backed Gull by broader wings, slightly paler upperparts (photo taken in cloudy conditions and possibly slightly underexposed, so gray tone is difficult to evaluate), more-extensive black on outer primaries (for example, shorter gray basal tongues on P8–P9). Harry J. Lehto. Tenerife, Canary Islands, 26 Feb. 1999.

26.22 ADULT BREEDING YELLOW-LEGGED GULL. Note dusky bases to secondaries and inner primaries (paler than Lesser Black-backed, duskier than Herring), extent of black wingtip, bill size and shape, and yellow legs. Theo Bakker. Essaouira, Morocco, 2 Mar. 1999.

26.23 FIRST-CYCLE YELLOW-LEGGED GULL. Perhaps not always distinguishable from Lesser Black-backed Gull but averages bulkier with broader wings, stouter bill, and less dark barring at bases of outer rectrices. Harry J. Lehto. La Palma, Canary Islands, 10 Sept. 1998.

26.24 FIRST-CYCLE YELLOW-LEGGED GULL *(L. M. MICHA-HELLIS).* Perhaps not always distinguishable from Lesser Black-backed Gull but averages bulkier with stouter bill and broader wings; also averages paler inner primaries and less dark barring at bases of outer rectrices; in addition, note extensive scapular and upperwing-covert molt, atypical of Lesser Black-backed Gull at this date. Killian Mullarney. Lesvos, Greece, 5 Oct. 1998.

26.25 SECOND-CYCLE YELLOW-LEGGED GULL *(L. M. ATLANTIS),* **STARTING PB2 MOLT (INNER PRIMARIES SHED).** Bulkier and broader winged than Lesser Black-backed Gull with less dark barring at bases of outer rectrices. Steve N. G. Howell. San Miguel, Azores, 27 Apr. 2002.

26.26 FIRST-CYCLE (BEHIND) AND SECOND-CYCLE YELLOW-LEGGED GULL. On second cycle note medium gray back and poorly contrasting paler inner primaries. First cycle very like Lesser Black-backed Gull, but note mostly white bases to outer rectrices and extensive post-juvenal scapular molt. Antero Topp. Madeira, Oct. 1998.

26.27 SECOND-CYCLE (LEFT) AND ADULT (RIGHT) YELLOW-LEGGED GULL. Averages bulkier and broader winged than Lesser Black-backed Gull, with slightly paler upperparts; adult also has more-extensive black in wingtip. Harry J. Lehto. Tenerife, Canary Islands, 26 Feb. 1999.

26.28 SECOND-CYCLE YELLOW-LEGGED GULL (PRESUMED *L. M. MICHAHELLIS*). Note medium gray upperparts and poorly contrasting paler inner primaries. Distinguished from hybrid European Herring Gull × Lesser Black-backed Gull with caution, but legs of this individual were fairly bright yellow, atypical of hybrids. Steve N. G. Howell. Chew Valley Lake, England, 5 May 2003.

26.29 THIRD-CYCLE YELLOW-LEGGED GULL (PROBABLY CANTABRICAN TYPE). Distinguished from American Herring Gull by medium gray upperparts with more-contrasting white trailing edge to wings. Annika Forsten. Peniche, Portugal, 27 Mar. 2001.

27.1 ADULT NONBREEDING LESSER BLACK-BACKED GULL (PROBABLY _L. F. GRAELLSII_) IN PB MOLT (P8–P10 OLD). Note slaty gray upperparts (and gray tone relative to Laughing Gull), yellowish legs, distinct head and neck streaking, and bill size and shape; also relatively late primary molt timing (typical of individuals that migrate well south). Dusky-flecked eye is atypical. Greg W. Lasley. Port Aransas, Texas, 8 Nov. 1988.

27.2 ADULT NONBREEDING LESSER BLACK-BACKED GULL (POSSIBLY _L. F. INTERMEDIUS_). Note same features as photo 27.1; upperparts look dark relative to Laughing Gull (compare with photo 27.1). Extensive black bill markings may indicate a fourth-cycle bird. Greg W. Lasley. Corpus Christi, Texas, 14 Feb. 1990.

27.4 ADULT BREEDING LESSER BLACK-BACKED GULL (_L. F. GRAELLSII_). Note slaty gray upperparts, yellow legs, bill size and shape, pale eye with reddish orange orbital ring, and relatively long wing projection. Steve Young. Skomer Island, Wales, June 2002.

27.3 ADULT NONBREEDING LESSER BLACK-BACKED GULL (_L. F. INTERMEDIUS_). Note same features as photo 27.1 but upperparts noticeably darker. Theo Bakker. Essaouira, Morocco, 2 Mar. 1999.

27.5 JUVENILE LESSER BLACK-BACKED GULL. A fairly typical individual. Note relatively slender build and slender black bill, long and pointed wing projection, whitish ground color to head and underparts, relatively narrow pale edgings on upperparts, and dark bases to greater coverts, typically widest on outer feathers. Bruce Mactavish. St. John's, Newfoundland, 28 Oct. 1991.

27.6 JUVENILE LESSER BLACK-BACKED GULL. Note same features as photo 27.5, but this individual is browner overall on head and underparts and brown back has bleached to a warmer tone. Bruce Mactavish. St. John's, Newfoundland, 23 Oct. 1991.

27.7 FIRST-CYCLE LESSER BLACK-BACKED GULL (CENTER) WITH TWO FIRST-CYCLE AMERICAN HERRING GULLS. Note smaller size and relatively slender build, slender black bill, and whitish head and chest contrasting with dark upperparts. Jon Dunn. Brownsville, Texas, 6 Jan. 1992.

27.8 FIRST-CYCLE LESSER BLACK-BACKED GULL. Note relatively slender build and slender black bill (which, as with this individual, can show pinkish at base by late winter), and long pointed wing projection. This bird has undergone extensive post-juvenal molt on the head, body, and scapulars (also some upperwing coverts), which contrast with the bleached, browner upperwing coverts. Bruce Hallett. Eleuthera, Bahamas, 18 Mar. 2003.

27.9 FIRST-CYCLE LESSER BLACK-BACKED GULL (PROBABLY *L. F. GRAELLSII*). A fairly typical late-winter individual. Note relatively slender build with long wing projection, relatively slender black bill, and some slaty post-juvenal scapulars. Killian Mullarney. Porto, Portugal, 1 Apr. 2001.

27.10 FIRST-CYCLE LESSER BLACK-BACKED GULL. Note relatively slender build with long wing projection, slender black bill (often showing some pink basally by spring), and overall brownish gray aspect to post-juvenal scapulars. Marshall J. Iliff. Mustang Island, Texas, 2 Apr. 2002.

27.11 FIRST-CYCLE LESSER BLACK-BACKED GULL (SAME BIRD AS PHOTO 27.31). Note same features as photo 27.10. Steve N. G. Howell. Cape Hatteras, North Carolina, 20 May 2004.

27.12 SECOND-CYCLE LESSER BLACK-BACKED GULL COMPLETING PB2 MOLT (P9–P10 OLD). Note whitish head and underparts contrasting with relatively dark, variegated brownish gray upperparts; also relatively long wing projection and bill size and shape (relatively stout on this individual). Rik Winters. Wijster, Netherlands, 20 Aug. 2000.

27.13 SECOND-CYCLE LESSER BLACK-BACKED GULL. A fairly typical individual (probably *L. f. graellsii*) completing PB2 molt/starting PA2 molt (outer primaries not quite fully grown but median coverts, and perhaps some scapulars, are A2 plumage. Note relatively slender build and bill (with pale tip, diffuse pinkish base), whitish head and underparts contrasting with variegated brownish gray upperparts. Bruce Mactavish. St. John's, Newfoundland, 14 Oct. 1999.

27.14 SECOND-CYCLE LESSER BLACK-BACKED GULL, APPARENTLY IN PA2 MOLT (DARKNESS OF GRAY ON UPPERPARTS MAY INDICATE *L. F. INTERMEDIUS*). Note relatively slender build and bill (with pale tip, diffuse pinkish base), whitish head and chest contrasting with dark upperparts that include fresh (and incoming?) dark slaty A2 feathers contrasting with frayed, brownish B2 feathers. Bruce Hallett. Nassau, Bahamas, 25 Jan. 2002.

27.15 SECOND-CYCLE LESSER BLACK-BACKED GULL (PROBABLY *L. F. GRAELLSII*). Note relatively slender build, bill size and shape, and whitish head and underparts contrasting with variegated gray-and-brown upperparts. Note how appearance changes strikingly between late winter (this bird) and spring (see photos 27.16–27.18). Annika Forsten. Figuera da Foz, Portugal, 29 Mar. 2001.

27.16 SECOND-CYCLE LESSER BLACK-BACKED GULL (*L. F. GRAELLSII*). Note relatively slender build and bill, yellowish flesh legs, and whitish head and underparts contrasting with overall dark upperparts, including extensively slaty back. Steve N. G. Howell. Chew Valley Lake, England, 5 May 2003.

27.17 SECOND-CYCLE LESSER BLACK-BACKED GULL (*L. F. GRAELLSII*). Note same features as photo 27.16, although this individual is more "advanced," with atypically boldly patterned B2 upperwing coverts. Steve N. G. Howell. Chew Valley Lake, England, 5 May 2003.

27.18 SECOND-CYCLE LESSER BLACK-BACKED GULL *(L. F. GRAELLSII).* Note same features as photo 27.16, but PA molt has included most upperwing coverts and tertials. Distinguished from third cycle by pattern of inner primaries (see photo 27.34 of same bird); also note bare-part colors (compare with photo 27.22). Steve N. G. Howell. Chew Valley Lake, England, 5 May 2003.

27.19 THIRD-CYCLE LESSER BLACK-BACKED GULL. Note overall structure, bill size and shape (pattern typically regresses from second summer; compare with photos 27.17–27.18), and legs often flesh colored through third winter. Distinguished from second cycle by more-uniform upperparts, mostly white tail, and primary pattern (visible in flight). Bruce Mactavish. St. John's, Newfoundland, 10 Jan. 2000.

27.20 THIRD-CYCLE LESSER BLACK-BACKED GULL. Note same features as photo 27.19. Killian Mullarney. Wexford, Ireland, 27 Jan. 1999.

27.21 THIRD-CYCLE LESSER BLACK-BACKED GULL. Note same features as photo 27.19, although darker upperparts of this bird may indicate *L. f. intermedius.* Bruce Hallett. Grand Bahama, Bahamas, 22 Feb. 1999.

27.22 THIRD-CYCLE LESSER BLACK-BACKED GULL, BREEDING ASPECT. Distinguished from adult by brownish upperwing coverts, dark tertial centers, and reduced white markings on outer primaries, and from advanced second cycle by primary pattern (seen in flight); also note bare-part colors (yellow legs not visible here; compare with photo 27.18). Steve N. G. Howell. Cardiff, Wales, 14 May 1998.

27.23 ADULT LESSER BLACK-BACKED GULL (PRESUMED *L. F. GRAELLSII*). Note slaty gray upperparts with contrasting black wingtips (compare apparent difference in upperwing tone with photo 27.24, taken with overhead sun), wingtip pattern, and yellow legs. Killian Mullarney. Wexford, Ireland, Dec. 1998.

27.24 ADULT LESSER BLACK-BACKED GULL *(L. F. GRAELLSII).* Note slaty gray upperparts with contrasting black wingtips (compare apparent difference in upperwing tone with photo 27.23, taken in low-angle light). Marshall J. Iliff. Cape Hatteras, North Carolina, 14 Feb. 1999.

27.25 ADULT BREEDING LESSER BLACK-BACKED GULL *(L. F. GRAELLSII),* STARTING PB MOLT (P1 ON RIGHT WING HAS BEEN SHED). Note dusky gray bases to secondaries and primaries merging with moderate demarcation into black wingtips; also yellow legs and relatively late primary molt. Distinguished from Kelp Gull (see photo 28.33) by narrower and more-pointed wings, narrower white trailing edge to secondaries and inner primaries. Killian Mullarney. Wexford, Ireland, 19 July 2000.

27.26 ADULT BREEDING LESSER BLACK-BACKED GULLS (*L. F. FUSCUS;* NOT RECORDED IN NORTH AMERICA), STARTING PB MOLT (P1 SHED). Note slaty blackish upperparts with indistinct wingtip contrast and reduced white in outer primaries (compare with photo 27.23). Distinguished from Kelp Gull (for example, photos 28.29–28.30) by lighter build, more-slender bill, and narrower white trailing edge to wings. Steve N. G. Howell. Tampere, Finland, 10 Aug. 2002.

27.27 FIRST-CYCLE LESSER BLACK-BACKED GULL. Note blackish remiges lacking pale panel on inner primaries, plain dark bases to outer greater coverts, and contrast between white uppertail coverts (with relatively sparse barring) and broad blackish distal tail band. Theo Bakker. Wijster, Netherlands, 30 Sept. 2000.

27.28 FIRST-CYCLE LESSER BLACK-BACKED GULL. Note same features as photo 27.27, as well as black-barred white bases to outer rectrices; fully spread primaries can show a paler panel on inners (as on this sunlit bird) but still much less contrasting than typical of Herring Gull. W. Edward Harper. Sacramento, California, 24 Nov. 2003.

27.29 FIRST-CYCLE LESSER BLACK-BACKED GULL. Note overall dark wings, above and below, with little trace of paler inner primary panel; also contrasting white tail coverts, overall whitish head and underparts, and bill size and shape. This individual has a typical, fairly wide distal black tail band (compare with photo 27.30). Steve N. G. Howell. Chew Valley Lake, England, 5 May 2003.

27.30 SECOND-CYCLE LESSER BLACK-BACKED GULL, STARTING PB2 MOLT (P1–P2 SHED). Note same features as photo 27.28; this individual has a relatively narrow distal black tail band (compare with photo 27.29), suggesting Yellow-legged Gull (but note relatively heavy basal barring). Steve N. G. Howell. Chew Valley Lake, England, 5 May 2003.

27.31 FIRST-CYCLE LESSER BLACK-BACKED GULL (SAME BIRD AS PHOTO 27.11). Note dark remiges with indistinct paler panel on inner primaries, plain dark bases to greater coverts, and contrast between overall whitish uppertail coverts and broad blackish distal tail band. Steve N. G. Howell. Cape Hatteras, North Carolina, 20 May 2004.

27.32 SECOND-CYCLE LESSER BLACK-BACKED GULL *(L. F. GRAELLSII).* Note relatively narrow and pointed wings and slaty gray back; distinguished from third cycle by immature pattern of inner and middle primaries (see photo 27.35). Killian Mullarney. Wexford, Ireland, 2 May 1998.

27.33 SECOND-CYCLE LESSER BLACK-BACKED GULL *(L. F. GRAELLSII).* Note slaty gray upperparts (visible on lower back), overall dark underwings (accentuated by shadow), and immature pattern of inner primaries on upperwing. Steve N. G. Howell. Cardiff, Wales, 3 May 2003.

27.34 SECOND-CYCLE LESSER BLACK-BACKED GULL *(L. F. GRAELLSII)*, A RELATIVELY "ADVANCED" INDIVIDUAL (SAME BIRD AS PHOTO 27.18). Note slaty gray upperparts and bill size and shape; reduced black in tail, like this, is not rare in second-cycle Lesser Black-backed. Distinguished from third cycle by immature pattern of inner and middle primaries (compare with photo 27.36). Steve N. G. Howell. Chew Valley Lake, England, 5 May 2003.

27.35 THIRD-CYCLE LESSER BLACK-BACKED GULL *(L. F. GRAELLSII)*, STARTING PB3 MOLT (P1–P2 NEW AND ADULTLIKE IN PATTERN, P3 GROWING; MANY WHITE UNDERWING COVERTS PROBABLY NEW, COMPARE WITH PHOTO 27.32). Note relatively long and pointed wings, overall dusky underside to remiges, and how bill and legs can brighten through summer (compare with photos 27.16–27.18). Aged by adultlike pattern of middle primaries; also note relatively extensive blackish in tail and narrow whitish trailing edge to secondaries (compare with photos 27.36–27.37). Killian Mullarney. Wexford, Ireland, 19 July 2000.

27.36 THIRD-CYCLE LESSER BLACK-BACKED GULL *(L. F. GRAELLSII)* COMPLETING PB3 MOLT (P10 NOT FULLY GROWN). Distinguished from adult by brownish upperwing coverts, reduced white on outer primaries, extensive blackish on alula, primary coverts, and bases of outer secondaries, dusky on underwing coverts. Killian Mullarney. Wexford, Ireland, 20 Oct. 1998.

27.37 THIRD-CYCLE TYPE BREEDING LESSER BLACK-BACKED GULL *(L. F. GRAELLSII)*. Distinguished from adult by reduced white (for example, no mirrors) and more extensive black (extending in to P4) on primaries; also note black on bill. Steve N. G. Howell. Chew Valley Lake, England, 5 May 2003.

28.1 ADULT BREEDING KELP GULLS (FEMALE BEHIND; *L. D. DOMINICANUS*). Note bill size and shape, slaty blackish upperparts, and greenish yellow legs; legs vary from greenish (photo 28.4) to yellow (photo 28.3). Steve N. G. Howell. Concon, Valparaíso, Chile, 26 Oct. 2002.

28.2 ADULT BREEDING KELP GULL *(L. D. DOMINICANUS)*. Note same features as photo 28.1. Eye color varies from dark (like this bird) to pale (photo 28.3). Steve N. G. Howell. Concon, Valparaíso, Chile, 26 Oct. 2002.

28.3 ADULT BREEDING KELP GULL *(L. D. DOMINICANUS)*. Note same features as photo 28.1; also yellow orbital ring (which varies from yellow to reddish orange). Eye color varies from pale (like this bird) to dark (photo 28.2). Steve N. G. Howell. Concon, Valparaíso, Chile, 26 Oct. 2002.

28.4 ADULT BREEDING KELP GULL *(L. D. DOMINICANUS)*. Birds in southern South America, like this individual, average shorter bills and more-greenish legs than birds in central and northern Chile (photos 28.1–28.3). Mike Danzenbaker. Ushuaia, Tierra del Fuego, Argentina, 19 Dec. 2000.

28.5 ADULT BREEDING KELP GULL *(L. D. AUSTRINUS)*. Note relatively short, and thus stout-looking, bill and yellow legs typical of Antarctic populations; also less-blackish, more-slaty, upperparts. Steve N. G. Howell. South Georgia, 26 Nov. 2002.

28.6 JUVENILE KELP GULL *(L. D. AUSTRINUS).* Note extensive scaly and notched edgings on upperparts, dusky flesh legs. Greg W. Lasley. Hannah Point, Antarctica, 31 Jan. 1998.

28.7 JUVENILE KELP GULL *(L. D. DOMINICANUS).* Note extensive scaly and notched edgings on upperparts, dusky flesh legs (note bill longer than Antarctic birds, compare with photos 28.6, 28.8). Kelp Gull is the only large white-headed gull in South America, where identification of juveniles is therefore straightforward. Most-similar Northern Hemisphere species is Lesser Black-backed Gull, which is less thickset with longer wing projection and less stout bill. Steve N. G. Howell. Ushuaia, Tierra del Fuego, Argentina, 11 Mar. 2005.

28.8 FIRST-CYCLE KELP GULL *(L. D. AUSTRINUS).* Note post-juvenal molt on mantle and scapulars; also compare relatively short bill with South American subspecies (photo 28.7). Steve N. G. Howell. South Georgia, 25 Mar. 2002.

28.9 FIRST-CYCLE JUVENILE KELP GULL, STILL IN ALMOST FULL JUVENAL PLUMAGE *(L. D. DOMINICANUS).* Like many northern gulls, some southern Kelp Gulls retain most or all juvenal plumage through the winter (and compare with photo 28.14). Note dusky flesh legs; head has bleached whitish. Enrique Couve. Fuerte Bulnes, Magallanes, Chile, Aug. 2002.

28.10 FIRST-CYCLE KELP GULL, A TYPICAL FIRST-SPRING BIRD IN CENTRAL CHILE *(L. D. DOMINICANUS).* Note bill size and shape, whitish head and chest, dusky gray-brown A1 scapulars, and dull-flesh legs. Steve N. G. Howell. Concon, Valparaíso, Chile, 26 Oct. 2002.

28.11 FIRST-CYCLE KELP GULLS, FAIRLY TYPICAL FIRST-SPRING BIRDS (L. D. DOMINICANUS). Note bill size and shape, whitish head and chest, and variation in scapular patterns. Steve N. G. Howell. Concon, Valparaíso, Chile, 26 Oct. 2002.

28.12 FIRST-CYCLE KELP GULL (L. D. DOMINICANUS). Note bill size (relatively small on this individual) and shape, overall dusky brown aspect, and dull-flesh legs. Steve N. G. Howell. Concon, Valparaíso, Chile, 26 Oct. 2002.

28.13 FIRST-CYCLE KELP GULL (L. D. DOMINICANUS). Some individuals of more northerly populations replace upperwing coverts in PA1 molt; also note more strongly bleached white head and underparts, and relatively advanced bill pattern (compare with photos 28.10–28.12). Steve N. G. Howell. Arica, Tarapacá, Chile, 22 Oct. 1999.

28.14 FIRST-CYCLE KELP GULL (L. D. DOMINICANUS). Some individuals of more southerly populations retain juvenal plumage through late winter (see photo 28.9) and then attain slaty blackish A1 back feathers; plumage is otherwise bleached juvenal. Steve N. G. Howell. Punta Arenas, Magallanes, Chile, 30 Oct. 2002.

28.15 FIRST-CYCLE KELP GULL (L. D. AUSTRINUS). First-year Antarctic and Falkland birds average darker overall than Chilean birds (for example, photos 28.10–28.11). Steve N. G. Howell. Stanley, Falkland Islands, 23 Nov. 2002.

28.16 SECOND-CYCLE KELP GULL *(L. D. AUSTRINUS)* IN PB2 MOLT (P5 HAS BEEN SHED). Note relatively stocky shape and short bill. Eric Preston. South Georgia, 9 Jan. 2003.

28.17 SECOND-CYCLE KELP GULL *(L. D. DOMINICANUS)* COMPLETING PB2 MOLT (OUTER PRIMARIES NOT FULLY GROWN). A relatively pale individual (compare with photos 28.18–28.19); note grayish green legs. Steve N. G. Howell. Río Grande, Tierra del Fuego, Argentina, 9 Feb. 1999.

28.18 SECOND-CYCLE KELP GULL *(L. D. DOMINICANUS)*, COMPLETING PB2 MOLT (P9–P10 OLD). A darker and more boldly patterned individual (compare with photo 28.17). Steve N. G. Howell. Ushuaia, Tierra del Fuego, Argentina, 9 Feb. 1999.

28.19 SECOND-CYCLE KELP GULL *(L. D. DOMINICANUS)*, COMPLETING PB2 MOLT (P10 NOT FULLY GROWN) AND STARTING PA2 MOLT (SOME MEDIAN COVERTS HAVE BEEN SHED). A more "advanced" individual (compare with photos 28.17–28.18) with slaty blackish upperparts, bicolored bill. Steve N. G. Howell. Ushuaia, Tierra del Fuego, Argentina, 11 Mar. 2005.

28.20 SECOND-CYCLE KELP GULL *(L. D. DOMINICANUS)*. A fairly typical midwinter individual. Note slaty blackish back and dull greenish flesh legs; no median coverts were replaced in fall in the PA2 molt (compare with photo 28.19). Enrique Couve. Punta Arenas, Magallanes, Chile, Aug. 2002.

28.21 SECOND-CYCLE KELP GULL (L. D. DOMINICANUS). A fairly typical individual but with more advanced bill pattern than photo 28.20, and pale gray-green legs. Steve N. G. Howell. Puerto Montt, Llanquihue, Chile, 5 Sept. 1997.

28.22 SECOND-CYCLE KELP GULL (L. D. DOMINICANUS). A typical second-summer individual. Note slaty blackish back, variegated brownish upperwing coverts, and fleshy yellowish legs. Steve N. G. Howell. Concon, Valparaíso, Chile, 26 Oct. 2002.

28.23 SECOND-CYCLE KELP GULL (L. D. DOMINICANUS). A typical second-summer individual; note same features as photo 28.22. Mike Danzenbaker. Ushuaia, Tierra del Fuego, Argentina, 19 Dec. 2000.

28.24 THIRD-CYCLE KELP GULL (L. D. AUSTRINUS) IN PB3 MOLT (P9–P10 OLD). Distinguished from adult by bill pattern, duller legs, and extensive dusky head and neck markings (which average heavier than on *L. d. dominicanus*). Steve N. G. Howell. South Georgia, 25 Mar. 2002.

28.25 THIRD-CYCLE KELP GULL (L. D. DOMINICANUS). Distinguished from adult by bill pattern, brownish upperwing coverts, lack of white tips to outer primaries, black in tail, and duller legs. Steve N. G. Howell. Concon, Valparaíso, Chile, 26 Oct. 2002.

28.26 THIRD-CYCLE KELP GULL *(L. D. DOMINICANUS)*. Note same features as photo 28.25. Steve N. G. Howell. Concon, Valparaíso, Chile, 26 Oct. 2002.

28.27 THIRD-CYCLE TYPE KELP GULL *(L. D. DOMINICANUS)*. Distinguished from adult by brownish upperwing coverts and reduced white tips to outer primaries. Steve N. G. Howell. Concon, Valparaíso, Chile, 26 Oct. 2002.

28.28 ADULT KELP GULL *(L. D. DOMINICANUS)*. Note slaty blackish upperparts with poorly contrasting black wingtips, indistinct white tongue-tips on P6, and small white P10 mirror. Steve N. G. Howell. Concon, Valparaíso, Chile, 26 Oct. 2002.

28.29 ADULT BREEDING KELP GULL *(L. D. DOMINICANUS)*. Note same features as photo 28.28; also bill size and shape. Steve N. G. Howell. Concon, Valparaíso, Chile, 26 Oct. 2002.

28.30 ADULT KELP GULL *(L. D. DOMINICANUS).* Note same features as photo 28.28; some birds (like this individual) also have a small P9 mirror. Mike Danzenbaker. Ushuaia, Tierra del Fuego, Argentina, 19 Dec. 2000.

28.31 ADULT NONBREEDING KELP GULL *(L. D. AUSTRINUS)* IN PB MOLT (P9–P10 OLD, P7–P8 GROWING AND NOT VISIBLE). Note relatively large P10 mirror and P9 mirror (visible on closed wing), distinct white tongue-tips on P5–P6, and fine dusky head streaking of fresh basic plumage. Steve N. G. Howell. South Georgia, 25 Mar. 2002.

28.32 ADULT BREEDING KELP GULLS *(L. D. AUSTRINUS).* Relative to *L. d. dominicanus* (see photos 28.28–28.30) note stouter bill, yellow legs, bold white tongue-tips on P5–P7, larger white P10 mirror (or mirror-tip), and slightly paler, slaty gray upperparts with more-contrasting black wingtips. Steve N. G. Howell. Deception Island, Antarctica, 3 Dec. 2002.

28.33 ADULT KELP GULL *(L. D. AUSTRINUS)* STARTING PB MOLT (P1 SHED). Note white P9–P10 mirrors, relatively large white tongue-tips on P5–P7. Steve N. G. Howell. Elephant Island, Antarctica, 2 Dec. 2002.

28.34 JUVENILE KELP GULL (L. D. DOMINICANUS). Note lack of a distinct pale panel on inner primaries, mostly plain bases to greater coverts, and mostly black tail with limited white barring at bases of outer rectrices. Steve N. G. Howell. Ushuaia, Tierra del Fuego, Argentina, 11 Mar. 2005.

28.35 FIRST-CYCLE KELP GULL (L. D. DOMINICANUS). Note same features as photo 28.34. Steve N. G. Howell. Concon, Valparaíso, Chile, 26 Oct. 2002.

28.36 FIRST-CYCLE KELP GULL (L. D. DOMINICANUS). Note lack of a distinct pale panel on inner primaries, mostly plain bases to greater coverts, and bleached whitish head. Steve N. G. Howell. Concon, Valparaíso, Chile, 26 Oct. 2002.

28.37 FIRST-CYCLE KELP GULL (L. D. DOMINICANUS) WITH VERY WORN TIPS TO PRIMARIES AND RECTRICES AND RELATIVELY "ADVANCED" BILL. Note same features as photo 28.36. Steve N. G. Howell. Concon, Valparaíso, Chile, 26 Oct. 2002.

28.38 SECOND-CYCLE KELP GULL *(L. D. DOMINICANUS)*. Note overall dark upperwings, bill size and shape, and fleshy yellowish legs. Steve N. G. Howell. Concon, Valparaíso, Chile, 26 Oct. 2002.

28.39 SECOND-CYCLE KELP GULL *(L. D. DOMINICANUS)*. Note overall dark upperwings, slaty blackish back, and bill size and shape; distinguished from third cycle (photo 28.41) by pattern of middle primaries. Steve N. G. Howell. Concon, Valparaíso, Chile, 26 Oct. 2002.

28.40 SECOND-CYCLE KELP GULL *(L. D. DOMINICANUS)*. Note same features as photo 28.39. Steve N. G. Howell. Concon, Valparaíso, Chile, 26 Oct. 2002.

28.41 THIRD-CYCLE KELP GULL *(L. D. DOMINICANUS)*. Distinguished from adult by brownish upperwing coverts and browner outer primaries lacking white mirror; some birds have black in tail. Told from second cycle (photos 28.39–28.40) by adultlike pattern of inner and middle primaries. Steve N. G. Howell. Concon, Valparaíso, Chile, 26 Oct. 2002.

29.1 ADULT BREEDING GREAT BLACK-BACKED GULL. Distinctive: note stout bill with swollen gonys, slaty blackish upperparts, short wing projection, and pale flesh pink legs. Bruce Mactavish. St. John's, Newfoundland, 5 Feb. 2001.

29.2 ADULT GREAT BLACK-BACKED GULL (WITH AMERICAN HERRING GULLS). Distinctive: note same features as photo 29.1; also large size relative to Herring Gulls. Bill of nonbreeding birds often has a black subterminal mark. Bruce Hallett. Myrtle Beach, South Carolina, 28 Feb. 2000.

29.3 ADULT BREEDING GREAT BLACK-BACKED GULL STARTING PB MOLT (SOME MEDIAN COVERTS SHED, ALSO SOME INNER PRIMARIES SHED, NOT VISIBLE HERE). Distinctive: note same features as photo 29.1; worn plumage has a browner cast than fresh plumage (photo 29.1). Steve N. G. Howell. Salisbury Beach, Massachusetts, 28 June 1998.

29.4 JUVENILE GREAT BLACK-BACKED GULLS (WINGTIPS NOT FULLY GROWN). Distinctive: note stout bill with diffuse paler base, extensively whitish median underparts, and boldly checkered upperparts. Marshall J. Iliff. Little Bodkin Island, Maryland, 31 July 1997.

29.5 JUVENILE GREAT BLACK-BACKED GULL. Distinctive: note stout bill, low-sloping forehead, and whitish ground color to head and underparts; some birds, like this individual, retain juvenal plumage through their first winter. Rik Winters. Wijster, Netherlands, 8 Jan. 2000.

29.6 FIRST-CYCLE GREAT BLACK-BACKED GULL. Distinctive: note stout bill with diffuse paler base, extensively whitish head and underparts, boldly checkered upperparts (with post-juvenal scapulars), and tail pattern. Bruce Mactavish. St. John's, Newfoundland, 1 Jan. 2002.

29.7 FIRST-CYCLE GREAT BLACK-BACKED GULL WITH FIRST-CYCLE KUMLIEN'S GULL. Distinctive: note stout bill, extensively whitish head and underparts, short wing projection, and large overall size (relative to Kumlien's); also variable post-juvenal scapular patterns (compare with photo 29.6). Steve N. G. Howell. St. John's, Newfoundland, 4 Feb. 2002.

29.8 SECOND-CYCLE GREAT BLACK-BACKED GULL IN PB2 MOLT (P9–P10 OLD). Distinctive: note stout bill with diffuse pink base and pale tip, whitish head and underparts, and boldly checkered upperparts. Steve N. G. Howell. Salisbury Beach, Massachusetts, 28 June 1998.

29.9 SECOND-CYCLE GREAT BLACK-BACKED GULL. Note same features as photo 29.8. Bruce Mactavish. St. John's, Newfoundland, 14 Oct. 1999.

29.10 SECOND-CYCLE GREAT BLACK-BACKED GULL. Note same features as photo 29.8. Bruce Mactavish. St. John's, Newfoundland, 2 Feb. 2002.

29.11 SECOND-CYCLE GREAT BLACK-BACKED GULL. Note same features as photo 29.8. Rik Winters. Wijster, Netherlands, 6 Feb. 2000.

29.12 SECOND-CYCLE GREAT BLACK-BACKED GULL. Distinctive: a very bleached and "retarded" individual with limited slaty blackish in upperparts, compare with photo 29.13. Harry J. Lehto. Oulu, Finland, 1 June 1998.

29.13 SECOND-CYCLE GREAT BLACK-BACKED GULL. Distinctive: a more "advanced" individual with brighter bill and mostly slaty blackish back; compare with photo 29.12. Harry J. Lehto. Oulu, Finland, 1 June 1998.

29.14 THIRD-CYCLE GREAT BLACK-BACKED GULL STARTING PB3 MOLT (INNER PRIMARIES SHED, NOT VISIBLE HERE; SOME UPPERWING COVERTS PROBABLY B3). Distinctive: note stout bill, low-sloping forehead, short wing projection, and slaty blackish upperparts. Steve N. G. Howell. Salisbury Beach, Massachusetts, 28 June 1998.

29.15 THIRD-CYCLE GREAT BLACK-BACKED GULL COMPLETING PB3 MOLT (WINGTIPS NOT FULLY GROWN); AN AVERAGE INDIVIDUAL (COMPARE WITH PHOTOS 29.16–29.17). Distinctive: note stout, neatly tricolored bill, low-sloping forehead, and extensively dark slaty upperparts. Bruce Mactavish. St. John's, Newfoundland, 29 Oct. 1996.

29.16 THIRD-CYCLE GREAT BLACK-BACKED GULL; A "RETARDED" INDIVIDUAL (COMPARE WITH PHOTOS 29.15, 29.18). Distinctive: note stout, tricolored bill, low-sloping forehead, and boldly patterned upperparts; distinguished from second cycle by bill pattern and overall dark greater coverts. Tony Leukering. Cape May, New Jersey, 12 Nov. 1993.

29.17 THIRD-CYCLE GREAT BLACK-BACKED GULL; A "RETARDED" INDIVIDUAL (COMPARE WITH PHOTOS 29.15, 29.18). Note same features as photo 29.16; also white primary tips. Rik Winters. Wijster, Netherlands, 25 Dec. 2002.

29.18 THIRD-CYCLE GREAT BLACK-BACKED GULL; AN "ADVANCED" INDIVIDUAL (COMPARE WITH PHOTOS 29.15–29.17). Distinctive: note stout, neatly tricolored bill, low-sloping forehead, and mostly slaty blackish upperparts. Tony Leukering. Cape May, New Jersey, 15 Nov. 1993.

29.19 THIRD-CYCLE GREAT BLACK-BACKED GULL, ALTERNATE PLUMAGE; A MORE "RETARDED" INDIVIDUAL (COMPARE WITH PHOTO 29.20). Distinctive: note stout bill, short wing projection, pale flesh pink legs. Harry J. Lehto. Turku, Finland, 24 Apr. 1997.

29.20 THIRD-CYCLE GREAT BLACK-BACKED GULL, ALTERNATE PLUMAGE; A MORE "ADVANCED" INDIVIDUAL (COMPARE WITH PHOTO 29.19). Note same features as photo 29.19. Harry J. Lehto. Turku, Finland, 5 June 1998.

29.21 ADULT GREAT BLACK-BACKED GULL. Distinctive: note slaty blackish upperparts with large white P10 tip and large P9 mirror. Bruce Mactavish. St. John's, Newfoundland, 25 Feb. 2001.

29.22 ADULT NONBREEDING GREAT BLACK-BACKED GULL.
Distinctive: note same features as photo 29.21;
fine dusky head streaking of basic plumage is
visible on this individual. Bruce Mactavish.
St. John's, Newfoundland, 1 Jan. 2002.

29.23 ADULT NONBREEDING GREAT BLACK-BACKED GULL.
Distinctive: note same features as photo 29.21,
plus the very long and broad wings. From below,
black wingtip blends into slaty gray bases of inner
primaries and secondaries. Kevin T. Karlson. Cape
May, New Jersey, Dec. 2002.

29.24 JUVENILE GREAT BLACK-BACKED GULL. Distinctive:
note boldly checkered upperparts, poorly contrasting paler panel on inner primaries, and white
rump and tail with wavy black distal bands. Larry
Sansone. Cape May, New Jersey, 13 Sept. 1999.

29.25 FIRST-CYCLE GREAT BLACK-BACKED GULL. Distinctive: note whitish head and chest, boldly checkered upperparts, poorly contrasting paler panel on
inner primaries, and white rump and tail with
broken black distal band. Michael D. Stubblefield.
Montauk Point, New York, Dec. 2000.

29.26 FIRST-CYCLE GREAT BLACK-BACKED GULL. Distinctive: note very long and broad wings, overall whitish head and underparts, and tail pattern. Kevin T. Karlson. Cape May, New Jersey, Dec. 2002.

29.27 SECOND-CYCLE GREAT BLACK-BACKED GULLS IN PB2 MOLT. Distinctive: note long and broad wings, overall whitish head and underparts, variable (juvenal) tail patterns, and stout bills. Steve N. G. Howell. Cape Hatteras, North Carolina, 22 May 2003.

29.28 SECOND-CYCLE GREAT BLACK-BACKED GULL. Distinctive: note checkered upperparts, poorly contrasting paler panel on inner primaries, and white rump and tail with broken black distal band. Distinguished from first cycle (photos 29.24–29.25) by more clean-cut pattern on P5–P6, small whitish mirror on P10, whiter wing-linings, contrasting median coverts, and bill pattern. Michael D. Stubblefield. Point Lookout, New York, Mar. 2002.

29.29 SECOND-CYCLE GREAT BLACK-BACKED GULL. Distinctive: note very long and broad wings, thickset whitish body, and stout bill. Distinguished from first cycle (photo 29.25) by more clean-cut pattern on P5–P6, lack of neat dark barring on undertail coverts, and distinct pale bill tip. Bruce Mactavish. St. John's, Newfoundland, 9 Feb. 2003.

29.30 THIRD-CYCLE GREAT BLACK-BACKED GULL IN PB3 MOLT.
Note tail patten and slaty blackish back; aged by
pattern on P4–P6. Steve N. G. Howell. Cape
Hatteras, North Carolina, 22 May 2004.

29.31 THIRD-CYCLE GREAT BLACK-BACKED GULL. Distinctive: note stout bill and slaty blackish upperparts.
Tony Leukering. Cape May, New Jersey, 16 Nov.
1993.

29.32 THIRD-CYCLE GREAT BLACK-BACKED GULL. Distinctive: note slaty blackish upperparts, broad wings
with large white mirror and white tip to P10, and
small P9 mirror (at least on left wing). Harry J.
Lehto. Turku, Finland, 17 Apr. 1997.

29.33 THIRD-CYCLE GREAT BLACK-BACKED GULL. Distinc-
tive: note very long and broad wings, large white
P10 mirror, flesh pink legs, and stout bill. Kevin T.
Karlson. Cape May, New Jersey, Dec. 2002.

30.1 ADULT NONBREEDING SLATY-BACKED GULL COMPLETING PB MOLT (OUTER PRIMARIES NOT FULLY GROWN). Note relatively parallel-edged and dull-colored bill, pale eye with reddish pink orbital ring, brownish head and neck streaking, slaty gray upperparts, broad white tertial crescent, and pink legs. Steve Heinl. Ketchikan, Alaska, 28 Oct. 1993.

30.2 ADULT BREEDING SLATY-BACKED GULL WITH ADULT VEGA GULL (SITTING, RIGHT) AND ADULT GLAUCOUS GULL (STANDING BEHIND). Note stout but relatively parallel-edged bill, dark slaty gray upperparts; the eye of this bird is atypically dark. Bruce Hallett. Nome, Alaska, early June 2001.

30.3 ADULT BREEDING SLATY-BACKED GULL. Note relatively parallel-edged bill, pale eye with pink orbital ring, slaty gray upperparts, and bright pink legs; white primary tips and tertial crescent are reduced in worn plumage. Mike Danzenbaker. Aomori Prefecture, Japan, July 1997.

30.4 JUVENILE SLATY-BACKED GULL. Note bill shape, overall dark brownish aspect with relatively fine pale markings on greater coverts, and brownish black wingtip with narrow whitish fringes to the primary tips. Harry J. Lehto. Hokkaido, Japan, 24 Aug. 1997.

30.5 FIRST-CYCLE SLATY-BACKED GULL. Note stout blackish bill, short wing projection, fairly plain greater coverts, brownish black wingtip, and bright pink legs. Geoff Carey. Choshi, Japan, 12 Nov. 1999.

30.6 FIRST-CYCLE SLATY-BACKED GULL. Note stout blackish bill, short wing projection, fairly plain greater coverts (wing coverts and tertials already quite worn; compare with photo 30.7), and brownish black wingtip; head and neck have bleached to whitish. Geoff Carey. Choshi, Japan, 13 Nov. 1999.

30.7 FIRST-CYCLE SLATY-BACKED GULL, LARGELY IN RELA-TIVELY FRESH JUVENAL PLUMAGE (COMPARE WITH PHOTO 30.6), WHICH HAS BLEACHED OVERALL TO A SLIGHTLY WARM BROWN. Note stout blackish bill, fairly plain greater coverts, brownish black wingtip, and bright pink legs. Geoff Carey. Choshi, Japan, 16 Mar. 1999.

30.8 FIRST-CYCLE SLATY-BACKED GULL. Note stout blackish bill, bleached whitish head and neck with warm brown streaking, bleached whitish greater coverts, and bright pink legs. Annika Forsten. Pohang, South Korea, 16 Feb. 2002.

30.9 FIRST-CYCLE SLATY-BACKED GULL. Note fairly stout, parallel-edged bill, bleached whitish head and underparts, and bleached whitish greater coverts. Mike Danzenbaker. Aomori Prefecture, Japan, 29 Mar. 1998.

30.10 FIRST-CYCLE SLATY-BACKED GULL IN BLEACHED PLUMAGE. Note bill size and shape, pattern of A1 scapulars, bleached white wing-covert panel contrasting with brown skirt and wingtip. Yoshiaki Watanabe. Choshi Chiba, Japan, 1 May 2001.

30.11 SECOND-CYCLE SLATY-BACKED GULL IN BLEACHED PLUMAGE, STARTING PB2 MOLT (INNER PRIMARIES SHED, SEE PHOTO 30.27 OF SAME BIRD). Note same features as photo 30.10. Gary H. Rosenberg. Barrow, Alaska, 22 June 1995.

30.12 SECOND-CYCLE SLATY-BACKED GULL IN PB2 MOLT (P8–P10 OLD, SEE PHOTO 30.28 OF SAME BIRD). Note bill size and shape, incoming slaty gray on back, and whitish mottling on scapulars. Bruce Mactavish. Inuvik, Northwest Territories, 5 Aug. 2002.

30.13 SECOND-CYCLE SLATY-BACKED GULL COMPLETING PB2 MOLT (OUTER PRIMARIES NOT FULLY GROWN). Note bill size (relatively small on this individual) and shape, incoming slaty gray on back, and whitish mottling on scapulars; eye can be dark or pale at this age. Kimball L. Garrett. Nome, Alaska, 14 Sept. 2002.

30.14 SECOND-CYCLE SLATY-BACKED GULL. Note bill size and shape, incoming slaty gray on back, and bright pink legs. Yoshiaki Watanabe. Hokkaido, Japan, 8 Dec. 2000.

30.15 SECOND-CYCLE SLATY-BACKED GULL. Note bill size and shape, pale eye, slaty gray back, whitish upperwing coverts, and bright pink legs; primaries relatively pale on this individual. Yoshiaki Watanabe. Hokkaido, Japan, 13 Feb. 2001.

30.16 SECOND-CYCLE SLATY-BACKED GULL. Note same features as photo 30.15, but primaries more typically blackish. Mike Danzenbaker. Aomori Prefecture, Japan, 1 Mar. 1998.

30.17 THIRD-CYCLE SLATY-BACKED GULL IN PB3 MOLT. Note bill size and shape (some birds have brighter, more adultlike bills; see photos 30.31–30.32), pale eye, and contrast between incoming slaty gray coverts and bleached B2 coverts. Cameron D. Eckert. Whitehorse, Yukon Territory, 18 July 2003.

30.18 THIRD-CYCLE SLATY-BACKED GULL COMPLETING PB3 MOLT (OUTER PRIMARIES NOT FULLY GROWN). Distinguished from adult by brownish on upperwing coverts and tertials, reduced white tips to primaries, and bill pattern. Kimball L. Garrett. Nome, Alaska, 14 Sept. 2002.

30.19 THIRD-CYCLE SLATY-BACKED GULL (SAME BIRD AS PHOTO 30.33). Distinguished from adult by brownish on upperwing coverts and tertials, reduced white tips to primaries, and black on tail; also note bill pattern. Steve Heinl. Ketchikan, Alaska, 30 Oct. 1993.

30.20 ADULT NONBREEDING SLATY-BACKED GULL. Note slaty gray upperparts, broad white trailing edge to wings, and bill size and shape. Lack of white tongue-tips on P8–P9 may indicate fourth-cycle plumage. Distinguished from adult Western Gull by distinct white tongue-tips on P6–P7. Mike Danzenbaker. Aomori Prefecture, Japan, 21 Feb. 1999.

30.21 ADULT SLATY-BACKED GULL. Note gray underside to primaries with blackish limited largely to subterminal bands on P6–P9; unlike photo 30.20, this bird shows bold white tongue-tips and mirrors through outer primaries. Steve Heinl. Ketchikan, Alaska, 29 Mar. 1997.

30.22 ADULT BREEDING SLATY-BACKED GULL. Note slaty gray upperwing, bold pattern of white tongue-tips and mirrors on outer primaries, and bill size and shape. Bruce Hallett. St. Lawrence Island, Alaska, early June 2001.

30.23 FIRST-CYCLE SLATY-BACKED GULL. Note broad wings, pale inner primary panel continuing out as pale tongues on inner webs of outer primaries, mostly blackish tail, and stout blackish bill. Geoff Carey. Choshi, Japan, 11 Nov. 1999.

30.24 FIRST-CYCLE SLATY-BACKED GULL. Note overall relatively plain, gray-brown aspect, broad wings, pale inner primary panel continuing out as pale tongues on inner webs of outer primaries, and mostly blackish tail. Geoff Carey. Chumunjin, South Korea, 30 Nov. 2000.

30.25 FIRST-CYCLE SLATY-BACKED GULL. Note bright pink legs and pale markings on bases of outer rectrices; pattern on upperside of far wing is obscured by shadow. Geoff Carey. Hokkaido, Japan, 2 Feb. 1999.

30.26 FIRST-CYCLE SLATY-BACKED GULL. Note pale inner primary panel continuing out as pale tongues on inner webs of outer primaries, bleached whitish greater coverts contrasting with dark secondary bar. Yoshiaki Watanabe. Choshi Chiba, Japan, 24 Mar. 2001.

30.27 SECOND-CYCLE SLATY-BACKED GULL STARTING PB2 MOLT (SAME BIRD AS PHOTO 30.11). Note two-tone pattern on outer primaries (inner primaries shed), bleached whitish greater coverts contrasting with dark secondary bar, and mostly dark tail. Gary H. Rosenberg. Barrow, Alaska, 22 June 1995.

30.28 SECOND-CYCLE SLATY-BACKED GULL IN PB2 MOLT (P8–P10 OLD; SAME BIRD AS PHOTO 30.12). Note incoming slaty gray on upperparts and faded two-tone pattern on outer primaries; distinguished from third cycle by retained juvenal flight feathers, pattern of inner primaries (especially P5–P6, which lack a well-defined adultlike pattern; see photos 30.34–30.35). Bruce Mactavish. Inuvik, Northwest Territories, 5 Aug. 2002.

30.29 SECOND-CYCLE SLATY-BACKED GULL. Pattern of remiges suggests first cycle, with paler tongues on outer primaries; note contrastingly different pattern of P1–P2, presumably molted during a more "advanced" hormonal peak. Annika Forsten. Pohang, South Korea, 16 Feb. 2002.

30.30 THIRD-CYCLE SLATY-BACKED GULL STARTING PB3 MOLT (P5–P10 OLD). Two-tone pattern of primaries (note pattern on P5–P6 versus photo 30.34–30.36) suggests first cycle. Martin Hale. Kuril Islands, Russia, 1 June 2003.

30.31 THIRD-CYCLE SLATY-BACKED GULL STARTING PB3 MOLT (P5–P10 OLD; SAME BIRD AS PHOTO 30.32). Bleached whitish greater coverts and two-tone pattern of primaries (note pattern on P5–P6 versus photos 30.34–30.36) suggest first cycle. Steve N. G. Howell. Kamchatka, Russia, 23 June 2003.

30.32 THIRD-CYCLE SLATY-BACKED GULL STARTING PB3 MOLT (P5–P10 OLD; SAME BIRD AS PHOTO 30.32). Note pattern on middle primaries (for example, P5–P6 versus photo 30.35) and bill shape; extensive brown on wing-linings and belly also typical of second-summer birds. Steve N. G. Howell. Kamchatka, Russia, 23 June 2003.

30.33 THIRD-CYCLE SLATY-BACKED GULL (SAME BIRD AS PHOTO 30.19). Distinguished from adult by brownish upperwing coverts, reduced white in outer primaries, and black on tail; also note bill pattern. Steve Heinl. Ketchikan, Alaska, 4 Nov. 1993.

30.34 THIRD-CYCLE TYPE SLATY-BACKED GULL. Distinguished from adult by brownish on wing-linings, reduced white in outer primaries, and black spot on R6. Steve Heinl. Ketchikan, Alaska, 29 Jan. 1994.

30.35 FOURTH-CYCLE SLATY-BACKED GULL STARTING PB4 MOLT (P4–P10 OLD). Note pattern on outer primaries (for example, adultlike P4–P5 versus photo 30.30), and bill shape. Distinguished from adult by gray-brown upperwing coverts, and black in tail (which can be all white). Martin Hale. Kuril Islands, Russia, 1 June 2003.

30.36 FOURTH-CYCLE SLATY-BACKED GULL STARTING PB4 MOLT (P5–P10 OLD). Note pattern on middle primaries (for example, P5–P6 versus photo 30.32), and bill shape. Distinguished from adult by reduced white in outer primaries, black in tail, brownish on wing-linings, and black on bill. Steve N. G. Howell. Kamchatka, Russia, 23 June 2003.

31.1 ADULT NONBREEDING WESTERN GULL *(L. O. WYMANI)* IN PB MOLT (P8–P10 OLD). Note stout, relatively bulbous-tipped bill (tinged pinkish basally), yellow orbital ring, and slaty gray upperparts. Dusky head and neck streaking is often heaviest at this stage of molt (and rarely if ever heavier than on this individual, which may be a fourth-cycle bird), and head usually becomes whiter by the time primary molt completes. Steve N. G. Howell. Bahía Asunción, Baja California Sur, Mexico, 22 Sept. 2002.

31.2 ADULT BREEDING WESTERN GULL (PRESUMED *L. O. WYMANI).* Note stout and bright bill, slaty gray upperparts, and yellow orbital ring; eye varies from pale to dark. Some birds, like this individual, can have yellow-tinged legs, mainly during spring (compare with more typical photo 31.3). Kimball L. Garrett. Mission Bay, California, 10 Mar. 2000.

31.4 FIRST-CYCLE WESTERN GULL (PRESUMED *L. O. WYMANI)* STARTING MOLT (ONE POST-JUVENAL SCAPULAR VISIBLE). Note overall dark brownish aspect, narrow skirt, and bulbous-tipped bill. Steve N. G. Howell. Bahía Asunción, Baja California Sur, Mexico, 23 Sept. 2002.

31.3 ADULT BREEDING WESTERN GULL *(L. O. WYMANI)* IN WORN PLUMAGE (WHITE PRIMARY TIPS MOSTLY ABSENT). Note same features as photo 31.2. Steve N. G. Howell. Islas San Benitos, Baja California, Mexico, 3 July 1999.

31.5 FIRST-CYCLE WESTERN GULL (PRESUMED *L. O. WYMANI)*, AN "ADVANCED" INDIVIDUAL. Note stout and bulbous-tipped bill, distinct skirt, relatively short wing projection. Bleached whitish head and underparts and pink-based bill suggest "retarded" Yellow-footed Gull, which is best separated by its generally whiter underparts and (not visible here) sparser dark bars on tail coverts. Steve N. G. Howell. El Sauzal, Baja California, 20 Feb. 1998.

31.6 SECOND-CYCLE WESTERN GULL (PRESUMED *L. O. WYMANI*). Note bulbous-tipped bill, whitish underparts and dirty-slaty upperparts of gray-type birds. Similar to first-cycle Yellow-footed Gull with extensive post-juvenal molt, but note less stout bill and more-rounded primaries. Steve N. G. Howell. Bahía Asunción, Baja California Sur, Mexico, 23 Sept. 2002.

31.7 SECOND-CYCLE WESTERN GULL (PRESUMED *L. O. WYMANI*). Note stout, bulbous-tipped bill, slaty gray on upperparts; head and underparts bleached whitish. Steve N. G. Howell. El Sauzal, Baja California, 20 Feb. 1998.

31.8 THIRD-CYCLE WESTERN GULL (PRESUMED *L. O. WYMANI*) COMPLETING PB3 MOLT (P10 NOT FULLY GROWN). Distinguished from adult by reduced white tips to outer primaries, brownish cast to upperwings, bill pattern, and dark in tail. Steve N. G. Howell. Bahía Asunción, Baja California Sur, Mexico, 23 Sept. 2002.

31.9 THIRD-CYCLE WESTERN GULL (PRESUMED *L. O. WYMANI*). Distinguished from adult by reduced white tips to outer primaries, brownish cast to upperwings, and black on bill. Steve N. G. Howell. El Sauzal, Baja California, 20 Feb. 1998.

31.10 ADULT WESTERN GULL (L. O. OCCIDENTALIS). Note slaty gray upperparts and pink legs. Distinguished from Slaty-backed Gull by narrower white trailing edge to wings, mostly black P8–P9, and indistinct, narrow whitish tongue-tips on P6–P8. Steve Heinl. Florence, Oregon, 6 Dec. 1994.

31.11 ADULT BREEDING WESTERN GULL (PRESUMED L. O. OCCIDENTALIS). Note slaty gray upperparts (versus darker upperwings with less-contrasting black wingtips of southern *wymani*; photo 31.12) and pink legs. Distinguished from Slaty-backed Gull by narrower white trailing edge to wings, mostly black P7–P9, and blackish underside to wingtip. Steve N. G. Howell. Bolinas, California, 21 Apr. 2003.

31.12 ADULT-TYPE WESTERN GULL (PRESUMED L. O. WYMANI). Note dark slaty gray upperparts (versus paler upperwings with more-contrasting black wingtips of nominate *occidentalis*; see photo 31.11). Distinguished from Slaty-backed Gull by narrower white trailing edge to wings and mostly black P7–P9. Blackish marks on alula and primary coverts may indicate a fourth-cycle bird; also note subterminal black on P4. Larry Sansone. Near Newport, California, 11 Jan. 2003.

31.13 ADULT WESTERN GULL. Note slaty gray bases to secondaries and inner primaries, pink legs. Distinguished from Slaty-backed Gull by extensively blackish underside to P8–P10; also note white head and bright bill (black line on mandible is garbage) in winter. Steve N. G. Howell. Monterey Bay, California, 15 Dec. 2003.

31.15 FIRST-CYCLE WESTERN GULL. Note same features as photo 31.14 but head has bleached to whitish, back includes grayer post-juvenal feathers, and inner primaries have bleached paler. Mike Danzenbaker. Monterey Bay, California, 15 Jan. 2000.

31.14 FIRST-CYCLE WESTERN GULL. Note overall dark brown aspect, broad wings, lack of a contrasting pale panel on inner primaries, black tail, barred tail coverts, and stout bill. Larry Sansone. Monterey, California, 17 Sept. 2002.

31.16 FIRST-CYCLE WESTERN GULL. Note overall dark brown aspect, broad wings, lack of a distinctly contrasting (translucent) pale panel on inner primaries, and heavily barred tail coverts. Steve N. G. Howell. Monterey Bay, California, 18 Oct. 1998.

31.17 SECOND-CYCLE WESTERN GULL. Note broad wings, slaty gray back, stout bill, and diffuse paler panel on inner primaries. Larry Sansone. Los Angeles, California, 22 Feb. 2003.

31.18 SECOND-CYCLE WESTERN GULL. Note same features as photo 31.17. Steve N. G. Howell. Bolinas, California, 21 Apr. 2003.

31.19 SECOND-CYCLE WESTERN GULL COMPLETING PB2 MOLT (P10 NOT FULLY GROWN). Note broad wings, dark wing-linings, and stout bill. Distinguished from first cycle (photo 31.16) by smudgier plumage, lack of distinct dark bars on tail coverts, and bill pattern. Steve N. G. Howell. Monterey Bay, California, 19 Sept. 1998.

31.20 THIRD-CYCLE WESTERN GULL. Note broad wings with mostly black outer primaries, slaty upperwing coverts, stout and bright bill, and flesh pink legs. Steve N. G. Howell. Bolinas, California, 21 Apr. 2003.

31.21 THIRD-CYCLE WESTERN GULL. Note same features as photo 31.20. Steve N. G. Howell. Bolinas, California, 15 Apr. 2003.

31.22 THIRD-CYCLE WESTERN GULL. Distinguished from adult by dusky marks on wing-linings, reduced white P10 mirror, and black in tail. Steve N. G. Howell. Monterey Bay, California, 18 Oct. 1998.

32.1 ADULT NONBREEDING YELLOW-FOOTED GULL COMPLETING PB MOLT (P10 OLD). Note stout bill, slaty gray upperparts, and yellowish legs and feet (typically dullest and tinged flesh at height of PB molt); also note limited dusky clouding on head (often strongest at this stage of molt), and fresh white primary tips (compare with photo 32.2). Kenneth Z. Kurland. Salton Sea, California, Sept. 2002.

32.2 ADULT BREEDING YELLOW-FOOTED GULL. Note stout and bulbous-tipped bill (relatively small on this presumed female) with large red gonydeal spot, yellow orbital ring, slaty gray upperparts, and yellow legs. White primary tips of fresh plumage (compare with photo 32.1) are typically much reduced by midwinter. Steve N. G. Howell. Puerto Peñasco, Sonora, Mexico, 21 Jan. 2003.

32.3 ADULT BREEDING YELLOW-FOOTED GULL. Note same features as photo 32.2, although larger bill suggests a male. Steve N. G. Howell. San Felipe, Baja California, Mexico, 16 Apr. 2004.

32.4 JUVENILE YELLOW-FOOTED GULL. Note stout and bulbous-tipped bill with dull-flesh basal two-thirds, extensively white belly and vent, and pale flesh legs. Kenneth Z. Kurland. Salton Sea, California, July 2000.

32.5 JUVENILE YELLOW-FOOTED GULL. Note same features as photo 32.4. Kenneth Z. Kurland. Salton Sea, California, July 2001.

32.6 FIRST-CYCLE YELLOW-FOOTED GULL. Juvenal plumage quite worn, especially on hindneck, with limited post-juvenal molt starting on face and back (compare with photo 32.7). Distinguished from Western Gull by paler head and underparts, more distinctly two-tone bill; also note relatively plain greater coverts, and pale flesh legs. Kenneth Z. Kurland. Salton Sea, California, Sept. 2002.

32.7 FIRST-CYCLE YELLOW-FOOTED GULL. In striking contrast to the individual in photo 32.6, this bird has already undergone extensive post-juvenal molt, with most of the head, neck, sides, back, and upperwing coverts replaced; also note bicolored bill, pale flesh legs. Kenneth Z. Kurland. Salton Sea, California, Sept. 2000.

32.9 FIRST-CYCLE YELLOW-FOOTED GULL. A moderately pigmented bird with retained juvenal upperwing coverts. Note very stout and bulbous-tipped bill, extensively white median underparts, and pale flesh legs. Steve N. G. Howell. Puerto Peñasco, Sonora, Mexico, 20 Jan. 2003.

32.8 FIRST-CYCLE YELLOW-FOOTED GULL. Occasional dark-pigmented individuals with little or no post-juvenal molt of upperwing coverts can resemble some Western Gulls: note clean white vent and (not visible here) white tail coverts with only sparse dark bars. Steve N. G. Howell. Puerto Peñasco, Sonora, Mexico, 21 Jan. 2003.

32.10 FIRST-CYCLE YELLOW-FOOTED GULL. A classic bird with mostly white head and underparts (bleached post-juvenal feathers) and extensive replacement of upperwing coverts; also note bill size and shape, pale flesh legs. Steve N. G. Howell. Puerto Peñasco, Sonora, Mexico, 21 Jan. 2003.

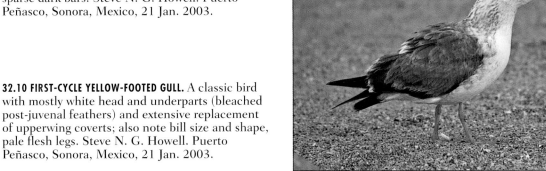

32.11 FIRST-CYCLE YELLOW-FOOTED GULL. Another classic bird with extensively white head and underparts and extensive post-juvenal molt of upperparts. Steve N. G. Howell. Puerto Peñasco, Sonora, Mexico, 21 Jan. 2003.

32.12 SECOND-CYCLE YELLOW-FOOTED GULL. By spring, bill usually pale flesh pink with black tip, eyes can be pale (but often dusky through second winter). Post-juvenal upperparts have bleached, and slaty gray scapulars probably represent start of PB2 molt (P1–P2 had been shed). Steve N. G. Howell. San Felipe, Baja California, Mexico, 16 Apr. 2004.

32.13 SECOND-CYCLE YELLOW-FOOTED GULL IN ADVANCED PB2 MOLT: P6 SHED AND P7–P10 OLD, MOST OF UPPERPARTS B2. Note bill size and shape, whitish head and underparts, and pale flesh legs. Steve N. G. Howell. San Felipe, Baja California, Mexico, 16 Apr. 2004.

32.14 SECOND-CYCLE YELLOW-FOOTED GULL IN PB2 MOLT (P9–P10 OLD). An unusually slender-billed individual. Most upperparts are fresh B2 feathers (compare with photo 32.13). Kenneth Z. Kurland. Salton Sea, California, June 2003.

32.15 SECOND-CYCLE YELLOW-FOOTED GULL COMPLETING PB2 MOLT (OUTER PRIMARIES NOT FULLY GROWN). PA2 molt under way (for example, incoming slaty median coverts). PA2 molt usually includes most of upperparts, which look fresh and slaty by midwinter (for example, photo 32.16). Kenneth Z. Kurland. Salton Sea, California, 8 Sept. 2003.

32.16 SECOND-CYCLE YELLOW-FOOTED GULL. A fairly typical midwinter bird. Note stout and bulbous-tipped bill, mostly slaty gray upperparts, yellow orbital ring, and fleshy yellow legs. Steve N. G. Howell. Puerto Peñasco, Sonora, Mexico, 21 Jan. 2003.

32.17 SECOND-CYCLE YELLOW-FOOTED GULL. Note same features as photo 32.16. The fresher and adultlike P5–P6 were apparently replaced in the PA2 molt (compare with photo 32.18), thus producing a pattern that suggests third cycles of other large dark-backed gulls. Steve N. G. Howell. Puerto Peñasco, Sonora, Mexico, 20 Jan. 2003.

32.18 SECOND-CYCLE YELLOW-FOOTED GULL WITH PRESUMED PA2 PRIMARY MOLT. Note white tip of P8, which is slightly less than half-grown, and contrast between more adultlike P1–P8 (new A2 feathers) and browner P9–P10 (old B2 feathers); some inner secondaries are also being molted. Steve N. G. Howell. Puerto Peñasco, Sonora, Mexico, 21 Jan. 2003.

32.19 SECOND-CYCLE YELLOW-FOOTED GULL. A relatively "retarded" individual with contrasting and worn B2 upperwing coverts (compare with photos 32.16–32.18). Distinguished from Western Gull mainly by bill size and shape; also note very white head and underparts, pale eye, and faint yellowish tinge to legs. Kimball L. Garrett. Bahía de Los Angeles, Baja California, Mexico, 11 Feb. 2003.

32.20 THIRD-CYCLE YELLOW-FOOTED GULLS (INNER PRIMARY MOLT JUST STARTING, NOT VISIBLE IN THESE PHOTOS). Typical (rear bird) or relatively "retarded" (front bird) appearance (compare with photo 32.21); bill brighter, with distinct red gonydeal spot relative to midwinter (see photos 32.16–32.17). Steve N. G. Howell. San Felipe, Baja California, Mexico, 16 Apr. 2004.

32.21 THIRD-CYCLE YELLOW-FOOTED GULL. Relatively advanced appearance (compare with photo 32.37 of same bird); extensive PA2 molt has included primaries out to P6 (note contrast between blacker, white-tipped P6 and browner, more-worn outer primaries). Steve N. G. Howell. San Felipe, Baja California, Mexico, 16 Apr. 2004.

32.22 PRESUMED THIRD-CYCLE YELLOW-FOOTED GULL IN PB3 MOLT (P9–P10 OLD). Distinguished from adult (see photo 32.1) by more-extensive dusky head markings and dull bill with distinct black subterminal band; also note reduced white on P10, dark eye. Kenneth Z. Kurland. Salton Sea, California, 8 Sept. 2003.

32.23 THIRD-CYCLE YELLOW-FOOTED GULL. Distinguished from adult by dark on bill, dusky eye, black in tail (see photo 32.38 of same bird). Steve N. G. Howell. Puerto Peñasco, Sonora, Mexico, 22 Jan. 2003.

32.24 THIRD-CYCLE YELLOW-FOOTED GULL. Distinguished from adult by dark on bill, faint dusky flecks on head, dusky eye, and pinkish hue to foot webbing. Note contrast in wingtip between fresh boldly white-tipped P4–P6 (apparently replaced in PA3 molt) and abraded P7–P10 (B2 feathers). Steve N. G. Howell. Puerto Peñasco, Sonora, Mexico, 23 Jan. 2003.

32.25 ADULT YELLOW-FOOTED GULL. Distinguished from Western Gull by slightly more-extensive black in wingtip and yellow feet. Steve N. G. Howell. Puerto Peñasco, Sonora, Mexico, 22 Jan. 2003.

32.26 ADULT YELLOW-FOOTED GULL. Distinguished from Western Gull by slightly more-extensive black in wingtip and yellow feet. Steve N. G. Howell. Puerto Peñasco, Sonora, Mexico, 22 Jan. 2003.

32.27 ADULT-TYPE YELLOW-FOOTED GULL. Relatively abraded primary tips and tail tip are common features of this species, which inhabits a region of strong sunlight. Steve N. G. Howell. San Felipe, Baja California, Mexico, 16 Apr. 2004.

32.28 JUVENILE YELLOW-FOOTED GULL. Note stout bill already with pale at base, white belly, and sparsely barred tail coverts. Kimball L. Garrett. El Golfo de Santa Clara, Sonora, Mexico, 23 July 1999.

32.29 FIRST-CYCLE YELLOW-FOOTED GULL. Note stout bill, mostly white underparts and uppertail coverts, and extensive post-juvenal molt of upperwing coverts. Steve N. G. Howell. Puerto Peñasco, Sonora, Mexico, 21 Jan. 2003.

32.30 FIRST-CYCLE YELLOW-FOOTED GULL. Note stout bill and mostly white underparts. Steve N. G. Howell. Puerto Peñasco, Sonora, Mexico, 22 Jan. 2003.

32.31 SECOND-CYCLE YELLOW-FOOTED GULL IN PB2 MOLT (P1 GROWING, P2–4 SHED, P5–P10 OLD). Note stout bill, pale flesh legs, white uppertail coverts, and rather advanced molt timing relative to Western Gull. Steve N. G. Howell. San Felipe, Baja California, Mexico, 16 Apr. 2004.

32.32 SECOND-CYCLE YELLOW-FOOTED GULL. A classic bird with uniform B2 primaries and tail. Note clean white uppertail coverts and yellowish feet. Relatively whitish wing-linings of second-cycle bird behind are typical. Steve N. G. Howell. Puerto Peñasco, Sonora, Mexico, 22 Jan. 2003.

32.33 SECOND-CYCLE YELLOW-FOOTED GULL. Note stout bill, uniform B2 primaries, but piebald tail, possibly including A2 feathers. Steve N. G. Howell. Puerto Peñasco, Sonora, Mexico, 22 Jan. 2003.

32.34 SECOND-CYCLE YELLOW-FOOTED GULL. Fresher and more adultlike P5–P6 on left wing, P5 on right wing, and mostly white tail presumably reflect extensive PA2 molt (see photos 32.17–32.18). Steve N. G. Howell. Puerto Peñasco, Sonora, Mexico, 20 Jan. 2003.

32.35 SECOND-CYCLE YELLOW-FOOTED GULL. Note fresher and more adultlike P1–P5 (presumably replaced in PA2 molt; see photo 32.18), which create upperwing pattern like third cycle of other large dark-backed gulls. Steve N. G. Howell. Puerto Peñasco, Sonora, Mexico, 21 Jan. 2003.

32.36 THIRD-CYCLE YELLOW-FOOTED GULL STARTING PB3 MOLT. A fairly typical bird at this date (compare with photo 32.37 of "advanced" type), with P1–P2 shed, most upperwing coverts replaced in PA molt, tail mixed black and white. Steve N. G. Howell. San Felipe, Baja California, Mexico, 16 Apr. 2004.

32.37 THIRD-CYCLE YELLOW-FOOTED GULL IN "ADVANCED" PLUMAGE, STARTING PB3 MOLT (P1 SHED; SAME BIRD AS PHOTO 32.21). Preceding PA2 molt produced adultlike flight feathers (see photo 32.18): inner primaries out to P6 (note contrast with browner and more-worn P7–P10), outer 4 secondaries, and tail. Told from subsequent plumage cycle (for example photo 32.39) by second-cycle outer primaries, primary coverts, and most secondaries. Steve N. G. Howell. San Felipe, Baja California, Mexico, 16 Apr. 2004.

32.38 THIRD-CYCLE YELLOW-FOOTED GULL. Distinguished from adult by dark on tail and primary coverts; also note dark on bill and dusky eye (see photo 32.23 of same bird). Steve N. G. Howell. Puerto Peñasco, Sonora, Mexico, 22 Jan. 2003.

32.39 THIRD-CYCLE TYPE YELLOW-FOOTED GULL. Distinguished from adult by dark on bill, slight brownish cast to upperwing coverts; from advanced second cycle by large P10 mirror and adultlike secondaries. Steve N. G. Howell. Puerto Peñasco, Sonora, Mexico, 22 Jan. 2003.

32.40 THIRD-CYCLE TYPE YELLOW-FOOTED GULL. Distinguished from adult by brownish cast to outer greater coverts and primary coverts and extensive black on outer primaries; also note dark spots on tail. Steve N. G. Howell. Puertecitos, Baja California, Mexico, 17 Apr. 2004.

33.1 ADULT NONBREEDING GLAUCOUS-WINGED GULL, COMPLETING PB MOLT (OUTER PRIMARIES NOT FULLY GROWN). Note stout bill, dark eye, smudgy quality to head and neck markings, and gray wingtips. Larry B. Spear. Dutch Harbor, Alaska, 2 Oct. 1982.

33.2 ADULT NONBREEDING GLAUCOUS-WINGED GULL. A heavily marked bird (compare with photo 33.3). Note same features as photo 33.1; also short wing projection. Steve N. G. Howell. Petaluma, California, 26 Dec. 2001.

33.3 ADULT NONBREEDING GLAUCOUS-WINGED GULL. A lightly marked bird (compare with photo 33.2). Note same features as photo 33.1; also short wing projection. Steve N. G. Howell. Petaluma, California, 27 Dec. 2001.

33.4 ADULT GLAUCOUS-WINGED GULL. Note stout bill, dark eye, and gray wingtips (close to maximum darkness for a pure bird); this banded bird came from a colony off the northwestern coast of Vancouver Island. Larry B. Spear. Charleston, Oregon, 5 Feb. 1982.

33.5 ADULT BREEDING GLAUCOUS-WINGED GULL. Note stout bill, pink orbital ring, and gray wingtips; some birds (<1 percent) have paler eyes, like this individual. Steve N. G. Howell. Seward, Alaska, 15 June 1999.

33.6 JUVENILE GLAUCOUS-WINGED GULL. Distinctive: note stout blackish bill, finely patterned upperparts, milky gray-brown wingtips concolorous with upperparts. Steve Heinl. Ketchikan, Alaska, 11 Sept. 2002.

33.7 JUVENILE GLAUCOUS-WINGED GULL. Note same features as photo 33.6, with wingtips paler on this individual. Larry B. Spear. Dutch Harbor, Alaska, 2 Oct. 1982.

33.8 FIRST-CYCLE GLAUCOUS-WINGED GULL STILL IN FAIRLY FRESH JUVENAL PLUMAGE. Note same features as photo 33.6. Steve N. G. Howell. Petaluma, California, 15 Dec. 2001.

33.9 FIRST-CYCLE GLAUCOUS-WINGED GULLS, MOSTLY IN JUVENAL PLUMAGE. Note same features as photo 33.6. The left-hand bird is relatively dark, at (or beyond?) the extreme for a pure bird. Steve N. G. Howell. Petaluma, California, 15 Dec. 2001.

33.10 FIRST-CYCLE GLAUCOUS-WINGED GULL. Whitish-looking wingtips of this individual simply reflect broad whitish tips to the outer primaries, which were otherwise typical milky gray-brown. Steve N. G. Howell. Petaluma, California, 21 Dec. 2001.

33.11 FIRST-CYCLE GLAUCOUS-WINGED GULL. Note stout dark bill, overall milky gray-brown aspect with marked contrast between bleached brown juvenal feathers and newer, grayish post-juvenal feathers; coarsely marked greater coverts are atypical and may reflect hybridization with Western Gull. Steve N. G. Howell. Inverness, California, 20 Dec. 1997.

33.12 FIRST-CYCLE GLAUCOUS-WINGED GULL. Note stout dark bill and overall frosty aspect (atypically checkered on this individual) with dusky wingtips. Steve N. G. Howell. Petaluma, California, 26 Dec. 2001.

33.14 FIRST-CYCLE GLAUCOUS-WINGED GULL. Distinctive: note stout dark bill and overall milky gray-brown aspect; head and chest have bleached to whitish. Steve N. G. Howell. Petaluma, California, 2 Jan. 2003.

33.13 FIRST-CYCLE GLAUCOUS-WINGED GULLS (SECOND-CYCLE RING-BILLED GULL IN FRONT). Note stout dark bill and overall milky aspect of right-hand bird. Left-hand bird has coarsely checkered upperwing coverts and relatively dark wingtip (for midwinter), which may reflect hybridization with Western Gull or Herring Gull. Steve N. G. Howell. Petaluma, California, 2 Jan. 2003.

33.15 FIRST-CYCLE GLAUCOUS-WINGED GULL. Distinctive: note stout dark bill and contrast between relatively dark A1 back and bleached white wings. White-winged birds in late winter invite confusion with Glaucous Gull, but that species has a bright pink, black-tipped bill. Steve N. G. Howell. Petaluma, California, 23 Mar. 2003.

33.16 FIRST-CYCLE GLAUCOUS-WINGED GULL. Note stout dark bill and overall milky aspect (little contrast between A1 scapulars and wings; compare with photo 33.15). Steve N. G. Howell. Petaluma, California, 23 Mar. 2003.

33.17 FIRST-CYCLE GLAUCOUS-WINGED GULL. Note stout dark bill and contrast between pale gray A1 scapulars and very bleached and abraded white wings. Steve N. G. Howell. Monterey, California, 15 May 1999.

33.18 SECOND-CYCLE GLAUCOUS-WINGED GULL COMPLETING PB2 MOLT (OUTER PRIMARIES NOT FULLY GROWN). Note stout bill and gray wingtips. Distinguished from first cycle by more-uniform upperparts and primary molt. Larry B. Spear. Dutch Harbor, Alaska, 3 Oct. 1982.

33.19 SECOND-CYCLE GLAUCOUS-WINGED GULL. Note stout bill, overall dirty aspect, brownish gray primaries, and short wing projection; distinguished from first cycle by more-uniform upperparts. Steve N. G. Howell. Petaluma, California, 26 Dec. 2001.

33.20 SECOND-CYCLE GLAUCOUS-WINGED GULL. Note same features as photo 33.19; some (pure?) birds, like this individual, have strongly bicolored bills, recalling Glaucous Gull. Steve N. G. Howell. Petaluma, California, 27 Dec. 2001.

33.21 SECOND-CYCLE GLAUCOUS-WINGED GULL. Note stout dark bill and contrast between pale gray A2 back and bleached wings; this bird hatched in 1980 on Kodiak Island, Alaska. Larry B. Spear. Florence, Oregon, 12 Feb. 1982.

33.22 SECOND-CYCLE GLAUCOUS-WINGED GULL (SAME BIRD AS PHOTO 33.36). Note stout bill and overall dirty aspect. Primaries and primary coverts are a little dark and suggest hybridism with Western Gull. Steve N. G. Howell. Bolinas, California, 3 Mar. 2003.

33.23 THIRD-CYCLE GLAUCOUS-WINGED GULL. Note stout bill and gray wingtips. Distinguished from second cycle by mostly gray upperparts and distinct white trailing edge to secondaries. Steve N. G. Howell. Petaluma, California, 21 Dec. 2001.

33.24 THIRD-CYCLE GLAUCOUS-WINGED GULL. Note same features as photo 33.23. Steve N. G. Howell. Petaluma, California, 2 Jan. 2003.

33.25 THIRD-CYCLE TYPE GLAUCOUS-WINGED GULL. An atypically pale-eyed individual, which, with relatively dark wingtips, might reflect hybridism with herring gull. Note same features as photo 33.23. Steve N. G. Howell. Petaluma, California, 2 Jan. 2003.

33.26 THIRD-CYCLE TYPE GLAUCOUS-WINGED GULL (SAME BIRD AS PHOTO 33.40). Note stout bill and gray wingtips. Distinguished from adult by retained black on bill at this date, lack of distinct white primary tips, and gray on tail. Steve N. G. Howell. Bolinas, California, 3 Apr. 2003.

33.27 ADULT NONBREEDING GLAUCOUS-WINGED GULL. Note gray wingtip markings (about maximum darkness for a presumed pure bird); also bill size and shape, dark eye. Mike Danzenbaker. Alviso, California, 8 Feb. 1997.

33.28 ADULT NONBREEDING GLAUCOUS-WINGED GULL. The relatively pale gray wingtip markings (accentuated by backlighting) and pale eye of this individual might reflect hybridization with Glaucous Gull. Louis R. Bevier. Santa Barbara, California, Jan. 1985.

33.29 ADULT NONBREEDING GLAUCOUS-WINGED GULL. Note gray underwings with white tongue-tips and mirrors, stout bill, and smudgy head and neck markings. Brian E. Small. Homer, Alaska, Mar. 2000.

33.30 ADULT NONBREEDING GLAUCOUS-WINGED GULL. Note same features as photo 33.29; some birds (like this one) have P9 plain gray. Brian E. Small. Homer, Alaska, Mar. 2000.

33.31 JUVENILE GLAUCOUS-WINGED GULL. Note broad wings, pale wingtips (which can vary greatly in appearance with light angle; compare with photo 33.32 of same bird), and stout bill. Eric Preston. Monterey Bay, California, 27 Oct. 2001.

33.32 JUVENILE GLAUCOUS-WINGED GULL. Note same features as photo 33.31 (of the same bird). Eric Preston. Monterey Bay, California, 27 Oct. 2001

33.33 JUVENILE GLAUCOUS-WINGED GULL. Note broad wings and translucent remiges; bill looks pale because of reflection. Steve N. G. Howell. Monterey Bay, California, 18 Oct. 1998.

33.34 FIRST-CYCLE GLAUCOUS-WINGED GULL. Bleached late-winter birds often look very white, inviting confusion with Glaucous Gull, but they lack the brightly two-tone bill of that species. John Sorensen. Monterey Bay, California, May 2000.

33.35 SECOND-CYCLE GLAUCOUS-WINGED GULL. Note broad wings, pale grayish wingtips. Distinguished from first cycle by plainer upperwings and mostly white uppertail coverts. Mike Danzenbaker. Off Santa Cruz, California, 29 Jan. 2000.

33.36 SECOND-CYCLE GLAUCOUS-WINGED GULL (SAME BIRD AS PHOTO 33.22) AND SECOND-CYCLE WESTERN GULL. Note broad wings and pale grayish wingtips (perhaps a little dark for a pure bird; compare with photo 33.37). Steve N. G. Howell. Bolinas, California, 3 Apr. 2003.

33.37 SECOND-CYCLE GLAUCOUS-WINGED GULL. Note broad wings, pale grayish primaries, and stout bill. Steve N. G. Howell. Bolinas, California, 21 Apr. 2003.

33.38 THIRD-CYCLE GLAUCOUS-WINGED GULL STARTING PB3 MOLT. Note incoming adultlike inner primaries. Also note broad wings, pale grayish wingtips, and stout bill (which can be more adultlike in color and pattern). Martin Hale. Outer Aleutians, Alaska, 8 June 2003.

33.39 THIRD-CYCLE GLAUCOUS-WINGED GULL. Note broad wings, pale grayish wingtips, and stout bill. Distinguished from second cycle (for example, photo 33.35) by extensively gray upperwings and adultlike inner primaries. Steve N. G. Howell. Point Reyes, California, 30 Jan. 2003.

33.41 FOURTH-CYCLE GLAUCOUS-WINGED GULL IN PB4 MOLT. Distinguished from adult by brownish cast to outer primaries and gray in tail. Steve N. G. Howell. Central Aleutians, Alaska, 27 June 2003.

33.40 THIRD-CYCLE TYPE GLAUCOUS-WINGED GULL. A relatively "advanced" individual (same bird as photo 33.26). Note broad wings and grayish wingtips. Distinguished from adult by brownish cast to outer primaries and gray in tail. Steve N. G. Howell. Bolinas, California, 3 Apr. 2003.

34.1 ADULT NONBREEDING GLAUCOUS GULL (PROBABLY *L. H. BARROVIANUS*) COMPLETING PB MOLT (P10 OLD). A relatively small-billed bird (pointing to a female; compare with photo 34.2) with bill depth at gonys greater than at base (compare with photos 34.0, 34.2). Bill larger than Iceland Gull, wing projection relatively short, and orbital ring orange. Steve Heinl. Ketchikan, Alaska, 17 Nov. 1994.

34.2 ADULT NONBREEDING GLAUCOUS GULL. Distinctive: note stout bill (relatively large on this bird, pointing to a male; compare with photo 34.1), short wing projection, and all-white wingtips. This bird shows a classic Glaucous Gull bill shape: stout overall, deepest at the base, and lacking a strong gonydeal expansion. Orbital ring of non-breeding birds (like base of bill) can be suffused pink, as on this individual. Brian E. Small. Homer, Alaska, Mar. 2000.

34.3 ADULT NONBREEDING GLAUCOUS GULL (*L. H. HYPER-BOREUS* BY RANGE) WITH ADULT KUMLIEN'S GULL AT REAR AND ADULT AMERICAN HERRING AT LEFT. Note same features as photo 34.2. Upperparts are noticeably paler than Kumlien's Gull but would be similar to Iceland Gull. Steve N. G. Howell. St. John's, Newfoundland, 2 Feb. 2002.

34.4 ADULT BREEDING GLAUCOUS GULLS (*L. H. BARROVIA-NUS*). Note relatively small bill of this subspecies; also note short wing projection and deep orange orbital ring. Bruce Mactavish. Barrow, Alaska, 23 May 2003.

34.5 JUVENILE GLAUCOUS GULL (PROBABLY *L. H. PALLIDIS-SIMUS* BY RANGE). Distinctive: note stout and brightly bicolored bill, short wing projection, and overall milky, finely patterned plumage (the buff plumage wash soon bleaches to white) with creamy white wingtips. Tony Leukering. St. Lawrence Island, Alaska, 26 Aug. 1999.

34.6 JUVENILE GLAUCOUS GULL. A relatively dark individual, perhaps clouded by hybridization with Herring Gull. Pure juvenile Glaucous Gulls can have dull bills when young, and some might be washed with this much brownish on the wingtips. Still, this bird's wingtips and, especially, tail are at (or beyond?) the extreme for a pure bird. Bruce Mactavish. Inuvik, Northwest Territories, 9 Sept. 2002.

34.7 JUVENILE GLAUCOUS GULL. Distinctive, with relatively stout, sharply bicolored bill and short wing projection. Horizontal pose accentuates relatively long-looking wingtip (compare with photo 34.8). Steve Heinl. Ketchikan, Alaska, 19 Oct. 1992.

34.8 JUVENILE GLAUCOUS GULL. Note same features as photo 34.7; more upright pose accentuates short wing projection. Steve Heinl. Ketchikan, Alaska, 7 Jan. 1995.

34.9 FIRST-CYCLE GLAUCOUS GULL (PROBABLY *L. H. HYPERBOREUS* BY RANGE). A relatively dark, thickset, and stout-billed individual (compare with photo 34.10). Note same features as photo 34.7; a few post-juvenal scapulars are visible. Bruce Mactavish. St. John's, Newfoundland, 1 Jan. 2002.

34.10 FIRST-CYCLE GLAUCOUS GULL (PROBABLY *L. H. HYPERBOREUS* BY RANGE). A relatively pale and small-billed individual (compare with photo 34.9). Distinguished from Kumlien's and Iceland Gulls by heavier build, relatively stout and brightly bicolored bill, and short wing projection; a few post-juvenal scapulars are visible. Bruce Mactavish. St. John's, Newfoundland, 24 Jan. 2001.

34.11 FIRST-CYCLE GLAUCOUS GULL. Bicolored bill can show pale tip by midwinter. Steve N. G. Howell. Puerto Peñasco, Sonora, Mexico, 23 Jan. 2003.

34.12 FIRST-CYCLE GLAUCOUS GULL (PROBABLY *L. H. HYPERBOREUS* BY RANGE). Some birds (like this individual) bleach to strikingly white by late winter. Bruce Mactavish. St. John's, Newfoundland, Mar. 1987.

34.13 FIRST-CYCLE (LEFT) AND SECOND-CYCLE (RIGHT) GLAUCOUS GULLS (PROBABLY *L. H. BARROVIANUS* BY RANGE). First-summer bird has bleached to almost pure white (brown mottling probably represents limited PA1 molt); second-summer bird has pale gray, A2 back. Inner primary molt has often started by June but is not discernible in this photo. Kevin T. Karlson. Prudhoe Bay, Alaska, June 1994.

34.14 SECOND-CYCLE GLAUCOUS GULL COMPLETING PB2 MOLT (OUTER PRIMARIES STILL GROWING). Note stout bicolored bill, white wingtips. Kimball L. Garrett. Nome, Alaska, 9 Sept. 2002.

34.15 SECOND-CYCLE GLAUCOUS GULL (PROBABLY *L. H. HYPERBOREUS* BY RANGE) WITH FIRST-CYCLE KUMLIEN'S GULLS. Note stout bicolored bill, short wing projection, and large size relative to Kumlien's Gulls; distinguished from first cycle by pale eye and upperwing pattern (see photo 34.29 of same bird). Steve N. G. Howell. St. John's, Newfoundland, 5 Feb. 2002.

34.16 SECOND-CYCLE GLAUCOUS GULL (PROBABLY *L. H. HYPERBOREUS* BY RANGE). Distinguished from first cycle by pale eye and diffuse dusky marks (not neat barring) on undertail coverts. Steve N. G. Howell. St. John's, Newfoundland, 2 Feb. 2002.

34.17 SECOND-CYCLE GLAUCOUS GULL (PROBABLY *L. H. HYPERBOREUS* BY RANGE). Distinguished from first cycle by pale eye and pale gray back. Bruce Mactavish. St. John's, Newfoundland, Apr. 1989.

34.18 SECOND-CYCLE GLAUCOUS GULL. Distinguished from first cycle (see photo 34.12) by pale eye and pale gray back. Bruce Hallett. Nome, Alaska, early June 2001.

34.19 THIRD-CYCLE GLAUCOUS GULL IN PB3 MOLT. Bill often brightens in mid- to late summer (see photos 34.18, 34.20). Bruce Mactavish. Inuvik, Northwest Territories, 7 Aug. 2002.

34.20 THIRD-CYCLE GLAUCOUS GULL (PROBABLY *L. H. HYPERBOREUS* BY RANGE). Distinguished from second cycle by extensive pale gray on upperwing coverts; note how bill color regresses from second summer. Bruce Mactavish. St. John's, Newfoundland, 9 Feb. 2003.

34.21 THIRD-CYCLE GLAUCOUS GULL (PROBABLY *L. H. BARROVIANUS* BY RANGE). Distinguished from second cycle by extensive pale gray on upperwing coverts and upperwing pattern (see photo 34.30 of same bird). Steve N. G. Howell. Bodega Bay, California, 4 Apr. 2000.

34.22 THIRD-CYCLE GLAUCOUS GULL. Distinguished from second cycle by extensive pale gray on upperwing coverts and adultlike secondaries. Peter LaTourrette. Nome, Alaska, 29 June 2000.

34.24 ADULT NONBREEDING GLAUCOUS GULL (PROBABLY *L. H. PALLIDISSIMUS* BY RANGE). Note pure white wingtips, stout bill, and pale eye. Mike Danzenbaker. Aomori Prefecture, Japan, 28 Feb. 1999.

34.23 ADULT BREEDING GLAUCOUS GULL. Note translucent white wingtips and stout bill. Bruce Hallett. Nome, Alaska, early June 2001.

34.25 FIRST-CYCLE GLAUCOUS GULL. Note stout, bicolored bill and overall whitish aspect with fine dusky markings. W. Edward Harper. Sacramento County, California, 16 Jan. 2001.

34.26 FIRST-CYCLE GLAUCOUS GULL (PROBABLY *L. H. PALLIDISSIMUS* BY RANGE). Note translucent white wingtips and stout, bicolored bill. Geoff Carey. Hokkaido, Japan, 3 Feb. 1999.

34.27 FIRST-CYCLE GLAUCOUS GULL (PROBABLY *L. H. PALLIDISSIMUS* BY RANGE). Note pure white wingtips and stout, bicolored bill. Mike Danzenbaker. Aomori Prefecture, Japan, 3 Mar. 1999.

34.28 FIRST-CYCLE GLAUCOUS GULL (PROBABLY *L. H. HYPERBOREUS* BY RANGE). Note stout, bicolored bill and strongly bleached plumage (brownish mottling indicates limited PA1 molt). Marshall J. Iliff. Bronwsville, Texas, 10 Apr. 1999.

34.29 SECOND-CYCLE GLAUCOUS GULL (SAME BIRD AS PHOTO 34.15). Relative to first cycle, upperwings plainer overall, secondaries average grayer and more speckled, and greater coverts and primary coverts lack dusky subterminal marks; also note contrasting median coverts and relatively rounded primaries. Steve N. G. Howell. St. John's, Newfoundland, 5 Feb. 2002.

34.30 THIRD-CYCLE GLAUCOUS GULL (SAME BIRD AS PHOTO 34.21). Relative to second cycle, inner primaries are adultlike in pattern. Steve N. G. Howell. Bodega Bay, California, 4 Apr. 2000.

35A.1 ADULT NONBREEDING KUMLIEN'S GULL. An individual with extensively slaty gray wingtips (stage 5 primary pattern, Howell and Mactavish 2003; compare with illus. 35a.7); also note deep pink legs and raspberry pink orbital ring. Steve N. G. Howell. St. John's, Newfoundland, 4 Feb. 2002.

35A.2 ADULT NONBREEDING KUMLIEN'S GULL. An individual with reduced slaty gray wingtip markings (stage 2 primary pattern; Howell and Mactavish 2003; compare with illus. 35a.7). Steve N. G. Howell. St. John's, Newfoundland, 5 Feb. 2002.

35A.3 ADULT NONBREEDING KUMLIEN'S GULL. An individual with reduced slaty gray wingtip markings (stage 1 primary pattern; Howell and Mactavish 2003; compare with illus. 35a.7). Steve N. G. Howell. St. John's, Newfoundland, 4 Feb. 2002.

35A.4 ADULT NONBREEDING PRESUMED KUMLIEN'S GULL. An individual with apparently unmarked white wingtips (stage 0 primary pattern; Howell and Mactavish 2003; compare with illus. 35a.7); Iceland Gull potentially separable by slightly paler gray upperparts (see photo 35b.2). Steve N. G. Howell. St. John's, Newfoundland, 4 Feb. 2002.

35A.5 ADULT NONBREEDING KUMLIEN'S GULL. An individual with fairly pale gray wingtip markings (stage 4 primary pattern; Howell and Mactavish 2003; compare with illus. 35a.7). Steve N. G. Howell. St. John's, Newfoundland, 4 Feb. 2002.

35A.6 ADULT NONBREEDING KUMLIEN'S GULL. An individual with dark slaty gray wingtip markings (stage 5 primary pattern; Howell and Mactavish 2003; compare with illus. 35a.7). Steve N. G. Howell. St. John's, Newfoundland, 4 Feb. 2002.

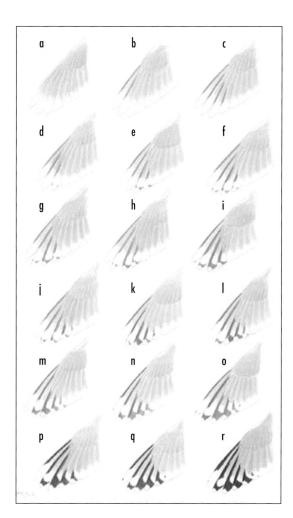

35A.7 VARIATION IN WINGTIP PATTERN OF ADULT KUMLIEN'S GULLS (A–O); TWO POSSIBLE KUMLIEN'S × THAYER'S HYBRIDS (P–Q); AND A TYPICAL THAYER'S GULL (R) FOR REFERENCE (FROM HOWELL AND MACTAVISH 2003). Of 345 birds studied in Newfoundland, 4 percent were type a (stage 0); 9 percent type b–c (stage 1); 11 percent type d–f (stage 2); 12 percent type g–i (stage 3); 55 percent type j–m (stage 4); 4 percent type n (stage 5); and 5 percent type o (stage 6). Painting by Martin T. Elliott.

35A.8 JUVENILE KUMLIEN'S GULL. A fresh-plumaged and relatively dark individual. Note small bill, frosty gray aspect including tertial centers and primaries, and overall structure, including relatively short legs. Bruce Mactavish. St. John's, Newfoundland, late Oct. 1990.

35A.9 FIRST-CYCLE KUMLIEN'S GULL. An average, fairly fresh-plumaged individual. Note small bill, checkered, frosty upperparts, and medium brown wingtips. Bruce Mactavish. St. John's, Newfoundland, 16 Nov. 1998.

35A.10 FIRST-CYCLE KUMLIEN'S GULL. An average midwinter individual. Note small bill, checkered, frosty upperparts, and whitish wingtips with fine and dusky shaft streaks. Bruce Mactavish. St. John's, Newfoundland, 5 Feb. 2001.

35A.11 FIRST-CYCLE KUMLIEN'S GULL. An average midwinter individual. Note small bill, checkered upperparts (contrast reduced by bleaching), and medium-brown subterminal areas on primaries. Bruce Mactavish. St. John's, Newfoundland, 5 Feb. 2001.

35A.12 JUVENILE KUMLIEN'S GULL. A fairly dark (and very small) midwinter individual. Note small bill, checkered, frosty upperparts, and medium brown wingtips. Steve N. G. Howell. St. John's, Newfoundland, 4 Feb. 2002.

35A.13 FIRST-CYCLE KUMLIEN'S GULL. An average midwinter individual. Note small bill, checkered, frosty upperparts, and pale brown wingtips with subterminal dark arrowhead marks. Steve N. G. Howell. St. John's, Newfoundland, 5 Feb. 2002.

35A.14 FIRST-CYCLE KUMLIEN'S GULL. A fairly pale midwinter individual with distinctly two-tone bill and obvious PA1 back molt. Note small bill, checkered, frosty upperparts, and medium brown wingtips with broad whitish primary tips. Steve N. G. Howell. St. John's, Newfoundland, 4 Feb. 2002.

35A.15 FIRST-CYCLE KUMLIEN'S GULL. A fairly pale midwinter individual; probably not safely separable from Iceland Gull. Note small bill, checkered, frosty upperparts, and whitish wingtips with subterminal dark arrowhead marks. Steve N. G. Howell. St. John's, Newfoundland, 4 Feb. 2002.

35A.16 FIRST-CYCLE PRESUMED KUMLIEN'S GULL. A moderately bleached, whitish midwinter individual; probably not safely separable from Iceland Gull. Note small bicolored bill and white wingtips. Steve N. G. Howell. St. John's, Newfoundland, 4 Feb. 2002.

35A.17 FIRST-CYCLE PRESUMED KUMLIEN'S GULL. A strongly bleached, whitish midwinter individual with distinctly two-tone bill; probably not safely separable from Iceland Gull. Note small bill and white wingtips. Steve N. G. Howell. St. John's, Newfoundland, 4 Feb. 2002.

35A.18 SECOND-CYCLE PRESUMED KUMLIEN'S GULL STARTING PB2 MOLT (P1–P2 SHED, NOT VISIBLE HERE). A strongly bleached first-summer bird; not safely separable from Iceland Gull. Note slender, mostly dark bill. Steve N. G. Howell. Salisbury Beach, Massachusetts, 28 June 1998.

35A.19 SECOND-CYCLE KUMLIEN'S GULL. A typical individual; note bicolored bill, pale gray on upperparts, and dusky primaries. Bruce Mactavish. St. John's, Newfoundland, 8 Dec. 1999.

35A.20 SECOND-CYCLE KUMLIEN'S GULL. A typical individual; note bicolored bill, pale gray on upperparts, and medium-brown primaries. Bruce Mactavish. St. John's, Newfoundland, 23 Dec. 1999.

35A.21 SECOND-CYCLE KUMLIEN'S GULL. A "retarded" individual; told from first cycle by pale freckling on greater coverts and tertials; also note bicolored bill, pale eye. Steve N. G. Howell. St. John's, Newfoundland, 5 Feb. 2002.

35A.22 SECOND-CYCLE KUMLIEN'S GULL. A fairly pale individual; note bicolored bill and pale gray primaries. Steve N. G. Howell. St. John's, Newfoundland, 4 Feb. 2002.

35A.23 SECOND-CYCLE PRESUMED KUMLIEN'S GULL. A "retarded" and very white individual; probably not safely separable from Iceland Gull. Told from first cycle by pale freckling on greater coverts and tertials; also note bicolored bill, pale eye. Steve N. G. Howell. St. John's, Newfoundland, 4 Feb. 2002.

35A.24 THIRD-CYCLE KUMLIEN'S GULL. A relatively "retarded" individual; note small bill and dusky wingtips. Told from second cycle by adultlike inner primaries (visible in flight); also note bill pattern. Bruce Mactavish. St. John's, Newfoundland, Dec. 1995.

35A.25 THIRD-CYCLE KUMLIEN'S GULL. A typical individual; note small bill and dusky wingtips. Bruce Mactavish. St. John's, Newfoundland, 23 Dec. 1999.

35A.26 THIRD-CYCLE KUMLIEN'S GULL (SAME BIRD AS PHOTO 35A.42). Distinguished from adult by brownish suffusion to upperwing coverts; also note bill pattern, dark eye. Steve N. G. Howell. St. John's, Newfoundland, 4 Feb. 2002.

35A.27 THIRD-CYCLE TYPE KUMLIEN'S GULL. A relatively "advanced" individual. Distinguished from adult by brownish subterminal freckling on visible primary covert; also note bill pattern, dark eye. Bruce Mactavish. St. John's, Newfoundland, 20 Dec. 2001.

35A.28 ADULT NONBREEDING KUMLIEN'S GULL. A typical individual, with stage 4 primary pattern (compare with illus. 35a.7); backlighting from snow makes wingtip markings look deceptively dark. Steve N. G. Howell. St. John's, Newfoundland, 4 Feb. 2002.

35A.29 ADULT NONBREEDING KUMLIEN'S GULL. A typical individual, with stage 4 primary pattern (compare with illus. 35a.7); note on underwing how dark markings show mainly as a narrow subterminal band. Steve N. G. Howell. St. John's, Newfoundland, 4 Feb. 2002.

35A.30 ADULT NONBREEDING KUMLIEN'S GULL. An individual with stage 2 primary pattern (compare with illus. 35a.7). Steve N. G. Howell. St. John's, Newfoundland, 4 Feb. 2002.

35A.32 ADULT NONBREEDING KUMLIEN'S (OR ICELAND?) GULL. An individual with stage 0 primary pattern (see illus. 35a.7) and apparently very pale gray upperparts; not safely distinguishable from Iceland Gull. Steve N. G. Howell. St. John's, Newfoundland, 4 Feb. 2002.

35A.31 ADULT NONBREEDING KUMLIEN'S GULL. An individual with stage 2 primary pattern (compare with illus. 35a.7). Bruce Mactavish. St. John's, Newfoundland, 5 Jan. 2000.

35A.33 ADULT NONBREEDING KUMLIEN'S GULL. A well-marked individual, with stage 5 primary pattern (compare with illus. 35a.7). Bruce Mactavish. St. John's, Newfoundland, 13 Jan. 1993.

35A.34 FIRST-CYCLE KUMLIEN'S GULLS. Typical individuals, with darker outer webs to outer primaries. Steve N. G. Howell. St. John's, Newfoundland, 5 Feb. 2002.

35A.35 FIRST-CYCLE KUMLIEN'S GULL. A typical individual, with darker outer webs to outer primaries strongest on P7–P9. Steve N. G. Howell. St. John's, Newfoundland, 4 Feb. 2002.

35A.36 FIRST-CYCLE KUMLIEN'S GULL. A typical individual, with darker outer webs to outer primaries strongest on P8–P9 and lack of a dark secondary bar; relatively dark tail band on this individual suggests Thayer's Gull. Steve N. G. Howell. St. John's, Newfoundland, 4 Feb. 2002.

35A.37 FIRST-CYCLE PRESUMED KUMLIEN'S GULL. A bleached, worn, and overall white individual; not safely distinguishable from Iceland Gull. Steve N. G. Howell. St. John's, Newfoundland, 5 Feb. 2002.

35A.38 SECOND-CYCLE KUMLIEN'S GULL. A fairly dark-winged individual; note dark on outer webs of outer primaries strongest on P8–P9. Bruce Mactavish. St. John's, Newfoundland, Jan.

35A.39 SECOND-CYCLE KUMLIEN'S GULL (WITH FOURTH-CYCLE TYPE ON WATER BEHIND). A fairly pale-winged individual; primaries washed pale brown and tail probably too dark for Iceland Gull. Distinguished from first cycle by overall plainer upperwings; also note bicolored bill. Steve N. G. Howell. St. John's, Newfoundland, 4 Feb. 2002.

35A.40 SECOND-CYCLE KUMLIEN'S GULL. A fairly pale-winged individual; note ghosting of adultlike pattern in outer primaries. Steve N. G. Howell. St. John's, Newfoundland, 4 Feb. 2002.

35A.41 THIRD-CYCLE KUMLIEN'S GULL. A fairly pale-winged and "retarded" individual; distinguished from second cycle by adultlike inner primaries; also note bill pattern, pale eye. Steve N. G. Howell. St. John's, Newfoundland, 3 Feb. 2002.

35A.42 THIRD-CYCLE KUMLIEN'S GULL (SAME BIRD AS PHOTO 35A.26). Distinguished from adult by brownish suffusion to upperwings and extensive dusky in tail; also note bill pattern. Steve N. G. Howell. St. John's, Newfoundland, 4 Feb. 2002.

35B.1 ADULT PRESUMED ICELAND GULL. Distinguished from Glaucous Gull by more petite build, smaller bill, and relatively longer wing projection; greenish bill base also atypical of Glaucous; perhaps not possible to rule out white-winged Kumlien's Gull. Larry Sansone. Bodega Bay, California, 15 Jan. 1985.

35B.2 ADULT NONBREEDING PRESUMED ICELAND GULL (FRONT) WITH ADULT KUMLIEN'S GULLS (BEHIND). Distinguished from white-winged Kumlien's Gull by paler gray upperparts, apparent in direct comparison (difference accentuated here by different angle of Kumlien's Gull). Jon Dunn. St. John's, Newfoundland, 25 Jan. 2003.

35B.3 ADULT ICELAND GULL. Distinguished from Glaucous Gull by more petite build, smaller bill, relatively longer wing projection, and reddish orbital ring. Chris Batty. Ayr, Scotland, 29 Mar. 2003.

35B.4 ADULT BREEDING *LARUS* SP. Identified in the field as a "dwarf" Glaucous Gull, but Iceland Gull difficult to eliminate based on this photo; note small bill, relatively long wing projection, and reddish orbital ring. Bruce Mactavish. Inuvik, Northwest Territories, 1 June 2002.

35B.5 JUVENILE PRESUMED ICELAND GULL (SAME BIRD AS PHOTO 35B.10). An extremely white individual for this early date; note dainty build and relatively small bill with diffuse pinkish base. Cameron D. Eckert. Whitehorse, Yukon Territory, 24 Oct. 1998.

35B.6 FIRST-CYCLE ICELAND GULL. A typical individual mostly still in full juvenal plumage. Like all large gulls, plumage at this age is highly variable but note white wingtips (here with faint dusky subterminal marks) and overall structure. Distinguished from Glacuous Gull by petite build and small, dull bill; from Kumlien's Gull by geographic range (and upperwing pattern, visible in flight, see photo 35b.11). R. L. Pitman. Disko Bay, Greenland, 9 Mar. 2000.

35B.7 SECOND-CYCLE ICELAND GULL. Like all large gulls, plumage at this age is highly variable, but note whitish wingtips and overall structure. Distinguished from Glacuous Gull by petite build, small bill, and long wing projection. Perhaps not safely distinguishable from pale Kumlien's Gull (and note pale brownish wash to wingtip). Told from first cycle by pale freckling on tertials, relatively rounded primaries, and contrasting median coverts; also note bill pattern (this individual aged as a first cycle by Malling Olsen 2003, photo 247). Harry J. Lehto. Helsinki, Finland, 30 Dec. 1990.

35B.8 ADULT NONBREEDING ICELAND GULL. Distinguished from Glacuous Gull by lighter overall build and smaller bill. Upperparts in the field were noted as very pale gray, similar to Glacuous Gull (and thus presumably too pale for Kumlien's Gull). Killian Mullarney. Njarövíkurfitjar, Iceland, 16 Mar. 2003.

35B.9 ADULT ICELAND GULL, ALMOST CLEANLY WHITE HEADED. Note same features as photo 35b.8. Killian Mullarney. Njarövíkurfitjar, Iceland, 16 Mar. 2003.

35B.10 JUVENILE PRESUMED ICELAND GULL (SAME BIRD AS PHOTO 35B.5). Note evenly pale primaries, overall whitish aspect, and bill size and shape. Cameron D. Eckert. Whitehorse, Yukon Territory, 24 Oct. 1998.

35B.11 FIRST-CYCLE ICELAND GULL. Told from Glaucous Gull by small bill without bright two-tone contrast and from Kumlien's Gull (see photos 35a.34–35a.36) by lack of contrast between inner and outer primaries. Steve Young. Fraserburgh, Scotland, Jan. 1993.

35B.12 THIRD-CYCLE ICELAND GULL. Distinguished from Glaucous Gull by lighter overall build and smaller bill; from adult Iceland by dusky brown markings on wing-linings and underparts; and from second cycle by adultlike inner primaries; also note bill pattern. Killian Mullarney. Njarövíkurfitjar, Iceland, 16 Mar. 2003.

35B.13 THIRD-CYCLE TYPE ICELAND GULL. Distinguished from Glaucous Gull by lighter overall build and smaller bill; from adult Iceland by brownish wash to upperwing coverts; also note bill pattern. Killian Mullarney. Njarövíkurfitjar, Iceland, 16 Mar. 2003.

36.1 ADULT NONBREEDING THAYER'S GULL. Distinguished from Herring Gull by more slender bill; dark eye (pale on up to 20 percent of Thayer's) with raspberry pink orbital ring; typically bolder white primary tips on slaty blackish (not jet-black) wingtips (but wingtips of Thayer's often look simply black unless seen alongside truly black-winged species); also, legs average richer pink and upperparts slightly darker and bluer than Herring Gull. Steve N. G. Howell. Petaluma, California, 8 Dec. 2003.

36.2 ADULT NONBREEDING THAYER'S GULLS. Distinguished from Herring Gull by same features as photo 36.1. Note difference in bill size between presumed female (left) and presumed male. Steve N. G. Howell. Tomales Bay, California, 29 Dec. 2002.

36.4 ADULT NONBREEDING THAYER'S GULL. A relatively small-billed (probably female) and pale-eyed bird (compare with photo 36.0). Other than eye color, separated from Herring Gull by same features as photo 36.1; and note extensively whitish underside to P10. Steve N. G. Howell. Tomales Bay, California, 29 Dec. 2002.

36.3 ADULT NONBREEDING THAYER'S GULLS. Right-hand bird has dark slaty (versus slaty blackish) wingtips at the pale extreme for presumed pure Thayer's wintering in central California; also note P9 (displaced) is extensively white with a narrow dark subterminal band, and P6 has a broken dark subterminal band. Distinguished from Herring Gull by same features as photo 36.1. Steve N. G. Howell. Tomales Bay, California, 29 Dec. 2002.

36.5 ADULT BREEDING THAYER'S GULL, ALTERNATE PLUMAGE. Distinguished from Herring Gull by same features as photo 36.1. Bruce Mactavish. Inuvik, Northwest Territories, 1 June 2002.

36.6 JUVENILE THAYER'S GULL IN FRESH PLUMAGE. A relatively dark and sooty-brown individual. Note the relatively slender blackish bill, relatively short legs, and blackish brown wingtips (which, atypically on this individual, lack distinct whitish edging to the primary tips; compare with photos 36.7–36.8). Cameron D. Eckert. Whitehorse, Yukon Territory, 24 Sept. 2003.

36.7 JUVENILE THAYER'S GULL IN FRESH PLUMAGE. A brightly checkered individual. Note relatively slender blackish bill and blackish brown wingtips with narrow whitish edging to the primary tips. Cameron D. Eckert. Whitehorse, Yukon Territory, 25 Sept. 2003.

36.8 JUVENILE THAYER'S GULLS. Relatively pale and dark individuals in fresh plumage. Note overall structure, bill size and shape, and blackish brown wingtips with narrow whitish edging to the primary tips; also note the solidly dark-centered tertials relative to Kumlien's Gull. Cameron D. Eckert. Whitehorse, Yukon Territory, 4 Oct. 2003.

36.9 JUVENILE THAYER'S GULL (IN CENTER, PREENING) AMID A MASS OF FIRST-CYCLE LARGER GULLS (MAINLY GLAUCOUS-WINGED GULLS, BUT WITH AMERICAN HERRING GULL AND WESTERN GULL IN FOREGROUND). A typical midwinter individual. Note contrasting, frosty upperparts relative to duller and more-finely spotted Glaucous-winged Gulls; also note whitish fringes to blackish brown primaries, dark tail band, and relatively small size. Steve N. G. Howell. Petaluma, California, 15 Dec. 2001.

36.10 JUVENILE THAYER'S GULL (RIGHT) AND FIRST-CYCLE GLAUCOUS-WINGED GULL (LEFT). Typical midwinter individual. Note slender bill, brownish black wingtips, and neat, frosty upperpart patterning of Thayer's (contrasting with dark tertial bases). Glaucous-winged is larger and bigger billed with a shorter wing projection, finer and more-speckled upperpart patterning, and paler wingtips that tend to be concolorous with the upperparts. Steve N. G. Howell. Petaluma, California, 15 Dec. 2001.

36.11 FIRST-CYCLE THAYER'S GULL (PA1 MOLT OF SOME SHORTER SCAPULARS HAS STARTED). A typical midwinter individual. Note relatively slender bill, brownish black wingtips with fine whitish primary edging, and neat, frosty upperpart patterning. Steve N. G. Howell. Petaluma, California, 27 Dec. 2001.

36.12 FIRST-CYCLE THAYER'S GULL. This individual has more-boldly checkered (less scaly) scapulars (compare with photos 36.10–36.11). Note same features as photo 36.11, and small bill relative to first-cycle Western Gull behind. Steve N. G. Howell. Petaluma, California, 15 Dec. 2001.

36.13 FIRST-CYCLE THAYER'S GULL. This individual has smudgier, less-brightly marked upperparts (accentuated by some PA1 molt of scapulars). Note same features as photo 36.11; bill typically shows some dull flesh basally by early winter. Steve N. G. Howell. Petaluma, California, 21 Dec. 2001.

36.14 FIRST-CYCLE THAYER'S GULL. In somewhat bleached plumage, starting PA1 molt. Note relatively slender bill, dark brown wingtip with fine whitish primary edging, and fairly plain A1 scapulars. Steve N. G. Howell. Puerto Peñasco, Sonora, Mexico, 22 Jan. 2003.

36.15 FIRST-CYCLE THAYER'S GULL. Still mostly or entirely in juvenal plumage, which is not overly bleached (compare with photo 36.16). Compare medium dark brown of exposed wingtip (pale primary tips accentuated by bleaching) with dark brown of more protected primary bases. Steve N. G. Howell. Petaluma, California, 26 Mar. 2004.

36.16 FIRST-CYCLE THAYER'S GULL. Bleached plumage fairly typical of late-winter individuals, at least those wintering in sunnier latitudes. Compare medium brown of exposed wingtip with dark brown of more-protected primary bases, and note relatively fine and diffuse pattern of A1 scapulars. Steve N. G. Howell. Petaluma, California, 26 Mar. 2004.

36.17 FIRST-CYCLE THAYER'S GULLS WITH VARIABLE PA1 MOLT OF SCAPULARS. Note overall structure, bill size and shape, and variable patterning of A1 scapulars. Steve N. G. Howell. Petaluma, California, 8 Apr. 1997.

36.18 FIRST-CYCLE THAYER'S GULL IN VERY BLEACHED PLUMAGE (SECOND-CYCLE CALIFORNIA GULL BEHIND). Overall whitish appearance invites confusion with Kumlien's Gull, but note that exposed primary bases are relatively dark; in flight a dark secondary bar was distinct (that is, an area more protected from bleaching). Steve N. G. Howell. Petaluma, California, 11 Apr. 1997.

36.19 SECOND-CYCLE THAYER'S GULL. In "retarded" plumage (contrasting median coverts may be A2 feathers). Note relatively slender bicolored bill and brownish black wingtips with fine whitish primary tips. Steve Heinl. Ketchikan, Alaska, 9 Oct. 1992.

36.20 SECOND-CYCLE THAYER'S GULL. In "advanced" plumage (gray back may include B2 and A2 feathers). Note same features as photo 36.19. Steve Heinl. Ketchikan, Alaska, 24 Oct. 1992.

36.21 SECOND-CYCLE THAYER'S GULL. Note same features as photo 36.19. Distinguished from first cycle by plainer upperparts, finely marked greater coverts, and strongly bicolored bill. Steve N. G. Howell. Petaluma, California, 15 Dec. 2001.

36.22 SECOND-CYCLE THAYER'S GULL. A typical individual. Note same features as photo 36.19. Distinguished from Herring Gull by smaller bill and two-tone pattern of outer primaries (not visible here; compare with photos 36.41–36.42); also note relatively short legs, dark eye. Steve N. G. Howell. Petaluma, California, 15 Dec. 2001.

36.23 SECOND-CYCLE THAYER'S GULL. Note bill size and shape, dark brown wingtips (relatively pale for a second-cycle bird) with fine whitish primary tips. Distinguished from first cycle by plainer upperparts mixed with gray, finely marked greater coverts, and strongly bicolored bill. Steve N. G. Howell. Tomales Bay, California, 29 Dec. 2002.

36.24 SECOND-CYCLE THAYER'S GULL. Note bill size and shape and brownish black wingtips with fine whitish primary tips. Steve N. G. Howell. Petaluma, California, 4 Mar. 1998.

36.25 SECOND-CYCLE THAYER'S GULL. Note same features as photo 36.24; also note trace of raspberry pink orbital ring. Brian E. Small. Churchill, Manitoba, early July 1988.

36.26 THIRD-CYCLE THAYER'S GULL. Note bill size and shape, dark eye, brownish black wingtips, and relatively bright pink legs. Best separated from a small Herring Gull by spread wingtip pattern (see photos 36.46–36.47 of the same bird). Steve N. G. Howell. Puerto Peñasco, Sonora, Mexico, 23 Jan. 2003.

36.27 THIRD-CYCLE THAYER'S GULL. Note same features as photo 36.26 and pattern on underside of P10. Tail varies from mostly white (like this) to extensively dark (photo 36.28). Best separated from small Herring Gull by spread wingtip pattern. Steve N. G. Howell. San Francisco, California, 25 Feb. 2004.

36.28 THIRD-CYCLE THAYER'S GULL. Note same features as photo 36.26. Best separated from small Herring Gull by spread wingtip pattern. Peter LaTourrette. Almaden Lake, California, 11 Mar. 2000.

36.29 THIRD-CYCLE THAYER'S GULL. Note bill size and shape, dark eye. Distinguished from adult by brownish on wing coverts and tertials, reduced white primary tips, and bill pattern. R. A. Behrstock/Naturewide Images. Churchill, Manitoba, 4 June 1989.

36.30 THIRD-CYCLE TYPE THAYER'S GULL. Note bill size and shape, dark eye. Distinguished from adult by black on primary coverts and reduced white primary tips. Brian E. Small. Churchill, Manitoba, early July 1988.

36.31 ADULT NONBREEDING THAYER'S GULL. Limited white in wingtip (compare with photo 36.36); completing PB molt (inner secondaries, and perhaps P10, still growing). Note white tongue-tips on P7–P8, white mirror on P9, and white tip to P10; also bill size and shape, dark eye. W. Edward Harper. Sacramento County, California, 27 Nov. 2002.

36.32 ADULT NONBREEDING THAYER'S GULL. Note bill size and shape, dark eye, white tongue-tips on P7–P8, and white tongue-mirror on P9. Steve N. G. Howell. Tomales Bay, California, 24 Dec. 2002.

36.33 ADULT NONBREEDING THAYER'S GULL. Note white tongue-tips on P7–P8 and white tongue-mirror on P9; also bill size and shape, dark eye. Mike Danzenbaker. Off Santa Cruz, California, 16 Jan. 2000.

36.34 ADULT NONBREEDING THAYER'S GULL. Note pale gray underside to primaries with whitish tongue-tips, and dark slaty restricted to a leading stripe on P10 and subterminal bands on P6–P9; also bill size and shape, dark eye. Steve N. G. Howell. Monterey Bay, California, 17 Dec. 1999.

36.35 ADULT NONBREEDING THAYER'S GULL. Note pale gray underside to primaries with dark slaty restricted to subterminal bands on P5–P10; also bill size and shape, dark eye. Mike Danzenbaker. Off Santa Cruz, California, 29 Jan. 2000.

36.36 ADULT NONBREEDING THAYER'S GULL (LEFT) AND ADULT CALIFORNIA GULL (RIGHT). This Thayer's has extensive white in the wingtip (compare with photo 36.31); also note blackish (versus black) markings on upperside of outer primaries (compare with California Gull's black wingtip) and mostly pale gray underside to primaries. Steve N. G. Howell. Point Reyes, California, 30 Jan. 2003.

36.37 FIRST-CYCLE THAYER'S GULL. Note distinct two-tone contrast on outer primaries (contrast usually at the shaft, but compare with photo 36.39), dark secondary bar, and broad dark distal band on spread tail. Mike Danzenbaker. Monterey, California, 26 Oct. 1996.

36.38 FIRST-CYCLE THAYER'S GULL. Note distinct two-tone contrast on outer primaries so that pale inner primary panel bleeds out into outer primaries; also dark secondary bar. Steve N. G. Howell. Petaluma, California, 27 Dec. 2001.

36.39 FIRST-CYCLE THAYER'S GULL. Note distinct two-tone contrast on outer primaries, but dark on outer primaries of this individual bleeds slightly on to inner web (compare with photos 36.37–36.38); also note finely barred pattern of A1 scapulars. Steve N. G. Howell. Puerto Peñasco, Sonora, Mexico, 22 Jan. 2003.

36.40 FIRST-CYCLE THAYER'S GULL (SAME BIRD AS PHOTO 36.41). Note two-tone outer primaries, dark secondary bar, and broad distal tail band. Steve N. G. Howell. Monterey Bay, California, 15 Dec. 2003.

36.41 FIRST-CYCLE THAYER'S GULL (SAME BIRD AS PHOTO 36.40). From below, wingtips look silvery gray (but this varies with lighting) with narrow dark tips to outer primaries. Steve N. G. Howell. Monterey Bay, California, 15 Dec. 2003.

36.42 SECOND-CYCLE THAYER'S GULL. Upperwings suggest first cycle but plainer overall, and secondary bar often less contrasting; note distinctive two-tone pattern on outer primaries. Mike Danzenbaker. Monterey Bay, California, 12 Jan. 2002.

36.43 SECOND-CYCLE THAYER'S GULL (WITH FIRST-CYCLE AND ADULT THAYER'S). Note same features as photo 36.42. Steve N. G. Howell. Tomales Bay, California, 23 Dec. 2001.

36.44 SECOND-CYCLE THAYER'S GULL (WITH CALIFORNIA GULL BEHIND). Note same features as photo 36.42. Steve N. G. Howell. Petaluma, California, 11 Dec. 2003.

36.45 THIRD-CYCLE THAYER'S GULL. Distinguished from adult by brownish on primary coverts, dark tail marks, reduced white in wingtip, and bill pattern. Steve N. G. Howell. Off Bodega, California, 20 Nov. 1998.

36.46 THIRD-CYCLE THAYER'S GULL (SAME BIRD AS PHOTOS 36.26, 36.47). Two-tone contrast on outer primaries of this bird is relatively muted, but note whitish tongue-tips on P7–P9 breaking up dark wingtip, and typical Thayer's pattern on underwing (compare with photo 36.34). Steve N. G. Howell. Puerto Peñasco, Sonora, Mexico, 23 Jan. 2003.

36.47 THIRD-CYCLE THAYER'S GULL (SAME BIRD AS PHOTOS 36.26, 36.46). Note bill size and shape, dark eye, and distinctive underwing pattern (compare with photo 36.34). Steve N. G. Howell. Puerto Peñasco, Sonora, Mexico, 23 Jan. 2003.

H1.1 ADULT NONBREEDING GLAUCOUS-WINGED × WESTERN GULL HYBRID. Most like Western Gull but upperparts a little pale and wingtips dark gray; also note dusky smudging on head and neck, dark bill marks. Steve N. G. Howell. Monterey, California, 24 Jan. 2004.

H1.2 ADULT NONBREEDING PRESUMED GLAUCOUS-WINGED × WESTERN GULL HYBRID. Wingtips and upperparts too dark for Glaucous-winged; upperparts and wingtips too pale for Western; note pink orbital ring and diffuse dusky smudging on head and neck. Upperparts probably a shade too dark for hybrid Glaucous-winged × American Herring Gull. Steve N. G. Howell. Petaluma, California, 11 Dec. 2003.

H1.3 ADULT NONBREEDING GLAUCOUS-WINGED × WESTERN GULL HYBRID, RESEMBLING WESTERN GULL (ADULT HYBRID AND FIRST-CYCLE GLAUCOUS-WINGED GULL BEHIND). Upperparts slightly pale for Western (apparent in direct comparison) and orbital ring mixed pink and yellow; also note dark eye, bill shape. Steve N. G. Howell. Petaluma, California, 21 Dec. 2001.

H1.4 ADULT BREEDING GLAUCOUS-WINGED × WESTERN GULL HYBRID, RESEMBLING GLAUCOUS-WINGED GULL. Wingtips and upperparts slightly too dark for Glaucous-winged (apparent in direct comparison); also note bright orange-yellow bill. Steve N. G. Howell. Fort Bragg, California, 11 May 2003.

H1.5 JUVENILE GLAUCOUS-WINGED × WESTERN GULL HYBRID. An intermediate individual. Wingtips and tail too dark for Glaucous-winged, too pale for Western. Bruce Hallett. Near Seattle, Washington, 4 Sept. 1996.

H1.6 FIRST-CYCLE GLAUCOUS-WINGED × WESTERN GULL HYBRID. An intermediate individual apparently still in juvenal plumage. Note same features as photo H1.5. Jon Dunn. Santa Barbara, California, 14 Nov. 1988.

H1.7 FIRST-CYCLE GLAUCOUS-WINGED × WESTERN GULL HYBRID. An intermediate individual with some post-juvenal molt on head and back. Note same features as photo H1.5. Steve N. G. Howell. Monterey, California, 24 Jan. 2004.

H1.8 FIRST-CYCLE GLAUCOUS-WINGED × WESTERN GULL HYBRIDS. Left-hand bird similar to Western Gull but wingtips and tail dark brown (not blackish); right-hand bird resembles Glaucous-winged but wingtips and tail too dark; distinguished from Thayer's Gull by structure and bill shape. Steve N. G. Howell. Petaluma, California, 21 Dec. 2001.

H1.9 FIRST-CYCLE PRESUMED GLAUCOUS-WINGED × WESTERN GULL HYBRID (WITH FIRST-CYCLE GLAUCOUS-WINGED GULL BEHIND). Plumage tones similar to a dark Glaucous-winged but coarsely checkered upperparts typical of Western. Steve N. G. Howell. Petaluma, California, 21 Dec. 2001.

H1.10 SECOND-CYCLE GLAUCOUS-WINGED × WESTERN GULL HYBRID. An intermediate individual completing PB2 molt (wingtips not fully grown). Wingtips and tail too dark for Glaucous-winged, too pale for Western. Bruce Hallett. Newport, Oregon, 5 Sept. 2001.

H1.11 SECOND-CYCLE GLAUCOUS-WINGED × WESTERN GULL HYBRID. An intermediate individual. Note same features as photo H1.10. Steve N. G. Howell. Bolinas, California, 31 Dec. 2001.

H1.12 SECOND-CYCLE GLAUCOUS-WINGED × WESTERN GULL HYBRID (SAME BIRD AS PHOTO H1.24; SECOND-CYCLE WESTERN GULL BEHIND). Similar to Western Gull but back and wingtip too pale; also note relatively pale and bleached upperwing coverts. Steve N. G. Howell. Bolinas, California, 3 Apr. 2003.

H1.13 THIRD-CYCLE GLAUCOUS-WINGED × WESTERN GULL HYBRID, COMPLETING PB3 MOLT (P9–P10 OLD). Overall suggests Glaucous-winged but note incoming blackish primaries. Steve N. G. Howell. Bodega Bay, California, 24 Aug. 1998.

H1.14 THIRD-CYCLE GLAUCOUS-WINGED × WESTERN GULL HYBRID, AN INTERMEDIATE INDIVIDUAL. Upperparts too pale for Western, wingtips too blackish for Glaucous-winged. Jon Dunn. Santa Barbara, California, 14 Nov. 1988.

H1.15 THIRD-CYCLE GLAUCOUS-WINGED × WESTERN GULL HYBRID. Overall suggests Western but upperparts and wingtips too pale (apparent in direct comparison). Steve N. G. Howell. Bolinas, California, 31 Dec. 2001.

H1.16 ADULT NONBREEDING GLAUCOUS-WINGED × WESTERN GULL HYBRID COMPLETING PB MOLT (P10 OLD, P9 SHED, P8 GROWING). Upperparts too pale for Western Gull, and note extensive dusky clouding on head, typical of Glaucous-winged. Steve N. G. Howell. Off Fort Bragg, California, 15 Oct. 2003.

H1.17 ADULT NONBREEDING GLAUCOUS-WINGED × WESTERN GULL HYBRID. Suggests Western Gull but wingtips too pale and poorly contrasting. Steve N. G. Howell. Bolinas, California, 3 Jan. 2002.

H1.18 ADULT NONBREEDING GLAUCOUS-WINGED × WESTERN GULL HYBRID. Suggests Western Gull but upperparts, especially wingtips, too pale; also note mostly gray underside to wingtip and extensive dusky head markings. Steve N. G. Howell. Monterey Bay, California, 24 Jan. 2004.

H1.19 ADULT NONBREEDING GLAUCOUS-WINGED × WESTERN GULL HYBRID. Extensively gray (rather than blackish, typical of Western) underside to outer primaries suggests Slaty-backed Gull, but white tongue-tips on P7–P9 restricted to absent, and note bright bill. Steve N. G. Howell. Monterey Bay, California, 15 Dec. 2003.

H1.20 JUVENILE GLAUCOUS-WINGED × WESTERN GULL HYBRID. Suggests Glaucous-winged Gull but wingtip pattern and tail too dark (more apparent when the bird was viewed at rest). Eric Preston. Monterey Bay, California, 16 Oct. 2002.

H1.21 FIRST-CYCLE GLAUCOUS-WINGED × WESTERN GULL HYBRID. Suggests a washed-out Western Gull; hybrids often show a pale inner primary panel, suggesting Herring Gull (but note bill size and shape, broad wings). Steve N. G. Howell. Bolinas, California, 1 Apr. 2003.

**H1.22 FIRST-CYCLE PRESUMED GLAUCOUS-WINGED ×
WESTERN GULL HYBRID.** An intermediate individual,
with upperwing pattern suggesting Thayer's Gull;
but note extensively dark tail (no white patterning
at base of outer rectrices) and stout bill. Distinguished from hybrid Glaucous-winged × Herring
Gull by structure. Steve N. G. Howell. Monterey
Bay, California, 24 Jan. 2004.

**H1.23 SECOND-CYCLE GLAUCOUS-WINGED × WESTERN GULL
HYBRID, AN INTERMEDIATE INDIVIDUAL.** Tail and secondaries too dark for Glaucous-winged, primaries too
pale for Western. Steve N. G. Howell. Bolinas,
California, 1 Apr. 2003.

**H1.24 SECOND-CYCLE GLAUCOUS-WINGED × WESTERN GULL
HYBRID (SAME BIRD AS PHOTO H1.12).** Resembles
Western Gull but back and upperwings slightly too
pale. Steve N. G. Howell. Bolinas, California,
1 Apr. 2003.

**H1.25 THIRD-CYCLE GLAUCOUS-WINGED × WESTERN GULL
HYBRID.** Suggests Glaucous-winged Gull but
wingtip and tail markings too dark. Steve N. G.
Howell. Monterey Bay, California, 15 Dec. 2003.

H2.1 ADULT NONBREEDING GLAUCOUS-WINGED × AMERICAN HERRING GULL HYBRID. Wingtips too dark for Glaucous-winged, and note pale eye; distinguished from Herring Gull by overall thickset structure, pink orbital ring, and smudgy (not streaked) head and neck markings. Steve Heinl. Ketchikan, Alaska, 29 Dec. 1994.

H2.2 ADULT NONBREEDING GLAUCOUS-WINGED × AMERICAN HERRING GULL HYBRID AND ADULT RING-BILLED GULL (LEFT). Wingtips too dark for Glaucous-winged; distinguished from Herring Gull by pink orbital ring, dark eye, and wingtip pattern (visible in flight). Steve N. G. Howell. Petaluma, California, 2 Jan. 2003.

H2.3 ADULT BREEDING GLAUCOUS-WINGED × AMERICAN HERRING GULL HYBRID. Wingtips too dark for Glaucous-winged, and note pale eye; distinguished from Herring Gull by dark gray wingtips. Steve Heinl. Anchorage, Alaska, 15 May 1996.

H2.4 ADULT BREEDING GLAUCOUS-WINGED × AMERICAN HERRING GULL HYBRID. Wingtips too dark for Glaucous-winged; told from Herring Gull by blackish (not black) wingtips, medium gray upperparts, darker eye, and pink orbital ring. Steve Heinl. Anchorage, Alaska, 15 May 1996.

H2.5 FIRST-CYCLE *LARUS* SP., PERHAPS GLAUCOUS-WINGED × AMERICAN HERRING GULL HYBRID. Overall suggests Herring Gull but note stucture, with broad wings showing as a skirt, relatively short wing projection, and stout bill, all typical of Glaucous-winged. Plumage also relatively plain, and note upperwing pattern (see photo H2.19 of same bird). Matches Slaty-backed Gull in many ways, thus highlighting an unresolved identification conundrum. Steve N. G. Howell. Bolinas, California, 27 Dec. 2003.

**H2.6 FIRST-CYCLE PRESUMED GLAUCOUS-WINGED ×
AMERICAN HERRING GULL HYBRID.** Wingtips and
secondaries too dark for Glaucous-winged, too
pale for Herring. Overall structure, streaked head
and neck markings, and location all point to
Herring (rather than Western) parentage. Steve
Heinl. Ketchikan, Alaska, 3 Mar. 2003.

**H2.7 FIRST-CYCLE PRESUMED GLAUCOUS-WINGED ×
AMERICAN HERRING GULL.** Overall suggests Herring
Gull and at rest would probably be passed off as
that species, albeit a slightly bleached late-winter
bird. Upperwing pattern, with two-tone outer
primaries, points to a hybrid (see photo H2.20 of
the same bird). Steve N. G. Howell. Bolinas,
California, 31 Mar. 2004.

**H2.8 SECOND-CYCLE PRESUMED GLAUCOUS-WINGED ×
AMERICAN HERRING GULL HYBRID.** Wingtips too dark for
Glaucous-winged. Difficult to rule out Glaucous-
winged × Western Gull hybrid but pale gray tone
of back feathers and bicolored bill more typical of
Herring Gull. Steve N. G. Howell. Petaluma,
California, 18 Dec. 1997.

**H2.9 SECOND-CYCLE PRESUMED GLAUCOUS-WINGED ×
AMERICAN HERRING GULL HYBRID.** Resembles Glaucous-
winged but note relatively slender bill, pale eye,
and streaked (versus smudged) head and neck, all
suggesting Herring Gull. Steve N. G. Howell.
Petaluma, California, 2 Jan. 2003.

H2.10 SECOND-CYCLE GLAUCOUS-WINGED × AMERICAN HERRING GULL HYBRID. Note same features as photo 2.8. Steve Heinl. Ketchikan, Alaska, 3 Mar. 2003.

H2.11 THIRD-CYCLE GLAUCOUS-WINGED × AMERICAN HERRING GULL HYBRID. Distinguished from hybrid Glaucous-winged × Western Gull by bill structure and paler upperparts; from Thayer's Gull by bill structure. Steve N. G. Howell. Petaluma, California, 2 Jan. 2003.

H2.12 THIRD-CYCLE GLAUCOUS-WINGED × AMERICAN HERRING GULL HYBRID. An intermediate individual. Distinguished from hybrid Glaucous-winged × Western Gull by bill structure. Steve Heinl. Ketchikan, Alaska, 17 Feb. 2003.

H2.13 ADULT NONBREEDING GLAUCOUS-WINGED × AMERICAN HERRING GULL HYBRID. Distinguished from Herring Gull by smoky gray bases to inner primaries and dark eye, and from Vega Gull by paler upperparts (not visible here); also note lack of distinct white tongue-tips on P6–P8. Steve N. G. Howell. Monterey Bay, California, 17 Dec. 2001.

H2.14 ADULT NONBREEDING GLAUCOUS-WINGED × AMERICAN HERRING GULL HYBRID. Distinguished from Thayer's Gull by broad wings and stout bill, also note reduced white on P9. Steve N. G. Howell. Petaluma, California, 2 Jan. 2003.

**H2.15 ADULT NONBREEDING GLAUCOUS-WINGED ×
AMERICAN HERRING GULL HYBRID.** Wingtips slightly too
pale for Herring Gull (and see photo H2.16 of
same bird). Steve N. G. Howell. Puerto Peñasco,
Sonora, Mexico, 23 Jan. 2003.

**H2.16 ADULT NONBREEDING GLAUCOUS-WINGED ×
AMERICAN HERRING GULL HYBRID.** Wingtips slightly too
pale for Herring Gull (see photo H2.15 of same
bird); also note smoky gray bases to underside of
inner primaries, dark eye, and deep pink orbital
ring. Steve N. G. Howell. Puerto Peñasco, Sonora,
Mexico, 23 Jan. 2003.

**H2.17 FIRST-CYCLE PRESUMED GLAUCOUS-WINGED ×
AMERICAN HERRING GULL HYBRID.** Distinguished from
Thayer's Gull by broad wings with indistinct
secondary bar and stout bill and from Western
hybrid by Herring-like head and bill structure,
pale bill base. Steve N. G. Howell. Monterey Bay,
California, 15 Oct. 2001.

**H2.18 FIRST-CYCLE PRESUMED GLAUCOUS-WINGED ×
AMERICAN HERRING GULL HYBRID.** Distinguished from
hybrid Glaucous-winged × Western Gull by
pinkish on bill base and broadly banded tail, both
typical of Herring Gull. Steve N. G. Howell.
Monterey Bay, California, 21 Dec. 1998.

**H2.19 FIRST-CYCLE *LARUS* SP., PERHAPS GLAUCOUS-WINGED
× AMERICAN HERRING GULL HYBRID.** Overall suggests
Herring Gull but note broad wings (compare with
photo H2.5 of same bird) and relatively washed-
out upperwing pattern with extensive pale panel
on inner primaries. Matches Slaty-backed Gull in
most features and might be that species, thus
highlighting an unresolved identification conundrum. Steve N. G. Howell. Bolinas, California,
27 Dec. 2003.

**H2.20 FIRST-CYCLE PRESUMED GLAUCOUS-WINGED ×
AMERICAN HERRING GULL.** Overall suggests Herring
Gull (at rest could be passed off as that species;
see photo H2.7 of the same bird) but reduced dark
in outer primaries (for example, two-tone pattern
on dorsal wingtip) points to a hybrid. Steve N. G.
Howell. Bolinas, California, 31 Mar. 2004.

**H2.21 SECOND-CYCLE GLAUCOUS-WINGED × AMERICAN
HERRING GULL HYBRID.** Distinguished from Herring
Gull by paler wingtips (with diffuse two-tone
pattern) and secondaries; from Thayer's Gull by
broader wings, stouter bill. Steve N. G. Howell.
Monterey Bay, California, 24 Jan. 2004.

**H2.22 SECOND-CYCLE GLAUCOUS-WINGED × AMERICAN
HERRING GULL HYBRID.** Note same features as photo
H2.21. Steve N. G. Howell. Point Reyes, Califor-
nia, 30 Jan. 2003.

**H2.23 THIRD-CYCLE GLAUCOUS-WINGED × AMERICAN
HERRING GULL HYBRID.** Distinguished from Herring
Gull by paler wingtips and dark eye; from Thayer's
Gull by stouter bill and broader wings with no
distinct contrast on underside of outer primary
tips; also note reduced white in outer primaries.
Steve N. G. Howell. Monterey Bay, California,
17 Dec. 2001.

H3.1 ADULT NONBREEDING GLAUCOUS × AMERICAN HERRING GULL HYBRID WITH AMERICAN HERRING GULLS. Note dark slaty (not black) dorsal wingtips and mostly white underside to far wingtip; also, upperparts are slightly paler than Herring Gull, and dusky head markings are reduced. Willie D'Anna. Niagara Falls, New York, 3 Jan. 2003.

H3.2 ADULT BREEDING GLAUCOUS × AMERICAN HERRING GULL HYBRID. Distinguished from Herring Gull by dark slaty wingtips with extensive white patterning. Bruce Mactavish. Inuvik, Northwest Territories, 24 June 2002.

H3.4 JUVENILE GLAUCOUS × AMERICAN HERRING GULL HYBRID. Distinguished from Herring Gull by brown wingtips and from Thayer's Gull by larger, bicolored bill and paler primaries. Bruce Mactavish. Inuvik, Northwest Territories, 9 Sept. 2002.

H3.3 FLEDGLING GLAUCOUS × AMERICAN HERRING GULL HYBRID (PRIMARIES NOT FULLY GROWN) OF KNOWN MIXED PAIR. Wingtips washed too dusky for pure Glaucous Gull; bill of fledgling Glaucous can be dull like this but soon changes to brightly bicolored. Larry B. Spear. Tuk, Northwest Territories, 31 Aug. 1984.

H3.5 FIRST-CYCLE PRESUMED GLAUCOUS × AMERICAN HERRING GULL HYBRID. Suggests a dark Glaucous Gull with brown-washed primaries; Glaucous-winged Gull parentage perhaps difficult to eliminate but shows no obvious Glaucous-winged traits. Distinguished from Kumlien's Gull by much larger size (evident in the field) and relatively long bill. Steve N. G. Howell. Petaluma, California, 27 Dec. 2001.

H3.6 FIRST-CYCLE PRESUMED GLAUCOUS × AMERICAN HERRING GULL HYBRID. Distinguished from Herring Gull by dark brown (not blackish) wingtips, stout-based bill (shape typical of Glaucous), and wingtip pattern (see photo H3.16 of same bird). Steve N. G. Howell. Puerto Peñasco, Sonora, Mexico, 22 Jan. 2003.

H3.7 FIRST-CYCLE GLAUCOUS × AMERICAN HERRING GULL HYBRID, MOSTLY IF NOT ENTIRELY IN JUVENAL PLUMAGE. Distinguished from Herring Gull by dark brown (not blackish) wingtips and overall frosty whitish aspect; also note brightly bicolored bill. Bruce Mactavish. St. John's, Newfoundland, 17 Jan. 1993.

H3.8 FIRST-CYCLE GLAUCOUS × AMERICAN HERRING GULL HYBRID. Distinguished from Herring Gull by dark brown wingtips and tail, deep-based (Glaucous-shaped) and brightly bicolored bill. Bruce Mactavish. St. John's, Newfoundland, 29 Jan. 2003.

H3.9 FIRST-CYCLE GLAUCOUS × AMERICAN HERRING GULL HYBRID (SAME BIRD AS PHOTO H3.17). Distinguished from Herring Gull by dark brown wingtips and overall whitish aspect; also note brightly bicolored bill. Bruce Mactavish. St. John's, Newfoundland, 11 Mar. 2001.

H3.10 SECOND-CYCLE PRESUMED GLAUCOUS × AMERICAN HERRING GULL HYBRID. Suggests Glaucous Gull but P8–P10 washed brown; hybrid Glaucous × Glaucous-winged Gull perhaps difficult to eliminate, but this bird shows no obvious Glaucous-winged traits. Steve N. G. Howell. Petaluma, California, 24 Dec. 1998.

H3.11 SECOND-CYCLE GLAUCOUS × AMERICAN HERRING GULL HYBRID. Distinguished from Herring Gull by blackish brown wingtips, dark brown tail, and overall whitish aspect. Marshall J. Iliff. Prince William County, Virginia, mid-Jan. 2002.

H3.12 SECOND-CYCLE GLAUCOUS × AMERICAN HERRING GULL HYBRID. Distinguished from Herring Gull by dark brown wingtips and tail. Bruce Mactavish. St. John's, Newfoundland, 2 Feb. 2003.

H3.13 THIRD-CYCLE TYPE PRESUMED GLAUCOUS × AMERICAN HERRING GULL HYBRID, COMPLETING PB MOLT (OUTER PRIMARIES NOT FULLY GROWN). Distinguished from Herring Gull by slaty (not black) wingtips, and from adult by dusky tertial marks; also note bill pattern. Hybrid Glaucous × Vega Gull probably cannot be eliminated from this photo. Kimball L. Garrett. Nome, Alaska, 14 Sept. 2002.

H3.14 THIRD-CYCLE TYPE GLAUCOUS × AMERICAN HERRING GULL HYBRID. Distinguished from Glaucous Gull by dusky wingtip markings; also note extensive dusky head and neck mottling. Bruce Mactavish. St. John's, Newfoundland, Dec. 2000.

H3.15 ADULT GLAUCOUS × AMERICAN HERRING GULL HYBRID. Distinguished from Herring Gull by restricted dark slaty (not black) wingtip markings and from Thayer's Gull by paler upperparts, reduced dark on P6, and bigger bill; also note staring pale yellow eye. Note growing P10 on far wing is noticeably shorter than on near wing. George L. Armistead/VIREO. Off Brielle, New Jersey, 19 Dec. 1997.

H3.16 FIRST-CYCLE PRESUMED GLAUCOUS × AMERICAN HERRING GULL HYBRID (SAME BIRD AS PHOTO H3.6). Distinguished from Herring Gull by dark brown wingtips with extensively pale inner webs to outer primaries. Steve N. G. Howell. Puerto Peñasco, Sonora, Mexico, 22 Jan. 2003.

H3 17 FIRST-CYCLE GLAUCOUS × AMERICAN HERRING GULL HYBRID (SAME BIRD AS PHOTO H3.9). Distinguished from Herring Gull by dark brown wingtips with extensively whitish inner webs, overall whitish aspect. Bruce Mactavish. St. John's, Newfoundland, 11 Mar. 2001.

H4.1 ADULT BREEDING PRESUMED GLAUCOUS × GLAUCOUS-WINGED GULL HYBRID. Resembles Glaucous Gull but note dusky wingtip markings, dusky eye, and deep pink orbital ring. Bruce Hallett. Nome, Alaska, early June 2001.

H4.2 FIRST-CYCLE PRESUMED GLAUCOUS × GLAUCOUS-WINGED GULL HYBRID. Resembles Glaucous Gull but with relatively short and dusky bill. Yoshiaki Watanabe. Choshi Chiba, Japan, 24 Dec. 2000.

H4.3 SECOND-CYCLE PRESUMED GLAUCOUS × GLAUCOUS-WINGED GULL HYBRID. Resembles Glaucous Gull, but note extensive and messy dark bill tip; also dark eye, medium gray scapulars, and bill shape. Steve N. G. Howell. Petaluma, California, 25 Feb. 1998.

H4.4 THIRD-CYCLE PRESUMED GLAUCOUS × GLAUCOUS-WINGED GULL HYBRID. Resembles Glaucous Gull but wingtip washed dusky. Larry B. Spear. At sea near Pribilof Islands, Alaska, Mar. 1983.

H4.5 THIRD-CYCLE TYPE PRESUMED GLAUCOUS × GLAUCOUS-WINGED GULL HYBRID COMPLETING PB MOLT (OUTER PRIMARIES NOT FULLY GROWN). Resembles Glaucous Gull, but note pale gray subterminal bands on primaries; distinguished from adult by bill pattern and brownish wash on greater coverts. Kimball L. Garrett. Nome, Alaska, 14 Sept. 2002.

H4.6 ADULT NONBREEDING PRESUMED GLAUCOUS × GLAUCOUS-WINGED GULL HYBRID. Resembles Glaucous Gull but white wingtip area reduced and clouded with faint gray distal markings. Larry B. Spear. At sea near Pribilof Islands, Alaska, Mar. 1983.

H4.7 ADULT NONBREEDING PRESUMED GLAUCOUS × GLAUCOUS-WINGED GULL HYBRID. Resembles Glaucous Gull but white wingtip area reduced and relatively sharply defined from medium gray upperwings; also note extensive dusky clouding on head, atypical of Glaucous. Larry B. Spear. At sea near Pribilof Islands, Alaska, Mar. 1983.

H5.1 ADULT NONBREEDING POSSIBLE THAYER'S GULL × KUMLIEN'S/ICELAND GULL HYBRID, COMPLETING PB MOLT (OUTER PRIMARIES NOT FULLY GROWN). This individual has appreciably paler wingtips than typical Thayer's Gulls (see photos 36.1–36.6). Its eye color, bill shape, and bill color are equally good for Kumlien's as for Thayer's. Perhaps not safely distinguishable from the dark-winged extreme of adult Kumlien's Gull (for example, 35a.7), but note dark subterminal band on P5, below the tertials. Steve Heinl. Ketchikan, Alaska, 19 Oct. 1992.

H5.2 FIRST-CYCLE PRESUMED THAYER'S × KUMLIEN'S/ICELAND GULL HYBRID. Relatively pale overall for Thayer's Gull at this season, with a tendency to subterminal arrowhead marks on outer primaries, extensive white on scapulars, pale and checkered tertials, and a very weak dark secondary bar (visible in flight); wingtips relatively dark for a Kumlien's/Iceland Gull. Steve N. G. Howell. Petaluma, California, 18 Dec. 1997.

H5.3 FIRST-CYCLE POSSIBLE THAYER'S × KUMLIEN'S/ICELAND GULL HYBRID. Relatively pale overall for a Thayer's Gull at this season (for example, medium-brown primary bases, pale tertial centers), although structure typical of Thayer's. Whether birds like this represent pure Thayer's Gulls remains to be determined. Steve N. G. Howell. Petaluma, California, 27 Dec. 2001.

H5.4 FIRST-CYCLE POSSIBLE THAYER'S × KUMLIEN'S/ICELAND GULL HYBRID. Relatively pale and milky overall for Thayer's Gull at this season (for example, medium-brown tertial centers); solidly dark brown wingtips atypical of Kumlien's Gull. Whether birds like this represent pure Kumlien's Gulls remains to be determined. Steve N. G. Howell. St. John's, Newfoundland, 4 Feb. 2002.

H5.5 FIRST-CYCLE *LARUS* SP. (STANDING; SAME BIRD AS PHOTO H5.6) AND THAYER'S GULL (SITTING; A RELATIVELY SMALL AND SMALL-BILLED INDIVIDUAL). Such birds would not be questioned as Kumlien's Gulls in Newfoundland, but when they occur in California they cause difficulties. All features of this bird are matched by presumed Kumlien's Gulls in Newfoundland, and its wingtips (which are not excessively bleached) and secondaries are too pale for Thayer's; but could it be a hybrid Kumlien's × Thayer's Gull? Steve N. G. Howell. Petaluma, California, 26 Mar. 2004.

H5.6 FIRST-CYCLE *LARUS* SP. (SAME BIRD AS PHOTO H5.5). This bird falls within the range of variation in Kumlien's Gull, but in California such birds cause difficulties because of the specter of potential hybridization between Kumlien's and Thayer's Gulls. Steve N. G. Howell. Petaluma, California, 26 Mar. 2004.

H5.7 SECOND-CYCLE POSSIBLE THAYER'S × KUMLIEN'S/ ICELAND GULL HYBRID. Relatively pale overall for a Thayer's Gull at this season, especially wingtips; bill relatively stout and long for a Kumlien's Gull. From this photo alone, Glaucous × Herring Gull hybrid difficult to rule out, but field observations of size and structure supported identification as a Thayer's-like bird. Steve Heinl. Ketchikan, Alaska, 14 Nov. 1992.

H5.8 THIRD-CYCLE PRESUMED THAYER'S × KUMLIEN'S/ ICELAND GULL HYBRID. Too much white in wingtips for Thayer's Gull; bill relatively large and eye dark for Kumlien's/Iceland Gull. Greg W. Lasley. Churchill, Manitoba, 21 June 1988.

**H6.1 ADULT NONBREEDING PRESUMED AMERICAN HERRING ×
GREAT BLACK-BACKED GULL HYBRID (SAME BIRD AS PHOTO
H6.2).** Resembles Great Black-backed Gull in shape
and wingtip pattern, but upperparts slaty gray,
hindneck with relatively extensive dusky streaking,
bill slightly less swollen at gonydeal expansion,
and eye staringly pale. Bruce Mactavish. St. John's,
Newfoundland, 2 Feb. 2003.

**H6.2 ADULT NONBREEDING PRESUMED AMERICAN HERRING ×
GREAT BLACK-BACKED GULL HYBRID (SAME BIRD AS PHOTO
H6.1).** Resembles Great Black-backed Gull in shape
and wingtip pattern, but upperparts slaty gray
(suggesting Lesser Black-backed Gull). Bruce
Mactavish. St. John's, Newfoundland, 2 Feb.
2003.

**H7.1 ADULT NONBREEDING PRESUMED AMERICAN HERRING ×
LESSER BLACK-BACKED GULL HYBRID.** Resembles Lesser
Black-backed Gull but slightly paler slaty gray
above, stockier overall with stouter bill, and
pinkish cast to legs. Bruce Mactavish. St. John's,
Newfoundland, 4 Feb. 2003.

**H7.2 ADULT NONBREEDING PRESUMED AMERICAN HERRING ×
LESSER BLACK-BACKED GULL HYBRID.** Note same features
as photo H7.1. Bruce Mactavish. St. John's,
Newfoundland, 22 Feb. 2001.

**H7.3 THIRD-CYCLE TYPE PRESUMED AMERICAN HERRING ×
LESSER BLACK-BACKED GULL HYBRID (SAME BIRD AS PHOTO
H7.4).** Resembles Lesser Black-backed Gull but
paler slaty gray above, stockier overall with stouter
bill, and pinkish legs. Marshall J. Iliff. Salisbury
Landfill, Maryland, 11 Jan. 2000.

**H7.4 THIRD-CYCLE TYPE PRESUMED AMERICAN HERRING ×
LESSER BLACK-BACKED GULL HYBRID (SAME BIRD AS PHOTO
H7.3; AMERICAN HERRING GULL TO LEFT).** Resembles
Lesser Black-backed Gull but paler slaty gray
above (compare with American Herring Gull to
left). Distinguished from adult by black on primary
coverts and alula; also note bill pattern. Marshall J.
Iliff. Salisbury Landfill, Maryland, 11 Jan. 2000.

H10.1 ADULT NONBREEDING GLAUCOUS × GREAT BLACK-BACKED GULL HYBRID (SAME BIRD AS PHOTO H10.4).
Resembles Great Black-backed Gull but slightly paler above and with solidly white wingtips. Bruce Mactavish. St. John's, Newfoundland, 29 Feb. 2004.

H10.2 FIRST-CYCLE GLAUCOUS × GREAT BLACK-BACKED GULL HYBRID. Resembles Great Black-backed Gull but frostier overall with paler wingtips. Bruce Mactavish. St. John's, Newfoundland, 18 Mar. 2001.

H10.3 SECOND-CYCLE OR THIRD-CYCLE GLAUCOUS × GREAT BLACK-BACKED GULL HYBRID. Resembles Great Black-backed Gull but with paler gray on upperparts and paler wingtips. Bruce Mactavish. St. John's, Newfoundland, 29 Jan. 2003.

H10.4 ADULT NONBREEDING GLAUCOUS × GREAT BLACK-BACKED GULL HYBRID (SAME BIRD AS PHOTO H10.1).
Resembles Great Black-backed Gull but slightly paler above and with solidly white wingtips. Bruce Mactavish. St. John's, Newfoundland, 29 Feb. 2004.

H12.1 FIRST-CYCLE PRESUMED GLAUCOUS × VEGA GULL HYBRID. Resembles Glaucous × American Herring Gull hybrid but photographed in Japan; also note rich pink legs. Yoshiaki Watanabe. Hokkaido, Japan, 18 Dec. 2001.

H12.2 THIRD-CYCLE PRESUMED GLAUCOUS × VEGA GULL HYBRID (SAME BIRD AS PHOTO H12.3). Resembles Glaucous × American Herring Gull hybrid but photographed in Japan; also note rich pink legs. Yasuhiro Kawasaki. Hokkaido, Japan, 15 Feb. 1996.

H12.3 THIRD-CYCLE PRESUMED GLAUCOUS × VEGA GULL HYBRID (SAME BIRD AS PHOTO H12.2). Resembles Glaucous × American Herring Gull hybrid but photographed in Japan; aged by adultlike inner and middle primaries. Yasuhiro Kawasaki. Hokkaido, Japan, 15 Feb. 1996.

H12.4 THIRD-CYCLE TYPE PRESUMED GLAUCOUS × VEGA GULL HYBRID (SAME BIRD AS PHOTO H12.5). Resembles Glaucous × American Herring Gull hybrid but photographed in Japan. Yoshiaki Watanabe. Hokkaido, Japan, 10 Feb. 2001.

H12.5 THIRD-CYCLE TYPE PRESUMED GLAUCOUS × VEGA GULL HYBRID (SAME BIRD AS PHOTO H12.4) AND ADULT SLATY-BACKED GULL. Resembles Glaucous × American Herring Gull hybrid but photographed in Japan; note resemblance of under-wingtip pattern to washed-out adult Thayer's Gull. Yoshiaki Watanabe. Hokkaido, Japan, 10 Feb. 2001.

H13.2 FIRST-CYCLE POSSIBLE SLATY-BACKED × VEGA GULL HYBRID. Atypical for Slaty-backed are the extensively pale tail base, relatively dark outer primaries, and relatively coarse pale checkering on greater coverts; atypical of Vega Gull are the stout blackish bill, broad wings, relatively broad dark tail band, and relatively dingy tail base and uppertail coverts. Geoff Carey. Choshi, Japan, 11 Nov. 1999.

H13.1 FIRST-CYCLE POSSIBLE SLATY-BACKED × VEGA GULL HYBRID. Dark distal tail band relatively narrow for Slaty-backed, and wings also look relatively narrow; distinguished from Vega Gull by stout blackish bill, overall dusky brownish aspect to underparts, and washed-out pattern on underside of primary tips. Geoff Carey. Choshi, Japan, 13 Nov. 1999.

H13.3 SECOND-CYCLE POSSIBLE SLATY-BACKED × VEGA GULL HYBRID. The gray back feathers look a little pale for Slaty-backed, and the bird's head and bill structure also look atypical of pure Slaty-backed. Yoshiaki Watanabe. Hokkaido, Japan, 20 Jan. 2001.

H14.1 FIRST-CYCLE PRESUMED GLAUCOUS-WINGED × SLATY-BACKED GULL HYBRID. Resembles a Glaucous-winged × Western Gull hybrid but photographed in Korea. Annika Forsten. Pohang, South Korea, 16 Feb. 2002.

H14.2 FIRST-CYCLE PRESUMED GLAUCOUS-WINGED × SLATY-BACKED GULL HYBRID. Outer primaries too pale for Slaty-backed, too dark for Glaucous-winged; difficult to separate from Glaucous-winged × Western Gull hybrid except by range. Geoff Carey. Choshi, Japan, 11 Nov. 1999.

H14.3 SECOND-CYCLE PRESUMED GLAUCOUS-WINGED × SLATY-BACKED GULL HYBRID. Distinguished from Glaucous-winged by dark wingtips and pale eye; from Slaty-backed by dark brown wingtips, extensive dusky smudging on head and underparts, and medium gray tone of scapulars. Yoshiaki Watanabe. Hokkaido, Japan, 15 Feb. 2001.

SPECIES
ACCOUNTS

TERNLIKE GULLS
MASKED GULLS
(SUBGENUS *Chroicocephalus*)

In the Americas five species of small to medium-sized gulls are in this distinctive group, which Crochet et al. (2000) recommended placing in the genus *Chroicocephalus*: Bonaparte's, Black-headed, Gray-hooded, Brown-hooded, and Andean Gulls. Bills are generally slender and pointed. Adults have red to black bills and reddish legs. Alternate-plumaged adults of typical species have a "mask" (or partial hood) with narrow white postocular crescents; the mask does not extend down the nape, and it ranges in color from blackish to pale gray. Adult upperwings are pale gray with a bold white leading wedge, but they lack a white trailing edge. All species attain adult plumage in their second or third cycle. Juvenal plumages have the head and neck white overall with a brownish cap, dark ear-spot, and a gingery to brown hindcollar; the wings have a dark ulnar bar and reduced white forewing flash. Preformative molts quickly produce an adultlike gray back, and first prealternate molts can produce a solid, adultlike hood in some species, although a partial hood is more common.

ADULT BREEDING BONAPARTE'S GULL. PP. 49, 302

ADULT BREEDING BLACK-HEADED GULL. PP. 53, 306

ADULT BREEDING GRAY-HOODED GULL WITH NONBREEDING FRANKLIN'S GULLS (BEHIND) AND BELCHER'S GULL (LEFT). PP. 56, 309

ADULT BREEDING BROWN-HOODED GULLS *(L. M. GLAUCODES).* PP. 59, 312

ADULT BREEDING ANDEAN GULL. PP. 64, 316

LENGTH 12.3–13.8 IN. (31–35 CM)

PHOTOS 1.0–1.16; GULL TOPOGRAPHY, 1.27; BLACK-HEADED GULL, 2.2, 2.3; LITTLE GULL, 6.6

IDENTIFICATION SUMMARY

A small, dainty, two- or three-cycle gull widespread in N. America. Bill slender and pointed; at rest, tail tip falls between tips of P6 and P7, usually nearer P6. Adult has black bill, orange-red to flesh pink legs, bold white leading wedge on upperwings; slaty blackish hood in alternate plumage, dark ear-spot in basic. First-cycle has dark ulnar bar and tail band. Much rarer Black-headed Gull is the only similar species likely in the same range as Bonaparte's: Black-headed is larger with a stouter, reddish to pinkish bill, dark underside to the middle primaries; adult alternate has dark brown hood. First-cycle Little Gull is smaller with smaller bill, dark cap, more solidly blackish tertials, blackish M pattern on upperwings.

TAXONOMY

Monotypic, although eastern-breeding birds average slightly larger than western-breeding birds.[1]

STATUS AND DISTRIBUTION

N. America, wintering to n. Mexico. Vagrant to Europe, w. Africa, Hawaii, and Japan.

Breeding. Breeds (May–Aug.) from w. Alaska (se. Seward Peninsula and base of Alaska Peninsula), Yukon, and s.-cen. B.C. east across Canada to Ont. and cen. Que.; has also nested locally in e. Que. (Magdalen Is.), probably nw. Me.,[2] and perhaps Wisc.

Nonbreeding. Distribution complex. Overall, a fairly common to abundant (especially on Great Lakes) migrant in eastern half of N. America (including e. Great Plains) and also along Pacific Coast. Uncommon to rare from w. Great Plains through Great Basin, with seasonal occurrences in these regions mirroring those elsewhere.

Fall movements begin early, and birds reach southern portions of Prairie Provinces, Great Lakes region, and Bay of Fundy during July–

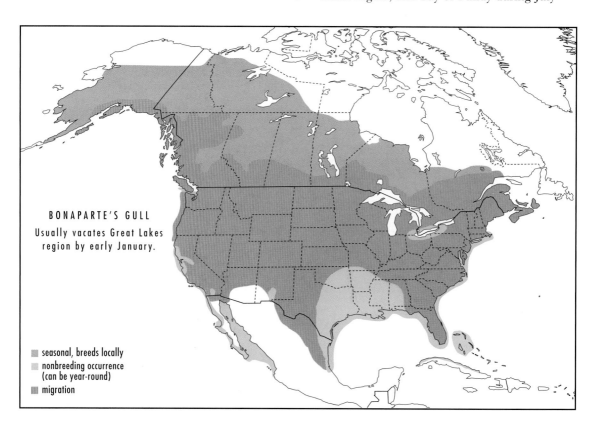

BONAPARTE'S GULL

Usually vacates Great Lakes region by early January.

▪ seasonal, breeds locally

▪ nonbreeding occurrence (can be year-round)

▪ migration

Aug. Within Great Lakes region there is a bi-modal fall passage.[3,4,5,6] The first influx peaks in Aug. and dissipates during Sept., the direction of dispersal mainly east to the Atlantic seaboard.[7] During this early peak, while numerous in Great Lakes region and Bay of Fundy, only small numbers are found farther south, and no more than casual south of Ohio R. Stronger and more widespread movement starts late Sept. in n. Great Lakes region, and early to mid-Oct. farther south. Peak movements during this second wave occur late Sept.–Oct. in n. Great Lakes region, and by late Oct.–Nov. over much of the rest of e. N. America. Main movements into Ky. and Tenn. typically start late Oct., into Fla. not usually until Nov. Rare visitor (mainly Sept.–Nov., casual at other seasons) north to Nfld., very rare to Lab. On Pacific Coast, a few early fall migrants (including juveniles) occur late July–Aug. south to cen. Calif., but main migration and arrival of wintering birds Oct.–Nov.

The bulk of the Bonaparte's Gull population spends the "winter period" (Oct.–Nov. to Feb.–Mar.) on Lake Erie, Lake Ontario, and along the Atlantic Coast from Mass. south through Mid-Atlantic states. During early winter, bulk of population is on Great Lakes, but once the lakes start to freeze birds move south and east, mostly to the coast. In mild winters, large numbers can remain in s. Great Lakes region through mid-Jan., occasionally later (and small numbers overwinter locally in some years). On Atlantic Coast, fairly common to common from Mass. to Fla. (rarely to the Keys), and along Gulf of Mex. coast to ne. Mex. Also winters locally in moderate to large numbers on large inland lakes and reservoirs in s. Great Plains and Gulf States. In winter, rare north to N.S., casual to Nfld.; rare to casual south to cen. Mex. and along coasts to Yucatán Peninsula, Belize, and cen. Panama. Uncommon to rare in winter (mainly Nov. to Feb.–Mar.) on Bermuda and locally in n. West Indies, accidental in Lesser Antilles.

In the West, fairly common to uncommon but local in winter (Oct.–Nov. to Mar.) from cen. Calif. to Pacific Coast of Baja Calif. Peninsula and Gulf of Calif., Mex.; also locally common in w. Wash. (Puget Sound), but rare in coastal Oregon and sw. B.C. Casual in winter north to se. Alaska, rare south along Pacific Coast to Colima, Mex., exceptionally to El Salvador and Costa Rica.

Spring departures from wintering areas mainly late Feb.–Apr. Northbound influxes typically start late Feb.–early Mar. on Mid-Atlantic Coast, mid-Mar. in Tenn., late Mar.

on Great Lakes, early Apr. on e. Great Plains, and mid-May in Prairie Provinces, with arrival on breeding grounds usually in late May. Peak movements in Midwest and e. Great Plains mid- to late Apr., extending to mid-May in Great Lakes region; and late Mar. to mid-Apr. in Mid-Atlantic region, late Apr. to mid-May in the Northeast. Rare after mid-Apr. in Fla., and after late Apr. on Gulf of Mexico Coast, but a few birds can linger into June. Rare after early May in Tenn. and Ky., and after late May to early June in s. Great Lakes region. Nonbreeders (mainly immatures) oversummer irregularly in Great Lakes region (where numbers vary from a few birds to hundreds) and locally in New England, with usually only a few birds elsewhere in east interior and along Atlantic Coast south of New England.

On Pacific Coast, northbound influxes start late Mar. in Oregon; late Mar. to early Apr. in coastal, mid-Apr. in interior, and early May in ne. B.C.; and late Apr. to mid-May in coastal Alaska. Peak Pacific Coast movements are Apr. to mid-May. Small to moderate numbers of oversummering birds (mainly immatures) linger in Pacific States, including interior regions, with fewer in interior west states. Casual visitor (late May to June, mid- to late Aug.) north to Bering Sea Is.

FIELD IDENTIFICATION

SIMILAR SPECIES

In N. America, Bonaparte's is a distinctive gull likely to be confused only with larger and much rarer Black-headed Gull. Attention to a few key points, such as bill size, bill color, and pattern on the underside of the primaries, should readily separate these two species. Also see first-cycle Little Gull. In S. America, where no overlap is likely, Brown-hooded, Gray-hooded, and Andean Gulls are all larger with heavier bills and different wing patterns.

BLACK-HEADED GULL (widespread but rare in N. America) is larger and bulkier with relatively broader wings; stouter, reddish to pink-based bill; appreciably longer legs; blackish wedge on underside of middle primaries; and slightly paler gray upperparts (Kodak 4–5) — so white leading wedge to upperwings slightly less contrasting. Calls of Black-headed lower pitched and less buzzy than Bonaparte's. Adult alternate Black-headed has dark brown hood (attained Feb.–Apr. in N. Atlantic, a month or so earlier than Bonaparte's) with relatively thinner white postocular crescent and dark reddish legs; adult basic has paler smoky gray hindneck wash, reddish legs. First-cycle Black-headed averages a less-distinct ulnar bar; mostly white outer primary coverts and oblique black medial stripes on outer primaries create a more striking white leading wedge.

LITTLE GULL (widespread but rare in N. America) smaller with smaller bill; relatively shorter and blunter-tipped wings lack white leading wedge. Adult slightly paler gray above (Kodak 4.5–5.5); at rest shows whitish wingtips; dark underwings striking in flight; alternate hood lacks white eye-crescents. First-cycle has black M pattern on upperwings with more contrasting white trailing edge to secondaries and inner primaries; at rest note smaller bill, shorter wing projection, and almost solidly dark tertials (broadly edged pale gray on typical Bonaparte's).

HABITAT AND BEHAVIOR

Estuaries, harbors, river mouths, inshore waters and straits, tidal rips, sewage ponds and outfalls, lakes, rivers, marshes, plowed and flooded fields, etc. Nests solitarily and in loose colonies around lakes and marshes in the boreal forest zone, with nests usually placed in conifers.[8] Often in flocks, locally up to a few thousand birds in migration and winter, feeding over tidal rips, sewage ponds, etc., when it associates readily with other gulls (especially smaller species), terns, and water birds such as loons and grebes. Flight graceful and buoyant, rather ternlike; feeds on small invertebrate prey, taken near water surface from hovering and dipping flight and while swimming or walking in shallows; also feeds in plowed and wet fields, scavenges at sewer outfalls, and hawks insects in flight.

DESCRIPTION AND MOLT

Adult Cycle. Complete PB molt (July–Oct.) produces adult basic plumage: head, neck, and underparts white, clouded smoky gray on hindneck, with dark ear-spot, two dusky bands across crown (that can be reduced by bleaching and wear), and dusky smudge around eye that offsets white postocular crescent; underparts sometimes with a pink flush. Upperparts pale gray (Kodak 5–6), wingtips black with small white tips out to P9, and often showing a white strip along bottom half of wingtip, especially when slightly spread. Uppertail coverts and tail white. IN FLIGHT: upperwing has white leading wedge with narrow black distal band on middle to outer primaries, black outer web to P10; underwings white with black trailing edge to middle and outer prima-

ries, primaries translucent when backlit. Eyes dark, bill black, often with some dull reddish basally, legs flesh pink to reddish pink. Partial PA molt (Mar.–May) produces adult alternate plumage: attains slaty blackish hood with white postocular crescent; underparts more often have pink flush. Orbital ring dark reddish, bill black, legs pinkish orange to orangered. Occasional aberrant individuals have alternate-like hoods in midwinter.

First Cycle. Juvenile (late July–Oct.): head, neck, and underparts white with crown, face, and hindcollar mottled and washed cinnamon brown, typically with a darker brown ear-spot. Back mottled cinnamon brown, with pale-edged scapulars. Upperwings pale gray with mottled brown ulnar bar, variable brownish subterminal marks, and whitish tips to other secondary coverts; tertials dark brown, edged pale gray; wingtips black with fine white primary tips (often lost by wear). IN FLIGHT: upperwings pale gray with mottled dark brown ulnar bar, blackish distal band on secondaries and primaries, white leading edge to alula and median primary coverts; dark streaks on outer primary coverts and basal outer webs of P8–P10 reduce prominence of white leading wedge, but pale gray from inner primaries continues out almost unbroken through white subterminal tongues on P8–P10. Occasional aberrant individuals have extensive dark upperwing markings so white leading wedge absent.[9,10] Underwings whitish overall with a narrow blackish trailing edge, primaries translucent when backlit. Tail white with narrow blackish subterminal band not extending to outer web of R6. Bill black, often with some dull pale flesh basally, legs pale flesh pink. Partial PF molt (late Aug.–Nov.) starts within a month of fledging, soon produces formative plumage similar to adult basic on head, neck, and back. At rest note dark brown tertial centers, brown on upperwing coverts; some birds retain residual brown mottling on lower hindneck into midwinter. Legs pale flesh pink. Partial PA1 molt (Mar.–May; can include rectrices) produces first alternate plumage: usually has partial hood of slaty blackish mottling; rarely if ever attains a complete, solid hood and some birds have basiclike head pattern. Legs pink. Some birds attain gray tertials and all-white central rectrices (rarely, whole tail[11]).

Second Cycle. Attains adultlike plumage by complete PB2 molt (mainly June–July to Aug.–Sept.), but some second-cycle birds distinguishable by blackish marks on alula, primary coverts, tertials, and tail; also average more black on inner primaries and often with black medial edging to outer webs of P8–P9, reduced white tips to outer primaries (out to P7/P8), and paler flesh pink legs (at least into early winter). Some second-alternate birds may have basiclike head patterns in summer.[12]

HYBRIDS

None reported.

NOTES

1. Braune 1987; 2. Braune 1989; 3. Brock 1997; 4. McPeek and Adams 1994; 5. Peterjohn 2001; 6. Wormington 2003; 7. Braune 1989; 8. Burger and Gochfeld 2002; 9. Grant 1986; 10. White 1999; 11. CAS specimen 17328 (14 May); 12. Howell pers. obs.

LENGTH 14.5–17 IN. (36–42.5 CM)
PHOTOS 2.0–2.13

IDENTIFICATION SUMMARY

A two- or three-cycle gull of Eurasia, rare to casual in most of N. America but locally fairly common in Atlantic Canada. Bill slender and medium length; at rest, tail tip falls between tips of P6 and P7, usually nearer P6. Adult has deep red bill and legs, bold white leading wedge on upperwings; dark brown hood in alternate plumage, dark ear-spot in basic. First cycle has dark ulnar bar and tail band. Bonaparte's Gull is the only similar American gull likely in the same areas as Black-headed: Bonaparte's is smaller with a slender black bill, translucent white underside to the primaries. In S. America, where no overlap is likely, compare with Brown-hooded, Gray-hooded, and Andean Gulls (under Rarer Species).

TAXONOMY

Two subspecies recognized[1] or species considered monotypic.[2] Nominate *ridibundus* breeds from Europe east to cen. Siberia (and presumably in ne. N. America); *sibiricus,* which averages larger, bigger billed, and has later molt timing, breeds in e. Siberia (and presumably ranges to Alaska). Brown-hooded Gull has been considered conspecific.[3]

STATUS AND DISTRIBUTION

Widespread in Eurasia. Local in e. N. America (presumably nominate *ridibundus*); migrants in Alaska (and probably those south along Pacific Coast) presumably *sibiricus*; vagrant to Hawaii.

Breeding. Breeds (May–Aug.) in N. America mainly in Nfld. (first noted nesting 1977), and probably also s. Lab.[4,5] Small numbers also breed in Gulf of St. Lawrence region, Que.; has also nested, or attempted to nest, in N.S.,[6] Me.,[7] and Mass.;[8] may have bred nw. Iowa or adjacent Minn. Its spread across the Atlantic took place during twentieth century: first bred Iceland in 1911 and has bred w. Greenland since 1960.

Nonbreeding. In Alaska, rare in spring (mainly May–June, a few into summer) in w. and cen.

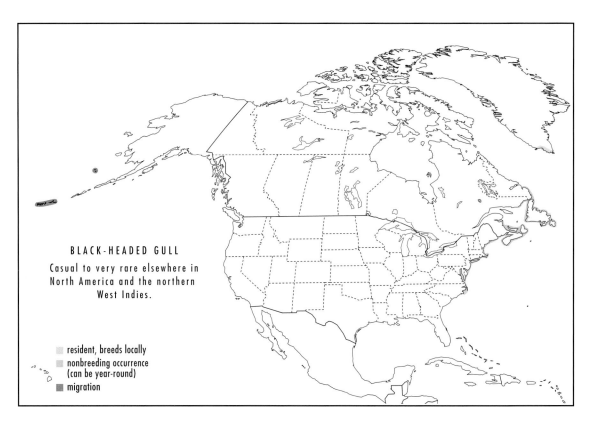

BLACK-HEADED GULL

Casual to very rare elsewhere in North America and the northern West Indies.

■ resident, breeds locally
■ nonbreeding occurrence (can be year-round)
■ migration

Aleutians and Pribilofs; very rare farther north in Bering Sea and Seward Peninsula. Casual (late Aug.–Oct.) on St. Lawrence Is., Pribilofs, Aleutians, Alaska Peninsula, and (mainly Sept.–Apr.) along Pacific Coast of N. America from s. coastal Alaska south to Calif.

Locally fairly common in winter (mainly Oct.–Apr.) in Nfld.; uncommon to rare and local along St. Lawrence Seaway and Atlantic Coast south to N.J., very rarely to N.C. Casual farther south along Atlantic Coast to Fla., uncommon in Bermuda, rare to casual (mainly Nov.–May; a few summer records) in n. and e. West Indies and south to Trinidad.[9] In the interior, casual in Great Lakes region (mainly mid-Nov.–mid-Jan., mid-Mar.–early May); casual at best in migration (mainly Sept.–Nov., mid-Mar.–mid-Apr.) west to Great Plains and south to Tenn., and casual in winter (mainly Nov./Dec.–Feb./Mar.) from Texas east through Gulf States, exceptionally south (Feb.) to s. Veracruz, Mex. Also casual (June–July) on sw. Hudson Bay.

FIELD IDENTIFICATION

SIMILAR SPECIES
In N. America, Black-headed is a reasonably distinctive gull likely to be confused only with smaller and much commoner Bonaparte's Gull. Attention to a few key points, such as bill size, bill color, and pattern on the underside of the primaries, should readily separate these two species. Similar species in S. America unlikely to overlap in range (discussed under Rarer Species).

BONAPARTE'S GULL (widespread in N. America) smaller and daintier with relatively narrower wings; a more slender black bill; appreciably shorter legs; white underwings with translucent primaries; and slightly darker gray upperparts (Kodak 5–6)—so white leading wedge to upperwings slightly more contrasting on adult. Calls of Black-headed less buzzy than Bonaparte's. Adult alternate Bonaparte's has blackish hood (attained in Apr.–May, that is, a month or so later than typical of n. Atlantic Black-headeds) with relatively bolder white postocular crescent, and orange-red legs; adult basic has darker smoky gray hindneck wash, flesh pink legs. First-cycle Bonaparte's averages a darker ulnar bar; dark streaks on outer primary coverts and basal outer webs of P8–P10 reduce prominence of white leading wedge, but pale gray from inner primaries continues out almost unbroken through white subterminal tongues on P8–P10, creating subtly different pattern from Black-headed.

RARER SPECIES
These three masked gulls of S. America are unlikely to overlap in range with Black-headed Gull.

BROWN-HOODED GULL (s. S. America) similar in size and structure to Black-headed; also shares dark brown hood in alternate plumage; upperparts average paler (Kodak 3.5–4.5). Note wingtip patterns: adult Brown-hooded has narrower black subterminal bands across middle and outer primaries (with larger white tips) so wingtips at rest look mostly white, or black with bold white tips; undersides of P9 and P10 on Brown-hooded have white restricted to distal half of P9 and P10 (rather than white extending to primary coverts, as on Black-headed). First-cycle Brown-hooded at rest typically has larger white primary tips; upperwing patterns of the two species similar (and variable) but underwing of Brown-hooded has white on outer primaries restricted to a mirror-band (versus white stripes extending to bases of primary coverts on Black-headed). Brown-hooded averages narrower black distal tail band.

GRAY-HOODED GULL (local in w. and e. S. America) averages slightly larger and broader winged with slightly longer and heavier bill. All post-juvenal plumages slightly darker gray above (Kodak 5–6), with black wingtips at rest, overall duskier underwings. Adult Gray-hooded has pale eyes, extensively black wingtips (obvious at rest and in flight); basic head pattern typically more diffuse, alternate hood pearl gray. First-cycle Gray-hooded has extensively and solidly black wingtips, typically a fainter dusky ear-spot.

ANDEAN GULL (Andes and Pacific Coast of S. America) larger and bulkier but with relatively smaller bill, slightly paler gray upperparts (Kodak 3.5–4.5). Adult upperwing has white leading wedge broken by broad black medial stripes on outer 3 primaries; underside of outer primaries black with broad white mirror-band on outer 3 primaries. Bill and legs blackish to dark red; alternate plumage has brownish black hood. First-cycle Andean has blackish bill and legs, alternate hood mottled blackish; upperwing has a larger and more solid white mirror-band (usually on outer 3 primaries) bordered basally by a broader black medial band; underside of primaries dark with white mirror-band.

HABITAT AND BEHAVIOR
Estuaries, harbors, river mouths, sewage outfalls and ponds, inshore waters, lakes, rivers, marshes, plowed and flooded fields, etc. Nests

colonially and also solitarily on open or partly vegetated ground near water, such as marshes, on islands in lakes, etc.; in N. America, usually in association with other water birds.[10] Found singly or in small groups, associating readily with other gulls (especially Bonaparte's), terns, and water birds. Feeds on small invertebrate prey, taken near water surface from hovering and dipping flight and while swimming or walking in shallows; also feeds in plowed and wet fields, scavenges at sewage outfalls, and hawks insects in flight.

DESCRIPTION AND MOLT

PB molts in w. Europe[11] average earlier than in e. Asia,[12,13] as do PA molts.[14]

Adult Cycle. Complete PB molt (late May/late July–Sept./Nov.) produces adult basic plumage: head, neck, and underparts white, clouded pale smoky gray on hindneck, with dark ear-spot, two dusky bands across crown (that can be reduced by bleaching and wear), and dusky smudge around eye that offsets white postocular crescent; underparts sometimes with a pink flush. Upperparts pale gray (Kodak 4–5), wingtips black with white tips out to P9, and often a white strip along bottom half of wingtip, especially when slightly spread. Extent of black pigmentation on outer primaries (for example, P9) decreases, on average, with age.[15] Uppertail coverts and tail white. IN FLIGHT: upperwing has white leading wedge with narrow black distal band on middle to outer primaries; from below, white leading edge contrasts with black wedge across middle primaries; wing-linings pale gray. Eyes dark, bill red with blackish tip (exceptionally, all-blackish[16]), legs red. Partial PA molt (Jan.–Apr.) produces adult alternate plumage: attains dark brown to blackish brown hood with white postocular crescent. Orbital ring dark red to purplish red, bill and legs dark red to red.

First Cycle. Juvenile (July–Sept.): head, neck, and underparts white with crown, face, and hindcollar mottled and washed cinnamon brown, typically with a darker brown ear-spot. Back mottled cinnamon brown, with pale-edged scapulars. Upperwings pale gray with mottled cinnamon brown ulnar bar, variable brownish subterminal marks and whitish tips to other secondary coverts; tertials dark brown, edged pale gray; wingtips black with fine white primary tips (often lost by wear). IN FLIGHT: upperwings pale gray with mottled brown ulnar bar; blackish distal band on secondaries and primaries; and bold white leading wedge broken by variable black medial stripes on outer primaries and forming white mirror-band on outer 2 primaries. Underside of primaries dark overall with less-extensive white leading wedge than on adult, and middle primaries slightly paler than on adult; wing-linings whitish. Tail white with narrow blackish subterminal band not extending to outer web of R6. Bill and legs flesh, bill tipped black. Partial PF molt (Aug.–Oct., sometimes includes upperwing coverts) starts within a month of fledging, soon produces formative plumage similar to adult basic on head, neck, and back, but hindneck clouding may average darker. At rest note dark brown tertial centers, brown on upperwing coverts. Bill and legs flesh to pinkish orange, bill tipped black. Partial PA1 molt (Feb.–Apr./May; can include rectrices) produces first alternate plumage: usually attains partial hood of brown mottling and speckling, but some birds have basiclike head pattern and others develop full, adult-like alternate hood. Some birds attain gray tertials and all-white central rectrices (rarely, whole tail[17]). Bill ranges from orange with black tip to overall dark red; legs dull dusky flesh to dark reddish.

Second Cycle. Attains adultlike plumage by complete PB2 molt (mid-May/mid-July–Aug./Sept.) but some second-cycle birds distinguishable by blackish marks on alula, primary coverts, and tertials; also average more black on inner primaries and more often show fine black medial edging to outer webs of P8–P9 and average paler, more orange-red legs.[18] Some second-alternate birds may have basiclike head patterns in summer.[19]

HYBRIDS

Presumed with Ring-billed Gull[20] and Laughing Gull[21] in N. America. Presumed with Common Gull[22,23] and Mediterranean Gull (*L. melanocephalus*)[24] in Europe.

NOTES

1. AOU 1957; 2. Vaurie 1965; 3. Hellmayr 1932; 4. Finch 1978; 5. Montevecchi et al. 1987; 6. Lock 1981; 7. Drennan et al. 1987; 8. Holt et al. 1986; 9. ffrench and White 1999; 10. Montevecchi et al. 1987; 11. Walters 1978; 12. AMNH specimens; 13. BM specimens; 14. M. T. Elliott pers. comm.; 15. Allaine and Lebreton 1990; 16. Larkin 1999; 17. Grant 1986; 18. M. T. Elliott pers. comm.; 19. Howell pers. obs.; 20. Weseloh and Mineau 1986; 21. Sibley 1994; 22. Balten et al. 1993; 23. Moskoff and Bevier 2002; 24. Langman 2000

LENGTH 15.3–17.7 IN. (39–45 CM)
PHOTOS 3.0–3.12

IDENTIFICATION SUMMARY

A medium-sized, two- or three-cycle gull resident locally on both coasts of S. America. Bill fairly long and slender, wings relatively broad; at rest, tail tip falls between tips of P6 and P7, usually nearer P6. Adult has deep red bill and legs, pale eyes, bold white leading wedge inside large black wingtip with white mirror-band on outer 2 primaries; dusky underwings

GRAY-HOODED GULL

resident, breeds locally
nonbreeding occurrence
(can be year-round)

with white mirror-band on outer 2 primaries; pearl gray hood in alternate plumage, dusky ear-spot in basic. First cycle has dark ulnar bar and tail band. Andean Gull (Pacific Coast in Peru and Chile) larger and bulkier with relatively smaller bill, paler upperparts, and pale wing-linings; alternate hood blackish. Brown-hooded Gull (overlaps in e. S. America) slightly smaller and narrower winged with paler upperparts, pale wing-linings; alternate hood dark brown. See Similar Species section for details to separate immatures; and see Black-headed Gull of N. America (unlikely to overlap in range).

TAXONOMY

Nominate New World subspecies averages slightly larger, paler dorsally, and with fainter basic head markings and average larger white mirror-band than *poiocephalus* of Africa.[1] Also known as Gray-headed Gull.[2]

STATUS AND DISTRIBUTION

Local in S. America and Africa.

Uncommon to fairly common but local breeding resident (mainly Apr.–Sept.) along Pacific Coast of S. America and locally up to 40 km inland,[3] from s. Ecuador (2° south) to s. Peru (17° south),[4,5] ranging north rarely to n. Ecuador (1° north) and south rarely (mainly May–Oct.) to n. Chile (18° south);[6,7,8] also a report from Panama. Accidental in Galápagos Is. (Aug. 1978).[9]

Uncommon to fairly common but local breeding resident (Sept.–Apr., less common in winter) in e. Argentina (s. Santiago del Estero south to Buenos Aires).[10] Ranges north in winter (mainly May–Oct.; locally to 1,000 m in Andean foothills)[11] to nw. Argentina, Uruguay, and s. Brazil (22°S),[12] casually to Paraguay. Accidental visitor to Falkland Is. (Mar. 1992)[13] and (geographic origin uncertain) in Fla. (Dec. 1998).[14]

FIELD IDENTIFICATION

SIMILAR SPECIES

Distinctive in most of Pacific Coast range (but compare with Andean Gull); in e. S. America occurs commonly alongside Brown-hooded Gull. Also see Black-headed Gull of N. America (unlikely to overlap in range).

BROWN-HOODED GULL (s. S. America) averages slightly smaller and narrower winged with slightly smaller bill; all ages dark eyed. Juvenile averages paler and often less-extensive brown markings on head and upperparts. All post-juvenal plumages slightly paler gray

above (Kodak 3.5–4.5) than Gray-hooded (noticeable in direct comparison) with whitish to pale gray underwing coverts. Adult Brown-hooded (nominate *maculipennis*) has bolder white primary tips at rest (obvious in fresh plumage), bolder white leading wedge on upperwing with narrow black subterminal band on outer primaries, darker ear-spot in basic, and dark brown hood in alternate. First-cycle Brown-hooded has distinct white primary tips on closed wingtip, variable white mirror-band or tongue-streaks in smaller black wingtip area, and typically a darker ear-spot.

ANDEAN GULL (Andes and Pacific Coast of S. America) larger and bulkier with relatively smaller bill; all ages dark eyed. Juvenile averages paler and less-extensive brown markings on head and upperparts. All post-juvenal plumages slightly paler gray above (Kodak 3.5–4.5), with broader white mirror-band across outer 3 primaries in blackish underwingtip, whitish underwing coverts. Adult Andean has blackish to dark red bill and legs; also told readily by upperwing pattern: extensive white leading wedge and wingtip with black medial stripes on outer primaries; alternate hood blackish. First-cycle Andean has blackish bill and legs, broader pale tertial edgings, and wingtip pattern similar to adult (and thus unlike Gray-hooded).

HABITAT AND BEHAVIOR

Breeds in small colonies on islands and dikes in freshwater and saline lagoons. Pacific population mostly coastal, found singly or in small groups at coastal lagoons, fishing harbors, river mouths, and sandy beaches. Atlantic population occurs along coasts but also ranges along rivers to inland lakes, marshes, and rubbish dumps. Associates readily with other gulls including Brown-hooded, which it tends to dominate at dumps in Argentina.[15] Feeds on small invertebrate prey, taken near water surface while swimming or walking in shallows, by dunking head under with wings held raised; also scavenges at dumps and harbors and picks food from surface in dipping flight.

DESCRIPTION AND MOLT

Adult Cycle. Complete PB molt (mainly July–Jan. in the West, Dec.–Mar. in the East) produces adult basic plumage: head, neck, and underparts white with typically faint dusky smudging on head, strongest around eye and in band across nape between dusky ear-spots; hindneck and neck sides cloudy pale gray (rarely noticeable in bright sunlight), separated from hood area by white nape band. Upperparts pale gray (Kodak 5–6), wingtips black with fine white tips to primaries (underside of closed wingtip black with white mirror-band). Uppertail coverts and tail white. IN FLIGHT: note diagnostic wing pattern: upperwings gray with bold white leading wedge inside black wingtip, white mirror-band on outer 2 primaries. Underwings dark overall: smoky gray underwings blend into blackish wingtip with white mirror-band on outer 2 primaries. Eyes pale lemon with dark red orbital ring, bill and legs reddish. Partial PA molt (mainly Jan.–Mar. in the West, June–Aug. in the East) produces adult alternate plumage: attains pearl gray hood (darkest at rear and bleaching to whitish on forehead and throat) with narrow white postocular crescent; white primary tips often wear off. Bare parts brighter red.

First Cycle. Juvenile (mainly June–Nov. in the West, Jan.–Mar. in the East): head, neck, and underparts white with crown, face, and hind-collar mottled and washed cinnamon brown to brown. Back mottled cinnamon brown to brown, with pale-edged scapulars. Upperwings gray with mottled cinnamon brown ulnar bar, variable brownish subterminal marks and whitish tips to other coverts; tertials dark brown, narrowly edged pale grayish; wingtips black with small whitish primary tips. IN FLIGHT: wing pattern suggests adult with more black and less white: upperwings gray with mottled cinnamon brown ulnar bar, blackish distal band on secondaries and inner primaries runs into extensive blackish wingtip; white leading wedge inside blackish wingtip often broken by 2 narrow dark bars (primary coverts range from mostly white to mostly blackish). Pale gray wing-linings merge into blackish remiges. Tail white with narrow black subterminal band (at times reduced to black spots) not extending to outer web of R6. Eyes dark, bill and legs dull pinkish, bill tipped black. Partial PF molt (timing varies) starts within a month of fledging, soon produces formative plumage similar to adult basic but ear-spot and head markings can be darker (especially on Argentine birds). At rest note all-black underside to wingtips, dark brown tertials, and brown on upperwing coverts. Bill and legs pinkish flesh to orange-flesh, bill tipped black. Partial PA1 molt (timing varies) often extensive (can include some, possibly all, rectrices), produces first alternate plumage: head varies from dirty whitish with variable dusky clouding to having a solid gray hood, like adult. Some birds attain white central rectrices and gray tertials. Eyes dark, bill and legs pinkish red, bill tipped black.

Second Cycle. Attains adultlike plumage by complete PB2 molt (timing varies), but some presumed second-cycle birds distinguishable by 1–2 tertials and some secondaries with brownish basal smudges; may average more black and less white in wingtips. Eyes often dark and bill averages duller reddish to pinkish red, tipped black.

HYBRIDS
Probably with Hartlaub's Gull (*L. hartlaubii*) in S. Africa.[16]

NOTES
1. Dwight 1925; 2. Grant 1986; 3. Schulenberg and Parker 1981; 4. Duffy et al. 1984; 5. Hughes 1970; 6. Howell pers. obs.; 7. B. Knapton pers. comm.; 8. Peredo and Amado 1995; 9. Jones 2000; 10. M. Pearman unpubl. data; 11. Ibid.; 12. Belton 1984; 13. Curtis 1994; 14. McNair 1999; 15. Howell pers. obs.; 16. Williams 1989

LENGTH 14–16 IN. (35.5–40.5 CM)
PHOTOS 4.0–4.21

IDENTIFICATION SUMMARY

This two- to three-cycle gull is widespread in s. S. America, especially along and near coasts. Bill slender and medium length; at rest, tail tip falls between tips of P6 and P7, usually nearer P6. Adult has deep red bill and legs, bold white leading wedge on upperwings; dark brown hood in alternate plumage, dark ear-spot in basic. First cycle has dark ulnar

BROWN-HOODED GULL

a. *L. m. glaucodes*
b. *L. m. maculipennis*

b.

?

?

a.

a.

resident, breeds locally
nonbreeding occurrence
(can be year-round)
? possible nonbreeding range

bar and tail band. Andean Gull (locally sympatric in central Chile) larger and bulkier with relatively smaller bill; alternate hood blackish. Gray-hooded Gull (overlaps in e. S. America) slightly larger and broader winged with darker upperparts, smoky gray wing-linings; alternate hood gray. See Similar Species section for details to separate immatures. Black-headed Gull of N. America does not overlap in range.

TAXONOMY

Two subspecies: nominate *maculipennis*, breeding in e. S. America from s. Brazil to n. Argentina, and *glaucodes*, breeding from s. Argentina and the Falklands up the Pacific Coast to cen. Chile. Breeding distributions and potential contact zone of the two taxa in e. Argentina not well known,[1] confounded by similarity in plumage of second-cycle *glaucodes* and adult *maculipennis*. Although Dwight[2] considered these subspecies invalid (the differences purportedly due to age), large series of specimens[3] consistently show extensive black in the wingtips of both adult and first-cycle *maculipennis* unlike the more white-winged adult and first-cycle *glaucodes*, and species status has even been suggested for these two taxa.[4] Brown-hooded has also been considered conspecific with Black-headed Gull.[5]

STATUS AND DISTRIBUTION

Endemic to s. S. America.

L. m. glaucodes. Fairly common to common but local breeder (mainly Nov.–Mar.) and mostly resident (SL-500 m, locally to 800 m and wandering higher) from Falklands and Tierra del Fuego north to cen. Chile (Valdivia), thence fairly common to uncommon and local (mainly near coast) north to Valparaíso, Chile; northern limit of occurrence along east coast of Argentina around Valdés Peninsula.[6,7] Some winter withdrawal (Mar.–Sept.) from southern areas, such as Tierra del Fuego, when more widespread and numerous in cen. Chile; probably occurs northward in Argentina. Ranges north rarely (mainly May–Aug.) at least to Coquimbo, Chile (30° south),[8] accidental in n. Chile (18° south)[9] and probably s. Peru (Sept.–Nov. 2002).[10] Other reports on n. coast of Chile[11] require confirmation; most are likely in error and reflect confusion with Andean or Gray-hooded Gulls. Murphy[12] mentioned sight reports north to Peru but considered them unsatisfactory; unrecorded for Peru by Parker et al.[13] A recent report[14] has since been withdrawn by the observer.[15] A report from South Georgia has been ques-

tioned.[16] A report of *glaucodes* from se. Brazil[17,18] pertains to a nominate *maculipennis* with extensive white on P10 (but typical patterning on P6–P9).[19]

L. m. maculipennis. Fairly common to common but local breeder (mainly Sept.–Feb.) and mostly resident on Atlantic Slope from Rio Grande do Sul, Brazil, south to Buenos Aires, Argentina; southern limit of regular occurrence (Nov.–Jan.) on e. coast of Argentina appears to be Chubut, with one specimen reported from Tierra del Fuego.[20] More widespread in winter when it ranges north rarely (mainly May–Aug.; but no recent records from Brazil[21]) to e. Brazil (casually to 10° south),[22] casually to se. Paraguay.

FIELD IDENTIFICATION

SIMILAR SPECIES

Distinctive in most of its range but locally sympatric with Andean Gull in cen. Chile, and in e. S. America occurs commonly alongside Gray-hooded Gull. Black-headed Gull of N. America does not overlap in range.

ANDEAN GULL (Andes and Pacific Coast of S. America) larger and bulkier with relatively smaller and dark bill. Adult has black wingtips at rest with small white primary tips; in flight, upperwing has extensive white leading wedge with black medial stripes on outer 3 primaries. Adult basic has blackish to dark red bill and legs, smaller dark ear-spot than Brown-hooded; adult alternate has brownish black hood, typically darker red bill and legs than Brown-hooded. First-cycle Andean has blackish bill and legs, alternate hood mottled blackish; note overall size and structure. Wing patterns similar and perhaps not always distinguishable: Andean averages broader black medial and subterminal bands, larger white mirror-band usually on outer 3 primaries; often lacks white tips to outer primaries.

GRAY-HOODED GULL (local in w. and e. S. America) averages slightly larger and broader winged, with slightly longer and heavier bill. Juvenile Gray-hooded averages darker and more-extensive brown markings on head and upperparts. All post-juvenal plumages slightly darker gray above (Kodak 5–6; noticeable in direct comparison) with black wingtips at rest, overall duskier underwings. Adult Gray-hooded has pale eyes, extensively black wingtips (obvious at rest and in flight); basic head markings weaker and more diffuse, alternate hood pearl gray. First-cycle Gray-hooded has small, dull whitish primary tips on closed wingtips, extensively black wingtip lacks white mirror-band, and typically fainter dusky head markings.

HABITAT AND BEHAVIOR

Estuaries, sandy and stony intertidal, inshore waters, lakes, rivers, marshes, plowed and flooded fields, sewage outfalls, etc. Nests colonially and also solitarily in marshes and around lakes, on raised ground or in reed beds; locally in association with other water birds. Found singly or more often in groups, locally in flocks of up to a few thousand birds, associating readily with other gulls, terns, and water birds. Feeds on small invertebrate prey, taken near water surface from hovering and dipping flight and while swimming or walking in shallows; also feeds in plowed and wet fields, scavenges at sewage outfalls, and hawks insects in flight.

DESCRIPTION AND MOLT

L. m. glaucodes (Tierra del Fuego and Falklands north to cen. Chile and s. Argentina).

Adult Cycle. Complete PB molt (mainly Dec./ Jan.–Mar./Apr.) produces adult basic plumage: head, neck, and underparts white with small dark ear-spot; often has dusky smudges in front of eye and across crown that offset white postocular crescent; underparts sometimes with a pink flush. Upperparts pale gray (Kodak 3.5–4.5), wingtips white with 3 to 4 black notches along top of closed primaries (underside of closed wingtip white). Uppertail coverts and tail white. IN FLIGHT: note diagnostic upperwing pattern: white leading wedge with variable black subterminal marks on middle primaries; from below, white wingtip contrasts with black wedge across bases of outer primaries; shadowed underwing often looks dusky with bold white tip; wing-linings pale gray. Eyes dark; orbital ring, bill, and legs red to dark red, bill possibly with darker tip on some birds. Partial PA molt (mainly July–Sept.) produces adult alternate plumage: attains dark brown to blackish brown hood with white postocular crescent; underparts more often have pink flush. Bare parts brighter red, bill lacks black tip.

First Cycle. Juvenile (mainly Jan.–Mar.): head, neck, and underparts white, with crown, face, and hindcollar mottled and washed cinnamon brown, typically with a darker brown ear-spot. Back mottled cinnamon brown, with pale-edged scapulars. Upperwings pale gray with mottled cinnamon brown ulnar bar, and variable brownish subterminal marks and whitish tips to other coverts; tertials dark brown, edged pale grayish; wingtips black

with distinct white primary tips. IN FLIGHT: upperwings pale gray with mottled cinnamon brown ulnar bar, blackish distal band on secondaries and primaries, and bold white leading wedge broken by variable oblique black band across outer primaries that isolates white mirror-band on outer 1–3 primaries. Underside of wingtip dark overall with white mirror-band on outer 1–3 primaries; wing-linings whitish. Tail white with narrow and often incomplete blackish subterminal band not extending to outer web of R6 (rarely, tail can be all white[23]). Bill and legs pinkish, bill tipped black. Partial PF molt (mainly Jan.–May) starts within a month of fledging, soon produces formative plumage similar to adult basic. At rest note black wingtips with white primary tips, dark brown tertial centers, and brown on upperwing coverts. Bill and legs pinkish to red, bill tipped black. Partial PA1 molt (mainly Aug.–Oct.) produces first alternate plumage: usually attains partial hood of brown mottling and speckling, but some birds have basiclike head pattern and others develop solid dark brown hood. Some birds attain gray tertials. Bill usually becomes red, tipped black; legs red.

Second Cycle. Attains adultlike plumage by complete PB2 molt (mainly Oct.–Feb.), but many second-cycle birds have extensive subterminal black on middle and outer primaries (forming black-and-white banded wingtip at rest), and some have black medial stripes on outer primaries and black bill tip (bill probably becomes all red in second summer).

L. m. maculipennis (n. Argentina north to s. Brazil).

Resembles *glaucodes* but with more-extensive black on primaries, and molts average a month or so earlier (reflecting more northerly distribution and earlier breeding season).

Adult Cycle. Wingtip typically has fairly broad, complete black subterminal bands on P6–P9 and a broken to complete subterminal black band on P10 (up to 10 percent of birds lack subterminal black on P10[24,25]). At rest, closed wingtips range from black with small white tips (that can be lost by wear) to boldly banded black-and-white.

First Cycle. Outer primaries average more-extensive black than *glaucodes,* with small white tips often lost through wear; P8–P10 typically mostly black with reduced whitish subterminal streaks only on P9–P10, primary coverts can be mostly blackish, tipped white (mostly white on typical *glaucodes*); subterminal blackish tail band averages wider.

Second Cycle. May average broader black subterminal bands and smaller white tips on middle and outer primaries than adult, but confirmation needed from known-age birds.

HYBRIDS

None reported.

NOTES

1. M. Pearman pers. comm.; 2. Dwight 1925; 3. AMNH and BM specimens; 4. Belton 1984; 5. Hellmayr 1932; 6. Howell pers. obs.; 7. M. Pearman pers. comm.; 8. Howell pers. obs.; 9. A. Jaramillo photo (1st cycle bird at Arica, Tarapacá, 10 May 1986); 10. T. Schulenberg pers. comm.; 11. Johnson 1972; 12. Murphy 1936; 13. Parker et al. 1982; 14. Clements and Shany 2001; 15. T. Schulenberg pers. comm.; 16. Prince and Croxall 1996; 17. AMNH 321229bis (July); 18. Belton 1984; 19. Howell pers. obs.; 20. M. Pearman pers. comm.; 21. J. F. Pacheco pers. comm.; 22. Murphy 1936; 23. Howell pers. obs.; 24. AMNH and BM specimens; 25. Howell pers. obs.

LENGTH 16.5–19 IN. (42–48 CM)
PHOTOS 5.0–5.13

IDENTIFICATION SUMMARY
This medium-sized, two-cycle gull nests at Andean lakes from s. Colombia to cen. Chile; nonbreeders range to the Pacific Coast. Large and heavy bodied for a masked gull but with relatively small bill; at rest, tail tip falls between tips of P6 and P7, usually nearer P6. Adult has dark red to blackish bill and legs, broad white mirror-band across outer 3 pri-

ANDEAN GULL

▨ resident, breeds locally
▨ seasonal, breeds locally
▨ nonbreeding occurrence
(can be year-round)

maries; brownish black hood in alternate plumage, dark ear-spot in basic. First cycle has dark ulnar bar and tail band. Brown-hooded Gull (locally sympatric in cen. Chile) smaller and slimmer with relatively larger bill; alternate hood dark brown. Gray-hooded Gull (locally sympatric on Pacific Coast) slightly smaller and slimmer with darker upperparts, smoky gray wing-linings; alternate hood gray. See Similar Species section for details to separate immatures. Black-headed Gull of N. America does not overlap in range.

TAXONOMY
Monotypic.

STATUS AND DISTRIBUTION
Endemic to w. S. America.

Generally a fairly common to common but somewhat local resident (breeding mainly May–Sept./Nov. south to n. Chile, Sept./Nov.–Jan. in cen. and s. Chile) in puna zone of Andes (mainly 3,000–4,600 m) from cen. Peru and w. Bolivia south to nw. Argentina and n. Chile; uncommon to locally fairly common in Andean páramo zone from n. Peru north to s. Colombia (1° north),[1] and south in Andes (down to 1,200 m or lower in the south) to n. Aísen, Chile (44°30′ south). Some birds resident in most of breeding range, but also an uncommon to locally fairly common migrant (mainly Apr.–Oct.) to coasts of Peru[2,3] and n. Chile,[4,5] uncommon to rare along Chilean coast south at least to Santiago (33°30′ south).[6] Casual visitor to Amazonian Ecuador.

FIELD IDENTIFICATION

SIMILAR SPECIES
Distinctive in most of its range, but locally sympatric with Brown-hooded Gull in cen. Chile and with Gray-hooded Gull on Pacific Coast of Peru and n. Chile. Also see Black-headed Gull of N. America (unlikely to overlap in range).

BROWN-HOODED GULL (s. S. America) markedly smaller and less bulky, only two-thirds the size of Andean but with relatively larger and longer bill. Adult and second-cycle Brown-hooded (glaucodes) told readily by wingtip pattern: bold white leading wedge extends to wingtips (wingtips at rest mostly white or banded black-and-white) versus black-edged white mirror-band of Andean (wingtips at rest mostly black, narrowly tipped white); bill and legs red, alternate hood brown. First-cycle Brown-

hooded has bill and legs pinkish to red with bill tipped black, alternate hood mottled brown; note overall size and structure. Wing patterns similar and perhaps not always distinguishable: Andean averages broader black medial and subterminal bands, larger white mirror-band usually on outer 3 primaries; often lacks white tips to outer primaries.

GRAY-HOODED GULL (local in w. and e. S. America) smaller and less bulky, about two-thirds the size of Andean but with relatively larger and longer bill. Juvenile Gray-hooded averages darker and more-extensive brown markings on head and upperparts. All post-juvenal plumages slightly darker gray above (Kodak 5–6) with overall dusky underwings. Adult Gray-hooded has pale eyes, red bill and legs; also told readily by wingtip pattern: white leading wedge inside black wingtip with white mirror-band on outer 2 primaries; alternate hood pearl gray. First-cycle Gray-hooded has pinkish bill (tipped black) and legs, narrow pale tertial edgings; extensively black wingtip lacks white mirror-band.

HABITAT AND BEHAVIOR
Breeds in colonies and scattered pairs at lakes and bogs from páramo and barren puna to austral forest zone, feeding at lakes, bogs, and nearby farmland. Nonbreeding birds range to river mouths and sandy beaches along the Pacific Coast, feeding in plowed and grassy fields, marshes. Associates readily with other water birds; coastal migrants occur singly or in groups up to 50 or more birds that tend to stay together within larger aggregations of Gray Gulls and other gulls. Feeds on insects and other small invertebrates picked from near water surface or ground, both from flight and while walking or swimming; also preys upon eggs and small young of other water birds[7] and scavenges scraps around ski resorts in winter.

DESCRIPTION AND MOLT
Adult Cycle. Complete PB molt (mainly July–Oct. in the north, Jan.–Apr. in the south) produces adult basic plumage: head, neck, and underparts white with small black ear-spot; black smudge in front of eye often offsets white postocular crescent. Upperparts pale gray (Kodak 3.5–4.5); at rest, wingtips black with 3 to 4 small white tips and white subterminal stripe visible along bottom edge of closed primaries (showing as large white mirror on underside of closed wingtip). Uppertail coverts and tail white. IN FLIGHT: note diagnostic upperwing pattern: extensive white leading

wedge and wingtip with black tips to middle and outer primaries, black medial stripes on outer 3 primaries; from below, wingtip blackish with solid, broad white mirror-band on outer 3 primaries, becoming white tongues on middle primaries. Eyes dark, bill and legs black or with dark red to purplish hue. Partial PA molt (mainly Jan.–Mar. in the north, July–Sept. in the south) produces adult alternate plumage: attains brownish black hood with white postocular crescent; underparts sometimes with a pink flush. Bill and legs dark red; orbital ring dark red and inconspicuous.

First Cycle. Juvenile (mainly Sept.–Feb.): head, neck, and underparts white, with crown, face, and hindcollar mottled and washed cinnamon brown to brown, typically with a darker ear-spot. Back mottled cinnamon brown, with pale-edged scapulars. Upperwings pale gray with mottled cinnamon brown ulnar bar, variable brownish subterminal marks and whitish tips to other coverts; tertials dark brown, broadly edged pale gray; wingtips black with white primary tips. IN FLIGHT: upperwings pale gray with mottled brown ulnar bar, blackish distal band on secondaries and primaries, and bold white leading wedge broken by oblique black medial band across outer primaries, isolating white mirror-band on outer 3 primaries. Underside of wingtip dark overall with white mirror-band on outer 3 primaries. Tail white with narrow black subterminal band (at times reduced to black spots) not extending to outer web of R6. Bill and legs blackish. PF molt (mainly Oct.–May) starts within a month of fledging, soon produces formative plumage similar to adult basic on head, neck, and back. At rest note blackish wingtips (usually lacking white tips), dark-centered tertials, and brown on upperwing coverts. Partial PA1 molt (mainly Mar.–Oct.) produces first alternate plumage: typically attains partial hood of blackish mottling and speckling, but some may have basiclike head pattern; some birds attain white central rectrices and gray tertials. Black bill can become tinged reddish. Apparently attains adult plumage by complete PB2 molt (mainly July–Mar.), although outer primaries may average more black, less white, than adult, and some possible second-cycle birds have black shaft streaks on outer primary coverts. The so-called second-summer plumage of Fjeldsa and Krabbe[8] refers to first alternate.

HYBRIDS
None reported.

NOTES
1. Strewe 2000; 2. Hughes 1970; 3. Pearson and Plenge 1974; 4. Howell pers. obs.; 5. Johnson 1967; 6. Howell pers. obs.; 7. Johnson 1967; 8. Fjeldsa and Krabbe 1990

SMALL GULLS
(SUBGENUS *Hydrocoloeus*)

This subgroup consists of two distinctive species: Little Gull and Ross's Gull, the latter usually separated in the monotypic genus *Rhodostethia*. Chu (1998) noted that both species could be placed in the genus *Hydrocoloeus*. These are the smallest gulls, with small heads and small slender black bills; adults have red legs. In alternate plumage, Little has a blackish hood, lacking white eye-crescents, whereas Ross's has only a blackish neck ring.

The adult wings have a white trailing edge and are overall pale gray above, smoky gray below. Adult plumage is attained in the second or third cycle. Juvenal plumage features a dark cap, dark hindcollar, and prominent dark M pattern on the upperwings. Preformative molts produce an adultlike pale gray back; first prealternate molts can produce a fairly extensive (rarely complete) dark hood on Little Gull and a dark collar on Ross's Gull.

ADULT BREEDING LITTLE GULL. PP. 68, 320

ADULT BREEDING ROSS'S GULL. PP. 71, 323

LENGTH 10.2–11.5 IN. (26–29 CM)
PHOTOS 6.0–6.15

IDENTIFICATION SUMMARY

This diminutive, two- or three-cycle gull is the smallest gull in the world. It occurs mainly in Eurasia but is a rare and local breeder in ne. N. America and rare to casual elsewhere in the Americas. Bill slender and pointed; at rest, tail tip falls between tips of P6 and P7. Adult has black bill, reddish legs, pale gray upperwings, and sooty gray underwings; blackish hood in alternate plumage, dark cap and earspot in basic. First cycle has blackish M pattern on upperwings. Very small size eliminates most other gulls. Bonaparte's (with which Little is often seen) is larger, with longer and more pointed wings and white leading wedge to outer wing; nonbreeding plumages lack dark cap. Also see Ross's Gull and first-cycle Black-legged Kittiwake.

TAXONOMY

Monotypic. Crochet et al.[1] recommended revalidating the genus *Hydrocoloeus* for Little Gull. Chu[2] noted that including both Little and Ross's Gulls in *Hydrocoloeus* would reflect their phylogeny.

STATUS AND DISTRIBUTION

Local in Eurasia and e. N. America.

Breeding. Breeds or has bred (May–Aug.) in Great Lakes region and vicinity of Hudson/James Bay. First detected nesting 1962 in Oshawa area bordering Lake Ontario, Ont.[3] Since then has nested locally elsewhere in Great Lakes region in s. Que., s. Ont., n. Mich., e. Wisc., and sw. Minn.; also in n. Man. (Hudson Bay). Nesting not confirmed in N. America since 1989, and appears to have declined as a breeding species in Great Lakes region. But numbers of migrants and winter visitors in some parts of e. N. America have declined only slightly from peak counts in 1970s, indicating that Little Gulls still breed in N. America, perhaps in lowlands of Hudson/James Bay region, where coverage is poor.[4]

Nonbreeding. Migrates (mainly Aug.–Nov., Mar.–May) primarily in Great Lakes region,

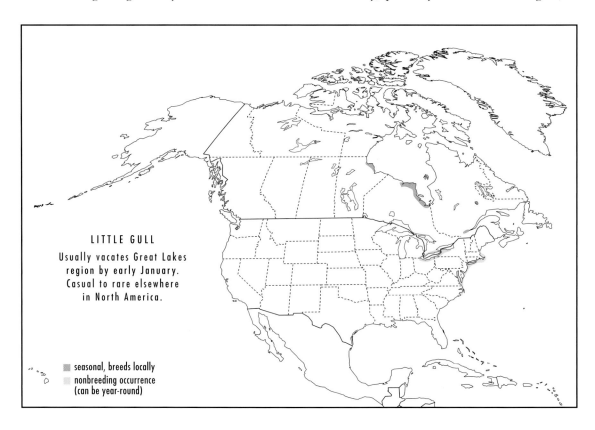

LITTLE GULL
Usually vacates Great Lakes region by early January. Casual to rare elsewhere in North America.

■ seasonal, breeds locally
▫ nonbreeding occurrence (can be year-round)

where a bimodal peak occurs in fall: a small movement late July–early Sept. and a marked peak late Oct.–early Dec.,[5] when seasonal totals locally have surpassed 100 individuals, for example, on n. shore of Lake Erie (Long Point)[6] and Lake Ontario (especially Rochester, N.Y.).[7] Usually departs this region during Dec.–early Jan., although a few can remain later, especially in warmer winters. Rare migrant in New England (mainly Aug.–Nov., Mar.–May) and on Mid-Atlantic Coast (mainly Nov.–Dec., late Feb.–May); very rare north (mainly June–Nov.) to s. N.B. and N.S., casual north (mainly July–Aug.) to Nfld. Casual during migration periods north to Greenland (late Apr.–mid-June), in Midwest away from Great Lakes region, and (mainly late Aug.–early Nov., Apr.–June) on Great Plains, north and west through Prairie Provinces. In the Northwest and Calif., casual during migration (mainly late July–Nov., Mar.–June) with a few records (mainly late Apr.–June) north to s. coastal Alaska and s. Yukon.

Winters (mid-Nov./Dec.–Mar./Apr.) primarily on Mid-Atlantic Coast; movements closely follow those of Bonaparte's Gull, with which Little Gulls usually associate. In mild winters some birds linger on e. Great Lakes, but in most years they eventually move to the coast; generally rare to locally uncommon over this region. Casual to very rare in winter north along coast to Mass. and exceptionally N.B.; in the Southeast (on coast and large inland reservoirs, west to Tex.); and in the West (mainly w. Wash. and Calif.). Accidental in Bermuda (late Nov.–mid-Mar.), s. Veracruz, Mex. (Jan.–Feb.), and on Pacific Coast of Colombia (Jan.–Feb.).[8]

FIELD IDENTIFICATION

SIMILAR SPECIES

In N. America, Little Gull is distinctive by virtue of its small size, although it might be confused with much commoner Bonaparte's Gull, with Ross's Gull (a high Arctic species), and perhaps with much larger first-cycle Black-legged Kittiwake. Chippering and fairly quiet single-note *kek* calls of Little are quite distinct from raspy calls of Bonaparte's Gull.

BONAPARTE'S GULL (widespread in N. America) slightly larger and longer billed, with relatively longer and more-pointed wings. Adult slightly darker gray above (Kodak 5–6), at rest on the water shows mostly black wingtips, underwings bright whitish; alternate hood has white postocular crescent. First cycle lacks dark cap (after juvenal plumage) and has browner and less contrasting dark ulnar bar, broader pale gray tertial edgings, upperwings lack bold black **M** pattern but have white leading wedge and bolder black trailing edge.

ROSS'S GULL (rare in Arctic regions) similar in most plumages but has shorter and blunter-tipped bill, longer and more-pointed wings, long and graduated tail; some plumages strongly flushed pink on head and underparts. Adult has broader white trailing edge to upperwing extending only to inner primaries, lacks dark hood (alternate plumage has narrow black neck ring, basic lacks dark cap). First cycle has brighter white trailing triangle on upperwing; grayer underwing coverts highlight white trailing edge, black tail tip often most prominent on elongated central rectrices.

BLACK-LEGGED KITTIWAKE (mainly northern oceans) much larger with longer, more pointed, and relatively narrower wings, stouter and longer bill (developing pale base by midwinter), and relatively shorter, dark legs. Juvenile from first-cycle Little Gull by extensive, bright whitish trailing triangle to upperwings, black hindcollar (often retained through winter, but note that traces of Little's dark juvenal hindcollar can form a similar pattern through early winter), and lack of dark cap.

HABITAT AND BEHAVIOR

Lakes, river mouths, sewage ponds and outfalls, estuaries, tidal rips, inshore waters, rivers, etc. Nests solitarily or in small groups, in marshes and around lakes, at times in association with other water birds. In N. America, mainly found singly or in small groups, most often in association with flocks of Bonaparte's Gulls. Flight fluttery and ternlike, dipping down to pick from the water surface, at times pattering its feet on the surface and hanging into the wind, recalling a storm-petrel; also feeds by picking while walking and swimming and by flycatching in flight.

DESCRIPTION AND MOLT

Adult Cycle. Complete PB molt (July–Oct./Nov.) produces adult basic plumage: head, neck, and underparts white with dark cap and ear-spot; often has dusky smudges around eyes; underparts sometimes with a pink flush. Upperparts pale gray (Kodak 4.5–5.5), extending as a partial collar onto sides of chest; broad white primary tips create mostly whitish primary projection; uppertail coverts and tail white. IN FLIGHT: upperwings pale gray with white trailing edge slightly broader on outer primaries; underwings sooty gray with paler lesser coverts (underwings often appear blackish when shadowed), white trailing edge and tips. Eyes dark, bill blackish, legs reddish to dull flesh. Partial PA molt (Mar.–May) produces adult alternate plumage: attains blackish hood (lacking white eye-crescents), underparts more often flushed pink. Orbital ring dark, bill black or with dull brown to red hue, legs red to orange-red.

First Cycle. Juvenile (late July–Nov.): head, neck, and underparts white with blackish brown cap, ear-spot, eye smudges, and hindneck collar extending to chest sides. Back mottled blackish brown, with pale-edged scapulars. Upperwings pale gray with mottled brownish black ulnar bar; tertials brownish black, narrowly fringed pale gray to whitish; wingtips black with white to pale gray primary tips. IN FLIGHT: upperwings pale gray with bold blackish M pattern, variable dark secondary bar, white trailing edge to secondaries and inner primaries, and white tongue-streaks visible on spread outer primaries; rare variants have mostly dark upperwings. Underwings pale gray to whitish overall with narrow black trailing edge to outer primaries, narrow dusky subterminal secondary band (can be very indistinct). Tail white with blackish distal band often not extending to R6. Bill blackish, legs flesh pink. Partial PF molt (late Aug.–Nov./ Dec.) produces formative plumage similar to adult basic on head, neck, and back, but brown-barred juvenal rump feathers often retained. At rest note blackish tertials and upperwing coverts, black-and-white wingtip;

some birds retain residual dark hindcollar mottling into midwinter. Partial PA1 molt (Mar.– May, often includes rectrices) produces first alternate plumage: usually has partial hood of blackish mottling, rarely attains full hood, and some birds have mostly basiclike head pattern but with more-extensive gray on hindneck; cap and hindneck can be slaty and underparts may attain a pink flush. Some birds attain gray tertials and all-white central rectrices (rarely whole tail[9]). Legs pink to pinkish red.

Second Cycle. Complete PB2 molt (June/July– Sept./Oct.) produces second basic plumage: some birds may be indistinguishable from adult basic but many have variable blackish subterminal marks on outer primaries, sometimes also on alula and primary coverts; lesser and median underwings coverts often paler than adult, pale gray to whitish. Partial PA2 molt (Feb.–May) into second alternate plumage: usually attains complete blackish hood like adult, but some show whitish speckling on face and chin; some attain basiclike head pattern.[10] Attains adult plumage by complete PB3 molt (July–Oct.).

HYBRIDS
None reported.

NOTES

1. Crochet et al. 2000; 2. Chu 1998; 3. Tozer and Richards 1974; 4. Weseloh 1987; 5. Peterjohn 2001; 6. Weseloh 1994; 7. Levine 1998; 8. Blokpoel et al. 1984; 9. Grant 1986; 10. Ibid.

LENGTH 12.5–14.2 IN. (32–36 CM)
IMAGES 7.0–7.13

IDENTIFICATION SUMMARY

This small two- or three-cycle gull is a beautiful and sought-after inhabitant of Arctic regions; it occurs rarely south to the lower 48 states in winter. Bill small, slender, and relatively blunt; wings and tail relatively long, the tail tip strongly graduated; at rest, tail tip falls around tip of P7. Head and underparts of all post-juvenal plumages often have pink flush (which can be diluted in bright sunlight but appear intense under cloudy skies). Adult has black bill, red legs, pale gray upperwings, and smoky gray underwings; thin black neck ring in alternate plumage, dark ear-spot in basic. First-cycle has blackish M pattern on upperwings. Small size and long graduated tail eliminate other gulls, but see Little Gull and juvenile Sabine's Gull.

TAXONOMY

Monotypic. Chu[1] proposed that, to reflect phylogeny better, Ross's and Little Gulls be placed in the genus *Hydrocoloeus* or that all gulls be merged into *Larus*, as done by Moynihan.[2]

STATUS AND DISTRIBUTION

Local in Arctic regions.

Breeding. Breeds very locally (June–Aug.) in n. Canada, with nesting first confirmed in late 1970s and 1980s on sw. Hudson Bay,[3] and in Cheyne Is., Nunavut. Also breeds locally in w.-cen. and n. Greenland. Main nesting range along and near Arctic coast of Russia from Kolyma Delta west to Taimyr Peninsula.

Nonbreeding. Post-breeding dispersal starts July–Aug. from breeding grounds in ne. Siberia, whence birds move east into Chukchi Sea and continue east into w. Beaufort Sea during late Sept.–early Oct., returning west to Chukchi Sea mainly mid- to late Oct.,[4] followed by movement south into nw. Bering Sea (late Oct.–Dec.).[5] In some years, incursions occur into interior of nw. Alaska (for example, late Sept. 1983[6]). Best known in fall from vicinity of Point Barrow (late July–early Nov.) with peak numbers late Sept.–mid-Oct., when an estimated 20,000–40,000 birds occur in n. Alaska waters.[7] In n. Atlantic region, locally common (Aug.–Sept.) in pack-ice between Greenland and Svalbard.[8]

Winter distribution probably linked to extent of pack-ice, thus showing marked interannual variation. Main winter grounds (Dec.–Apr.) apparently in n. Pacific basin from Bering Sea south to waters north of Japan. In n. Atlantic to Arctic Ocean, poorly known except for extralimital records, although the relatively large numbers of these (for example, in nw. Europe) suggest a substantial wintering population somewhere.

Northbound movements in this species appear to be mainly overland (May–early June) from Gulf of Anadyr and n. Sea of Okhotsk to n. Siberian coasts.[9] Small numbers range east irregularly (late May–June; mainly immatures) to ne. Bering Sea (for example, St. Lawrence Is.), and casual in w. and cen. Aleutians. Arrival on breeding grounds late May–mid-June.

Casual nonbreeding visitor south into cen. Canada (mainly mid-Apr.–early June, from s. Manitoba east to Ontario) and U.S. (mainly mid-Oct.–mid-May), where most records are in Midwest (mainly late Oct.–mid-Jan.) and Northeast (mainly Dec.–Apr.), north to Nfld., with records from as far south as ne. Colo., Mo., and Del. Much rarer in the Northwest, with only a handful of records (late Oct.–early Mar.) from sw. B.C. south to Ore. and Idaho; also a late July juvenile in n. Yukon.

FIELD IDENTIFICATION

SIMILAR SPECIES

Ross's is a distinctive gull by virtue of its small size, long and graduated tail, and long wings—which create an elongated, tapered rear end on swimming and standing birds. At a distance it might be confused with Little Gull; see also juvenile Sabine's Gull and Bonaparte's Gull (with which southern vagrant Ross's may be found).

LITTLE GULL (widespread but rare) similar in most plumages but has slightly longer and more pointed bill, shorter and blunter wings, and a "normal" squared tail; some plumages can be flushed pink on head and underparts. Adult has narrower white trailing edge to wings extending to wingtip, dark hood in alternate plumage, and dark cap in basic. First cycle has duller and less extensive whitish trailing triangle on upperwing (with dark secondary bar), black tail tip forms an even band—versus black tip to elongated central rectrices on Ross's.

BONAPARTE'S GULL (widespread in N. America) larger with longer and more pointed bill, broader wings, and short squared tail. First cycle has white leading wedge and black trailing edge to upperwing.

SABINE'S GULL (also breeds Arctic region). Juvenile Sabine's has extensively brown upperparts and bold white trailing edge to upperwing similar to rarely seen juvenile Ross's Gull, but note Ross's long and graduated tail, gray leading edge to innerwing, more extensive white postocular area, and smaller bill; on resting birds note Ross's smaller bill, long primary projection, and that its greater coverts are usually paler and grayer than the brown upperparts.

HABITAT AND BEHAVIOR

In the Arctic region, most often seen along coasts and at coastal lagoons, river mouths, nearby freshwater marshes, and in winter around sea ice; vagrants occur at sewage ponds and outfalls, river mouths, lakes, and other areas where small gulls (especially Bonaparte's) concentrate. Nests in solitary pairs and small colonies, in marshes and around small lakes in tundra, at times in association with other water birds such as Arctic Terns.[10,11] In N. America, mainly found singly or in small groups. Flight buoyant and strong with fairly deep wingbeats; dips down to pick from the water while hovering or lands briefly; also feeds by picking while walking and swimming.

DESCRIPTION AND MOLT

Adult Cycle. Complete PB molt (late June/July–Sept./early Oct.) produces adult basic plumage: head, neck, and underparts white with dark ear-spot, gray wash on crown; often has dusky smudges around eyes and can have traces of a narrow dark neck ring. Upperparts pale gray (Kodak 3.5–4.5), extending on to sides of chest as a partial, smoky gray collar that often offsets white head; narrow scapular and tertial crescents, uppertail coverts, and tail white. White areas of plumage can have a variable pink flush. IN FLIGHT: upperwings pale gray with broad white trailing edge to secondaries and inner primaries, blackish outer web to P10; underwings smoky gray (appearing darker when shadowed) with broad white trailing edge to secondaries and inner primaries. Eyes dark, bill black, legs dark red to orange-red. Partial PA molt (Mar.–May) produces adult alternate plumage: head white

with neat black neck ring; "white" areas of plumage often flushed brighter pink. Orbital ring brightens to red, legs bright orange-red.

First Cycle. Juvenile (late July–Sept., rarely retained into winter): lores, variable postocular area, lower face, foreneck, and underparts white with dark brown collar at neck sides. Crown, auriculars, neck sides, hindneck, and back dark sooty brown; scaly cinnamon buff to pale buffy gray tips on back boldest on scapulars. Upperwings pale gray with broad, brownish black ulnar bar; tertials brownish black, narrowly edged buff to whitish; wingtips at rest black with white primary tips; white tongue-tips on P5–P7 often show as white patches on closed wingtip. IN FLIGHT: upperwings show striking white trailing triangle suggesting Sabine's Gull (formed by secondaries, greater coverts, inner and middle primaries) contrasting with blackish brown lesser and median coverts, black leading wedge; white tongue-streaks visible on spread outer primaries, and leading edge of inner lesser coverts pale gray. Underwings pale gray (appearing darker when shadowed) with broad white trailing edge translucent when backlit, and narrow black trailing edge to outer primaries. Uppertail coverts and tail white, dusky tips to longest uppertail coverts rarely visible; R1 with bold black subterminal band, R2–R3/R4 with narrower black subterminal marks. Bill blackish, legs flesh. Partial PF molt (late Aug.–Oct./Nov.) produces formative plumage similar to adult basic on head, neck, and back but may average more-extensive dusky gray on crown, and brown-barred juvenal rump feathers and some hindcollar mottling can be retained. At rest note blackish tertials and upperwing coverts, black-and-white wingtip. Legs flesh pink to reddish. Partial PA1 molt (Mar.–May, can include rectrices) produces first alternate plumage: usually attains partial to complete narrow black neck ring, loses dark ear-spot; some birds may attain mostly basiclike head pattern. Underparts often have a variable pink flush. Some birds attain all-white central rectrices, sometimes whole tail.[12] Legs red to orange-red.

Second Cycle. Attains adultlike plumage by complete PB2 molt (late June/July–Sept.) although some second-cycle birds distinguishable by dark marks on alula, primary coverts, lesser wing coverts, and tertials; legs average duller, at least through second winter. Also may have broader whitish tips to outer primaries and, in alternate plumage, may attain variably basiclike head pattern; more study needed.

HYBRIDS
None reported.

NOTES

1. Chu 1998; 2. Moynihan 1959; 3. Chartier and Cooke 1980; 4. Divoky et al. 1988; 5. Degtyaryev et al. 1987; 6. Osborne and Osborne 1986; 7. Divoky et al. 1988; 8. Boertmann 1994; 9. Degtyaryev et al. 1987; 10. Chartier and Cooke 1980; 11. Cramp and Simmons 1983; 12. Howell pers. obs. (early June bird shot by locals at St. Lawrence Is., Alaska)

KITTIWAKES
(GENUS *Rissa*)

This subgroup includes two oceangoing species, the Black-legged and Red-legged Kittiwakes, often separated in the genus *Rissa*. These are medium-sized, long-winged gulls with relatively small slender to stubby bills and short legs. The short legs, along with the hind toe reduced to a stub, are adaptations for cliff nesting. Adult bills are plain yellow, legs black or red. Adult alternate plumages lack a hood, and upperwings are gray with a white trailing edge and black tips. Kittiwakes are three-cycle gulls. The juvenal plumage is unusual among gulls in lacking brown, that is, the back starts out gray, and Red-legged also lacks black on the tail, virtually unique among first-cycle gulls. Juvenal kittiwakes have dark hindcollars and ear-spots and a black leading wedge to the outer wing, contrasting with a broad pale trailing edge. Juvenal plumage is retained into winter, and first prealternate molts are often limited in extent.

ADULT BLACK-LEGGED KITTIWAKE, ALTERNATE PLUMAGE *(R. T. POLLICARIS)*. PP. 75, 327

ADULT BREEDING RED-LEGGED KITTIWAKE. PP. 79, 331

LENGTH 16–18 IN. (41–46 CM)
PHOTOS 8.0–8.17, I.26, 9.2, 9.5–9.6, 9.14.

IDENTIFICATION SUMMARY

This elegant, medium-sized, three-cycle gull is a circumpolar breeder, locally common in the N. Pacific and N. Atlantic; southward it occurs mainly as a pelagic winter visitor, reaching nw. Mexico and e. U.S. Bill medium length with a slight gonydeal expansion, tail slightly cleft (most marked on first-cycle birds), legs short. At rest, tail tip falls between

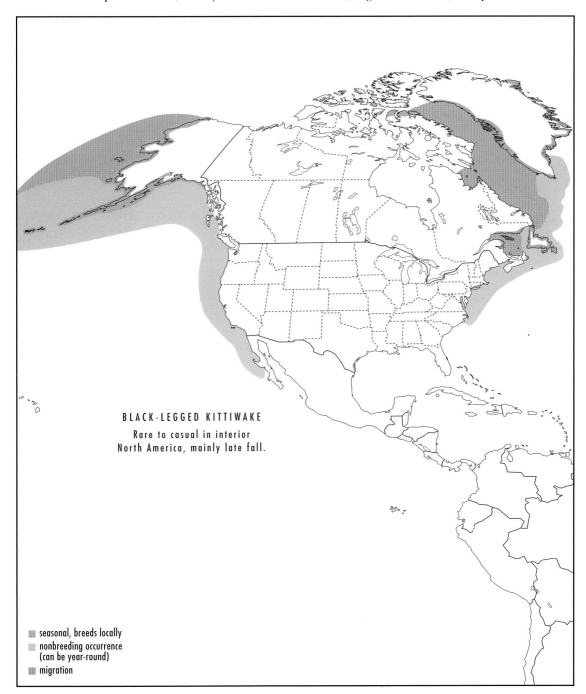

BLACK-LEGGED KITTIWAKE
Rare to casual in interior
North America, mainly late fall.

▨ seasonal, breeds locally
▨ nonbreeding occurrence
   (can be year-round)
▨ migration

tips of P6 and P7. Adult has medium gray upperparts (Kodak 6.5–8; see Taxonomy), black wingtips (lacking white mirrors) and, in basic plumage, a dark ear-spot and dusky hindneck. Juvenile has gray back and black M pattern on upperwings. PA1 variable, starting Sept.–Feb. All ages have dark eyes; juvenile has dusky legs, becoming black by adult cycle; orbital ring red.

Medium size, narrow wings, medium gray back, short black legs, plain yellow bill, and brown eyes are a distinctive combination among adults of regularly occurring New World gulls. In N. Pacific, Red-legged Kittiwake is slightly smaller with short bill, darker gray upperparts, and red legs. Also see adult Mew Gull (white wingtip mirrors, yellowish legs). First-cycle distinguished from Little Gull by larger size, contrasting white trailing triangle to upperwing, and black hindcollar. See Similar Species section for more detailed identification criteria.

TAXONOMY
Two subspecies are generally recognized,[1,2] although some authors consider the species monotypic.[3] Nominate *tridactyla* breeds in the N. Atlantic region, and *pollicaris* breeds in the N. Pacific region. *Pollicaris* averages slightly larger and longer billed, slightly darker above (Kodak 7–8 versus 6.5–7.5 in *tridactyla*), has more-extensive black in the wingtip, and more often has a rudimentary hind claw. Chardine[4] discussed variation within nominate *tridactyla*, noting that *tridactyla* and *pollicaris* might qualify as phylogenetic species.

STATUS AND DISTRIBUTION
N. Pacific and N. Atlantic oceans; vagrant to Hawaii.

Breeding. Breeds (May–Aug./Sept.; *R. t. pollicaris*) in nw. and w. Alaska, including Bering Sea Is. and Aleutians, and from s. coastal Alaska and offshore is. south to se. Alaska (Glacier Bay and vicinity). *P. t. tridactyla* breeds (late Apr./May–Aug./Sept.) from Canadian Arctic Archipelago, Greenland, and Lab. south to Gulf of St. Lawrence and Bay of Fundy. Breeding population and range in Gulf of St. Lawrence (Que.) has expanded greatly in recent decades (from 11 colonies with 43,000 pairs in 1975 to 46 colonies with 83,957 pairs in 1991[5]).

Nonbreeding. In Pacific region, southbound movements in the far North (for example, Beaufort Sea) begin by late Aug., whereas departure from colonies off s. coastal Alaska is mid-Aug.–mid-Sept.; still fairly common into Oct. in n. Bering Sea, with some lingering to Nov. Migration apparently starts off B.C. by late Aug., and some appear off Ore. by early Sept.; early fall movements in the Northwest may be largely coastal,[6] with appearances offshore (where best known) later in fall. Arrival off cen. Calif. usually after mid-Oct., and off s. Calif. after early to mid-Nov. Peak movements in coastal B.C. Sept., and off Calif. mid-Nov. and later.

In Atlantic region, departure from Arctic Canada and Greenland Aug.–Sept. with fall staging near Grand Banks. Earliest arrivals in New England are late Aug. and in Mid-Atlantic region mid-Sept. but usually late Oct. with main arrivals during mid-Nov.–Dec. In interior N. America, rare to casual (mainly late Oct.–Dec., exceptionally from Aug. and through winter) in the East; casual (mainly Nov.–Jan., exceptionally through winter in Southwest) in the West; most interior records are of first-cycle birds.

Winters (mainly Oct./Nov.–Mar./Apr.) in Pacific region from s. Bering Sea south to off n. Calif., irregularly (absent some years, fairly common others; mainly Nov.–Mar.) south to off Baja Calif., Mex., casually to Gulf of Calif. and south to Jalisco, Mex.;[7] accidental (July) in cen. Peru.[8] In Atlantic region, winters from off sw. Greenland and Atlantic Canada south to N.C. and Bermuda, rarely to cen. Fla.; very rare to casual along Gulf of Mex. coast west to n. Tamaulipas, Mex., casual (Dec.–Mar.) south to Bahamas and exceptionally to n. and e. West Indies, Belize, and Trinidad.[9]

Northbound movement along Pacific Coast mainly mid-Mar.–Apr., some lingering later. Arrival at colonies in s. coastal Alaska mid- to late Mar.[10] but not until mid- to late May on Seward Peninsula. In Atlantic, northbound movement from s. wintering areas evident late Feb. to mid-Mar., and most have departed waters off New England by mid-Apr. Arrival at colonies in Gulf of St. Lawrence is Mar., in Nfld. early–mid-Apr., and in Greenland Mar.–May. In Canadian Arctic, only low densities present on breeding grounds until mid-June. There is a scattering of spring records from interior N. America (where strictly casual; mostly Mar.–mid-May).

Nonbreeders (mainly immatures) oversummer irregularly off Pacific Coast of N. America south to Calif., especially after flight years. In Atlantic, oversummering birds occur irregularly south to Cape Cod, casually to Md. Common to abundant in summer and fall in Chukchi Sea and w. Beaufort Sea, rarely reaching Yukon coast. In Canadian Arctic, ranges west to Victoria Is. and casual in summer (mid-June–mid-July) on sw. Hudson Bay.

FIELD IDENTIFICATION

SIMILAR SPECIES

The only regularly occurring and potentially similar species in the Americas are Red-legged Kittiwake, Sabine's Gull, first-cycle Little Gull, and adult Mew Gull. Also see adults of much rarer Common Gull and Kamchatka Gull.

Adult Cycle. Distinctive. Note medium size, long and narrow wings, medium gray upperparts with paler primary bases accentuating "dipped-in-ink" black wingtips, short black legs, plain yellow bill. RED-LEGGED KITTIWAKE (Bering Sea) averages smaller with steeper forehead, stubby bill, bright red legs, more uniform and darker gray upperparts (Kodak 8.5–9.5) with more-contrasting white trailing edge to upperwing, and smoky gray underside to remiges—so black wingtip contrasts less, both above and below; head-on in flight, gray marginal coverts do not show up, unlike white marginal coverts on Black-legged. Wingbeats often slightly jerkier, less smoothly buoyant than Black-legged.

MEW GULL (w. N. America) shares medium gray upperparts (Kodak 6–7.5), dark eyes, and plain yellow bill but has shorter and more rounded wings with bold white mirrors on P9–P10, longer yellowish legs.

First Cycle. Distinctive. Note medium size, long and narrow wings, bold black M pattern on upperwings, black tail band, and short dark legs.

RED-LEGGED KITTIWAKE lacks black ulnar bar and tail band, has slightly darker gray upperparts; legs become orange-red by spring. Underside of outer primaries smoky gray, so black wingtip contrasts less.

SABINE'S GULL (Arctic breeder, pelagic migrant) noticeably smaller in direct comparison, with relatively shorter and less slender wings, forked tail, and finer bill. Upperwing pattern of first-cycle Black-legged Kittiwake can suggest Sabine's Gull, especially at long range, but note kittiwake's black ulnar bar and clean white underwings with only a small black wingtip; juvenile Sabine's has darker, brownish upperparts, and subsequent plumages lack black tail band.

LITTLE GULL (widespread but rare) much smaller with shorter and blunter-tipped wings, slender black bill, and relatively longer, flesh-colored legs; secondary bar and inner primary coverts dark (pale on kittiwake), so upperwing lacks extensive and bright white trailing triangle; Little also lacks black hindcollar (traces of dark juvenal hindcollar can form similar pattern through early winter) but has dark cap.

Second Cycle. Second-cycle Black-legged Kittiwake looks much like adult and differs from other species in the same respects as do adults.

RARER SPECIES

Adult Cycle. Common Gull (casual to rare in ne. N. America) and Kamchatka Gull (casual in w. Alaska) share medium gray upperparts, dark eyes, and plain yellow bill but have relatively shorter and broader wings, with bold white mirrors on P9–P10, and longer yellowish legs.

HABITAT AND BEHAVIOR

Breeds colonially on sea cliffs and locally, at least in N. Atlantic, on waterside buildings that provide surrogate cliffs. Rarely seen from shore south of breeding range, where it occurs at river mouths, freshwater lakes near the coast, on beaches, ice floes, etc. Flight buoyant and agile, wheeling easily in windy conditions. Winter wrecks occur periodically, perhaps driven by food shortages (especially in the Pacific), when birds can be blown onshore and even a short distance inland, and then linger on beaches and at river mouths. Often social and associates readily with other seabirds, including in mixed-species feeding flocks at schooling fish. Forages over shelf and offshore waters, concentrating locally along edges and leads in sea ice, both in winter and summer.[11] Feeds mainly in flight by shallow plunge-dives or by picking food from near the sea surface. Laughing or honking calls of flocks can suggest small geese, and rhythmic *ketewehk ketewehk* calls resulted in its onomatopoeic name.

DESCRIPTION AND MOLT

R. t. tridactyla (N. Atlantic Ocean)

Adult Cycle. Complete PB molt (June–Oct./Dec., sometimes protracted into Jan./Feb.[12]) produces adult basic plumage: head, neck, and underparts white with dusky gray hindcollar, variable dark patch on auriculars, and variable dusky smudges from eyes up over crown. Back and upperwings medium gray (Kodak 6.5–7.5) with paler primary bases often fading to whitish distally, strongly offsetting clean-cut black wingtips (black on outer web of P10 extends to primary coverts); narrow and inconspicuous white scapular and tertial crescents. Uppertail coverts and tail white. White trailing edge to secondaries becomes indistinct on inner primaries, with fine white tips out to P8—often lost by wear so P7–P10 wingtip typically looks solidly black; P6 has black subterminal band framed in white (often shows as a black spot both in flight and on perched birds); P5 has limited black marks on up to 40 percent of birds and can rarely have a narrow black subterminal band.[13] Underwings show black wingtips contrastingly clean-cut from pale gray primary bases. Eyes dark brown, orbital ring reddish (to blackish in fall and winter); bill unmarked yellow to greenish yellow; legs blackish. Partial PA molt (Jan./Feb.–Apr.) produces adult alternate plumage: head and neck clean white, although birds in nonbreeding condition may attain basiclike head patterns.[14] Orbital ring orange-red, bill brighter yellow with small orange-red gape, legs black (very rarely orange-yellow to red[15]).

First Cycle. Juvenile (July–Jan.): head, neck, and underparts white with variable dark smudging around eyes, smoky gray wash to nape; blackish ear-spot and hindcollar often appear as a double "collar." Upperparts medium gray with fine whitish edgings in fresh plumage, variable fine dark bars on mantle and rump (rarely visible), mottled black ulnar bar, black shaft streaks on tertials, and black wingtips (P6 tipped white in fresh plumage). Uppertail coverts and slightly cleft tail white with black distal tail band not usually reaching outer web of R6. IN FLIGHT: boldly patterned black, white, and gray. Black ulnar bar and black leading wedge form an open M pattern on upperwings; whitish outer greater coverts, secondaries, and inner primaries form variably contrasting white triangle on trailing edge of upperwing; underwings whitish with black wingtip. Eyes dark brown, bill blackish, legs blackish to brownish flesh. PA1 molt (late Sept.–Apr./May; does not include upperwing coverts but may include central rectrices in late winter or spring) produces first alternate plumage: much like juvenile but most birds show little or no trace of blackish hindcollar by mid- to late winter, ear-spot duller, and hindneck washed dusky gray. Bill often develops pale grayish or greenish yellow base by late winter.

Second Cycle. Complete PB2 molt (May–Sept.) into second basic plumage. Resembles adult basic but black wingtip slightly more extensive, especially on outer webs of P8–P9, and primary coverts and alula usually with some black marks; exceptionally, tail can show small black marks.[16] Bill greenish yellow, usually with variable dark marks, especially on culmen and tip. Partial PA2 molt (Feb.–May) produces second alternate plumage: head and neck typically become clean white but some have variable dusky hindneck wash and dark ear-spot; orbital ring becomes reddish in summer; bill unmarked yellow or with fine dark tip. Attains adult plumage by third prebasic molt (June–Sept./Oct.).

R. t. pollicaris (N. Pacific Ocean)
Averages slightly larger and longer billed than nominate *tridactyla* with slightly darker upperparts (Kodak 7–8); juvenile may average thicker black hindcollar but critical study lacking of possible first-cycle differences. Adult has more-extensive black wingtip, and P5 has black subterminal band on about 40 percent of birds (only about 10 percent lack black on P5).[17] Breeding season averages later, as does molt cycle:[18] adult PB molt starts late June–late Sept., completes Nov.–Jan. in most years but can be suspended or protracted into May or later;[19] adult PA molt mainly Mar.–May. Juvenal plumage usually retained into winter and PA1 molt mostly Jan./Feb.–May (so, for example, dark double "collar" can be retained through spring); PB2 molt mainly mid-May/June–Sept./Oct.

HYBRIDS
None reported.

NOTES

1. Chardine 2002; 2. Dwight 1925; 3. Vaurie 1965; 4. Chardine 2002; 5. Brousseau 1996; 6. Contreras 2003; 7. Howell et al. 2001; 8. Haase 1993; 9. ffrench and White 1999; 10. Isleib and Kessel 1973; 11. Baird 1994; 12. Weir et al. 1996; 13. Chardine 2002; 14. CAS specimen 31280 (5 July); 15. Coulson 1959; 16. Grant 1986; 17. Chardine 2002; 18. Howell unpubl. data; 19. Howell and Corben 2000d

LENGTH 15.5–17 IN. (39–43 CM)
IMAGES 9.0–9.14

IDENTIFICATION SUMMARY

A very local, medium-small three-cycle gull of the Bering Sea. Bill relatively short and stubby with slight gonydeal expansion, tail slightly cleft (most marked on first-cycle birds), legs short. At rest, tail tip falls at or slightly beyond tip of P6. Adult has pale slaty gray upperparts (Kodak 8.5–9.5), black wingtips (lacking white mirrors), and, in basic plumage, a dusky ear-spot and hindneck collar. Juvenile has gray back and broad white trailing edge to upperwings. PA1 poorly known. All ages have dark eyes; juvenile has dark legs, becoming bright red by adult cycle; orbital ring red.

Medium-small size, pale slaty back, all-black wingtips, short red legs, plain yellow bill, and brown eyes are a distinctive combination among adults of regularly occurring New World gulls. Black-legged Kittiwake is slightly larger with longer and more slender bill, paler gray upperparts, more-contrasting black wingtips, and black legs. First cycle distinguished from adult Sabine's Gull by larger size, thick bill, and less-extensive white trailing edge to upperwing.

TAXONOMY
Monotypic.

STATUS AND DISTRIBUTION
Local breeder on islands in the Bering Sea region.

Breeding. Breeds (mid-June–Sept.) in Pribilofs (St. Paul, St. George, and Otter Is.) and very locally in Aleutians (Buldir, Bogoslof, and Fire Is.); also on Commander Is., Russia. Most of world population has traditionally nested on Pribilofs, but populations there have declined 50 percent since mid-1970s; conversely, populations in Aleutians increased between mid-1970s and early 1990s.[1]

Nonbreeding. Distribution poorly known. Presumed to winter (Oct.–Mar.) well offshore in n. Pacific Ocean but few supporting records (no doubt due to poor coverage), and also north to pack-ice in Bering Sea.[2] Casual (late Nov.–Mar., late June–mid-Aug.) south to Wash. and Ore. with most winter records involving birds salvaged on beaches or even up

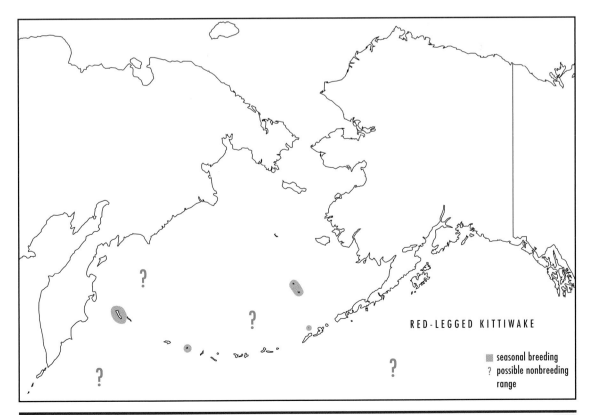

RED-LEGGED KITTIWAKE

■ seasonal breeding
? possible nonbreeding range

to 50 km inland, exceptionally (Feb.) south to Calif. Returns to breeding islands Apr.–early May, and rare (June–early Aug.) in Bering Sea well away from breeding islands north to St. Lawrence Is., east to Bristol Bay. A Sept. report from se. Alaska[3] is not credible.

Extralimital records inland along Yukon R. in Alaska (early July, below Kandik) and cen. Yukon (mid-Oct., near Forty Mile); and in s. Nevada (early July).

FIELD IDENTIFICATION

SIMILAR SPECIES

Distinctive. Note medium to small size, relatively stubby bill, pale slaty upperparts; adult has "dipped-in-ink" black wingtips, short red legs; first cycle has broad white trailing edge to upperwing, lacks black ulnar bar and tail band. Laughing calls distinctly squeakier than Black-legged Kittiwake.

BLACK-LEGGED KITTIWAKE slightly larger with more sloping forehead, longer bill, black legs, slightly paler gray upperparts (Kodak 7–8) and whitish underwings—so black wingtips more contrasting both above and below; head-on in flight, white marginal coverts show up, unlike gray marginal coverts on Red-legged. First cycle has black ulnar bar and black tail band. Wingbeats often slightly smoother, less jerky, than Red-legged.

SABINE'S GULL smaller and slimmer in direct comparison, with slender black bill, forked tail. Upperwing pattern of first-cycle Red-legged Kittiwake suggests Sabine's Gull, but white trailing triangle less extensive, bases of outer primaries gray.

HABITAT AND BEHAVIOR

Breeds colonially on sea cliffs, often in same areas as Black-legged Kittiwakes, and the two species are readily seen together around colonies, on adjacent coasts, at river mouths, and freshwater lakes near coast. Forages in summer mainly over deeper waters beyond the continental shelf; winter habits almost unknown, presumed over deep pelagic waters of N. Pacific.[4] Flight similar to Black-legged Kittiwake but wingbeats jerkier and slightly more hurried. Associates readily with other seabirds, including in mixed-species feeding flocks at schooling fish. Feeds mainly in flight by shallow plunge-dives or by picking food from near the sea surface.

DESCRIPTION AND MOLT

Molt timings poorly known (for example, when PB molts finish, when PA1 molt starts).

Adult Cycle. Complete PB molt starts late July–late Sept., perhaps completes Nov.–Jan. in most birds, but Feb.–Mar. on vagrants in Calif.;[5,6] on some (presumably nonbreeding) birds, primary molt can be arrested in winter or protracted into spring and summer, even overlapping with start of next PB molt.[7] Adult basic plumage: head, neck, and underparts white with dusky mottled hindcollar, dark patch on auriculars merging into dusky gray band over crown, and dusky smudges around eyes. Back and upperwings pale slaty gray (Kodak 8.5–9.5) with black wingtips (black on outer web of P10, sometimes also P9, extends to primary coverts); narrow white scapular and tertial crescents. Uppertail coverts and tail white. White trailing edge to secondaries and inner primaries well defined with fine pale gray tips on P7–P9/P10—at any distance, P7–P10 wingtip looks solidly black; P5 usually has black subterminal mark on outer web. Underwings show black wingtips contrastingly with dusky gray underside to inner primaries and secondaries; wing-linings pale smoky gray. Eyes dark brown, orbital ring reddish (blackish in fall and winter?); bill unmarked yellow to greenish yellow; legs red. Partial PA molt (*Mar.–May*) produces adult alternate plumage: head and neck clean white; possibly with traces of basiclike pattern in nonbreeders. Orbital ring orange-red, bill brighter yellow with small orange-red gape, legs bright orange-red.

First Cycle. Juvenile (late Aug.–*Feb./Mar.*): head, neck, and underparts white with variable dark smudging around eyes, faint smoky gray wash to nape; blackish ear-spot and mottled blackish hindcollar can appear as a double "collar." Upperparts pale slaty gray with fine whitish edgings in fresh plumage, scattered dark spots on lesser coverts, and black wingtips with distinct whitish tips out to P6/P7. Uppertail coverts and tail white. IN FLIGHT: upperwing pale slaty gray with contrasting black leading wedge and broad white trailing edge formed by secondaries, broad tips of inner primaries, and tips of greater coverts; underwings whitish with smoky gray marginal coverts, primary coverts, and outer primary bases, blackish wingtips. Eyes dark brown, bill blackish, legs blackish to dull brownish flesh. PA1 molt (*Feb./Mar.–May*; does not include upperwing coverts) produces first alternate plumage: much like juvenile but head and neck whiter overall, most birds show little or no trace of blackish hindcollar, and ear-spot duller. By late winter or spring, bill develops greenish yellow base, legs become orange to orange-red.

Second Cycle. Complete PB2 molt (late May/

June–Sept./Oct.) into second basic plumage. Resembles adult basic but black wingtip slightly more extensive, especially on outer webs of P8–P9; P5 usually with complete black subterminal band, and primary coverts and alula often with some black marks. Bill greenish yellow, usually with dark tip. Partial PA2 molt (*Mar.–May*) produces second alternate plumage: head and neck typically become clean white, but some have variable dusky hindneck wash and dark ear-spot; orbital ring becomes reddish in summer; bill unmarked yellow or with fine dark tip; legs average duller than adult. Attains adult plumage by third prebasic molt (starting June/July, earlier than adult PB molt).

HYBRIDS
None reported.

NOTES
1. Byrd et al. 1997; 2. Everett et al. 1989; 3. Siegel-Causey and Meehan 1981; 4. Byrd and Williams 1993; 5. CAS specimen 88973 (13 Feb.); 6. LACM specimen 109199 (28 Feb.); 7. CAS specimen 13928 (7 Aug.; P9 is 95 percent grown, P10 is an old and worn adult feather, P1 is newly shed)

FORK-TAILED GULLS
(SUBGENUS *Xema*)

Moynihan (1959) included two distinctive species in this subgroup: Swallow-tailed Gull and, provisionally, Sabine's Gull. The former is usually placed in a monotypic genus, *Creagrus*, the latter sometimes in the monotypic genus *Xema* (AOU 1998). Crochet et al. (2000) considered that Ivory Gull was the closest living relative to Sabine's Gull. Swallow-tailed and Sabine's share boldly tricolored upperwings with a large white trailing triangle and forked tails; and breeding adults have blackish hoods (lacking white eye-crescents), red orbital rings, and pale-tipped bills. Beyond this, however, they are quite different: Swallow-tailed is a large, broad-winged gull that breeds on the Equator, Sabine's is a small long-distance migrant that breeds in the Arctic. Sabine's is a two-cycle gull with a complete preformative molt and partial first prealternate molt. The first-cycle molts of Swallow-tailed Gull are undescribed.

ADULT BREEDING SABINE'S GULL. PP. 83, 335

ADULT BREEDING SWALLOW-TAILED GULL. PP. 86, 339

LENGTH 12.5–14 IN. (32–35.5 CM)
PHOTOS 10.0–10.14

IDENTIFICATION SUMMARY

This small, elegant, two-cycle hooded gull is mostly pelagic away from its Arctic breeding grounds. Bill small and slender, tail moderately forked; at rest, tail tip falls between tips of P7 and P8. The striking wing pattern and forked tail, in combination with small size, are diagnostic, but see first-cycle kittiwakes and juvenile Ross's Gull. With alternate-plumaged adults at rest, compare with other small hooded species (see Similar Species). Juveniles migrate south to the nonbreeding grounds before molting.

TAXONOMY

Four subspecies described,[1] but some authors consider the species monotypic.[2] Nominate *sabini* (breeds n. Alaska and Arctic Canada east to Greenland; migrant off Pacific and Atlantic coasts) is the smallest and palest race; *palearctica* (breeds n. Russia from Taimyr Peninsula east to New Siberian Is.; possibly migrates off Pacific Coast) slightly larger and darker than *sabini*; *tschuktschorum* (breeds ne. Siberia and Wrangel Is.; probably migrates off Pacific Coast) similar to *palearctica* but averages darker above; and *woznesenskii* (breeds w. Alaska; migrates off Pacific Coast) averages darker still. AOU[3] combined *palearctica* with *sabini* but recognized *woznesenskii*. Sometimes placed in the genus *Larus*.[4]

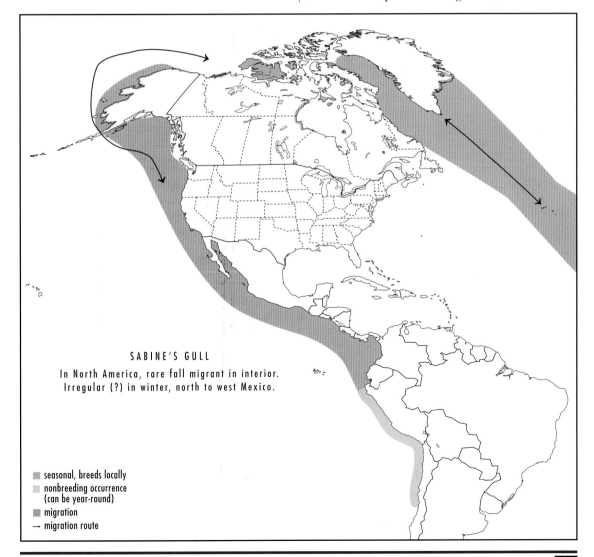

SABINE'S GULL

In North America, rare fall migrant in interior.
Irregular (?) in winter, north to west Mexico.

▨ seasonal, breeds locally
▨ nonbreeding occurrence
(can be year-round)
▨ migration
→ migration route

High-latitude Holarctic breeder; nonbreeding grounds mainly in Humboldt Current off w. S. America and Benguela Current off S. Africa.

Breeding. Breeds (late May/June–mid-July/Aug.) in w. Alaska (south to the Alaska Peninsula), n. Alaska, on Arctic coast of nw. Mackenzie, in Canadian Arctic Archipelago, and in n. and e.-cen. Greenland.

Nonbreeding. In fall, birds from Alaska (and w. to cen. Arctic Siberia) and Mackenzie migrate south through e. Pacific Ocean, whereas birds from the Canadian Arctic generally migrate across Davis Strait to Greenland, thence across n. Atlantic Ocean and south to S. Africa. Small numbers also migrate south overland across N. America, mainly in the West.

Southbound movements of adults in w. Alaska start late July–early Aug. with juveniles from Aug., a few lingering into Oct., exceptionally Nov. Rare fall transient (mid-July–Sept.) in e. Aleutians. Common to fairly common off Pacific Coast of N. and Middle America (mainly late July–Oct. with a peak during mid-Aug.–mid-Oct.; earlier in the north, later in the south); most depart N. American waters in Oct., very few linger into Nov., exceptionally to mid-Dec.

In interior N. America rare in fall (except the Southeast, where casual at best); overall more numerous in Great Basin and Great Plains than Great Lakes region. Most records are Sept. (especially mid- to late month), with gradual falling off into Oct. Some birds appear as early as July–Aug., and a few linger into Nov., exceptionally Dec.

Off Atlantic Coast of N. America, rare to casual in fall (mostly late Aug.–early Oct., some from July and into Nov., exceptionally later), with very few records south of Outer Banks, N.C. Casual at best (Oct.–Nov.) off Middle America from ne. Yucatán Peninsula[5] to Panama, and unrecorded in West Indies.[6]

Wintering areas incompletely known and may show interannual variation. Main winter grounds (Oct.–Mar.) are in Humboldt Current off Peru and n. Chile (mainly 5–20° south);[7,8,9] uncommon to rare s. to cen. Chile (to near 37° south). Locally (irregularly?) fairly common in winter off w. Mex.,[10] and molting winter birds photographed off El Salvador.[11] In N. America, almost unknown in winter, with well-documented winter records from Lake Erie (a long-staying immature, Jan. 1989–Nov. 1990) and Fla. (late Nov.–mid-Jan.); also Yucatán, Mex. (Feb.). Winter reports from N. Pacific (B.C. south to Calif.) require substantiation.

Northbound migration starts Mar.–Apr., and fairly common to common off Pacific Coast of Cen. America (mainly late Mar.–Apr.) and N. America (mainly late Apr.–May, exceptionally from late Mar.). Peak movements off w. N. America are mid- to late May, with smaller numbers into early June, and a scattering of later June records. Rare migrant (mid- to late May) in e. Aleutians, casual (late May–early July) in cen. and w. Aleutians. Arrival on southern breeding grounds in w. Alaska can be late Apr.–early May, but mainly later in May; farther north, for example, on Seward Peninsula, arrives late May, and in Canadian Arctic and Greenland usually arrives early June (a few in late May). Nonbreeding birds (mainly immatures) range north to Calif. (mainly June/July–Oct.[12]), moving north after main adult migrations; nonbreeding immatures probably also occur off Middle and S. America during Apr.–Aug.[13,14]

Casual at best (late Apr.–early June) in interior N. America, mainly in the West, with most records from Prairie Provinces; rare (late May–early July) on sw. Hudson Bay. Casual (late Apr.–mid-June) off Atlantic Coast of N. America from s. Fla. north to Lab. with a few nonbreeders summering (late June–July) in nw. Atlantic.[15]

FIELD IDENTIFICATION

SIMILAR SPECIES

Adult Cycle. Adult Sabine's Gull distinctive but confusion possible with some species, mainly if seen poorly and at long range (particularly first-cycle kittiwakes in flight); also note birds at rest.

BLACK-LEGGED KITTIWAKE noticeably larger in direct comparison, with squared tail, larger bill. First-cycle upperwing pattern suggests adult Sabine's Gull, especially at long range, but less contrasting; note kittiwake's black ulnar bar, black tail tip, clean white underwings with only small black wingtips, and overall size and structure.

RED-LEGGED KITTIWAKE larger in direct comparison, with thick bill, squared tail. First-cycle upperwing pattern suggests adult Sabine's Gull, but white trailing triangle less extensive, bases of outer primaries gray.

FRANKLIN'S GULL at rest is slightly larger with slightly thicker bill (often orange tipped on nonbreeding birds); all ages have bold white eye-crescents, and nonbreeding birds have a well-defined half-hood; upperwing pattern in flight quite different from Sabine's, but wingtip pattern at rest similar.

BONAPARTE'S GULL at rest is slimmer overall with more-slender, all-black bill, pale gray upperparts (Kodak 5–6), mostly black wingtips (and very different upperwing pattern from Sabine's), reddish legs; alternate has white eye-crescents.

BLACK-HEADED GULL at rest is slightly larger with longer, reddish bill, pale gray upperparts (Kodak 4–5), mostly black wingtips (and very different upperwing pattern from Sabine's), reddish legs; alternate has dark brown (not slaty) hood with white eye-crescents.

LITTLE GULL at rest is smaller with smaller, more-slender, and all-black bill, pale gray upperparts (Kodak 4.5–5.5), pinkish to red legs; adult has mostly white wingtips (and very different upperwing pattern from Sabine's).

SWALLOW-TAILED GULL has overall similar plumage but is much larger and broader winged with more deeply forked tail, longer bill, and more-extensive white upperwing panels; should not be confused with Sabine's Gull.

First Cycle. Juvenile Sabine's Gull (plumage retained through fall migration) also distinctive, but see juvenile Ross's, Little, and Franklin's Gulls.

ROSS'S GULL juvenile (rarely seen) has extensively dark brown upperparts and bold white trailing edge to upperwing similar to Sabine's, but note Ross's strongly graduated tail with black-tipped central rectrices, gray leading edge to innerwing, smaller bill; on resting birds note Ross's smaller bill, more extensive white postocular area, long primary projection; greater coverts often grayer than brown upperparts.

LITTLE GULL juvenile in flight has bold upperwing pattern but lacks juvenile Sabine's striking white trailing triangle; note Little's gray leading edge to innerwing, dark secondary bar, and more extensive white face; on resting birds, note Little's smaller bill, more extensive white on face and neck, and pale gray greater coverts.

FRANKLIN'S GULL juvenile typically has blackish half-hood and paler hindneck, but some heavily pigmented birds (mainly July–Aug.) have head and hindneck dark brownish, suggesting Sabine's; note stouter bill, blackish legs, bolder white tips to outer primaries, and, in flight, very different wing pattern.

HABITAT AND BEHAVIOR

Pelagic away from Arctic breeding grounds. Breeds on low-lying tundra and marshy areas, often near the coast; in summer, singles or migrant groups can be seen associating with groups of terns and other gulls at nearby river mouths, lagoons, and beaches. In migration and winter mostly pelagic except storm-blown birds along coasts, and fall migrants at interior lakes in w. N. America. Rarely seen from mainland coasts of N. America (more often seen from shore off Cen. and S. America), singly or in small groups. Most are offshore where fall flocks off California can number up to 1,000–2,000 birds[16] and winter flocks off S. America locally in hundreds.[17] Associates with feeding flocks of other seabirds; picks food from near sea surface in dipping flight and while swimming and walking in shallows. Flight buoyant and ternlike, low to fairly high over the water.

DESCRIPTION AND MOLT

Adult Cycle. Complete PB molt (late July/Aug.–Mar. starts with head during migration, and body molt mostly completed Dec.–Jan.; primary molt mainly Dec.–Mar.) produces adult basic plumage: head, neck, and underparts white with dark slaty hindcollar and ear-spot, variable dark mottling on nape, smoky gray wash on sides of neck; sometimes shows pink flush to underparts. Upperparts gray (Kodak 7–9) with narrow white scapular crescent; uppertail coverts and tail white. Wingtips black with bold white primary tips; white upperwing panel sometimes shows at rest along bottom edge of closed wing. IN FLIGHT: note strikingly tricolored upperwing pattern: white triangle on trailing edge of wings (formed by secondaries, greater coverts, and inner primaries) contrasts sharply with black leading wedge and gray inner coverts; white tongue-streaks in black outer primaries visible on fully spread wings. Underwings white with dark wingtips and subterminal secondary band. Orbital ring reddish to grayish, bill black with yellow tip, legs pale flesh to blackish. Partial PA molt (mainly Mar.–Apr., overlapping with end of PB primary molt) produces adult alternate plumage: attains dark slaty hood demarcated by black collar but with no pale eye-crescents. White primary tips can wear off by late summer or fall; often shows pink flush on underparts. Orbital ring bolder, bright red on breeding birds, yellow bill tip more sharply demarcated, legs black to dusky flesh.

First Cycle. Juvenile (mainly Aug.–Dec.): lores, variable circumorbital area, lower face, foreneck, and underparts white. Crown, head and neck sides, hindneck, and back sooty brown to gray-brown (rarely brownish gray) with neat scaly pattern of narrow subterminal dark bands and buffy white tips boldest on scapulars, upperwing coverts, and tertials. Uppertail coverts and tail white, tail with black distal band typically not reaching outer web of R6. Wingtips blackish with narrow white primary tips. Upperwings patterned like adult but inner coverts gray-brown like back. Bill black, legs flesh. Protracted and typically complete PF molt (head and body mainly Oct./Nov.–Dec./Jan.; primaries mainly Dec./Jan.–Mar./Apr.) produces formative plumage similar to adult basic but perhaps with more extensive dark shawl on hindneck. Bill black or with variable yellowish tip; legs dark to flesh. Some birds (mainly vagrant and perhaps sick individuals, such as those wintering north of main nonbreeding range) have retarded or partial PF molt, limited to head and back feathers by Apr.[18,19]. Partial PA1 molt (Apr.–May) produces head and neck pattern variably intermediate between adult basic and alternate; some may attain full hoods indistinguishable from adult alternate, but confirmation needed from known-age birds.

Second Cycle. Attains adult basic plumage by complete PB2 molt on similar schedule to adult cycle. However, some adult-type birds have P10 or P9–P10 browner without bold white tips, and these birds also usually have a subterminal black band on P5 and lack white tips to the primary coverts; they occasionally have dusky fringes to some rectrix tips and dark smudges on the tertials. Most adults, by contrast, have black outer primaries with bold white tips, usually lack a black subterminal band on P5, and have small white tips to the primary coverts. The former may be second-cycle birds, but confirmation needed from known-age birds.

HYBRIDS
None reported.

NOTES

1. Portenko 1939; 2. Vaurie 1965; 3. AOU 1957; 4. Cramp and Simmons 1983; 5. Howell et al. 2001; 6. Raffaele et al. 1998; 7. Chapman 1969; 8. Mackiernan et al. 2001; 9. Post 1971; 10. Howell and Engel 1993; 11. Grant 1986; 12. Howell pers. obs.; 13. Chapman 1969; 14. Howell and Engel 1993; 15. Lambert 1973; 16. Howell pers. obs.; 17. Chapman 1969; 18. Rosche and Hannikman 1989; 19. Vinicombe and Cottridge 1996 (plate 37, no. 6).

11. SWALLOW-TAILED GULL *Creagrus furcatus*

LENGTH 22–24 IN. (56–61 CM)
PHOTOS 11.0–11.10, I.31

IDENTIFICATION SUMMARY

This large, spectacular, and unmistakable pelagic gull of the E. Tropical Pacific breeds mainly on the Galápagos Is. Bill long, slightly droop-tipped, and pointed, with slight gonydeal expansion. Wings long and broad, tail medium long and forked; at rest, tail tip falls about equal with tip of P7. All plumages have bold white triangle on upperwings; breeding adult has blackish slate hood, bright red orbital ring.

SWALLOW-TAILED GULL

resident, breeds locally
nonbreeding occurrence
(can be year-round)

Taxonomy

Monotypic. Occasionally placed in the genus *Larus*.[1]

Status and Distribution

Endemic to the e. Tropical Pacific Ocean off w. S. America.

Locally common breeder on Galápagos Is., Ecuador (breeding year-round but with local synchrony[2,3]); also breeds Isla Malpelo, Colombia (estimated 50 pairs[4]). Ranges at sea over offshore waters from s. Colombia to cen. Peru (mainly 3° north to 12° south[5]), less commonly (mainly Dec.–June) south to cen. Chile, around 33° south,[6,7] and irregularly north to Gulf of Panama (around 6° north; Apr.,[8] July); also reported off se. Costa Rica (Mar.)[9] and exceptionally north to Calif. (Mar., June).[10]

Field Identification

Similar Species

Should be unmistakable; compare with much smaller Sabine's Gull, which shares similar upperwing pattern and forked tail.

Habitat and Behavior

Breeds on rocky islands with cliffs, nesting on steep slopes, lava ledges, in crevices and caves. Notably confiding at breeding grounds, often seen standing and displaying on cliff tops and making short flights along cliffs. Pelagic and mainly nocturnal feeder, picking marine organisms from near sea surface. Occurs singly or in small groups, at times in loafing flocks on the ocean up to several hundred birds,[11] and may associate with mixed-species aggregations of other seabirds. Direct flight with easy shallow wingbeats; usually seen sitting on sea or investigating ships and fishing boats briefly during day; typically does not follow ships during day but will accompany ships at night, perhaps attracted to lights on board.[12] Usually silent at sea although sometimes utters shrill chippering calls at night; at nesting islands, calls include guttural rattles, wheezy or creaky brays, and high, shrill, screechy chippers, all very distinct from other gull species.

Description and Molt

Adult Cycle (9–10 months). Complete PB molt after breeding (timing varies) produces adult basic plumage: white head, with black "mascara" eye-patch and dusky ear-spot, merges into smoky gray neck collar and pale smoky gray lower neck and chest, rest of underparts white; head may show variable dusky clouding and streaking on nape and throat. Upperparts medium gray (Kodak 7–8) with narrow white edgings to longest scapulars forming fine white braces; uppertail coverts and tail white; wingtips black with small white primary tips. Appearance transforms in flight: upperwings mostly bright white, contrasting sharply with gray panel on inner wing coverts, black outer webs and tips to outer primaries and primary coverts; underwings white overall, outer primaries with dusky leading edge and narrow black trailing edge; wing-linings often look smoky gray in contrast to broad, translucent white trailing wedge. Eyes dark brown with reddish orbital ring, bill black with pale gray tip, legs and feet pink. PB molt occurs mainly at sea after breeding, although inner primaries can be dropped before young fledge, and outer primaries often complete growth at start of breeding cycle, after alternate head plumage is attained.[13] Partial PA molt (timing varies) produces adult alternate plumage: attains blackish slate hood with bright white "saddle spot" at culmen base and small white spot below gape. Orbital ring bright red, legs and feet brighter, pink to reddish pink, pale gray bill tip bolder.

First Cycle. Juvenile: head, neck, and underparts white with blackish eye-patch, dusky gray-brown ear-spot, and variable dusky brown mottling at sides of chest. Upperparts dark sooty brown with scaly, pale gray to buffy white edgings (often looking boldly dappled or spotted overall); rump typically plain gray or with dark distal mottling. Uppertail coverts and tail white with black distal tail band not extending to outer web of R6, longest uppertail coverts sometimes with dark subterminal marks. Wingtips black, often with fine white tips out to P5–P6. Upperwing pattern overall similar to adult but with dark ulnar bar, more-extensive dark on primary coverts and outer primaries, and often dark subterminal bands on inner primaries; variable dusky subterminal marks on outer webs of secondary bases rarely visible. Eyes blackish, bill black, legs dusky dull-flesh to pinkish. Immature molts and plumages undescribed. May attain adultlike basic plumage following first complete molt, at end of first cycle, but with more-extensive dark on primary coverts. Second alternate perhaps has partial "hood" of dark spotting and streaking.

HYBRIDS
None reported.

NOTES
1. Blake 1977; 2. Hailman 1964; 3. Snow and Snow 1967; 4. Pitman et al. 1995; 5. Pitman 1986; 6. Johnson 1972; 7. Mackiernan et al. 2001; 8. L. B. Spear and D. G. Ainley unpubl. data; 9. Jones 2003b; 10. Rottenborn and Morlan 2000; 11. Mackiernan et al. 2001; 12. Howell pers. obs.; 13. Ibid.

IVORY GULL
(GENUS *Pagophila*)

The distinctive Ivory Gull is the sole member of this subgroup. It is a medium-sized high-Arctic species (*Pagophila* means "ice-loving") with fairly long, pointed, and broad-based wings and a relatively long, slightly graduated tail. Its medium-sized, slightly tapered bill is greenish, tipped orange. Its relatively short legs are black, and its toes have distinct claws.

The adult plumage is entirely ivory-white, the juvenal plumage white with a dark-smudged face and black spots on the upperparts, wings, and tail. Ivory is a two-cycle gull that apparently lacks a prealternate molt; juveniles molt directly into adult plumage by a complete molt in their second cycle.

ADULT (LEFT) AND FIRST-CYCLE (RIGHT) IVORY GULLS AT CARCASS WITH FIRST-CYCLE GLAUCOUS GULL (AT REAR).
PP. 88, 343

LENGTH 17–19 IN. (43–48 CM)
PHOTOS 12.0–12.7

IDENTIFICATION SUMMARY
  This unique, medium-sized, two-cycle Arctic
gull is rarely seen away from sea ice and is often very tame. Bill medium size and slightly
tapered; legs fairly short and toes with well-
developed claws; wings fairly long, pointed,
and broad based; at rest, tail tip falls about
equal with tip of P7. Should be unmistakable: plumage overall ivory-white, first cycle
marked with variable black on face, upperparts, and tips of flight feathers; bill greenish
with orange to yellow tip, legs black.

TAXONOMY
  Monotypic. Has been placed in the genus
Larus.[1]

STATUS AND DISTRIBUTION
  Holarctic breeder, mainly north of Arctic Cir-
cle, winters mainly along pack-ice edge.
  Breeding. Breeds very locally (mid-June–
Sept.) in Canadian High Arctic on Ellesmere,
Seymour, Devon, Baffin, and Perley Is.; also
locally in n. and se. Greenland. Recent data
suggest significant population decreases in
Canadian populations.[2]
  Nonbreeding. Movements closely tied to pack-
ice and thus prone to considerable interan-
nual variation in timing and location. Move-

ment away from breeding colonies mainly
during Sept. In Chukchi Sea, large eastern
passage noted on south side of Wrangel Is.
during Sept.–Oct./Nov. with late Oct.–Nov.
movement south into Bering Sea; irregular in
Beaufort Sea, but late Oct. counts of 50–75
birds have been made at Point Barrow. Canadian breeders move east into Baffin Bay in
Oct., and in Nov.–Dec. head south into Davis
Strait. During Sept., large numbers occur off
e. Greenland.
  Winters (Nov./Dec.–Mar./Apr.) in and
around pack-ice in Bering Sea, Lab. Sea, and
Davis Strait (probably also off e. Greenland),
ranging south irregularly (mainly Jan.–Feb.)
to Nfld. Spring movements poorly known, but
in nw. Bering Sea moves north during late
Mar.–Apr. with small numbers (mainly immatures) still present late May–early June in
most years, when recorded east to St. Lawrence Is. and Seward Peninsula. Arrival on
breeding grounds mainly Apr.–early June; also
an early June report from sw. Hudson Bay.
  Away from its normal range in Alaska, casual in Pribilofs (late winter), on s. coast
(mid-Apr.–early May), and in Southeast (mid-
July–early Nov.). Elsewhere in w. N. America,
casual at best (late Oct.–Feb.) from s. Yukon
south to Wash., exceptionally (early Jan.) to s.
Calif. and Colo. Better known as a vagrant in
the East: casual (late Oct.–early Apr., mainly
Dec.–Jan.) from s. Man. east through Great

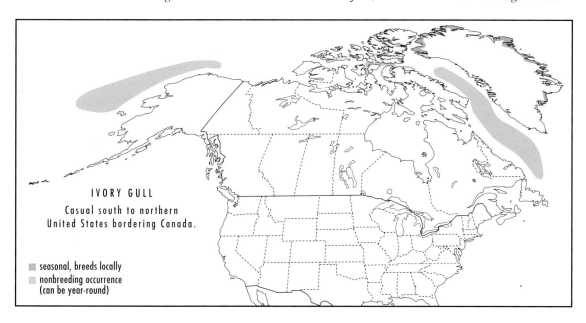

IVORY GULL
Casual south to northern
United States bordering Canada.

■ seasonal, breeds locally
■ nonbreeding occurrence
  (can be year-round)

Lakes region to s. Que., exceptionally (mid-Feb.) south to Tenn.; and casual (mid-Oct.–mid-Apr., mainly late Dec.–early Feb.) from Maritime Provinces south to N.J.

FIELD IDENTIFICATION

SIMILAR SPECIES

Should be unmistakable (more likely to be confused with all-white feral pigeons than with other gulls), but beware leucistic or albino individuals of any gull species. Some first-summer Glaucous and Iceland Gulls can bleach to almost all white but are larger with longer pink legs, larger bills (bicolored pink-and-black on Glaucous, dark with a flesh base on Iceland), and typical large-gull structure and flight.

HABITAT AND BEHAVIOR

Rarely far from ice except for vagrant individuals that wander south in winter. Singles and small groups feed in association with sea ice and on nearby beaches, rarely sitting on the sea. Flight buoyant and graceful, wheeling and sailing proficiently in windy conditions. Breeds in small to medium-sized colonies (5–300 pairs) on rocky and stony substrates, from cliffs and nunataks to gravel terraces, sometimes in association with other gulls such as Black-legged Kittiwakes and Glaucous Gulls.[3] Feeds by surface-seizing and shallow plunging from standing on ice or from hovering flight over water; also picks from water while swimming,[4] and commonly scavenges at carcasses, when notably bold and often aggressive. Usually associates only loosely with other gulls except when scavenging. Mostly silent but calls include high, shrill whistles (recalling Arctic Tern *Sterna paradisaea*) given by birds fighting over carrion.[5]

DESCRIPTION AND MOLT

Adult Cycle. Complete PB molt (Mar.–Sept., interrupted during height of breeding season; molt of outer 1–2 primaries rarely suspended over winter[6]) produces adult basic plumage: plumage entirely ivory-white, some birds with yellowish staining to the primary shafts. Eyes dark, narrow orbital ring black to red in winter and rarely noticeable, but red and more noticeable on breeding birds; bill gray-green with orange to yellow-orange tip, legs and feet black. No evidence of prealternate molt, and no seasonal change in appearance.

First Cycle. Juvenile (mid-Aug./Sept.–Mar./Apr.): plumage ivory-white overall with variable dark sooty blotching on face and throat, scattered dusky spots on rest of head, back, and underparts, highly variable blackish distal spots on upperwing coverts, tertials, and flight feathers. Some birds are mostly white overall with dark face, and black spots largely restricted to flight feathers; others have extensive dark spotting on upperparts. Eyes dark, orbital ring grayish, bill darker gray-green basally than adult with yellow-orange tip and often dusky distal marks from late winter to spring. Attains adult basic plumage by complete PB2 molt (Apr.–Aug.[7]). Adultlike birds with dusky flecking on head, above eyes, may be second basic, but confirmation for known-age birds is lacking.

HYBRIDS

None reported.

NOTES

1. Moynihan 1959; 2. Mallory et al. 2003; 3. Haney 1993; 4. B. Mactavish pers. comm.; 5. Ibid.; 6. Howell 2001c; 7. Ibid.

"TYPICAL" GULLS
HOODED GULLS
(GENUS *Larus*, IN PART)

This subgroup includes three species in the Americas: Laughing, Franklin's, and Lava Gulls. These are medium-sized gulls with moderately thick bills; their bills and legs range from black to red. In alternate plumage they have a black hood, which extends down the nape, and white eye-crescents. The adult upperwings are dark gray with a white trailing edge to the secondaries and inner primaries.

Outer primaries range from mostly black in Lava to black-and-white in Franklin's. Adult plumage is attained in the third cycle. Juvenal plumages are brownish overall, the upperparts with scaly pale edgings. Preformative molts produce an adultlike gray back, and first prealternate molts typically produce partial hoods.

BREEDING ADULT FRANKLIN'S GULL (BEHIND) AND LAUGHING GULL. PP. 95, 350; 91, 346

ADULT BREEDING LAVA GULLS. PP. 98, 354

LENGTH 15–17 IN. (38–43 CM)
PHOTOS 13.1–13.17; 1.5, 14.0

IDENTIFICATION SUMMARY

A medium-sized, three-cycle gull breeding on the coasts of e. N. America and w. Mex., occurring south to n. S. America. Bill relatively long and slightly droop-tipped, with a slight to moderate gonydeal expansion; wings relatively long; at rest, tail tip falls from around tip of P6 to between tips of P6 and P7. Adult has slaty gray upperparts (Kodak 8–9), black wingtips with small white primary tips; alternate has deep red bill and legs, blackish hood with white eye-crescents; basic has blackish bill and legs, dusky auricular mask. First cycle has dusky hindneck, black distal tail band. Franklin's Gull, the only potentially similar species, is slightly smaller with blunter-tipped wings, a shorter bill, thicker white eye-crescents; adult has bold black-and-white wingtip pattern; non-breeding plumages have dark half-hood; first cycle lacks dusky hindneck, black tail band does not extend to tail sides.

TAXONOMY

Noble[1] proposed recognition of two races: nominate *atricilla* from the West Indies, which averages smaller than *L. a. megalopterus* of the American mainland. Dwight[2] and AOU[3] did not recognize *megalopterus,* but Parkes[4] considered it valid, and *megalopterus* was recognized by Burger and Gochfeld.[5]

STATUS AND DISTRIBUTION

Widespread in warmer regions of the Americas. Vagrant to Europe, W. Africa, and across Pacific Ocean as far as Japan and Australia.

Breeding. Breeds locally (Apr.–July/Aug.) in Pacific region from n. Gulf of Calif. south to Colima, Mex., irregularly north to Salton Sea, se. Calif. In Atlantic region, breeds (Apr./May–July/Aug.) along coasts from e. Me. south to Fla., along Gulf of Mex. coast from s.

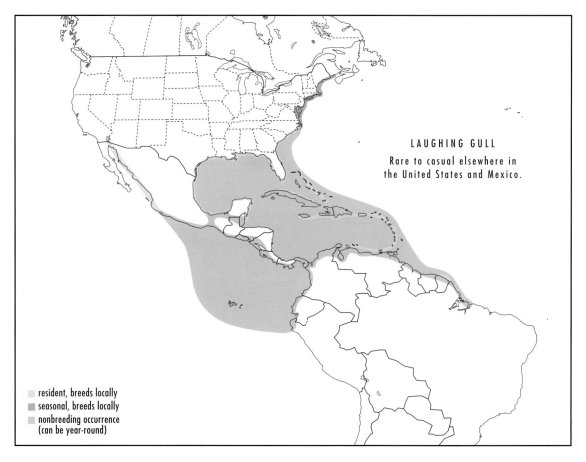

LAUGHING GULL
Rare to casual elsewhere in
the United States and Mexico.

resident, breeds locally
seasonal, breeds locally
nonbreeding occurrence
(can be year-round)

U.S. to Yucatán Peninsula, Mex. and locally in Caribbean region from Bahamas to islands off n. coasts of Venezuela and French Guiana. Nonbreeding birds widespread through most of breeding range in summer (Apr.–Aug.). Also two small recent colonies inland in s. Texas, east to Lake Amistad, Val Verde Co.,[6] and has nested on islands off N.S. and N.B. A few attempt to breed in s. Great Lakes region (for example, Ohio and Wisc.) and some may hybridize with Ring-billed Gulls.[7]

Breeding populations in N. America (especially New England and Mid-Atlantic region) severely depleted in late nineteenth and early twentieth centuries due to human persecution, but since rebounded. More-recent declines from New England and Mid-Atlantic region presumed due to southward breeding expansion of Great Black-backed and Herring Gulls.[8]

Nonbreeding. Fairly common to common (mainly Aug./Sept.–Mar./Apr.; smaller numbers in nonbreeding range May–July) along Pacific Coast from Sinaloa, Mex., south to n. Peru, uncommon to rare and local north to Gulf of Calif. and coasts of Baja Calif. Sur; rare to casual south to n. Chile (Aug.–Dec.)[9,10] and north (mainly Feb.–Sept.) to Pacific Coast of Calif., casually (May–Sept.) to Wash. Uncommon to fairly common (mainly May–Nov.) to Salton Sea and casual (mainly Apr.–Sept., but scattered records year-round) inland elsewhere throughout the West, where recorded north to Wash. and Mont., exceptionally north to sw. Hudson Bay (July–Aug.). Rare wanderer offshore in the e. Tropical Pacific Ocean (mainly Oct.–May), reaching Clipperton Atoll, Cocos Is., and Galápagos. In Latin America, away from Pacific Coast lowlands, regular wanderer inland (mainly Sept.–Apr.; to 3,000 m) from cen. Mex. to Guatemala; casual to rare inland (Nov.–Jan.; to 3,500 m) in Andes and Amazonian lowlands of Ecuador and Peru;[11] and casual w. Brazil.[12]

Migrates in e. U.S. along coast, tidal rivers, and estuaries. In fall, peak movements from New England to Mid-Atlantic Coast late Aug.–Sept., but small numbers linger to late Dec.–early Jan., mainly south from N.J. Generally common nonbreeding visitor (Aug./Sept.–Mar./Apr.) on Atlantic Coast from S.C. to Fla. (where many also winter inland), throughout Gulf of Mex. and Caribbean region, and along coasts of Middle America to n. coast of S. America. Rare east to ne. Brazil; accidental Rio Grande do Sul, se. Brazil. Small numbers winter north to Outer Banks of N.C., but very rare or casual farther north

in midwinter (late Jan.–Feb.). Casual inland in winter in Midwest, north to s. Great Lakes. Rare in winter in Bermuda (where uncommon at other seasons). First spring migrants detected early Mar. in Mid-Atlantic region, late Mar. in New England. Main movements on Atlantic Coast of U.S. Apr.–early May, and rare nonbreeding visitor (mainly May–July) north to Nfld., casually (late June, early Nov.) to Greenland. Rare but increasing visitor (mainly late Apr.–May, casual to rare through summer and fall) in interior e. U.S. and s. Canada, especially s. Great Lakes region. Tropical disturbances can push small to moderate numbers inland and north along coast to Atlantic Canada (exceptionally, thousands occurred in N.S. after Hurricane Gladys in 1968[13]).

FIELD IDENTIFICATION

SIMILAR SPECIES

Laughing Gull is a fairly distinctive species and in much of its range there are no regularly occurring similar species. Franklin's Gull (breeding in interior N. America, wintering along coasts of w. S. America) is the only potentially similar species. Attention to a few key points, such as bill size and shape, wing-tip pattern, and first-cycle tail pattern, usually allows ready separation of these two species. Also, calls of adult Franklin's Gull tend to be higher and more yelping, less crowing, than those of adult Laughing Gull.

FRANKLIN'S GULL slightly smaller (noticeable in direct comparison) with shorter and more-rounded wings, shorter legs, and shorter bill that lacks droop-tipped look of Laughing Gull; all plumages have thicker white eye-crescents, pale gray tail. Adult Franklin's has large white primary tips (which can be abraded in midsummer), a white medial band inside the black wingtips, pale gray bases to the underside of the outer primaries (very different from blackish underwing wedge of Laughing). Adult basic Franklin's has a well-defined blackish half-hood offsetting bold white eye-crescents. First-cycle Franklin's has a blackish half-hood offsetting bold white eye-crescents, a paler to whitish hindneck, whiter chest and underparts, grayish greater coverts, whitish underwings (lacking strong dusky tips to axillars), broader white tips to grayer inner primaries, and its narrower black tail band does not reach the tail sides (a pattern shown by some first-winter Laughing Gulls that replace outer rectrices). First-summer (and second-summer) Franklin's Gulls have slaty gray upperparts, and their wingtip pattern (when lacking the white medial band) can suggest adult or second-cycle Laughing Gull (latter, in alternate plumage, can have partial hood suggesting immature Franklin's); note structural features, and that the black underwing-tip of Franklin's is much more restricted and contrasts sharply with the pale gray primary bases.

HABITAT AND BEHAVIOR

Mainly coastal, also inland and offshore. Beaches, estuaries, harbors, coastal lagoons, river mouths, inshore waters, parking lots, garbage dumps, lakes, rivers, and marshes; often follows fishing boats and ferries. Nests colonially on low sandy and rocky islands along and near the coast, and in saltmarshes, at times in association with other water birds. Often in flocks, locally up to a few thousand birds in migration and winter; associates readily with other gulls, terns, and water birds such as pelicans and cormorants. Flight fairly strong and agile, readily snatches bread and scraps in midair. Feeds on small invertebrate prey, taken near water surface from hovering and shallow dives, scavenges readily, and also hawks insects in flight.

DESCRIPTION AND MOLT

Adult Cycle. Complete PB molt (June/July–Sept./Nov.) produces adult basic plumage: head, neck, and underparts white with dusky mottled auricular mask, variable dusky mottling over crown and around nape, white eye-crescents, and faint dusky wash to hindneck and chest sides. Upperparts slaty gray (Kodak 8–9) with narrow white scapular and tertial crescents, black wingtip with small white primary tips out to P9. Rump and tail white. IN FLIGHT: slaty gray upperwing has black leading wedge (black on outer webs of P8–P10 extends to primary coverts; P5 usually lacks black subterminal marks), white trailing edge to secondaries narrows on inner primaries and breaks into small white tips on outer primaries; from below, blackish wingtip blends into dusky gray inner primaries and secondaries; wing-linings whitish. Eyes dark; bill blackish with reddish orange tip to culmen, sometimes dull reddish at base; legs blackish. Partial PA molt (Jan./Feb.–Apr.) produces adult alternate plumage: attains slaty blackish hood with white eye-crescents; underparts can have a pink flush; white primary tips can wear off. Orbital ring red, bill deep reddish to bright red (sometimes with a dark subterminal band), legs dark purplish to deep red.

First Cycle. Juvenile (June/July–Oct.): head, neck, chest, and sides brownish with white eye-crescents, whitish throat, and variable whitish grizzling and tipping, especially on crown and chest; belly to undertail coverts white. Upperparts brown with scaly buff (fading to whitish) edgings to scapulars and upperwing coverts; scapulars sometimes with paler centers; tertials dark brown to blackish brown with whitish edging, wingtips black with narrow whitish tips out to P7/P8. Remiges blackish, becoming paler and browner on inner primaries, with white tips to secondaries fading out on inner primaries. White tail coverts and pale grayish to whitish tail base contrast with broad black distal tail band, narrowly tipped whitish. IN FLIGHT: brownish overall with white belly to tail coverts, blackish flight feathers with white secondary tips and contrasting white uppertail coverts. Underwings overall dusky brownish to whitish, washed and mottled brownish. Eyes dark, bill blackish (sometimes with fine pale tip and dull-flesh hue basally), legs blackish. Partial PF molt (late July/Aug.–Nov./Dec.; often includes upperwing coverts, sometimes tertials) produces formative plumage: head whitish with pattern similar to heavily marked adult basic (dusky-mottled auricular mask, variable dusky mottling on crown and nape); neck, chest, and sides grayish, often mixed with retained brown juvenal feathers; back slaty gray, contrasting with faded pale brownish upperwing coverts, or some upperwing coverts and tertials replaced by slaty gray, adultlike feathers; wingtips faded and browner. Some birds replace one to all rectrices with white feathers during Dec.–Feb., possibly as part of PA1 molt (Jan.–Apr.), which produces first alternate plumage: some birds attain a mottled, slaty blackish hood, others attain a basiclike pattern; tail varies from black to white, often with a mixed, piano-key pattern in late winter.

Second Cycle. Complete PB2 molt (late May/June–Aug./Oct.) produces second basic plumage: resembles adult basic but neck, chest, and sides variably washed gray to solidly smoky gray; black in primaries more extensive (P5 and sometimes P4 with subterminal black), alula and primary coverts often streaked black, underwing coverts sometimes with dark flecks, and secondaries and tail can have black subterminal marks (rarely forming a partial tail band); 57 percent of second-cycle birds from New York had at least partial tail bands.[14] Partial PA2 molt (Jan./Feb.–Apr.) produces second alternate plumage: resembles adult alternate except for wing and tail differences; some birds have only a mottled hood or half-hood and variable dusky hindneck wash; white primary tips often wear off. Bill and legs average duller reddish. Adult plumage attained by complete PB3 molt (June/July–Sept./Oct.), but up to 4 percent of third-cycle birds have dark tail markings.[15]

HYBRIDS

Reported with Ring-billed Gull,[16] presumed with Black-headed Gull,[17] and possibly with Gray-hooded Gull in Senegal.[18]

NOTES

1. Noble 1916; 2. Dwight 1925; 3. AOU 1957; 4. Parkes 1952; 5. Burger and Gochfeld 1996; 6. Lockwood 2001; 7. Peterjohn 2001; 8. Burger 1996; 9. Hoogendoorn 1993; 10. Howell pers. obs.; 11. O'Donnell and González 2003; 12. Williams 1995; 13. Tufts 1986; 14. Belant and Dolbeer 1996; 15. Ibid.; 16. Henshaw 1992; 17. Sibley 1994; 18. Erard et al. 1984

LENGTH 13.3–15 IN. (34–38 CM)
PHOTOS 14.0–14.15, 3.0

IDENTIFICATION SUMMARY

A medium-small, three-cycle gull breeding in the prairies of interior N. America; nonbreed- ing range along the Pacific Coast of S. America. Bill medium size with slight gonydeal expansion; wings slightly rounded; at rest, tail tip falls between tips of P6 and P7. Adult has slaty gray upperparts (Kodak 8–9) with a white band inside the black wingtips; alter-

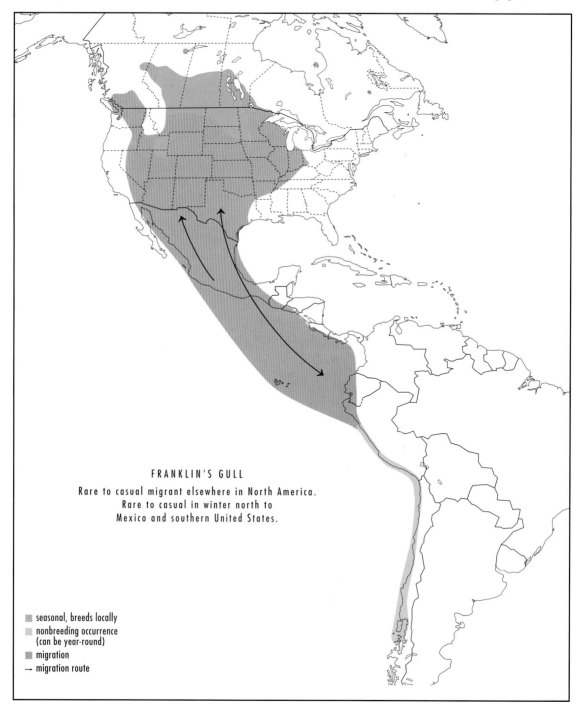

FRANKLIN'S GULL

Rare to casual migrant elsewhere in North America.
Rare to casual in winter north to
Mexico and southern United States.

▨ seasonal, breeds locally
▨ nonbreeding occurrence
  (can be year-round)
▨ migration
→ migration route

nate has red bill and legs, blackish hood with thick white eye-crescents; basic has blackish bill and legs, well-defined blackish half-hood. First cycle has whitish hindneck, narrow black distal tail band not reaching tail sides. Laughing Gull is the main confusion species. It is slightly larger with longer and more-pointed wings, a longer and stouter, droop-tipped bill, and narrower white eye-crescents; adult Laughing has mostly black wingtips; nonbreeding plumages have a dusky auricular mask; first cycle has dusky hindneck, wider black tail band extending to tail sides. Also see Sabine's Gull.

TAXONOMY
Monotypic.

STATUS AND DISTRIBUTION
Breeds interior w. N. America, winters Humboldt Current coasts of Peru and Chile. Vagrant to Europe, W. Africa, and across Pacific Ocean as far as Japan and Australia.
Breeding. Breeds (May–Aug.) from cen. Alberta and s. Man. south to s.-cen. Mont., N. D., nw. Minn., and ne. S.D. Isolated nesting colonies south and west to e. Ore., Nev., and ne. Utah. Has nested south to ne. Calif., n. Colo., Neb., Kans., and nw. Iowa. Breeding range shifted west and south through 1900s. Large numbers of nonbreeders occur locally in summer away from core nesting areas, for example, in e.-cen. B.C., cen. Man., and Colo.
Nonbreeding. Ranges (mainly Nov.–Mar.) along Humboldt Current coast of S. America from cen. Peru to cen. Chile (mainly 10–35° south; where common to locally abundant); irregularly fairly common to uncommon south to Chiloé and Golfo de Corcovado (43° south), thence rare south into Chilean fjords and casual (mainly Jan.) south to Beagle Channel (54° south).[1,2] Uncommon (Dec.–Feb.) north along Pacific Coast of S. America to Ecuador, and rare in e. and coastal Argentina, south to Santa Cruz (46° south).[3,4] Rare to casual in winter north to w. Mex. and e. Tex. Occasional winter records elsewhere in U.S., north to the s. Great Lakes and Long Is., N.Y.
Common to abundant southbound migrant (mainly Aug.–Nov.) along its main migration corridor: south through Great Plains (mainly Aug.–Oct.; departs Prairie Provinces by Oct.) to Gulf of Mex. coastal lowlands from s. Tex. and e. Mex. (mainly mid-Oct.–Nov.) south to Veracruz, crossing Isthmus of Tehuantepec, and thence south and southeast along Pacific Coast and over offshore waters (rare in Colombia but regular in and around Galápagos)

to Humboldt Current. Fall migration begins late July, but mainly Aug.; peaks on n. and cen. Great Plains Sept.–early Oct. and a bit later on s. Great Plains, where large numbers occur late Oct. even into early Nov. (for example, an amazing concentration of 750,000 birds at Lake Texhoma, n.-cen. Tex., 4 Nov. 1971[5]), with lingerers into Dec. From s. Great Plains migration appears rapid (nonstop?) to Humboldt Current, where large numbers arrive early Nov.
Northbound migration (mainly Mar.–May) follows a similar route in reverse, although shifting slightly west from Mex. north: birds start leaving the Humboldt Current region in late Feb.–Mar., and most pass north through Mex. in Mar.–Apr. Spring arrivals in U.S. as early as late Feb.–early Mar. north to Neb. and S.D., but not in any numbers until late Mar., with peak movements late Apr.–early May and arrival on breeding grounds mainly May. Nonbreeders rare to casual (May–Sept.) from cen. Chile[6,7] north through Middle America, and (June–July) nearly continent wide in N. America.
Uncommon to very rare migrant west of the Rockies (away from breeding areas). Rare in fall (mainly Aug.–early Sept.) north to se. Alaska, casual (mainly May–July) north to w. Aleutians, Pribilofs, Nunavut, n. Man., and Greenland. Uncommon to rare migrant in midwestern states and Ont., occasionally more numerous in fall (for instance, after strong cold fronts). Casual to very rare along Atlantic Coast from Nfld. to Fla., and (mainly Sept.–Dec.) in Caribbean and along mainland coasts from Yucatán Peninsula, Mex., south to Panama and Venezuela. Casual to rare (mainly Oct.–Nov., Mar.; to 4,000 m) in Andes from Ecuador to Bolivia[8,9] and in s. Amazonian Peru.[10] Accidental off Atlantic Coast of se. Brazil[11] and at South Georgia.[12]

FIELD IDENTIFICATION

SIMILAR SPECIES
Franklin's Gull is a fairly distinctive species. Laughing Gull (mainly coastal, from e. N. America and Mex. south to S. America), and Sabine's Gull (as a fall migrant in the interior West) are usually the only species to consider. Attention to a few key points, such as bill size and shape, wingtip pattern, and first-cycle hindneck and tail pattern, usually allows ready identification. Also, calls of adult Laughing Gull tend to be lower and more crowing, less yelping, than those of adult Franklin's Gull.
LAUGHING GULL slightly larger (noticeable in direct comparison) with longer, more-pointed,

and proportionately narrower wings, longer legs, and a longer, slightly droop-tipped bill; all plumages have narrower white eye-crescents. Adult has small white primary tips and a black leading wedge above and below (very different from the white medial band between black wingtips and pale gray outer primary bases of adult Franklin's) and all-white tail. Adult basic Laughing has a dusky auricular mask. First-cycle Laughing also has a dusky auricular mask, plus a dusky hindneck and chest, browner greater coverts, narrower white tips to inner primaries, more dusky mottling on underwing (especially axillar tips), and a broader black tail band that reaches the tail sides. First-summer (and second-summer) Franklin's Gulls have slaty gray upperparts and their wingtip pattern (when lacking the white medial band) can suggest second-cycle or adult Laughing Gull: note structural features and that the black underwing-tip of Franklin's is much more restricted and contrasts sharply with the pale gray primary bases.

SABINE'S GULL smaller and more petite with a finer bill. Adult Sabine's has bill usually tipped yellow; lacks white eye-crescents, and alternate-plumage hood dark slaty gray; in flight, its diagnostic upperwing pattern is striking. Juvenile Sabine's has more solidly brown hindneck and brown, scaly upperparts retained through fall migration, reduced white tips to outer primaries, flesh legs, plus diagnostic and striking upperwing pattern, forked tail; from below in flight, note dark band across secondary bases.

HABITAT AND BEHAVIOR

Interior, coastal, and pelagic. Beaches, estuaries, harbors, river mouths, inshore waters, plowed and flooded fields, garbage dumps, lakes, rivers, and marshes. Nests colonially in freshwater marshes, building platform nests on floating weed mats and in emergent vegetation, at times in association with other water birds. In migration and winter, associates readily with other gulls, terns, and water birds on beaches, rocky coasts, at river mouths, etc. Often in the company of Laughing Gulls in Texas and Mexico, and of Gray Gulls and Elegant Terns in Peru and Chile. In migration, occurs in spectacular flocks of up to tens of thousands, with silvery lines streaming north and south along and near the coast. Flight fairly strong with measured, bouyant wingbeats. Feeds on small invertebrate prey taken near water surface from hovering, shallow dives, and while swimming; also pokes in wet

and disturbed ground, scavenges at sewage outfalls, fish plants, and dumps, and adeptly hawks insects in flight.

DESCRIPTION AND MOLT

Unusual among birds in having two complete molts a year, although PA molts can be incomplete, at least in some years (probably reflecting winter food shortages related to El Niño events).

Adult Cycle. Complete PB molt (late June/July–mid-Sept./Oct.) produces adult basic plumage: head, neck, and underparts white with variable, blackish-mottled half-hood setting off bold white eye-crescents; underparts sometimes with a pink flush. Upperparts slaty gray (Kodak 8–9) with white scapular and tertial crescents, black wingtips (black on outer web of P10 reaches primary coverts) with bold white primary tips out to P10. Rump and uppertail coverts white, tail pale smoky gray (often looks whitish). IN FLIGHT: slaty gray upperwing has variable white medial band across base of black wingtip (P5 usually lacks subterminal black), and P10 often has white mirror or mirror-tip; white trailing edge to secondaries and inner primaries breaks into discrete white tips on outer primaries; from below, blackish wingtip usually separated from smoky gray bases to remiges by white medial band; wing-linings whitish. Eyes dark; bill blackish with reddish orange tip to culmen; legs blackish. Complete (rarely incomplete, with outer 1–2 primaries retained[13]) PA molt (late Nov./Dec.–Mar./Apr.) produces adult alternate plumage: attains slaty blackish hood with bold white eye-crescents; underparts often have a pink flush, which can be striking on spring migrants, and wingtip averages more-extensive white, for example, on P9–P10. Orbital ring reddish pink, bill red, often with a blackish subterminal ring, legs dark reddish.

First Cycle. Juvenile (July–Sept.): head, neck, and underparts white with blackish-mottled half-hood setting off white eye-crescents; neck and chest sides mottled and washed dusky brownish. Lower hindneck and upperparts dark brown with scaly buff (fading to whitish) edgings to scapulars and upperwing coverts; greater coverts usually plainer and grayer; tertials dark brown to blackish brown with whitish edging, wingtips black with white tips out to P9/P10. Remiges blackish, becoming paler and grayer on inner primaries, with white tips to secondaries and inner primaries. White tail coverts and pale smoky gray tail with contrasting black distal tail band tipped whitish and narrowest at edges, not extending to outer web of R6. IN FLIGHT: head and underparts white with blackish half-hood, upperparts brown with grayer greater coverts, blackish remiges with fairly broad white tips to secondaries and inner primaries, whitish rump and tail with contrasting black distal band. Underwings overall whitish with dusky gray remiges, blackish wingtips, and distinct white trailing edge to secondaries and inner primaries. Eyes dark, bill blackish, legs dark, dull flesh to blackish. Partial PF molt (Aug.–Nov./Dec.) produces formative plumage: attains mostly gray back, head and underparts often slightly cleaner and whiter (rarely with pink flush), wing coverts bleach to plainer brownish and white primary tips can abrade. Complete to incomplete PA1 molt (Dec./Jan.–Mar./May; 2–3 juvenal outer primaries often retained; rarely, few or no primaries molted) produces first alternate plumage: overall resembles adult basic but black in wingtips more extensive, typically extending to primary coverts on outer webs of P9–P10, white medial band absent or reduced to white tonguetips on P6–P7; P5 typically with a subterminal black mark; primary coverts and alula often with black streaks, and secondaries and tail can have black subterminal marks. Some birds develop a more complete hood, but forehead and lores heavily mottled whitish. Bill black or with orange tip to culmen.

Second Cycle. Complete PB2 molt (June–Sept./Oct.) produces second basic plumage: resembles adult basic but averages more black and less white in wingtip, with white medial band narrower to almost absent; "retarded" birds attain wingtip pattern like first alternate with black marks on primary coverts, whereas "advanced" birds perhaps inseparable from adult. Complete to incomplete PA2 molt (Dec.–Mar./Apr.) produces second alternate plumage: resembles adult alternate but some have less white in wingtip; some may have white flecking in black hood. Bill and legs average darker. Adult plumage attained by complete PB3 molt (late June/July–Sept./Oct.).

HYBRIDS
With Ring-billed Gull[14] and Gray-hooded Gull.[15]

NOTES

1. Babarskas and Chebez 1999; 2. Marín and Couve 2001; 3. Devillers and Terschuren 1977; 4. M. Pearman pers. comm.; 5. Pulich 1988; 6. D. J. Evans pers. comm.; 7. Howell pers. obs.; 8. Fjeldsa and Krabbe 1986; 9. Fjeldsa and Krabbe 1990; 10. T. S. Schulenberg pers. comm.; 11. Almeida 2003; 12. Reid 1998; 13. BM specimens; 14. Weseloh 1981; 15. Erard et al. 1984

LENGTH 17.5–19 IN. (44–48 CM)
PHOTOS 15.0–15.9; I.33

IDENTIFICATION SUMMARY

Restricted to coasts of Galápagos Is., Ecuador, where no similar species occur. A medium-sized, three-cycle gull whose structure recalls a large Laughing Gull. Dark overall with black bill and legs, adult and older immature have contrasting dark hood and whitish eye-crescents.

TAXONOMY

Monotypic.

STATUS AND DISTRIBUTION

The world's rarest gull, with population probably fewer than 300 pairs.[1] Endemic to the Galápagos Is., Ecuador (around 0° latitude), where local and mostly sedentary, although nonbreeding birds wander among the islands. Breeds year-round on a 9–12 month cycle, but most eggs probably laid May–Oct.[2]

FIELD IDENTIFICATION

SIMILAR SPECIES

Unmistakable in its very limited range. Gray Gull (unrecorded in Galápagos but could occur) is more lightly built with longer and thinner bill, lacks contrasting pale uppertail coverts and pale eye-crescents of Lava Gull.

HABITAT AND BEHAVIOR

Coastal. Rocky and sandy coasts, harbors, and fish-cleaning areas. Solitary nester on low islets or near saline lagoons.[3] Found singly, in pairs, or loose aggregations up to 20–30 birds at feeding sites such as fishing harbors. Bold and confiding when scavenging, running around one's feet, but wary in vicinity of nest. Rarely if ever alights on water. Varied crowing and laughing calls reminiscent of Laughing Gull.

DESCRIPTION

Adult Cycle (9–12 months). No strong seasonal difference in adult plumages. Complete PB molt (timing varies) produces adult basic plumage: sooty blackish to brownish black hood (with white eye-crescents and pale gray mottling on throat) contrasts with dark slaty neck, which blends into slaty blue-gray underparts; undertail coverts whitish. Upperparts dark slaty gray (Kodak 9.5–10.5) with narrow whitish scapular crescent and bolder white tertial crescent; uppertail coverts contrastingly pale gray (obvious in flight) with dusky central stripe. Upperwings dark slaty, becoming black on wingtips, with white trailing edge to secondaries and narrower whitish tips out to P7/P8; underwings dark. Tail smoky gray with pale gray outermost rectrices. Eyes brown with reddish orbital ring, bill black with red to orange-red gape and maxilla tip, legs blackish. Partial PA molt (overlaps in timing with completion of PB primary molt) produces adult alternate plumage: cleaner-cut and more solidly blackish hood has bolder white eye-crescents. Breeding adults have more prominent red orbital ring and gape.

First Cycle. Juvenile: Dark sooty brown overall with grayish eye-crescents not contrasting. Back, upperwing coverts, and tertials with pale buffy brown to gray-brown scaly edgings that bleach to whitish; slight contrast of darker head, neck, and chest with slightly grayer underparts; undertail coverts pale gray to whitish. Forehead and chin can bleach paler. Uppertail coverts pale grayish with dusky central stripe. Flight feathers blackish with narrow pale grayish tips to secondaries and inner primaries; tail tip faintly paler but soon wears away; bases of outer rectrices paler and grayer, visible from below and on fully spread tail; underwings dark. Eyes dark brown, bill and legs blackish. PF molt (often includes upperwing coverts and tertials) probably starts within a month or so of fledging, produces formative plumage: head, neck, back, upperwing coverts, and underparts sooty to slaty gray, darkest on head and neck which have messy cut-off from gray chest; eye-crescents pale gray to whitish; scapular crescents indistinct; tertials with fairly broad, pale brownish tips. PA1 molt (may include upperwing coverts but rarely tertials) produces first alternate plumage: much like formative plumage but head and neck can be more contrastingly blackish with whiter eye-crescents; slaty gray upperparts often contrast slightly with relatively faded, brownish gray tertials. One to all rectrices often replaced in first cycle: new rectrices smoky gray with dark speckling and variable dark subterminal marks that can form a broad dark distal band on inner rectrices. Primaries often faded brown and heavily worn; exceptionally, 1–2 outer primaries can be replaced in first cycle.[4] Orbital ring can become dull pinkish, maxilla tip dull reddish.

Second Cycle. Complete PB2 molt produces second basic plumage: similar to first alternate but more uniformly sooty gray above with more contrasting blackish head and neck; cleaner whitish scapular and tertial crescents; eye-crescents often duller, pale gray to whitish; new black primaries relatively broad and rounded with pale gray tips out to P5/P6. Upperwings dark slaty with black wingtips and pale gray to whitish trailing edge to blackish secondaries. Tail variable: typically smoky gray with variable dark mottling distally (on some forming broad dark distal band on inner rectrices) and R6 mostly pale gray; on others mostly blackish with some gray basally on outer rectrices, R6 mostly pale. Eyes brown,

orbital ring gray to pinkish, bill and legs black, often with reddish maxilla tip. Overlapping partial PA2 molt produces second alternate plumage: head and body similar to alternate adult but plumage averages duller and browner; note flight feathers. Some birds may replace one or more rectrices in PA2 molt. Orbital ring, gape, and maxilla tip red. Adult plumage probably attained by complete PB3 molt, but birds with black on alula, dark mottling on carpal region, dark secondary bases, and slight brownish cast overall may be third cycle.

HYBRIDS
None reported.

NOTES

1. Snow and Snow 1969; 2. Ibid.; 3. Ibid.; 4. CAS specimen 1840

PRIMITIVE WHITE-HEADED GULLS
(GENUS *Larus*, IN PART)

We place six medium-sized to medium-large species in this "catch-all" subgroup, while recognizing that they are probably not all closely related: Heermann's, Gray, Dolphin, Belcher's, Olrog's, and Black-tailed Gulls. Moynihan considered the White-headed Gulls (subgenus *Larus*) simply to comprise Dolphin Gull as one subgroup, and all the others as a second subgroup, although he commented on the similarities of Dolphin, Belcher's, Olrog's, and Black-tailed Gulls. He treated Heermann's and Gray Gulls as "white-hooded gulls" (subgenus *Xema*), but we consider it more useful to group these two species here; Crochet et al. (2000) also allied these two species with the *Larus* assemblage. Bills vary from notably thick to slender, and adult bills and legs range from black or red to yellow. Adults of this so-called primitive group collectively show various characters often associated with immature plumage, including black in the tail, an extensive dark hood in basic plumage, and mostly black wingtips lacking white spots or mirrors. Adult upperwings are slaty to blackish with a white trailing edge and black tips. Adult plumage is attained in the third or fourth cycle. Juvenal plumages vary from mostly dark brown to a more conventional pattern of prominent pale edgings on dark upperparts. First prealternate molts are generally quite extensive.

ADULT BREEDING HEERMANN'S GULL.
PP. 102, 357

ADULT BREEDING GRAY GULL. PP. 107, 360

ADULT BREEDING DOLPHIN GULL.
PP. 110, 363

ADULT BREEDING BELCHER'S GULL.
PP. 114, 366

ADULT BREEDING OLROG'S GULL WITH CHICKS. PP. 118, 369

ADULT BREEDING BLACK-TAILED GULL.
PP. 121, 372

LENGTH 18–20 IN. (45.5–50.5 CM)
PHOTOS 16.0–16.21, I.34–I.35

IDENTIFICATION SUMMARY

This attractive, medium-sized, four-cycle gull breeds in nw. Mexico and is a regular post-breeding visitor north along the Pacific Coast to s. Canada, casually to se. Alaska. Bill average in depth with slight gonydeal expansion; tail tip falls between tips of P6 and P7 at rest. All ages are dark slaty gray to sooty brown overall with black legs. Alternate adult has a clean white head and mostly red bill; immature bills are pinkish to reddish basally. No other all-dark gull occurs regularly in its range.

TAXONOMY
Monotypic.

STATUS AND DISTRIBUTION
Endemic to w. N. America.

Breeding. Breeds (Apr.–July) and partly resident in the Gulf of Calif., Mex., with 95 percent of the nesting population on Isla Rasa (which has 300,000–400,000 adults[1]), and south locally to n. Jalisco and off Pacific Coast of cen. Baja Calif. Peninsula. Has nested on 19 islands in w. Mex., but during 1999 to 2000 bred on only 12 islands there.[2] Since 1979, a few pairs have attempted nesting in coastal cen. Calif. (San Luis Obispo Co. north to San Francisco Co.);[3] in 1990, hybridized with California Gull in Nevada.[4]

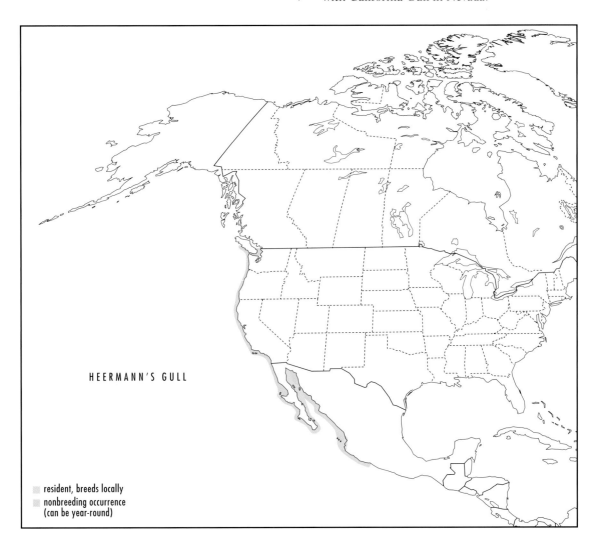

HEERMANN'S GULL

resident, breeds locally
nonbreeding occurrence
(can be year-round)

Nonbreeding. Post-breeding dispersal (mainly June–Nov.) mostly north along Pacific Coast of N. America, regularly north to sw. B.C. (mainly s. Vancouver Is.); also south to cen. Mex., where uncommon to fairly common south to Colima, rare or casual south to Oaxaca and Guatemala. Fairly common to common (mainly May–Feb.) along both coasts of Baja Calif. Peninsula (casual inland). Northbound movement in Calif. and Ore. evident by June (a few birds in May), with numbers increasing dramatically after mid-June; peak numbers on cen. Calif. coast mid-July–Nov. Farther north, a few appear in sw. B.C. by June–early July, with peak numbers in coastal Wash. and sw. B.C. Aug.–mid-Oct., after which there is rapid southward withdrawal. Casual (Aug.–Sept.) north to se. Alaska. Often remains common in Ore. and n. Calif. until mid-Nov., in s. Calif. into Feb. Rare north of cen. Calif. after Dec., although some nonbreeders remain in cen. and s. Calif. through spring. Uncommon more than about 50 km offshore. Casual inland in Wash., along coastal slope of Ore. (west of the Cascades), and Calif. (late Aug.–mid-Nov.), exceptionally in small flocks.

Well away from the coast, most frequently found at Salton Sea (where rare; mainly mid-Apr.–early Oct., casually into winter), with scattering of records (Apr.–Oct.) elsewhere in se. Calif. (north to at least Mono Co.) and north to Nev. Casual (mainly Sept.–Nov.) along Colo. R. north to Lake Mead (Ariz./Nev.), and elsewhere in Ariz.

Accidental (mainly Aug.–Dec.) east in N. America to Great Lakes, Va., Fla., and s. Tex., with some individuals remaining many months, for example, Aug. 1979 to Nov. 1981 in Mich./Ohio, Nov. 1999 to Sept. 2000 in Ont., and Oct. 2000–Aug. 2004 or later in Fla.

FIELD IDENTIFICATION

SIMILAR SPECIES

Uniformly dark plumage, black legs, and red to pinkish bill base diagnostic. First-cycle California Gull and Black-tailed Gull approach Heermann's in overall darkness and have pink, black-tipped bills—but both have pinkish legs, less solidly dark plumage overall with obvious white on tail coverts, bolder pale patterning on wing coverts, and variegated A1 scapulars.

JAEGERS (genus *Stercorarius*) can be mistaken for Heermann's Gull, and vice versa, especially because Heermann's Gulls often chase and kleptoparasitize gulls and terns—but usually this confusion is short lived. Jaegers have white flashes at the base of the underside of their primaries (occasional adult Heermann's have a white patch on the upperwing, but on the primary coverts), immatures often have distinct barring on their underwings, and most have elongated and projecting central rectrices.

GRAY GULL (Pacific Coast of S. America) averages smaller and slimmer overall with more-slender black bill in all ages, adult is paler and more-uniform gray overall (upperparts paler); adult tail has variable gray basally and lacks bold white tip of adult Heermann's.

HABITAT AND BEHAVIOR

Coastal. Sandy and rocky coasts, river mouths, coastal lagoons, fishing harbors. Rarely occurs more than a kilometer inland but ranges over inshore waters, mostly within 50 km of shore. Nests mainly on rocky islands and islets, locally in dense colonies. Nonbreeding birds often in flocks (locally up to a few thousand birds), associating readily with other gulls and water birds. Feeds commonly by scavenging (when often bold and aggressive for its size), also forages in intertidal and surface waters for marine invertebrates, and often seen in association with Brown Pelicans—which Heermann's Gulls routinely kleptoparasitize.

DESCRIPTION AND MOLT

Adult Cycle. Complete PB molt (May/mid-June–Sept./Oct.) produces adult basic plumage: head, neck, and underparts gray, head speckled and mottled dark slaty to brownish with whitish-grizzled forehead and lores, white eye-crescents, and whitish throat. Upperparts darker, slaty gray (Kodak 10–11.5) with bold whitish scapular crescent, broad whitish tertial tips, and pale gray uppertail coverts. Flight feathers blackish, tail boldly tipped pale gray to white, secondaries and inner primaries boldly tipped white, with narrower whitish tips out to about P7. Some adults (< 1 percent) have a variable number of white primary coverts forming a bold white patch on the upperwing. Underwings dark. Eyes brown to pale grayish with narrow gray to reddish orbital ring, legs blackish. Bill red to bright red with black distal third and small whitish to pale reddish tip, sometimes a small greenish area at mandible base during height of molt. Partial PA molt (*Sept./Oct.*–Jan./Feb.) produces adult alternate plumage: head becomes clean bright white, orbital ring bright red, bill brighter overall and averages reduced distal black. In years of reduced breeding effort (due to food shortages), some birds may attain variable dusky gray mottling on head in alternate plumage. Slaty plumage often bleaches to brownish by summer, so birds undergoing PB molt show a mixture of clean slaty gray and faded brown feathers.

First Cycle. Juvenile (July–Sept.): dark sooty brown overall, slightly paler on underparts, with smoky gray throat. Upperparts with scaly buff edgings—varying individually from very broad to fairly narrow; subscapular and tertial tips can bleach to form pale crescents. Flight feathers blackish, secondaries, inner primaries, and tail narrowly tipped buffy white, which often wears away. IN FLIGHT: dark brown overall with blackish flight feathers, bleached upperwing coverts sometimes forming a paler mid-wing panel; underwings dark. Eyes dark, legs blackish. Bill blackish with dull flesh base, becoming dull flesh pink with black tip. Variable PA1 molt (Sept.–Mar.) often includes upperwing coverts and, in tropical populations, can include primaries.[5] First alternate plumage: head, neck, chest, and flanks dark sooty brown, often mixed with faded juvenal feathers; eye-crescents brown to pale gray and throat whitish; some birds attain whitish flecks in face. Back and variable number of upperwing coverts and tertials dark sooty gray-brown, new subscapulars and tertials tipped pale gray. Retained juvenal wing coverts often bleach to a contrasting pale panel. Bill flesh pink with black tip, often some gray-green basally.

Second Cycle. Complete PB2 molt (Apr.–Aug.) produces second basic plumage: dark sooty brown to gray-brown overall, often with head and neck darker sooty brown; throat smoky gray, eye-crescents brownish to pale gray. Subscapulars and tertials broadly tipped whitish, uppertail coverts mottled smoky gray. Flight feathers blackish; secondaries, inner primaries, and tail narrowly tipped whitish (often lost by wear). Eyes dark brown with narrow gray orbital ring, legs blackish. Bill pinkish orange with gray-green to bluish green base and black distal third with fine pale tip. Partial PA2 molt (Aug.–Mar.; usually includes some upperwing coverts, often some tertials, sometimes inner rectrices) produces second alternate plumage: grayer overall than second basic. Head varies from dark sooty brown with whitish throat and eye-crescents to variably mottled whitish (some may attain mostly white head, perhaps especially in good food years). Some birds attain boldly white-tipped inner rectrices, most often R1. Bill often brightens in spring to orange-red with black distal third and fine pale tip, some still with blue-gray base; most-retarded birds have pinkish bill with black tip, similar to first alternate; orbital ring reddish to bright red.

Third Cycle. Complete PB3 molt (May–Sept.) produces third basic plumage: variably intermediate between B2 and adult basic. Retarded birds dark sooty overall with dark sooty hood variably grizzled whitish in face and on crown, pale gray to whitish eye-crescents. Advanced birds brownish gray overall, darker above, with head coarsely mottled dark brown, throat whitish, face grizzled white and with white eye-crescents. Scapular crescent white and tertials broadly tipped pale gray to white. Flight feathers brownish black, tail boldly tipped pale gray to white, secondaries boldly tipped white, with narrower white tips out to about P5. Eyes brown to pale brown with narrow gray to greenish orbital ring, legs blackish. Bill reddish orange to red with greenish base, black distal third tipped ivory. Partial PA3 molt (Sept.–Feb./Mar.) into third alternate plumage: overall grayer and adultlike, head clean white or with variable dark mottling. Some probably indistinguishable from alternate adult: note flight feathers average browner with narrower white tips to tail and secondaries. Orbital ring becomes red, bill bright red with black distal third and pale tip. Adult plumage attained by complete PB4 molt (May/June–Sept./Oct.).

HYBRIDS
With California Gull.[6]

NOTES

1. Mellink 2001; 2. Ibid.; 3. Roberson et al. 2001; 4. Chisholm and Neel 2003; 5. Howell and Wood 2004; 6. Chisholm and Neel 2003

LENGTH 16.5–18.5 IN. (42–47 CM)
PHOTOS 17.0–17.15

IDENTIFICATION SUMMARY

This attractive, medium-sized, three-cycle gull is unmistakable in its normal range — the desert coasts of western S. America. Bill fairly slender with a slight gonydeal expansion; at rest, tail tip about equal with or slightly longer than tip of P6. All plumages mostly dark (breeding adult has white head) with black bill and black legs.

GRAY GULL

■ seasonal, breeds locally
▨ nonbreeding occurrence
(can be year-round)

Taxonomy

Monotypic.

Status and Distribution

Endemic to w. S. America.

Breeds (Oct./Nov.–Feb./Mar.) inland in Atacama Desert of n. Chile and ranges along coasts north to Colombia, south to s.-cen. Chile. Common nonbreeding resident along desert coasts from cen. Peru (about 7° south) to n. Chile, south to Coquimbo (30° south). Ranges south commonly (Mar.–Sept., irregularly in smaller numbers Oct.–Feb.) to Golfo de Arauco (37° south), thence uncommon to fairly common and irregular (mainly Mar.–Sept.) to Valdivia (40° south), rarely to Golfo de Penas (47° south). Ranges north commonly (mainly May–Aug.) to Guayas, s. Ecuador (2° south), rarely to n. Ecuador and s. Colombia, casually north to Gulf of Panama (Nov.–Feb.) and Cocos Is., Costa Rica (May; 5° north). Accidental in La. (Dec. 1987).[1] Reports from Falkland Is.[2] and S. Orkneys hypothetical.[3]

Southward and northward incursions vary in timing and numbers, probably related to success of breeding season and strength of El Niño events.[4,5] During strong El Niños can have near-complete breeding failure.[6]

Field Identification

Similar Species

None in its normal range, but beware the possibility of melanistic or oiled gulls.

HEERMANN'S GULL (Pacific Coast of N. America) averages larger and bulkier with darker upperparts, thicker bill pinkish with black tip in first cycle, becoming bright red in adult; adult has black tail with bold white tip.

LAVA GULL (sedentary on Galápagos Is.) similar in overall size but stockier, averages darker gray overall with dark hood (and pale eye-crescents) at all ages, black bill stouter with more marked gonydeal expansion and often a fine reddish tip.

Habitat and Behavior

Mainly coastal. Sandy beaches, rocky coasts, river mouths, inshore waters; generally avoids muddy intertidal. Nests colonially inland on remote, stony desert plains of Atacama Desert, commuting to and from coast to feed. Often in flocks, locally to a few thousand birds, and associates readily with other gulls, terns, pelicans, etc., loafing and roosting on coastal rocks. Feeds on small crustaceans in wave-washed zone of sandy beaches, running back and forth after receding and advancing waves like Sanderlings or hanging low over the water into stiff onshore breezes, dropping and lifting off into wind with ebb and flow of waves; also scavenges at fishing boats and fish plants and feeds over schooling fish with terns, boobies, and pelicans.

Description

Adult Cycle. Complete PB molt (mainly Jan.–June) produces adult basic plumage: smoky gray overall (upperparts Kodak 8.5–9.5), slightly paler below, with variably solid, brownish hood; forehead, lores, and narrow eye-ring pale gray to whitish. Remiges blackish with bold white trailing edge to secondaries fading out on inner primaries. Tail gray with variable black subterminal band and white to pale gray tip. Bill and legs black (gape bright orange). Partial PA molt (mainly July–Sept.; may include rectrices) produces adult alternate plumage: white to whitish head contrasts with gray neck, head often with faint smoky wash and whiter eye-ring. Molts more protracted and less regular during El Niño breeding failures,[7] and some nonbreeding birds may attain variable dusky mottling on head in alternate plumage.[8]

First Cycle. Juvenile (Feb.–May): brown overall, slightly paler below and often with paler forehead, throat, and eye-ring; scapulars and upperwing coverts with scaly buff edgings, uppertail coverts tipped buff; flight feathers brownish black; secondaries and tail narrowly tipped buffy white. Partial PA1 molt (mainly Apr.–Sept.; often includes upperwing coverts and tertials) produces first alternate plumage: new feathers of head, body, and upperwings brownish gray, fading to browner, and contrasting with bleached brown to creamy juvenal feathers.

Second Cycle. Complete PB2 molt (mainly Oct./Nov.–Feb./Mar.) produces second basic plumage: smoky gray overall with variable brownish cast (especially to upperwings) and a browner hood (extending down to upper neck) with paler forehead and indistinct pale eye-ring. Remiges brownish black with narrower white secondary tips than adult; tail blackish with narrow pale gray to whitish tip; some birds with grayish tail base visible mainly when tail spread. Partial PA2 molt (mainly Mar.–Sept.; often includes upperwing coverts and may include rectrices) produces second alternate plumage: many birds similar to adult alternate but upperwings browner, white secondary tips narrower, and some retain brownish hood markings; note tail pattern. Apparently attains adult plumage by complete PB3 molt (mainly Nov.–Apr.) but third basic may average a more-extensive and less neatly defined brownish hood than adult, and black distal tail band may average broader; confirmation needed from known-age birds.

HYBRIDS
None reported.

NOTES

1. Muth 1988; 2. Cawkwell and Hamilton 1961; 3. Mazar B. and Pearman 2001; 4. Howell pers. obs.; 5. Ridgely and Greenfield 2001; 6. Guerra et al. 1988; 7. Ibid.; 8. Howell pers. obs.

LENGTH 16–18 IN. (41–46 CM)
PHOTOS 18.0–18.16

IDENTIFICATION SUMMARY

A distinctive, medium-sized, and fairly stocky three-cycle gull found along coasts of s. S. America and the Falkland Is. Bill very deep and swollen on adult, more slender on first-cycle birds; tail relatively long with tip falling at or slightly past tip of P7 at rest. Adult has pearl gray head and underparts (with dark head in basic), dark slaty upperparts, lipstick red swollen bill and red legs; juvenile dark sooty brown overall with whitish belly, clean

DOLPHIN GULL

■ resident, breeds locally

white rump and tail with neat black tail band, dull flesh bill base and legs; immature has dark head, pinkish bill tipped black. Should be unmistakable in its range; compare with nonbreeding and immature Belcher's and Olrog's Gulls.

TAXONOMY
Monotypic. Sometimes placed in the monotypic genus *Leucophaeus* (see Burger and Gochfeld[1]).

STATUS AND DISTRIBUTION
Endemic to s. S. America.
   Fairly common resident (breeds Oct.–Mar.) in Falklands (estimated 3,000–6,000 pairs[2]), fairly common to uncommon from Tierra del Fuego north locally to Punta Tombo, Argentina (44° south), and to Isla Chiloé[3] and Isla Doña Sebastiana,[4] Chile (41–42° south); possibly more common in n. areas in winter (Apr.–Sept.), when casual north to Concepción, Chile.[5] Casual visitor (Feb.–Apr.) to S. Georgia.

FIELD IDENTIFICATION

SIMILAR SPECIES
   None in its normal range. Immature and nonbreeding adult Belcher's Gull and Olrog's Gull, of Chilean and Argentine coasts, respectively, are larger and rangier in build with longer yellow legs, longer yellowish bills with black-and-red distal markings; first-cycle immatures have more-variegated upperparts and extensive dark hoods down to chest; adults have broad black distal tail bands.

HABITAT AND BEHAVIOR
   Coastal, often near seabird and seal colonies. Rocky shorelines, stony to muddy and sandy intertidal areas, sewage outfalls; also nearby freshwater lakes and fields. Breeds mainly in small, usually tightly packed colonies (up to a few hundred pairs) on inshore islets and on higher ground of beaches and marshes, often in association with other gulls and South American Terns. Mainly found in small groups or singly, locally in flocks of up to a few hundred birds. Associates readily with other gulls and water birds. Feeds mainly by scavenging but also forages in intertidal shallows.

DESCRIPTION AND MOLT
   Adult cycle. Complete PB molt (mainly Jan./Feb.–May/June) produces adult basic plumage: head pale gray with narrow white eye-ring and variable hood of dark slaty mottling

and speckling (appearing from Feb. or Mar. onward); neck and underparts pearl gray, becoming whitish on undertail coverts; wing-linings pale gray. Back and upperwings dark slaty gray (Kodak 12.5–13.5), becoming black on remiges, with white scapular crescents and very broad white trailing edge to secondaries and inner primaries; rump and tail whitish. Eyes pale lemon with red orbital ring, bill and legs deep red to pinkish red. Partial PA molt (mainly July–Sept.) produces adult alternate plumage: head becomes clean pearl gray with narrow white eye-ring; head often fractionally darker than neck with trace of neck-ring contrast often visible. Bare parts brighter.
   First Cycle. Juvenile (Feb.–May): head, neck, and chest sooty gray-brown, becoming whitish on lower underparts with flanks mottled sooty. Upperparts dark sooty gray-brown with narrow and poorly contrasting brown edgings, bold white scapular crescent; remiges black with broad white trailing edge to secondaries and inner primaries. Wing-linings off whitish, mottled dusky. Rump and tail white with broad black subterminal tail band not reaching sides. Bill notably more slender than adult, blackish with dull flesh at base; legs dull, dark flesh; eyes dark brown. Partial PA1 molt (Mar.–Sept.; not including wing coverts) produces variable first alternate plumage: hood dark brownish slate to sooty brown with pale mottling on face and throat, whitish eye-crescents; back mostly to solidly dark slaty in contrast to worn brown upperwing coverts; neck and underparts pale smoky gray, or with variable brownish mottling on neck and chest. Eyes brown to pale brown, bill thicker (but less swollen than adult), pink with black to blackish red tip, legs pink to dusky brownish flesh.
   Second Cycle. Complete PB2 molt (mainly Oct.–Mar.) produces second basic plumage: hood dark sooty gray with pale mottling on face and throat, white eye-crescents. Upperparts dark slaty with broader white trailing edge to remiges, variable brown cast to upperwing coverts; primaries black with smaller white tips than adult; tail all white. Underparts pearl gray. Bare parts similar to first summer, although bill may average deeper pink. Partial PA2 molt (Mar.–Sept.) produces second alternate plumage: similar to adult alternate but head with variable dusky to brownish mottling (ranging from basiclike hood to almost unmarked), upperwings browner. Bill less swollen than adult, pinkish red to red with black subterminal band, legs pinkish red to red, eyes pale yellowish. Some second-cycle

birds (or perhaps retarded third-cycle?) have adultlike head and bill: note smaller white primary tips, brown wash to upperwing coverts, and any dark marks on bill. Adult plumage attained by complete PB molt (mainly Dec.–Apr./May), although some third-basic birds distinguishable by dark distal bill markings, which are probably lost by third summer; white trailing edge to secondaries and white primary tips may average narrower in third cycle than in adult.

HYBRIDS
None reported.

NOTES

1. Burger and Gochfeld 1996; 2. Woods and Woods 1997; 3. Marín et al. 1989; 4. Espinosa and von Meyer H. 1999; 5. Johnson 1967

LENGTH 17.7–21.2 IN. (45–54 CM)
PHOTOS 19.0–19.19, 3.0

IDENTIFICATION SUMMARY

This striking, medium-large, rather lanky three-cycle gull is a local resident along desert coasts of Peru and n. Chile. Bill relatively long and fairly stout, legs relatively long; at rest, tail tip falls between tips of P6 and P7. Adult has slaty black upperparts with broad white trailing edge to wings, whitish head and underparts (with dark hood in basic), white tail with broad black subterminal band; dark eyes, yellow bill with black subterminal band and red tip, yellow legs. First cycle has dark head and neck, variegated upperparts, bold black tail band, pale flesh to yellow legs and bill, with black-and-red bill tip.

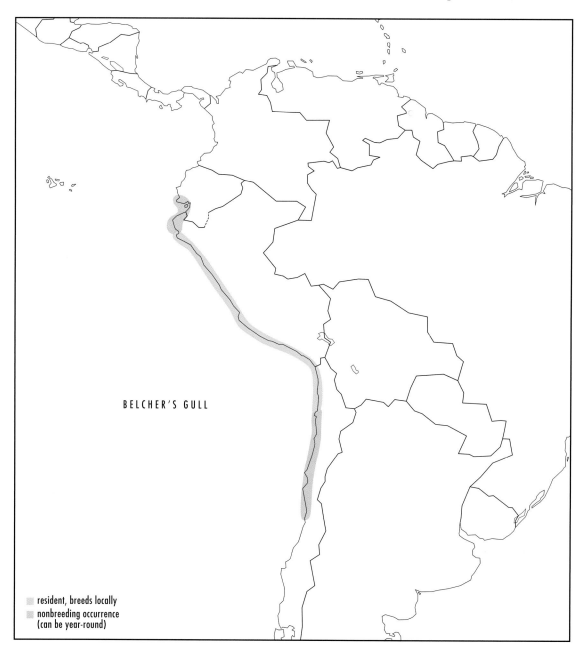

BELCHER'S GULL

▧ resident, breeds locally
▧ nonbreeding occurrence
    (can be year-round)

In its range, Belcher's Gull is reasonably distinctive, but adults could be confused with Kelp Gull, which is larger and stockier with a stouter bill lacking a black subterminal band, lacks black tail band, eyes often pale. Third-cycle Kelp Gull can have black on tail but not in a neat, broad band; note bill shape, overall size and structure. Olrog's Gull (Atlantic Coast of S. America) does not overlap, but vagrants should be separated with caution from Belcher's Gull (see Rarer Species).

TAXONOMY

Monotypic. Has been considered conspecific with Olrog's Gull (*L. atlanticus*) of Atlantic Coast of S. America,[1] but the two are now generally considered separate species.[2] The combined species is known as Band-tailed Gull (*L. belcheri*), a name that has been used only for Belcher's Gull.[3]

STATUS AND DISTRIBUTION

Endemic to w. S. America.

Fairly common to uncommon and somewhat local breeding resident (breeding mainly Oct.–Mar., but some birds may nest year-round) on coast and inshore islands from Piura, n. Peru, south to Atacama, n. Chile (6–21° south). Casual to rare nonbreeding visitor (mainly May–Sept.) south to cen. Chile (30–33° south),[4,5] north to s. Ecuador (Jan.) and cen. Panama (May, Aug., Dec.). Accidental in Calif. (Aug.–Jan.),[6] casual in Fla. (3–4 records, Sept.–Jan., June).

Reports (Mar.–Apr.) from Falklands[7] may pertain to this species or to Olrog's Gull. Reports south to Isla Chiloé[8] presumed in error.[9]

FIELD IDENTIFICATION

SIMILAR SPECIES

KELP GULL (widespread in S. America). Non-flying adult and second-cycle Belcher's might be confused with Kelp Gull, but Belcher's is smaller and rangier in build with longer (and often brighter colored) legs, longer and less heavy bill (tipped black and red), dark eyes, and blacker upperparts lacking white in wingtips; neat black tail band of Belcher's conspicuous in flight. First-cycle Kelp Gull lacks hooded effect shown by Belcher's, bill mostly blackish.

RARER SPECIES

OLROG'S GULL (Atlantic Coast of S. America) about 15 percent larger than Belcher's with relatively shorter legs, longer wings, and stouter bill. Adult Olrog's has slaty blackish (less brownish) upperparts with broader white trailing edge to secondaries, slightly narrower black tail band, neck and underparts lack smoky gray wash, orbital ring reddish; adult basic has a dusky hood of dense dark speckling rather than a solid dark hood. First cycle told by structure (especially stouter bill); whitish forehead and lores on paler, sooty brown hood of Olrog's distinct from the darker brown, more-solid hood of Belcher's. Underparts of Olrog's often more extensively dark brownish, down to legs, but uppertail coverts mostly white with sparse dark marks (heavily spotted and barred dark brown on first-cycle Belcher's). Second cycle told by structure (especially bill), white hindneck collar (pale gray on Belcher's), and average blacker upperparts and whiter underparts.

DOLPHIN GULL (s. S. America) smaller and stockier with shorter and thicker bill, shorter legs. First- and second-cycle plumages have dark upperparts and dark hood that might suggest Belcher's, and first-cycle has neat black tail band; note structure, pink to red bill with black tip, dull flesh to reddish legs, pale smoky gray neck and underparts.

BLACK-TAILED GULL (E. Asia, casual in N. America) markedly smaller and slimmer overall with shorter legs; adult and older immatures have paler, slaty gray upperparts (Kodak 8–9.5), pale eyes. Adult also has broader and more even-width black tail band with wider white tip. First cycle dark brown overall with flesh pink legs and black-tipped bill.

HABITAT AND BEHAVIOR

Coastal and inshore waters. Rocky coasts, stony to sandy intertidal, fishing harbors, sewage outfalls. Nests colonially on inshore islands and islets, less often on mainland coast. Elsewhere found singly or in groups up to 50 or so birds, associating readily with other gulls, terns, and water birds. Feeds by foraging in the intertidal; picking fish from near the sea surface, such as in association with feeding flocks of Inca Terns and other seabirds; scavenging from fishing boats; stealing eggs, and preying upon seabird chicks.[10]

DESCRIPTION AND MOLT

Adult Cycle. Complete PB molt (mainly Dec./Jan.–Apr./May) produces adult basic plumage: dark slaty hood with white eye-crescents and whitish mottling (mainly on throat and lores) contrasts with white neck and underparts, which are clouded smoky gray on neck and chest. Upperparts slaty brownish black

(Kodak 14–16) with narrow white scapular and tertial crescents. Rump and tail white with broad black subterminal tail band widest on central rectrices and bordered white. Upperwings slaty brownish black, becoming black on wingtips, with broad white trailing edge to secondaries fading out narrowly on inner primaries. Underwings whitish with smoky gray clouding, becoming blackish on wingtips, white on trailing edge of secondaries. Eyes dark with narrow yellowish orbital ring, bill chrome yellow with red tip and broad black subterminal band, legs chrome yellow. Partial PA molt (mainly June–Aug.) produces adult alternate plumage: head becomes clean white, contrasting subtly with smoky washed neck and chest (contrast bleached out in bright sun); bare parts brighten with red bill tip larger and black subterminal bill band often reduced to a black wedge on the maxilla.

First Cycle. Juvenile (mainly Jan.–Apr.): head, neck, and chest dark sooty brown with narrow whitish eye-crescents and whitish flecking in face, variable whitish or "floury" veiling on chest; flanks mottled sooty brown, belly and undertail coverts white. Upperparts dark brown with broad, scaly, buff to whitish edgings creating an overall scaly or scalloped pattern; uppertail coverts white with variable, typically fairly heavy, dark brownish markings. Tail brownish black with a narrow white tip, white bases to outer rectrices, and mostly whitish outer web to R6. Remiges blackish (to dark brown on inner primaries) with narrow white tips from secondaries to middle or outer primaries (soon abrading on exposed primaries); underwings dusky gray-brown. Eyes dark, bill flesh pink with clean-cut black tip or subterminal band, legs flesh pink. Wearing of pale tips soon creates browner and more uniform appearance, and variable PA1 molt (mainly Mar./Apr.–Oct./Nov.; often including wing coverts and tertials) produces first alternate plumage: head, neck, and chest dark sooty brown with dull whitish to pale gray eye-crescents, whitish grizzling on lores and throat; hoary pale gray hindcollar between dark brown hood and mantle. Some birds retain much of their juvenal upperparts, which become worn, warm brown with narrow pale gray to whitish edgings. Others undergo extensive molt of new scapulars, upperwing coverts, and tertials, which are dark brown with pale buffy gray edgings (earlier molted and similar to juvenal feathers but fresh in contrast to worn primaries) to dark slaty (later-molted feathers). Bill horn flesh to yellow with broad black tip or subterminal ring and red tip, legs dull flesh to greenish yellow.

Second Cycle. Complete PB2 molt (mainly Oct./Nov.–Mar./Apr.) produces second basic plumage: dark slaty brownish hood extends down to chest, separated from brownish black back by pale gray hindcollar; whitish eye-crescents and pale mottling on face and throat. Upperwings mixed slaty brownish black and brownish, with narrower and duller white trailing edge than adult. Tail band slightly wider, less clean-cut, and more brownish black than adult, with narrower white tip; whitish basal areas often washed gray. Bill yellowish flesh to yellow with broad black subterminal band and red tip, legs dull fleshy yellow to yellow. Partial PA molt (mainly May–Oct.) into second alternate plumage: head and neck on some birds become whitish (with pale smoky wash to hindneck and chest), similar to adult or with some dark speckling and mottling on head; other birds appear to attain dark hoods, less extensive than second basic. Upperparts similar to adult but usually with some browner upperwing coverts. Bare parts often as bright as adult although bill averages more black, less red. Adult plumage apparently attained by complete PB3 molt (Nov.–Apr.), although some B3 birds may have some brownish upperwing coverts and hood may average more extensive on foreneck and chest; some nonbreeders may attain basiclike hoods in alternate plumage; confirmation needed from known-age birds.

HYBRIDS
None reported.

NOTES
1. Blake 1977; 2. Devillers 1977; 3. AOU 1998; 4. A. Jaramillo pers. comm.; 5. Murphy 1936; 6. Rottenborn and Morlan 2000; 7. Woods 1988; 8. Pearman 1995; 9. Howell 1996; 10. Murphy 1936

LENGTH 19.7–23.7 IN. (50–60 CM)
PHOTOS 20.0–20.14

IDENTIFICATION SUMMARY

This striking, medium-large, three-cycle gull is a local coastal inhabitant of Argentina. Bill relatively long and stout, legs relatively long; at rest, tail tip falls between tips of P6 and P7. Adult has slaty black upperparts (Kodak 15–17) with very broad white trailing edge to wings, whitish head and underparts (with dusky flecked head in basic), white tail with broad black subterminal band; dark eyes, red orbital ring, yellow bill with black subterminal band and red tip, yellow legs. First cycle has dark head and neck, variegated upperparts, bold black tail band, pale flesh to yellow legs and bill, with black-and-red bill tip.

OLROG'S GULL

resident, breeds locally
nonbreeding occurrence
(can be year-round)

In its range, Olrog's Gull is reasonably distinctive, but adults could be confused with Kelp Gull, which is stockier with a stouter bill lacking black subterminal band, lacks black tail band, eyes often pale. Third-cycle Kelp Gull can have black on tail but not in a neat, broad band; note bill shape, overall size and structure. Also see Belcher's Gull and Black-tailed Gull (see Belcher's Gull account, under Rarer Species).

TAXONOMY

Monotypic. Has been considered conspecific with Belcher's Gull (*L. belcheri*) of Pacific Coast of S. America,[1] but the two are now generally considered separate species.[2] The combined species is called Band-tailed Gull (*L. belcheri*).

STATUS AND DISTRIBUTION

Endemic to se. S. America.

Local breeding resident (breeding Sept.–Jan.) in coastal Argentina from s. Buenos Aires to s. Chubut (39–45° south), with population estimated at 2,300 pairs in 10 colonies,[3] although in 1999 a previously unknown colony with 1,635 active nests was found in Bahía Blanca.[4] Ranges south (mainly Dec.–Jan.?) to Santa Cruz (48° south), possibly to Tierra del Fuego (55° south),[5] and north regularly in winter (mainly Apr.–Nov.) to Uruguay,[6] casually to s. Brazil[7] and exceptionally inland to Cordoba, Argentina (Mar.).[8]

Reports (Mar.–Apr.) from Falklands[9] may pertain to this species or to Belcher's Gull; a report from South Georgia[10] is in error.[11]

FIELD IDENTIFICATION

SIMILAR SPECIES

KELP GULL. Non-flying adult and second-cycle Olrog's might be confused with Kelp Gull but average slightly smaller and rangier in build with longer and less heavy bill (tipped black and red), dark eyes, and blacker upperparts lacking white in wingtips but with broader white trailing edge to secondaries; neat black tail band of Olrog's conspicuous in flight. First-cycle Kelp Gull lacks hooded effect shown by Olrog's, bill mostly blackish.

DOLPHIN GULL (s. S. America) rarely overlaps in range. Smaller and stockier with shorter and thicker bill, shorter legs. First- and second-cycle plumages have dark upperparts and dark hood that might suggest Olrog's, and first cycle has neat black tail band; note structure, pink to red bill with black tip, dull flesh to reddish legs, pale smoky gray neck and underparts.

RARER SPECIES

See Belcher's Gull (w. S. America).

BLACK-TAILED GULL (E. Asia, casual in N. America) markedly smaller and slimmer overall with shorter legs; adult and older immatures have paler, slaty gray upperparts (Kodak 8–9.5), pale eyes. First cycle dark brown overall with flesh pink legs and black-tipped bill.

HABITAT AND BEHAVIOR

Coastal and inshore waters. Favors estuaries, mud flats, harbors, and adjacent rocky coasts; specializes in eating small crabs, less often scavenges. Nests colonially on low sandy islands in coastal bays and estuary complexes, typically in association with Kelp Gulls.[12] Elsewhere found singly or in groups up to 50 or so birds that associate with other gulls and terns, although Olrog's Gulls often keep somewhat separate, such as at the edge of mixed-species flocks.

DESCRIPTION

Adult Cycle. Complete PB molt (mainly Nov./Dec.–Mar.) produces adult basic plumage: head, neck, and underparts white with variable dark slaty speckling on head forming a partial dusky hood (appearing from Dec./Jan. onward), darkest at lower edges, with white eye-crescents and with forehead, lores, and throat mostly unmarked white. Upperparts slaty black (Kodak 15–17) with white scapular and tertial crescents. Rump and tail white with broad black subterminal tail band bordered white. Upperwings slaty black with very broad white trailing edge to secondaries fading out narrowly on inner primaries. Underwings whitish, becoming blackish on wingtips, with secondaries translucent when backlit. Eyes dark with narrow reddish orbital ring, bill chrome yellow with red tip and broad black subterminal band, legs chrome yellow. Partial PA molt (mainly Apr.–June/July) produces adult alternate plumage: head molts to clean white; bare parts brighten, and black subterminal bill band may become reduced.

First Cycle. Juvenile (mainly Dec.–Mar.): head, neck, and chest sooty gray-brown with narrow whitish eye-crescents and extensively whitish forehead, lores, and throat, variable whitish or "floury" veiling on chest; flanks mottled sooty brown, belly and undertail coverts white. Upperparts dark brown with broad, scaly, sandy gray to whitish edgings creating an overall dappled or spotted pattern; greater coverts often appear as a pale panel; tertials dark brown with narrow buffy white edging and broader whitish tips; uppertail coverts white with sparse brownish markings;

tail brownish black with a narrow white tip, white bases to outer rectrices, and mostly whitish outer web to R6. Remiges blackish (to gray-brown on inner primaries) with narrow white tips from secondaries to middle or outer primaries (soon abrading on exposed primaries); underwings dusky. Eyes dark, bill flesh pink to yellowish flesh with clean-cut black tip or subterminal band, legs flesh pink to yellowish flesh. Wearing of pale tips soon creates browner and more uniform appearance, and variable PA1 molt (Dec./Feb.–Aug./Sept.; can include wing coverts) produces first alternate plumage: head, neck, and chest (down to legs) dark gray-brown with dull whitish to pale gray eye-crescents, whitish forehead, lores, and throat; hoary pale gray hindcollar between gray-brown hood and mantle. Some birds may retain most or all juvenal upperparts, which become worn, warm brown with narrow pale gray to whitish edgings; others undergo extensive molt of new scapulars, upperwing coverts, and tertials. Bill horn flesh to yellowish with broad black tip or subterminal band and red tip, legs dull flesh to yellow-olive.

Second Cycle. Complete PB2 molt (mainly Sept./Oct.–Jan./Feb.) produces second basic plumage: dark slaty brown hood extends down to chest, separated from slaty black back by whitish hindcollar; white eye-crescents, whitish forehead and throat. Upperwings mixed slaty black and brownish with narrower and duller white trailing edge than adult. Tail band slightly wider and less clean-cut than adult with narrower white tip. Bill flesh-yellow to greenish yellow with broad black subterminal band and red tip, legs flesh-yellow to greenish yellow. Partial PA molt (mainly Mar./Apr.–July/Aug.) into second alternate plumage: head and neck of some birds become mostly white, similar to adult or with some dark speckling on head; other birds appear to attain dark hoods, less extensive than second basic. Bare parts often as bright as adult although bill may average more black, less red. Adult plumage apparently attained by complete PB3 molt (Oct./Nov.–Mar.), although fresh-plumaged third basic may average more heavily marked dusky hood than adult;[13] and some birds may have a few brownish upperwing coverts.

HYBRIDS
None reported.

NOTES

1. Blake 1977; 2. Devillers 1977; 3. Yorio et al. 1997; 4. Delhey et al. 2001; 5. Collar et al. 1992; 6. Escalante 1966; 7. Collar et al. 1992; 8. Yzurieta 1995; 9. Woods 1988; 10. Blake 1977; 11. Prince and Croxall 1996; 12. Yorio et al. 1997; 13. Howell pers. obs.

LENGTH 17–20 IN. (43–51 CM)
PHOTOS 21.0–21.21

IDENTIFICATION SUMMARY

This medium-sized four-cycle gull of ne. Asia is a vagrant to N. America, with records scattered from Alaska to Belize. Bill relatively long and parallel-edged with slight to moderate gonydeal expansion. At rest, tail tip falls at or slightly beyond tip of P6, so wing projection relatively long. Adult has slaty gray upperparts (Kodak 8–9.5) with black wingtips (lacking white mirrors), broad black subterminal tail band, and, in basic plumage, fairly diffuse dusky head and hindneck streaking. Juvenile dark brown overall with mostly blackish tail. PA1 variable, starting Sept.–Oct. Subsequent ages variable in appearance. First cycle has flesh pink legs becoming yellow by adult cycle; adult eyes pale lemon, orbital ring red.

Medium size, slaty gray upperparts, broad black subterminal tail band, pale eyes, yellowish legs, and black bill ring with red tip are a distinctive combination among adults of New World gulls. Mostly dark brown and dark-tailed first cycle told from California Gull by longer bill and contrasting white uppertail coverts. In S. America, Belcher's and Olrog's Gulls larger with blacker upperparts. See Similar Species section for more detailed identification criteria.

TAXONOMY

Monotypic. Has been known as Temminck's Gull.[1]

STATUS AND DISTRIBUTION

Coasts of ne. Asia, vagrant to N. America.

Nonbreeding. Casual visitor to w. Alaska (late May–mid-July) and s.-coastal and se. Alaska (mid-June–Oct.), exceptionally (Aug.–Jan.) along Pacific Coast to B.C., Wash., Calif.,[2,3,4,5] and Sonora, Mex. (June).[6] Casual in interior N. America from N.T. east to w. Great Lakes (June–July),[7,8] along Atlantic Coast of e. N. America from Nfld. south to Va. (mainly Apr.–Oct. in Atlantic Canada, July–Apr. in U.S.),[9] exceptionally (Feb.–Mar.) in s. Tex. and Belize.

FIELD IDENTIFICATION

SIMILAR SPECIES

Black-tailed Gull is a distinctive species, perhaps most likely to be confused with California Gull.

Adult Cycle. Note medium size, slaty gray upperparts, long bill with black-and-red tip, pale eyes, yellow legs, and broad black subterminal tail band. In N. America, compare with California Gull and larger Lesser Black-backed Gull. Also see Belcher's and Olrog's Gulls (S. America).

CALIFORNIA GULL (w. N. America) is paler gray above (Kodak 5–7.5) with dark eyes, bold white tips and mirrors on outer primaries, and all-white tail.

LESSER BLACK-BACKED GULL (widespread) larger with relatively shorter bill, wingtips have white mirrors on P10 or P9–P10, and tail all white.

First Cycle. Distinctive; note size and structure, bill length and pattern, and overall dark brown aspect with contrasting white tail coverts and black tail.

HEERMANN'S GULL (w. N. America) uniformly dark brown (lacking contrasting white tail coverts) with smaller bill (duller flesh basally) and black legs.

CALIFORNIA GULL has overall paler and grayer head and underparts, lacks white eye-crescents, often has more-variegated upperparts, tail coverts more heavily barred dark brown, and tail not solidly black.

Second Cycle. Distinctive, although at this age it might be more easily confused with California Gull than at other ages; note long bill, white eye-crescents, black tail, tone of gray on upperparts, and upperwing pattern.

CALIFORNIA GULL has relatively shorter bill that lacks red at tip, dusky markings on head and underparts (including wing-linings) are more mottled and streaky, less diffuse, gray on upperparts is paler, eyes are dark brown without white eye-crescents, and paler inner 3–4 primaries form contrasting panel on upperwing (uniformly dark on Black-tailed).

Third Cycle. Third-cycle Black-tailed Gull looks much like adult, which see for differences from other species; some third-cycle Lesser Black-backed Gulls have black in the tail, but this does not form a neat, broad subterminal band.

RARER SPECIES

Adult Cycle. Belcher's Gull and Olrog's Gull (S. America) were formerly considered conspecific under the name Band-tailed Gull; they share a broad black subterminal tail band, yellow legs, and yellow bill with black-and-red tip. But otherwise they look quite different from Black-tailed Gull, being markedly larger and bulkier with longer legs and stouter bills, slaty blackish upperparts (Kodak 14–17), dark eyes, and often brighter yellow legs and bills; basic (and immature) plumages have dark mottled hoods.

HABITAT AND BEHAVIOR

Much as other medium-sized gulls, with which it is likely to be found (several N. American records have been with Mew, Ring-billed, and California Gulls); scavenges readily at dumps and fishing harbors.

DESCRIPTION AND MOLT

Adult Cycle. Complete PB molt (June/July–Oct./Nov.) produces adult basic plumage: head, neck, and underparts white; head and neck with variable (usually moderate) dusky clouding and mottling, often concentrated on hindneck. Back and upperwings slaty gray (Kodak 8–9.5) with black wingtips (black on outer web of P6/P7–P10 extends to primary coverts; P4 typically has black on outer web); white scapular and tertial crescents; and small white tips to outer primaries. White trailing edge to secondaries (usually hidden at rest) and inner primaries breaks into discrete white tips on outer primaries. Uppertail coverts and tail white with broad, clean-cut subterminal black tail band that does not extend to outer web of R6; closed tail from below shows limited black due to long white undertail coverts and white outer web to R6. Underwings show blackish wingtips merging into smoky gray, white-tipped inner primaries and secondaries. Eyes pale lemon, orbital ring red (can be gray to pinkish in winter). Bill yellow to greenish yellow with broad black subterminal band adjoining orange-red gonydeal spot and tip. Legs yellow to greenish yellow. Partial PA molt (Sept./Oct.–Mar./Apr.) produces adult alternate plumage: head and neck clean white; white primary tips often lost through wear. Orbital ring red, legs brighter yellow; bill bright yellow with larger red gonydeal spot, and reduced subterminal black mark.

First Cycle. Juvenile (late July–*Nov.*): dark brown overall with scaly buff (bleaching to whitish) edgings to upperparts, becoming white on vent and tail coverts, which have sparse dark bars and spots; forehead, lores, throat, and eye-crescents often bleach to whitish. Tertials blackish brown with whitish edging, and wingtips black. Flight feathers black to brownish black, tail and secondaries narrowly tipped whitish. IN FLIGHT: dark brownish overall with blackish flight feathers and contrasting white tail coverts; underwings dark. Eyes dark, bill starts out mostly dark but becomes flesh pink with clean-cut black tip by fall; legs flesh to flesh pink. PA1 molt (*Sept.–Apr.*; often include upperwing coverts) produces first alternate plumage: face and chest bleach to whitish, often offsetting a dusky hood and hindneck shawl (suggesting adult-basic pattern), white eye-crescents often less contrasting by spring, and some grayish feathers attained on head and body. A1 scapulars and wing coverts variable, ranging from dark brown with pale edging, to brownish gray with dark anchor patterns, to fairly plain grayish. Eyes brown, bill flesh pink with clean-cut black tip, sometimes showing a yellowish cast and pale reddish tip by spring; legs flesh pink.

Second Cycle. Complete PB2 molt (*late May/June*–late Aug./Sept.) into second basic plumage. Head, neck, and underparts whitish with variable dusky brown clouding and mottling heaviest on hindneck and across chest; forehead, lores, throat, and eye-crescents whitish; vent and tail coverts white with no to few dark marks. Upperparts mixed dusky brown and gray, some feathers with contrasting pale edgings. Flight feathers blackish with narrow whitish tips to secondaries, inner primaries, and tail; white basal corners to outer rectrices visible on spread tail. Wing-linings whitish with variable dusky clouding. Eyes brown to pale lemon, bill flesh pink to gray-green with black distal third and usually a reddish tip, legs flesh pink to gray-green. Partial PA2 molt (*Sept.–Apr.*; often includes upperwing coverts) produces second alternate plumage: head, neck, and underparts white, variably streaked and mottled dusky (often bleaching and wearing to mostly white by summer), back becomes mostly plain gray, and many birds attain some gray upperwing coverts, especially median coverts. By spring and summer, orbital ring may show reddish; bill greenish to yellow with broad black subterminal band, red tip, and often a trace of orange-red gonydeal blush. Legs flesh to gray-green, sometimes becoming yellow-green in summer.

Third Cycle. Complete PB3 molt (*late May/June*–Sept./Oct.) produces third basic plumage: overall resembles adult basic but averages more dusky streaking and mottling on head and neck; white tips to wingtips smaller or absent; some upperwing coverts often washed brownish; tertials can have brown centers. Wingtip pattern averages more extensively black than adult, with variable blackish on primary coverts and alula, sometimes black on P3. Underwings may have slight dusky clouding on coverts. Bare parts similar to adult but bill and legs average more greenish yellow through winter. Partial PA3 molt (*Sept./Oct.–Mar./Apr.*) into third alternate plumage: head and neck clean white, white tips to outer primaries can be lost by wear; best aged by wingtip pattern. Bill and legs brighten in late winter, often indistinguishable from adult by summer. Adult plumage attained by complete PB4 molt (*June–Sept./Oct.*).

HYBRIDS
None reported.

NOTES
1. Dwight 1925; 2. Anon 2003; 3. Heinl 1997; 4. Lethaby and Bangma 1998; 5. Wahl et al. 2005; 6. Garrett and Molina 1998; 7. ABA 2002; 8. Anon 2003; 9. Lethaby and Bangma 1998

SMALL WHITE-HEADED GULLS
(GENUS *Larus*, IN PART)

Two species (Mew Gull and Ring-billed Gull) can be separated from the large white-headed gulls by virtue of smaller overall size and, in adults, lack of a red gonydeal spot; the Mew Gull can be further divided into three subspecies groups (see below). These are medium-sized gulls with slender to "average" bills that have a slight gonydeal expansion. Adult bills and legs are yellow, the Mew's bill unmarked,

the Ring-billed's with a black subterminal ring. The adult upperwings are gray with a white trailing edge and black tips marked with white spots. Basic plumages have dusky streaking and mottling on the head and neck. Both are three- or four-cycle gulls. Juvenal plumage is patterned brownish overall, and the first prealternate molt usually produces a gray back.

ADULT NONBREEDING MEW GULL. PP. 127, 377

ADULT NONBREEDING COMMON GULL. PP. 133, 381

ADULT NONBREEDING KAMCHATKA GULL. PP. 136, 385

ADULT NONBREEDING RING-BILLED GULL. PP. 139, 388

The Mew Gull complex comprises four taxa of medium-sized three-cycle gulls that breed in the n. Holarctic from Europe east through Asia and into w. N. America; no taxa of this complex breed in e. N. America or Greenland. The AOU (1998) treated these taxa as conspecific but comprising three subspecies groups: the Common Gull *L. [canus] canus* (including nominate *canus* breeding in W. Asia and *heinei* breeding in cen. Asia), the Kamchatka Gull *L. [canus] kamtschatschensis* (breeding in E. Asia), and the Mew Gull or Short-billed Gull *L. [canus] brachyrhynchus* (breeding in nw. N. America). We treat these three groups in separate accounts: Mew Gull is the common taxon in N. America; Common Gulls and Kamchatka Gulls are rare to casual visitors to ne. N. America and w. Alaska, respectively.

Differences among the taxa are subtle, but many first-cycle and adult individuals are identifiable in the field. N. American Mew Gulls are smallest, adults have bold white wingtip markings, and first-cycle birds are dusky overall with mostly dark tails. Common Gulls are intermediate in size, adults have more black in their wingtips than Mew Gull, and first-cycle birds are paler overall than Mew, with a white tail base and contrasting black tail band. Kamchatka Gulls are largest and bulkiest; adults have a wingtip pattern close to Common Gull, and first-cycle birds appear variably intermediate between Common and Mew.

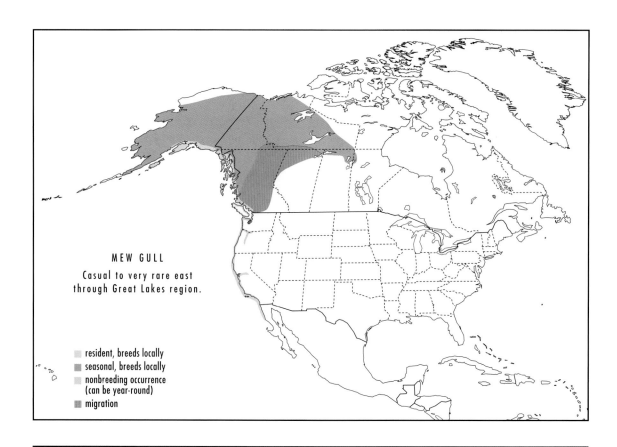

MEW GULL

Casual to very rare east through Great Lakes region.

■ resident, breeds locally
■ seasonal, breeds locally
□ nonbreeding occurrence (can be year-round)
■ migration

22A. MEW GULL *Larus [canus] brachyrhynchus*

LENGTH 16.2–19 IN. (41–48 CM)
PHOTOS 22A.0–22A.28, 23.29–23.30

IDENTIFICATION SUMMARY

A medium-small yellow-legged gull of w. N. America. Common breeder in Alaska and nw. Canada, wintering mainly along the Pacific Coast from s. Alaska to n. Baja Calif. Bill medium small and often slightly tapered, relatively slender with a slight gonydeal expansion. At rest, tail tip falls between tips of P6 and P7. Adult has medium gray upperparts (Kodak 6–7.5) with black wingtips (white mirrors on outer 2 primaries) and, in basic plumage, fairly smudgy and mottled dusky head and neck markings. Juvenile dusky gray-brown overall with dark tail. PA1 variable, starting Sept.–Jan. Second cycle variably intermediate between first cycle and adult. First cycle has flesh legs, becoming yellow by adult cycle; adult eyes brownish; orbital ring red.

Medium-small size, medium gray back, yellowish legs, plain yellowish bill, and brown eyes are a distinctive combination among adults of regularly occurring New World gulls. Especially see larger and longer-billed Ring-billed and California Gulls, which also have yellow legs as adults. Adult Ring-billed is paler gray above with black bill ring, pale eyes; adult California has black-and-red subterminal bill band. First-cycle Mew attains mostly gray back in first winter; note its size and structure (especially of the bill), mostly dark tail, mostly pale gray greater coverts, and dusky underwings. See Similar Species section for more-detailed identification criteria.

TAXONOMY

See introduction to the Mew Gull complex. Sometimes known as Short-billed Gull.

STATUS AND DISTRIBUTION

Western N. America; accidental in Hong Kong.[1]

Breeding. Breeds (May–Aug.) from Alaska (sparingly to foothills on n. side of Brooks Range) and Yukon south to w. B.C. (including Vancouver Is.), east to se. Northwest Territories and n. Saskatchewan. Has nested (unsuccessfully) in ne. Man.

Nonbreeding. Migrates along coast and through interior portions of Alaska and nw. Canada, including ne. B.C. and n. Alta. Substantial southern movements in n. areas (for example, Yukon) start early July. First fall arrivals can occur late July in Ore., Aug.–Sept. in n. and cen. Calif., early Sept. in the e. Aleutians, and mid-Oct. at the southern end of the regular winter range (San Diego Co., Calif.). Main arrival, however, not until mid-Oct. in coastal Ore. and n. Calif., Nov. in the Willamette Valley, Ore., and in coastal cen. and s. Calif. In the North (for example, w. Alaska, Yukon), most southward migration is over by late Aug., with small flocks until mid-Sept., some birds lingering exceptionally into Oct.

Winters (Oct./Nov.–Mar./Apr.) from e. (rarely cen.) Aleutians, Alaska Peninsula (north to Bristol Bay), Kodiak Is., and s. coastal Alaska commonly south along and near Pacific Coast to cen. Calif., thence uncommon to locally fairly common south to s. Calif., uncommon and local in n. Baja Calif. Winters locally inland in B.C. and Pacific states, notably in Willamette Valley, Ore., and Delta region of Sacramento Valley, Calif. Rare farther inland in e. portions of Pacific states, south locally to Salton Sea, and rare or casual (mid-Nov.–Feb.) in n. Gulf of Calif. and Baja Calif. Sur.

Casual (mainly Nov.–Mar.) in interior w. states, s. portions of Prairie Provinces, Great Plains (annual e. Colo.), Tex., and entire Great Lakes region and s. Que. (late Sept.–May; mainly late Oct.–Mar.). Exceptional records (mainly winter) from Atlantic Coast in N.B., Mass., and Va. Some records published as "Mew Gulls" from New England south to Mid-Atlantic states do not distinguish between Mew Gull and Common Gull.

Departure from Pacific Coast wintering areas of U.S. mainly Mar.–mid-Apr.; a few linger into May; very rare or casual through summer period, including at Salton Sea. Arrival in n. areas typically from mid-Apr. (s. Yukon) to early May at n. edges of the breeding range. Rarely reaches Arctic coast (mainly in summer) of Alaska, Yukon, Northwest Territories, and Nunavut. Also rare in nw. Man. (late Apr.–late May) and s. interior B.C. (mainly Mar.–May, Aug.–Sept.). Casual in ne. Man. (June–July), Pribilofs (late May–June), and St. Lawrence Is. (late Aug.).

SIMILAR SPECIES

Mew Gull is generally distinctive in its normal range; note medium-small size, rounded head, small, slender, and relatively short bill, brownish eyes at all ages. Ring-billed Gull and California Gull are the only commonly occurring and potentially similar species; also note adult Black-legged Kittiwake. See Common Gull and Kamchatka Gull under Rarer Species.

Adult Cycle. Note medium gray back, yellowish legs, plain yellowish bill.

RING-BILLED GULL (widespread in N. America) averages larger with longer, stouter, and blunter-tipped bill, less rounded head. Bill has distinct black ring year-round, eyes staring pale lemon, upperparts paler (Kodak 4–5) with narrower and less contrasting white scapular and tertial crescents, basic head and neck markings finer and more distinct. In flight has smaller white mirrors on P9–P10, small and poorly contrasting white tongue-tips out to P8, and less contrasting white trailing edge to wings.

BLACK-LEGGED KITTIWAKE (breeds n. N. America, pelagic elsewhere) shares medium gray upperparts (Kodak 6.5–8), dark eyes, and plain yellow bill but has narrower and more pointed wings with clean-cut black wingtips (lacking white mirrors), short black legs.

CALIFORNIA GULL (mainly w. N. America) often occurs alongside Mew Gulls in winter. California is appreciably larger with a longer, stouter, and blunter-tipped bill (that has a red gonydeal spot as well as a variable black subterminal band) and a longer wing projection. California has more black in the wingtip and lacks such distinct white tongue-tips on P7–P8. Basic head and neck markings of California tend to be coarser and less diffuse, often concentrated on lower hindneck.

First Cycle. Note overall dusky brownish aspect, flesh pink bill with black tip, and mostly dark tail; does not replace wing coverts in PA1 molt.

RING-BILLED GULL averages larger with longer, stouter, and blunter-tipped bill, less rounded head. Plumage whiter overall (especially on underparts) with white tail base and broad black distal band (but tail pattern sometimes overlaps with Mew Gull), white underwings with variable dusky markings, little or no barring on tail coverts, broader and pale-notched tips to upperwing coverts (often creating a more checkered, rather than scaly, pattern), less even-width (more notched) tertial edgings, and less-distinct whitish tips to closed primaries; PA1 molt can include upperwing

coverts. Some second-cycle Mew Gulls with solid black tail band might suggest first-cycle Ring-billed; note lack of distinct dark secondary bar, greenish bill base and legs.

CALIFORNIA GULL larger and bigger billed; upperparts more variegated (PA1 molt often includes upperwing coverts) with notched pale tips to tertials; does not attain mostly gray back until second cycle. First-cycle Mew distinguished from second-cycle California by size, pale gray greater coverts (dark brownish on California), and lack of green or blue-gray hue to bill and legs; also note different tail and primary patterns.

Second Cycle. RING-BILLED GULL averages larger with longer, stouter, and blunter-tipped bill, less rounded head. Upperparts paler gray with less-contrasting white scapular and tertial crescents; upperwings with small P10 mirror and no P9 mirror, less-contrasting white trailing edge; eyes often pale.

CALIFORNIA GULL can appear similar to first-cycle Mew (see above). Second-cycle Mew distinguished from third-cycle California by smaller size, small bill, and shorter wings, but plumage and bare parts similar: California more often has black bill ring and can have some orange-red at gonys, Mew Gull usually has black subterminal marks on P4 (sometimes outer web of P3), whereas P3–P4 typically lack black on California.

RARER SPECIES

Adult Cycle. COMMON GULL (casual to rare in ne. N. America) averages larger and longer billed with average paler upperparts (Kodak 5–6.5 on nominate *canus*) and darker eyes, but best identified by wingtip pattern. On Common Gull, white tips to the inner primaries are narrower than the broad white secondary tips (white tips more even width throughout on Mew); the outer primaries have more-extensive black (extending to primary coverts on P8/P9–P10) with smaller P9–P10 mirrors and rarely any white tongue-tip on P8 (which can, instead, have a white mirror—reflecting the more extensive black portion of the primary); and P4 usually lacks black (often present on Mew). At rest, the wingtip difference may be seen as more-extensive gray on the primary bases of Mew Gull, and the white P8 tongue-tip of Mew often shows above the edge of P7. Basic Mew Gulls have smudgier and more-diffuse dusky head and neck mottling and often lack a dusky bill ring (usually shown by Common Gull). Beware presumed third-cycle Mew Gulls with relatively extensive black in wingtips, which may suggest Common Gull.

KAMCHATKA GULL (casual in w. Alaska) averages

larger, bulkier, and broader winged with longer and stouter bill, average darker upperparts (Kodak 6.5–8) and paler eyes; perhaps best identified by wingtip pattern. On Kamchatka Gull, white tips to the inner primaries are narrower than the broad white secondary tips (white tips more even width throughout on Mew); the outer primaries have more-extensive black (extending to primary coverts on P8/P9–P10) with smaller P9–P10 mirrors and narrower white tongue-tip out to P7, rarely to P8. At rest, the wingtip difference may be seen as more-extensive gray on the primary bases of Mew Gull, and the white P8 tongue-tip of Mew often shows above the edge of P7. Basic Mew Gulls have smudgier and more-diffuse dusky head and neck mottling and often lack a dusky bill ring.

First Cycle. COMMON GULL averages slightly larger and longer billed. Plumage whiter overall (especially on underparts) with white tail base and contrasting black distal band, overall whitish underwings with variable dusky markings, little or no dark barring on tail coverts, and on average less extensive dark subterminal marks on inner primaries (so inner primary panel more contrasting). Some second-cycle Mew Gulls with gray saddle and black tail band can suggest first-cycle Common; note lack of distinct dark secondary bar, greenish bill base and legs.

KAMCHATKA GULL averages larger, bulkier, and broader winged with longer and stouter bill but may overlap with large male Mew Gull. Plumage characters variably overlap with Mew Gull; critical study needed to elucidate diagnostic features. Tail base typically whiter or less strongly washed dusky, with broad, clean-cut blackish distal band, and less heavily barred tail coverts; but some may have mostly dark tail, similar to Mew Gull—and some Mews have tail similar to typical Kamchatka; head and underparts average more whitish streaking and mottling, and inner primaries average less-extensive dark subterminal marks on inner primaries (so inner primary panel more contrasting); underwings less uniform than Mew, typically with darker covert tips forming dark bars.

Second Cycle COMMON GULL averages slightly larger and longer billed, but diagnostic identification criteria still need elucidation. Common often has an all-white tail (Mew usually has dark tail marks, and birds with extensive dark markings are unlikely to be Common Gulls); advanced-type Mew Gull wing patterns with bold white tongue-tip on P8 not shown by Common Gull; Common Gull's dusky head and neck markings may also aver-

age finer and less extensive. Second-cycle Common can resemble adult Mew in smudgy head and neck markings, black on P4; but note reduced white in outer primaries, overall structure, bill size and shape.

KAMCHATKA GULL averages larger, bulkier, and broader winged with longer and stouter bill, but diagnostic identification criteria still need elucidation. Kamchatka Gull more often keeps a pinkish bill base into midwinter (usually greenish on Mew).

HABITAT AND BEHAVIOR
Winters mainly along coasts and also locally inland. Occurs in wide range of intertidal habitats, including beaches, estuaries, and rocky coasts, also farmland, flooded fields, reservoirs, duck ponds, sewage ponds, and dumps; rarely ranges more than 5–10 km offshore. Nests usually in colonies, from tundra and inland marshes to sea cliffs, locally in conifer trees.[2] Nonbreeding birds often in flocks of up to a few hundred birds, locally in thousands, associating readily with other gulls and water birds. Flight buoyant and agile. Feeds mainly by picking while walking, or picks from near water surface while swimming and in flight.

DESCRIPTION AND MOLT
Adult Cycle. Complete PB molt (June/mid-July–Sept./Oct.) produces adult basic plumage: head, neck, and underparts white with smudgy and diffuse dusky mottling and streaking on head, neck, and sometimes sides of chest, often heaviest on hindneck. Back and upperwings medium gray (Kodak 6–7.5) with black wingtips (black on outer web of P10 extends to primary coverts); fairly contrasting white scapular and tertial crescents; and white tips to outer primaries. Fairly broad white trailing edge to secondaries and inner primaries breaks into discrete white tips on outer primaries; P5–P8 typically have distinct white tongue-tips and black subterminal bands, and P9–P10 have large white mirrors; P4 often has variable black subterminal marks. Uppertail coverts and tail white. Underwings show blackish wingtips (with P9–P10 mirrors) demarcated from smoky gray, white-tipped inner primaries and secondaries. Eyes brown to pale greenish yellow with dark flecking, orbital ring reddish (often gray to dull pinkish in midwinter). Bill yellowish to gray-green overall or greenish with a yellow tip, sometimes with a narrow (usually indistinct) dusky subterminal ring. Legs yellowish to gray-green. Partial PA molt (*Feb.*–Apr./May) produces adult alternate plumage: head and neck clean white;

white primary tips can be reduced through wear. Orbital ring red, legs and bill brighter yellow, bill lacks dark subterminal marks.

First Cycle. Juvenile (mid-July–Jan.): dusky brown to gray-brown overall. Head indistinctly streaked whitish and throat whitish; vent and undertail coverts whitish with distinct dark brown barring. Upperparts (including tertials) gray-brown with scaly buff (bleaching to whitish) edgings, the greater coverts typically plainer and grayer. Uppertail coverts whitish with distinct brown barring. Remiges blackish to brownish black with contrasting pale gray panel on inner primaries; secondaries and inner primaries tipped whitish, outer primaries with narrow whitish edging visible at rest; P10 rarely with indistinct small pale mirror. Tail variable: pale gray (bleaching to whitish) basally with variable dusky clouding and dark mottling, blackish brown distally in a broad band; looks solidly dark on most birds, but some lightly marked birds have pale base with broad, blackish brown distal band. IN FLIGHT: dusky gray-brown overall with blackish remiges except for dark-tipped pale gray inner primary panel, paler uppertail coverts; underwings dusky brown overall. Eyes dark brown, bill blackish with dull flesh base, usually becoming flesh to flesh pink with variable blackish tip by early winter; legs dull flesh to flesh pink. PA1 molt (Sept.–Mar./Apr.; does not include upperwing coverts or tertials) produces first alternate plumage: head, neck, and underparts white with variable dusky brown streaking and mottling, often fairly dusky through winter but bleaching to overall whitish by spring. A1 scapulars mostly plain grayish. In late winter and spring, upperwing coverts can bleach to a whitish panel, contrasting with gray back; bleaching can also increase prominence of any P10 mirror. Eyes brown. Bill flesh pink with black tip, sometimes becoming greenish in spring; legs flesh to flesh pink.

Second Cycle. Complete PB2 molt (late May/June–Sept.) into second basic plumage. Overall resembles adult basic but averages heavier dark streaking on head, neck, and chest; wingtips black to brownish black with at most only fine whitish tips, often lost by wear; upperwing coverts often with variable brown wash or markings (mostly gray-brown, contrasting with gray saddle on some birds); tertials sometimes with dark centers; black in wingtip more extensive, including alula and primary coverts, with P10 mirror smaller and P9 mirror sometimes absent, white tongue-tips on P5–P8 reduced; tail often has some black distal markings (12 percent of birds have a solid black subterminal band, 13 percent have all-white tails[3]); underwings mostly white with variable dusky mottling on coverts. Eyes brown to dirty pale yellowish, bill typically greenish with black tip or broad distal band (but some birds have flesh-based bill), legs gray-green to grayish flesh. Partial PA2 molt (*Feb.*–Apr./May; may include upperwing coverts?) produces second alternate plumage: head and neck typically become clean white; differs from adult primarily in wing and tail markings; orbital ring becomes reddish in summer; bill and legs brighten to yellow, often similar to adult but with variable black distal marks on bill. Attains adultlike plumage by third prebasic molt (June–Sept.), but presumed third-cycle birds average more black and less white in wingtips (for example, white tips on P5–P7 reduced, absent on P8–P10), more often show black on primary coverts.

HYBRIDS

Mew/Common Gull (unidentified taxon) possibly with Ring-billed Gull.[4]

NOTES

1. Carey and Kennerley 1996; 2. Moskoff and Bevier 2002; 3. Howell and McKee 1998; 4. M. O'Brien pers. comm. (photos 23.29–23.30)

LENGTH 16.5–19.7 IN. (42–50 CM)
PHOTOS 22B.0–22B.14, 23.29–23.30

IDENTIFICATION SUMMARY

Casual to rare visitor to e. N. America from Europe. Bill medium length and relatively slender, with slight gonydeal expansion. At rest, tail tip falls between tips of P6 and P7. Adult has medium gray upperparts (Kodak 5–7; see Taxonomy) with black wingtips (white mirrors on outer 2–3 primaries) and, in basic plumage, fairly neat and spotted dusky head and neck markings. First cycle has white tail with clean-cut blackish distal band. PA1 variable, starting Aug.–Dec. Second cycle variably intermediate between first cycle and adult. First cycle has flesh legs, becoming yellow by adult cycle; adult eyes brownish; orbital ring red. See Similar Species/Rarer Species for distinctions from Ring-billed, Mew, and other taxa.

TAXONOMY

See introduction to the Mew Gull complex. *L. c. heinei,* breeding in cen. Asia but occurring in migration and winter west to Europe[1] and probably east to coastal China and n. Japan,[2,3,4] averages larger overall and darker above (Kodak 5.5–7 versus 5–6.5) but much overlap;[5,6,7] lone birds probably not safely identifiable in the field. Intergrades between *heinei* and Kamchatka Gull reported from cen. e. Siberia.[8]

STATUS AND DISTRIBUTION

Northern Eurasia. European range has increased in the past 50 years, with Iceland colonized in 1955 and the population there increasing rapidly; N. American records seem to have increased in tandem with this expansion.[9]

Nonbreeding. In N. America, status clouded by difficulties in distinguishing Mew Gull from Common Gull. Common Gulls (presumably all nominate *canus*) are known in N. America mainly from Atlantic Canada (mid-Sept.–early May, mainly late Oct.–Apr., casually through the summer), and most frequent in Nfld. (where rare but regular); thence rare to casual south to Mass., and casual (mainly Dec.–Mar.) south to Outer Banks, N.C. Casual visitor (June–early Dec.) to Greenland.

FIELD IDENTIFICATION

SIMILAR SPECIES

Most similar to Ring-billed Gull. Also see Mew Gull, adult Black-legged Kittiwake, and, under Rarer Species, California Gull and Kamchatka Gull.

Adult Cycle. Note medium size, medium gray back, yellowish legs, plain yellowish bill, brown eyes.

RING-BILLED GULL (widespread in N. America) averages larger with longer, slightly stouter, and blunter-tipped bill that has a distinct black ring year-round, eyes staring pale lemon, upperparts paler (Kodak 4–5) with narrower and less contrasting white scapular and tertial crescents. In flight has smaller white mirrors on P9–P10, small and poorly contrasting white tongue-tips out to P8, and less contrasting white trailing edge to upperwings. Basic head and neck markings average finer and more streaked.

MEW GULL (w. N. America) averages smaller and shorter billed, with average darker upperparts (Kodak 6–7.5) and paler eyes; perhaps best identified by wingtip pattern. On Mew Gull, white tips to the inner primaries are broad like the secondary tips (narrower on Common); the outer primaries have less extensive black (extending to primary coverts only on P10) with larger P9–P10 mirrors and typically bold white tongue-tips out to P8; P4 often has some black. At rest, the wingtip difference may be seen as more-extensive gray on the primary bases of Mew Gull, and the white P8 tongue-tip of Mew often shows above the edge of P7. Mew Gulls in winter have smudgier and more-diffuse dusky head and neck mottling, and often lack a dusky bill ring. Beware presumed third-cycle Mew Gulls with relatively extensive black in wingtips, which may suggest Common Gull.

BLACK-LEGGED KITTIWAKE (breeds n. N. America, pelagic elsewhere) shares medium gray upperparts (Kodak 6.5–8), dark eyes, and plain yellow bill, but has narrower and more pointed wings with clean-cut black wingtips (lacking white mirrors), short black legs.

First Cycle. Plumage more similar to Ring-billed Gull than to Mew Gull.

RING-BILLED GULL averages larger with longer, stouter, and blunter-tipped bill, less rounded head. Note tail and upperwing pattern: Ring-billed tends to have less-solid tail band often washed dusky basally and broken with whitish distally, whereas Common typically has solid black distal band; but some Ring-billeds may match Common Gull in this respect; upperwing pattern of Ring-billed overall more contrasting, with blacker outer primaries and paler, silvery gray inner primaries and greater coverts. Other features similar to Common Gull but back slightly paler gray, rarely creating a distinct saddle effect; upperwing coverts have broader, pale-notched tips (often creating a more checkered, rather than scaly, pattern); tertials tend to be darker with wider and more-notched pale edgings; and dusky head and neck markings tend to be less coarsely mottled, more finely streaked on head.

MEW GULL averages slightly smaller and shorter billed. Plumage dusky brownish overall (especially on underparts) with dark tail, dusky underwings, strong barring on tail coverts, and on average more-extensive dark subterminal marks on inner primaries. Some second-cycle Mew Gulls with gray saddle and black tail band can suggest first-cycle Common; note lack of distinct dark secondary bar, mostly gray tertials, greenish bill base and legs.

Second Cycle. RING-BILLED GULL averages larger and stouter billed, often with a less rounded head. Eyes often pale and black bill ring more sharply defined. Upperparts slightly paler gray with less contrasting white scapular and tertial crescents; upperwings with average smaller P10 mirror (lacking P9 mirror), and less contrasting white trailing edge; tail and secondaries more often have dark marks.

MEW GULL averages slightly smaller and shorter billed but diagnostic identification criteria still need elucidation. Mew usually has dark tail marks, and birds with extensive dark markings unlikely to be Common Gulls; advanced-type Mew Gull wing patterns with bold white tongue-tip on P8 probably not shown by Common Gull; and Mew Gull's head and neck markings may average coarser, blurrier, and more extensive.

RARER SPECIES

Adult Cycle. CALIFORNIA GULL (mainly w. N. America) larger with a longer and stouter bill (that has a red gonydeal spot as well as a variable black subterminal band), and longer wing projection; upperparts average darker gray (Kodak 6–7.5 in smaller nominate race). California has more black in the wingtip (especially on P6–P7, which typically lack distinct white tongue-tips). Basic head and neck markings of California tend to be coarser.

KAMCHATKA GULL (casual in w. Alaska) averages larger and bulkier with longer and stouter bill, average darker upperparts (Kodak 6.5–8), and paler eyes, but conclusive identification criteria require elucidation. Kamchatka Gull also averages smaller white P9–P10 mirrors, more often has broader white tongue-tips on P5–P7/P8, and sometimes has black on P4, but some may overlap with Common Gull in wingtip pattern. Basic Kamchatka Gull also has heavier and coarser dusky head and neck markings than typical of Common Gull.

First Cycle. CALIFORNIA GULL larger and longer billed; upperparts more variegated (PA1 molt often includes upperwing coverts) with notched pale tips to tertials; does not attain mostly gray back until second cycle. First-cycle Common Gull distinguished from second-cycle California by size, pale gray greater coverts (dark brownish on California), and lack of green or blue-gray hue to bill and legs; also note different tail and primary patterns.

KAMCHATKA GULL averages larger and bulkier with longer and stouter bill, is duskier and more brownish overall in first winter, suggesting a large Mew Gull at rest but with more-extensive whitish streaking and mottling below; gray saddle often incomplete in midwinter (with retained juvenal scapulars); tail base washed brownish but can bleach to whitish; note stronger barring on tail coverts, overall duskier underwings.

Second Cycle. CALIFORNIA GULL might appear similar to first-cycle Common (see above); second-cycle Common distinguished from third-cycle California by smaller size, smaller bill, and shorter wings, but plumage and bare parts can be similar: California averages darker gray above (Kodak 6–7.5 in smaller nominate race), more often has black bill ring, and can have some orange-red at gonys; Common Gull usually has black subterminal marks on P4 (sometimes outer web of P3), whereas P3–P4 typically lack black on California.

KAMCHATKA GULL averages larger, bulkier, and broader winged with longer and stouter bill, but diagnostic identification criteria need elucidation. Kamchatka Gull more often keeps a pinkish bill base into midwinter (usually greenish on Common), upperwing and tail patterns average more "retarded," and head and neck markings probably average coarser and more extensive.

HABITAT AND BEHAVIOR

Nonbreeding habitat and habits much like Mew Gull. In N. America usually found singly, most often with Ring-billed Gulls but locally (in Newfoundland) associates with Black-headed Gulls.

DESCRIPTION AND MOLT

Prebasic molts in Europe[10] average earlier than Mew Gull in N. America.

Adult Cycle. Complete PB molt (mid-May/mid-July–Sept./Oct.) produces adult basic plumage: head, neck, and underparts white; head and neck typically with fairly fine dusky spotting and streaking often heaviest on hindneck (rarely can have a dark-streaked "hood"). Back and upperwings pale medium gray (Kodak 5–7) with black wingtips (black on outer web of P9–P10, sometimes P8–P10, extends to primary coverts; P4 typically lacks black); fairly contrasting white scapular and tertial crescents; and white tips to outer primaries. Fairly broad white trailing edge to secondaries narrows on inner primaries and breaks into discrete white tips on outer primaries; P5–P7 typically have distinct white tongue-tips and black subterminal bands, and P9–P10 have large white mirrors, often with a smaller mirror on P8. Uppertail coverts and tail white. Underwings show blackish wingtips (with P8/P9–P10 mirrors) demarcated from smoky gray, white-tipped inner primaries and secondaries. Eyes dark brown (exceptionally pale lemon[11]), orbital ring reddish (often gray to dull pinkish in midwinter). Bill gray-green to yellowish, often greenish with a yellow tip, and usually with a narrow dark subterminal ring. Legs yellowish to gray-green. Partial PA molt (*Jan.*–Mar./Apr.) produces adult alternate plumage: head and neck clean white; white primary tips can be reduced through wear. Orbital ring red, legs and bill brighter yellow, bill lacks dark subterminal marks.

First Cycle. Juvenile (late July–Dec.): dusky brown to gray-brown overall. Head, neck, chest, and sides streaked and mottled whitish; vent and undertail coverts white with sparse dark brown bars on tail coverts. Upperparts (including tertials) gray-brown with scaly buff (bleaching to whitish) edgings, the greater coverts typically plainer and grayer. Uppertail coverts white with sparse dark spots and bars. Remiges blackish with contrasting pale gray panel on inner primaries; secondaries and inner primaries tipped whitish, outer primaries with fine pale edgings; P10 rarely with indistinct small pale mirror. Tail white with clean-cut blackish distal band narrowing on outer rectrices and often not extending to outer web of R6; sometimes with dark extending basally on outer webs. IN FLIGHT: dusky gray-brown overall with blackish remiges except for pale gray inner primary panel, white uppertail coverts and tail base with black distal tail band; underwings whitish with variable dusky mottling often forming bars on coverts. Eyes dark brown, bill blackish with dull flesh base, usually becoming flesh to flesh pink with variable blackish tip by early winter; legs dull flesh to flesh pink. PA1 molt (Sept.–Mar./Apr.; does not include upperwing coverts or tertials) produces first alternate plumage: head, neck, and underparts white with variable dusky brown streaking and mottling, often bleaching to overall whitish by late winter. A1 scapulars mostly plain grayish. In late winter and spring, upperwing coverts can bleach to a whitish panel; bleaching can also increase prominence of any P10 mirror. Eyes brown. Bill flesh pink with black tip, sometimes becoming greenish in spring; legs flesh to flesh pink.

Second Cycle. Complete PB2 molt (May/June–Sept.) into second basic plumage. Overall resembles adult basic but averages heavier dark streaking on head, neck, and chest; wingtips black with at most only fine whitish tips, often lost by wear; lesser coverts can have some brown mottling; tertials sometimes with dark centers; black in wingtip more extensive, including alula and primary coverts, with P10 mirror smaller and P9 mirror sometimes absent; tail can have limited black distal markings (often all white); underwings white with little or no dusky mottling on coverts. Eyes dark brown, bill typically greenish with black tip or broad distal band (but some birds have flesh-based bill), legs gray-green to grayish flesh. Partial PA2 molt (*Feb.*–Apr./May; may include upperwing coverts?) produces second alternate plumage: head and neck typically become clean white; differs from adult primarily in wing and tail markings; orbital ring becomes reddish in summer; bill and legs brighten to yellow, often similar to adult but with variable black distal marks on bill. Attains adult plumage by third prebasic molt (June–Sept./Oct.), but third-cycle birds may average more black and less white in wingtips, more often show black on primary coverts.

HYBRIDS

Presumed with Black-headed Gull[12] and Mediterranean Gull (*L. melanocephalus*);[13] possibly with Ring-billed Gull.[14] Mew/Common Gull (unidentified taxon) possibly with Ring-billed Gull.[15]

NOTES

1. Hein and Martens 2002; 2. Carey and Kennerley 1996; 3. Dunn pers. obs.; 4. Howell pers. obs.; 5. BM specimens; 6. Cramp and Simmons 1983; 7. Hein and Martens 2002; 8. Cramp and Simmons 1983; 9. Moskoff and Bevier 2002; 10. Walters 1978; 11. Koerkamp 1987; 12. Moskoff and Bevier 2002; 13. Pullan and Martin 2004; 14. Kehoe 1992; 15. M. O'Brien pers. comm. (photos 23.29–23.30)

IDENTIFICATION SUMMARY

Casual to rare visitor to w. Alaska from Asia. Bill medium length with slight gonydeal expansion. At rest, tail tip falls between tips of P6 and P7. Adult has medium gray upperparts (Kodak 6.5–8) with black wingtips (white mirrors on outer 2–3 primaries) and, in basic plumage, fairly coarse and heavy dusky head and neck markings. First cycle has whitish tail with broad blackish distal band. PA1 variable, starting Sept.–Feb. Second cycle variably intermediate between first cycle and adult. First cycle has flesh pink legs, becoming yellow by adult cycle; adult eyes dirty pale lemon to brownish; orbital ring red. See Similar Species/Rarer Species for distinctions from Mew, Ring-billed, and Common Gulls.

TAXONOMY

See introduction to the Mew Gull complex. Intergrades between Kamchatka Gull and Common Gull (*L. c. heinei*) reported from cen. e. Siberia.[1]

STATUS AND DISTRIBUTION

E. Asia; accidental in Hawaii.

Nonbreeding. In N. America, a rare spring (May–mid-June) and casual fall (Sept.–mid-Oct., late Nov.) migrant in the w. Aleutians; a June bird at Skagul, cen. Aleutians, probably also this subspecies.[2] Casual north (mid-May–early June, Aug.) to the Bering Sea, including the Pribilofs and St. Lawrence Is.

FIELD IDENTIFICATION

SIMILAR SPECIES

Mew Gull is the main species to eliminate when confronted with a possible Kamchatka Gull, but also see Ring-billed and California Gulls. Also note Common Gull (rare winter visitor, e. N. America) under Rarer Species account of that taxon.

Adult Cycle. MEW GULL (w. N. America) averages smaller, less thickset, and shorter billed with average paler upperparts (Kodak 6–7.5); perhaps best identified by wingtip pattern. On Mew Gull, white tips to the inner primaries are broad like the secondary tips (narrower on Kamchatka); outer primaries have less-exten-

sive black (extending to primary coverts only on P10) with larger P9–P10 mirrors and typically bold white tongue-tips out to P8. At rest, the wingtip difference may be seen as more-extensive gray on the primary bases of Mew Gull, and the white P8 tongue-tip of Mew often shows above the edge of P7. Mew Gulls in winter have smudgier and more-diffuse dusky head and neck mottling and often lack a dusky bill ring (often shown by Kamchatka Gull). Beware presumed third-cycle Mew Gulls with relatively extensive black in wingtips, which may suggest Kamchatka Gull.

RING-BILLED GULL (widespread in N. America but not in w. Alaska) has slightly stouter, blunter-tipped bill with distinct black ring year-round, staring pale lemon eyes, and paler upperparts (Kodak 4–5) with narrower and less contrasting white scapular and tertial crescents. In flight has small and poorly contrasting white tongue-tips out to P8, and less contrasting white trailing edge to upperwings. Basic head and neck markings finer and more streaked.

BLACK-LEGGED KITTIWAKE (breeds n. N. America, pelagic elsewhere) shares medium gray upperparts (Kodak 6.5–8) and plain yellow bill but has narrower and more pointed wings with clean-cut black wingtips (lacking white mirrors), short black legs.

CALIFORNIA GULL (mainly w. N. America) is larger with a longer and heavier bill (that has a red gonydeal spot as well as a variable black subterminal band), a longer wing projection, and dark eyes. California has more black in the wingtip (especially on P6–P7, which typically lack distinct white tongue-tips). Basic head and neck markings of California tend to be more streaked and often concentrated on the lower hindneck.

First Cycle. Note medium size, bill size and shape, broad blackish distal tail band, and dusky wash to tail base.

MEW GULL averages smaller, slighter, and narrower winged with shorter and thinner bill, but some may overlap with a small Kamchatka Gull. Plumage characters variably overlap with Kamchatka Gull and critical study needed to elucidate diagnostic features. Tail base of Mew typically darker, more strongly washed dusky, and so lacks broad, clean-cut blackish distal band often shown by Kamchatka—but some birds overlap in tail pattern.

Mew has tail coverts more heavily barred brown, head and underparts average duskier than Kamchatka, and inner primaries average more-extensive dark subterminal marks.

RING-BILLED GULL typically much more whitish overall in first winter, PA1 molt usually produces pale gray back by early winter and can include upperwing coverts; upperwing pattern more contrasting with blacker outer primaries and paler, silvery gray inner primaries and greater coverts; underwings whitish overall. Tail pattern can be similar to Kamchatka Gull although blackish distal band usually less solid, averaging narrower and with whitish internal markings distally; upperwing coverts have broader, pale-notched tips (often creating a more checkered, rather than scaly, pattern); and white tail coverts have little or no barring.

CALIFORNIA GULL larger and longer billed; upperparts more variegated (PA1 molt often includes upperwing coverts) with notched pale tips to tertials; does not attain mostly gray back until second cycle. First-cycle Kamchatka distinguished from second-cycle California by smaller size, pale gray greater coverts (dark brownish on California), and lack of green or blue-gray hue to bill and legs; also note different tail and primary patterns.

Second Cycle. MEW GULL averages smaller with smaller bill, but diagnostic identification criteria still need elucidation. Kamchatka Gull more often keeps a pinkish bill base into midwinter (usually greenish on Mew).

RING-BILLED GULL has upperparts paler gray with less contrasting white scapular and tertial crescents; upperwings have average smaller P10 mirror (lacking P9 mirror), and less contrasting white trailing edge; bill has more clean-cut black ring.

CALIFORNIA GULL might appear similar to first-cycle Kamchatka (see above); second-cycle Kamchatka distinguished from third-cycle California by smaller size, smaller bill, and shorter wings, but plumage and bare parts can be similar: California more often has black bill ring and can have some orange-red at gonys, Kamchatka Gull usually has black subterminal marks on P4 (sometimes outer web of P3), whereas P3–P4 typically lack black on California.

HABITAT AND BEHAVIOR

Nonbreeding habitat and habits much as Mew Gull, with which it could occur.

DESCRIPTION AND MOLT

Adult Cycle. Complete PB molt (mid-June/mid-July–mid-Sept./early Nov.) produces adult basic plumage: head, neck, and underparts white; head and neck typically with fairly coarse dusky spotting and streaking often heaviest on hindneck. Back and upperwings medium gray (Kodak 6.5–8) with black wing-tips (black on outer webs of P9–P10, sometimes also P8, extends to primary coverts); fairly contrasting white scapular and tertial crescents; and white tips to outer primaries. Uppertail coverts and tail white. Fairly broad white trailing edge to secondaries narrows on inner primaries and breaks into discrete white tips on outer primaries; P5–P7, sometimes also P8, have narrow white tongue-tips and black subterminal bands; P9–P10 have white mirrors. Underwings show blackish wingtips (with P9–P10 mirrors) demarcated from smoky gray, white-tipped inner primaries and secondaries. Eyes dirty pale lemon (flecked dusky) to brownish, orbital ring reddish (often gray to dull pinkish in midwinter). Bill gray-green to yellowish, often greenish with a yellow tip and variable dusky subterminal ring. Legs yellowish to gray-green. Partial PA molt (*Feb.–Apr./May*) produces adult alternate plumage: head and neck clean white; white primary tips can be reduced through wear. Orbital ring red, legs and bill brighter yellow, bill lacks dark subterminal marks.

First Cycle. Juvenile (late July–Feb.): dusky brown to gray-brown overall. Head, neck, and underparts streaked and mottled whitish, becoming white on vent and undertail coverts, which have dark brown bars. Upperparts (including tertials) gray-brown with scaly buff (bleaching to whitish) edgings, the greater coverts typically plainer and grayer. Uppertail coverts white with distinct brown barring. Remiges blackish with contrasting pale gray panel on inner primaries; secondaries and inner primaries tipped whitish, outer primaries with narrow pale edging visible at rest. Tail whitish based with broad blackish distal band and variable dusky wash basally; can look all dark when closed. IN FLIGHT: dusky gray-brown overall with blackish remiges except for pale gray inner primary panel, contrasting whiter uppertail coverts and tail base with broad blackish distal tail band; underwings whitish to washed pale brownish with extensive dusky markings on coverts. Eyes dark brown, bill blackish with dull flesh base, usually becoming flesh to flesh pink with variable blackish tip by early winter; legs flesh to flesh pink. PA1 molt (Sept.–Apr.; does not include upperwing coverts or tertials) produces first alternate plumage: head, neck, and underparts white with variable dusky brown streaking and mottling, often bleaching to overall whitish by late winter. A1 scapulars mostly plain grayish. In late winter and spring, upperwing coverts can bleach to a whitish panel. Eyes brown. Bill flesh pink with black tip; legs flesh to flesh pink.

Second Cycle. Complete PB2 molt (late May/June–late Aug./Sept.) into second basic plumage. Overall resembles adult basic but averages heavier dark streaking on head, neck, and chest; wingtips black with at most only fine whitish tips, often lost by wear; upperwing coverts often with variable brown wash or markings (mostly gray-brown, contrasting with gray saddle on some birds); tertials sometimes with dark centers; black in wingtip more extensive, including alula and primary coverts with P10 mirror smaller and P9 mirror sometimes absent; tail often has some black distal markings (varies from all white to having an almost solid black subterminal band); underwings white, usually with slight dusky mottling on coverts. Eyes brown to dirty pale lemon, bill flesh pink to greenish with black tip or broad distal band, legs flesh pink to gray-green. Partial PA2 molt (*Feb.–Apr./May;* may include upperwing coverts?) produces second alternate plumage: head and neck typically become clean white; differs from adult primarily in wing and tail markings; orbital ring becomes reddish in summer; bill and legs brighten to yellow, often similar to adult but with variable black distal marks on bill. Attains adult plumage by third prebasic molt (June–Sept.), but third-cycle birds may average more black and less white in wingtips and more often show black on primary coverts.

HYBRIDS
None reported.

NOTES
1. Cramp and Simmons 1983; 2. Gibson and Byrd unpubl.

LENGTH 17.3–20.5 IN. (44–52 CM)
PHOTOS 23.0–23.30; I.36, H2.2

IDENTIFICATION SUMMARY

This common and widespread three-cycle yellow-legged gull is perhaps the most familiar gull in N. America, with nonbreeders occurring south to Middle America. Bill medium sized with a slight gonydeal expansion, relatively slender on some females (especially first-cycle birds). At rest, tail tip falls between tips of P6 and P7. Adult has pale gray upperparts (Kodak 4–5) with black wingtips (white mirrors on outer 1–2 primaries) and, in basic plumage, fine dusky head and neck streaking. Juvenile pale gray-brown overall with white tail and broad blackish distal tail band. PA1 variable, starting Aug.–Dec. Second cycle variably intermediate between first cycle and adult. First cycle has flesh pink legs, becoming yellow by adult cycle; adult eyes staring pale lemon; orbital ring orange-red.

Medium size, pale gray back, yellow legs, black bill ring, and pale eyes are a distinctive combination among adults of regularly occurring New World gulls. In the West, note Mew Gull and California Gull, which also have yellow legs as adults (both are darker gray above and have dark eyes). First cycle attains mostly pale gray back in first winter (and can resemble second-cycle Herring Gull or California Gull) and has white tail base with sharply contrasting blackish distal band, mostly pale gray greater coverts, and mostly whitish underwings. See Similar Species for more-detailed identification criteria; for separation from Common and Kamchatka Gulls, see under those taxa.

TAXONOMY

Monotypic.

STATUS AND DISTRIBUTION

Mid-latitude N. America, wintering to Middle America. Vagrant to Europe, W. Africa, and Hawaii.

Breeding. Breeds (late Apr./May–July/Aug.) from sw. N.T., s. B.C., ne. Calif., and n. Nev.

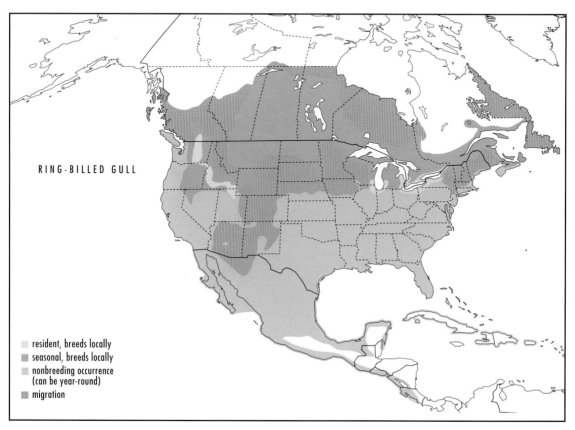

RING-BILLED GULL

- resident, breeds locally
- seasonal, breeds locally
- nonbreeding occurrence (can be year-round)
- migration

east across n. N. America to s. James Bay, s. Lab., Nfld., s. Great Lakes region, ne. N.B., and P.E. Is. Has nested w. Neb., and, since mid-1970s, w. Wash. Largely disappeared from Great Lakes region and other areas during latter part of nineteenth century due to human persecution. Recolonization occurred by 1920s, populations in Great Lakes/St. Lawrence R. region exploded during 1960s and 1970s,[1] and today Ring-billed may be the most populous gull in N. America.

Nonbreeding. Migrates nearly throughout N. America where common to abundant in many regions. Local dispersal away from breeding areas begins by late June, and juveniles have been recorded mid-July from as far south as se. Calif. Fall migration becomes more widespread during mid-July–Aug., when pronounced movement to areas south of breeding range takes place. Arrivals in Southeast typically Sept., earlier in the West (by mid-July), but summering nonbreeders make it difficult to distinguish new arrivals, unless juveniles. Peak numbers on Great Plains and in Great Lakes region occur Oct.–Nov., with large numbers remaining into Dec. Main arrival in more s. wintering areas (for example, Gulf of Mex. coast) is Oct. North of breeding range, uncommon to fairly common in fall in se. Alaska (late July–mid-Oct., most late Aug.–early Sept.), casual farther north to sw., s. coastal, and cen. Alaska, exceptionally to Arctic coast of n. Alaska; regular in small numbers on sw. Hudson Bay (summer) and accidental (late Nov.) in Greenland.

Winters (Sept./Oct.–Mar./Apr.) coastally throughout U.S. and in interior from Idaho, w. Mont., n. Utah, S.D. (Missouri R.), s. Great Lakes region, s. Que., s. N.B. and N.S. (rarely north to Nfld., casually to s.-coastal Alaska) south to cen. Mex., n. Yucatán Peninsula, and n. West Indies; also common in Bermuda. Uncommon to rare south along Pacific Coast from sw. Mex. to Costa Rica; casually to cen. Panama and exceptionally to Colombia and Ecuador. Casual in interior from s. Mex. to Guatemala, and rare to casual south in Atlantic region to s. West Indies, cen. Panama, and n. Venezuela,[2] exceptionally to Amazonian Brazil.[3]

Northward movement begins by mid-Feb. and pronounced by early Mar. in nearly all regions of U.S. and se. Canada, with arrival in Prairie Provinces typically late Mar. Peak movements take place during Mar. over much of N. America, during mid-Apr.–mid-May in n. Great Lakes region and Prairie Provinces.

Oversummering nonbreeders are regular (uncommon to locally common) along Pacific, Atlantic, and Gulf of Mex. coasts south to n. Mex., in Great Lakes region, and at Salton Sea. Summers locally elsewhere, especially on larger lakes and rivers. In general, away from arid regions of the West, rarest in summer in interior Southeast.

FIELD IDENTIFICATION

SIMILAR SPECIES

A generally common and distinctive medium-sized species, especially in the East. In the West, compare with Mew and California Gulls; also see Common Gull (rare winter visitor, e. N. America) and Kamchatka Gull (casual w. Alaska) under those taxa.

Adult Cycle. Note yellow legs, pale gray upperparts, clean-cut black bill ring, and staring pale eyes. Mew Gull and California Gull are the only potentially similar yellow-legged taxa—both have darker gray upperparts and darker eyes, different bill patterns.

MEW GULL (mainly w. N. America) averages smaller and rounder headed; more slender and pointed yellow bill lacks bold black ring (can have narrow dark ring in winter), eyes brownish, upperparts darker (Kodak 6–7.5) with more-contrasting white scapular and tertial crescents; legs in winter often greenish. In flight has larger white mirrors on P9–P10, larger and more contrasting white tongue-tips out to P8, and more-contrasting white trailing edge to upperwings. Winter head and neck markings more smudgy and mottled than Ring-billed.

CALIFORNIA GULL (mainly w. N. America) larger with longer and stouter bill (which has a red gonydeal spot as well as a variable black subterminal band), dark eyes, and darker upperparts (Kodak 6–7.5 on smaller nominate race, Kodak 5–6 on larger *albertaensis* race). White scapular and tertial crescents and trailing edge to upperwing more contrasting; nominate *californicus* in particular has more-extensive black wingtip. Overhead in flight, California shows smoky gray bases to remiges (pale gray to whitish on Ring-billed, but beware effects of lighting). Winter head and neck markings coarser and more mottled, often concentrated on hindneck.

First Cycle. Note medium size, flesh pink bill with black tip or distal black band, overall contrasting appearance, and white tail with broad black distal band. PA1 molt can include upperwing coverts (not replaced in the Mew Gull complex).

MEW GULL averages smaller and finer billed, often with a more rounded head. Plumage duskier brownish overall (especially on underparts) with mostly dark tail (rarely matched by Ring-billed), dusky underwings, strong brown barring on tail coverts, more even-width (not notched) tertial edgings, fuller and darker centers to upperwing coverts (creating scaly rather than checkered pattern) and usually more-distinct whitish fringes to closed primaries. Some second-cycle Mew Gulls with solid black tail band might suggest first-cycle Ring-billed; note lack of distinct dark secondary bar, greenish bill base and legs.

CALIFORNIA GULL generally larger, darker, and browner than Ring-billed Gull with a longer bill that is rarely as bright pink; does not attain mostly gray back until second cycle. First-cycle Ring-billed distinguished from second-cycle California by pale gray back, mostly pale gray greater coverts (dark brownish on California), and lack of green or blue-gray hue to legs; also note different tail and primary patterns.

AMERICAN HERRING GULL and other large white-headed gulls should be eliminated by size. Aside from much larger size, second-cycle Herring Gull distinguished from first-cycle Ring-billed by shape, especially its stouter bill with a more distinct gonydeal expansion, more-rounded primary tips; also note second-cycle Herring's dark brownish greater coverts, more finely peppered whitish tertial markings, more extensively dark tail, and usually messier and browner appearance overall.

Second Cycle. MEW GULL averages smaller and finer billed, often with a more rounded head. Upperparts darker gray with more-contrasting white scapular and tertial crescents; upperwings with larger P10 or P9–P10 mirrors and more contrasting white trailing edge; eyes brown.

CALIFORNIA GULL similar to first-cycle Ring-billed (see above). Second-cycle Ring-billed distinguished from third-cycle California by smaller size and shorter wings; upperparts paler gray with poorly contrasting scapular and tertial crescents; white trailing edge to upperwing poorly contrasting; eyes often pale; and primaries lack distinct white tips at rest and distinct P9–P10 mirrors (often shown by third-cycle California).

HABITAT AND BEHAVIOR
Widespread and adaptable: readily found on beaches, at lakes, duck ponds, parking lots, fishing harbors, dumps, fields, and along rivers; rarely seen far offshore. Nests mainly co-

lonially, typically on low, sparsely vegetated islands in lakes. Nonbreeding birds often in flocks (locally up to thousands of birds), associating readily with other gulls and water birds. Feeds by picking while walking and from the water surface while swimming and in flight, regularly scavenges, and notably agile at snatching bread in flight; also soars on thermals to catch flying insects.

DESCRIPTION AND MOLT
Adult Cycle. Complete PB molt (late May/June–late Sept./Oct.) produces adult basic plumage: head, neck, and underparts white; head and neck with variably extensive, typically fine dusky streaking and spotting. Back and upperwings pale gray (Kodak 4–5) with black wingtips (black on outer web of P9–P10, and sometimes P8, extends to primary coverts; P4 lacks black); indistinct white scapular and tertial crescents; and white tips to outer primaries. White trailing edge to secondaries narrows on inner primaries and breaks into discrete white tips on outer primaries; P6–P8 typically have narrow and poorly contrasting white tongue-tips and black subterminal bands, and P10 or P9–P10 have distinct white mirrors; P5 has variable black subterminal marks. Uppertail coverts and tail white. Underwings show blackish wingtips (with P10 or P9–P10 mirrors) sharply demarcated from pale gray, white-tipped inner primaries and secondaries. Eyes staring pale lemon, orbital ring reddish (often dark gray in midwinter). Bill yellowish with bold black subterminal ring; reddish gape often apparent from midwinter on. Legs yellowish to bright yellow. Partial PA molt (Jan.–Mar./Apr.) produces adult alternate plumage: head and neck clean white; white primary tips can be lost through wear. Orbital ring red to orange-red, legs and bill brighter yellow, bill with orange-red gape.

First Cycle. Juvenile (late July–Dec.): head, neck, and underparts white, variably streaked and spotted brownish, often with chevrons on sides and flanks, and unmarked on median underparts; undertail coverts with sparse dark brown bars. Upperparts dark brown to gray-brown with buff (bleaching to whitish) edgings, the greater coverts typically plainer and grayer; upperpart markings scaly to checkered overall. Tertials blackish brown with coarsely notched white tips and distal edging. Uppertail coverts white with sparse dark spots and bars. Remiges blackish to brownish black with contrasting pale gray panel on inner primaries; secondaries and inner primaries tipped whitish, outer primaries with narrow whitish tips visible at rest (often lost through wear). Tail variable: whitish based (bleaching to white), typically with contrasting blackish distal band, often with variable dark wash or markings basally (most heavily marked birds look dark tailed); blackish distal band sometimes broken subterminally by whitish marks and often not extending to outer web of R6. IN FLIGHT: fairly pale brownish gray above with blackish remiges except for contrasting pale gray inner primary panel (rarely dull), bold white tail base with broad blackish distal band; underwings whitish overall with variable, usually sparse, dark markings on coverts. Eyes dark brown, bill flesh pink with typically fairly clean-cut black tip; legs flesh to flesh pink. PA1 molt (Aug.–Mar./Apr.; often includes upperwing coverts, sometimes tertials) produces first alternate plumage: head, neck, and underparts white with variable dusky brown streaking and spotting on head, neck, chest, and sides, tending to chevrons on sides and flanks; underparts often bleach to overall whitish by late winter. A1 scapulars and upperwing coverts mostly pale gray, often with variable brown markings and whitish fringes when fresh. In late winter, blackish to blackish brown wingtips and worn, dark brown tertials often contrast with bleached whitish panel on upperwing coverts. Eyes brown (can become medium pale by late winter); bill flesh pink with black tip, often attains fine pale tip by midwinter; some late-winter birds have broad black subterminal bill ring and pinkish yellow bill; legs flesh pink.

Second Cycle. Complete PB2 molt (late Apr./May–late Aug./Sept.) into second basic plumage. Overall resembles adult basic but averages heavier dark streaking on head, neck, and chest; wingtips black with at most only fine whitish tips, often lost by wear; lesser co-

verts may have some brown mottling; tertials sometimes with dark centers; black in wingtip more extensive (P4 sometimes with subterminal blackish), including alula and primary coverts, with P10 mirror smaller and P9 mirror absent; tail often has some black distal markings (varies from all white to having a solid black subterminal band). Eyes pale lemon to dark brown, bill typically greenish yellow with black subterminal ring wider than adult (but some birds have pink bill like first cycle, others have almost adultlike bill), legs grayish green to flesh. Partial PA2 molt (Jan./Feb.–Apr.; often includes upperwing coverts) produces second alternate plumage: head and neck typically become clean white during Mar.–Apr.; differs from adult primarily in wing and tail markings. Eyes pale lemon to dull lemon, orbital ring becomes orange-red in summer; bill and legs brighten to yellow, often similar to adult but black ring averages wider. Attains adult plumage by third prebasic molt (May/June–Sept./Oct.), but third-cycle birds average more black and less white in wingtips, more often show black on primary coverts.[4]

HYBRIDS

With Franklin's Gull[5] and presumed with Common Black-headed Gull;[6] possibly with Common Gull,[7] Mew/Common Gull,[8] and California Gull;[9] reported with Laughing Gull.[10]

NOTES

1. Ludwig 1974; 2. Fairbank 2002; 3. Sick 1979; 4. Blokpoel et al. 1985; 5. Weseloh 1981; 6. Weseloh and Mineau 1986; 7. Kehoe 1992; 8. M. O'Brien pers. comm. (photos 23.29–23.30); 9. Dunn and Howell pers. obs. (photos 23.26–23.28); 10. Henshaw 1992

LARGE WHITE-HEADED GULLS
(GENUS *Larus*, IN PART)

These are a group of mostly Northern Hemisphere gulls that includes relatively recently evolved and evolving taxa, with numerous uncertainties at the species level. In the Americas we treat 13 species: California Gull, Herring Gull (including American Herring Gull, European Herring Gull, and Vega Gull), Yellow-legged Gull, Lesser Black-backed Gull, Kelp Gull, Great Black-backed Gull, Slaty-backed Gull, Western Gull, Yellow-footed Gull, Glaucous-winged Gull, Glaucous Gull, Iceland Gull (including Kumlien's Gull), and Thayer's Gull. Note, though, that rapid-paced recent advances in our understanding of gull taxonomy (largely through genetic analyses) indicate that this arrangement does not accurately reflect species limits (see introduction to the Herring Gull complex, p. 401). Also note that hybridization is frequent among some species of large white-headed gulls, especially in western N. America.

Males are larger than females, often strikingly so, such that almost all species overlap in terms of measurements (see table 1 in Introduction).

Bills are medium to large, with a moderate to distinct gonydeal expansion in several species, but females and immatures have smaller and more slender bills than adult males. Adult bills are yellow with a reddish gonydeal spot and sometimes black distal marks or a black subterminal ring, especially on nonbreeding birds. Adult legs and feet range from pink to yellow. Legs of all first-cycle birds are pinkish, their bills all black or with a pinkish base. Adult upperwings of most species range from pale gray to slaty blackish with a white trailing edge and a blackish tip with white spots; three species have gray to white wingtips. Basic plumages have variable dusky streaking and mottling on the head and neck. These are ostensibly four-cycle gulls with a notorious range of individual variation in immature plumages. Juvenal plumage is brownish overall with scaly and notched pale patterning on the upperparts. First prealternate molts range from limited (or even absent) to extensive. In most species, adultlike back color is first attained in the second plumage cycle.

ADULT NONBREEDING CALIFORNIA GULL (PRESUMED *L. C. CALIFORNICUS*). PP. 150, 395

ADULT NONBREEDING AMERICAN HERRING GULL. PP. 159, 402

ADULT NONBREEDING EUROPEAN HERRING GULLS. PP. 170, 410

ADULT NONBREEDING VEGA GULL. PP. 175, 412

ADULT NONBREEDING YELLOW-LEGGED GULL. PP. 180, 417

ADULT NONBREEDING LESSER BLACK-BACKED GULL *(L. F. GRAELLSII)*. PP. 187, 422

ADULT BREEDING KELP GULL *(L. D. DOMINICANUS)*. PP. 196, 428

ADULT NONBREEDING GREAT BLACK-BACKED GULL. PP. 205, 434

ADULT NONBREEDING SLATY-BACKED GULL. PP. 213, 438

ADULT NONBREEDING WESTERN GULL. PP. 221, 442

ADULT YELLOW-FOOTED GULL. PP. 226, 448

ADULT NONBREEDING GLAUCOUS-WINGED GULL. PP. 235, 453

ADULT NONBREEDING GLAUCOUS GULL. PP. 244, 458

ADULT NONBREEDING KUMLIEN'S GULL. PP. 251, 463

ADULT NONBREEDING ICELAND GULL. PP. 260, 468

ADULT NONBREEDING THAYER'S GULL. PP. 263, 471

Determining a bird's age can be important in identification. But doing so can be difficult because of extensive individual variation, particularly in second- and third-cycle plumages. Plumage and bare-part colors and patterns are related to hormonal levels, which vary greatly among individuals. In one experiment, American Herring Gull embryos injected with testosterone resulted in a very advanced-looking juvenal plumage and in essentially "adult plumage" being attained by the second prebasic molt (Boss 1943)! Variation under normal conditions is less extreme, and some guidelines for aging large gulls are noted below; also see the discussion of molt and changing appearance in the introduction (pp. 33–44). Important points to check include the shape of the primary tips (relatively tapered on first-cycle birds, more rounded on subsequent cycles), pattern of the tail coverts (neatly barred on first-cycle birds), and pattern on the inner and middle primaries (for separating second- and third-cycle birds).

First-cycle birds generally have relatively tapered primary tips (which often become worn by late in the first cycle), distinct and neatly patterned dark barring on the tail coverts, and uniformly patterned upperwing coverts (except for a few species that frequently replace coverts in their PA1 molt, namely Califor-nia, Yellow-legged, Lesser Black-backed, and Yellow-footed Gulls). Post-juvenal scapulars vary greatly in pattern depending on when they are molted relative to a bird's hormonal development: in general, earlier-molted feathers tend to be browner and more juvenal-like, later feathers grayer and more adultlike.

Second-cycle birds have more-rounded primary tips, less neatly patterned dark barring or markings on the tail coverts, and less uniformly patterned upperwing coverts (often with PA2 median coverts contrasting in freshness and pattern). Their inner and middle primaries typically have patterns that resemble first-cycle birds (very rarely, one or two inner primaries can be more advanced and adultlike in pattern).

Third-cycle birds often resemble adults much more than they do second-cycle birds, but "retarded" third-cycle plumages can be similar to second-cycle in some species (especially American Herring, Glaucous-winged, Glaucous, and Iceland Gulls). Perhaps the best aging character is the pattern of the inner and middle primaries (P1–P6), which are generally adultlike in pattern (for example, gray with broad, clean white tips to the inner primaries, and with adultlike markings on the middle primaries), versus the immature-like pattern typical of second-cycle birds.

LENGTH 18–23 IN. (45.5–58 CM)

PHOTOS 24.0–24.41; I.1–I.4, I.8, I.36, 23.26–23.28, 36.38

IDENTIFICATION SUMMARY

A medium-sized to medium-large, relatively long-winged, yellow-legged gull of w. N. America. Breeds mainly in the interior, winters mainly on the Pacific Coast. Bill medium sized (relatively slender on some females, especially first-cycle birds) and overall parallel edged with a slight gonydeal expansion. At rest, tail tip falls at or slightly beyond tip of P6, so wing projection is relatively long. Adult has pale gray to medium gray upperparts (Kodak 5–7.5; see taxonomy) with black wingtips (white mirrors on outer 2 primaries) and, in basic plumage, fairly extensive dusky head and neck streaking. Juvenile brownish overall with mostly blackish tail. PA1 variable, starting Aug.–Jan. Subsequent ages variable in appearance. All ages have dark brown eyes; first cycle has pinkish legs becoming yellowish by adult cycle; adult orbital ring red.

Medium size, pale gray to medium gray back, dark brown eyes, yellowish legs, and black bill ring with a red gonydeal spot are a distinctive combination among adults of regularly occurring New World gulls. Mostly dark brown and black-tailed first cycle told from Western Gull, Herring Gull, and Thayer's Gull by more slender and narrow-winged build, flesh pink bill with clean-cut black tip, and from the last two also by lack of a pale inner primary panel and by dark-based greater coverts. See Similar Species and Rarer Species sections for fuller identification criteria.

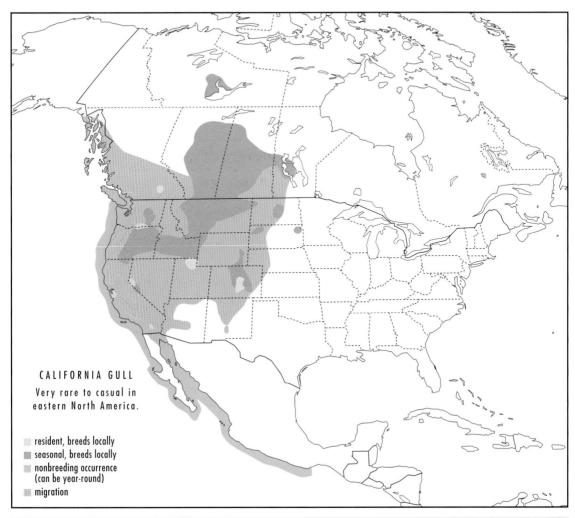

CALIFORNIA GULL

Very rare to casual in eastern North America.

▫ resident, breeds locally
▨ seasonal, breeds locally
▨ nonbreeding occurrence (can be year-round)
▨ migration

Taxonomy

Two subspecies recognized:[1] nominate *californicus*, breeding mainly in Great Basin from cen. Calif. east and northeast to Colo. and s. Mont.; and *albertaensis*, breeding in n. Great Plains from ne. Mont. north to Northwest Territories, east to N.D. Nonbreeding distributions of the subspecies not well known. Nominate birds average smaller (adults 19–21.7 in.; 48–55 cm) and darker gray above (Kodak 6–7.5), *albertaensis* averages larger (adults 20–23 in.; 51–58 cm) and paler gray above (Kodak 5–6).

Status and Distribution

Breeds w. N. America, winters w. U.S. and nw. Mex. Vagrant to Hawaii.

Breeding. Breeds (mid-Apr.–mid-July/Aug.; nominate *californicus*) locally from s.-cen. B.C. (Okanagan Lake), e. Wash., e. and cen. Ore., and e. Calif. (south to Mono Lake) e. to n. Utah, se. Wyo., and cen. Colo. Isolated colonies in w.-cen. Calif. (s. San Francisco Bay since 1980s[2]) and se. Calif. (Salton Sea since 1990s[3]). *L. c. albertaensis* breeds (May–Aug.) from Great Slave Lake in the N.T., e. Alb., and Sask. south to sw. Man. and ne. S.D. Intergradation between subspecies probably occurs in Mont.[4]

Nonbreeding. Both subspecies occur throughout main nonbreeding range, from se. Alaska to nw. Mex. (perhaps with *albertaensis* averaging a more southerly winter distribution), but data are insufficient to determine details of subspecies' relative abundance or distribution. In fall, birds head west and northwest to the Pacific Coast and then drift south through the winter before heading north in spring along the coast and overland.[5,6]

Fall movements begin by early July from Wash. to Calif. and by mid-July in most other regions but not until Aug. in Prairie Provinces. Peak numbers occur mid-Aug.–early Sept. in the interior West, Sept.–Oct. on the coast. Ranges north commonly (mid-July–Nov. with peak numbers late Aug.–early Sept.) along coast north to se. Alaska and through s. third of B.C. Fall withdrawal south to wintering areas usually late Oct.–early Nov.

Winters commonly (Oct./Nov.–Mar./Apr.) from sw. B.C. south along Pacific Coast, including well offshore, to Baja Calif. Peninsula and Gulf of Calif., thence irregularly rare to fairly common south to Colima, Mex., rare or casual (Jan.–Mar.) south to s. Mex. and El Salvador;[7] accidental w. Ecuador. Also winters inland from s.-cen. B.C. (uncommon) locally south to e. and cen. Ore., in w.-cen. Nev., Calif. (especially Central Valley and Salton Sea), w. Neb., along Front Range, Colo., and rarely in w. Tex. Along Pacific Coast, large numbers commute daily to interior valleys where they are often the commonest gull. Generally rare or even casual in winter elsewhere in West but has been recorded as far north as se. Alaska.

In e. N. America, generally casual to rare but increasing in Midwest, Great Lakes region, Mid-Atlantic states, Southeast, and on Gulf of Mex. coast from ne. Mex.[8] east to Fla. Has been recorded most frequently from se. Ont. (over 30 records; Oct.–early Jan., Mar.–June), including an incubating female in a Ring-billed Gull colony near Toronto in 1981 and 1982. Midwest records (south to Mo. and Ky.) scattered in July–May (mostly Sept.–late Nov. and late Mar.–mid-May); casual in interior Southeast since 2000 (mainly Jan.–Feb.). On Mid-Atlantic coast, now annual Chesapeake Bay region and Outer Banks, N.C. Farthest ne. records (Oct.–Dec., Feb.–Apr.) are from se. N.Y. and Mass.

Northbound movements in Calif. start Feb. on cen. coast, mid-Feb.–Mar. in interior. Arrival at breeding grounds in e. Calif. and e. Ore. by mid-Mar., continuing into Apr. On coast and in s. interior of B.C., movement evident by mid-Mar., peaking early Apr. From w. Great Plains (for example, w. Neb.) north through s. Alta. arrivals evident mid–late Mar., but not until mid-Apr. in sw. Man. Spring movement continues throughout w. N. America into May. Nonbreeding visitor (late May–July) along Pacific Coast from s. B.C. south to nw. Mex. (more commonly from cen. Calif. north), and at Salton Sea; also uncommon in se. Alaska, rare in interior West well away from breeding areas, and casual north to s. coastal Alaska and sw. Hudson Bay, exceptionally to Arctic coast of Alaska.

Field Identification

Similar Species

California Gull spans the medium to large size range and might be confused both with three-cycle, small white-headed gulls and with four-cycle, large white-headed gulls. Note its long wings, relatively long and parallel-edged bill, and dark eyes at all ages.

Adult Cycle. Distinctive. Note medium size, long and pointed wings, medium gray upperparts with broad-based black wingtip patch, dark eyes, black bill ring (reduced on breeding birds) with a red gonydeal spot, and greenish to yellow legs.

RING-BILLED GULL (widespread) smaller with shorter and slimmer bill (that lacks red gonydeal spot), staring pale lemon eyes, and pale gray upperparts (Kodak 4–5) with less contrasting white scapular and tertial crescents. Overhead in flight, Ring-billed shows mostly white underwings, less extensive and narrower-based black wingtip patch, and lacks smoky gray bases to remiges of California. Winter head and neck markings finer and more streaked.

MEW GULL (w. N. America) appreciably smaller with smaller, plain yellow bill and shorter wing projection. Mew has less black in the wingtip and typically larger white tongue-tips on P7–P8. Basic head and neck markings of Mew tend to be more diffuse, or smudgy.

LESSER BLACK-BACKED GULL (widespread, but rare in West) averages larger with slightly stouter bill, slaty gray upperparts (Kodak 9–13), and pale eyes; legs yellow to fleshy yellow, lacking gray-green hues often shown by California; black wingtips contrast less on darker upperwings, and underwings show darker bases to remiges.

AMERICAN HERRING GULL, THAYER'S GULL, and other large gulls with pale gray to medium gray upperparts have pink legs. Occasional Herring Gulls with yellow legs can suggest *albertaensis* California Gull but average larger and bulkier with shorter wing projection, deeper gonys; Herring also has staring pale eyes, slightly paler upperparts (Kodak 4–5), more tapered black wingtip wedge (often with only a small P10 mirror in w. N. America), underwing lacks smoky gray secondary bases, and bill has less distinct black distal band in winter.

First Cycle. California Gull is a fairly distinctive but notoriously variable species, and observers in the West should learn it well. Features to note are the relatively long, narrow, and pointed wings, fairly long and parallel-sided bill that is strongly bicolored pink-and-black, pinkish legs with a variable blue-gray hue to the tibia and joints, solidly dark primaries and blackish tail, and frequently extensive PA1 molt that often includes upperwing coverts and tertials.

RING-BILLED GULL averages smaller and shorter billed; told readily from first-cycle California by much more contrasting and whiter overall appearance: for example, pale gray inner primary panel, whitish underwings, and white rump and tail with broad black distal band; attains pale gray back in first winter. First-cycle Ring-billed distinguished from second-cycle California by pale gray back, pale gray greater coverts (dark brownish on California), and brighter pink bill and legs, lacking green or blue-gray hues; also note different tail and primary patterns.

MEW GULL smaller and shorter billed, but first-cycle plumages can resemble second-cycle California Gull. Distinguished from second-cycle California by size, pale gray greater coverts (dark brownish on California), contrasting pale gray panel on inner primaries.

AMERICAN HERRING GULL (widespread) averages larger with shorter wing projection, slightly broader and less crooked wings in flight, and less parallel-edged bill that is rarely strongly two-toned in midwinter; its pinker legs lack a bluish hue to the tibia and joints. Herring Gull typically has a contrasting pale panel on the inner primaries, the bases of its greater coverts are less often solidly dark brown, and its tail (especially in the West) often has more-extensive pale barring at the basal corners. PA1 molt averages later (especially in the West) and only exceptionally includes upperwing coverts.

THAYER'S GULL (mainly w. N. America) similar in overall size but often looks relatively shorter legged and has shorter wing projection. Most winter birds told readily by mostly dark bill, which is also relatively shorter with deeper gonys than California. Thayer's typically retains juvenal plumage through midwinter and has browner, less blackish wingtips; in flight, the pale inner primary panel and barred tail base of Thayer's are distinctive.

WESTERN GULL (w. N. America) larger and bulkier with stouter, slightly bulbous-tipped, black bill, broader wings (often showing a skirt at rest), and shorter wing projection. Plumage can be very similar to California, but head and neck usually more solidly dark and sootier brown; bill mostly black (develops pinkish at base in midwinter but does not attain sharply two-tone pattern of California). A1 scapulars typically have blackish centers and grayish to pale brownish edgings (a pattern rare on California).

HEERMANN'S GULL (w. N. America) more uniformly dark brown (lacking contrasting whitish tail coverts) with smaller bill (duller flesh basally) and black legs.

LESSER BLACK-BACKED GULL has relatively shorter, all-black bill that starts to show some flesh at base only in late winter; averages colder and grayer overall than California. Upperparts (including tertials) average narrower pale edgings; juvenal plumage often retained into winter, but PA1 molt can include upperwing coverts. Uppertail coverts and tail base contrastingly white with clean-cut, black distal tail band.

Second Cycle. California Gull usually attains a mostly to solidly medium gray back by early in its second winter. Thus, second-cycle California can suggest third-cycle plumages of large white-headed gulls *and* first-cycle plumages of small white-headed gulls. Note that it has a medium gray back, dark eyes, and often a gray-green hue to bill and tibia.

MEW GULL in first cycle can resemble second-cycle California (see above). Second-cycle Mew distinguished from third-cycle California by smaller size, smaller bill, and shorter wings, but plumage and bare parts similar: California more often has black bill ring and can have some orange-red at gonys; Mew usually has black subterminal marks on P4 (sometimes outer web of P3), whereas P3–P4 typically lack black on California.

RING-BILLED GULL in first cycle can resemble second-cycle California (see above). Second-cycle Ring-billed distinguished from third-cycle California by smaller size and shorter wings; paler gray upperparts with poorly contrasting scapular and tertial crescents; poorly contrasting white trailing edge to upperwing; eyes often pale; and primaries lack distinct white tips at rest and distinct P9–P10 mirrors (often shown by third-cycle California).

AMERICAN HERRING GULL averages larger and bulkier with shorter wing projection, stouter bill; pink legs and bill base lack greenish or bluish hues, and bill rarely so neatly two-toned; eyes often pale; pale panel on upperwing more extensive (on inner 5–6 primaries versus usually 3–4 on California); gray back feathers paler (Kodak 4–5).

THAYER'S GULL typically lacks well-defined saddle, and gray of upperparts averages paler (Kodak 5–6), but some could closely resemble California in plumage: note Thayer's shorter wing projection, less parallel-edged bill, and pink legs lacking blue-green hues. In flight, extensive pale inner primary panel and two-tone outer primaries of Thayer's distinctive.

WESTERN GULL larger and bulkier with shorter wing projection, stouter bill bulbous tipped; pink legs lack the greenish or bluish cast often shown by California; bill rarely so neatly two-toned; and gray on upperparts darker (Kodak 8–11).

LESSER BLACK-BACKED GULL has extensively blackish bill in winter, more-variegated upperparts, and eyes often pale; gray in upperparts darker (Kodak 9–13); lacks strongly contrasting pale panel on inner primaries.

Third Cycle. AMERICAN HERRING GULL and LESSER BLACK-BACKED GULL differ in much the same ways as do adults (see above and relevant accounts); note California's bill size and shape, medium gray upperparts, dark eyes, and gray-green to yellowish legs.

RARER SPECIES

See above under Similar Species for summary of characters for each plumage cycle of California Gull. Also see Common Gull (rare in winter, e. N. America), Kamchatka Gull (casual, w. Alaska), and Black-tailed Gull (casual N. America).

Adult Cycle. YELLOW-LEGGED GULL (casual e. N. America) larger and bulkier with heavier bill, although *atlantis* subspecies averages shorter legged and longer winged, suggesting California in shape. Upperparts medium gray (Kodak 6–8) and orbital ring reddish, like California, but eyes pale lemon, bill has reduced or no black distal marks, basic head streaking finer and more restricted (mostly on the head).

First Cycle. VEGA GULL (n. Pacific), Yellow-legged Gull, and European Herring Gull (casual e. N. America) all average larger and with structure more like American Herring Gull. All have contrastingly white uppertail coverts and tail base with clean-cut black distal tail band; mostly dark bills through the winter; Vega and European Herring also have distinct pale inner primary panels.

KELP GULL (S. America) larger and bulkier with broader wings, shorter wing projection, stouter bill distinctly swollen at gonys; bill mostly black through first cycle and legs dusky flesh.

Second Cycle. YELLOW-LEGGED GULL averages larger and bulkier with stouter bill and deeper gonys; plumage can be similar to California but bill rarely neatly two-toned and lacks any greenish hues, eyes usually pale by summer; inner primaries lack strongly contrasting pale panel.

VEGA GULL averages larger and bulkier with stouter bill and deeper gonys; plumage can be similar to California but bill rarely neatly two-toned and lacks greenish hues, legs flesh pink; pale panel on inner primaries more extensive.

Third Cycle. YELLOW-LEGGED GULL and VEGA GULL differ in much the same ways as do adults (see above and relevant accounts). Note California's long wings, bill size and shape, dark eyes, and gray-green to yellowish legs.

HABITAT AND BEHAVIOR

Widespread and adaptable. Nonbreeding birds common at beaches, estuaries, river mouths, lakes, parking lots, fields, duck ponds, fishing harbors, dumps, etc., also ranging offshore to 50 km or more from mainland. In summer also occurs from taiga bogs to desert shrublands. Nests colonially, mainly on islands in lakes and rivers. Nonbreeding birds often in flocks (locally up to a few thousand birds), associating readily with other gulls and water birds. Feeds mainly on a wide range of invertebrates, but also fish and small mammals, and commonly scavenges.

DESCRIPTION AND MOLT

L. c. californicus (breeds Great Basin and south).

Adult Cycle. Complete PB molt (June/early July–mid-Sept./Oct.) produces adult basic plumage: head, neck, and underparts white; head, neck, and sometimes upper chest with variable (usually moderate to heavy) dusky streaking and mottling, often concentrated on hindneck. Upperparts medium gray (Kodak 6–7.5) with black wingtips (black on outer webs of P8/P9–P10, sometimes P7, extends to primary coverts); white scapular and tertial crescents; and white tips to outer primaries. Uppertail coverts and tail white. White trailing edge to secondaries (usually hidden at rest) and inner primaries breaks into discrete white tips on outer primaries; P5–P7 can have narrow white tongue-tips, P4 typically lacks black; P9–P10 (rarely just P10) have distinct white mirrors, which on P10 can merge into white tip. Underwings show blackish wingtips (with P9–P10 mirrors) cleanly demarcated from smoky gray white-tipped inner primaries and secondaries. Eyes dark brown (very rarely dull pale lemon[9]), orbital ring red (often dark gray in winter and pinkish in transition). Bill yellowish (sometimes pinkish to greenish basally through midwinter, and with orange-red gape from late winter) with orange-red gonydeal spot adjoining black subterminal band. Legs yellow to greenish yellow, often paler and more greenish during height of PB molt. Partial PA molt (*Sept.*–Mar./Apr.) produces adult alternate plumage: head and neck clean white (usually by Mar.); white primary tips can be lost through wear. By spring (and on some birds by mid-Jan.), orbital ring orange-red, legs brighter yellow to orange-yellow; bill bright yellow with orange-red gape, larger red gonydeal spot, and reduced subterminal black mark (black rarely lacking in midsummer[10]).

First Cycle. Juvenile (July–Dec.): highly variable, but most birds fairly dark gray-brown overall. Head, neck, and underparts variably streaked and mottled whitish, becoming whitish on vent and undertail coverts, which are barred dark brown; many birds have forehead, lores, and chin bleached to creamy, and some have foreneck and underparts mostly creamy or dusky pale cinnamon. Upperparts with buff (bleaching to dull whitish) scaly and notched edgings, the outer greater coverts often with

unmarked (or lightly marked) bases. Tertials blackish brown with notched whitish tips and distal edging, and usually a pale brown subterminal patch. Uppertail coverts whitish with strong dark brown barring. Flight feathers black to brownish black, narrowly tipped whitish, with inner primaries at most only slightly paler, not forming a distinct pale panel; whitish tips to outer primaries visible at rest (often lost through wear). Tail blackish to blackish brown with limited whitish barring on inner webs of outer rectrices (rarely visible except when spread) and whitish ribbing on outer web of R6; some birds have a subterminal band of small whitish marks creating a lace-tipped effect. IN FLIGHT: brownish to gray-brown overall with contrasting blackish flight feathers and usually a plain dark band across bases of greater coverts; underwings gray-brown with inner primaries looking paler when backlit; tail coverts strongly barred. Eyes dark, bill starts out blackish but soon attains flesh basally, typically flesh pink with fairly clean-cut blackish tip by late fall (a few birds keep dark bill at least through Oct.); legs dusky flesh to flesh pink. PA1 molt (Aug.–Apr./May; often includes upperwing coverts, sometimes tertials) produces first alternate plumage: head, neck, chest, and flanks smoky gray-brown to sooty gray, often mixed with bleached juvenal feathers, and with variable whitish streaking and mottling; face and chest often bleach to whitish. A1 scapulars highly variable, ranging from dark brown with pale gray edging (early-molted feathers) to fairly plain medium gray (late-molted feathers); a common pattern of first-winter birds is a variegated, brown-and-gray back that features numerous anchor-patterned scapulars. By late winter, lesser coverts often bleach to a whitish carpal panel. Bill flesh pink basally with clean-cut black tip; legs flesh pink, often with a blue-gray hue to tibia by midwinter.

Second Cycle. Complete PB2 molt (May/June–late Aug./Sept.) into second basic plumage. Head, neck, and underparts whitish with variable dusky brown streaking and mottling, tail coverts white with dark bars absent (or limited mainly to longest coverts). Upperparts variegated brown and gray, many birds with some plain gray back feathers; greater coverts and tertials dark brown overall with whitish distal speckling. Flight feathers blackish with a variably contrasting gray-brown to pale gray panel on inner 3–5 primaries, P10 sometimes with a small whitish mirror; outer rectrices more extensively white basally, with bases speckled and marbled white (sometimes with one or more white or mostly white feathers by late winter, perhaps attained by PA2 molt). Wing-linings whitish with brown mottling to mostly brownish. Eyes dark brown, bill flesh pink to bluish flesh with black distal third and a fine pale tip, legs flesh pink to bluish flesh. Partial PA2 molt (Sept.–Apr.; often includes some upperwing coverts, possibly one or more rectrices) produces second alternate plumage: head, neck, and underparts white, variably streaked and mottled dusky (often bleaching and wearing to mostly white by summer), back becomes mostly plain gray, and many birds attain some gray upperwing coverts, especially median coverts. Orbital ring brightens to orange or pinkish red in summer. Bill often fleshy blue-green by winter, with broad black distal band and small pale tip, sometimes a blush of orange at gonys; by midsummer bill often brightens to yellow with a reddish gonydeal spot and black distal marks. Legs flesh to bluish flesh, sometimes becoming yellowish flesh in summer.

Third Cycle. Complete PB3 molt (late May/June–Sept./Oct.) produces third basic plumage. Overall resembles adult basic but averages more dusky streaking and mottling on head, neck, and chest; wingtips average smaller white tips; some upperwing coverts often washed brownish; tertials can have dark brown centers. Tail often has black distal marks (varies from all white to having a subterminal black band). Wingtip pattern averages more black and less white than adult, with variable blackish on primary coverts and alula; P9–P10 mirrors smaller. Underwings often have some dusky mottling on coverts. Eyes dark brown (rarely pale dusky lemon); bill pale greenish to gray-green with broad black subterminal band, often some orange-red at gonys, and sometimes tinged pinkish basally; legs pale gray-green, sometimes tinged flesh. Partial PA3 molt (*Sept.*–Mar./Apr.) into third alternate plumage: dark markings on head and neck reduced to absent; white tips to outer primaries can be lost by wear. Bill and legs brighten in late winter, often indistinguishable from adult by summer. Adult plumage attained by complete PB4 molt (June–Sept./Oct.) but some presumed fourth-cycle birds retain signs of immaturity on alula, primary coverts, and tail.

L. c. albertaensis (breeds n. Great Plains).

Very similar to nominate *californicus;* many birds probably not safely identified to subspecies in the field. Averages 5–12 percent larger than *californicus* in linear dimensions (especially bill length and depth) and 27 percent greater in body mass;[11] adult averages paler gray on upperparts (Kodak 5–6 versus 6–7.5 in *californicus*).

In describing the subspecies *albertaensis*, Jehl[12] noted more-extensive pale gray tongues on the outer primaries, which King[13] attempted to expand upon: on average, *albertaensis* has longer basal gray tongues on P7–P10 than does *californicus*, creating a relatively less extensive black wingtip (black on outer web of P7–P8 often does not reach primary coverts). Other average differences include larger white P9–P10 mirrors on *albertaensis*, which may more often show a solid white tip to P10, and a greater tendency in *albertaensis* to have narrow white tongue-tips on P5–P7. However, given individual variation and overlap in characters,[14] field identification of lone birds based simply on wingtip pattern is inadvisable. Identification of *albertaensis* is best based on its bulkier dimensions, bigger bill, and paler upperparts (often noticeable in direct comparison with *californicus*, but difficult to appreciate on sunny days); wingtip pattern is a supporting feature. No plumage differences known in first-cycle birds;[15] upperpart tone may be helpful for second- and third-cycle birds (with *albertaensis* being slightly paler) but confirmation desirable from birds of known natal origin.

HYBRIDS

With American Herring Gull in Colo.;[16] possibly with Ring-billed Gull.[17]

NOTES
1. Jehl 1987; 2. Shuford and Ryan 2000; 3. Ibid.; 4. Jehl 1987; 5. Dunn and Howell pers. obs.; 6. Pugesek et al. 1999; 7. Komar 2001; 8. King 2001; 9. Howell pers. obs.; 10. Ibid.; 11. Jehl 1987; 12. Ibid.; 13. King 2000; 14. Ibid.; 15. Jehl 1987; 16. Chase 1984; 17. Dunn and Howell pers. obs. (photos 23.26–23.28)

The Herring Gull complex of the Holarctic constitutes one of the most problematic issues in contemporary avian taxonomy. Many of the taxa involved appear to have diverged relatively recently, such that isolating mechanisms between them are still being established, and interbreeding occurs to varying degrees. Differences in mantle tone, wingtip pattern, bare-part colors, and displays suggest that several taxa behave as species—but these differences have evolved more quickly than differences detectable by some genetic studies; furthermore, similarities in external morphology and plumage do not necessarily reflect close genetic affinities.[1,2,3,4,5] Yésou[6] provided a useful review of the taxonomic history of this complex.

Herring Gull and Lesser Black-backed Gull have long been treated as separate species due to contact with little interbreeding in western Europe, but the situation with other northern-breeding taxa of the complex is less clear-cut. From two to five species are recognized by different authors: American Herring Gull *L. [a.] smithsonianus*, European Herring Gull *L. [a.] argentatus* (including *argenteus*), Lesser Black-backed Gull *L. fuscus* (including *graellsii* and *intermedius*), West Siberian Gull *L. [f.] heuglini* (including *taimyrensis*), and Vega Gull *L. [a.] vegae* (including *birulai*). Related taxa breeding across the mid-latitude regions of Eurasia (from west to east: *atlantis*, *michahellis*, *armenicus*, *cachinnans*, *barabensis*, and *mongolicus*) probably include at least three species: Yellow-legged Gull *L. michahellis* (including *atlantis*), Armenian Gull *L. armenicus*, and Caspian Gull *L. cachinnans*. The taxa *barabensis* and *mongolicus* appear more closely related to northern taxa than to other southern taxa.[7,8] Some authors[9] still unite most or all of the southern taxa as Yellow-legged Gull *L. cachinnans*, but the *cachinnans* group is distinct from the *michahellis* group,[10,11,12,13,14] and these two groups are best treated as separate species.

In N. America, American Herring Gull *L. [a.] smithsonianus* is the only widespread taxon, and Vega Gulls *L. [a.] vegae* breed in nw. Alaska. European Herring Gulls and Yellow-legged Gulls are casual or rare visitors to e. N. America. American Herring Gull, European Herring Gull, and Vega Gull are best treated as distinct species,[15,16] although not yet recognized as such by the American Ornithologists' Union; we treat them here in separate accounts.

NOTES

1. Crochet et al. 2002; 2. Crochet et al. 2003; 3. de Knijff et al. 2001; 4. Liebers et al. 2001; 5. Liebers et al. 2004; 6. Yésou 2002; 7. Liebers et al. 2001; 8. Liebers et al. 2004; 9. AOU 1998; 10. Crochet et al. 2002; 11. de Knijff et al. 2001; 12. Klein and Buchheim 1997; 13. Liebers et al. 2001; 14. Liebers et al. 2004; 15. Crochet et al. 2002; 16. Liebers et al. 2004

LENGTH 22–26.3 IN. (56–67 CM)
PHOTOS 25A.0–25A.53; I.6, I.17–I.18, I.21, I.37, I.42–I.43, 24.21, 25B.2

IDENTIFICATION SUMMARY

The most widespread, large, pink-legged gull in N. America, common in much of the East, more local and less common in the West. Bill fairly stout and parallel edged, relatively slender on some females (especially first-cycle birds). Gonydeal expansion usually distinct but bill not bulbous tipped. At rest, tail tip falls between tips of P6 and P7. Adult has pale gray upperparts (Kodak 4–5, averaging slightly paler on birds breeding in e. N. America) with black wingtips (white mirrors on outer 1–2 primaries) and, in basic plumage, extensive dusky head and neck streaking and mottling. Juvenile dark brown overall with

mostly blackish tail. PA1 variable, starting Sept.–Feb. Subsequent ages variable in appearance. All ages have pink legs; adult eyes staring pale lemon; orbital ring yellow-orange.

Large size, pale gray back, black wingtips, pink legs, and pale eyes with yellow-orange orbital ring are a distinctive combination among adults of regularly occurring New World gulls. Mostly dark brown and dark-tailed first-cycle plumage distinct among large gulls in the East, but in the West note especially Western Gull (stockier and broader winged, black bill more bulbous tipped, lacks distinct pale inner primary panel), Thayer's Gull (slighter in build with more slender bill, outer primaries contrastingly pale on inner webs), and California Gull (more slender and narrower winged, bill typically flesh pink with

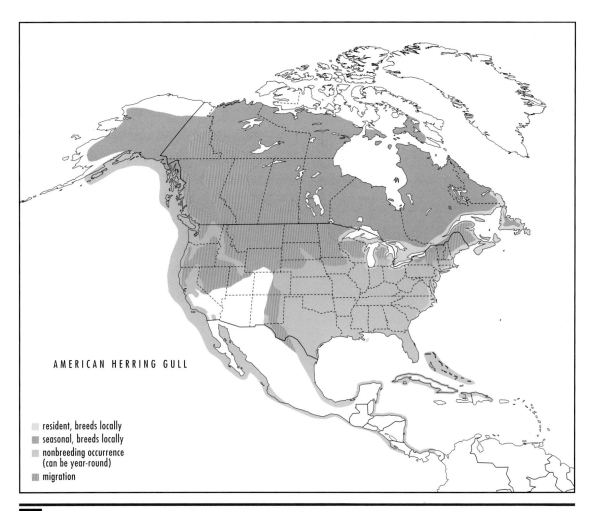

AMERICAN HERRING GULL

- resident, breeds locally
- seasonal, breeds locally
- nonbreeding occurrence (can be year-round)
- migration

clean-cut black tip, lacks distinct pale inner primary panel). See Similar Species and Rarer Species accounts for details.

TAXONOMY

See introductory section to the Herring Gull complex. Crochet et al.[1] and Liebers et al.[2] found that *smithsonianus* is not closely related to European Herring Gull and should be treated as a separate species, often known as American Herring Gull (see review by Yésou[3]); *smithsonianus* is also called Hudsonian Gull.[4] Traditionally, *smithsonianus* has been considered insufficiently different (based on morphology and plumage) to warrant even subspecific recognition from European Herring Gull.[5] Measurements of *smithsonianus* and nominate *argentatus* are not statistically different,[6] but adults of these two taxa are distinguished by the gray tone of their upperparts. In addition, adults within N. America exhibit variation in adult wingtip pattern and perhaps other characters,[7] suggesting that more than one New World subspecies may be distinguishable.

STATUS AND DISTRIBUTION

N. America, wintering to Middle America. Vagrant to w. Europe and Hawaii.

Breeding. Breeds (May–Aug.) from much of Alaska (except the w. coast, n. slope, Aleutian Is., and southeast), Yukon, and s.-cen. B.C. east through Canada to Lab. and Nfld., south to cen. Minn., entire Great Lakes region, various lakes from N.Y. to N.H., and along Atlantic Coast from Maritimes south to S.C. During twentieth century, breeding range has greatly expanded in Great Lakes region and south along Atlantic Coast. Since late 1980s, breeding reported on Chandeleur Is., La.,[8] and in Cameron Co., s. Tex.[9]

Nonbreeding. In nw. N. America, fall movement begins by mid-July in s. Yukon, Aug. in interior B.C. and Alta., mid-Sept. in the Northwest (a few as early as Aug.), and Oct. in Calif. (a few by mid-Sept.). Arrives around mid-Sept. in cen. Great Plains. In e. N. America, away from breeding areas, southbound movement evident by early July from as far south as Ohio R., but not widespread until Aug.–Sept. By Oct., has arrived continentwide, with marked increase during mid–late Oct. Peak numbers are not reached in Great Lakes region until Nov.–Dec. Numbers decline in many n. regions (such as the Yukon) during Sept., but often numerous into Oct., with last birds departing by mid-Nov. Typically departs Prairie Provinces by mid-Dec., and great majority vacate n.

Great Lakes region during coldest winter periods.

Fairly common to locally common in winter (mainly Oct.–Apr.) along and near Pacific Coast from sw. Alaska to nw. Mex. (uncommon along much of immediate coast in range of Glaucous-winged and Western Gulls), but overall far less numerous in w. N. America than in the East. Also fairly common well offshore in n. Pacific (out to 1,000 km[10]). Uncommon to rare south to cen. w. Mex., and rare to casual (mainly Nov.–Apr.) south to Costa Rica and cen. Panama. Farther south on Pacific Coast, reported as accidental in Colombia and in Peru.[11] On Atlantic Coast, common to fairly common in winter (mainly Oct.–Apr.) from Nfld. south to Fla., Gulf of Mex., and locally in n. West Indies; thence uncommon to rare south through Caribbean and along mainland coasts to cen. Panama, casually to n. Venezuela.

Also winters in interior N. America (where prefers large lakes) locally throughout the West north to s.-cen. B.C., from cen. Great Plains and s. Great Lakes region south through Tex., and in the Southeast. Scarcest in the Southwest, where generally rare except Salton Sea (where common).

Northward movement occurs along Pacific Coast Feb.–May, peaking late Mar.–Apr. In Great Lakes region, strong movement evident by late Feb., peaking Mar. in most areas, and continuing into Apr. in more n. areas. A few arrive in Prairie Provinces by early Mar., with more general arrival late Mar., and peak Apr.–early May. Arrival in s. Yukon and on sw. Hudson Bay is early Apr., with peak movements late Apr. in s. Yukon, May–early June on sw. Hudson Bay. Spring departures from most regions in N. America are by late May, but some birds oversummer.

In w. N. America, rare to casual in summer on coast and at Salton Sea. Ranges north and west (mainly June–Sept.) to Arctic coast of Alaska, Seward Peninsula, and Bering Sea Is. Summering nonbreeders occur in small to moderate numbers along s. Atlantic Coast and along entire Gulf of Mex. coast, but very rare or casual inland in e. N. America south of Ohio R. and on Great Plains. Has been collected in Greenland, and "Herring Gulls" have bred w. Greenland, but which taxon is unspecified.[12]

FIELD IDENTIFICATION

SIMILAR SPECIES

Because of hybridization, especially in w. N. America, determining where a pure Herring

Gull starts and a hybrid stops can be difficult, if not impossible, in the field; see hybrid American Herring Gull accounts (pp. 482–485).

Adult Cycle. Distinctive in e. N. America, except for vagrants (see Rarer Species, below), but in the West compare with Thayer's Gull and in w. Alaska with Vega Gull. Also see hybrid American Herring Gull accounts (pp. 482–485). Note pale gray upperparts, clean-cut black wingtips, pale eyes, and structure. East Coast types (see Description) have more white in wingtips, whereas West Coast types (see Description) usually have more black in wingtip and a white mirror only on P10.

THAYER'S GULL (winters w. N. America) averages smaller and, especially, slimmer billed; upperparts average slightly darker (Kodak 4.5–6; differences rarely apparent in sunny conditions). Wingtip patterns can overlap with *smithsonianus*, but dark areas on Thayer's wingtips are slaty black (Kodak 14.5–17), not jet black as on Herring (Kodak 18–19), and are largely restricted to the tips and outer webs—so underwingtip of Thayer's looks mostly silvery gray, not blackish as on typical Herring. Thayer's eyes are usually dirty yellowish to brown, rarely staring pale lemon, its orbital ring purplish pink, and its legs often richer pink than Herring. On winter adults the dusky head and neck markings of Thayer's are often more mottled, less streaked, and the bill rarely has distinct dark distal marks often shown by Herring. In w. N. America, where most Thayer's winter, adult Herring rarely has a white mirror on P9, and its upperwingtip is more solidly black than almost all Thayer's.

CALIFORNIA GULL (w. N. America) usually told readily by dark eyes and gray-green (nonbreeding) to bright yellow (breeding) legs, but beware some spring Herring Gulls with yellowish legs. California averages smaller with relatively longer and narrower wings, slimmer bill, and darker upperparts (Kodak 5–6 on larger *albertaensis* subspecies of California Gull could overlap with Herring). Wingtip of California has more-extensive and blunter-based black patch and averages more white in outer primaries than typical Herring Gulls wintering in the West; underwing shows dusky gray secondary bases, and bill has more-distinct black subterminal band.

VEGA GULL (w. Alaska) similar in size and shape but upperparts noticeably darker (Kodak 7–8), eyes often darker, orbital ring reddish, black wingtip area averages more extensive, and underwing shows duskier secondary bases.

HYBRID GLAUCOUS-WINGED GULL × WESTERN GULL (w. N. America) can suggest Herring Gull when

paler gray upperparts (around Kodak 6) combine with blackish wingtips. Aside from slightly darker upperparts note bulkier structure, especially broader wings (with short wing projection, usually distinct skirt) and more bulbous-tipped bill of hybrids. Also, blackish to slaty wingtips less clean cut, eyes often dusky (but can be pale, although usually more greenish white than pale yellow), and orbital ring often mixed pink and yellow.

First Cycle. American Herring Gull is common but notoriously variable, and it should be learned thoroughly. In e. N. America the only other regular dark-winged large gulls are Great Black-backed and rarer Lesser Black-backed. In the West, several potentially similar species occur; also see hybrid American Herring Gull accounts (pp. 482–485). Features to note are the relatively long and narrow wings; relatively parallel-sided bill with variable pinkish basally; blackish to brownish black wingtips and tail; and a pale upperwing panel on the inner 5–6 primaries. Relative to other N. Atlantic species, relatively plain brownish underparts of American Herring are distinctive. East Coast types (see Description) average earlier PA1 molt and typically have more solidly blackish tail, whereas West Coast types (see Description) molt later on average and often have whitish at tail base.

THAYER'S GULL averages smaller with a more slender bill that generally has a less distinct gonydeal expansion and often shows slightly steeper and more rounded forehead. Plumage overall slightly to distinctly paler than Herring Gull, blackish brown to medium brown wingtips usually have distinct whitish fringes, upperparts often with coarser and more checkered, or marbled, pale patterning. Inner webs of outer primaries more extensively pale so that pale inner primary panel on upperwing bleeds into distinctly two-tone outer primaries; underside of outer primaries paler, more silvery gray (but can be reflectively pale on Herring). Tail typically dark brown (blackish to blackish brown on Herring). Some darkly pigmented Thayer's can be very similar to Herring Gull (or hybrids), and problem birds may not be identifiable.

GREAT BLACK-BACKED GULL (e. N. America) larger and more massive overall with more bulbous-tipped bill. Head and underparts whiter and upperparts more boldly checkered; uppertail coverts and tail contrastingly white with clean-cut black distal tail banding; underwings paler brownish overall, contrasting with white body; upperwings rarely with distinct pale panel on inner primaries.

LESSER BLACK-BACKED GULL (widespread but rare

in West) averages smaller and slimmer with narrower wings, longer wing projection, and slimmer, all-black bill. Upperparts (including tertials) average narrower pale edgings. Primaries overall dark with no or very indistinct paler panel on inners; bases of greater coverts more often solidly dark brown. Uppertail coverts and tail base contrastingly white with clean-cut, black distal tail band.

CALIFORNIA GULL averages smaller with longer wing projection (tail tip about equal with tip of P6), narrower and more crooked wings in flight, and more parallel-sided bill that, by Oct., is typically flesh pink with a clean-cut black tip (also shown by some Herrings); its pinkish legs often have a bluish hue on the tibia and joints. Primaries overall dark with no or very indistinct paler panel on inners, bases of greater coverts more often solidly dark brown. PA1 molt generally extensive (often includes upperwing coverts) and earlier than Herring Gull.

WESTERN GULL (w. N. America) larger and bulkier with a stouter, rather bulbous-tipped bill, broader wings (often shows a skirt). Dark sooty brownish overall, A1 scapulars typically have blackish centers and grayish to pale brownish edgings (not the barred pattern common on Herring), primaries overall dark with no or very indistinct paler panel on inners, tail solidly blackish; typically does not get whitish-headed look common on first-winter Herring Gull.

VEGA GULL can look very similar (and perhaps not always safely distinguishable) but underparts average paler overall and does not attain strongly bicolored bill. Tail coverts and tail base whiter with less-extensive dark barring, tail has narrower blackish distal band than most American Herring Gulls.

SLATY-BACKED GULL (n. Pacific) averages heavier bodied and broader winged. Has plainer and paler greater coverts, A1 scapulars typically with dark shaft streaks or dark centers (like Western Gull) rather than paler gray with dark cross-barring or anchor patterns (typical of Herring). Outer primaries have more-extensive and more-contrasting pale on inner webs (so pale inner primary panel contrasts less strongly and spread upperwing often shows pale tongue-streaks on outer primaries). Whiter-looking tail coverts have sparser dark marks and often contrast more strongly with mostly dark tail.

YELLOW-FOOTED GULL (Gulf of Calif.) larger and bulkier with much stouter, bulbous-tipped bill, broader wings (often shows a skirt at rest). Belly and tail coverts white with sparse dark bars, A1 scapulars typically darker and

more uniform than Herring (and PA1 often includes upperwing coverts and tertials), primaries overall dark with no or very indistinct paler panel on inners, tail solidly blackish.

HYBRID GLAUCOUS-WINGED GULL × WESTERN GULL more thickset with broader wings (usually showing a skirt), stouter and more bulbous-tipped bill; can show pale panel on inner primaries suggesting Herring but outer primaries generally paler (dark brown versus blackish); tail solidly dark (often barred basally on Herring); A1 scapulars tend to have dark centers or be diffusely patterned, lacking bold bars common on Herring.

Second Cycle. Second-cycle American Herring Gull notoriously variable in appearance; note size and structure, especially of the bill, pale panel on inner primaries, and mostly dark outer primaries; also see hybrid American Herring Gull accounts (pp. 482–485).

THAYER'S GULL can be very similar but averages smaller with a less stout bill, often shows a more rounded forehead. Best plumage feature is paler inner webs of outer primaries — pale inner primary panel on upperwing blends outward into two-tone pattern on outer primaries, unlike more solidly dark outer primaries on Herring; tail often has less-extensive, and browner, dark markings than Herring.

GREAT BLACK-BACKED GULL larger with stouter and more swollen-tipped blackish bill that often has bold creamy tip; tail white with narrower and less solid black distal band; scapulars more variegated, often with some dark slaty gray.

LESSER BLACK-BACKED GULL slimmer and longer winged; less stout and mostly black bill often boldly tipped creamy. Upperparts distinctly darker, upperwing lacks contrasting pale panel on inner primaries, tail averages less black, and uppertail coverts whiter overall.

CALIFORNIA GULL averages smaller and slimmer with longer wing projection, slimmer and more parallel-edged bill; legs and bill usually with greenish or bluish hues and bill sharply two-toned; eyes dark; pale panel on upperwing smaller (typically on inner 3–4 primaries versus 5–6 on Herring); and gray back feathers darker (Kodak 5–7.5).

VEGA GULL perhaps not always safely separable, but any plain gray on upperparts slightly darker, and tail averages less-extensive black (more like third-cycle American Herring).

WESTERN GULL more thickset with broader wings, stouter and more bulbous-tipped bill, upperparts usually with some to extensive slaty gray, and upperwings lack strongly contrasting pale panel on inner primaries.

SLATY-BACKED GULL averages heavier bodied and

broader winged. Usually shows some dark slaty gray in the upperparts by late winter, and pale inner webs of outer primaries create a Thayer's-like pattern.

HYBRID GLAUCOUS-WINGED GULL × WESTERN GULL more thickset with broader wings, stouter and more bulbous-tipped bill, upperparts often with some to extensive medium gray, and dark areas of primaries and tail generally diluted, without a strongly contrasting pale panel on inner primaries.

Third Cycle. Thayer's Gull, California Gull, Vega Gull, and hybrids differ in much the same ways as do adults (see above and relevant accounts).

RARER SPECIES

Also see hybrid American Herring Gull accounts (pp. 482–485, 490).

Adult Cycle. YELLOW-LEGGED GULL (casual e. N. America) similar in overall size and structure, although *atlantis* subspecies averages shorter legged and longer winged than Herring (more like Lesser Black-backed). Note slightly darker gray upperparts (Kodak 6–7 on *michahellis*, 7–8.5 on *atlantis*), reddish orbital ring, yellowish legs, relatively reduced dusky head streaking in winter (mostly on head), more extensive black wingtip, and earlier molt timing (so looks whiter headed in winter).

EUROPEAN HERRING GULL (casual e. N. America). Nominate *argentatus* similar in size and shape to *smithsonianus* but differs in slightly darker upperparts (Kodak 5.5–7), wingtips generally show extensive white areas, P5 often lacks black marks, and some birds have fleshy yellow to yellowish legs. Race *argenteus* averages smaller than *smithsonianus* but upperparts similar in tone (Kodak 4–5), and these two taxa not separable given present knowledge concerning variation in American Herring Gull. Some reliable differences in wingtip patterns may exist between these taxa, but this needs further study incorporating birds from throughout N. America.[13] Adult-type *smithsonianus* can show blackish tertial spots, not known in European Herring Gulls.[14]

First Cycle. YELLOW-LEGGED GULL has whiter head and underparts, brighter white uppertail coverts and tail base with narrower black distal tail band (more like Lesser Black-backed Gull), overall dark primaries with indistinct paler panel on inners, more solidly dark bases of greater coverts, blackish bill, and averages narrower tertial edgings. PA1 in nominate *michahellis* often includes upperwing coverts and even tertials by early winter.

EUROPEAN HERRING GULL paler and frostier overall, typically with paler underparts not strongly washed brown, whiter tail coverts and tail base more sparsely barred brown, tail with narrower dark distal band, and inner primaries with less-extensive dark subterminal marks. Outer primaries of some nominate *argentatus,* at least, have more-extensive paler inner webs and may show pale tongue-streaks, as opposed to more solidly dark outer primaries typical of American Herring.

KELP GULL (S. America) has dull, dusky flesh legs, lacks contrasting pale panel on inner primaries, and has more sparsely barred and more-contrasting white uppertail coverts.

Second Cycle. YELLOW-LEGGED GULL typically has less contrasting pale panel on inner primaries, any plain gray on upperparts is slightly darker, greater coverts typically paler overall and more coarsely patterned (often fairly dark brownish overall on American Herring), and tail averages less-extensive black (more like third-cycle American Herring).

EUROPEAN HERRING GULL averages less-extensive black on tail (more like many third-cycle American Herrings) and greater coverts typically paler overall and more patterned (often fairly dark brownish overall on American Herring), but some individuals may overlap in pattern; also note slightly darker gray upperparts of nominate *argentatus*. Study needed of distinguishing features.

KELP GULL has distinctly darker upperparts, upperwing lacks contrasting pale panel on inner primaries, and tail averages less black (more like third-cycle Herring); winter bill often black, tipped creamy, becoming adultlike by summer; legs dusky flesh to dull greenish.

Third Cycle. Yellow-legged Gull and European Herring Gull differ in much the same ways as do adults (see above and relevant accounts); both lack extensive brownish mottling on underparts, which is often shown by American Herring. European Herring rarely if ever has solidly blackish tertial centers and well-defined blackish marks on the secondaries (shown by many third-cycle American Herring Gulls), and averages bolder white tips to outer primaries.[15]

HABITAT AND BEHAVIOR

Widespread and adaptable. In the East this is the common large "seagull" found on beaches, at estuaries, fishing harbors, dumps, and parking lots, ranging offshore over shelf waters and inland to lakes, rivers, farmland, etc. It is also common around the Great Lakes and locally on larger lakes and rivers in the interior. On the West Coast it is more local than in the

East, favoring inland areas and offshore waters rather than the immediate coast (where Western and Glaucous-winged Gulls dominate). Nests colonially or in scattered pairs on inshore coastal islands and islets, islands in lakes, locally on buildings. Nonbreeding birds often in flocks (locally up to a few thousand birds), associating readily with other gulls and water birds. Feeds commonly by scavenging; also forages in intertidal and surface waters for marine invertebrates, and preys on eggs and young birds.

DESCRIPTION AND MOLT

Molts of migrants in w. N. America average up to a month or so later than those of populations breeding in e. N. America.[16] Some average plumage differences within populations also occur, at least in first-cycle birds. We discuss these differences below under so-called West Coast types and East Coast types, while recognizing that this simplifies the distribution of the plumage types; more study is needed on patterns of plumage variation in American Herring Gulls. Based on specimens, birds breeding on the Great Lakes and the New England coast average slightly paler (nearer Kodak 4.5; n = 20) than Alaska breeders and birds wintering in Calif. (nearer Kodak 5; n = 30), but such differences not likely to be noticeable in the field.

Adult Cycle. Complete PB molt (June/July–Nov./Jan.) produces adult basic plumage: head, neck, and underparts white; head, neck, and sometimes upper chest with variable (usually moderate to heavy) dusky streaking and mottling. Upperparts pale gray (Kodak 4–5) with black wingtips (black on outer web of P10 and sometimes P9 extends to primary coverts; P4 sometimes with limited black); white scapular and tertial crescents; and white tips to outer primaries. Uppertail coverts and tail white. White trailing edge to secondaries (often hidden at rest) and inner primaries breaks into discrete white tips on outer primaries; P5–P8 typically have narrow white tonguetips and black subterminal bands, and P10 has distinct white mirror; P10 mirror largest on ne. coastal populations, and these also often have a P9 mirror rarely seen on West Coast migrants.[17,18] Birds wintering in e. Canada also average less black in wingtips than those wintering on Great Lakes[19] and in w. N. America.[20] Underwings typically show blackish wingtips (with P10 or P9–P10 mirrors, white tongue-tips out to P8) cleanly demarcated from pale gray, white-tipped inner primaries and secondaries; however, some birds

in e. Canada have relatively washed-out underside to wingtip. Eyes staring pale lemon (rarely flecked dusky, especially in the West,[21] and exceptionally dull olive; perhaps indicating hybridism?), orbital ring orange to yellow-orange (can be dark gray in winter and pinkish in transition). Bill yellow (often pinkish to greenish basally in winter) with orange-red to red gonydeal spot and, in winter, often a dark distal band. Legs flesh pink, often paler during later stages of PB molt. Partial PA molt (Oct.–Mar./Apr.) produces adult alternate plumage: head and neck clean white (usually by Feb./Mar. on East Coast, by Mar./Apr. on West Coast); white primary tips can be lost through wear. By spring, orbital ring yellow-orange to reddish orange, legs brighter flesh pink (becoming lemon yellow on some birds during at least Mar.–Apr.[22]), bill bright lemon yellow with red gonydeal spot, lacking dark distal marks.

First Cycle. Juvenile (Aug.—Feb.): dark brown to medium gray-brown overall. Head, neck, and underparts variably streaked and mottled whitish, becoming whitish on vent and undertail coverts, which have broad, sooty brown bars. Upperparts with buff (bleaching to dull whitish) scaly and notched edgings and markings, the outer greater coverts often with unmarked (or lightly marked) bases. Upperpart markings typically scaly to checkered, often fairly contrasting and neatly marked in fresh plumage (through late winter on some birds). Tertials darker, blackish brown with notched whitish tips and distal edging. Uppertail coverts whitish with strong dark barring. Flight feathers black to brownish black, secondaries and tail narrowly tipped whitish, outer primaries with narrow whitish tips visible at rest (lost through wear). Pale panel on inner primaries distinctive on spread wing but varies from strongly contrasting (usually) to poorly contrasting on some heavily pigmented birds; outer primaries blackish with paler edging to inner webs not reaching shaft. Tail variable: most East Coast types and some West Coast types have almost solidly blackish tail with limited whitish barring on inner webs of outer rectrices (rarely visible) and whitish ribbing on outer web of R6.[23] Many West Coast types and some East Coast types have extensive whitish barring on tail base (mainly on inner webs) so tail has a blackish distal band (best seen from below or with tail fully spread).[24] IN FLIGHT: dark brownish to gray-brown overall with blackish flight feathers except for pale inner primary panel, variable whitish barring at tail base; underwings medium to dark brown with inner primaries appearing as a paler panel when backlit; underside of primaries can look reflectively pale; tail coverts strongly barred whitish. Eyes dark, bill blackish with variable dull flesh on basal two-thirds, and by midwinter some birds have flesh pink bill with fairly clean-cut blackish tip; legs dusky flesh to flesh pink. PA1 molt (Sept.–May; exceptionally includes upperwing coverts) produces first alternate plumage: head, neck, chest, and flanks smoky gray-brown to sooty gray, often mixed with bleached juvenal feathers and with variable whitish streaking and mottling; head often bleaches to whitish. A1 scapulars range from brownish gray to pale gray, typically with a broad dark basal wedge or median band and often with a narrow dark subterminal band or anchor pattern; late-molted scapulars can be fairly plain grayish with fine dusky vermiculations or a dark shaft streak. A common pattern of first-winter birds is a grayish back with slightly checkered dark barring mixed with brown juvenal scapulars. In late winter, blackish to blackish brown wingtips and worn, dark brown tertials often contrast with worn and bleached upperwing covert panel. Bill dull flesh to flesh pink basally with black tip and sometimes a fine pale horn tip; legs flesh pink; eyes dark.

Second Cycle. Complete PB2 molt (Apr./May–late Sept./Nov.) into second basic plumage. Some birds bleach strikingly by early summer, before PB2 is very advanced, and new B2 feathers can look contrastingly dark. Mottled brown and pale brown overall with variable whitish streaking and mottling on head, neck, and underparts; undertail with variable brown barring and mottling, less neat than first-cycle barring; some birds have scattered gray on back; uppertail coverts mostly white with sparse dark markings; head and chest of some birds bleach by midwinter. Relative to first cycle, greater coverts and blackish brown tertials typically have finer, more-peppered whitish distal markings; median and lesser coverts often more coarsely barred. Flight feathers similar to first cycle but wingtips and tail often blacker; inner primaries average grayer and more contrasting, rarely with 1–2 broadly white-tipped feathers; wingtips with narrow whitish tips and, very rarely, a small, diffuse P10 mirror; outer rectrices with white basal corners more streaked, less barred than first cycle. Wing-linings medium brown to whitish with fairly heavy brown mottling. Eyes brownish to pale lemon, bill typically flesh pink with black distal third and pale horn tip

(sometimes dull, like first winter), legs flesh pink. Partial PA2 molt (Sept.–Apr./May; often includes some upperwing coverts) produces second alternate plumage: head, neck, and underparts white, mottled and streaked dusky (sometimes bleaching and wearing to mostly white by summer), back can become mostly pale gray in contrast to faded upperwing coverts; some birds attain a few gray upperwing coverts, especially median coverts. Eyes pale lemon to brownish, orbital ring can be yellow-orange in summer. Through winter, bill typically pinkish basally, blackish distally with pale tip and sometimes a blush of reddish at gonys; in summer, some birds have yellowish bill with reddish gonydeal smudge and black distal band. Legs flesh pink.

Third Cycle. Complete PB3 molt (May/June–Nov./Dec.) produces third basic plumage: highly variable. Some retarded plumages resemble second cycle but average more gray on upperparts; note adultlike gray inner primaries with broad white tips, blackish subterminal bands on middle primaries, usually less black in tail. More advanced plumages variably resemble basic adult but average more dusky streaking and mottling on underparts; upperwing coverts often washed or variably mottled brownish; tertials typically with dark brown to blackish centers; white tips to remiges narrower. Tail varies from all white to blackish (up to 30 percent have mostly blackish tails like second cycle, 13 percent have all-white tails[25]); tail often extensively blackish but, relative to second-cycle birds, with more white at basal corners and distally. Wingtip pattern averages more black and less white than adult, with variable blackish on primary coverts and alula; P9 typically lacks mirror, and P10 mirror small or absent. Underwings have some dusky mottling on coverts. Eyes pale lemon (rarely dusky); bill flesh pink with black distal band and pale tip, often with some reddish at gonys; legs flesh pink. Partial PA3 molt (Sept.–Mar./May) into third alternate plumage: dark markings on head and neck reduced to absent; bill brighter and may be indistinguishable from adult or have dark distal marks. White tips to outer primaries often lost by wear. Adult plumage attained by complete PB4 molt (May/June–Dec.) but many fourth-cycle birds retain signs of immaturity on alula, primary coverts, and tail.[26]

HYBRIDS

Hybridizes commonly with Glaucous-winged Gull in s.-cen. Alaska, and south locally to s. British Columbia;[27,28,29,30] with Glaucous Gull in nw. Canada[31] and presumably ne. Canada;[32] and presumably with Great Black-backed Gull.[33] Extralimital cases of hybridization with California Gull in Colorado,[34] Kelp Gull in Louisiana,[35] and presumed with Lesser Black-backed Gull in e. N. America[36] (and see pp. 490).

NOTES

1. Crochet et al. 2002; 2. Liebers et al. 2004; 3. Yésou 2002; 4. Yésou 2003; 5. Voous 1959; 6. Threlfall and Jewer 1978; 7. Jonsson and Mactavish 2001; 8. Purrington 1994; 9. Farmer 1990; 10. Sanger 1970; 11. Krabbe et al. 2001; 12. Boertmann 1994; 13. Adriaens and Mactavish 2004; 14. Lonergan and Mullarney 2004; 15. Ibid.; 16. Howell pers. obs.; 17. Jonsson and Mactavish 2001; 18. Macpherson 1961; 19. Jonsson and Mactavish 2001; 20. Howell pers. obs.; 21. Ibid.; 22. Ibid.; 23. Ibid.; 24. Ibid.; 25. Poor 1946; 26. Ibid.; 27. R. J. Cannings pers. comm.; 28. Merilees 1974; 29. Patten 1980; 30. Williamson and Peyton 1963; 31. Spear 1987; 32. B. Mactavish pers. comm.; 33. Foxall 1979; 34. Chase 1984; 35. Dittman and Cardiff 2005; 36. McWilliams and Brauning 2000

LENGTH 20–26.3 IN. (51–67 CM)
PHOTOS 25B.0–25B.23

IDENTIFICATION SUMMARY
Casual visitor to e. N. America from Europe. The counterpart of American Herring Gull in w. Europe, and generally similar in appearance. First cycle has whiter uppertail coverts and tail with broad blackish distal tail band; identification criteria for subsequent ages not well known but some adults are slightly darker gray above than American Herring Gull. Study needed of potential wingtip pattern differences.

TAXONOMY
See introductory section on the Herring Gull complex. Two subspecies generally recognized in w. Europe, and both probably occur in N. America: larger nominate *argentatus* of n. Europe (22–26.3 in.; 56–67 cm), which is similar in measurements to American Herring Gull but darker above; and smaller *argenteus* of w. Europe (20–24.7 in.; 51–63 cm), which averages smaller than American Herring Gull but is similar in upperpart tone.[1] Some authors have considered variation within European populations clinal such that no subspecies could be recognized, with American Herring Gull also not diagnosable as a taxon.[2] Recent genetic work, however, has shown American Herring Gull to be quite distinct from European Herring Gull.[3,4]

STATUS AND DISTRIBUTION
Nw. Europe, wintering to s. Europe.
In N. America, known only as a rare to casual winter visitor (mainly Nov.–Apr.) in the East. Most records are from Nfld. (where annual, Nov.–Apr., mainly Jan.–Feb.[5]). Casual elsewhere, with records from N.S.,[6] e. Ont.,[7] e. Mass., N.J., and Md.[8] (photo 25b.16). Vagrant to Greenland (possibly increasing), and "Herring Gulls" have bred w. Greenland, but which taxon is unspecified.[9]

FIELD IDENTIFICATION

SIMILAR SPECIES
Second-cycle and older plumages very similar to widespread American Herring Gull and many perhaps not safely separable in the field, pending critical studies of individual varia-

tion. First-cycle plumages can often be distinguished,[10] and see Lesser Black-backed Gull and Yellow-legged Gull. Except for first-cycle tail pattern, differs from other taxa in much the same respects as does American Herring Gull (which see).

Adult Cycle. AMERICAN HERRING GULL similar in size and shape to *argentatus* but upperparts slightly paler (Kodak 4–5), averages larger than *argenteus* but upperparts similar in tone. Wingtip patterns may show some differences, but reliable criteria need elucidation, and so far have only been proposed in the context of distinguishing adult American Herring Gull in Europe.[11] Adult-type *smithsonianus* can show blackish tertial spots, not known in European Herring Gulls.[12]

First Cycle. AMERICAN HERRING GULL typically has heavy dark barring on uppertail and undertail coverts, tail base more heavily barred or tail mostly blackish brown; thus, European Herring Gull has whiter-looking uppertail coverts and tail base with broad, blackish distal tail band, perhaps never matched by American Herring. Other features probably overlap, but European Herring Gull often looks relatively pale and frosty overall, rarely if ever matching the overall dark brown aspect of many American Herrings (especially on underparts); greater coverts more usually barred and checkered overall, lacking darker basal area often shown by American Herring; dark subterminal marks on inner primaries average less extensive; and does not show flesh pink bill with fairly clean-cut blackish tip shown by some American Herrings.

Second and subsequent cycles. AMERICAN HERRING averages more black on tail, and second-cycle often has more solidly dark brownish greater coverts (typically paler overall and more patterned on European Herring), but some individuals may overlap in pattern. Gray of upperparts averages paler than nominate *argentatus* (Kodak 4–5 versus Kodak 5.5–7) but upperpart tones of immatures less consistent than those of adults. Third-cycle American Herring often has solidly dark to blackish tertial centers, secondaries can show blackish marks (both features rarely if ever found on European Herring), and P6–P10 average smaller white tips.[13]

HABITAT AND BEHAVIOR

Likely to be found anywhere American Herring Gulls occur and probably with that taxon.

DESCRIPTION AND MOLT

Adult Cycle. Much like American Herring Gull (*smithsonianus*). Until variation in each taxon is fully appreciated, many birds probably not safely identified in the field. Molt in w. Europe averages earlier than American Herring Gull, but this may not be reflected by vagrants. Complete PB molt mainly mid-May/mid-July–Oct./mid-Dec.[14,15,16] Upperparts of nominate *argentatus* (Kodak 5.5–7) average noticeably darker than *smithsonianus* (Kodak 4–5). Wingtips of nominate *argentatus* typically have white-tipped P10 and lack black on P5, whereas *argenteus* more often has black subterminal band on P10 and some black on P5; but noticeable geographic variation occurs within wingtip patterns of *argenteus*.[17] Legs typically flesh pink but, especially on *argentatus*, can be pale yellowish.

First Cycle. Juvenile (Aug.–Feb.): gray-brown to brown overall, averaging paler than many *smithsonianus*. Head, neck, and underparts variably streaked and mottled whitish, becoming whitish on vent and undertail coverts, which have relatively sparse brown markings. Upperparts with buff (bleaching to dull whitish) scaly and notched edgings and markings, the greater coverts rarely with unmarked (or lightly marked) bases like *smithsonianus*. Tertials darker, blackish brown with notched whitish tips and distal edging. Uppertail coverts dingy whitish with relatively sparse dark markings. Flight feathers blackish, secondaries and tail narrowly tipped whitish, outer primaries with narrow whitish tips visible at rest. Contrasting pale panel on inner primaries distinctive on spread wing; outer primaries blackish with broad paler edging to inner webs not reaching shaft. Tail with extensive whitish base, barred and spotted dark, and with broad, blackish brown distal band. IN FLIGHT: gray-brown overall with blackish remiges except for pale inner primary panel, whitish uppertail coverts and tail with broad blackish tail band; underwings medium-pale brown to medium brown with inner primaries appearing as paler panel when backlit; underside of primaries can look reflectively pale with narrow dark tips. Eyes dark, bill blackish with variable dull flesh on basal two-thirds; legs dusky flesh to flesh pink. PA1 molt (Aug.–May; rarely includes upperwing coverts) produces first alternate plumage: molt generally extensive and early (mainly Aug.–Oct.) in most British *argenteus*, averages later (starting between Sept. and Mar.) in nominate *argentatus*, which can keep juvenal plumage through winter, like some *smithsonianus*. Post-juvenal upperparts typically pale grayish to pale brownish with coarse blackish brown barring. Bill dull flesh to flesh pink basally with black tip and sometimes a fine pale horn tip; legs flesh pink; eyes dark.

Second and subsequent cycles. PB2 molt in w. Europe mainly Apr./May–late Aug./early Oct.[18,19] Similar to American Herring Gull but second cycle averages less black on tail, third cycle more often lacks black on tail and has paler and more-diffuse brown tertial centers Gray of upperparts averages slightly darker gray on nominate *argentatus*.

HYBRIDS

With Glaucous Gull in Iceland,[20] Lesser Black-backed Gull in Europe,[21,22,23] Yellow-legged Gull (*L. michahellis*) in w. Europe.[24,25] Presumably with Caspian Gull (*L. cachinnans*) in Poland[26,27] and Great Black-backed Gull in n. Europe.[28,29]

NOTES

1. Threlfall and Jewer 1978; 2. Voous 1959; 3. Crochet et al. 2002; 4. Liebers et al. 2004; 5. B. Mactavish pers. comm.; 6. Gosselin and Pittaway 2002; 7. Ibid.; 8. M. J. Iliff photos; 9. Boertmann 1994; 10. Lonergan and Mullarney 2004; 11. Adriaens and Mactavish 2004; 12. Lonergan and Mullarney 2004; 13. Ibid.; 14. Barth 1974; 15. Howell pers. obs.; 16. Walters 1978; 17. Coulson et al. 1982; 18. Howell pers. obs.; 19. Walters 1978; 20. Ingolfsson 1987 21.; M. T. Elliott pers. comm.; 22. Harris et al. 1978; 23. Tinbergen 1929; 24. Garner 1997; 25. Yésou 1991; 26. Faber et al. 2001; 27. G. Neubauer pers. comm.; 28. H. J. Lehto and H. Lehto photos; 29. Malling Olsen and Larsson 2003

LENGTH 21.7–26.3 IN. (55–67 CM)

PHOTOS 25C.0–25C.20, I.19

IDENTIFICATION SUMMARY

This large pink-legged gull replaces American Herring Gull in nw. Alaska. Size and structure similar to American Herring Gull but adults medium gray on upperparts (Kodak 7–8 versus 4–5). First cycle averages paler and grayer overall with less-extensive brown barring on tail coverts, and whitish tail has broad blackish distal band. Subsequent ages best separated from American Herring Gull by medium gray upperparts. All ages have pink legs; adult eyes olive to dirty pale lemon, orbital ring orange-red.

TAXONOMY

See introductory section on the Herring Gull complex. Quite distinct from American Herring Gull and better treated as a separate species, Vega Gull *L. vegae*.[1,2,3] Western populations of *vegae* may average slightly paler above and are sometimes separated as the subspecies *birulai* (breeding from New Siberian Is. west to Taimyr Peninsula[4]). Dement'ev and Gladkov[5] considered individual variation too great to warrant recognition of *birulai*. The taxon *mongolicus* (breeding in e. cen. Asia) is sometimes included with Vega Gull, in which case *L. vegae* may be called East Siberian Gull.[6] Vega Gull has also been treated as conspecific with Slaty-backed Gull.[7]

STATUS AND DISTRIBUTION

Ne. Asia, ranging to nw. Hawaiian Is. and w. Alaska.

Breeding. Breeds in N. America only on St. Lawrence Is., Bering Sea, where fairly common in summer (May–Sept.), but in 1977 a mixed pair (Vega and Glaucous) raised young at Bluff on s. side of Seward Peninsula.[8]

Nonbreeding. Rare fall (mid-Sept.–mid-Oct.) and casual spring (late Apr.–mid-June) migrant through w. Aleutians (where casual in winter). Occurs casually in cen. Aleutians (sightings year round), and there are two records (Feb., June) from e. Aleutians. Spring arrival on St. Lawrence Is. late Apr.–early May with more general arrival mid–late May.[9] Uncommon to rare nonbreeding summer visitor on Seward Peninsula, with numbers increasing late summer to fall (especially Aug.–Sept.,

a few remaining until mid-Oct.); casual north to Arctic coast of Alaska (late May 2003)[10] and Pribilof Is. (Sept. 2003).[11]

Away from Alaska, specimens have been reported from B.C.[12] and Ore.,[13] but former pertains to hybrid Glaucous-winged × Western Gull or Glaucous-winged × American Herring Gull,[14] and latter warrants critical examination. Other reports from Ore.[15] are unconfirmed. Almost certainly overlooked in winter in w. N. America, with several Dec.–Mar. records of presumed Vega Gulls from cen. Calif.[16,17,18] Accidental s. Tex. (Mar. 2000).[19]

FIELD IDENTIFICATION

SIMILAR SPECIES

In w. Alaska the main confusion species is Slaty-backed Gull. Elsewhere this taxon should be distinguished with caution from American Herring Gull and hybrids (and see hybrid Vega Gull accounts; p. 492), and Rarer Species when dealing with potential vagrants.

Adult Cycle. Note medium gray upperparts with contrasting black wingtips, rich pink legs.

SLATY-BACKED GULL (n. Pacific) averages bulkier and broader winged with stouter bill. Upperparts darker, slaty gray (Kodak 9.5–11.5; but Vega Gulls against ice and snow can look deceptively dark backed) with less contrasting black wingtips above and below; white trailing edge to secondaries broader; eyes usually pale.

AMERICAN HERRING GULL (widespread but rare in w. Alaska) has paler upperparts (Kodak 4–5) with less contrasting white scapular and tertial crescents, black wingtips often less extensive, underwings whiter without dusky gray bases to inner primaries and secondaries, eyes pale lemon with yellow-orange orbital ring, legs often paler flesh pink.

HYBRID GLAUCOUS-WINGED GULL × AMERICAN HERRING GULL (w. N. America) can closely resemble Vega Gull but upperparts slightly paler (Kodak 5–6) and wingtips blackish (versus black); also averages heavier in build with broader wings and more bulbous-tipped bill.

First Cycle. Note size and structure similar to American Herring Gull, primary pattern, and tail pattern; also see hybrid Vega Gulls (p. 492).

SLATY-BACKED GULL averages bulkier and broader

winged with stouter bill. Has plainer and paler greater coverts (especially when bleached), A1 scapulars typically have dark shaft streaks or dark centers (like Western Gull) rather than paler gray with dark cross-barring or anchor patterns (typical of Vega). Outer primaries have more-extensive and more-contrasting pale on inner webs, so pale inner primary panel contrasts less and spread upperwing often shows pale tongue-streaks on outer primaries. Whiter looking tail coverts have relatively sparse dark marks, and tail often has broader and browner dark distal area.

AMERICAN HERRING GULL typically darker and browner overall with darker underparts and heavier dark barring on tail coverts; usually has more extensive dark on tail, but some may overlap in tail pattern with darkest-tailed Vega Gulls; dark subterminal marks on inner primaries average more extensive; Vega does not show flesh pink bill with fairly clean-cut blackish tip shown by some American Herrings. Identification criteria need study.

HYBRID GLAUCOUS-WINGED GULL × AMERICAN HERRING GULL variably resembles washed-out Vega Gull (primaries usually dark brown) but is often more thickset with broader wings and a stouter bill with more swollen gonys; in flight, pale inner primary panel may bleed into outer primaries, which are often more extensively pale on inner webs than Vega, and tail often more solidly dark with more heavily barred and less contrasting uppertail coverts.

HYBRID GLAUCOUS GULL × AMERICAN HERRING GULL (mainly n. latitudes) can resemble washed-out Vega Gull overall but with dark primaries similar to pure Vega; bill often more clean-cut pink-and-black like Glaucous. In flight, pale panel on inner primaries usually bleeds into outer primaries, which are more extensively pale on inner webs than Vega, and tail may be more solidly plain.

THAYER'S GULL (winters w. N. America) averages smaller with a more slender bill that generally has less gonydeal expansion, often shows a steeper and more rounded forehead. Dark brown to blackish brown wingtips usually have distinct whitish fringes. Inner webs of outer primaries more extensively pale so that pale inner primary panel on upperwing bleeds into distinctly two-tone outer primaries; underside of outer primaries paler, more silvery gray (but can be reflectively pale on Vega); uppertail coverts more heavily barred and tail dark brown with limited whitish barring basally.

Second Cycle. SLATY-BACKED GULL averages bulkier and broader winged. Plumage generally darker, usually with some slaty gray on the back by late winter; pale inner webs of outer primaries create a Thayer's-like pattern.

AMERICAN HERRING GULL perhaps not always safely separable but any plain gray on upperparts slightly paler, tail averages more-extensive black, and greater coverts often more solidly dark brown (typically paler overall and more patterned on Vega).

HYBRID GLAUCOUS-WINGED GULL × AMERICAN HERRING GULL variably resembles washed-out Vega Gull (primaries usually dark brown) but is often more thickset with broader wings and a stouter bill with more swollen gonys; in flight, pale inner primary panel may bleed into outer primaries, which are often more extensively pale on inner webs than Vega, and tail often more solidly dark.

HYBRID GLAUCOUS GULL × AMERICAN HERRING GULL can resemble washed-out Vega Gull overall but with dark primaries similar to pure Vega. In flight, pale panel on inner primaries usually bleeds into outer primaries, which are more extensively pale on inner webs than Vega.

THAYER'S GULL averages smaller with less stout bill. Best plumage feature is paler inner webs of outer primaries—so pale inner primary panel on upperwing blends into two-tone pattern on outer primaries, unlike more solidly dark outer primaries of Vega.

Third Cycle. Slaty-backed Gull, American Herring Gull, and hybrid Glaucous-winged Gull × American Herring Gull differ in much the same way as do adults (see above).

RARER SPECIES

Adult Cycle. HYBRID GLAUCOUS-WINGED GULL × WESTERN GULL (w. N. America) can resemble Vega Gull in upperpart tone (Kodak 6–8) and perhaps in wingtip pattern but is bulkier and broader winged with more bulbous-tipped bill; orbital ring varies from chrome yellow to pinkish.

WESTERN GULL (w. N. America) bulkier and broader winged with more bulbous-tipped bill (that is usually bright in winter); upperparts slightly to distinctly darker (Kodak 8–11) with less contrasting black wingtips that have reduced white markings; basic plumage has reduced dusky head and neck markings; orbital ring chrome yellow.

EUROPEAN HERRING GULL (casual e. N. America) typically has paler gray upperparts (Kodak 4–7) but darkest *argentatus* may overlap with Vega, black wingtips often less extensive (especially *argentatus*); eyes pale lemon with yellow-orange orbital ring.

YELLOW-LEGGED GULL (casual e. N. America) has yellow legs, pale eyes, lacks heavy dusky head and neck streaking in basic plumage, but upperparts (Kodak 6–8.5) can be same tone as Vega, and wingtip patterns can be similar.

HYBRID AMERICAN HERRING GULL × LESSER BLACK-BACKED GULL not well known. European Herring Gull hybrids intermediate between parent species with medium gray upperparts similar to Vega (around Kodak 7), but legs yellowish flesh to pale yellow, orbital ring orange to orange-yellow.

First Cycle. HYBRID GLAUCOUS-WINGED GULL × WESTERN GULL bulkier with broader wings, stouter and more bulbous-tipped bill; can show pale panel on inner primaries suggesting Vega but outer primaries generally paler (dark brown versus blackish); tail solidly dark with more heavily barred and less contrasting uppertail coverts; A1 scapulars tend to have dark centers or be diffusely patterned, lacking bold bars common on Vega.

WESTERN GULL bulkier with broader wings, stouter and bulbous-tipped bill; overall darker and more brownish, A1 scapulars tend to have dark centers or be diffusely patterned, lacking bold bars common on Vega. Lacks contrasting pale panel on inner primaries and tail solidly blackish with more heavily barred and less-contrasting uppertail coverts.

LESSER BLACK-BACKED GULL (widespread, but rare in West) averages smaller and slimmer with narrower wings, longer wing projection, and slimmer, all-black bill. Upperparts (including tertials) average narrower pale edgings. Primaries overall dark with no or very indistinct paler panel on inners, bases of greater coverts more often solidly dark brown.

CALIFORNIA GULL (w. N. America) averages smaller with longer wing projection, narrower and more crooked wings in flight, and more parallel-sided bill that, by October, is typically flesh pink with a clean-cut black tip. Primaries overall dark with no distinct pale panel on inners, bases of greater coverts often solidly dark brown, and tail all blackish.

GREAT BLACK-BACKED GULL (e. N. America) larger and more massive overall with more bulbous-tipped bill; upperparts more checkered overall, inner primaries duller and not forming a distinct pale upperwing panel, tail white with narrow and wavy black distal band.

YELLOW-FOOTED GULL (Gulf of California) bulkier with broader wings, stouter and bulbous-tipped bill; lower underparts often mostly white. PA1 often includes upperwing coverts, and A1 upperparts tend to be dark overall (lacking bold pattern common on Vega). Lacks contrasting pale panel on inner primaries and tail solidly blackish with more-contrasting, sparsely barred white tail coverts.

YELLOW-LEGGED GULL has overall dark primaries with indistinct paler panel on inners, more-solidly dark bases to greater coverts, blackish bill, and averages narrower tertial edgings. PA1 in nominate *michahellis* often includes some upperwing coverts and tertials by early winter.

EUROPEAN HERRING GULL appears very similar overall and perhaps not safely told from Vega at this age; study needed.

Second Cycle. HYBRID GLAUCOUS-WINGED × WESTERN GULL bulkier with broader wings, stouter and more bulbous-tipped bill, dark areas of primaries and tail average more diluted.

WESTERN GULL bulkier with broader wings, stouter and more bulbous-tipped bill, upperparts usually with some to extensive slaty gray, and upperwings have weaker pale panel on inner primaries.

LESSER BLACK-BACKED GULL slimmer and longer winged; bill less stout and mostly black, often boldly tipped creamy. Upperparts darker and upperwing lacks contrasting pale panel on inner primaries.

CALIFORNIA GULL averages smaller and slimmer with longer wing projection, slimmer and more parallel-edged bill; legs and bill have greenish or bluish hues by winter, and bill sharply two-toned; pale panel on upperwing smaller (typically on inner 3–4 primaries versus 5–6 on Vega).

GREAT BLACK-BACKED GULL larger with stouter and more bulbous-tipped bill; blackish bill often has bold creamy tip.

YELLOW-LEGGED GULL has less-contrasting pale panel on inner primaries and legs generally yellowish by second summer; otherwise, very similar to Vega Gull; study needed.

EUROPEAN HERRING GULL perhaps not always safely separable, but any plain gray on upperparts slightly paler; study needed.

Third Cycle. Western Gull, European Herring Gull, Yellow-legged Gull, and hybrids differ in much the same ways as do adults (see above).

HABITAT AND BEHAVIOR

Mainly coastal in Alaska, but also ranges inland a short distance to dumps and freshwater lakes. Readily associates with other gulls, and habits much like American Herring and other large gulls. Calls lower pitched, harsher, and less laughing than American Herring Gull.[20]

DESCRIPTION AND MOLT

Adult Cycle. Complete PB molt (June/July–Dec./Jan. or later) produces adult basic plumage: head, neck, and underparts white; head, neck, and sometimes upper chest with variable (usually moderate to heavy) dusky streaking and mottling often heaviest on hindneck. Upperparts medium gray (Kodak 7–8) with black wingtips (black on outer web of P9–P10 extends most or all of the way to primary coverts; P4 sometimes with limited black), contrasting white scapular and tertial crescents; and white tips to outer primaries. Uppertail coverts and tail white. White trailing edge to secondaries (often hidden at rest) and inner primaries breaks into discrete white tips on outer primaries; P5–P7, sometimes P5–P8, have white tongue-tips, and P9–P10 (sometimes only P10) have white mirrors. Underwings show black wingtips (with P9–P10 mirrors) cleanly demarcated from pale smoky gray, white-tipped inner primaries and secondaries. Eyes olive to dirty pale lemon (rarely if ever unmarked, staring pale lemon), orbital ring orange-red to deep orange. Bill yellowish (can be pinkish to greenish basally in winter) with orange-red to red gonydeal spot and rarely a dark distal mark. Legs rich pink, perhaps paler during height of PB molt. Partial PA molt (*Oct.–Mar./May*) produces adult alternate plumage: head and neck clean white (rarely before Mar./Apr.); white primary tips may be lost through wear. By spring, orbital ring red to orange-red, legs brighter, bill bright lemon yellow with red gonydeal spot, lacks dark distal marks.

First Cycle. Juvenile (Aug.–Feb.): gray-brown to brown overall, averaging paler and grayer than many American Herring Gulls. Head, neck, and underparts variably streaked and mottled whitish, becoming whitish on vent and undertail coverts, which have brown bars. Upperparts with buff (bleaching to dull whitish) scaly and notched edgings and markings, the greater coverts rarely with unmarked (or lightly marked) bases. Tertials blackish brown with notched whitish tips and distal edging. Uppertail coverts whitish with relatively sparse dark markings. Flight feathers blackish, secondaries and tail narrowly tipped whitish, outer primaries with narrow whitish tips visible at rest (lost through wear). Contrasting pale panel on inner primaries visible on spread wing; outer primaries blackish with paler edging to inner webs not reaching shaft. Tail typically with extensive whitish base, barred and spotted dark, and with broad, blackish brown distal band. IN FLIGHT: gray-brown overall with blackish remiges except for pale inner primary panel, whitish uppertail coverts and tail with broad blackish distal band; underwings medium to dark brown with inner primaries ap-

pearing as paler panel when backlit; underside of primaries can look reflectively pale. Eyes dark, bill blackish with variable dull-flesh on basal two-thirds; legs dusky flesh to rich pink. PA1 molt (*Sept.–May*; rarely includes upperwing coverts) produces first alternate plumage: head, neck, chest, and flanks gray-brown, often mixed with bleached juvenal feathers, and with variable whitish streaking and mottling; head and chest often bleach to mostly whitish. A1 scapulars typically pale grayish with dark bars to anchor patterns. From late winter through summer, blackish to blackish brown wingtips and worn, dark brown tertials often contrast with bleached whitish upperwing covert panel. Bill dull flesh to flesh pink basally with black tip, and sometimes a fine pale horn tip; legs rich pink; eyes dark.

Second Cycle. Complete PB2 molt (mainly June–Nov./Dec.) into variable second basic plumage. Some birds bleach strikingly by early summer, before PB2 is very advanced, and new B2 feathers can look contrastingly dark. Head, neck, and underparts whitish with variable brown streaking on head and neck, brown mottling on belly, few to no brown marks on tail coverts; some have gray mixed in on mantle and scapulars. Upperwing coverts broadly edged whitish, often forming a contrasting pale panel, and blackish brown tertials typically with finer, more peppered, whitish distal markings than juvenile. Tail white with variable blackish distal band usually spotted and broken with whitish. Flight feathers similar to first cycle but wingtips and tail often blacker, wingtips with narrow whitish tips, and grayer inner primaries more contrastingly pale. Wing-linings medium brown. Eyes brownish to dirty pale lemon, bill typically flesh pink with black distal third and pale horn tip (sometimes dull, like first-winter bird), legs rich pink. Partial PA molt (*Oct.–Apr./May*; often includes some upperwing coverts) produces second alternate plumage: head, neck, and underparts mottled dusky and whitish (usually bleaching and wearing to mostly white by summer), back often becomes mostly medium gray in contrast to mostly whitish upperwing coverts; some birds attain a few medium gray upperwing coverts, especially median coverts. Eyes brownish to dirty pale lemon, orbital ring can be yellow-orange in summer. Through winter, bill typically pinkish basally, blackish distally with pale tip and sometimes a blush of reddish at gonys; in summer some birds have yellowish bill with reddish gonydeal spot and black distal band.

Third Cycle. Complete PB3 molt (mainly June–Dec.) produces third basic plumage: highly variable. Some retarded plumages resemble second cycle but with more gray on upperparts, reduced black (and more white) on outer primaries, adultlike inner primaries, less black in tail. More advanced plumages typical, resemble basic adult but average more dusky streaking and mottling on chest and sides; upperwing coverts often washed or variably mottled brownish; tertials typically with dark brown centers; white tips to remiges narrower. Tail varies from all white to having broken blackish distal band. Wingtip pattern averages more black and less white than adult with variable blackish on primary coverts; P9 typically lacks mirror, and P10 mirror smaller. Underwings have some dusky mottling on coverts. Eyes similar to adult; bill flesh pink with black distal band and pale tip, often with some reddish at gonys; legs rich pink. Partial PA3 molt (*Sept.*–Apr./May) into third alternate plumage: dark markings on head and neck reduced to absent; bill brightens and by summer may be indistinguishable from adult or have dark distal marks. White tips to outer primaries often lost by wear. Adult plumage attained by complete PB4 molt (June–Dec.) but some fourth-cycle birds may retain signs of immaturity on alula, primary coverts, and tail.

HYBRIDS
With Slaty-backed Gull in ne. Kamchatka[21] and with Glaucous Gull[22] (and see p. 492).

NOTES
1. Crochet et al. 2002; 2. Liebers et al. 2004; 3. Yésou 2002; 4. Peters 1934; 5. Dement'ev and Gladkov 1969; 6. Yésou 2002; 7. Vaurie 1965:735; 8. Kessel 1989; 9. Ibid.; 10. B. Mactavish photos; 11. D. Lovitch photos; 12. Campbell et al. 1990; 13. Bayer 1989; 14. Howell 2003c; 15. Marshall et al. 2003; 16. Howell pers. obs.; 17. A. Jaramillo pers. comm.; 18. S. C. Rottenborn pers. comm.; 19. W. Sekula and M. Reid pers. comm. (photos); 20. Howell pers. obs.; 21. Vaurie 1965:735; 22. Kessel 1989

LENGTH 21–26.3 IN. (53–67 CM)
PHOTOS 26.0–26.29

IDENTIFICATION SUMMARY

This large yellow-legged gull is a casual visitor to e. N. America from Europe. Adult overall intermediate in appearance between Herring Gull and Lesser Black-backed Gull. Bill fairly stout and parallel edged (more so on nominate *michahellis*); gonydeal expansion varies from slight to moderate. Adult upperparts medium gray to pale slaty gray (Kodak 6–8.5; see Taxonomy) with fairly extensive black wingtips (white mirrors on outer 1–2 primaries) and, in basic plumage, relatively limited dusky streaking mainly on head. Juvenile brown overall with contrasting white tail base and black distal tail band. Subsequent ages variable in appearance. First cycle has black bill, flesh legs become yellow by adult cycle; adult eyes pale lemon; orbital ring reddish. Breeding and molt cycles average 1–2 months earlier than American and European Herring Gulls.

Should be identified with great care in N. America, and note the potential of hybrid American Herring Gull × Lesser Black-backed Gull. *L. m. atlantis* suggests *graellsii* Lesser Black-backed Gull but slightly bulkier and broader winged; adult slightly paler above with underside of inner primaries and secondaries paler smoky gray; reduced dusky streaking on head and neck in basic. First-cycle *atlantis* also similar to *graellsii* but inner webs of inner primaries average paler, white tail base typically lacks distinct black barring at sides. Adult *michahellis*, by contrast, suggests American Herring Gull overall but upperparts slightly darker with more-extensive black wingtips, duskier underside to remiges, reduced dusky streaking on head and hindneck in basic (often white headed by midwinter), yellowish legs, red orbital ring. First-cycle *michahellis* often suggests Great Black-backed Gull in its whitish head and underparts, boldly checkered and spangled upperparts. See Similar Species and Rarer Species sections for details.

TAXONOMY

See introductory section to the Herring Gull complex (p. 401). Two widely recognized taxa in w. Europe: the smaller (21–24 in.; 53–61 cm), shorter-legged, and darker-backed (Kodak 7–8.5) *atlantis* of the Azores (Atlantic Yellow-legged Gull), which was once treated as a race of Lesser Black-backed Gull;[1] and the larger (21.7–26.3 in.; 55–67 cm), longer-legged, and paler-backed (Kodak 6–7) nominate *michahellis* of the Mediterranean region (Mediterranean Yellow-legged Gull), which was once treated as a race of Herring Gull.[2] Birds breeding along Atlantic coasts from nw. Spain to Morocco (including so-called Cantabrican Yellow-legged Gull in nw. Spain), and on the Canary Is. and Madeira may represent one or more unnamed taxa of Yellow-legged Gull.[3,4,5] Pending more study of the complex, in the descriptions below we provisionally include Cantabrican birds with *michahellis*, and birds from the Canary Is. and Madeira with *atlantis*.

Yellow-legged Gull was considered conspecific with Herring Gull[6] but now split by AOU[7] and others as *Larus cachinnans* because of sympatry with limited interbreeding in France.[8] But *michahellis* is very distinct from true *cachinnans*,[9,10,11,12] and the two are best regarded as a separate species: Yellow-legged Gull *L. michahellis* and Caspian Gull *L. cachinnans*. The latter breeds in se. Europe and cen. Asia and seems an unlikely candidate for vagrancy to N. America.

STATUS AND DISTRIBUTION

S. Europe and islands off nw. Africa, including Azores.

Casual nonbreeding visitor (mainly Oct./Dec.–Mar./Apr.; also June and Aug. records from Que.) to e. N. America from Atlantic Canada (mainly Nfld.) south to Mid-Atlantic coast,[13] exceptionally Tex. (Jan.–Apr. 2004). An Aug. specimen from Que. has been referred to Azorean *L. m. atlantis*;[14] provenance of other birds uncertain.

FIELD IDENTIFICATION

SIMILAR SPECIES

The main confusion species in N. America are Lesser Black-backed Gull and American Herring Gull. Also see hybrid American Herring Gull × Lesser Black-backed Gull and European Herring Gull (under Rarer Species).

Adult Cycle. Note medium gray tone of upperparts (intermediate between American

Herring Gull and Lesser Black-backed Gull), yellowish legs, and, in winter, little or no dusky head streaking and relatively bright bill. Long-call harsher and more grating than American Herring Gull.

LESSER BLACK-BACKED GULL (widespread, but generally rare away from East Coast) overall smaller with more slender bill, narrower and relatively longer wings and shorter legs (especially than nominate *michahellis*). Upperparts slightly to distinctly darker (Kodak 9–11) with less contrasting and slightly less extensive black wingtips (for example, longer gray basal tongues on P8–P9); molt timing late (by 1–4 months); heavier dusky head and neck streaking in basic retained later.

AMERICAN HERRING GULL (widespread) paler above (Kodak 4–5) with less extensive black wingtips that often have more white (at least in ne. N. America), flesh pink legs, yellow-orange orbital ring, and, in winter, heavier dusky head and neck streaking, and often a duller and more pinkish bill with more-distinct dark distal marks but no red on maxilla or gape (shown by many Yellow-leggeds). Molts usually 1–2 months later than Yellow-legged.

First Cycle. *Atlantis* can suggest American Herring or Lesser Black-backed Gull, whereas nominate *michahellis* can recall Great Black-backed Gull. Mediterranean *michahellis*, at least, often has fairly extensive PA1 molt that includes upperwing coverts and even tertials by early winter, unlike American Herring Gull.

LESSER BLACK-BACKED GULL perhaps not always safely distinguishable. Nominate *michahellis* larger and bulkier than Lesser with blockier head, stouter bill, and longer legs; PA1 molt averages earlier and more extensive with new feathers often paler gray and barred, similar to Herring Gull; note indistinct pale inner primary panel (poorly marked birds overlap with Lesser), and tail base averages more-extensively and plainer white at sides than Lesser. Race *atlantis* structurally more similar to Lesser but averages bulkier and broader winged; first-cycle plumages relatively dark and similar to Lesser; study needed.

GREAT BLACK-BACKED GULL larger and bulkier with stouter bill, but plumage can look similar to *michahellis*; note narrower tail band more broken by wavy white barring, slightly paler inner primaries, paler greater coverts (with coarse pale barring), and later and less-extensive molt (with much juvenal plumage often retained into winter).

AMERICAN HERRING GULL typically browner overall with less contrasting uppertail coverts and tail; often has some flesh at bill base; inner primaries show as contrasting pale panel; PA1 molt rarely includes upperwing coverts.

Second Cycle. YELLOW-LEGGED GULL often shows yellowish legs by second summer, when back has moderate to extensive medium gray.

LESSER BLACK-BACKED GULL averages smaller and slimmer than nominate *michahellis* with more slender bill, generally darker on head and underparts in winter, and upperparts often show darker slaty gray. Race *atlantis* very similar to Lesser Black-backed but slaty gray on back slightly paler; study needed.

GREAT BLACK-BACKED GULL larger and more massive with stouter, swollen-tipped bill. More "retarded" upperparts often have some dark slaty gray, blackish distal tail band typically narrower and less solid, inner primaries average paler overall, and eyes usually darker.

AMERICAN HERRING GULL typically has more contrasting pale panel on inner primaries, any plain gray on upperparts slightly paler, and tail averages more extensively black (rarely solidly black on Yellow-legged).

Third Cycle. Much like adult but legs can be fleshy yellow, upperwing coverts mixed with brownish, white wingtip markings reduced. See adult cycle for differences from other species, especially Lesser Black-backed Gull.

RARER SPECIES

Adult Cycle. Note medium gray to pale slaty gray upperparts, yellowish legs, Herring Gull-like structure.

CALIFORNIA GULL (w. N. America) averages smaller and slighter in build, upperparts similar in tone (Kodak 5–7.5) and wingtips extensively black but eyes dark; legs often greenish yellow on nonbreeding birds; bill has blackish subterminal band (very rarely absent in summer), and winter birds have extensive dusky head and neck streaking heaviest on hindneck.

HYBRID AMERICAN HERRING GULL × LESSER BLACK-BACKED GULL might be quite similar to *atlantis* Yellow-legged Gull (for example, upperparts around Kodak 7), but field identification criteria unknown. Hybrid European Herring Gull × Lesser Black-backed Gull in Europe typically have orangish orbital ring, yellowish flesh legs,[15] and molt later (more like Lesser Black-backed Gull[16]), so they usually lack streaking when Mediterranean *michahellis* show streaking in late summer. Hybrids have distinct dusky head and neck streaking in winter, sometimes lost by Jan. or Feb., but this is similar to Cantabrican *michahellis*[17] and to *at-*

lantis; and molt timing of vagrants may differ from source populations.

EUROPEAN HERRING GULL (casual e. N. America). Nominate *argentatus* averages paler gray above (Kodak 5.5–7), but darkest birds overlap with *michahellis*, less-extensive black wingtips often have more white on P9–P10, legs usually flesh pink (but can be yellowish), orbital ring typically yellow-orange, and, in winter, has heavier dusky head streaking and more often shows dark distal bill markings. Molts 1–2 months later than Yellow-legged.

VEGA GULL (w. Alaska) similar in size, shape, and upperpart tone (Kodak 7–8) to nominate *michahellis* (averages larger and bulkier than *atlantis*) but has rich pink legs, averages larger white tongue-tips out to P7/P8, and more often has P9 mirror; also note darker eyes.

First Cycle. CALIFORNIA GULL develops black-tipped, pinkish bill by October; tail mostly black with limited whitish barring at base.

HYBRID AMERICAN HERRING GULL × LESSER BLACK-BACKED GULL might be quite similar to *atlantis* Yellow-legged Gull, but field identification criteria unknown.

EUROPEAN HERRING GULL has more-contrasting pale panel on inner primaries, duller whitish uppertail coverts and tail base with less sharply contrasting blackish distal tail band. Also averages broader and more-notched pale distal edging to tertials, more evenly barred greater coverts, and usually shows some pinkish at bill base. Nominate *michahellis* often whiter on head and underparts by early to midwinter, and PA1 often includes some upperwing coverts.

KELP GULL (S. America) averages bulkier with a stouter bill, more-swollen gonys, broader black tail band, darker underwing coverts. PA1 molt averages less extensive with new feathers usually plainer, not boldly barred and checkered; legs average duskier and duller flesh. Note potential differences in primary molt timing of source populations, but these may be modified on vagrants.

HYBRID KELP GULL × AMERICAN HERRING GULL not well described; potential differences from Yellow-legged include stouter, bulbous-tipped bill, extensively black tail, duller flesh legs.

VEGA GULL has more-contrasting pale panel on inner primaries, more boldly barred greater coverts, and pale distal edging to tertials averages bolder, more notched; usually shows some pinkish at bill base.

THAYER'S GULL (mainly w. N. America) averages smaller with a less stout bill; PA1 molt later and less extensive (not including upperwing coverts); brownish black wingtips usually have distinct whitish tips and fringes. Upperwing has contrasting pale panel on inner primaries, and outer primaries pale on inner webs; uppertail coverts heavily barred brown and tail mostly dark.

SLATY-BACKED GULL (n. Pacific) averages bulkier and broader winged. Has paler greater coverts, A1 scapulars typically with dark shaft streaks or dark centers. Upperwing shows distinct pale panel on inner primaries, and outer primaries have contrasting pale on inner webs. Tail mostly dark.

WESTERN GULL and YELLOW-FOOTED GULL (both w. N. America) told by larger size and heavier build with stouter and swollen-tipped bills, solidly black tails.

Second Cycle. YELLOW-LEGGED GULL often shows yellowish legs by second summer, when back has moderate to extensive medium gray to pale slaty gray.

CALIFORNIA GULL averages smaller and slimmer with longer wing projection, slimmer and more parallel-edged bill; legs and bill often have greenish or bluish hues, and bill sharply two-toned; eyes dark; upperwing has pale panel on inner 3–4 primaries.

HYBRID AMERICAN HERRING GULL × LESSER BLACK-BACKED GULL might be quite similar to *atlantis* Yellow-legged Gull, but field identification criteria unknown.

EUROPEAN HERRING GULL has more-contrasting pale panel on inner primaries, any plain gray on upperparts slightly paler.

KELP GULL bill averages stouter with deeper gonys, legs typically dull flesh to greenish, any plain gray on upperparts (obvious by second alternate) is slaty blackish.

HYBRID KELP GULL × AMERICAN HERRING GULL not well described; potential differences from Yellow-legged include stouter, bulbous-tipped bill, more extensively black tail, duller flesh to greenish legs.

VEGA GULL has more-contrasting pale panel on inner primaries and legs rich pink in second summer, upperwing coverts average brighter and bolder patterning; study needed of distinguishing features.

THAYER'S GULL averages smaller with a less stout bill. Best plumage feature is overall paler upperwings, with pale panel on inner primaries blending into two-tone pattern on outer primaries.

SLATY-BACKED GULL averages bulkier and broader winged. Plumage usually has some slaty gray in the upperparts by late winter; upperwing has pale inner primary panel and pale inner webs of outer primaries, creating a Thayer's-like pattern.

WESTERN GULL bulkier and broader winged with stouter, more bulbous-tipped bill; upperparts usually with some to extensive slaty gray; legs flesh pink.

Third Cycle. California Gull and Vega Gull differ in much the same ways as do adults (see above).

HABITAT AND BEHAVIOR

Much as American Herring Gull, with which it is likely to be found in N. America.

DESCRIPTION AND MOLT

L. m. atlantis (breeds Atlantic is.).

Adult Cycle. Complete PB molt (May/June–Oct./Nov.) produces adult basic plumage: head, neck, and underparts white; head and neck with variable (often light) dusky streaking typically concentrated in half-hood and on lower hindneck; streaking most distinct during Aug.–Nov. and many birds mostly white headed in midwinter (Dec.–Feb.). Upperparts medium gray to pale slaty gray (Kodak 7–8.5, averaging paler on birds of Madeira and Canary Is.[18]) with moderately extensive black wingtips (black on outer web of P10 and often P9 extends to primary coverts; P4 can have a small black mark), white scapular and tertial crescents; and white tips to outer primaries. Uppertail coverts and tail white. White trailing edge to secondaries (usually hidden at rest) and inner primaries breaks into discrete white tips on outer primaries; P5/P7 can show narrow whitish tongue-tips, P10 has distinct white mirror, and up to 20 percent of Azores adults (n = 30[19]) have small P9 mirror. Underwings show black wingtips (with P10 or P9–P10 mirrors) demarcated from pale smoky gray, white-tipped inner primaries and secondaries, which form a dusky subterminal band on underwings. Eyes pale lemon, orbital ring red to orange-red. Bill yellow (often fairly bright) with large orange-red to red gonydeal spot (that often bleeds slightly onto maxilla), and sometimes dark distal marks. Legs yellow to flesh-yellow. Partial PA molt (*Sept./Oct.–Feb./Mar.*) produces adult alternate plumage: head and neck clean white (usually by Jan./Feb.); white primary tips reduced through wear. Orbital ring red, legs brighter yellow. Bill bright yellow with orange-red gonydeal spot, loses any dark distal marks, and orange-red gape more prominent.

First Cycle. Juvenile (July/Aug.–*Jan.*): dark brown to medium gray-brown overall. Head, neck, and underparts whitish, variably streaked and mottled gray-brown, becoming white on vent and undertail coverts, which have variable dark barring. Upperparts with buff (bleaching to dull whitish) scaly and notched edgings and markings, the outer greater coverts typically with rather plain, dark bases. Tertials blackish brown with notched whitish tips and distal edging. Uppertail coverts white with sparse dark markings. Remiges blackish with narrow whitish tips to secondaries and inner primaries; outer primaries with fine paler tips visible at rest (lost through wear), inner primaries with slightly paler inner webs forming indistinct paler panel on spread upperwing. Tail base white with sparse blackish markings, sharply demarcated from broad black distal tail band; outer web of R6 ribbed to edged white and tail narrowly tipped white. IN FLIGHT: dark brownish overall with blackish flight feathers, indistinct paler panel on inner primaries, dark bar on greater-covert bases, and contrasting white uppertail coverts and tail base; underwings medium to dark brown. Eyes dark; blackish bill can show dull brownish base and fine pale tip by late winter; legs dusky flesh to flesh pink. PA1 molt (Sept.–Apr.; can include upperwing coverts) produces first alternate plumage: head, neck, and chest often bleach to mostly whitish with variable dusky brown streaking and spotting; A1 scapulars and upperwing coverts range from pale brownish with dark anchor marks, and dark brownish with broad paler edgings (earlier-molted feathers) to mostly grayish, often with dark shaft streaks (later-molted feathers). Eyes brown, orbital ring dull-flesh in summer. Bill black with variable dull-flesh basally in first summer and often a pale horn tip; legs flesh pink.

Second Cycle. Complete PB2 molt (Apr./May–Sept./Oct.) into second basic plumage. Head, neck, and underparts whitish with variable dusky streaking and mottling typically heaviest at half-hood and on belly. Upperparts dark brown with paler edgings and sometimes a mix of gray back feathers; upperwing coverts less uniformly marked than first cycle, and tertials often with broader whitish edging and notching; uppertail coverts mostly white. Remiges similar to first cycle but averages a wider white trailing edge to secondaries and paler inner primaries, which usually form an indistinct paler panel; tail ranges from extensively black to variably mixed with white; base less neatly marked than first cycle. Underwings dark with paler inner primaries when backlit. Eyes brownish to dirty pale lemon; bill typically flesh basally, black distally with a pale horn tip, legs flesh pink to yellowish flesh. Partial PA2 molt (*Sept.–Mar./Apr.*; often includes some upperwing coverts) produces second alternate plumage: head, neck, and underparts white, variably streaked and mottled dusky (often bleaching and wearing to mostly white by summer), back typically becomes mostly pale slaty gray in contrast to faded upperwing coverts; some birds attain a few plain gray upperwing coverts, especially median coverts. Eyes pale lemon to dusky, orbital ring reddish in summer. Through winter, bill typically pinkish basally, blackish distally with a pale tip and sometimes a blush of red at gonys; in summer, bill typically yellow with reddish gonydeal smudge and black distal band. Legs yellowish.

Third Cycle. Complete PB3 molt (May/June–Oct./Nov.) produces third basic plumage. Some "retarded" plumages resemble second cycle but with more gray on upperparts, less black in tail. More advanced-looking plumages typical, and variably resemble basic adult but with heavier dusky streaking and spotting on head and neck, typically forming a grayish streaked hood;[20] upperwing coverts may be washed brownish; tertials can show dark centers; white tips to remiges narrower. Tail often all white[21] but some have blackish distal markings. Blackish wingtip pattern averages more extensive and browner, with less white than adult; variable blackish on primary coverts and alula; P9 typically lacks mirror, and P10 mirror smaller to absent. Underwings have some dusky mottling on coverts. Eyes pale lemon; bill flesh pink with variable black median band and markings, and pale tip, often with some reddish at gonys; legs yellow to yellowish flesh. Partial PA3 molt (*Sept.–Feb./Mar.*) into third alternate plumage: dark markings on head and neck reduced to absent; bill brighter and often indistinguishable from adult or with faint dark distal marks. White tips to outer primaries often lost by wear. Adult plumage attained by complete PB4 molt (May/June–Oct./Nov.).

L. m. michahellis (breeds Mediterranean region).

Upperparts of adults and older immatures paler, medium gray (Kodak 6–7). Mediterranean birds larger, longer-legged, and bulkier overall than *atlantis* with stouter bill and earlier molt timing; but some mainland Atlantic Coast birds more similar in structure to *atlantis*; Cantabrian birds of nw. Spain look somewhat intermediate between Mediterranean Yellow-legged Gull and European Herring Gull.

Adult Cycle. Complete PB molt (May–Sept./Nov.) produces adult basic plumage. Similar to *atlantis* but upperparts paler, medium gray, averages less-extensive dusky head streaking, eyes average darker yellow. Bare parts similar to *atlantis*. Basic head streaking on Mediterranean birds most distinct during Aug.–Oct.; most become white headed by Nov.–Dec.; Cantabrian birds average later molt and more-extensive dusky streaking in basic (extending down hindneck), often retained through Jan.[22]

First Cycle. Juvenile (July–Sept./Oct.): similar to *atlantis* but head, neck, and underparts whiter, often bleaching to whitish by Sept.; inner primary panel averages paler on upperwing. PA1 more rapid and averages more extensive (late July–Mar./Apr.), often including numerous upperwing coverts and even tertials by Sept./Oct.; but Cantabrian birds molt later and often replace no upperwing coverts.[23] A1 scapulars typically pale grayish with dark anchor marks or broad subterminal bars.

Second Cycle. Complete PB2 molt (Apr.–Aug./Sept.) and partial PA2 (Sept.–Mar.). Basic head, neck, and underparts whiter overall than *atlantis*, new gray feathers in back average paler, medium gray, and inner primary panel on upperwing slightly more distinct.

Third Cycle. Differs from *atlantis* in same respects as does adult *michahellis*.

HYBRIDS

Has bred with Lesser Black-backed Gull and European Herring Gull in w. Europe,[24,25,26] Kelp Gull in Mauritania,[27] and presumably with Caspian Gull (*L. cachinnans*) in Poland.[28]

NOTES

1. Dwight 1925; 2. Cramp and Simmons 1983; 3. Dubois 2001; 4. Dubois and Yésou 1984; 5. Yésou 2002; 6. Cramp and Simmons 1983; 7. AOU 1998; 8. Yésou 1991; 9. Crochet et al. 2002; 10. de Knijff et al. 2001; 11. Klein and Buchheim 1997; 12. Liebers et al. 2001; 13. ABA 2002; 14. Wilds and Czaplak 1994; 15. Harris et al. 1978; 16. M. T. Elliott pers. comm.; 17. A. Bermejo pers. comm.; 18. Malling Olsen and Larsson 2003; 19. Howell pers. obs.; 20. Dubois 2001 21. Howell pers. obs.; 22. A. Bermejo pers. comm.; 23. Ibid.; 24. Cottaar 2004; 25. Garner 1997; 26. Yésou 1991; 27. Pineau et al. 2001; 28. Faber et al. 2001

LENGTH 19.7–24.3 IN. (50–62 CM)
PHOTOS 27.0–27.37

IDENTIFICATION SUMMARY

This medium large, relatively long-winged, dark-backed and yellow-legged gull is an increasingly common visitor to N. America from Europe. Medium-sized bill relatively slender or slightly tapered, with depth at base often slightly greater than depth at gonys; gonydeal expansion slight to moderate. At rest, tail tip falls at or just beyond tip of P6. Adult upperparts pale slaty gray to slaty blackish (Kodak 9–15; see Taxonomy) with black wingtips (white mirrors on outer 1–2 primaries) and, in basic plumage, fairly extensive dusky head and neck streaking often densest around the eyes. Juvenile brownish overall (often whiter on head and underparts) with contrasting white uppertail coverts and tail base, broad black distal tail band. PA1 variable, starting Sept.–Feb. Subsequent ages variable in appearance. First cycle has black bill, pale flesh pink legs, becoming yellow by adult cycle; adult eyes staring pale lemon; orbital ring orange-red.

LESSER BLACK-BACKED GULL
Very rare to casual elsewhere
in North America,
western Mexico, and the
West Indies.

seasonal, breeds locally
nonbreeding occurrence
(can be year-round)

Medium-large size, slaty gray upperparts, yellow legs, and pale eyes with reddish orbital ring are a distinctive combination among adults of regularly occurring New World gulls (but see Rarer Species, below). First-cycle plumage has distinctive upperwing and tail pattern relative to other large gulls in the East (see Great Black-backed and Herring Gulls); in the West note stouter-billed and dark-tailed Western and Yellow-footed Gulls, and pale-billed California Gull.

TAXONOMY

See introductory section to the Herring Gull complex (p. 401). Some authors[1] include the taxa *heuglini* and *taimyrensis* within Lesser Black-backed Gull, but numerous studies support the separation of these taxa from *L. fuscus*.[2,3] Thus, the three subspecies of Lesser Black-backed Gull (*fuscus, intermedius,* and *graellsii*) all breed in Europe. *L. f. graellsii* (breeds w. Europe, including Iceland) is by far the commonest taxon seen in N. America:[4] it is the largest and bulkiest subspecies, with slaty gray upperparts (Kodak 9–11) and relatively contrasting black wingtips that have relatively large white mirrors and primary tips. Scandinavian breeding race *intermedius* has darker slaty gray upperparts (Kodak 11–13) and poorly contrasting black wingtips with smaller white mirrors and primary tips. Nominate *fuscus,* breeding mainly in Finland (unrecorded—and unlikely—in N. America) averages smaller, slimmer, and longer winged than other races with slaty blackish upperparts (Kodak 13–15) poorly contrasting with black wingtips, which typically have a small P10 mirror and very small white primary tips; basic plumage has indistinct dusky head streaking.

STATUS AND DISTRIBUTION

Nw. Europe, wintering south to Africa, ranging to N. America.

Breeding. Breeds w. Greenland (since 1990, perhaps by 1986), but not (yet) confirmed N. America. First bred Iceland in late 1920s.

Nonbreeding. Has increased dramatically in N. America, especially since 1980 and in the East; first N. American record (excluding Greenland) Sept. 1934 in N.J.[5] Winters (mainly Sept.–Apr.) rarely to uncommonly (very locally fairly common) from Nfld. and s. Great Lakes region south along Atlantic Coast to s. Fla., in Bermuda, Bahamas, and along Gulf of Mex. coast from Fla. to Tamaulipas and n. Yucatán Peninsula, Mex. Rare to casual north to Lab., s. to cen. Panama and

through West Indies south to Tobago and n. Venezuela;[6,7] accidental in Argentina.[8] Maximum counts (up to 25–100 or more birds) are from Mass. south to Fla., with maxima of 200+ birds in Bucks Co., Pa., 500+ in Broward Co., Fla. Rare and very local in interior e. N. America away from Great Lakes region (annual on large lakes in w. Ky.). Farther west, largely casual on Great Plains south to w. Tex., but small numbers now winter annually in e. Colo. Casual (mainly Oct.–Mar.) in B.C. and Pacific states. Also casual (mid-Nov.–Feb.) in Sonora, Mex., possibly Costa Rica, and accidental in Ecuador. Many winter records involve birds returning to localities year after year.

Fall movement over most of e. N. America begins by mid–late Aug., becoming pronounced by late Oct.; earliest Calif. record mid-Sept. Records largely lacking after mid-Dec. from n. Great Lakes region and n. Great Plains (where mainly recorded mid-Sept.– early Nov., late Apr.–May). Away from wintering areas, casual elsewhere in Colo. and now annual (fall and spring) in w. Neb. Scattered but increasing records (mainly late fall through winter) elsewhere in the West (for example, Idaho, Utah), but still unrecorded in some states (such as Ore., Nev., Ariz.). Over most regions, spring sightings involve lingering wintering birds (which usually depart Mar.), although some Feb.–early May movement often evident in Atlantic Coast wintering regions.

Oversummering birds rare to locally uncommon along Atlantic Coast from Canada south to Fla., casually Gulf of Mex. coast west to Tex. and Great Lakes region. Ranges north casually (May–July) to Yukon, Hudson Bay, and James Bay, and (Aug.–Sept.) to se. Alaska.

FIELD IDENTIFICATION

SIMILAR SPECIES

Note relatively long, narrow, and pointed wings and slender bill, distinct from broader-winged and stouter-billed Herring Gull.

Adult Cycle. Adult distinctive among regularly occurring N. American gulls; note medium-large size, relatively slender bill, slaty gray upperparts, and yellow legs.

GREAT BLACK-BACKED GULL (ne. N. America) much larger and more massive with relatively shorter wing projection, stout bill swollen at gonys, slaty blackish upperparts (Kodak 13–15), flesh pink legs, more white in wingtips (P10 usually extensively white-tipped), lightly streaked head in winter. But beware some small female, presumed fourth-cycle Great Black-backeds, which can have relatively extensive dusky head streaking.[9]

CALIFORNIA GULL (w. N. America) averages smaller and lighter in build with dark eyes; paler upperparts (Kodak 5–7.5) have more sharply contrasting black wingtips with more white; underwings have less contrasting dusky bases to remiges; legs often greenish yellow on nonbreeding birds.

YELLOW-FOOTED GULL (nw. Mex.) larger and bulkier with broader wings, shorter wing projection, very stout and bulbous-tipped bill, yellow orbital ring, and vestigial dusky head smudging in basic plumage.

WESTERN GULL (w. N. America) occasionally has yellowish legs as adult (normally flesh pink), but averages larger and bulkier with broader wings, shorter wing projection, stouter bill with bulbous tip, yellow orbital ring, and reduced basic head streaking; eyes often dusky.

SLATY-BACKED GULL (n. Pacific) typically larger and bulkier with stouter bill, broader wings, rich pink legs, wider white trailing edge to wing, and more-extensive white in wingtips (for example, white tongue-tips usually distinct out to P8).

First Cycle. Note medium-large size, long-winged shape, slender black bill, relatively uniform dark primaries on upperwing, dark bases to outer greater coverts, and contrasting white tail base with well defined black distal tail band.

AMERICAN HERRING GULL (widespread) averages larger and bulkier with broader and blunter-tipped wings, shorter wing projection, stouter bill. Underparts overall uniform brownish, more heavily dark-barred uppertail coverts contrast less with brownish black tail, head often bleaches to contrastingly whiter in first winter, bill often has some flesh at base, paler inner primaries show as more-contrasting pale panel on upperwing.

GREAT BLACK-BACKED GULL much larger and bulkier with stouter bill; head and underparts average whiter, upperparts more brightly and coarsely checkered: for example, boldly patterned greater coverts; black tail band narrower and less solid, mixed with wavy white barring.

CALIFORNIA GULL develops black-tipped pinkish bill by Oct., tail mostly black with limited whitish barring at base and tail coverts not contrastingly whiter; upperparts (including tertials) often with broader and more-notched whitish edgings in juvenal plumage; A1 scapulars often boldly spangled or checkered.

WESTERN GULL and YELLOW-FOOTED GULL typically larger and bulkier with stouter, bulbous-tipped bill, broader wings, shorter wing projection, solidly black tail, and average bolder whitish tertial tips; Western Gull also has more uniformly brownish underparts.

SLATY-BACKED GULL typically larger and bulkier with stouter bill, plumage often paler overall with mostly plain and overall pale greater coverts; distinct pale panel on inner primaries blends into two-tone outer primaries.

THAYER'S GULL (winters w. N. America) slightly stockier with structure similar to small Herring Gull; bill shows dull flesh basally by early winter, upperparts typically with bolder and "frosty" patterning, brownish black wingtips usually have distinct whitish fringes. Upperwing has contrasting pale panel on inner primaries blending into two-tone outer primaries; uppertail coverts heavily barred brown and tail mostly dark brown.

Second Cycle. Note medium-large size, long-winged shape, slender bill, and overall dark aspect to upperparts, which often contrast with whitish head and chest. Second-fall and winter birds can suggest first cycle, whereas second-summer birds often strikingly different and adultlike in several characters.

CALIFORNIA GULL has strongly bicolored bill (flesh pink to greenish basally in winter), dark brown eyes, much paler underwing coverts, incoming medium gray upperparts, gray-green to flesh legs; upperwing typically has pale panel on inner 3–4 primaries.

AMERICAN HERRING GULL averages larger and bulkier with broader and blunter wings, shorter wing projection, stouter bill. Upperparts have incoming pale gray (Kodak 4–5), upperwing has contrasting pale inner primaries, legs flesh pink.

GREAT BLACK-BACKED GULL much larger and bulkier with stout bill; upperparts often more boldly variegated and with incoming feathers darker, slaty blackish; wing-linings paler; eyes average darker and legs paler fleshy.

WESTERN GULL typically larger and bulkier with stouter, bulbous-tipped bill, broader wings, shorter wing projection, mostly black tail, flesh pink legs.

YELLOW-FOOTED GULL has much more advanced looking plumage, more like third-cycle Lesser Black-backed, from which told by structure (especially bill), yellow orbital ring.

SLATY-BACKED GULL typically larger and bulkier with stouter bill, broader wings, brighter pink legs. Upperwing has pale panel on inner primaries.

THAYER'S GULL typically has dull flesh pink bill,

tipped blackish, upperparts paler overall with incoming pale gray. Upperwing has contrasting pale panel on inner primaries and two-tone outer primaries.

Third Cycle. Much like adult but legs can be yellowish flesh, upperwing coverts often mixed with brownish, white wingtip markings reduced, and bill more extensively blackish in winter (but adults often with appreciable black on bill in winter). See adult cycle for differences from other species.

Rarer Species

Adult Cycle. Relatively distinctive, but see Kelp Gull and hybrid Kelp × American Herring Gull. Also see Yellow-legged Gull, European Herring Gull, and Vega Gull (differences given under those taxa). Note structure (especially bill) and gray tone of upperparts.

KELP GULL (S. America) averages larger and bulkier with stouter bill (deeper at gonys than base), greenish yellow legs, virtually unstreaked head in basic; eyes often dusky. Upperparts slaty blackish (Kodak 12.5–15.5), darker than most Lesser Black-backeds in N. America but similar to nominate *fuscus* (unrecorded N. America).

HYBRID KELP GULL × AMERICAN HERRING GULL (Gulf of Mexico) bulkier with stouter bill. F1 hybrid much like Lesser Black-backed in plumage but underside of middle primaries paler gray, contrasting more sharply with blackish wingtip; legs greenish yellow.

First Cycle. Note structure, especially of the bill, and upperwing pattern. Also see Vega Gull and European Herring Gull under those accounts.

KELP GULL similar in plumage but note structural features under adult cycle, especially stout bill deeper at gonys, shorter wing projection; Kelp averages broader black tail band and duller, duskier flesh legs.

HYBRID KELP GULL × AMERICAN HERRING GULL bulkier with stouter, bulbous-tipped bill (more like Kelp in structure); tail may average more extensively black and legs duller flesh (needs study).

Second Cycle. Often shows yellowish legs by second summer, when back has moderate to extensive slaty gray of adultlike tone.

KELP GULL. Note structural features, especially stouter bill; legs dusky flesh to greenish yellow, and incoming back feathers darker slaty blackish.

HYBRID KELP GULL × AMERICAN HERRING GULL. Note structural features; potential differences include more extensively black tail, duller flesh to greenish legs (needs study).

Third Cycle. Much like adult but legs can be yellowish flesh, upperwing coverts often mixed with brownish, white wingtip markings reduced, and bill more extensively blackish in winter. See adult cycle for differences from other species.

Habitat and Behavior

Much like American Herring Gull and other large gulls, with which Lesser Black-backed occurs regularly, but often more aerial and maneuverable in flight than Herring Gulls. Frequents beaches, dumps, fishing harbors, lakes, parking lots, fields, etc., and ranges offshore over shelf waters. Feeds commonly by scavenging; also forages in intertidal and surface waters for marine invertebrates.

Description and Molt

L. f. graellsii (breeds w. Europe).

Adult Cycle. Complete PB molt (late May/early Aug.–Nov./Mar., can be suspended or protracted over winter) produces adult basic plumage: head, neck, and underparts white; head, neck, and sometimes chest with variable dusky streaking and spotting, which is often most concentrated around eyes and on hindneck. Back and upperwings slaty gray (Kodak 9–11) with extensive black wingtips (black on outer web of P10, usually P9–P10, extends to primary coverts; P4 sometimes and P3 rarely with black subterminal mark, mainly on outer web); white scapular and tertial crescents; and white tips to outer primaries. Uppertail coverts and tail white. White trailing edge to secondaries (usually hidden at rest) and inner primaries breaks into discrete white tips on outer primaries; P5–P7 can have narrow whitish tongue-tips, P10 has distinct white mirror, and around 50 percent of birds have P9 mirror.[10,11] Underwings show black wingtips (with white mirrors and narrow whitish tongue-tips) merging with moderate demarcation into white-tipped, dusky gray inner primaries and secondaries, which form a dusky subterminal band on underwings. Eyes pale lemon, orbital ring reddish. Bill yellowish (often fairly bright) with orange-red to red gonydeal spot and typically a variable blackish distal mark or band. Legs yellow (ranging from orange-yellow to fleshy yellow). Partial PA molt (Oct.–Mar./Apr.) produces adult alternate plumage: head and neck clean white (rarely before Mar.); white primary tips reduced through wear. Orbital ring orange-red to orange, legs brighter orange-yellow. Bill bright yellow with orange-red gonydeal spot, which can bleed on to maxilla; loses dark distal marks, and orange-red gape more prominent.

First Cycle. Juvenile (Aug.–Feb.): dark brown to medium gray-brown overall. Head, neck, and underparts whitish, variably streaked and mottled gray-brown, becoming white on vent and undertail coverts, which have relatively sparse dark bars; head streaking often concentrated as a broad dark mask. Upperparts with cinnamon-buff (bleaching to dull whitish), relatively narrow scaly and notched edgings and markings, the greater coverts typically with unmarked (or lightly marked) bases. Upperpart markings typically scaly to slightly notched, contrasting and neatly marked in fresh plumage (through late winter on some birds). Tertials blackish brown with narrow whitish distal edging and variable notches. Uppertail coverts white with variable (but rarely heavy) dark markings, contrasting appreciably with blackish tail band. Remiges blackish with narrow whitish tips to secondaries and browner, slightly paler inner primaries; outer primaries with fine whitish tips visible at rest (often lost through wear). Tail base white with black barring, sharply demarcated from broad black distal tail band; outer web of R6 ribbed to edged white and tail narrowly tipped white. Some birds have mostly blackish tail with very limited white basally.[12] IN FLIGHT: dark brownish overall with blackish flight feathers, dark bar on greater covert bases, and contrasting white uppertail coverts and tail base; underwings dark. Eyes dark; bill black, by late winter sometimes attaining dull flesh basally and a fine pale tip; legs dusky flesh to flesh pink. PA1 molt (Sept.–Apr.; often includes upperwing coverts from midwinter on) produces first alternate plumage: head, neck, and underparts often bleach to mostly whitish with variable dusky brown streaking and mottling; A1 scapulars and upperwing coverts range from pale brownish with dark anchor marks or dark brownish with broad paler edgings (earlier-molted feathers) to mostly grayish, often with dark shaft streaks (later-molted feathers). Bill black with variable dull flesh basally in first summer and often a pale horn tip (rarely dull flesh pink with a black distal third); legs flesh pink.

Second Cycle. Complete PB2 molt (late Apr./May–late Sept./Nov.) into variable second basic plumage. Head, neck, and underparts whitish with variable dusky streaking and mottling, at times with dark streaks concentrated around eyes and some birds with more solid dusky mottling on belly. Upperparts dark brown with variegated paler edgings and typically a mix of slaty gray back feathers; upper-

wing coverts more coarsely marked than first cycle and tertials often with broader whitish edging and notching; uppertail coverts mostly white. Remiges similar to first cycle but with wider white trailing edge to blacker secondaries and paler brownish to gray-brown inner primaries; wing-linings dark brown to medium brown. Tail white with variable (sometimes broken) blackish subterminal band. Eyes dark brownish to dirty pale lemon, bill typically flesh pink basally, black distally with a pale horn tip, legs flesh pink to yellowish flesh. Partial PA2 molt (Sept.–Apr.; often includes some upperwing coverts, probably rectrices on some birds) produces second alternate plumage: head, neck, and underparts white, variably streaked and mottled dusky (often bleaching to mostly white by summer), back typically becomes mostly slaty gray in contrast to faded upperwing coverts; some birds attain a few slaty gray upperwing coverts, especially median coverts. Tail more often with white feathers and less-solid blackish band than B2. Eyes pale lemon to dusky; orbital ring can be reddish in summer. By summer, some birds develop a yellow bill with reddish gonydeal mark and black distal band. Legs flesh pink to flesh-yellow.

Third Cycle. Complete PB3 molt (May/June–Nov./Jan.) produces third basic plumage. Some retarded plumages resemble second cycle but upperparts darker and more solidly gray, tail with less black (often all white); note adultlike inner and middle primaries. More advanced appearance typical, variably resembling adult basic but averaging more dusky streaking on head and neck; upperwing coverts usually washed or variably mottled brownish; tertials typically with dark centers; white tips to remiges narrower. Tail varies from all white to having a broken blackish subterminal band. Wingtip pattern averages more black and less white than adult, with variable blackish on primary coverts and alula; P9 typically lacks mirror, and P10 mirror smaller or absent. Underwings have some dusky mottling on coverts. Eyes pale lemon; bill regresses from bright second-summer colors to mostly blackish with dull flesh basally and a large creamy tip; legs yellowish flesh to yellow. Partial PA3 molt (Sept.–Mar./Apr.) into third alternate plumage: dark markings on head and neck reduced to absent; bill brightens and may be indistinguishable from summer adult or have dark subterminal marks; legs brighter yellow. White tips to outer primaries often lost by wear. Adult plumage attained by complete PB4 molt (May–Dec.).

L. f. intermedius (breeds Scandinavia).

Similar overall to *graellsii*, but adult and older immatures have darker slaty gray upperparts (Kodak 11–13), white mirrors and tips to outer primaries average smaller, and narrow whitish tongue-tips on P5–P7 average less indistinct. Molt timing similar to *graellsii*; PA1 molt (presumably of longer-distance migrants) apparently can include variable number of primaries (like many nominate *fuscus*).[13]

L. f. fuscus (breeds Finland, unrecorded in N. America).

Similar overall to *intermedius* but upperparts darker, slaty blackish (Kodak 13–15), often with a brownish cast when bleached, and white in outer primaries reduced. Many individuals are long-distance migrants that have late and extensive, sometimes complete, molts in their first winter—so plumage of first-summer birds looks relatively advanced, with extensive dark on upperparts and fresh primaries, in other words similar to second-cycle *graellsii* and most second-cycle *intermedius*. Adult prebasic molt also relatively late and occurs mostly on nonbreeding grounds, after migration. See Jonsson[14] for more details, but note timing and extent of molt reflects migration distance rather than taxon.[15,16]

HYBRIDS

With European Herring Gull[17,18] and Yellow-legged Gull.[19,20] Presumably in N. America with American Herring Gull.[21]

NOTES

1. AOU 1998; 2. Liebers and Helbig 2002; 3. Yésou 2002; 4. Post and Lewis 1995b; 5. Post and Lewis 1995a; 6. Fairbank 2002; 7. ffrench and White 1999; 8. Steullet and Deautier 1939; 9. M. T. Elliott pers. comm.; 10. Ibid.; 11. Howell pers. obs.; 12. M. T. Elliott pers. comm.; 13. R. Winters unpubl. data; 14. Jonsson 1998; 15. Howell 2001a; 16. R. Winters unpubl. data; 17. Harris et al. 1978; 18. Tinbergen 1929; 19. Cottaar 2004; 20. Yésou 1991; 21. McWilliams and Brauning 2000

LENGTH 21–25 IN. (53–63 CM)
PHOTOS 28.0–28.41

IDENTIFICATION SUMMARY
A large, black-backed, yellow-legged gull of circumpolar range in the Southern Hemi- sphere; also called Dominican Gull and Southern Black-backed Gull. In our region, common in s. S. America, ranging casually to N. America. Bill stout with distinct gonydeal expansion and variably bulbous tip. Tail tip at rest falls between tip of P6 and P7 on S.

KELP GULL
Breeds inland locally in Patagonia.
Casual north to the United States.

resident, breeds locally
nonbreeding occurrence
(can be year-round)

American birds, around P7 tip on Antarctic birds. Adult has slaty blackish upperparts (Kodak 12.5–15.5; see Taxonomy), greenish yellow to gray-green legs, limited dusky head markings in basic plumage; wingtips black with small P10 mirror in S. America, larger P10 mirror in Antarctic Peninsula. Juvenile gray-brown overall with contrasting white uppertail coverts, black tail. Subsequent ages variable in appearance. First cycle has black bill developing pinkish at base, dull flesh legs. Adult eyes greenish white to olive-brown, orbital ring orange.

In S. America, adult Belcher's and Olrog's Gulls have blackish upperparts and yellowish legs, but both have black tail bands and black subterminal bill rings. In N. America, blackish upperparts and yellowish legs fairly distinctive, but see dark-mantled Lesser Black-backed Gulls (slighter in build with longer wing projection and more slender bill, which often looks deeper at base than gonys). See Similar Species and Rarer Species sections for more details and identification of immatures.

TAXONOMY

Jiguet[1] proposed recognition of five subspecies, with others possible pending critical revision: nominate *dominicanus* in (at least e.) S. America (type specimen from Brazil), *austrinus* in S. Shetland Is. and Antarctic Peninsula, *vetula* in S. Africa,[2] *judithae* on Subantarctic Indian Ocean is., and *melisandae* on Madagascar. Based on overall similarities in structure, bare-part colors, and wingtip pattern, we provisionally group birds from w. S. America with *dominicanus* and birds from the Falkland Is. and S. Georgia with *austrinus*. Overall, Antarctic and Subantarctic birds (including Falklands) have shorter and relatively stouter bills, n. populations (S. America and S. Africa) have longer and relatively more slender bills;[3,4] subspecies differ only slightly in darkness of upperparts, these being darker and browner in northern populations, paler and more slaty on southern populations.[5,6] Wingtip patterns vary by subspecies, with n. populations averaging less white.[7] Eye color variable (pale to dark) in S. America; typically pale on Antarctic, Subantarctic, and Madagascar birds; and typically dark in S. Africa. Orbital ring color reported as red in many populations[8,9] but typically deep orange on breeding adults of S. America and Antarctic Peninsula, varying to orange-yellow in cen. Chile and orange-red on Subantarctic and Antarctic populations.[10] Slight average differences in w. S. America unlikely to warrant subspecific recognition: s. breeders average shorter and stouter billed, whereas n. breeders average brighter yellowish legs.[11]

STATUS AND DISTRIBUTION

Circumpolar and expanding its range in the Southern Hemisphere, vagrant to N. America.

L. d. dominicanus. Common resident (breeds mainly Oct.–Mar. in South and along Pacific Coast, June–Nov. in Uruguay and Brazil) from Falklands and Tierra del Fuego north to cen. Chile (around 33° south) and Argentina (around 37° south), thence a fairly common to uncommon and local breeding resident north to n. Peru and s. Brazil (22° south); local resident (since 1990s) in s. Ecuador.[12] Commonest along and near coast but ranges inland (locally to 1,000 m elevation in Andean foothills of Chile, occasionally to 2,000 m in Argentina[13]), especially in cen. and s. Chile and Argentina. Some winter withdrawal from s. areas (mainly Apr.–Oct.) when commoner and more widespread north at least to s. Peru[14] and s. Brazil. Reported without details as accidental in Galápagos Is.[15]

Small numbers reached Gulf of Mex. in late 1980s and 1990s, with breeding reported in La.,[16] possible in Yucatán, Mex.[17] Casual nonbreeding visitor (mainly Sept.–Apr.) since mid-1990s along Gulf of Mex. coast from La. to s. Tex.,[18] ne. Mex., and n. Yucatán Peninsula[19,20] and in s. Caribbean.[21] Accidental in e. U.S. with records from Great Lakes region and Mid-Atlantic Coast.[22]

L. d. austrinus. Local resident (breeding Oct./Nov.–Feb./Mar.) on Scotia Arc Is. and Antarctic Peninsula; latter populations partly migratory, some birds reaching s. S. America in winter.[23]

FIELD IDENTIFICATION

SIMILAR SPECIES

In S. America, Kelp Gull is the only large white-headed gull that occurs regularly, so usually identified readily. Compare with adult and second-cycle Belcher's and Olrog's Gulls.

Adult Cycle. BELCHER'S GULL (coastal Peru to n. Chile) and Olrog's Gull (coastal Argentina) overall rangier in build than Kelp Gull with longer bills, longer, bright yellow legs, dark eyes, and no white tips and mirrors on outer primaries; in flight, note their clean-cut, subterminal black tail bands and broader white trailing edge to the secondaries. Basic plumages have variable dark hoods. Belcher's averages smaller than Kelp Gull, but Olrog's similar in size.

First Cycle. Belcher's and Olrog's Gulls have pale flesh bill with black tip, more solidly dark brown head and neck, relatively longer and paler flesh legs.

Second Cycle. Belcher's and Olrog's Gulls have longer bill, longer and brighter fleshy-yellow to yellow legs. Second-cycle Kelp can lack white outer primary mirrors and have black tail band, and second-cycle Olrog's and Belcher's have narrower white trailing edge to wings than adult. Both told from Kelp Gull by clean-cut black tail band (neat pattern not matched by Kelp), red bill tip; also note dark eyes; second-basic plumages have extensive dark hoods.

RARER SPECIES

Adult Cycle. In Middle and N. America, note Kelp Gull's yellowish to greenish legs, stout bill, and slaty blackish upperparts (Kodak 14–15.5) that contrast little with black wingtips; also note hybrid Kelp Gull × American Herring Gull (pp. 490–491).

LESSER BLACK-BACKED GULL (widespread). Kelp Gull much blacker above than the *graellsii* subspecies of Lesser Black-backed Gull, which accounts for most New World records. Blackish-backed subspecies of Lesser are rare (*intermedius*; Kodak 11–13) or unrecorded (nominate *fuscus*; Kodak 13–15) in the Americas. Lesser more lightly built and slimmer overall with relatively longer and narrower wings, relatively slender bill, narrower white trailing edge to secondaries, and, typically, brighter yellow to fleshy yellow legs; adult basic *graellsii* and *intermedius* have distinct dusky head and neck streaking, and bills often have blackish distal marks.

YELLOW-FOOTED GULL (Gulf of California) has slaty gray upperparts (Kodak 9–10.5) contrasting with black wingtips, stouter bill, chrome yellow orbital ring, bright yellow legs, and narrower white trailing edge to secondaries.

GREAT BLACK-BACKED GULL (e. N. America) more massive overall with stouter bill, flesh pink legs, narrower white trailing edge to secondaries, and more white in wingtips.

WESTERN GULL (w. N. America) has slaty gray upperparts (Kodak 8–11) contrasting with black wingtips, flesh pink legs, chrome yellow orbital ring, and narrower white trailing edge to secondaries.

SLATY-BACKED GULL (n. Pacific) has slaty gray upperparts (Kodak 9.5–11.5) contrasting with black wingtips, rich pink legs, more white in

wingtip; basic adult has extensive dusky head and neck streaking.

First Cycle. Note structure (especially bill), tail pattern, upperwing pattern, and dusky flesh legs. Also see Yellow-legged Gull, Vega Gull, and European Herring Gull (differences noted under those taxa).

LESSER BLACK-BACKED GULL similar in plumage but note structural features under adult cycle, especially longer wingtips and slender bill with less distinct gonydeal expansion. Lesser Black-backed averages narrower black tail band, legs average paler flesh, less dusky.

AMERICAN HERRING GULL (widespread) has flesh pink legs, contrasting pale panel on inner primaries, more heavily dark-barred and less contrasting uppertail coverts.

GREAT BLACK-BACKED GULL larger and bulkier with stouter bill; head and underparts average whiter and upperparts more coarsely checkered; black tail band narrower and broken by wavy white barring; legs paler flesh pink.

WESTERN GULL and YELLOW-FOOTED GULL have almost solidly black tails without white barring and ribbing at basal corners; legs typically brighter, flesh pink; Yellow-footed also has deeper bill and Western averages denser dark barring on uppertail coverts. Some tropical populations of Kelp Gull molt upperwing coverts and bleach to whitish on head and underparts in first cycle, thus looking similar to Yellow-footed: note bill shape, leg color, and tail pattern, and that upperwing of Kelp averages darker brown, less prone to fading.

SLATY-BACKED GULL often paler overall with mostly plain and overall pale greater coverts; distinct pale panel on inner primaries blends into two-tone outer primaries; legs bright pink.

Second Cycle. Note dusky flesh to chalky olive legs, and structure (especially bill).

LESSER BLACK-BACKED GULL similar overall in plumage but note structural features under adult cycle, especially more slender bill, long wing projection; Lesser averages narrower black tail band and brighter fleshy yellow legs.

GREAT BLACK-BACKED GULL. Besides structure, upperparts (including upperwing coverts) often paler and more variegated, legs flesh pink, tail has narrower and diffusely peppered black distal band.

YELLOW-FOOTED GULL averages stouter bill, paler flesh to fleshy yellow legs, smudgier dusky markings on head, neck, and underparts, and has incoming slaty gray on upperparts.

WESTERN GULL has smudgier dusky markings on head, neck, and underparts, flesh pink legs, incoming slaty gray on upperparts.

SLATY-BACKED GULL has bright flesh pink legs, contrasting pale inner primary panel; in second summer, slaty gray back often contrasts strongly with very pale upperwing coverts.

AMERICAN HERRING GULL averages less stout bill, has pale inner primary panel, flesh pink legs, and incoming pale gray on upperparts.

Third Cycle. Much like adult but legs often duller and more greenish or grayish, upperwing coverts mixed with brownish, white wingtip markings reduced. See adult cycle for differences from other species, especially Lesser Black-backed and Yellow-footed Gulls.

HABITAT AND BEHAVIOR

Coasts, harbors, estuaries, dumps, sewage outfalls, lakes, rivers, wet fields, ranging at least to 50 km offshore. Nests colonially or in scattered pairs on flat ground of rocky islets, higher ground of beaches, on cliffs, etc. Often in flocks (locally to a few thousand birds) at river mouths, harbors, and along beaches, associating readily with other gulls and water birds. Feeds commonly by scavenging; also forages in intertidal and surface waters for marine invertebrates, preys on eggs and young of seabirds and waterfowl.

DESCRIPTION AND MOLT

L. d. dominicanus (S. America).

Molt timings given below are for s. S. America (n. Chile to Patagonia and Tierra del Fuego) and presumably vary with different breeding cycles, such as in e. S. America, where adult prebasic molt can be expected Aug.–Jan.

Adult Cycle. Complete PB molt (timing varies with region, mainly Dec.–June in s. S. America) produces adult basic plumage: head, neck, and underparts white; head and hindneck with slight dusky clouding and spotting in fresh plumage (mainly Mar.–June; heaviest in s. birds, least in n. populations); usually looks overall white-headed. Upperparts slaty blackish (Kodak 14–15.5) with poorly contrasting black wingtips, bold white scapular and tertial crescents, and white tips to outer primaries. Upperparts more brownish, less slaty, when bleached. Uppertail coverts and tail white. Broad white trailing edge to secondaries (often shows as skirt) and narrower white trailing edge to inner primaries breaks into discrete white tips on outer primaries; P5–P6 typically (and P7 rarely) with narrow white tongue-tips; P10 has small to medium white mirror, and up to 5–10 percent of birds (n = 100)[24] have small white mirror on P9. Underwings show black wingtips (with white

primary tips and mirrors) blending into white-tipped, slaty gray inner primaries and secondaries, which form a dusky subterminal band on underwings; white secondary tips broad so that dark bases reduced to absent on inner secondaries. Eyes lemon-white to olive-brown, orbital ring orange (varies from orange-yellow to orange-red), bill yellow to orange-yellow with a large red gonydeal spot and rarely a narrow dusky tomium line at gonys; bill base often suffused pinkish during height of PB molt. Legs yellow to chalky yellowish green. Partial PA molt (mainly *May*–Oct. in s. S. America) produces adult alternate plumage: head and neck clean white (usually by June/July in s. S. America). Orbital ring, bill, and legs brighter; white primary tips can be lost through wear.

First Cycle. Juvenile (mainly Jan.–May in s. S. America): dark gray-brown to gray-brown overall, rarely dark sooty brown. Head, neck, and underparts variably streaked and mottled whitish, becoming white on vent and undertail coverts, which have dark bars and spots; head and foreneck may bleach to whitish with dark mask through eyes. Upperparts with pale buff (bleaching to whitish) scaly and notched edgings and markings, the greater coverts typically with unmarked (or lightly marked) bases. Tertials blackish brown with notched whitish tips. Uppertail coverts white with relatively sparse dark spots and bars. Flight feathers brownish black; browner inner webs of inner primaries form indistinct panel on spread upperwing, and paler inner edges to inner webs of middle and outer primaries can show as indistinct tongue-streaks on widely spread upperwing; secondaries narrowly tipped whitish; tail with white tip, whitish bars at basal corners, and often with white ribbing on outer web of R6. IN FLIGHT: gray-brown overall with blackish flight feathers, dark bar on greater-covert bases, and contrasting white uppertail coverts; underwings dark. Eyes dark, bill black, legs dull dusky flesh. Protracted and variable PA1 molt (mainly Mar.–Nov. in s. S. America; can include upperwing coverts and tertials on n. birds), in combination with bleaching and wear, produces first alternate plumage: head, neck, and underparts often bleach to mostly white (especially on n. populations); other birds attain brown-streaked and mottled head and underparts, usually with whiter head and chest. Post-juvenal scapulars (and upperwing coverts on some birds) mostly gray-brown to grayish with variable dark centers (ranging from shaft streaks to anchor marks) and pale tips, wingtips and tail fade to dark brown. Southerly wintering birds often retain juvenal plumage later and some (late-molting?) birds attain solidly slaty blackish scapulars. Bill blackish overall, usually with some flesh at base and sometimes a pale horn tip, rarely yellowish flesh with black distal third; legs grayish flesh.

Second Cycle. Complete PB2 molt (mainly Oct./Nov.–Mar./Apr. in s. S. America) into second basic plumage. Head, neck, and underparts white with variable dusky brown streaking and mottling (heaviest on southern birds). Upperparts more uniform than first cycle: mixed brownish and dark slaty, wing coverts in particular with paler edgings and bars creating variably scaly to checkered appearance; outer greater coverts usually solidly dark based and tertials blackish with broad, notched whitish tips. Wingtips blackish with fine pale fringes. Mostly white uppertail coverts contrast with mostly blackish tail; white rectrix bases average more extensive than first cycle. Upperwings similar to first cycle, but coverts more uniform, and averages more-distinct white trailing edge to blackish secondaries and browner inner primaries. Wing-linings medium to pale brown. Eyes brown to dull pale lemon, bill averages more-extensive pinkish at base and often has pale horn tip, legs dull flesh to dusky gray-green. Partial PA2 molt (mainly Apr.–Nov. in s. S. America) produces second alternate plumage: head, neck, and underparts become whiter (some clean white like adult), back becomes mostly slaty blackish in contrast to brownish upperwing coverts; some birds attain a few dark slaty upperwing coverts, especially median coverts. Eyes pale lemon to brownish; orbital ring can brighten to orange-yellow; bill typically becomes yellow with red gonydeal spot like adult and usually a black tip or subterminal band (some, however, retain pinkish bill with black distal band); legs gray-green to dull greenish yellow.

Third Cycle. Complete PB3 molt (mainly Dec.–May in s. S. America) produces third basic plumage: overall resembles adult but with more extensive dusky streaking on head, neck, and sometimes on chest; upperwings average browner with narrower white tips to remiges (wingtips at rest all black on some birds), white tongue-tips to P4–P5/P6, and sometimes small P10 mirror; often some black on tail (which varies from all white to extensively black). White wing-linings sometimes with brownish wash and flecks. Bare parts intermediate between second cycle and

adult. Partial PA3 molt (mainly June–Oct. in s. S. America) into third alternate plumage: dark markings on head and neck reduced to absent but browner areas on upperwings often more distinct because of bleaching; bill and orbital ring brighter, often indistinguishable from adult, or bill can have dark mark above red gonydeal spot, legs average more grayish or greenish. Adult plumage attained by complete PB4 molt.

L. d. austrinus (Falklands and Scotia Arc Is. to Antarctic Peninsula; see Taxonomy).

Resembles *domincanus* but with average shorter bill, shorter and blunter wing projection; molt schedule similar to s. Chile, but adult may average earlier start and more contracted molt (Nov./Dec.–Apr./May). Characters of different island populations require study.

Adult Cycle. Resembles *dominicanus* but upperparts average paler and slatier gray (Kodak 12.5–14), contrasting more with black wingtips, which have larger white P10 mirror (rarely an all-white tip[25]), more often a P9 mirror (on 15 percent of 50 birds[26]), and bolder white tongue-tips on P5–P7. Eyes greenish white (olive on <5 percent of 150 birds[27]), orbital ring orange to orange-red, legs yellow to greenish yellow.

First Cycle. Juvenile (mainly Jan.–May) similar to *dominicanus*. Partial PA1 molt averages less extensive (rarely if ever includes upperwing coverts or tertials); first alternate plumage averages browner overall, with more-distinct brownish streaking and mottling on head, neck, and underparts (but some birds have extensively white head and underparts).

Second Cycle. No consistent known differences from nominate *dominicanus* but second basic may average darker and browner overall, gray on upperparts may average paler, and, in second summer, may more often attain fully adultlike bill colors and yellower legs.

Third Cycle. Much like nominate *dominicanus* but third-basic plumage may average more extensive dark markings on head and neck, slaty gray on upperparts probably averages paler. Adult plumage attained by complete PB4 molt.

HYBRIDS
With American Herring Gull in La.,[28] Yellow-legged Gull in w. Africa.[29]

NOTES
1. Jiguet 2002; 2. Brooke and Cooper 1979; 3. Howell pers. obs.; 4. Jiguet 2002; 5. Howell pers. obs.; 6. Jiguet 2002; 7. Ibid.; 8. Ibid.;

9. Jiguet et al. 2001; 10. Howell pers. obs.;
11. Ibid.; 12. Haase 1996; 13. M. Pearman
pers. comm.; 14. Hughes 1970; 15. Harris
1982; 16. ABA 2002; 17. Howell et al. 1993;
18. ABA 2002; 19. Gee and Edwards 2000;
20. Howell et al. 2001; 21. Hayes et al. 2002;
22. ABA 2002; 23. Parmelee et al. 1977;
24. Howell pers. obs.; 25. Ibid.; 26. Ibid.;
27. Ibid.; 28. Dittman and Cardiff 2005;
29. Pineau et al. 2001

LENGTH 25–31 IN. (63.5–78.5 CM)
PHOTOS 29.0–29.33; I.9, I.16, I.30

IDENTIFICATION SUMMARY

A N. Atlantic species, fairly common in ne. N. America and ranging south to se. U.S. This very large, black-backed, pink-legged gull is the largest gull in the world, and males in particular are massive. Bill stout and heavy with distinct and slightly swollen gonydeal expansion. At rest, tip of tail falls around tip of P7. Forecrown often long and gently sloping. Adult has slaty blackish upperparts (Kodak 13–15), browner when worn; wingtips black with large white tip to P10, large white mirror on P9. Limited fine dusky streaking on head in basic plumage. Juvenile relatively pale to whitish on head, neck, and underparts; upperparts boldly checkered; tail white with narrow black distal band. PA1 variable, starting Sept.–Feb. Subsequent ages variable in appearance. All ages have flesh pink legs; adult eyes olive to dirty pale lemon; orbital ring reddish.

Large size, slaty blackish upperparts, large white P10 tip, and pale flesh pink legs are a distinctive combination among adults of regularly occurring New World gulls; and this is the only black-backed, pink-legged gull regular in the East (compare with Western Gull in w. N. America, Slaty-backed Gull in the n. Pacific). Large size, stout bill, whitish head and underparts, boldly checkered upperparts, and tail pattern distinctive in first cycle. See Similar Species and Rarer Species sections for more detail and other immature plumages.

TAXONOMY
Monotypic.

STATUS AND DISTRIBUTION
Ne. N. America and nw. Europe.
Breeding. Breeds (late Apr./May–Aug.) from s. Greenland, ne. Que., Lab., and Nfld. south along Atlantic Coast of N. America to N.C. and locally on ne. side of James Bay, Que. Also locally in small numbers on Lake Ont. and Lake Huron, in interior s. Que. (Lac St.

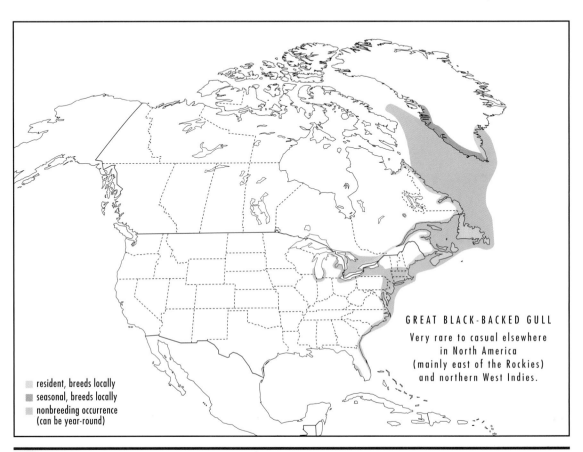

GREAT BLACK-BACKED GULL
Very rare to casual elsewhere
in North America
(mainly east of the Rockies)
and northern West Indies.

resident, breeds locally
seasonal, breeds locally
nonbreeding occurrence
(can be year-round)

Jean), N.Y./Vt. (Lake Champlain), and inland in Nfld., e. N.B., s. N.S., and, at least once, se. N.H. Breeding range has spread south along Atlantic Coast from Me. during twentieth century, and into Great Lakes, where first nested 1954 on Lake Huron.[1] Similarly, winter records in s. parts of nonbreeding range are increasing.

Nonbreeding. Southbound movements begin late Aug.–Sept. and become pronounced by late Oct.–Nov. Winters over much of breeding range (though withdraws south from n. Que. and Lab.) and south to Atlantic coastal Fla., more sparingly to s. Florida. Uncommon to locally fairly common (mainly Oct.–Mar., casual in summer) in Bermuda. Rare to locally uncommon (mainly Oct.–Mar.) in n. West Indies, casual in Yucatán Peninsula, Mex.;[2] perhaps accidental in Venezuela. A report from Belize[3] is hypothetical.[4] Northbound movements on Atlantic Coast mainly evident Mar.–Apr., and small numbers of nonbreeders oversummer nearly throughout the regular winter range, including south to Fla.

Widespread in winter in Great Lakes region with peak numbers late Nov.–early Jan., smaller numbers through winter: common to fairly common on e. Great Lakes, uncommon on Lake Michigan, and very rare Lake Superior, where it is a migrant. Casual or very rare (mainly Nov.–Mar.) in Midwest well away from Great Lakes and in e. states away from Atlantic coastal plain, with most inland records along Ohio and Mississippi Rs. or on large lakes. Very rare to casual in winter on Gulf of Mex. coast west to s. Tex. Casual migrant se. Man. (late Mar.–mid-June, late Sept.–mid-Nov.) and north to sw. Hudson Bay (mainly late May–early July) and Nunavut (July).[5]

Elsewhere in N. America, casual to very rare (mainly Nov.–Mar.) in interior Southeast and on Great Plains; exceptionally (Dec.–Apr.) west to s.-coastal Alaska, interior B.C., and Wash.[6]

FIELD IDENTIFICATION

SIMILAR SPECIES

Large size and massive bill usually distinctive, but smaller females might be confused with other species. This is the only black-backed, pink-legged gull normally found in e. N. America, where the other regularly occurring dark-winged large gulls are American Herring Gull and Lesser Black-backed Gull.

Adult Cycle. Note overall size, bill size and shape, slaty blackish upperparts, wingtip pattern, and leg color.

LESSER BLACK-BACKED GULL much smaller with slender bill, relatively longer and narrower wings, slaty gray upperparts (Kodak 9–13), yellowish legs, wingtips with less white (P10 has small white mirror, P9 often lacks mirror), head heavily streaked in basic.

First Cycle. Great Black-backed Gull's pale head and underparts, boldly checkered upperparts, and tail pattern, in combination with size and structure, render it distinctive.

AMERICAN HERRING GULL smaller with less stout bill, longer wing projection; darker and browner overall with less boldly checkered upperparts, pale inner primaries form distinct pale panel on upperwing, tail with wider and solid blackish distal band, bill often with more-distinct pinkish basally.

LESSER BLACK-BACKED GULL smaller and slimmer with slender bill, longer wing projection; head and underparts average browner, upperparts with narrower pale edgings; bases of greater coverts typically all dark; black tail band wider and more solid.

Second Cycle. Note large size and stout bill of Great Black-backed.

AMERICAN HERRING GULL often has some pale gray on upperparts, blackish distal tail band wider and more solid, eyes often pale, bill often extensively pink based but lacks bold creamy tip.

LESSER BLACK-BACKED GULL smaller and slimmer with slender bill, longer wing projection; upperparts less boldly variegated and often with slaty gray feathers; eyes average paler and legs brighter flesh to yellowish flesh.

Third Cycle. LESSER BLACK-BACKED GULL differs in much the same ways as does adult (see above), although legs can be fleshy, especially in winter.

RARER SPECIES

Several other species of large gulls might be confused with Great Black-backed but do not normally occur in the same geographic range.

Adult Cycle. Note Great Black-backed's overall large size, bill size and shape, slaty blackish upperparts, wingtip pattern, and flesh pink legs.

WESTERN GULL (w. N. America) has slaty gray upperparts (Kodak 8–11), less white in wingtips, typically brighter pink legs, brighter bill in winter (usually lacking dark marks), chrome yellow orbital ring.

SLATY-BACKED GULL (n. Pacific) has slaty gray upperparts (Kodak 9.5–11.5), brighter pink legs, different wingtip pattern, extensive basic head streaking.

KELP GULL (mainly S. America) has yellowish legs, slightly blacker upperparts (Kodak 14–15.5) with less white in wingtips, and broader white trailing edge to secondaries.

YELLOW-FOOTED GULL (Gulf of California) has slaty gray upperparts (Kodak 9–10.5), less white in wingtips, bright yellow to fleshy yellow legs, brighter bill in winter (usually lacking dark marks), chrome yellow orbital ring.

HYBRID KELP GULL × AMERICAN HERRING GULL not well known. Upperparts (at least of F1 hybrids) slaty gray and less blackish, legs can be flesh; note overall structure, bill size and shape, details of wingtip pattern.

First Cycle. Note Great Black-backed's overall size and shape, bill size and shape, upperwing pattern, and tail pattern. Also see Yellow-legged Gull (nominate *michahellis*; casual e. N. America), European Herring Gull (casual e. N. America), and Vega Gull (w. Alaska) under the accounts for those taxa.

KELP GULL (S. America) averages more-extensive dusky markings on head and underparts, upperparts plainer and darker (bases of greater coverts typically all dark), tail mostly black, legs dusky flesh.

SLATY-BACKED GULL more uniform brownish overall with mostly black tail, distinct pale panel on inner primaries, brighter flesh pink legs.

WESTERN GULL dark brownish overall with mostly black tail.

YELLOW-FOOTED GULL has darker and plainer upperparts (extensive PA1 molt often includes upperwing coverts), mostly black tail.

HYBRID KELP GULL × AMERICAN HERRING GULL not well known but darker overall, resembling Kelp Gull or Lesser Black-backed Gull in plumage.

Second Cycle. Note large size and stout bill of Great Black-backed. Also see Yellow-legged Gull, European Herring Gull, and Vega Gull under accounts for those taxa.

KELP GULL. Besides structure, upperparts often more solidly blackish slate, legs greenish yellow, tail usually with broader blackish distal band.

SLATY-BACKED GULL more uniform and darker overall with less boldly checkered upperparts, brighter pink legs; primaries with contrasting pale inner panel, tail more extensively blackish.

WESTERN GULL has plainer upperparts (often with some slaty gray), often dingier underparts, and extensive black tail band.

YELLOW-FOOTED GULL has plainer upperparts (with extensive slaty gray), extensively black or mixed black-and-white tail, flesh to yellow-flesh legs.

HYBRID KELP GULL × AMERICAN HERRING GULL resembles Lesser Black-backed Gull in plumage.

Third Cycle. Western Gull, Slaty-backed Gull, Yellow-footed Gull, and Kelp Gull all differ in much the same ways as do adults (see above and relevant accounts).

HABITAT AND BEHAVIOR

Mainly coastal but also on the Great Lakes. Found on beaches, at estuaries, fishing harbors, dumps, parking lots, and ranges over inshore waters (mainly within 50 km of land) and inland to lakes, rivers, farmland, etc. Nests in small colonies or in scattered pairs on inshore rocky islands, beach barrier islands, islets in lakes and rivers, and locally on rooftops. Nonbreeding birds often in small flocks up to 20–30 birds (locally up to a hundred or more), associating readily with other gulls and water birds. Feeds commonly by scavenging; also forages in intertidal and surface waters for marine invertebrates and preys on eggs, young and adult birds.

DESCRIPTION AND MOLT

Adult Cycle. Complete PB molt (June/July–Nov./Jan.) produces adult basic plumage: head, neck, and underparts white; crown and hindneck with variable (usually light) dusky streaking and flecking. Upperparts slaty blackish (Kodak 13–15) with black wingtips (black on outer web of P9–P10, sometimes also P8, extends to primary coverts; P5 sometimes with limited black), white scapular and tertial crescents, and white tips to outer primaries. Uppertail coverts and tail white. White trailing edge to secondaries and inner primaries breaks into discrete white tips on outer primaries; P6–P7 typically have narrow white tongue-tips and black subterminal bands, P9 has large white mirror (P8 rarely a small mirror), and P10 has large white tip. Underwings show black wingtips (with white P10 tip and mirrors, white tongue-tips out to P7) blending into white-tipped, slaty gray inner primaries and secondaries. Eyes olive to dull pale lemon, orbital ring reddish (can be dark gray to pinkish in winter). Bill yellow (often suffused pinkish basally in winter) with orange-red to red gonydeal spot and, in winter, usually a dark distal mark. Legs flesh pink, often paler during height of PB molt. Partial PA molt (*Oct.*–Mar./Apr.) produces adult alternate plumage: head and neck clean white (usually by Mar.); white primary tips reduced through wear. By spring, orbital ring reddish orange, legs average brighter flesh pink, bill brighter yellow with red gonydeal spot, and usually lacks dark distal marks.

First Cycle. Juvenile (Aug.–Feb.): head, neck, and underparts whitish with variable dusky brown streaking and mottling (often forming a dark eye-patch), becoming white on vent and undertail coverts, which have narrow dark bars. Upperparts dark brown with bold pale buff (bleaching to whitish) notched edgings and bars creating a contrasty, checkered appearance. Tertials blackish brown with coarsely notched whitish tips and edging. Uppertail coverts and tail white with broad black distal tail band typically watered down by internal, narrow white barring; tail base and uppertail coverts with fairly sparse dark bars. Remiges blackish with fine white tips to primaries in fresh plumage, narrow white secondary tips; inner webs of inner primaries variably paler and browner, forming poorly to moderately contrasting pale panel on spread upperwing. IN FLIGHT: head and underparts whitish, upperparts boldly checkered, with dark remiges; contrasting white uppertail coverts and tail with watered black distal tail band; underwings medium brown with grayer remiges that can look reflectively pale. Eyes dark, bill black, usually with some dull flesh basally; legs dull flesh to flesh pink. PA1 molt (Oct.–Apr./May; does not include upperwing coverts) produces first alternate plumage: head, neck, and underparts whiter. A1 scapulars range from dark brown with blackish centers and broad whitish edging to pale gray with black subterminal bars or anchor marks. Bill black with variable dull flesh basally, sometimes a fine pale horn tip; legs flesh pink to grayish flesh; eyes dark.

Second Cycle. Complete PB2 molt (late Apr./May–Sept./Oct.) into second basic plumage: often looks similar overall to first cycle. Head, neck, and underparts white with variable (usually sparse) dusky streaking on head, neck, and chest, diffuse dusky mottling on sides, and sparse dark bars on undertail coverts. Upperparts overall with boldly variegated pattern of blackish brown, whitish, and pale brown; greater coverts typically with fairly fine speckling and barring (unlike boldly barred first-cycle coverts); sometimes a few dark slaty feathers appear on back. Uppertail coverts and tail white with blackish distal tail band variably speckled and mixed with white; tail base and uppertail coverts with sparse dark bars. Remiges similar to first cycle but secondaries more broadly tipped white, inner primaries slightly paler and browner (often forming a pale panel), P10 can have a small white mirror. Underwings medium gray-brown, much like first cycle. Eyes dark to medium brown, bill typically dull flesh basally, black distally, with a distinct pale horn tip, legs flesh pink to grayish flesh. Partial PA2 molt (Sept.–Apr.; can

include some upperwing coverts) produces second alternate plumage: head, neck, and underparts whiter, back attains dark slaty feathers (from a few to forming a mostly solid saddle), upperwing coverts often bleach paler, and some birds attain one or more dark slaty median coverts. Eyes brownish olive to pale brown; in summer, orbital ring can brighten to orange, and some birds develop yellow bill with reddish gonydeal smudge and black subterminal band. Legs pale flesh to flesh pink.

Third Cycle. Complete PB3 molt (May/June–Oct./Nov.) produces variable third basic plumage: some retarded plumages resemble second cycle (but note greater coverts, bill pattern, and inner primaries), others overall quite adultlike. Head, neck, and underparts white with fine dusky streaking on head, neck, and chest. Upperparts dark slaty to blackish slate overall with variable extent of brownish and patterned wing coverts and tertials; some birds also with variegated scapulars. Wingtips black with narrow to distinct white tips to outer primaries. Tail white with variable, usually indistinct, dark-speckled distal band; rarely may be all white. Remiges similar in pattern to adult but often browner, with blackish on primary coverts and alula; P9 can lack mirror, and white tip to P10 often reduced to a mirror. Underwings have slight dusky mottling on coverts. Eyes dark to pale brownish; bill typically flesh pink with broad black subterminal band and creamy to pale horn tip; legs pale flesh to flesh pink. Partial PA3 molt (*Sept.*–Mar./Apr.) into third alternate plumage: dark markings on head and neck reduced to absent, upperparts become more solidly slaty on some birds; white tips to outer primaries often lost by wear. Orbital ring can brighten to orange, bill usually brightens and in summer may be indistinguishable from adult, but typically with dark distal marks. Adultlike plumage attained by complete PB4 molt (May/June–Nov./Dec.).

HYBRIDS
Presumably with American Herring Gull,[7,8] Glaucous Gull,[9,10] and European Herring Gull.[11]

NOTES
1. Ewins et al. 1992; 2. *NAB* 59:505 (2005); 3. Howell et al. 1992; 4. Jones 2002; 5. Couch 1977; 6. Wahl et al 2005; 7. Andrle 1972; 8. Jehl 1960; 9. B. Mactavish pers. comm. (see p. 491); 10. Wilson 1951; 11. H. J. Lehto and H. Lehto photos

LENGTH 22–26.3 IN. (56–67 CM)
PHOTOS 30.0–30.36; I.22–I.23, I.38–I.42, 25C.2

IDENTIFICATION SUMMARY

This large, dark-backed, pink-legged gull is a rare visitor to Alaska from Asia and occurs casually southward in N. America. Bill stout but relatively parallel edged, relatively slender on some females. At rest, tail tip falls about equal with, or slightly shorter than, tip of P7. Adult has dark slaty gray upperparts (Kodak 9.5–11.5); fairly extensive dusky brownish streaking on head and neck in basic plumage often concentrated around eyes. Juvenile medium brownish overall with mostly dark tail, relatively diffuse paler patterning, two-tone middle to outer primaries; plumage often bleaches strikingly over first winter. PA1 starts Oct.–Feb. Subsequent ages variable in appearance. All ages have pink legs; adult eyes pale lemon; orbital ring reddish.

No other dark-backed large gull occurs regularly in its northern range, so older immature and adult Slaty-backed Gull normally distinctive by virtue of dark slaty gray upperparts and pink legs, but see adult Vega Gull (medium gray upperparts contrast with black wingtips). Also see Western Gull (w. N. America) and Great Black-backed Gull (e. N. America). In first cycle also see Vega Gull, American Herring Gull, and note that various hybrids can resemble Slaty-backed Gull. See Similar Species and Rarer Species for details.

TAXONOMY

Usually considered monotypic, but subspecies *ochotensis* has been described from the Sea of Okhotsk, reportedly averaging darker above and slightly smaller overall than (nominate) *schistisagus*.[1] Has also been considered conspecific with Vega Gull because of interbreeding between the two in s. Koryakland.[2]

STATUS AND DISTRIBUTION

Ne. Asia, wintering south to Hong Kong, ranging to nw. Hawaiian Is. and w. Alaska.

Breeding. Has bred (1996–1997) in a Glaucous Gull colony at Cape Romanzof, w. Alaska,[3] and may have nested on occasion in w. Aleutians.[4]

Nonbreeding. In Alaska, generally rare in spring, summer, and fall on Bering and Chukchi coasts and on offshore islands in Bering

Sea. Becomes locally uncommon (for example, on Seward Peninsula and St. Lawrence Is.) in fall (Aug.–Sept.). Casual to very rare (mid-May–Aug.) on Beaufort Sea coast east to Prudhoe Bay. In w. Aleutians, rare in spring (late Apr.–early June), very rare or casual in summer and fall. In cen. and e. Aleutians and s.-coastal Alaska, very rare or casual at any season; rare (mid-Aug.–mid-Mar., mainly late Oct.–early Dec.) in se. Alaska.

Elsewhere in N. America, casual to very rare (July–early Sept.) in Yukon and (mainly Nov.–Mar.) from B.C. south to cen. Calif. Scattered records (mainly Nov.–Mar.) of third-cycle and adult birds elsewhere in N. America, mainly east to Great Lakes region and s. Que.,[5,6] and south to Colo., exceptionally to s. Tex. and s. Fla. Records from Atlantic Coast, and elsewhere in N. America, tainted by potential of hybridization with Vega and Glaucous-winged Gulls (see King and Carey[7]).

FIELD IDENTIFICATION

SIMILAR SPECIES

No other dark-backed large gull occurs regularly in the Bering Sea region, but beware Vega Gull, which can look deceptively dark-backed when seen against ice or snow. Vagrants need to be separated with care from a variety of potential confusion species and hybrids (see Rarer Species and accounts for Slaty-backed Gull hybrids, p. 492).

Adult Cycle. Note slaty gray tone of upperparts, wingtip contrast and pattern, and overall structure; also see Slaty-backed Gull hybrids (p. 492).

VEGA GULL (w. Alaska) averages lighter in build with more slender bill. Upperparts medium gray (Kodak 7–8) but can look darker against ice; note distinct contrast between upperparts and black wingtip, both perched and in flight, and more contrasting black wingtip on underwing; eyes olive to dirty pale lemon.

WESTERN GULL (w. N. America, regular in se. Alaska) has upperparts slightly paler or similar in shade (Kodak 8–11), but white primary tips smaller at rest, bill more bulbous-tipped and typically brighter in winter (orange-yellow, without dark distal marks), orbital ring yellow, eyes often dusky, and, in winter, has little or no dusky head and neck streaking.

Also note Western's narrower white trailing edge to secondaries, narrower and more-restricted whitish tongue-tips and mirrors on outer primaries, and blackish underside to wingtip.

HYBRID GLAUCOUS-WINGED GULL × WESTERN GULL (w. N. America) has paler upperparts (Kodak 6–8), typically a more bulbous-tipped bill, smaller white tongue-tips on outer primaries, and dusky (not brown-toned) and often smudgier basic head and neck markings.

First Cycle. Note overall size and structure, bill size and shape, two-tone pattern of outer primaries, relatively plain greater coverts.

VEGA GULL less thickset with narrower and relatively longer wings, less stout bill typically dull pinkish at base; some birds may overlap in size and overall shape with Slaty-backed. Plumage generally has more-contrasting patterning, notably, on greater coverts; tail base whiter with narrower and blacker distal band; A1 scapulars neatly marked with bars and anchor patterns; outer primaries darker on inner webs, so spread wingtips lack pale tongues of Slaty-backed. Bleached first-summer Vega Gulls often have blacker tertials; note scapular and tail patterns.

AMERICAN HERRING GULL (widespread) averages less thickset with narrower and relatively longer wings, averages less stout bill that is typically dull pinkish at base. Plumage generally darker and browner with bolder pale patterning, strongly barred tail coverts; outer primaries darker on inner webs, so spread wingtips lack pale tongues of Slaty-backed.

WESTERN GULL averages more thickset with more bulbous-tipped bill, plumage darker and browner overall, darker upperwings lack pale panel on inner to middle primaries, tail more solidly blackish.

THAYER'S GULL (w. N. America) smaller and more lightly built with narrower wings and smaller, less stout bill, shorter legs. Upperparts overall more brightly and boldly patterned. Wing and tail patterns similar to Slaty-backed but tail browner, and dark/light contrast on outer primaries averages stronger at shaft.

HYBRID GLAUCOUS-WINGED GULL × AMERICAN HERRING GULL (w. N. America). Slaty-backed upperwing typically has relatively plain and pale greater coverts, contrastingly pale inner primaries, and more-distinct inner web/outer web contrast on the outer primaries (at least in fresh plumage), but these features may be matched on hybrids; deep pink legs of some Slaty-backeds may be outside range of hybrids. Field characters need study.

HYBRID GLAUCOUS-WINGED GULL × WESTERN GULL averages bulkier and broader winged, with a more bulbous-tipped bill. Hybrids typically have more distinctly patterned greater coverts, less contrasting pale panel on inner primaries, and more uniformly dark tail.

Second Cycle. Note overall size and structure, bill size and shape, two-tone pattern of outer primaries, slaty gray incoming feathers on back.

VEGA GULL and AMERICAN HERRING GULL often more boldly barred on upperparts in fresh B2 with incoming medium (Vega) to pale (American Herring) gray on upperparts; inner primaries contrast more abruptly with blacker outer primaries, which lack strong two-tone pattern of Slaty-backed.

THAYER'S GULL paler overall with incoming back feathers pale gray. Wing and tail patterns similar to Slaty-backed but tail less blackish, and dark/light contrast on outer primaries averages stronger at shaft.

WESTERN GULL has more-uniform and darker upperwings with poorly contrasting pale inner primaries, lacks two-tone outer primaries of Slaty-backed.

HYBRID GLAUCOUS-WINGED GULL × AMERICAN HERRING GULL has blackish to dark brown wingtips and tail, incoming pale gray on upperparts. Field characters need study.

HYBRID GLAUCOUS-WINGED GULL × WESTERN GULL has more-uniform and often darker upperwing coverts, but primary pattern might approach Slaty-backed; incoming gray on upperparts paler (Kodak 6–8), wings and tail blackish to dark brown.

Third Cycle. Differences from Vega Gull, Western Gull, and hybrids much as adult cycle (which see); note wingtip pattern, bill size and shape, tone of upperparts, leg color.

RARER SPECIES

Also see Great Black-backed Gull, Kelp Gull, Lesser Black-backed Gull, and (as immatures) Yellow-legged Gull and European Herring Gull (differences given under those taxa).

Adult Cycle. Note slaty gray tone of upperparts, leg color, wingtip pattern, and overall structure, especially bill size and shape.

YELLOW-FOOTED GULL (Gulf of Calif.) has slaty upperparts similar to Slaty-backed but stouter bill more swollen tipped, legs yellow, wingtips more extensively blackish with no bold pattern of white tongue-tips. Prebasic molt averages 2–3 months earlier than Slaty-backed.

First Cycle. Note overall size and structure, bill size and shape, two-tone pattern of outer primaries, relatively plain greater coverts.

YELLOW-FOOTED GULL has more swollen-tipped bill, darker upperwings lack pale panel on inner primaries; PA1 molt often extensive, including upperwing coverts.

Second Cycle. Note overall size and structure, bill size and shape, two-tone pattern of outer primaries, incoming slaty gray feathers on upperparts.

YELLOW-FOOTED GULL has flesh to yellowish legs, upperparts mostly slate gray (like third-cycle Slaty-backed) but tail mostly black or mixed black-and-white, bill flesh to yellow with black distal third in winter. Prebasic molt averages 2–3 months earlier than Slaty-backed.

Third Cycle. Differs from other species in much the same respects as adult cycle (which see); note wingtip pattern, bill size and shape, tone of upperparts, leg color.

HABITAT AND BEHAVIOR

Much as other large gulls such as Glaucous, Vega, Glaucous-winged, and American Herring, with which it usually occurs at feeding and loafing areas.

DESCRIPTION AND MOLT

Dark areas of plumage in this species, such as upperwing coverts of first-cycle birds and basic head streaking of adults, seem especially prone to bleaching. However, the wide variation in adult upperpart tone attributed to this species by some authors[8] is presumably due to hybridization with other taxa.[9]

Adult Cycle. Complete PB molt (June/July–Dec./Jan.) produces adult basic plumage: head, neck, and underparts white; head, neck, and sometimes upper chest with variable dusky brown to warm brown streaking and mottling often concentrated around eyes. Upperparts dark slaty gray (Kodak 9.5–11.5) with black wingtips (black on outer webs of P9–P10, sometimes also P8, extends to primary coverts), broad white scapular and tertial crescents, and broad white tips to outer primaries. Uppertail coverts and tail white. Broad white trailing edge to secondaries (often shows as a skirt) and inner primaries breaks into discrete white tips on outer primaries; P5–P7/P8 have white tongue-tips; P10 or P9–P10 have white mirrors. Underwings show dark slaty to silvery black wingtips (with white primary tips, mirrors, and tongue-tips) blending into white-tipped, dusky gray inner primaries and secondaries, which form a dusky subterminal band on underwings. Eyes pale lemon (rarely dark), orbital ring reddish. Bill yellowish or variably fleshy at base with orange-red to red gonydeal spot and sometimes a dark distal mark. Legs rich pink, perhaps paler during height of PB molt. Partial PA molt (*Oct.–Mar./Apr.*) produces adult alternate plumage: head and neck clean white (rarely before Mar./Apr.). By spring, orbital ring, bill, and legs brighter, bill lacks dark distal marks; white primary tips reduced through wear.

First Cycle. Juvenile (*Aug.–Feb.*): medium brown to medium dark brown overall. Head, neck, and underparts variably streaked and mottled whitish, becoming white on vent and undertail coverts, which have brown barring. Upperparts with buff (bleaching to whitish) scaly and notched edgings, the greater coverts typically fairly plain or with variable, often fairly coarse but diffuse, distal whitish notching. Tertials dark brown with notched whitish tips and distal edging, the dark tertial bases merging with secondary bases that often show as a skirt. Uppertail coverts whitish with brown barring. Wingtips blackish (bleaching to dark brown) with narrow whitish fringes to tips; contrastingly darker than tertials. Outer primaries blackish brown with paler inner webs often forming a two-tone pattern on backlit spread wing, merging inward with pale inner primary panel. Secondaries blackish brown, tipped whitish. Tail blackish brown overall with narrow whitish tip; variable, wavy whitish bars and marbling at basal corners; often irregular white ribbing on outer web of R6; can show a broad, dark distal band from below. IN FLIGHT: brownish overall with mostly dark tail, dark secondary bar (often contrasting strongly with pale greater coverts in faded plumage), and pale inner to middle primary panel blending into outer primaries, which, when bleached, can show distinct two-tone pattern; underwings medium brown with remiges often reflectively pale. Eyes dark, bill blackish and often with some dull pinkish basally by midwinter, legs dusky flesh to flesh pink. PA1 molt (*Oct.–Apr./May*; does not include upperwing coverts) produces variable first alternate plumage: head, neck, and underparts often bleach to mostly whitish, with variable brownish (worn juvenal) to smoky gray (A1) streaking and mottling. A1 scapulars typically brownish to grayish (often fading to whitish) with dark centers or shaft streaks; less often with anchor patterns or subterminal bars. Blackish brown to dark brown wingtips contrast with faded upperwing coverts; greater coverts often bleach to a plain, whitish panel. Bill typically shows some dull-flesh to pinkish basally, sometimes a pale horn tip; legs flesh pink. Note: Some birds retain most or all juvenal plumage through late winter and can be very bleached, almost whitish in overall appearance except for flight feathers.

Second Cycle. Complete PB2 molt (May/June–Oct./Nov.) into second basic plumage. Head, neck, and underparts streaked and mottled whitish and dusky brown, often whiter overall on head and chest; undertail coverts with sparse dark bars. Upperparts medium dark gray-brown overall with diffuse whitish to pale brown edgings and tips to wing coverts and scapulars, often a few dark slaty scapulars and mantle feathers; tertials blackish brown to dark brown with broad whitish to marbled pale brownish tips. Wingtips blackish with fine pale fringes, most distinct out to P5/P6. White uppertail coverts have sparse dark marks and contrast with narrowly white-tipped, mostly blackish tail; outer rectrices with white basal corners more diffuse and speckled than first cycle. Upperwing pattern of remiges similar to first cycle, but outer primaries have more distinct pale tongues, inner primaries paler overall, secondaries average paler and do not always form a contrasting dark bar. Wing-linings medium brown with underside of remiges often reflectively pale. Eyes brown to pale grayish, bill averages more extensively pinkish at base than first cycle and often has small pale horn tip; sometimes extensively flesh pink on basal two-thirds with blackish tip or subterminal band. Legs flesh pink. Partial PA2 molt (Sept.–*Apr.*; can include some upperwing coverts) produces second alternate plumage: head, neck, and underparts whitish with variable dusky mottling and streaking, often concentrated as a dusky belly smudge; head, neck, and chest often bleach to mostly white. Back becomes mottled to almost solidly slaty gray in contrast to faded whitish and brownish upperwing coverts; some birds attain a few slaty gray upperwing coverts, especially median coverts. Eyes pale lemon to brown, orbital ring can be reddish. Through winter, bill typically pinkish basally, blackish distally; in summer some have a yellow bill with reddish gonydeal spot and black distal band. Legs flesh pink.

Third Cycle. Complete PB3 molt (May/June–Nov.) produces third basic plumage: resembles adult basic overall but with more extensive dusky streaking and mottling on head, neck, and underparts; upperwing coverts mixed slaty gray and brownish; white scapular and tertial crescents and tips to remiges narrower (but still broad); P10 mirror smaller and P9 mirror absent; smaller and more diffuse white tongue-tips on P5–P7/P8; white tail typically has fairly broad, often broken, blackish distal band but can be all white or with small dark subterminal marks; white wing-linings lightly washed and mottled with brownish. Bill ranges from adultlike with a blackish subterminal mark to pinkish with a black subterminal band. Partial PA3 molt (*Sept.*–Mar./Apr.) into third alternate plumage: dark markings on head and neck reduced to absent; bill brightens by summer and often indistinguishable from adult, or with dark distal marks. White tips to outer primaries can be lost by wear. Adult plumage attained by complete PB4 molt (June–Nov./Dec.) although some fourth-cycle birds probably show dusky marks on tail and less white in wingtips.

HYBRIDS

With Vega Gull in Siberia,[10] with Glaucous-winged Gull in Kamchatka and on Commander Is.[11,12,13]

NOTES

1. Vaurie 1965:735; 2. Ibid.; 3. McCaffery et al. 1997; 4. Gibson and Byrd unpubl. data; 5. Goetz et al. 1986; 6. Gustafson and Peterjohn 1994; 7. King and Carey 1999; 8. Gustafson and Peterjohn 1994; 9. King and Carey 1999; 10. Vaurie 1965:735; 11. Firsova and Levada 1982; 12. Grabovsky et al. unpubl. data; 13. King and Carey 1999

LENGTH 21–26 IN. (53.5–66 CM)
PHOTOS 31.0–31.22; I.13, I.41, I.44–I.77, 33.37

IDENTIFICATION SUMMARY
This large, dark-backed, pink-legged gull is common along the U.S. Pacific Coast, where its is characteristic of the California Current coastal upwelling ecosystem. Heavily built and broad-winged (typically showing a skirt at rest). Bill typically stout and bulbous tipped, but relatively slender on some females; compared to Glaucous-winged Gull, bill of Western often looks shorter and more bulbous-tipped. At rest, tail tip about equal with or slightly shorter than tip of P7. Adult has slaty gray upperparts (Kodak 8–11, see Taxonomy) and reduced dusky head and neck streaking in basic plumage. Juvenal dark brownish overall with solidly blackish tail. PA1 starts Sept.–Nov. Subsequent ages variable in appearance.

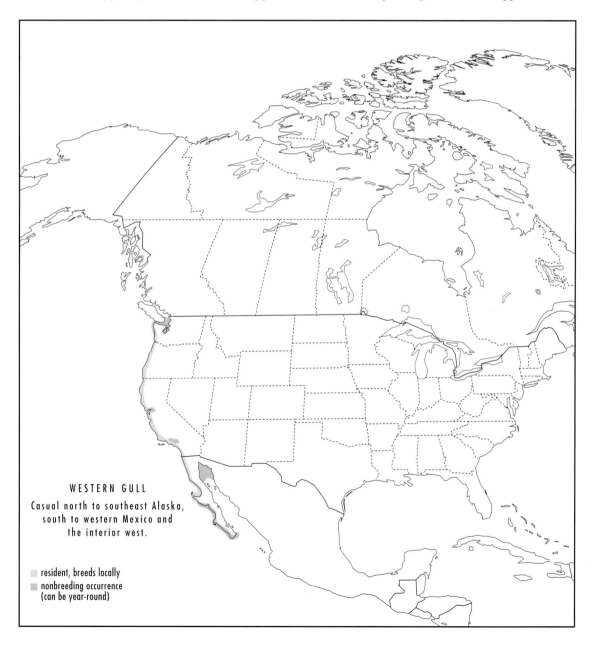

WESTERN GULL
Casual north to southeast Alaska, south to western Mexico and the interior west.

resident, breeds locally
nonbreeding occurrence (can be year-round)

All ages have pink legs; adult eyes pale to dusky; orbital ring chrome yellow.

No other large dark-backed gull occurs regularly in its range, so older immature and adult Western Gull normally distinctive by virtue of slaty gray upperparts and pink legs. Most similar species are Slaty-backed Gull (N. Pacific) and Yellow-footed Gull (Gulf of California). In first cycle also see Herring Gull, and note that hybrid Western × Glaucous-winged Gulls show various combinations of parental characters—and can also resemble other species (see hybrid account; pp. 479–481).

TAXONOMY

Two subspecies recognized, distinguished mainly by darkness of upperparts although southern birds average slightly smaller:[1] paler-backed (Kodak 8–9.5) nominate *occidentalis* (Northern Western Gull) and darker-backed (Kodak 9.5–11) *wymani* (Southern Western Gull). Subspecies boundary not well known,[2,3] and tone of upperparts somewhat clinal:[4] typical nominate *occidentalis* breeds from n. California south to San Mateo County (37–42° north), typical *wymani* from California Channel Is. south to n. Baja California Sur (27–34° north). Breeding birds in Monterey and San Luis Obispo counties (35–36.5° north) intermediate in upperpart tone (Kodak 9–10), whereas "Western Gulls" in Oregon and Washington paler above (Kodak 7–8) than typical *occidentalis*, perhaps reflecting introgression with Glaucous-winged Gull.[5]

Northern *occidentalis* hybridizes commonly with Glaucous-winged Gull in Washington and Oregon,[6,7,8] and some authors consider these taxa conspecific.[9] Yellow-footed Gull of Mexico formerly considered a subspecies of Western Gull.[10]

STATUS AND DISTRIBUTION

W. N. America; accidental in Hawaii.

Breeding. Common to fairly common resident (breeds Apr.–Aug.) on Pacific Coast and islands from s. Wash. (north to Cape Flattery) south to Baja Calif. Peninsula, Mex. (south to around 27° north). May breed sw. B.C., but distinguishing pure birds from hybrids with Glaucous-winged Gull is problematic. A few pairs have bred since 2001 in n. Sinaloa, Mex.[11]

Nonbreeding. Fairly common to rare nonbreeding visitor (year-round) north to sw. B.C. and Queen Charlotte Is., south (mainly Sept.–Apr.) to the tip of Baja Calif. Peninsula, Mex., and rare but increasing (year-round)

in n. Gulf of Calif. Rare visitor north to se. Alaska (mainly Sept.–Mar.), exceptionally north to Bristol Bay (June), and casual (Jan.–June) south along Pacific Coast of Mex. to Oaxaca.

Uncommon to rare in protected marine waters of Wash. away from the coast, ranging in fall and winter up Columbia R. to se. Wash.; rare inland in Ore. away from Columbia R. In Calif., generally increasing in inland valleys near the coast, especially in Los Angeles Co. Rare (mainly Sept.–Mar.) in Sacramento Valley and rare but increasing at Salton Sea. Casual in Calif. east of Sierra Nevada (scattered records year-round). Farther inland, casual at best (mainly Oct.–Dec.; also Apr.–May and July) with scattered reports east to s. Lake Michigan[12] and se. Tex. A bird that ranged from Ala. to Fla., 1977–1990, was thought by some to be a Western Gull,[13] but many believed it may have been a hybrid.[14]

FIELD IDENTIFICATION

SIMILAR SPECIES

Western Gull is the only dark-backed large gull normally found in its range, although first-cycle birds can be confused with other West Coast species. Also see hybrid Glaucous-winged Gull × Western Gull account (pp. 479–481).

Adult Cycle. Several species of dark-backed large gulls can be confused with Western Gull but have limited range overlap (see Rarer Species). Note leg color, darkness of upperparts, wingtip pattern, and overall structure; in winter, adult Western Gull typically has a bright yellow to orange-yellow bill that sets it apart from most other gulls at that season. Adult voice, including long-call, higher pitched than adult Yellow-footed Gull (but can be similar to second-cycle Yellow-footed).

YELLOW-FOOTED GULL (Gulf of California) has slaty gray upperparts (Kodak 9–10.5) similar to Southern Western Gull but bill thicker and more swollen tipped (often bulging slightly on culmen as well as distinctly at gonydeal expansion), legs yellow, red gonydeal spot typically larger (reflecting deeper bill of Yellow-footed). Wingtips of Yellow-footed more extensively blackish, often with blackish subterminal marks on P4. Prebasic molt averages 1–2 months earlier than Western Gull and white tips to outer primaries usually much reduced by wear in winter (bolder and fresher on Western).

SLATY-BACKED GULL (n. Pacific) has slightly darker upperparts (Kodak 9.5–11.5) than

Northern Western Gull, bill less bulbous tipped (and duller yellow in winter, often with flesh pink basally), orbital ring reddish, and head and neck with distinct brownish streaking in basic plumage. Also note Slaty-backed's broader white trailing edge to secondaries, bolder white tongue-tips and mirrors on outer primaries, and more silvery (less blackish) underside to wingtip (but see hybrid Glaucous-winged Gull × Western Gull).

LESSER BLACK-BACKED GULL (widespread, but rare in West) more lightly built and slimmer overall with relatively longer and narrower wings (tail tip falls around tip of P6), slender bill. Legs fleshy yellow to yellow. Adult basic has distinct dusky head and neck streaking, and its duller yellow to fleshy yellow bill often has blackish distal marks; orbital ring reddish.

First Cycle. Note overall size and structure, bill size and shape, overall dark brown aspect. Also see hybrid Glaucous-winged Gull × Western Gull account (pp. 479–481).

YELLOW-FOOTED GULL averages stouter and more swollen-tipped bill, but some are very similar in overall appearance to Southern Western Gull. PA1 molt of Western can include upperwing coverts and tertials on up to 10 percent of *wymani* (replaced on up to 90 percent of Yellow-footeds); tail coverts have denser dark barring on Western; legs average brighter pinkish on Western; belly more extensively and cleaner white on Yellow-footed. A few birds, however, may defy specific identification. From Oct.–Nov. onward, note that first-cycle Yellow-footed Gulls with extensive PA1 molt, including most upperwing coverts and tertials, recall fresh second-basic Western Gull and other species; note pointed juvenal primaries and all-black tail of first-cycle Yellow-footed, plus its deep and swollen-tipped bill.

CALIFORNIA GULL (w. N. America) averages smaller and more lightly built with relatively longer primary projection, narrower wings, slender bill usually sharply bicolored pink with black tip by early winter. Plumage can be very similar to Western but head and neck usually grizzled with whitish (not solidly dark as typical of Western), forehead and lores often bleach to whitish; A1 scapulars typically more variegated and often with distinct anchor marks (a pattern rare on Western).

AMERICAN HERRING GULL (widespread) less thickset with narrower wings, bill less stout and bulbous tipped, typically dull pinkish at base; A1 scapulars often boldly barred pale gray and blackish. Plumage overall gray-brown, less sooty brown than Western. In flight, note pale inner primary panel on upperwings, often more white at base of tail. First-cycle Herrings often have relatively clean-cut bleached whitish head rarely shown by Western.

THAYER'S GULL (mainly w. N. America) smaller with relatively slender bill, upperparts typically with bolder, frostier patterning, brownish black wingtips usually have distinct whitish tips and fringes. Upperwing has contrasting pale panel on inner primaries blending into two-tone outer primaries; tail mostly dark brown.

SLATY-BACKED GULL averages less bulbous-tipped bill, plumage paler overall, bill usually blackish through winter. Upperwings show pale panel on inner primaries blending into two-tone outer primaries, tail has white barring at base.

LESSER BLACK-BACKED GULL smaller and slimmer with long primary projection, relatively slender black bill; tail base barred white, with contrasting black distal tail band.

Second Cycle. Note overall size and structure, bill size and shape, pink legs, incoming slaty gray on upperparts. Also see hybrid Glaucous-winged Gull × Western Gull account (pp. 479–481).

YELLOW-FOOTED GULL has stouter and more swollen-tipped bill. Its advanced appearance often recalls third-cycle Western Gull, with more-uniform slaty upperparts than second-cycle Western; legs often yellowish. Distinguished from third-cycle Western by deeper and more swollen-tipped bill, usually fleshy yellow to yellow legs; tail mostly black or mixed black-and-white.

CALIFORNIA GULL smaller and slimmer with strongly bicolored bill (pink to gray-green basally), incoming medium gray on upperparts, paler gray-green to flesh legs; upperwing has contrasting pale panel on inner primaries.

AMERICAN HERRING GULL less thickset with narrower wings, less bulbous-tipped bill; upperparts usually with some to extensive pale gray, and upperwings have more contrasting pale panel on inner primaries.

THAYER'S GULL smaller with relatively slender bill, contrasting pale panel on inner primaries blending into two-tone outer primaries, and incoming pale gray on upperparts.

SLATY-BACKED GULL best told by upperwing pattern, with pale inner primary panel blending into two-tone outer primaries, paler secondaries with less-contrasting white trailing edge, and overall plainer and paler coverts, especially greater coverts; in second summer, upperwings of Slaty-backed often more bleached and paler, contrasting more with dark saddle than on Western.

LESSER BLACK-BACKED GULL slimmer and longer

winged with relatively slender bill; note white tail base with variable black distal band; legs often yellowish by summer.

Third Cycle. Differences much as adult cycle (which see).

RARER SPECIES

Adult Cycle. Note leg color, slaty gray tone of upperparts, wingtip pattern, and overall structure; in winter, Western Gull typically has a bright yellow to orange-yellow bill that sets it apart from most other gulls in its range. See Great Black-backed Gull and Kelp Gull (differences given under those species). Also see hybrid Glaucous-winged Gull × Western Gull account (pp. 479–481).

HYBRID KELP GULL × AMERICAN HERRING GULL. F1 hybrids probably less thickset overall, perhaps with less bulbous-tipped bill; legs yellow to greenish yellow.

HYBRID AMERICAN HERRING GULL × GREAT BLACK-BACKED GULL intermediate in size and structure between the parent species, with pale slaty upperparts and pinkish legs that could overlap Western Gull; orbital ring varies from yellow to red. Basic head streaking finer and perhaps more extensive in midwinter than Western, and wingtip averages more white: P10 has a large white mirror or white tip, P9 typically has a small white mirror, and there are white tongue-tips out to P7 or P8.

First Cycle. Note overall size and structure, bill size and shape, overall dark brown aspect. See Great Black-backed Gull, Kelp Gull, Vega Gull, European Herring Gull, and Yellow-legged Gull (differences given under those species). Also see hybrid Glaucous-winged Gull × Western Gull account (pp. 479–481).

HYBRID AMERICAN HERRING GULL × GREAT BLACK-BACKED GULL undescribed at this age but presumably intermediate in size and structure between the parent species; upperwings likely to be paler on inner primaries than Western, and tail less extensively blackish.

HYBRID KELP GULL × AMERICAN HERRING GULL poorly known but likely to differ in structure; plumage of F1 similar to Kelp Gull.

Second Cycle. Note overall size and structure, bill size and shape, pink legs, incoming slaty gray on upperparts. See Great Black-backed Gull, Kelp Gull, Vega Gull, European Herring Gull, and Yellow-legged Gull (differences given under those species). Also see hybrid Glaucous-winged Gull × Western Gull account (pp. 479–481).

HYBRID AMERICAN HERRING GULL × GREAT BLACK-BACKED GULL undescribed at this age but presumably intermediate in size and structure between the parent species; upperwings likely to be paler on inner primaries than Western, and tail less extensively blackish.

HYBRID KELP GULL × AMERICAN HERRING GULL likely to differ in structure; plumage similar to Lesser Black-backed Gull.

Third Cycle. Differences much as adult cycle (which see).

HABITAT AND BEHAVIOR

Coastal, favoring fishing harbors, beaches, river mouths, etc. Ranges inland a short distance to dumps, reservoirs, freshwater lakes, also over inshore waters, mainly within 50 km of shore. Nests on rocky islands and islets, coastal cliffs, harbor markers, and even houses. Nonbreeding birds often in flocks (locally to a few thousand birds), associating readily with other gulls and water birds. Feeds commonly by scavenging; also forages in intertidal and surface waters for marine invertebrates and preys on eggs and young birds, also on small adult seabirds at colonies (such as storm-petrels and auklets). Western and Glaucous-winged Gulls and their hybrids dominate coastal feeding sites, which helps explain why Herring Gulls do not winter commonly along the immediate coast in the range of Western Gulls.

DESCRIPTION AND MOLT

L. o. occidentalis (n. California and north).

Adult Cycle. Complete PB molt (mid-May/early July–Nov./Dec.) produces adult basic plumage: head, neck, and underparts white; head and neck with variable (usually slight) dusky clouding and streaking in fresh plumage. This dusky often wears away by early winter and is heaviest in northern birds (reflecting introgression with Glaucous-winged Gull?). Upperparts slaty gray (Kodak 8–9.5) with black wingtips (black on outer webs of P8–P10, sometimes P7–P10, extends to primary coverts), bold white scapular and tertial crescents, and white tips to outer primaries. Uppertail coverts and tail white. White trailing edge to secondaries (often shows as a skirt) and inner primaries breaks into discrete white tips on outer primaries; P5–P6 typically have narrow white tongue-tips, and P10 a white mirror; up to 5 percent or so of adults also have a small white P9 mirror.[15] Underwings show blackish wingtips (with white primary tips and mirrors) blending into white-tipped, dusky gray inner primaries and secondaries, which form a dusky subterminal band on underwings. Eyes lemon whitish to dull olive, orbital ring chrome yellow. Bill bright yellow to orange-yellow with reddish gonydeal spot and sometimes a small dusky mark at gonys; often suffused pinkish at base and with dark distal marks during height of PB molt; returns to bright yellow by early winter. Legs flesh pink, often paler during height of PB molt. Partial PA molt (Oct.–Feb.) produces adult alternate plumage: head and neck clean white (often by Dec./Jan.). By spring, orbital ring, bill, and legs brighter, bill lacks dark distal marks; white primary tips can be lost through wear. Legs of some birds (mainly Feb.–Apr.) become salmon-yellow although typically with pinkish joints and foot webbing.[16]

First Cycle. Juvenile (late July–Nov.): dark sooty brown overall, less often gray-brown and exceptionally very dark, blackish brown. Head, neck, and underparts variably mottled and streaked whitish, becoming white on vent and undertail coverts, which have fairly heavy dark barring; some birds have belly mostly veiled whitish, contrasting sharply with brown chest and flanks. Upperparts with buff (bleaching to whitish) scaly and notched edgings and markings, the greater coverts typically with unmarked (or lightly marked) bases. Tertials blackish brown with notched whitish tips and distal edging, the dark tertial bases merging with dark secondary bases that often show as a skirt. Uppertail coverts whitish with dark barring. Flight feathers blackish, secondaries and tail narrowly tipped whitish, tail with whitish bars at basal corners and often with white ribbing on outer web of R6. IN FLIGHT: dark brown overall (some with contrastingly whitish belly) with whitish uppertail coverts, blackish tail, blackish remiges with narrow white trailing edge to secondaries and poorly contrasting browner panel on inner primaries, and plain brown greater-covert bases; underwings dark but reflective underside of primaries can look silvery. Eyes dark, bill blackish and often with some dull pinkish basally, legs dusky flesh to flesh pink. PA1 molt (Sept./Nov.–Apr./May; exceptionally includes upperwing coverts) produces first alternate plumage: head, neck, chest, and flanks variably mixed sooty brown to gray-brown (new feathers) and paler brown to gingery brown (bleached juvenal feathers), the nape sometimes bleaching to whitish. By spring, some (early-molting?) birds have head, neck, and chest bleached dirty whitish; others at this season (late-molting or starting PB2?) are dark sooty overall. Back mottled dark brownish to sooty gray with pale edgings, the new scapulars ranging from dark sooty brown with blackish shaft streaks and broad pale buff edges (earlier-molted feathers) to dark slaty

with blacker shaft streaks and indistinct browner tips (some later-molted feathers). Blackish to brownish black wingtips contrast with worn brownish upperwing coverts (which can bleach to a whitish and pale brown panel), and outer primaries often show narrow bleached pale tips. Bill typically shows some dull-flesh to pinkish basally, sometimes a pale horn tip; legs flesh pink.

Second Cycle. Complete PB2 molt (Apr./May–Sept./Oct.) into second basic plumage. "Brown type" has head, neck, and underparts mottled dusky brown overall with variable whitish streaking and mottling. Upperparts more uniform than first cycle: mixed dark brown and gray-brown overall, wing coverts in particular with paler tips and bars creating variably scaly to checkered appearance; bases of greater coverts usually solidly patterned and tertials blackish with broad, marbled whitish tips. Wingtips blackish with fine pale fringes that can bleach to whitish. White uppertail coverts have sparse dark marks and contrast with mostly blackish tail; outer rectrices with white basal corners more diffuse and averaging more extensive than first cycle. Upperwings variably gray-brown with blackish wingtips and fairly broad whitish trailing edge to blackish secondaries and brown inner primaries. Underwings dark overall. Eyes dark brown to pale grayish, bill averages more extensively pinkish at base and often has small pale horn tip (sometimes extensively flesh pink on basal two-thirds, with diffusely defined blackish tip), legs flesh pink. "Gray type" (up to 20 percent of birds) has head, neck, and underparts whiter overall, back grayer, and bill typically pinkish with blackish tip or broad distal band. Gray and brown types represent extremes of variability; intermediates common. Partial PA2 molt (mid-Aug./Sept.–Apr.; usually includes some upperwing coverts) produces second alternate plumage: head, neck, and underparts whitish with variable dusky mottling and streaking (bleaching and wearing to mostly white), back becomes mostly slaty gray in contrast to faded brownish upperwing coverts; some birds attain a few slaty gray upperwing coverts, especially median coverts. Eyes pale lemon to brown, orbital ring often yellowish in summer. Through winter, bill typically pinkish basally, blackish distally; in summer often becomes yellow with red gonydeal spot and black distal band—advanced birds have adultlike bill, whereas retarded birds retain blackish bill with limited pinkish basally. Legs flesh pink.

Third Cycle. Complete PB3 molt (May–Oct.)

produces third basic plumage: resembles adult basic overall but with more dusky clouding and streaking on head, neck, and sometimes on chest; browner upperwing coverts; narrower white tips to remiges and smaller to absent P10 mirror (and no P9 mirror); often some blackish on tertial centers, primary coverts, and tail (which varies from all white to extensively black). Birds of this age more often look relatively dark slaty above than other ages (and suggest southern *wymani*), possibly due to the darkening effect of brown pigment in a slaty gray ground color. Underwings like adult but with some dusky on coverts. Bare parts like adult except bill regresses from yellow of second cycle to mostly pinkish and black during end of PB3 molt, often pink to yellow with black subterminal ring in midwinter. Partial PA3 molt (Sept.–Mar.) into third alternate plumage: dark markings on head and neck reduced to absent; bill brightens by summer and often indistinguishable from adult, or with dark distal marks. White tips to outer primaries often lost by wear. Adult plumage attained by complete PB4 molt (mid-May/June–Oct./Nov.).

L. o. wymani (s. California and south).

Molts average 1–2 weeks earlier than *L. o. occidentalis* but much overlap (and interannual variation).

Adult plumages similar to nominate *occidentalis* but upperparts slightly darker slaty gray (Kodak 9.5–11); less contrasting black wingtips have reduced whitish tongue-tips and rarely show subterminal black on P4. Most adults cleanly white headed by November. Eyes lemon whitish to dull olive, similar to *occidentalis*.

Based on comparison of nominate *occidentalis* in n. cen. California and *wymani* in Baja California,[17] several average differences occur in plumage and bare-part progression of immatures, with *wymani* overall more advanced in appearance (but molt timing similar). Thus first-winter *wymani* in some respects (such as bill color, whiter head and underparts) looks as much like Yellow-footed Gull as it does northern Western Gull.

First Cycle. Juvenile: No consistent differences noted. First alternate plumage averages more gray on upperparts, whiter head, neck, and underparts, and bill more often with extensive pink on basal two-thirds from first winter onward; on up to 10 percent of birds, PA1 molt can include a few to many upperwing coverts and some tertials.[18]

Second Cycle. In second basic plumage up to 80 percent of birds are "gray types" (versus up to 20 percent in *occidentalis*). Proportions of bill patterns appear "reversed" between immature *wymani* and *occidentalis*. Thus 75 percent of second-cycle *wymani* in Sept.–Oct. (n = 100) have flesh pink bill with blackish distal third and fine pale tip, while only 20 percent of *occidentalis* at the same season have this pattern. Conversely, 70 percent of second-cycle *occidentalis* in Sept.–Oct. (n = 100) have mostly black bill with limited pinkish at the base, versus only 10 percent of *wymani*.

Third Cycle. In third basic plumage, appearance averages more advanced than *occidentalis* with more fully slate gray upperparts and upperwings (less admixed with brown), tail more often all white. But up to 90 percent of third-cycle *wymani* in Sept.–Oct. (n = 50) have more "immature-like" chalky pink bill with black subterminal band or tip, and only 10 percent have yellowish bill with dark subterminal ring and orange-red gonydeal spot, this latter pattern typical of 50 percent of third-cycle *occidentalis* at this season (n = 50).

HYBRIDS

Interbreeds extensively with Glaucous-winged Gull;[19,20,21] see hybrid account (pp. 479–481).

NOTES

1. Bell 1996; 2. AOU 1957; 3. Roberson 2002; 4. Bell 1996; 5. Ibid.; 6. Bell 1997; 7. Hoffman et al. 1978; 8. Scott 1971; 9. Weber 1981; 10. AOU 1957; 11. González B. et al. 2003; 12. Wright and Komarek 1928; 13. Duncan 1982; 14. Stevenson and Anderson 1994; 15. Howell pers. obs.; 16. Ibid.; 17. Ibid.; 18. Ibid.; 19. Bell 1997; 20. Hoffman et al. 1978; 21. Scott 1971

LENGTH 22–26.5 IN. (56–67.5 CM)
PHOTOS 32.0–32.40

IDENTIFICATION SUMMARY

This large, dark-backed, yellow-legged gull is endemic as a breeder to the Gulf of California, Mexico, with post-breeding dispersal north to the Salton Sea, California. Heavily built and broad-winged; second-cycle and third-cycle plumages relatively advanced in appearance. Bill stout and slightly bulbous tipped, with moderate to distinct gonydeal expansion. At rest, tail tip falls between tips of P6 and P7. Adult has slaty gray upperparts (Kodak 9–10.5) and very limited dusky head and neck markings in fresh basic plumage. Juvenile dark brownish overall with solidly blackish tail, mostly white belly. PA1 typically extensive, starting late July–Sept. Subsequent ages variable in appearance. First cycle has pinkish legs, becoming yellow by adult cycle; adult eyes pale lemon; orbital ring chrome yellow.

No other large dark-backed gull occurs commonly in its range, and adult Yellow-footed Gull is distinctive by virtue of its slaty gray upperparts and yellow legs. Most similar species is Western Gull (rare but increasing in Gulf of California), which has pink legs; also see blackish-backed Kelp Gull of S. America (expanding northward). In first cycle also see Herring Gull.

TAXONOMY

Monotypic. Formerly considered a subspecies of Western Gull.[1]

STATUS AND DISTRIBUTION

Endemic to Gulf of Calif., Mex., ranging north to se. Calif.

Breeding. Fairly common to common resident (breeds Apr.–July) in Gulf of Calif. and

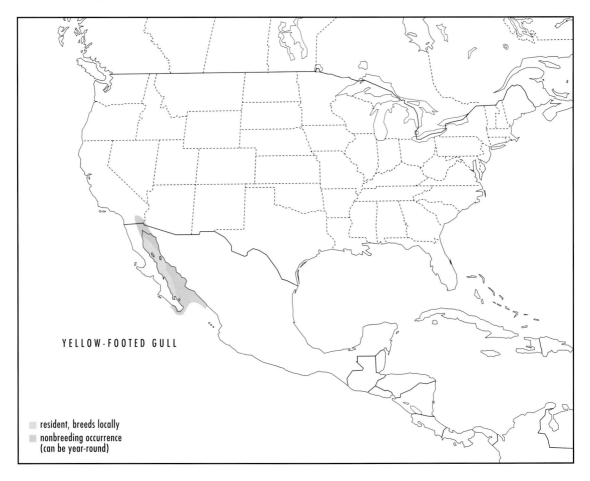

YELLOW-FOOTED GULL

resident, breeds locally
nonbreeding occurrence
(can be year-round)

along adjacent coasts of Baja Calif. Peninsula, Sonora, and n. Sinaloa, Mex., nesting on numerous islands in the Gulf (mainly 31°–24°30′ north).

Nonbreeding. Fairly common to common post-breeding visitor (mainly May–Sept.) north through Río Colo. drainage to Salton Sea (where rare during Oct.–Mar.). Casual inland elsewhere in sw. U.S. (late Apr.–early Dec.), north to e.-cen Calif., s. Nev., and n. Ariz./s. Utah. Casual nonbreeding visitor north (mainly June–Jan.) along Pacific Coast of Baja Calif. Peninsula to s. Calif., north to Los Angeles Co., and south (Nov.–May) along Pacific Coast of Mex. to Oaxaca. Photos of a putative Yellow-footed Gull from Tex.[2] look atypical of that species in structure, leg color, and delayed primary molt; we consider the record unconvincing.

FIELD IDENTIFICATION

SIMILAR SPECIES

WESTERN GULL the only large dark-backed gull normally found in range of Yellow-footed. In first cycle see Herring Gull. Yellow-footed calls notably lower pitched than Western Gull; note, though, that calls of immature Yellow-footed are higher pitched, more similar to adult Western Gull (but still deeper and throatier).

Adult Cycle. Note leg color, slaty gray tone of upperparts, wingtip pattern, and structure, especially bill size and shape.

WESTERN GULL (w. N. America) has slaty gray upperparts (Kodak 8–11) that overlap with Yellow-footed but bill less stout with smaller red gonydeal spot, legs flesh pink. Western often has narrow whitish tongue-tips out to P5/P6, P4 usually lacks black subterminal marks, and prebasic molt averages 1–2 months later than Yellow-footed, so white primary tips usually bolder through winter.

LESSER BLACK-BACKED GULL (widespread, but rare in West) more lightly built with relatively longer and narrower wings, slender bill. Legs fleshy yellow to yellow. Basic adult has distinct dusky head and neck streaking, and bill often has blackish distal marks.

First Cycle. Note bill size and shape, mostly white belly and undertail coverts.

WESTERN GULL generally has less stout bill, plumage often darker and browner overall but some birds very similar. PA1 molt of Western can include upperwing coverts and tertials on up to 10 percent of s. populations (replaced on up to 90 percent of Yellow-footeds); tail coverts have denser dark barring on Western;

legs average brighter pink on Western; belly more extensively and cleaner white on Yellow-footed. A few birds, however, may defy specific identification.

AMERICAN HERRING GULL (widespread) less thickset with narrower wings, less bulbous-tipped bill. Underparts overall brownish with extensive dark barring on tail coverts; often retains much juvenal plumage into winter, and A1 scapulars paler and more boldly marked than relatively dark and plain upperparts of Yellow-footed. In flight, note Herring's pale inner primary panel on upperwings; also often has more white at base of tail.

CALIFORNIA GULL (w. N. America) smaller and more lightly built with relatively longer primary projection, narrower wings, slender bill usually sharply bicolored pink with black tip by Oct.; A1 scapulars typically more variegated and often with distinct anchor marks.

LESSER BLACK-BACKED GULL smaller, slimmer, and longer-winged with slender black bill; lacks contrasting white belly; white tail base barred black.

Second Cycle. Note bill size and shape, leg color, incoming slaty gray on upperparts. From Oct.–Nov. onward, note that first-cycle Yellow-footed Gulls with extensive PA1 molt (including most upperwing coverts and tertials) recall fresh second-basic Western Gull and other species; note pointed juvenal primaries and all-black tail of first-cycle Yellow-footed, plus very stout bill. Second-cycle Yellow-footed, especially birds with PA molt of primaries and tail, much like third cycles of other dark-backed species.

WESTERN GULL has more retarded appearance in fresh plumage, usually with mostly brownish upperwing coverts; A2 often has mostly slaty back and contrastingly paler brown upperwing coverts. Distinguished from first-cycle Yellow-footed by rounded primaries, slightly wider white tail tip, and more extensive white tail base.

LESSER BLACK-BACKED GULL smaller with slender bill; more retarded in appearance than second-cycle Yellow-footed. Distinguished from first-cycle Yellow-footed by rounded primaries, white tail base with variable black distal band.

Third Cycle. Yellow-footed mostly adultlike in appearance (see Adult Cycle for distinctions from other species). However, second-cycle Yellow-footed can resemble third cycle of other large, dark-backed gulls; note its bill size and shape, flesh to yellow bill with a black tip, and fleshy yellow to yellow legs. Second-cycle Yellow-footed distinguished from third-cycle Western Gull by deeper, more swollen-tipped bill, fleshy yellow to yellow legs; often has more black in tail and more brownish on underwing coverts.

RARER SPECIES

Adult Cycle. Note leg color, slaty gray tone of upperparts, wingtip pattern, and structure, especially bill size and shape. See Kelp Gull, Slaty-backed Gull, and Great Black-backed Gull (differences given under those species).

HYBRID KELP GULL × AMERICAN HERRING GULL (Gulf of Mexico). F1 hybrids probably less thickset overall with narrower wings, average less stout bill. Legs greenish yellow to yellow, orbital ring orange, and wings show more contrasting black wingtip (on underwing blended fairly abruptly from smoky gray inner primaries and secondaries).

HYBRID AMERICAN HERRING GULL × GREAT BLACK-BACKED GULL intermediate in size and structure between the parent species with paler upperparts and flesh pink legs; orbital ring varies from yellow to red. Basic head streaking finer and more extensive in midwinter, and wingtip averages more white.

First Cycle. Note bill size and shape, mostly white belly and undertail coverts. See Kelp Gull, Slaty-backed Gull, Great Black-backed Gull, Vega Gull, European Herring Gull, and Yellow-legged Gull (differences given under those taxa).

HYBRID KELP GULL × AMERICAN HERRING GULL likely to differ in structure, plumage more similar to Kelp Gull.

HYBRID AMERICAN HERRING GULL × GREAT BLACK-BACKED GULL undescribed at this age, but presumably intermediate in size and structure between the parent species; upperwings likely to be paler on inner primaries than Yellow-footed, and tail less extensively blackish.

Second Cycle. Note bill size and shape, leg color, incoming slaty gray on upperparts. From Oct.–Nov. onward, note that first-cycle Yellow-footed Gulls with extensive PA1 molt, including most upperwing coverts and tertials, recall fresh second-basic plumage of other species; note pointed juvenal primaries and all-black tail of first-cycle Yellow-footed, plus its very stout bill. Second-cycle Yellow-footed, especially birds with PA molt of primaries and tail, much like third cycle of other dark-backed species. See Kelp Gull, Slaty-backed Gull, and Great Black-backed Gull (differences given under those species).

HYBRID KELP GULL × AMERICAN HERRING GULL likely to differ in structure, plumage similar to Lesser Black-backed Gull.

HYBRID AMERICAN HERRING GULL × GREAT BLACK-BACKED GULL undescribed at this age, but presumably intermediate in size and structure between the parent species; upperwings likely to be paler on inner primaries, and gray on upperparts paler.

HABITAT AND BEHAVIOR

Coasts and islands in Gulf of California, favoring rocky coasts, fishing harbors, beaches, river mouths, etc.; also in flooded fields around Salton Sea. Ranges inland to Salton Sea and other water bodies in Río Colorado drainage. Nests in small colonies (up to 30–40 pairs) and also as solitary pairs on islands and islets, usually within 30 m of the high-tide line.[3] Nonbreeding birds often in loose flocks, mainly of 20–50 birds (locally in hundreds in late summer and fall), associating readily with other gulls and water birds. Feeds commonly by scavenging; also forages in intertidal and surface waters for marine invertebrates and preys on eggs and young birds, also on small adult seabirds at their colonies.

DESCRIPTION AND MOLT

Adult Cycle. Complete PB molt (mid-Apr./May–Sept./Oct.) produces adult basic plumage: head, neck, and underparts white; head and neck with variable (usually slight) dusky clouding and streaking in fresh plumage; this dusky typically disappears by early winter. Upperparts slaty gray (Kodak 9–10.5) with extensively black wingtips (black on outer webs of P8–P10, sometimes also P7, extends to primary coverts, which may have blackish shaft streaks), bold white scapular and tertial crescents, and white tips to outer primaries. Uppertail coverts and tail white. White trailing edge to secondaries (often shows as a skirt) and inner primaries breaks into discrete white tips on outer primaries; P5 typically with a narrow whitish tongue-tip and P4 with dark subterminal marks; P10 with white mirror (P9 rarely with small white mirror). Underwings show blackish wingtips (with white primary tips and mirrors) blending into white-tipped, dusky gray inner primaries and secondaries, which form a dusky subterminal band on underwings. Eyes greenish white to olive, orbital ring chrome yellow to orange. Bill yellow to orange-yellow with large orange-red to red gonydeal spot; bill base may be suffused pinkish during height of PB molt (and bill may develop dark distal marks; perhaps mainly fourth-cycle birds?) but returns to bright yellow by early winter. Legs chrome yellow to fleshy yellow, the latter color especially at height of PB molt and on nonbreeding birds. Partial PA molt (*Sept.*–Jan./Feb.) produces adult alternate plumage: head and neck clean white (usually by Nov./Dec.). By spring, orbital ring, bill, and legs brighter; white primary tips greatly reduced by wear.

First Cycle. Juvenile (mid-June–mid-Sept.): dark gray-brown overall with contrasting white belly. Head, neck, chest, and flanks variably streaked and mottled whitish, often with a dark-faced effect; belly and vent clean white, undertail coverts white with brown bars mainly on longest feathers. Upperparts with cinnamon-buff (bleaching to whitish) scaly and notched edgings and markings, the greater coverts typically with unmarked bases forming a contrasting dark band. Tertials blackish brown with notched whitish tips and distal edging, the dark tertial bases merging with dark secondary bases that often show as a skirt. Uppertail coverts white with sparse dark spots and bars mainly on longest feathers. Flight feathers blackish, secondaries and inner primaries tipped whitish, tail with narrow whitish tip and sometimes slight whitish ribbing on bases of outer rectrices. IN FLIGHT: dark brown overall with striking white belly, contrasting whitish uppertail coverts, blackish tail, blackish remiges with narrow white trailing edge to secondaries and poorly contrasting browner panel on inner primaries, and plain brown greater-covert bases; underwings dark. Eyes dark, bill variably dull pinkish on basal two-thirds, black distally with fine pale tip; legs dusky flesh to pale flesh pink. PA1 molt (mid-July/Sept.–*Mar.*; often includes upperwing coverts, tail coverts, and tertials; only about 10 percent of birds molt no upperwing coverts; n = 50)[4] produces variable first alternate plumage: head, neck, and underparts white with variable dusky brown streaking mainly on head and hindneck; upperparts dark gray-brown to grayish with some paler edgings and often a few grayish feathers, especially scapulars. A1 scapulars vary from gray-brown with dark shaft streaks and paler tips (earlier-molted?) to overall grayish (later-molted?). New tertials typically have very broad white tips with a speckled dark-and-white border. Eyes brown to pale grayish, orbital ring dull flesh. Bill flesh to pinkish basally (especially on mandible), black distally with a pale horn tip; legs dull flesh to yellowish flesh.

Second Cycle. Complete PB2 molt (mid-Mar./mid-Apr.–Aug./Sept.) into variable second basic plumage. Head, neck, and underparts white with dusky streaking mainly on head and hindneck. Upperparts mostly slaty gray to gray-brown with white scapular and tertial crescents. Rump and uppertail coverts white. Remiges blackish with white trailing edge to secondaries and browner inner primaries; tail blackish with white at basal corners and whitish tip. Underwings with medium brown wing-linings, blackish wingtips blending into dusky inner primaries and secondaries. Eyes olive brown to pale lemon, orbital ring dark to fleshy yellow. Bill flesh to yellowish with black distal third and sometimes a fine pale tip. Legs pale flesh to fleshy yellow. Variable PA2 molt (Aug./Sept.–Feb./Mar.; often includes much of back, most upperwing coverts, and some to all rectrices; can include up to 8 inner primaries during *Oct.*–Dec./Jan.[5]) produces second alternate plumage: dusky streaking on head and neck reduced to absent by Mar./Apr., upperparts mostly slaty gray, sometimes with contrasting, faded brown upperwing coverts; tail often mixed black-and-white; new inner primaries slaty gray with bold white tips. Orbital ring yellow, bill flesh to yellow with black distal band (reduced to absent in summer) and often some red at gonys (most extensive in summer), legs fleshy yellow to yellow. Note that PA2 molt of tail and inner primaries produces appearance much like third cycle of other large white-headed gulls.

Third Cycle. Complete PB3 molt (Apr.–late Aug./Sept.) produces third basic plumage: resembles adult basic overall but dusky head and neck clouding average heavier in fall; wingtips average browner and have more extensive blackish, for example, on primary coverts and P4, with P10 mirror smaller to absent; tail often has small black spots.[6] Eyes average duller, pale olive to pale lemon, bill yellowish flesh with black subterminal band to yellow with orange-red gonydeal spot and black distal marks, legs fleshy yellow. Partial PA3 molt (*Sept.*–Feb.) into third alternate plumage (can include up to 6 inner primaries[7]): resembles adult alternate except for any differences in wing and tail patterns; bill adultlike by winter but often shows small black marks near tip (lost by summer?); some may be indistinguishable from adult. White tips to outer primaries often lost by wear. Adult plumage attained by complete PB4 molt (mid-Apr./May–Sept./Oct.).

HYBRIDS
None reported.

NOTES

1. AOU 1957; 2. Weeks and Patten 2000; 3. Spear and Anderson 1989; 4. Howell pers. obs.; 5. Howell pers. obs. (4/12 second-cycle birds and 1/5 third-cycle birds with inner primaries newly replaced or growing; Jan. 2003); 6. Howell pers. obs.; 7. Howell pers. obs. (4/12 second-cycle birds and 1/5 third-cycle birds with inner primaries newly replaced or growing; Jan. 2003)

LENGTH 22–26.3 IN. (56–67 CM)
PHOTOS 33.0–33.41; I.32, I.37, I.41, 36.10, 36.11

IDENTIFICATION SUMMARY

This large, gray-winged, pink-legged gull is common along the N. American Pacific Coast. Heavily built and broad-winged (typically showing a skirt at rest). Bill stout and bulbous tipped, but relatively slender on some females; compared to Western Gull, bill of Glaucous-winged often looks longer and less bulbous tipped. At rest, tail tip about equal with or slightly shorter than tip of P7. Adult has pale gray upperparts (Kodak 5–6) with medium gray wingtips (Kodak 6–8; averaging paler on northern populations) and, in basic plumage, extensive dusky head and neck mottling and clouding. Juvenile milky brown overall, including wingtips. PA1 variable in extent and timing, starts Oct.–Mar. Subsequent ages variable in appearance but never have blackish or contrastingly dark wingtips. All ages have pink legs; adult eyes dusky to pale; orbital ring pink.

No other large gray-winged gull occurs regularly in its range, so older immature and adult Glaucous-winged Gulls normally distinctive by virtue of their gray wingtips — but identification confounded by hybridization with Western, American Herring, and Glaucous Gulls, so field definition of "pure" Glaucous-winged Gull problematic. Most similar species in plumage is smaller Kumlien's Gull of N. Atlantic, and in first cycle compare with Thayer's Gull. See Similar Species and Rarer Species sections for details.

TAXONOMY

Monotypic, but breeding birds from N. British Columbia to w. Alaska average paler above than birds from s. British Columbia and Washington (perhaps reflecting introgression of latter with Western Gull).[1] Hybridizes extensively with Western Gull in Washington and Oregon,[2,3,4] and some authors consider these taxa conspecific.[5]

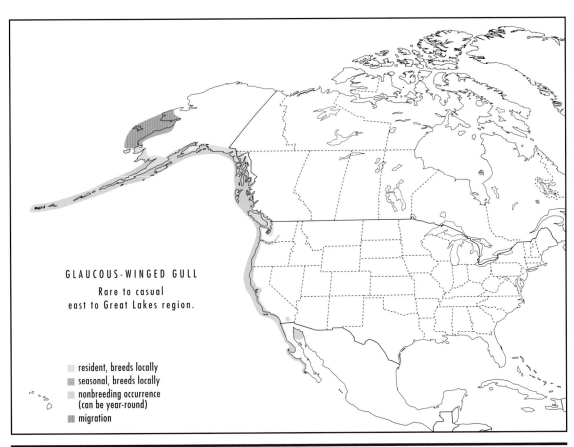

GLAUCOUS-WINGED GULL
Rare to casual
east to Great Lakes region.

■ resident, breeds locally
■ seasonal, breeds locally
■ nonbreeding occurrence
   (can be year-round)
■ migration

Nw. N. America and ne. Asia, ranging to Hawaii. Accidental in nw. Africa.[6]

Breeding. Breeds (May–Aug.) along coasts from w. Alaska (north to Cape Romanzof), Bering Sea is. (north to St. Matthew Is.), the Aleutians, and Alaska Peninsula south along Pacific Coast of N. America to nw. Ore. (south to Lane Co.). Also on inland lakes in sw. Alaska and Alaska Peninsula, and in small numbers inland along Columbia R. to The Dalles (in Ring-billed Gull and California Gull colonies), probably to north of Richland, Benton Co., Wash.[7] Has bred casually (apparently) on St. Lawrence Is. and Cape Denbigh in Norton Sound, Alaska.[8]

Nonbreeding. Southbound movements difficult to detect in n. regions where species resident, but evident by mid-Sept. from coastal Ore. south to cen. Calif., with main arrivals Oct.–Nov. In coastal s. Calif., arrivals usually after mid-Oct., with most Nov.–Dec.

Winters from sea-ice front zone in Bering Sea[9] south along coasts to Baja Calif., Mex. and also out to 1,000 km offshore in N. Pacific.[10] Common to fairly common along coasts from s. Alaska to cen. Calif. (mainly Oct.–Apr. south of breeding range), becoming uncommon to rare (mainly Nov.–Mar.) on Pacific Coast of Baja Calif. Peninsula and in n. Gulf of Calif. Casual (Nov.–Feb.) south to Islas Revillagigedo and Jalisco, Mex.,[11] exceptionally south to El Salvador (Jan.)[12] and to 4°40′ north 147° west in tropical Pacific Ocean (early Mar.).[13] Rare to locally uncommon inland (mainly Nov.–Apr.) in B.C. and Pacific states. Casual to locally rare (but with records increasing) farther inland in N. America,[14] but has been recorded (mostly Nov.–mid-Apr.) east and south to Wisc., Ill., Mo., Okla., Tex., and N.M., exceptionally to Nfld.[15]

Northward movement starts Feb.–Mar. in Calif., with most wintering birds gone by late Apr., some lingering into May and a few through the summer, especially from cen. Calif. north. Ranges north (May–Oct., mainly Aug.–Sept.) in Bering Sea in small numbers regularly to St. Lawrence Is. and Seward Peninsula. Rare inland in Yukon (mainly late Apr.–mid-May, casual in summer and fall). Casual in summer to Arctic coast of Alaska and sw. Hudson Bay.

FIELD IDENTIFICATION

SIMILAR SPECIES

Glaucous-winged Gull is the only large gray-winged gull normally found in its range and,

as such, it should be distinctive; see Rarer Species. However, because of frequent hybridization with Glaucous Gull in w. Alaska, with American Herring Gull in s. Alaska, and with Western Gull in Wash. and Ore., determining where a pure Glaucous-winged Gull starts and a hybrid stops may not be possible in the field, at least away from core breeding areas (see accounts for hybrids, pp. 479–487).

Adult Cycle. Note the problems inherent in defining a pure Glaucous-winged Gull (above), and see Glaucous-winged Gull hybrids (pp. 479–487).

THAYER'S GULL typically has slaty blackish wingtips quite different from Glaucous-winged, but some birds (hybrid Thayer's × Kumlien's?) have charcoal gray wingtips similar to dark or hybrid Glaucous-winged Gulls. Best separated by structure: Thayer's is smaller with a less stout bill, shorter legs, and proportionately longer and narrower wings (creating a relatively longer wing projection).

GLAUCOUS GULL has pure white wingtips, pale lemon eyes, orange orbital ring, and paler gray upperparts (Kodak 3–5); see account for hybrid Glaucous × Glaucous-winged Gull (pp. 486–487).

First Cycle. Note problems inherent in defining a pure Glaucous-winged Gull (above), and see Glaucous-winged Gull hybrids (pp. 479–487).

THAYER'S GULL averages smaller with a slender bill, longer wing projection, shorter legs. Wingtips of Thayer's medium dark brown to blackish brown, obviously darker than the upperparts. In flight, Thayer's typically has contrasting dark brown outer primaries (pale on inner webs), secondary bar, and tail—more contrasting than Glaucous-winged but similar to hybrids. From midwinter onward, wingtips of Thayer's often bleach and can be same tone as upperparts, that is, similar to Glaucous-winged. Note structural differences, especially Thayer's relatively slender bill and longer wing projection, and its dark secondary bar and darker tail (usually protected from bleaching).

GLAUCOUS GULL typically paler overall, often whitish (but beware bleached late-winter and first-summer Glaucous-wingeds), with whitish wingtips. Glaucous has flesh pink bill with clean-cut black tip—very different from mostly blackish bill of first-cycle Glaucous-winged.

SLATY-BACKED GULL in first-summer plumage can be very bleached, suggesting Glaucous-winged, but darker outer webs to outer primaries create more-distinct two-tone pattern than Glaucous-winged; dark brown secondary bar and tail of Slaty-backed tend not to fade as much as the exposed primaries and are distinct from paler and plainer pattern of pure Glaucous-winged—but similar to hybrid Glaucous-winged × American Herring Gulls.

Second Cycle. Note problems inherent in defining a pure Glaucous-winged Gull (above), and see Glaucous-winged Gull hybrids (pp. 479–487).

GLAUCOUS GULL whiter overall with white remiges, often has pale eyes; any incoming clear gray on back is usually paler. Clean-cut bill pattern (flesh pink basal two-thirds and black distal third with fine pale tip) may be shown by some second-winter Glaucous-wingeds, but these tend to have a more bulbous-tipped bill than Glaucous and also have dusky gray wingtips.

THAYER'S GULL averages smaller with a slender bill, longer wing projection, and blackish brown wingtips not prone to fading (unlike first-cycle birds), so should not be confused with Glaucous-winged, but see hybrids.

Third Cycle. Thayer's Gull differs as does adult (see above).

RARER SPECIES

KUMLIEN'S GULL (breeding ne. Canada, wintering N. Atlantic) is the most similar taxon in plumage to Glaucous-winged Gull but should be distinguished readily by size and structure. At one time, Kumlien's was called Lesser Glaucous-winged Gull; it is noticeably smaller than Glaucous-winged with a much smaller bill; it also has a relatively longer wing projection and shorter legs.

Adult Cycle. KUMLIEN'S GULL usually lacks dark bill markings in winter; eyes usually pale. Plumage can be very similar to Glaucous-winged but upperparts paler (Kodak 4–5) and rarely has gray subterminal marks on P5 that Glaucous-winged often shows.

First Cycle. KUMLIEN'S GULL typically has neater and more-contrasting checkering on upperparts, wingtips often paler (tending to whitish) with neat dark subterminal marks on outer primaries and primary coverts (unlike plainer milky brown on Glaucous-winged).

Second Cycle. KUMLIEN'S GULL typically has neater and more-contrasting dark barring on upperwing coverts, and eyes often pale by second winter.

Third Cycle. KUMLIEN'S GULL differs in same ways as adult (above) but may more often have gray subterminal band on P5.

HABITAT AND BEHAVIOR

Largely coastal, favoring rocky and muddy intertidal areas, fishing harbors, beaches, river mouths, etc. Ranges inland to dumps, reservoirs, freshwater lakes, also over inshore waters, mainly within 50–100 km of shore but locally to 500 km or more from land, mainly in winter. Nests on inshore rocky islands and islets, coastal cliffs, and locally on buildings. Nonbreeding birds often in flocks (locally to a few thousand birds), associating readily with other gulls and water birds. Feeds commonly by scavenging; also forages in intertidal and surface waters for marine invertebrates and preys on eggs and young birds, also on small adult seabirds at colonies. Glaucous-winged and Western Gulls and their hybrids dominate coastal feeding sites, which helps explain why Herring Gulls do not winter commonly along the immediate coast in the range of these species.

DESCRIPTION AND MOLT

Adult Cycle. Complete PB molt (late May/June–Nov./Dec.) produces adult basic plumage: head, neck, and underparts white; head, neck, and sometimes chest with variable (usually moderate to heavy) dusky mottling and clouding that is distinctly smudgy, usually not forming neat streaks. Upperparts pale gray (Kodak 5–6) with medium gray wingtips (Kodak 6–8; averaging paler on n. populations) usually including a subterminal band on P5 and extending most or all of the way to primary coverts on outer webs of P9–P10; bold white scapular and tertial crescents; and white tips to outer primaries. Uppertail coverts and tail white. White trailing edge to secondaries (often shows at rest) and inner primaries breaks into discrete white tips on outer primaries; white tongue-tips on P6–P8 and mirrors on P10 or P9–P10 typically form distinct white spots inside medium gray subterminal band. Underwings show pale smoky gray remiges with white trailing edge to secondaries and inner primaries continuing as a band of subterminal white spots across outer primaries; narrow gray subterminal band on white-tipped outer primaries. Eyes typically dark, but dusky pale lemon on up to 5 percent (n = 100),[16] orbital ring pink. Bill yellowish (often pinkish to greenish basally in winter; rarely orange-yellow[17]) with orange-red to red gonydeal spot and, in winter, usually a dark distal mark. Legs flesh pink, often paler during height of PB molt, and rarely bright orange-yellow.[18] Partial PA molt (Oct.–Mar./Apr.) produces adult alternate plumage: head and neck clean white (rarely before Mar.); white primary tips can be lost through wear. By spring, orbital ring, bill, and legs brighter; lemon yellow bill lacks dark distal marks.

First Cycle. Juvenile (Aug.–Feb.): medium gray-brown to brownish gray overall, often fading to pale milky brown by midwinter. Head, neck, and underparts variably mottled and streaked whitish, undertail coverts barred and spotted dark brown and whitish. Upperparts with buff (bleaching to dull whitish) scaly and notched edgings and markings, the outer greater coverts often less heavily marked and thus looking relatively plain. Upperpart markings relatively fine overall, scaly to speckled, at times with a muted lacy aspect, and rarely boldly checkered (which on some birds may indicate hybridism). Tertials with notched to speckled whitish tips and distal edging, the plain tertial bases merging with plain secondary bases that often show as a skirt. Uppertail coverts extensively spotted and barred brown and whitish. Flight feathers medium gray-brown to brownish gray, similar in tone to upperparts; inner webs of outer primaries slightly paler than darker tips and outer webs. Wingtips can be slightly darker than upperparts and typically have neat, narrow whitish edgings; inner primaries subtly paler than outers, with dark subterminal marks. Some birds have broad and diffuse whitish tips to outer primaries, which create contrastingly paler wingtips at rest—but such wings look typical in flight. Secondaries and tail indistinctly tipped whitish, tail with wavy whitish bars at basal corners and often with white ribbing or edging on outer web of R6. IN FLIGHT: milky gray-brown overall with no strongly contrasting patterns: often the tail is the darkest area of plumage, the primaries are translucent when backlit (narrow darker tips to the outer primaries show at close range), and upperwing can show a slightly darker secondary bar depending on the light angle; underwings milky gray-brown overall with remiges reflective silvery to translucent, depending on light angle. Eyes dark, bill black at first, often with some dull pinkish basally by midwinter, legs dusky flesh to flesh pink. PA1 molt (Oct.–Apr./May; exceptionally includes upperwing coverts) produces first alternate plumage: head, neck, chest, and flanks smoky gray-brown to sooty gray, often mixed with bleached juvenal feathers. Many birds have limited PA1 molt and by spring their head, neck, and chest become bleached whitish; the most extreme cases bleach all over to whitish except for a few A1 feathers that can look contrastingly dark. A1 scapulars range from brownish gray with a diffuse darker sub-

terminal band (earlier-molted feathers) to plain grayish or with only faint dusky vermiculations (some later-molted feathers). Wingtips often bleach to whitish and upperwing coverts to a whitish and pale brown panel. Bill typically shows some dull flesh to pinkish basally, sometimes a pale horn tip; legs flesh pink.

Second Cycle. Complete PB2 molt (late Apr./May–Oct./Nov.) into second basic plumage. Some birds bleach to strikingly white or whitish overall in summer, before PB2 is very advanced—and new B2 feathers look contrastingly dark. Some fresh B2 birds suggest juvenile: overall medium gray-brown with variable whitish mottling and streaking on head, neck, and underparts, undertail coverts typically messy milky brown and whitish with less distinct bars than first cycle; wing coverts and tertials usually plainer than first cycle; note more-rounded primaries. Other, more typical, B2 birds have adultlike gray feathers mixed in on back and tertials, plainer upperwing coverts and often slightly darker wingtips than first cycle. Head, neck, and chest often mostly white in midwinter with brownish belly. Flight feathers similar to first cycle but wingtips and tail often darker, medium gray or brownish gray, wingtips with narrow whitish edging; P10 rarely has a small, diffuse whitish mirror; outer rectrices with whitish basal corners. Uppertail coverts smudgy brown and whitish, not as distinctly barred as first cycle. Underwings milky brownish overall with remiges reflective silvery to translucent, depending on light angle. Eyes dark brown to grayish, bill averages more extensively pinkish at base and often has pale horn tip (sometimes extensively flesh pink on basal two-thirds by midwinter), legs flesh pink. Partial PA2 molt (Sept.–Apr. often includes some upperwing coverts) produces second alternate plumage: head, neck, and underparts mottled dusky and whitish (sometimes bleaching and wearing to mostly white by summer), back becomes mostly gray in contrast to faded, milky brownish upperwing coverts; some birds attain a few gray upperwing coverts, especially median coverts. Eyes brown to dusky pale lemon, orbital ring can become pinkish in summer. Through winter, bill typically pinkish basally, blackish distally; in summer can become yellowish with red gonydeal spot and black distal band; "retarded birds" retain blackish bill with limited pinkish basally. Legs flesh pink.

Third Cycle. Complete PB3 molt (May/June–Oct./Nov.) produces third basic plumage: resembles adult basic overall but probably averages more extensive dusky clouding and mottling on chest and sides; often washed brownish on upperwing coverts and tertials; wingtips may average darker and browner gray and outer primaries have smaller white tips; often has dusky wash on primary coverts and tail (which varies from all white to extensively dusky gray). White trailing edge to secondaries and inner primaries narrower than adult and wingtip pattern reduced: smaller white tongue-tips on P6–P7 only, P9 lacks mirror, and P10 mirror averages smaller—so row of white spots usually broken on P8–P9. Underwings have dusky brown mottling on coverts. Bill regresses to mostly blackish with some pinkish basally during end of PB3 molt and is often pinkish with black tip or subterminal band though midwinter; legs flesh pink. Partial PA3 molt (Sept.–Mar./Apr.) into third alternate plumage: dark markings on head and neck reduced to absent; bill brightens by summer and may be indistinguishable from adult or have dark distal marks. White tips to outer primaries often lost by wear. Adult plumage attained by complete PB4 molt (May/June–Nov.) although some fourth-cycle birds probably show dusky marks on tail and less white in wingtips.

HYBRIDS

Commonly with Western Gull in Washington and Oregon,[19,20,21] with American Herring Gull from s. Alaska to British Columbia,[22,23,24,25] and with Glaucous Gull in w. Alaska.[26,27,28] Also with Slaty-backed Gull in Kamchatka and on Commander Islands.[29,30,31]

NOTES

1. Bell 1996; 2. Bell 1997; 3. Hoffman et al. 1978; 4. Scott 1971; 5. Weber 1981; 6. Bakker et al. 2001; 7. Smith et al. 1997; 8. Verbeek 1993; 9. Kessel 1989; 10. Sanger 1970; 11. Howell et al. 2001; 12. Jones 2003a; 13. P. Unitt pers. comm. (photos); 14. Johnson et al. 1995; 15. NAB 59:231,370 (2005); 16. Howell pers. obs.; 17. Vermeer et al. 1963; 18. Verbeek 1993; 19. Bell 1997; 20. Hoffman et al. 1978; 21. Scott 1971; 22. R. J. Cannings pers. comm.; 23. Merilees 1974; 24. Patten 1980; 25. Williamson and Peyton 1963; 26. McCaffery et al. 1997; 27. Strang 1977; 28. Swarth 1934; 29. Firsova and Levada 1982; 30. Grabovsky et al. unpubl. data; 31. King and Carey 1999

LENGTH 21.5–29 IN. (55–74 CM)
PHOTOS 34.0–34.30, I.6, I.20, I.28

IDENTIFICATION SUMMARY

A large, white-winged, Arctic-breeding gull that occurs south to mid-latitudes in winter. Bill stout but relatively parallel sided (not bulbous tipped, except some females) with moderate gonydeal expansion; bill base often has slightly expanded culmen that creates distinctive shape (especially males), with depth at base greater than depth at gonydeal expansion. At rest, tail tip falls between tips of P7 and P8, so wing projection relatively short. Adult has pale gray upperparts (Kodak 3–5; see Taxonomy) with all-white wingtips. Juvenile pale creamy brown overall (often bleaches much whiter in first winter) with variable, usually fine, brownish markings, white to whitish wingtips. PA1 variable, starting Oct.–Apr. Subsequent ages somewhat variable in appearance but overall very pale with white wingtips. All ages have pink legs; adult eyes pale lemon and orbital ring orange.

Mostly distinctive but smaller females may be confused with Kumlien's and Iceland Gulls; also beware leucistic or albino individuals of other species. Adult Kumlien's and Iceland are smaller and less thickset with a smaller, more slender bill and a relatively longer wing projection; besides size and structure (especially bill), first-cycle Glaucous has a pink bill with a sharply demarcated black distal third, and white to whitish wingtips. Adult Glaucous-winged Gull has gray wingtip markings; bleached first-cycle Glaucous-winged Gull has blackish bill.

TAXONOMY

Recognition of four subspecies proposed by Banks,[1] although he provided no sample sizes (or conventional series of measurements). Malling Olsen and Larsson (2003) considered *leuceretes* (breeding in Canada) synonymous with *hyperboreus* (breeding w. Eurasia). Differences in all subspecies slight and clinal, except perhaps where largest and palest (*pallidissimus*) meets smallest and darkest (*barrovianus*) in Bering Sea region. Nominate *hyperboreus* breeds from Canada east through Greenland, Jan Mayan, and Spitzbergen to Taimyr Peninsula, Russia; *pallidissimus* from Taimyr Peninsula east to Siberia and Bering Sea Is.; and *barrovianus* in Alaska. In adults, *barrovianus* averages smallest, especially in bill, and darkest above (Kodak 4–5); *hyperboreus* averages larger and paler above (Kodak 3–4.5), and intergrades with *barrovianus* in w.

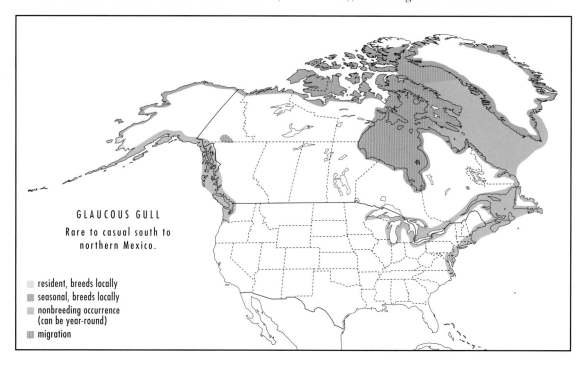

GLAUCOUS GULL
Rare to casual south to
northern Mexico.

- resident, breeds locally
- seasonal, breeds locally
- nonbreeding occurrence
  (can be year-round)
- migration

Canada; and *pallidissimus* averages largest overall and palest above (Kodak 3–4). Length (all ages combined) of *barrovianus* 21.5–24.8 in. (55–63 cm); *hyperboreus* 24.5–29 in. (62–74 cm); and *pallidissimus* 25.5–29 in. (65–74 cm). Relative to Eurasian *hyperboreus*, Canadian adults ("*leuceretes*") average slightly paler upperparts (Kodak 3–4 vs. 3.5–4.5) and less-extensive dusky head and neck markings in basic; first-cycle birds average whiter. Subspecies rarely distinguishable in the field (or even in specimens away from breeding grounds) except perhaps by differences in size and adult upperpart tone when typical *pallidissimus* are seen alongside typical *barrovianus*.[2]

STATUS AND DISTRIBUTION

High-latitude Holarctic, wintering south to mid-latitudes, casually to Hawaii. See Taxonomy for subspecies distributions.

Breeding. In N. America, breeds (June–Sept.) from w. Alaska (south to Bristol Bay and including islands in n. Bering Sea south to St. Matthew) and n. Alaska (locally inland to foothills of Brooks Range and upper Colville watershed), east along Arctic coast of Canada, including n. Canadian Arctic is. and Greenland, south to Belcher Is. in s. Hudson Bay, n. Que., and cen. Lab.

Nonbreeding. Southbound movements begin by late Aug. in the North (e.g., in s. Yukon) and most depart northern nesting areas during Sept., with some remaining through Nov. Arrival in se. Alaska usually early Oct., but can appear as early as late Aug. Across s. Canada and n. U.S., fall arrival typically Nov., often after mid-month, though a few appear by late Oct., exceptionally earlier. Remains numerous on s. Hudson Bay until mid-Nov., and in Prairie Provinces some remain into Dec.

Winters (mainly Nov./Dec.–Mar./Apr.) from s. Bering Sea (some north to St. Lawrence Is. and open leads off Point Hope in s. Chukchi Sea[3]), Hudson Bay (a few), s. Lab., and s. Greenland south to the Northwest, Great Lakes region, and coastal Northeast. Largely absent after early winter from interior Canada well away from coasts and Great Lakes. Elsewhere in U.S., rare in most regions (mainly late Dec.–Mar.), including Pacific Coast south to Calif., very rarely to Baja Calif. Sur and n. Gulf of Calif., Mex.; and along Atlantic Coast south to Fla.; very rare to casual on Gulf of Mex. coast (recorded south to n. Tamaulipas, Mex.[4]); casual at best in interior Southeast and Southwest. Casual in Bermuda (late Nov.–early Mar.).

Northbound migrants in coastal Calif. mainly Feb.–Mar., with arrivals on Seward Peninsula during late Apr., where fairly common by mid-May. Northbound movement mainly Mar.–Apr. on Great Lakes and in coastal Northeast, with some birds lingering into May. Peak spring movements on s. Hudson Bay mid-Apr.–early June, and arrival on Arctic coast usually May, with peak movements probably in mid-month. Summer records of nonbreeders frequent in coastal Canada with fewer on Great Lakes and U.S. coasts; oversummering birds have occurred casually as far south as s. Calif. and Fla.

FIELD IDENTIFICATION

SIMILAR SPECIES

Large size and overall white appearance distinctive, but always beware that leucistic or albino gulls of other species can suggest Glaucous Gull (check structure, especially of bill and wingtip); also see various Glaucous Gull hybrids (pp. 484–487, 491–492).

Adult Cycle. KUMLIEN'S GULL (ne. N. America) and ICELAND GULL (Greenland) notably smaller with smaller, shorter, and more slender bill, relatively longer and narrower wings, and longer wing projection (tail tip falls around tip of P7); bill in winter typically more greenish based or yellowish overall (often more pinkish based and with dark distal marks on Glaucous). Kumlien's Gull typically has medium gray wingtip markings and slightly but noticeably darker upperparts than *hyperboreus* subspecies of Glaucous (with which it usually occurs).

GLAUCOUS-WINGED GULL (w. N. America) has slightly darker upperparts (Kodak 5–6), gray subterminal marks on outer primaries, and pinkish orbital ring.

First Cycle. Besides size and structure (especially bill), note pink bill with sharply demarcated black distal third, white to whitish wingtips. See adult cycle for structural differences of other species; also see various Glaucous Gull hybrids (pp. 484–487, 491–492).

KUMLIEN'S GULL often has darker brownish primaries; white-winged birds told from Glaucous by size and structure, and bill rarely so cleanly two-toned (often mostly dark).

ICELAND GULL told by size and structure; bill rarely so cleanly two-toned (often mostly dark).

GLAUCOUS-WINGED GULL overall duskier in appearance with gray-brown wingtips, blackish bill. Bleached birds in spring can be very whitish, inviting confusion with Glaucous, but note blackish bill and solidly dusky tail of Glaucous-winged.

Second Cycle. Note large size, heavy build, stout bill, and short wing projection; also see various Glaucous Gull hybrids (pp. 484–487, 491–492).

KUMLIEN'S GULL usually has darker brownish primaries; white-winged birds told from Glaucous by size and structure, and bill averages duller, less cleanly two-toned.

ICELAND GULL told by size and structure; bill averages duller, less cleanly two-toned.

GLAUCOUS-WINGED GULL overall much duskier and smudgier in appearance with gray-brown wingtips, bill base variably pinkish (can be cleanly two-toned); eyes dark.

Third Cycle. Kumlien's, Iceland, Glaucous, Glaucous-winged, and hybrids all differ in much the same ways as do adults (see above and relevant accounts).

HABITAT AND BEHAVIOR

In winter found mainly on beaches, at estuaries, fishing harbors, dumps, and lakes, ranging over inshore waters and along rivers. Nests colonially or in scattered pairs on coastal islands, sea cliffs, islands in lakes, and on open tundra. Nonbreeding birds often in flocks (locally up to hundreds of birds in the north), associating readily with other gulls and water birds. Feeds commonly by scavenging; also forages in intertidal and surface waters for marine invertebrates and preys on eggs and young and adult birds.

DESCRIPTION AND MOLT

Adult Cycle. Complete PB molt (mid-May/June–Nov./Dec.) produces adult basic plumage: head, neck, and underparts white; head, neck, and sometimes upper chest with variable (but rarely heavy) dusky to brownish mottling and streaking. Upperparts pale gray (Kodak 3–5) with clean white wingtips and white trailing edge to secondaries (often shows as a skirt) and inner primaries. Uppertail coverts and tail white. Eyes pale lemon, orbital ring orange to pale flesh pink. Bill yellowish (often pinkish from fall into midwinter) with orange-red to red gonydeal spot and often a dark distal mark. Legs flesh pink, often slightly duller during height of PB molt. Partial PA molt (Oct.–Mar./Apr.) produces adult alternate plumage: head and neck clean white (rarely before Mar./Apr.). By spring, orbital ring brightens to orange or chrome yellow, varying to orange-red on some *pallidissimus*;[5] bill brightens to lemon yellow with red gonydeal spot, lacks dark distal marks.

First Cycle. Juvenile (Aug.–Apr.): pale brown to creamy overall, often with a buffy or pinkish cast in fresh plumage (soon fading to whitish). Head, neck, and underparts variably streaked and mottled whitish and pale brown, with distinct brownish bars on vent and undertail coverts. Upperparts marked with wavy brownish barring, checkering, and lacy patterning that varies from distinct and sharply patterned to muted and washed out (mainly from midwinter onward, when bleached). Uppertail coverts whitish with brownish barring. Tertials pale brown to whitish with darker brownish distal barring and notching. Wingtips vary from whitish to milky pale brown, often with fine brown subterminal chevrons or spots; similar in tone to, or paler than, upperparts. Tail pale brown to whitish with variable, wavy brown markings. IN FLIGHT: pale brownish to creamy overall with whiter wingtips; wing-linings medium to pale brownish. Eyes dark, bill of fledgling mostly dark but, usually by Sept., becomes flesh pink with clean-cut black distal third; legs flesh pink to flesh. PA1 molt (Oct.–Apr./May; does not include upperwing coverts) produces first alternate plumage. Note that many birds retain most or all juvenal plumage through Apr. and May and look bleached white overall by mid- to late winter. New A1 feathers on head, neck, chest, and flanks appear as variable dusky brownish mottling. A1 scapulars range from pale brown to grayish, typically with fine and often blurry darker bars or wavy markings. Bill can develop fine pale tip by midwinter.

Second Cycle. Complete PB2 molt (May/early June–Sept./Oct.) into second basic plumage. Some birds bleach strikingly by early summer, before PB2 is very advanced—and new B2 feathers can look contrastingly dark. Head, neck, and underparts white, variably mottled and streaked gray-brown, undertail coverts with sparser dusky bars than first cycle. Upperparts vary from whitish with diffuse, fine, and fairly sparse brownish barring and speckling to extensively but finely barred and checkered brown; some birds attain a few pale gray back feathers. Tertials whitish with variable brownish speckling and barring to pale gray-brown with speckled and notched whitish tips and edging. Wingtips whitish with indistinct fine dusky distal markings, often whiter overall than tertials. Upperwing pattern similar to first cycle but plainer overall and secondaries average grayer and more finely speckled; wing-linings whitish to washed pale brown. Tail whitish to pale brown, often with more-extensive and finer basal markings than first cycle;

tail mostly whitish on palest birds. Eyes pale lemon to brownish, bill flesh pink with black distal third and variable pale tip, legs flesh pink. Partial PA2 molt (*Sept.–Apr.*; often includes some upperwing coverts) produces second alternate plumage: head, neck, and underparts whiter, variably mottled dusky brown. Back more extensively gray in contrast to whitish or white upperwing coverts; some birds attain a few gray A2 upperwing coverts, especially median coverts. Orbital ring can be pinkish in summer. Through spring, bill typically pinkish basally, blackish distally with pale tip; by late summer some birds develop yellowish bill with reddish gonydeal smudge and black distal band. Legs flesh pink.

Third Cycle. Complete PB3 molt (May/June–Oct./Nov.) produces third basic plumage. Head, neck, and underparts white with variable dusky mottling and streaking. Upperparts pale gray, often mixed with brown-washed and whitish upperwing coverts. Rump and tail white with variable pale brownish distal tail markings (tail varies from all white to having a fairly broad pale brownish band). Remiges pale gray with poorly contrasting but fairly broad white tips, often with a brown wash to primary bases. Underwings white with sparse pale brown markings on coverts. Eyes pale lemon to dirty lemon; bill flesh pink with black distal band and pale tip; legs flesh pink. Partial PA3 molt (*Sept.–Mar./Apr.*) into third alternate plumage: dark markings on head and neck reduced to absent, upperparts can be more solidly pale gray. Eyes pale lemon, orbital ring reddish to orange; bill brightens and by summer can be indistinguishable from adult or have dark distal marks. Adult plumage attained by complete PB4 molt (May/June–Oct./Nov.).

HYBRIDS

With American Herring Gull in nw. Canada[6] and presumably ne. Canada;[7] with European Herring Gull in Iceland;[8] presumably with Vega Gull in e. Siberia and Bering Sea region[9] (and see p. 492); presumably with Glaucous-winged Gull in w. Alaska;[10,11,12] presumably with Great Black-backed Gull.[13,14]

NOTES

1. Banks 1986; 2. Howell pers. obs.; 3. Kessel 1989; 4. Gee and Edwards 2000; 5. Howell pers. obs.; 6. Spear 1987; 7. B. Mactavish pers. comm.; 8. Ingolfsson 1987; 9. Kessel 1989; 10. McCaffery et al. 1997; 11. Strang 1977; 12. Swarth 1934; 13. B. Mactavish pers. comm.; 14. Wilson 1951

The Iceland Gull complex comprises two or three taxa of large white-headed gulls that breed in Arctic Canada and Greenland: *glaucoides* (Iceland Gull, breeding in Greenland), *kumlieni* (Kumlien's Gull, breeding in ne. Canada), and perhaps *thayeri* (Thayer's Gull, breeding in n. Canada). Kumlien's Gull is generally treated as a subspecies of Iceland Gull (and almost all records of so-called Iceland Gulls in N. America are of this taxon), but the taxonomic status of Thayer's Gull has been subject to much debate.[1,2]

Recent field studies[3,4] support the distinctness of Thayer's Gull, which is treated as a full species by AOU,[5] and Browning[6] recommended that Thayer's, Kumlien's, and Iceland be recognized as separate species until proven otherwise. Snell[7] argued for the lumping of Iceland (including Kumlien's) and Thayer's, although his data (for example, his table 1) support the recognition of three distinct populations that correspond to Iceland, Kumlien's, and Thayer's. Most gull taxa are defined by morphological characters such as wingtip pattern, yet Snell's[8] criteria for defining these taxa are somewhat circular: for example, nominate Iceland Gulls can have gray in the wingtips simply because such birds breed in Greenland; why are these not simply extralimital Kumlien's Gulls, as with Glaucous-winged Gulls that breed in cen. California? Compounding the problem, studies on the breeding grounds where Kumlien's and Thayer's presumably interbreed have either: 1) been spurious;[9,10,11] or 2) failed to define variation in the characters of these taxa,[12,13] so the degree of reported interbreeding is impossible to assess. Hence, we can't learn how much Kumlien's and Thayer's interbreed until we can distinguish them, but we can't distinguish them because they appear to interbreed. Given this uncertainty, we treat the three taxa in separate accounts, with Thayer's Gull as a full species, but we recognize that much remains to be learned about this complex.

NOTES

1. Howell 1998; 2. Pittaway 1999; 3. Howell and Elliott 2001; 4. Howell and Mactavish 2003; 5. AOU 1998; 6. Browning 2002; 7. Snell 2002; 8. Ibid.; 9. Smith 1966; 10. Snell 1989; 11. Snell 1991; 12. Gaston and Decker 1985; 13. Snell 1989

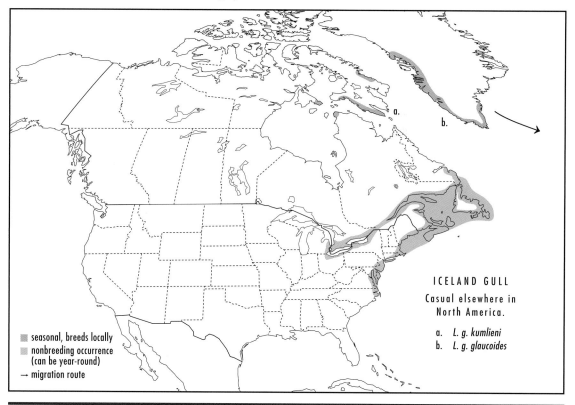

ICELAND GULL

Casual elsewhere in North America.

a. *L. g. kumlieni*
b. *L. g. glaucoides*

▨ seasonal, breeds locally
▨ nonbreeding occurrence (can be year-round)
→ migration route

LENGTH 19–24.5 IN. (48–62 CM)
IMAGES 35A.0–35A.41, I.29, 29.7, 34.15, 35B.3

IDENTIFICATION SUMMARY

A medium-large to medium-sized, pink-legged gull breeding in the Canadian Low Arctic and wintering mainly in the nw. Atlantic. Bill relatively short and slender, parallel edged with a shallow to moderate gonydeal expansion. At rest, tail tip falls between tips of P6 and P7. Adult has pale gray upperparts (Kodak 4–5) with variable wingtip pattern (Illus. 35a.7). Most birds have dark gray stripes and subterminal bands on the outer 4–5 primaries; a few birds are almost white winged (approaching Iceland Gull), and a few have darker wingtip markings (approaching Thayer's Gull). Juvenile medium brown to creamy overall with medium-brown to whitish wingtips. PA1 variable, starting Oct.–Apr. Subsequent ages variable in appearance. All ages have pink legs, often quite bright; adult eyes pale lemon to brownish, orbital ring purplish pink.

Adults mostly distinctive. Glaucous-winged Gull similar in plumage but much larger with longer and stouter bill, broad wings, short wing projection, slightly darker upperparts. White-winged adults most likely to be confused with Iceland Gull, which averages paler gray above with all-white wingtips, pale lemon eyes; Glaucous Gull notably larger and more massive with larger and thicker bill, relatively shorter wing projection, slightly paler gray upperparts, orange orbital ring. Dark-winged extremes similar to Thayer's Gull: note that Kumlien's averages paler gray above with slaty gray versus slaty blackish wingtips. See Similar Species section for more detailed identification criteria and separation from various hybrid combinations, all of which are larger and bigger billed than Kumlien's Gull.

First-cycle Kumlien's typically has brownish wash on outer primaries versus evenly pale primaries on Iceland. First-cycle Thayer's larger and darker with longer bill, blackish brown outer webs to outer primaries, contrasting dark secondary bar. Glaucous Gull larger with a stouter bill that is sharply bicolored (pink with a black tip), short wing projection, generally whiter primaries.

TAXONOMY

Kumlien's Gull was first described as a species,[1] later viewed as a hybrid between Thayer's Gull (then considered a race of Herring Gull) and Iceland Gull,[2,3] as a full species,[4] and as a subspecies of Iceland Gull.[5,6] It might yet prove to be a full species.[7,8,9] Field characters of adults based on wintering populations were proposed recently,[10] but critical studies on the breeding grounds are still needed. See introduction to the Iceland Gull complex.

STATUS AND DISTRIBUTION

Breeds ne. Canada, winters N. Atlantic (including Iceland), rarely to nw. Europe.

Breeding. Breeds (June–Aug.) in n. Canada on s. Baffin I. (north on e. coast to Home Bay and Broughton I.), e. Southampton I. (Bell Peninsula), and Coats I.; also Ungava Peninsula, nw. Que.

Nonbreeding. Southbound fall movements to Atlantic Canada can begin early Oct., but arrival there and coastal New England more regular after mid-Oct., with many more arriving Nov. On Great Lakes some arrive Nov. but most not until mid-Dec. or later. Arrivals on Mid-Atlantic Coast mainly Nov.–Dec.

Winters (Oct./Nov.–Mar./Apr.) mainly in Atlantic Canada (north to s. Lab.), with smaller numbers east to Greenland and south along Atlantic Coast of N. America to N.J., and in e. Great Lakes region. Rare (mainly Dec.–Mar.) south to Outer Banks, N.C., and on w. Great Lakes (very rare to casual on Lake Superior). Casual (mainly Dec.–Mar. in most areas, but mainly Nov.–early Dec. in Prairie Provinces) along Atlantic Coast south to Fla., on Gulf of Mex. coast west to s. Tex., in Midwest well away from Great Lakes, in interior Southeast, on Great Plains south to Colo., and in the Northwest.

Northbound movements begin by late Feb., with most departing s. parts of winter range during Mar., and n. parts during Apr.–May; a few birds remain into June, very occasionally through mid-Aug.–Sept. in New England and Atlantic Canada, making it difficult to determine fall arrival dates. Regular on sw. Hudson Bay in summer (mid-May–Oct., mostly late May–early June), and casual (Sept.–Oct.) along Arctic coast of Alaska and in s. Yukon.

"Iceland Gull" in Bermuda termed "frequent but rare" (Amos 1991) with about 7 recent fall records (late Nov.–late Dec.) and 10 spring records (late Feb.–early Apr.), but subspecies usually unspecified (at least 2 records of *kumlieni*).

SIMILAR SPECIES

In ne. N. America, the main confusion species are Glaucous Gull, Iceland Gull, and Thayer's Gull; also see hybrid Glaucous Gull × American Herring Gull. Other potentially similar species and hybrids occur mainly on the Pacific Coast of N. America (see Rarer Species).

Adult Cycle. GLAUCOUS GULL (n. latitudes) larger overall with longer and stouter bill, longer legs, and relatively shorter wing projection; upperparts paler gray (Kodak 3–4 in e. N. America) and wingtips all white. Bill often more pinkish based in winter and with dark distal marks; eyes pale lemon, orbital ring yellow-orange to reddish (can be pinkish in winter).

THAYER'S GULL (winters mainly on Pacific Coast of N. America) averages larger with longer and more hook-tipped bill, slightly longer and more pointed wing projection. Wingtip markings slaty blackish (Kodak 14.5–17) and often more extensive (on 5–6 outer primaries), upperparts slightly darker (Kodak 5–6). P10 and P5 can have complete dark subterminal bands, P9 mirror often restricted by continuous dark along the outer web, and slaty blackish medial area on P9 typically extends on to inner web. Presumed hybrids with Kumlien's look intermediate and not safely assigned to either taxon.

ICELAND GULL (apparently rare in N. America) similar in size and shape but averages paler upperparts (Kodak 3–4) and has all-white wingtips, pale lemon eyes. May interbreed with Kumlien's Gull, so some individuals not safely assigned to either taxon. An evaluation of variation in upperpart tone, wingtip pattern, eye color, and orbital ring color of adult Iceland Gulls is desirable; until then, field separation criteria from pale-winged Kumlien's should be considered tentative.

HYBRID GLAUCOUS GULL × AMERICAN HERRING GULL (widespread) best told by larger size and structure, especially longer and stouter bill, longer legs; birds with Glaucous Gull structure also have short wing projection. Bill often more pinkish based in winter and with dark distal marks. Orbital ring in summer yellow-orange (can be pinkish in winter). Critical study of wingtip patterns needed.

First Cycle. See adult cycle for structural differences between taxa.

GLAUCOUS GULL differs in larger size and structure, white to whitish wingtips, flesh pink bill with clean-cut blackish distal third.

THAYER'S GULL darker and browner overall with blackish brown to dark brown wingtips (with strong inner web/outer web contrast on P6–P10), dark secondary bar and tail, and more solidly and darker brown tertials. Presumed hybrids with Kumlien's look intermediate and not safely assigned to either taxon.

ICELAND GULL perhaps not safely separable from palest-winged Kumlien's. Iceland typically has evenly pale (whitish) primaries versus brown-washed outer primaries (especially outer webs) and whitish inners on Kumlien's—but bleaching by midwinter can render such distinctions moot. Iceland more often attains a distinct pinkish bill base in first winter, but a few Kumlien's overlap in this feature.

HYBRID GLAUCOUS GULL × AMERICAN HERRING GULL best told by size and structure, especially bill; often has Glaucous-like pinkish bill with black tip and Herring-like darker secondary bar.

Second Cycle. See adult cycle for structural differences between taxa.

GLAUCOUS GULL differs in larger size and structure; primaries evenly whitish without darker outer webs to outer primaries.

THAYER'S GULL averages longer bill and longer and more-pointed wingtips; its darker wingtips have distinct dark outer webs to P6–P10, and P5 often has a large dark distal mark (dark outer webs usually restricted to P7–P10 on Kumlien's). Presumed hybrids with Kumlien's look intermediate and are not safely assigned to either taxon.

ICELAND GULL perhaps not safely separable from palest-winged Kumlien's but typically has evenly pale (whitish) primaries versus brown-washed outer primaries (especially outer webs) and whitish inners on Kumlien's.

HYBRID GLAUCOUS GULL × AMERICAN HERRING GULL best told by size and structure, especially bill.

Third Cycle. Glaucous Gull, Thayer's Gull, Iceland Gull, and hybrid Glaucous Gull × American Herring Gull all differ in much the same ways as do adults (see above and relevant species accounts).

RARER SPECIES

All of these N. Pacific hybrids can resemble Kumlien's Gull in plumage, but all are larger and differ in structure. Also see Glaucous-winged Gull (differences noted under that species).

Adult Cycle. HYBRID GLAUCOUS-WINGED GULL × AMERICAN HERRING GULL (w. N. America) larger and bulkier overall with a bigger bill; some have broader wings with shorter wing projection (more like Glaucous-winged), orbital ring can show some yellowish (like Herring), and bill in winter often has dark distal marks. Study needed of wingtip patterns.

HYBRID GLAUCOUS-WINGED GULL × GLAUCOUS GULL (N. Pacific) larger and bulkier overall with a bigger bill, broader wings with shorter wing projection. Orbital ring may show some yellow-orange, and bill in winter often has dark distal marks. Study needed of wingtip patterns.

HYBRID GLAUCOUS-WINGED GULL × WESTERN GULL (w. N. America) larger and bulkier overall with a bigger bill, broader wings with shorter wing projection, and darker upperparts (Kodak 6–8). Orbital ring may show some yellow-orange, and bill in winter often has dark distal marks. Study needed of wingtip patterns.

First Cycle. See adult cycle for structural differences between taxa.

HYBRID GLAUCOUS-WINGED GULL × AMERICAN HERRING GULL best told by size and structure; more often has darker secondary bar and tail.

HYBRID GLAUCOUS-WINGED GULL × GLAUCOUS GULL best told by size and structure, especially large bill, short wing projection.

HYBRID GLAUCOUS-WINGED GULL × WESTERN GULL best told by size and structure, especially large bill, short wing projection.

Second Cycle. See adult cycle for structural differences between taxa.

HYBRID GLAUCOUS-WINGED GULL × AMERICAN HERRING GULL best told by size and structure; more often has darker secondary bar and tail.

HYBRID GLAUCOUS-WINGED GULL × GLAUCOUS GULL best told by size and structure, especially large bill, short wing projection.

HYBRID GLAUCOUS-WINGED GULL × WESTERN GULL best told by size and structure, especially large bill, short wing projection.

Third Cycle. Hybrids all differ in much the same ways as do adults (see above).

HABITAT AND BEHAVIOR

Breeds on cliffs and rocky islands in Canadian Arctic; adults winter mainly at sea and along the coast at fishing harbors, sewage outfalls, inlets, and beaches. First-winter birds (and, to an extent, other ages) also occur often at lakes, duck ponds, dumps, parking lots, and other habitats where large gulls occur. Non-breeding birds (especially adults) often in flocks (locally up to a few thousand birds, but more often 100–1,000 birds). Kumlien's Gulls associate readily with other gulls and water birds but, at least in winter, they often avoid feeding areas dominated by the larger American Herring and Glaucous Gulls. Feeds while swimming and in flight by picking and surface-plunging, and overall more aerial than

Glaucous Gull. In winter, feeds on marine invertebrates and fish in inshore and offshore waters, often along and around leads in sea ice;[11] also scavenges.

DESCRIPTION AND MOLT

Note: some Kumlien's-type birds have atypically dark wingtips (blackish gray on adult and third cycle, dark brown in first cycle and second cycle) and overall increased dark pigmentation in the flight feathers. Some of these are probably hybrids with Thayer's Gull (see pp. 488–489), but some may represent variation in pure Kumlien's, the limits of which have yet to be satisfactorily established.

Adult Cycle. Complete PB molt (June/July–Nov./Dec.) produces adult basic plumage: head, neck, and underparts white; head, neck, and sometimes upper chest with variable (usually moderate to heavy) dusky mottling and streaking. Upperparts pale gray (Kodak 4–5) with variable slaty gray wingtip markings (mostly Kodak 7–10). Most birds (about 70 percent) have slaty gray markings on P6–P10 or P7–P10 with complete dark subterminal bands on up to 3 primaries among P6–P9 and the most extensive dark markings on P8; P10 lacks a subterminal band and often has no subterminal gray markings; P9 has a white mirror typically extending across the outer web, and dark medial markings rarely extend onto the inner web. The least-marked wingtips (9 percent of birds) have gray stripes along the basal to medial portions of the outer web and shaft of 1–4 primaries among P7–P10, and some birds (about 4 percent) appear completely "white winged" in the field. The most extensively marked wingtips (5 percent of birds) have dark marks on the outer 6 primaries but rarely a distinct or complete subterminal band on P5. White trailing edge to secondaries (often hidden at rest) and inner primaries. Uppertail coverts and tail white. Underwings show a ghosting of variable upperwing pattern. Eyes pale lemon to brownish, orbital ring purplish pink to reddish. Bill yellowish (often greenish basally in winter) with orange-red to red gonydeal spot and rarely a dark mark at gonys. Legs bright flesh pink, perhaps duller during height of PB molt. Partial PA molt (Oct.–Mar./Apr.) produces adult alternate: head and neck clean white (rarely before Mar./Apr.); white primary tips can be lost through wear. By spring, orbital ring brightens, bill brightens to lemon yellow with red gonydeal spot, lacks dark distal marks.

First Cycle. Juvenile (Aug.–Apr.): medium

brown to creamy overall. Head, neck, and underparts variably streaked and mottled whitish and brownish, becoming whitish on vent and undertail coverts which have fairly broad brownish bars. Upperparts marked with typically fairly fine brownish barring, checkering, and lacy patterning that varies from distinct and sharply patterned to muted and washed out (mainly from midwinter onward, when bleached). Uppertail coverts whitish with brownish barring. Tertials pale brown to whitish with variable, typically fine patterning similar to upperparts. Wingtips vary from medium brown with narrow whitish edgings to whitish overall with fine brown subterminal chevrons or spots; typically similar in tone to upperparts. Spread primaries often show a slightly paler panel on inners; secondaries medium-pale brown to whitish, not contrasting on spread wing. Outer primary coverts plain pale brownish to whitish, often with slightly darker subterminal marks. Tail medium brown with whitish tip and whitish ribbing on outer web of R6; whitish marbling and barring basally on outer rectrices best seen when tail fully spread or from below. IN FLIGHT: pale brownish to creamy overall with variably darker, medium brown to pale brown outer webs to P7–P10 and broad, medium brown to pale brown distal tail band; inner secondaries sometimes slightly darker than upperwing coverts; wing-linings medium to pale brownish. Eyes dark, bill blackish, usually with variable dull flesh on basal two-thirds by early winter and sometimes flesh pink with fairly clean-cut blackish tip; legs flesh pink to flesh. PA1 molt (Oct.–Apr./May; does not include upperwing coverts) produces first alternate plumage. Note that some birds retain most or all juvenal plumage through Apr. and May and look bleached white overall. Head, neck, chest, and flanks variably mottled and streaked smoky grayish. A1 scapulars range from whitish to pale grayish, typically with fine, often blurry, darker bars or wavy markings that contrast with bleached brownish markings of juvenal scapulars. Bill typically blackish with dull flesh to flesh pink basally; legs flesh pink; eyes dark.

Second Cycle. Complete PB2 molt (May/June–Sept./Oct.) into second basic plumage. Some birds bleach strikingly by early summer, before PB2 is very advanced—and new B2 feathers can look contrastingly dark. Head, neck, and underparts white, variably mottled and streaked gray-brown; head and chest of some birds bleach to mostly whitish by midwinter. Upperparts vary from whitish with diffuse, fine, and fairly sparse brownish barring and speckling to extensively but finely barred and checkered brown; some birds have a few gray back feathers and others have a mostly pale gray back. Tertials whitish with variable brownish speckling and barring, to medium-pale gray-brown with speckled and notched whitish tips and edging. Wingtips medium gray-brown to whitish, not contrastingly darker than tertials. Upperwing pattern of remiges similar to first cycle, but inner primaries average paler and secondaries darker and grayer; outer primaries of darker-winged birds often show whiter tongues (and sometimes a faint P10 mirror) hinting at adult pattern. Distal tail band medium to pale gray-brown, often with more-extensive and finer whitish basal markings than first cycle; tail mostly whitish on palest birds. Wing-linings medium to pale gray-brown with underside of primaries often reflectively pale and showing a ghosting of upperwing pattern. Eyes pale lemon to brownish, bill typically flesh pink to pale greenish with black distal third and pale horn tip (sometimes duller, like first winter), legs flesh pink. Partial PA2 molt (Sept.–Apr.; often includes some upperwing coverts) produces second alternate plumage: head, neck, and underparts whiter, variably mottled dusky (sometimes bleaching and wearing to mostly white by summer), back more extensively gray in contrast to faded upperwing coverts; some birds attain a few gray upperwing coverts, especially median coverts. Orbital ring can be pinkish in summer. By summer, some birds have yellowish bill with reddish gonydeal smudge and black distal band.

Third Cycle. Complete PB3 molt (May/June–Oct.) produces third basic plumage. Head, neck, and underparts white with variable dusky streaking and mottling. Upperparts pale gray, usually with variable brown wash to upperwing coverts, brownish tertial centers. Rump and tail white with variable pale brownish distal tail markings (tail varies from all white to having a fairly broad, pale brownish band). Variable wingtip patterns mirror adult patterns (see above) but darker-winged birds have more-extensive grayish (to brownish gray) and less white than adult. Underwings mostly white with variable brown markings on coverts, outer primaries show ghosting of upperwing pattern. Eyes pale lemon to brownish; bill flesh to dull pale greenish with black distal band and pale tip; legs flesh pink. Partial PA3 molt (Sept.–Mar./Apr.) into third alternate plumage: dark markings on head and neck reduced to absent; bill brighter and can be indistinguishable from adult or have dark distal marks. White tips to outer primaries may be lost by wear. Adult plumage attained by complete PB4 molt (May/June–Oct./Nov.).

HYBRIDS

Presumably with Thayer's Gull[12,13] but extent of hybridization difficult to assess (see Taxonomy and introduction to Iceland Gull complex); seems possible with Iceland Gull in w. Greenland.[14]

NOTES

1. Brewster 1883; 2. AOU 1931; 3. Dwight 1925; 4. Taverner 1937; 5. AOU 1957; 6. Godfrey 1986; 7. AOU 1998; 8. Browning 2002; 9. Howell and Mactavish 2003; 10. Ibid.; 11. Snell 2002; 12. Gaston and Decker 1985; 13. Knudsen 1976; 14. Boertmann 2001

LENGTH 19–24.5 IN. (48–62 CM)
PHOTOS 35B.0–35B.13

IDENTIFICATION SUMMARY

See separate account for Kumlien's Gull, which is the regularly occurring subspecies of Iceland Gull in N. America. Nominate Iceland Gull is a medium-large to medium-sized, white-winged gull breeding in Greenland and wintering mainly in the N. Atlantic. Bill relatively short and slender, parallel edged with shallow to moderate gonydeal angle. At rest, tail tip falls between tips of P6 and P7. Adult has pale gray upperparts (Kodak 3–4) with white wingtips. Juvenile pale brown to creamy overall with pale brown to whitish wingtips. PA1 variable, starting Oct.–Apr. Subsequent ages somewhat variable in appearance but overall very pale with white wingtips. All ages have pink legs; adult eyes pale lemon and orbital ring pink to reddish.

Adult perhaps not always separable from pale-eyed and white-winged Kumlien's Gull but upperparts average paler gray. Glaucous Gull virtually identical in plumage but notably larger and more massive with larger and stouter bill, relatively shorter wing projection, orbital ring of birds in ne. N. America usually orange. First-cycle Iceland typically has uniformly pale primaries, whereas Kumlien's typically has a browner wash on the outer primaries. First-cycle Glaucous Gull larger with stouter bill that is more sharply bicolored (pink with a black tip), short wing projection.

TAXONOMY

Kumlien's Gull usually considered a subspecies of Iceland Gull[1,2] but may prove to be a full species.[3,4,5] Some authors[6,7] lump Thayer's Gull with Iceland Gull, based mainly on putative interbreeding of Thayer's and Kumlien's (but see Taxonomy sections in Kumlien's Gull and Thayer's Gull accounts, plus introduction to the Iceland Gull complex).

STATUS AND DISTRIBUTION

Breeds Greenland, winters N. Atlantic, vagrants reported to Japan.[8]

Breeding. Breeds (mid-May/June–Aug.) w. and se. Greenland, with population estimated at 80,000 pairs.[9]

Nonbreeding. Winters "abundantly" in open water off Greenland;[10] also winters Iceland and Faeroe Is., with much smaller numbers reaching nw. Europe (mainly Dec./Jan.–Mar.). Status in ne. N. America unclear given uncertainty of identification with regard to white-winged Kumlien's Gulls. Iceland Gull probably rare in winter (mainly Nov.–Mar.) in e. Nfld.,[11] perhaps elsewhere in Atlantic Canada. In e. Ont. there are three records (late Nov.–mid-Jan.) attributed to nominate *glaucoides*, including an adult specimen.[12] Sightings of adults with apparently pure white wingtips (but no details of upperpart gray tone) have occurred along Atlantic Coast south to N.Y.

In w. N. America, records attributed to nominate *glaucoides* include at least one from n. Alaska (Oct.),[13,14] one from s. Yukon (Oct.), and two from Calif. (late Dec.–Jan.).[15]

FIELD IDENTIFICATION

SIMILAR SPECIES

Kumlien's Gull and Glaucous Gull are the only potentially similar species.

Adult Cycle. An evaluation of variation in upperpart tone, wingtip pattern, eye color, and orbital-ring color of adult Iceland Gulls is desirable; until then, field separation criteria relative to pale-winged Kumlien's should be considered tentative. As with all white-winged gulls, beware the possibility of leucistic or albino individuals of other species.

KUMLIEN'S GULL (ne. N. America) similar in size and shape but averages darker upperparts (Kodak 4–5) and heavier dusky head and neck markings in winter; most have gray subterminal marks on the outer primaries, and many have dusky eyes. May interbreed with Iceland Gull, so some individuals not safely assigned to either taxon.

GLAUCOUS GULL (n. latitudes) larger overall with longer and stouter bill, longer legs, and relatively shorter wing projection (tail tip falls between tips of P7 and P8). Bill often more pinkish based in winter and with dark distal marks; orbital ring of breeding birds in ne. N. America orange to orange-yellow but can be pinkish in winter.

First Cycle. KUMLIEN'S GULL. Palest-winged Kumlien's perhaps not safely separable from Iceland but most have brown-washed outer primaries (especially outer webs) and whitish inners—but bleaching by midwinter can render such distinctions moot. Iceland more often attains a distinct pinkish bill base in first winter, but a few Kumlien's overlap in this feature.

GLAUCOUS GULL differs in larger size and structure, white to whitish wingtips, flesh pink bill with cleaner-cut blackish distal third.

Second Cycle. KUMLIEN'S GULL. Palest-winged Kumlien's perhaps not safely separable from Iceland, but most have brown-washed outer primaries (especially outer webs) and whitish inners.

GLAUCOUS GULL larger with short wing projection, bigger bill.

Third Cycle. Kumlien's Gull and Glaucous Gull differ in much the same ways as do adults (see above and relevant species accounts).

Habitat and Behavior

Much as Kumlien's Gull, with which Iceland Gull is likely to occur in N. America.

Description and Molt

Adult Cycle. Complete PB molt (June/July–Nov./Dec.) produces adult basic plumage: head, neck, and underparts white; head, neck, and sometimes upper chest with variable (usually moderate to light) dusky mottling and streaking. Upperparts pale gray (Kodak 3–4) with white wingtips and white trailing edge to secondaries (often hidden at rest) and inner primaries. Uppertail coverts and tail white. Eyes pale lemon, orbital ring pinkish to red. Bill yellowish (often greenish basally in winter) with orange-red to red gonydeal spot and rarely a dark distal mark. Legs bright flesh pink, perhaps duller during height of PB molt. Partial PA molt (Oct.–Mar./Apr.) produces adult alternate plumage: head and neck clean white (rarely before Mar./Apr.). By spring, orbital ring brighter reddish, bill bright lemon yellow with red gonydeal spot, lacks dark distal marks.

First Cycle. Juvenile (Aug.–Apr.): pale brown to creamy overall, often with buffy or pinkish cast in fresh plumage (soon fading to whitish). Head, neck, and underparts variably streaked and mottled whitish and pale brown, with distinct brownish bars on vent and undertail coverts. Upperparts marked with wavy brownish barring, checkering, and lacy patterning that varies from distinct and sharply patterned to muted and washed out (mainly from midwinter onward, when bleached). Uppertail coverts whitish with brownish barring. Tertials pale brown to whitish with darker brownish distal barring and notching. Wing-

tips vary from whitish to milky pale brown, often with fine brown subterminal chevrons or spots; similar in tone to, or paler than, upperparts. Tail pale brown to whitish with variable, wavy brown markings. IN FLIGHT: pale brownish to creamy overall with whiter wingtips; wing-linings medium to pale brownish. Eyes dark, bill of fledgling mostly dark but by first winter usually dull flesh with blackish distal third; legs flesh pink to flesh. PA1 molt (Oct.–Apr./May; does not include upperwing coverts) produces first alternate plumage. Note that many birds retain most or all juvenal plumage through Apr. and May and can be bleached white in overall appearance. New A1 feathers on head, neck, chest, and flanks appear as variable dusky mottling. A1 scapulars range from pale brown to grayish, typically with fine and often blurry darker bars or wavy markings. Bill often brightens to flesh with fairly clean-cut blackish distal third; can develop fine pale tip by midwinter.

Second Cycle. Complete PB2 molt (May–Sept./Oct.) into second basic plumage. Some birds bleach strikingly by early summer, before PB2 is very advanced—and new B2 feathers can look contrastingly dark. Head, neck, and underparts white, variably mottled and streaked gray-brown, undertail coverts with sparser dusky bars than first cycle. Upperparts vary from whitish with diffuse, fine, and fairly sparse brownish barring and speckling, to extensively but finely barred and checkered brown; some birds attain a few pale gray back feathers. Tertials whitish with variable brownish speckling and barring to pale gray-brown with speckled and notched whitish tips and edging. Wingtips whitish with indistinct fine dusky distal markings, often whiter overall than tertials. Upperwing pattern similar to first cycle but plainer overall and secondaries average grayer and more finely speckled; wing-linings whitish to washed pale brown. Tail whitish to pale brown, often with more-extensive and finer basal markings than first cycle; tail mostly whitish on palest birds. Eyes dirty pale lemon to brownish, bill flesh pink with black distal third and pale tip, legs flesh pink. Partial PA2 molt (Sept.–Apr.; often includes some upperwing coverts) produces second alternate plumage: head, neck, and underparts whiter, variably mottled dusky brown, back more extensively gray in contrast to whitish or white upperwing coverts; some birds attain a few gray upperwing coverts, especially median coverts. Orbital ring may be pinkish in summer. Through spring, bill typically pinkish basally, blackish distally with pale tip; by late summer some birds develop yellowish bill with reddish gonydeal smudge and black distal band.

Third Cycle. Complete PB3 molt (May/June–Oct.) produces third basic plumage. Head, neck, and underparts white with variable dusky mottling and streaking. Upperparts pale gray, often mixed with brown-washed and whitish upperwing coverts. Rump and tail white with variable pale brownish distal tail markings (tail varies from all white to having a fairly broad, pale brownish band). Remiges pale gray with poorly contrasting but fairly broad white tips, often with a brown wash to primary bases. Underwings white with sparse pale brown markings on coverts. Eyes pale lemon to dirty lemon; bill flesh pink with black distal band and pale tip; legs flesh pink. Partial PA3 molt (*Sept.*–Mar./Apr.) into third alternate plumage: dark markings on head and neck reduced to absent, back may become more solidly pale gray. Eyes pale lemon,

orbital ring may be reddish; bill brightens and can be indistinguishable from adult or have dark distal marks. Adult plumage attained by complete PB4 molt (May/June–Oct./Nov.).

HYBRIDS

None reported. Hybridization seems possible with Thayer's Gull in the Canadian High Arctic[16] and with Kumlien's Gull in w. Greenland.[17]

NOTES

1. AOU 1957; 2. Godfrey 1986; 3. AOU 1998; 4. Browning 2002; 5. Howell and Mactavish 2003; 6. BOU 1991; 7. Godfrey 1986; 8. Brazil 1991; 9. Boertmann 1994; 10. Ibid.; 11. Peters and Burleigh 1951; 12. Pittaway 1992; 13. Bailey et al. 1933; 14. D. D. Gibson pers. comm.; 15. Erickson and Hamilton 2001; 16. Howell and Mactavish 2003; 17. Boertmann 2001

36. THAYER'S GULL *Larus thayeri*

LENGTH 19.7–25 IN. (50–63.5 CM)
PHOTOS 36.0–36.47, I.11–I.12, I.24–I.25, I.37

IDENTIFICATION SUMMARY

A medium-large, dark-winged, pink-legged gull breeding in the Canadian High Arctic and wintering mainly along the N. American Pacific Coast. Bill relatively slender and parallel edged with moderate gonydeal expansion. Adult has pale gray upperparts (Kodak 5–6) with slaty blackish wingtips (typically with white mirrors or mirror-tongues on P9–P10, distinct white tongue-tips on P6–P8) and, in basic plumage, extensive dusky mottling and streaking on head and neck. Juvenile medium-dark brown overall with blackish brown wingtips and tail, pale inner webs to outer primaries. PA1 variable, starting Nov.–Apr. Subsequent ages variable in appearance. All ages have pink legs, often bright; adult eyes brownish to pale lemon, orbital ring purplish pink.

Most likely to be confused with American Herring Gull, hybrid Glaucous-winged × American Herring and Glaucous-winged × Western gulls, and dark-winged Kumlien's Gulls. Adult Thayer's distinguished from American Herring Gull by average smaller

size and more slender bill, eye color (rarely staring pale lemon like Herring), purplish pink orbital ring, slightly darker upperparts, and wingtip pattern: wingtips are slaty blackish (versus black) mainly on the outer webs so underwing looks silvery gray (not as extensively black as Herring) with blackish restricted to subterminal bands on the outer primaries; wingtips also have more-extensive white than typical of Herring Gulls in the West. Hybrids, however, can show these Thayer's Gull plumage characters and are best identified by structure (especially bill size and shape). Dark-winged Kumlien's Gull similar to Thayer's Gull: Note that Kumlien's averages paler gray above with slaty gray versus slaty blackish wingtips. See Similar Species section for more detailed identification criteria and separation from various hybrid combinations, all of which are larger and bigger billed than Thayer's.

First-cycle Thayer's Gull identified by size and structure (especially bill), blackish brown to dark brown outer primaries with dark outer webs and pale inner webs. Thayer's plumage characters can be shown by hybrids, however, so note size and structure relative to other gulls. Distinguished from Glaucous-winged

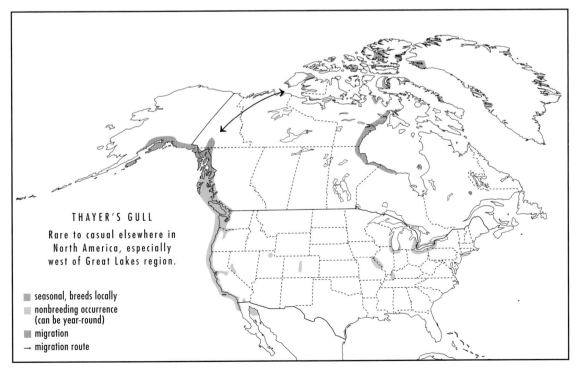

THAYER'S GULL
Rare to casual elsewhere in North America, especially west of Great Lakes region.

- seasonal, breeds locally
- nonbreeding occurrence (can be year-round)
- migration
- → migration route

and most Kumlien's Gulls by dark brown primaries contrasting darker than rest of upperparts, at least in fresh plumage. See Similar Species section for details.

TAXONOMY

Thayer's Gull was described as a species,[1] then lumped as a subspecies of Herring Gull based on perceived plumage intergradation in museum specimens.[2,3] Macpherson[4] showed that Herring and Thayer's bred sympatrically without interbreeding and restored Thayer's Gull to a full species while noting its similarity in several respects to Iceland and Kumlien's Gulls. Subsequent authors have treated Thayer's Gull as a full species[5,6,7,8] or as a subspecies of Iceland Gull.[9,10] Studies on the breeding grounds where Thayer's and Kumlien's presumably interbreed have either: 1) been spurious[11,12,13] or 2) failed to define the characters of the taxa,[14,15,16] so the degree of putative interbreeding is impossible to assess. Hence, we can't learn how much Thayer's and Kumlien's interbreed until we can distinguish them, but we can't distinguish them because they appear to interbreed. Field characters of adults based on wintering populations were proposed recently,[17] but critical studies on the breeding grounds are still needed.

STATUS AND DISTRIBUTION

Breeds n. Canada, winters w. N. America. Vagrants reported from Japan and w. Europe.

Breeding. Breeds (June–Aug.) in Arctic Canada from Banks Is. and s. Victoria Is. east to Southampton Is., Ellesmere Is., Devon Is., and e.-cen. Baffin Is., and on Arctic coast of Keewatin; has also bred nw. Greenland.

Nonbreeding. Southbound fall movement evident in sw. Hudson Bay and s. Yukon by early Aug. (peak movements early–mid-Sept.), in se. Alaska by late Aug. (peak movements mid–late Sept.). Uncommon fall migrant (mainly Aug.–Sept.) along Arctic coast of Alaska west to Point Barrow and casual in Bering Sea. On Pacific Coast, arrival in the Northwest may be as early as late Aug., but mostly mid-Oct.–Nov. In coastal Calif., a few arrive mid–late Oct., most during Nov. A juvenile reported from Salton Sea, 29 Sept.,[18] if correct, would be remarkable. In interior East and Great Lakes region, first fall arrivals typically mid-Oct., more often late Oct.–early Nov., exceptionally late Sept. From n. interior regions (for example, Prairie Provinces) most birds depart by late Nov. Migration route to Pacific Coast from Arctic breeding grounds unclear, perhaps a direct overland flight through Yukon and B.C. at high elevation.

Locally fairly common in winter (mainly Oct./Nov.–Mar./Apr.) from se. Alaska south along coast (fewer to inland valleys and reservoirs) to cen. Calif., rarely north to s. coastal Alaska (Kodiak Is.), rarely to uncommonly (mainly Dec.–Mar.) south to Baja Calif., casually to Baja Calif. Sur. Casual (late Sept.–May, mostly fall) in cen. and e. Aleutians. Small numbers also winter Salton Sea and n. Gulf of Calif., Mex.; casual in the Southwest. Rare in Great Basin, Great Plains, and Midwest, especially Great Lakes region (where more numerous on w. lakes; for example, outnumbers Kumlien's more than 3:1 on Indiana lakefront[19]), but also on lower Ohio and Miss. rivers and nearby large lakes. Rare to very rare south to Gulf of Mex. coast in Tex., casually south to n. Tamaulipas, Mex.[20] and east to Fla. Very rare to casual along Atlantic Coast of N. America (mainly Nov./Dec.–Mar.), with perhaps most records from Mid-Atlantic region, but also reported north to Nfld.,[21] south to Fla.

Spring movement evident in U.S. by Feb.; most depart wintering areas during Mar.–early Apr.; some remain into late Apr., very few into May. At least in some years, thousands of birds stage early–mid-May in se. Alaska (around Juneau), presumably before a direct overland flight to Arctic coast.[22] Common on sw. Hudson Bay late May–mid-June (some nonbreeders remain through summer). First arrivals on breeding grounds mid–late May, most not until June. Casual in winter range June–Aug. with exceptional summer records as far south as s. Calif. and Fla.

FIELD IDENTIFICATION

SIMILAR SPECIES

Thayer's Gull is medium-large, fairly long winged, and relatively slender billed, but its measurements overlap with most other large gulls, so identification should be based on a suite of characters. In particular, note overall size and structure (in comparison to gulls of known identity), especially bill size and shape, and wingtip pattern.

Adult Cycle. The main confusion species is American Herring Gull, but also consider hybrids. Note overall size and structure, pale gray upperparts, slaty blackish wingtips (which often look simply black in the field, unless compared to truly black-winged species), pink legs.

AMERICAN HERRING GULL (widespread) averages larger and, especially, stouter billed; slightly paler gray upperparts (Kodak 4–5) rarely apparent in sunny conditions. Wingtip patterns can overlap with Thayer's, but dark portions on Thayer's wingtips are slaty blackish (Kodak 14.5–17), not jet black as on Herring (Kodak 18–19), and are largely restricted to the tips and outer webs — so underwingtip of Thayer's looks mostly silvery gray with narrow dark trailing edge, not blackish as on most Herrings, especially those in the West. Thayer's eyes are usually dirty yellowish to brown, rarely staring pale lemon, its orbital ring purplish pink, and its legs often brighter pink than Herring. On winter adults, the dusky head and neck markings of Thayer's average more mottled, less streaked, and the bill rarely has distinct dark distal marks, which are often shown by Herrings.

KUMLIEN'S GULL (ne. N. America) averages slightly smaller with shorter and blunter-tipped bill, slightly shorter and blunter wing projection. Wingtip markings slaty gray (mainly Kodak 7–10) and often less extensive, upperparts slightly paler (Kodak 4–5). P10 rarely has dark subterminal marks, and P5 usually unmarked; P9 mirror usually crosses both webs and dark on medial portion of P9 rarely extends noticeably onto inner web. Presumed hybrids with Thayer's look intermediate and are not safely assigned to either taxon.

HYBRID GLAUCOUS-WINGED GULL × AMERICAN HERRING GULL (w. N. America) averages larger and bulkier with a bigger bill. Plumage and bare-part combinations can match Thayer's, so attention to size and structure important. Hybrids often have broader wings with shorter wing projection (more like Glaucous-winged), orbital ring may show some yellowish (like Herring), and bill in winter often has dark distal marks (uncommon on Thayer's); critical study needed of wingtip patterns.

HYBRID GLAUCOUS-WINGED GULL × WESTERN GULL (w. N. America) can suggest Thayer's Gull in plumage but tends to be darker above (mostly Kodak 6–8) and bill notably stouter, often with a swollen gonys; also note large overall size, broad wings, and relatively short wing projection. Hybrids rarely show extensive, neatly demarcated white on P9–P10. Behavior is also a clue: If you think you see a Thayer's Gull dominating feeding Western and Glaucous-winged gulls, then it's most likely a hybrid.

HYBRID GLAUCOUS GULL × AMERICAN HERRING GULL (widespread) larger with longer and stouter bill, paler gray upperparts, pale eyes, and orange orbital ring (can be pinkish in winter). Wingtip pattern might resemble Thayer's but range of variation poorly known; should be separable by size and structure, especially bill.

VEGA GULL (w. Alaska), larger and bulkier with stouter bill, upperparts slightly darker (Kodak 7–8), more extensive black wingtip contrasts below, orbital ring reddish.

GLAUCOUS-WINGED GULL (w. N. America) averages larger with proportionately shorter and broader wings, relatively shorter wing projection, and stouter bill. Thayer's typically has slaty blackish wingtips quite different from Glaucous-winged, but some birds (hybrid Thayer's × Kumlien's?) have charcoal gray wingtips similar to dark or hybrid Glaucous-winged Gulls. Best separated by structure.

First Cycle. First-cycle Thayer's Gull variable, with the main confusion species in regular winter range being American Herring Gull and Glaucous-winged Gull (especially compared to bleached Thayer's). Note size and structure (especially bill), and outer-primary patterns.

AMERICAN HERRING GULL averages larger with stouter bill that generally has more-marked gonydeal expansion, often shows shallower sloping forehead. Plumage slightly to distinctly darker overall than Thayer's, blackish to brownish black wingtips usually have indistinct or no whitish fringes, upperparts often have finer and less "frosty" pale patterning. Inner webs of outer primaries more extensively dark, so pale inner primary panel on upperwing contrasts more with more solidly dark outer primaries; underside of outer primaries darker (but can be reflectively pale). Some darkly pigmented Thayer's can be very similar to Herring Gull (or hybrids), and problem birds may not be identifiable.

GLAUCOUS-WINGED GULL averages larger and bulkier with stouter bill, but some male Thayer's approach small female Glaucous-winged. Wingtips of Glaucous-winged are pale to medium brown, similar in tone to upperparts, which typically have finer and less "frosty" patterning than Thayer's. In flight, Glaucous-winged looks plainer and less contrasting, without a dark secondary bar and contrasting two-tone outer primaries.

KUMLIEN'S GULL paler and milkier overall with medium brown to whitish wingtips (lacking strong inner web/outer web contrast on P6–P10), lacks distinct dark secondary bar and tail band, and tertials paler and more finely patterned. Some presumed hybrids with Thayer's look intermediate and are not safely assigned to either taxon.

VEGA GULL averages larger with a stouter bill that generally has a more marked gonydeal expansion; often shows a shallower sloping forehead. Blackish to brownish black wingtips usually have no or indistinct whitish fringes.

Inner webs of outer primaries more extensively dark so that pale inner primary panel on upperwing contrasts more with more solidly dark outer primaries; underside of outer primaries darker (but can be reflectively pale); uppertail coverts and tail base contrastingly white, barred blackish with contrasting black distal tail band.

CALIFORNIA GULL (w. N. America) similar in overall size but has longer and narrower wings with long wing projection. Almost all winter birds told readily by sharply bicolored pink-and-black bill (can be mostly dark into early winter), which is also relatively longer with only a slight gonydeal expansion. California has earlier and more extensive PA1 molt (often including wing coverts) and has blacker wingtips; in flight, note California's all-dark primaries (lacking a distinct pale inner panel) and solidly blackish tail.

WESTERN GULL (w. N. America) larger and bulkier with broad wings and stout, bulbous-tipped bill. Plumage generally darker and browner with black wingtips; upperwing lacks contrasting pale panel on inner primaries, and outer primaries solidly dark; tail solidly blackish.

HYBRID GLAUCOUS-WINGED GULL × AMERICAN HERRING GULL larger overall with longer and stouter bill, but plumage can overlap with Thayer's. Some presumed hybrids resemble Thayer's closely and may be difficult to identify without known species for size and structure comparison, but most hybrids are bulkier with larger bills.

HYBRID GLAUCOUS-WINGED GULL × WESTERN GULL. Besides structural differences (with broad wings and bill size/shape the most obvious), the following characters help separate hybrids from Thayer's—but a hybrid may resemble Thayer's Gull in each feature. Hybrids more often have the tertials, tail, and wingtips similar in tone; hybrids have more-diffuse contrast between outer and inner webs on the outer primaries; hybrids often have more solidly dark tails; hybrids often have more advanced molt timing, with extensive scapular molt under way by midwinter (and often with coarser A1 scapular patterns); and hybrids often have duller, dusky pinkish legs.

HYBRID GLAUCOUS GULL × AMERICAN HERRING GULL larger with longer and stouter bill that often has brighter pinkish basally. Wingtip and tail pattern might resemble Thayer's, but range of variation poorly known; should be separable by size and structure, especially bill.

SLATY-BACKED GULL (n. Pacific) should be separable by structure, being larger and bulkier with broad wings, shorter wing projection, longer legs, and stouter bill. Its plumage,

however, is similar to Thayer's, although the upperparts tend to be more uniform and less contrastingly patterned (suggesting a dark Glaucous-winged Gull), tail averages darker, and dark/light contrast on outer primaries averages less distinct at shaft.

LESSER BLACK-BACKED GULL (widespread, but rare in West) slimmer and longer winged with slender black bill, typically narrower pale edgings to upperparts (lacking boldly patterned or checkered look common to Thayer's). Upperwing lacks contrasting pale panel on inner primaries, and outer primaries solidly dark; underside of outer primaries darker (but can be reflectively pale); uppertail coverts and tail base contrastingly white, barred blackish, with contrasting black distal tail band.

Second Cycle. The main confusion species are American Herring Gull and Kumlien's Gull. Note size and structure, especially of the bill and head, and pattern of the outer primaries.

AMERICAN HERRING GULL averages larger with a stouter bill, often shows a shallower sloping forehead. Best plumage feature is more extensively dark inner webs of outer primaries, so pale inner primary panel on upperwing contrasts more with more solidly dark outer primaries; underside of outer primaries darker (but can be reflectively pale); tail of Herring often more extensively blackish and eye often pale at this age (rarely so on Thayer's).

KUMLIEN'S GULL averages slightly shorter bill and shorter, less pointed wingtips; wingtips overall paler with dark on outer webs usually restricted to P7–P10 and often boldest on P8–P9 (versus equally distinct dark outer webs to P6–P10 on Thayer's); tertials rarely as solidly dark brown as some Thayer's, and wingtips of many birds pale brown to whitish. Presumed hybrids with Thayer's look intermediate and are not safely assigned to either taxon.

VEGA GULL can look similar to Thayer's but averages larger with stouter bill; often has shallower sloping forehead. Best plumage feature is more extensively dark inner webs of outer primaries, so pale inner primary panel on upperwing contrasts more with more solidly dark outer primaries; underside of outer primaries darker (but can be reflectively pale).

HYBRID GLAUCOUS-WINGED × AMERICAN HERRING GULL best separated from Thayer's by structure, especially bigger bill; plumage characters need study.

HYBRID GLAUCOUS-WINGED GULL × WESTERN GULL best separated from Thayer's by structure, especially bigger bill; plumage characters need study.

CALIFORNIA GULL typically has well-defined gray

saddle, and gray of upperparts averages darker (Kodak 5–7.5), but some closely resemble Thayer's in plumage: note California's longer and blacker wing projection, more parallel-edged bill, and often a blue-green hue to the tibia. In flight, note restricted pale inner primary panel (usually on inner 3–4 primaries) and solidly dark outer primaries of California.

HYBRID GLAUCOUS GULL × AMERICAN HERRING GULL should be separable by size and structure, especially bill; wingtip and tail pattern might resemble Thayer's, but range of variation poorly known.

WESTERN GULL larger and bulkier with broad wings and stouter, bulbous-tipped bill. Plumage generally darker with black wingtips, usually with some slaty gray on upperparts by late winter; upperwing lacks strongly contrasting pale panel on inner primaries, and outer primaries solidly blackish.

SLATY-BACKED GULL should be separable by structure, being larger and bulkier with broad wings, shorter wing projection, longer legs, and stouter bill. Plumage generally darker overall, usually with some slaty gray on back by late winter, tail more blackish, and dark/light contrast on outer primaries averages weaker at shaft.

LESSER BLACK-BACKED GULL slimmer and longer winged; mostly black bill often boldly tipped creamy. Upperparts distinctly darker, upperwing lacks contrasting pale panel on inner primaries, and outer primaries solidly dark.

Third Cycle. American Herring Gull, Kumlien's Gull, California Gull, and hybrids differ in much the same ways as do adults (see above and relevant accounts); note Thayer's bill size and shape and two-tone outer primaries.

RARER SPECIES

Adult Cycle. HYBRID GLAUCOUS GULL × VEGA GULL (w. Alaska) larger with longer and stouter bill. Upperpart tone, eye color, orbital ring, and wingtip pattern may resemble Thayer's Gull, but range of variation poorly known; should be separable by size and structure, especially bill.

EUROPEAN HERRING GULL (casual e. N. America) typically larger and bulkier with stouter bill; wingtip pattern of some nominate *argentatus* very similar to Thayer's but usually with more black on underside of outer primaries. Note size, structure, pale eyes with yellow-orange orbital ring, and upperpart tone (Kodak 4–5 on *argenteus*, Kodak 5.5–7 on *argentatus*).

First Cycle. Also see Yellow-legged Gull (differences given under that species).

HYBRID GLAUCOUS GULL × VEGA GULL should be separable by size and structure, especially bill;

wingtip and tail pattern may resemble Thayer's, but range of variation poorly known.

EUROPEAN HERRING GULL averages larger with a stouter bill that generally has more-marked gonydeal expansion; often shows shallower sloping forehead. Inner webs of outer primaries more extensively dark, so that pale inner primary panel on upperwing contrasts more with more solidly dark outer primaries; underside of outer primaries darker (but can be reflectively pale); uppertail coverts and tail base contrastingly white, barred blackish, with contrasting black distal tail band.

Second Cycle. Also see European Herring Gull and Yellow-legged Gull (differences given under those taxa).

HYBRID GLAUCOUS GULL × VEGA GULL should be separable by size and structure, especially bill; wingtip and tail pattern may resemble Thayer's, but range of variation poorly known.

Third Cycle. European Herring Gull, Yellow-legged Gull, and hybrids differ in much the same ways as do adults (see above and relevant accounts); note Thayer's bill size and shape, and two-tone outer primaries.

HABITAT AND BEHAVIOR

Breeds on cliffs and rocky islands in Canadian High Arctic. Adults winter mostly along or near the coast at bays, estuaries, and river mouths; first-cycle birds (and, to a lesser extent, other ages) also occur at lakes, duck ponds, dumps, parking lots, and other habitats where large gulls occur. Nonbreeding birds (especially adults) often in flocks (locally up to a few hundred birds but more often 20–100 birds). Thayer's Gulls associate readily with other gulls and water birds but, at least in winter, they mostly avoid feeding areas dominated by the larger Western and Glaucous-winged Gulls. First-cycle birds often associate with groups of California Gulls at town and city parks with lakes, where they can be quite confiding. In winter, feeds on spawning fish in inshore waters and bays; also scavenges.

DESCRIPTION AND MOLT

Some adult and third-cycle putative or presumed Thayer's Gulls have slaty gray wingtips and others have mostly whitish wingtips with limited gray markings.[23,24] Some first-cycle and second-cycle Thayer's-like birds have pale brown wingtips and reduced dark pigmentation in the flight feathers. Some of these are probably hybrids with Iceland and Kumlien's Gulls, but some may represent variation in pure Thayer's, the limits of which have yet to be established.

Adult Cycle. Complete PB molt (June/July–Nov./Jan.) produces adult basic plumage: head, neck, and underparts white; head, neck, and sometimes upper chest with variable (usually moderate to heavy) dusky mottling and streaking. Upperparts pale gray (Kodak 5–6) with slaty blackish wingtips (black on outer web of P10 and sometimes P9 extends to primary coverts; P4 and sometimes P5 unmarked); white scapular and tertial crescents; and white tips to outer primaries. Uppertail coverts and tail white. White trailing edge to secondaries (often hidden at rest) and inner primaries breaks into discrete white tips on outer primaries; P5/P6–P8 have white tongue-tips and blackish subterminal bands, P9–P10 typically have white mirrors or mirror-tongues; on P9, blackish on medial portion extends onto inner web, and an unbroken narrow blackish line runs along outer web across mirror region; P10 usually has a partial to complete blackish subterminal band. Underwings show pale smoky gray remiges with white trailing edge to secondaries and inner primaries continuing as a band of white tongue-tips and mirrors across outer primaries, a narrow slaty blackish subterminal band on outer primaries, and a dark leading edge to P10. Eyes brownish to pale lemon, orbital ring purplish pink. Bill yellowish (often greenish basally in winter) with orange-red to red gonydeal spot and sometimes a dark mark at gonys. Legs pink, perhaps duller during height of PB molt. Partial PA molt (*Oct.–Feb./Apr.*) produces adult alternate plumage: head and neck clean white (rarely before Mar./Apr.); white primary tips can be lost through wear. By spring, orbital ring brightens, bill brightens to lemon yellow with red gonydeal spot and lacks dark distal marks, legs rich pink.

First Cycle. Juvenile (Aug.–Apr.): dark brown to medium gray-brown overall. Head, neck, and underparts variably streaked and mottled whitish, becoming whitish on vent and undertail coverts, which have broad sooty brown bars. Upperparts with buff (bleaching to dull whitish) scaly and notched edgings and markings, the greater coverts sometimes with lightly marked (or unmarked) bases. Upperpart markings typically scaly to checkered, often fairly contrasting and neatly marked, or frosty, in fresh plumage (through late winter on some birds). Uppertail coverts whitish with strong dark barring. Tertials dark brown to dark gray-brown with notched whitish tips and distal edging. Wingtips blackish brown, contrasting darker than tertials (and usually darker than tail), with whitish fringes or tips

usually distinct. Pale panel on inner primaries distinctive on spread upperwing; outer primaries blackish brown with paler inner webs reaching shaft and forming a two-tone pattern that merges inward with pale inner primary panel. Secondaries dark brown, tipped whitish. Outer primary coverts plain brownish with narrow whitish tips. Tail dark brown, usually slightly paler than wingtips with whitish tip and whitish ribbing on outer web of R6; whitish basal barring on outer rectrices best seen when tail fully spread or from below. IN FLIGHT: brownish to gray-brown overall with dark outer webs to outer primaries (varying from a solid panel when wings not fully spread to a two-tone pattern when spread), pale inner primary panel, contrasting dark secondary bar, and broad dark brown distal tail band; underwings medium brown with underside of primaries often reflectively pale. Eyes dark, bill blackish, usually with variable dull flesh on basal two-thirds by early winter; legs flesh to flesh pink. PA1 molt (Nov.–May; does not include upperwing coverts) produces first alternate plumage: head, neck, chest, and flanks smoky gray to sooty gray with variable whitish streaking and mottling, and often mixed with bleached juvenal feathers (juvenal head can bleach to mostly whitish). A1 scapulars range from brownish gray to medium pale gray, typically with fine dark bars or wavy markings and ranging from fairly plain grayish to having dark bars or anchor patterns. Bill blackish with dull flesh to flesh pink basally, sometimes a fine pale horn tip; exceptionally flesh pinkish with a blackish distal third;[25] legs flesh pink; eyes dark. Note that some birds retain most or all juvenal plumage through Apr. and can be very bleached, almost whitish in overall appearance, but note dark secondary bar and brownish tail, usually fairly protected from bleaching.

Second Cycle. Complete PB2 molt (May/June–Sept./Oct.) into second basic plumage. Some birds bleach strikingly by early summer, before PB2 is very advanced—and new B2 feathers can look contrastingly dark. Head, neck, and underparts variably mottled and streaked gray-brown and whitish; head and chest of some birds bleach to mostly whitish by midwinter. Upperparts vary from fairly boldly barred and checkered brown and whitish overall to a mostly grayish back contrasting with upperwing coverts that are barred and spotted gray-brown and whitish. Tertials dark brown to dark gray-brown with speckled and notched whitish tips and distal edging. Wingtips blackish brown, contrasting darker than tertials, with whitish fringes widest at tips. Upperwing pattern of remiges similar to first cycle, but inner primaries average paler and grayer, secondaries often paler and not forming a strong dark bar; P10 rarely has a small, diffuse mirror. Distal tail band blackish brown to dark brown with white tail base more sparsely and finely marked than first cycle. Wing-linings medium brown with underside of primaries often reflectively pale. Eyes brownish to pale, bill typically flesh pink to pale greenish with black distal third and pale horn tip (sometimes dull like first winter), legs flesh pink. Partial PA2 molt (*Sept.–Apr.*; often includes some upperwing coverts) produces second alternate plumage: head, neck, and underparts whiter, mottled dusky and whitish (sometimes bleaching and wearing to mostly white by summer), back more extensively gray in contrast to faded upperwing coverts; some birds attain a few gray upperwing coverts, especially median coverts. Eyes brownish to dirty pale lemon, orbital ring can be pinkish in summer. By summer, some birds have yellowish bill with reddish gonydeal smudge and black distal band. Legs flesh pink.

Third Cycle. Complete PB3 molt (May/June–Oct.) produces third basic plumage. Head, neck, and underparts white with variable dusky streaking and mottling. Upperparts pale gray, usually with variable brown wash to upperwing coverts, brown tertial centers. Rump and tail white with variable dark brown to blackish brown distal tail band (tail varies from all white to having a fairly broad dark band). Wingtips blackish brown to slaty blackish, usually with a white P10 mirror and sometimes a small P9 mirror; wingtips at rest show whitish to distinct white tips. Upperwings mostly gray, mixed with brown (especially on primary coverts), with dark outer webs to outer primaries (creating two-tone

pattern), 1–2 white mirrors, and white trailing edge to secondaries and inner primaries. Underwings mostly white with variable brown markings on coverts, outer primaries silvery gray with a dark subterminal band and whitish tongue-tips hinting at adult pattern. Eyes brownish to pale lemon; bill flesh to dull pale greenish with black distal band and pale tip; legs flesh pink. Partial PA3 molt (*Sept.–Mar./ Apr.*) into third alternate plumage: dark markings on head and neck reduced to absent; bill brightens in spring and in summer can be indistinguishable from adult or have dark distal marks. White tips to outer primaries may be lost by wear. Adult plumage attained by complete PB4 molt (May/June–Oct./Nov.), but fourth-cycle birds may retain signs of immaturity on alula, primary coverts, and tail.

HYBRIDS
Presumably with Kumlien's Gull,[26,27,28,29] but extent of hybridization difficult to assess (see Taxonomy, and introduction to Iceland Gull complex); hybridization seems possible with Iceland Gull in the Canadian High Arctic.[30]

NOTES
1. Brooks 1915; 2. AOU 1931; 3. Dwight 1917; 4. Macpherson 1961; 5. AOU 1973; 6. AOU 1998; 7. Browning 2002; 8. Howell and Elliott 2001; 9. BOU 1991; 10. Godfrey 1986; 11. Smith 1966; 12. Snell 1989; 13. Snell 1991; 14. Gaston and Decker 1985; 15. Snell 1989; 16. Snell 2002; 17. Howell and Elliott 2001; 18. Patten et al. 2003; 19. Brock 1997; 20. Gee and Edwards 2000; 21. Peters and Burleigh 1951; 22. Tobish 1996; 23. Parmelee and MacDonald 1960; 24. Snell 2002; 25. Howell pers. obs.; 26. Gaston and Decker 1985; 27. Knudsen 1976; 28. Snell 1989; 29. Snell 2002; 30. Howell and Mactavish 2003

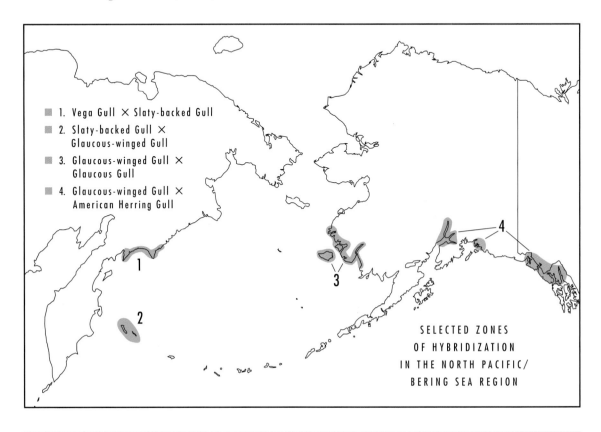

HYBRID GULLS

Hybridism in gulls varies from common (among some species) to rare or, in many species, unknown. Occasional oddball hybrids, such as between Laughing Gull and Ring-billed Gull, are confusing (photo I.5, p. 14), but they are rare enough that most observers will never encounter them. And hybridism among a few species might be commoner than recognized because hybrids may look similar to the parent species and not be recognized as hybrids (see photos 23.26–23.30). Hybridism among some of the large white-headed gulls is relatively common, and hybrids can cause identification problems. We have divided hybrids among the large white-headed gulls into two main groups: 1) the five most widespread and commonly seen presumed hybrids, which receive longer accounts; and 2) less common

and rarely seen hybrids, which we treat in shorter accounts. The latter group, for which only adults or near-adults have usually been described, can be subdivided into Atlantic hybrids and Pacific hybrids.

The commonest and most readily seen hybrids are in w. N. America, namely Glaucous-winged Gull × Western Gull and Glaucous-winged Gull × American Herring Gull. Less common, or at least less often seen by most observers, are Glaucous Gull × American Herring Gull hybrids and Glaucous Gull × Glaucous-winged Gull hybrids; and less well known are presumed Thayer's Gull × Kumlien's/Iceland Gull hybrids. In addition to these, six rarer Atlantic Coast hybrids and three rarer N. Pacific hybrids are discussed.

1. Vega Gull × Slaty-backed Gull
2. Slaty-backed Gull × Glaucous-winged Gull
3. Glaucous-winged Gull × Glaucous Gull
4. Glaucous-winged Gull × American Herring Gull

SELECTED ZONES
OF HYBRIDIZATION
IN THE NORTH PACIFIC/
BERING SEA REGION

WIDESPREAD HYBRIDS

H1. GLAUCOUS-WINGED GULL × WESTERN GULL
Larus glaucescens × *Larus o. occidentalis*

LENGTH 22–26.3 IN. (56–67 CM)
PHOTOS H1.1–H1.25 (PP. 274–279); I.8, I.43

IDENTIFICATION SUMMARY

This hybrid combination—sometimes called "Puget Sound Gull" or "Olympic Gull"—is common along the Pacific Coast of N. America, breeding from British Columbia south to Oregon. Nonbreeding migrants occur regularly south to s. California and north to se. Alaska. Hybrids show various combinations of parental plumage and structure[1] (see Glaucous-winged Gull and Western Gull accounts) and can also resemble other species, thus causing identification problems. The most common problems are distinguishing Glaucous-winged × Western hybrids from Slaty-backed and Thayer's Gulls, and they can also be difficult to separate from Glaucous-winged Gull × American Herring Gull hybrids (see Similar Species section for details).

Because hybrids span the range of characters between parental types it is difficult to establish where a pure Glaucous-winged Gull or Western Gull ends and a hybrid begins.[2] Many birds are clearly intermediate between the parent species, but other hybrids are more subtle. Some adults look like Western Gulls, but their backs are a shade too pale, their wingtips blackish (versus black), their orbital rings mixed yellow and pink, and, in basic plumage, their heads have relatively extensive and smudgy dark markings, and their bills are pale yellowish with dark distal marks. Others look like Glaucous-winged Gulls, but their wingtips are a shade too dark, their orbital rings mixed yellow and pink, and, in winter, they have bright bills typical of Western Gull. Most breeding hybrids from the Juan de Fuca Strait north look more similar to Glaucous-winged Gulls than to Western Gulls, most from the outer coast of cen.

Washington south look more similar to Western Gulls.[3]

First-cycle presumed hybrids also look variably intermediate between the parent species, and their wingtips tend to be some shade of medium brown or dark brown. Birds that look mostly like Glaucous-wingeds can have strongly checked upperparts typical of Western Gull, whereas birds that look mostly like Western Gulls can exhibit delayed PA1 molt and then attain relatively plain, medium gray scapulars typical of Glaucous-winged Gull. Second-cycle and third-cycle plumages are equally variable.

STATUS AND DISTRIBUTION

Common breeding resident along coasts from s. B.C. to cen. Ore. The hybrid zone extends from Puget Sound and Juan de Fuca Strait south to cen. Ore. (43–49° north) with some introgression north to Queen Charlotte Is. (54° north)[4] and occasional hybridization south to cen. Calif. (around 38° north).[5,6] Regular nonbreeding visitor (mainly Oct.–Mar.) north to se. Alaska, south to s. Calif., rarely to n. Baja Calif., and possibly to n. Sonora.[7] Status inland in w. N. America clouded by difficulties distinguishing hybrids from pure Glaucous-winged Gulls and by a general lack of interest in hybrids among birders. Small numbers winter inland at least to e. Ore.,[8] Central Valley of Calif., and n. Great Basin.[9]

Up to 75 percent of some Western Gull and Glaucous-winged Gull colonies in Wash. and Ore. comprise hybrids.[10,11,12] In cen. Calif. (Marin County), 15–25 percent of the wintering population of Western and Glaucous-winged Gulls typically show hybrid characters, and at some sites up to 50 percent appear to be hybrids.[13] Hybrids become progressively less common southward along the Calif. coast in winter.

SIMILAR SPECIES

Here we deal only with the commonest identification pitfalls caused by birds intermediate between the parent species. For hybrids that closely resemble the parent species, see differences from other species listed in the Glaucous-winged Gull and Western Gull accounts.

Adult Cycle. THAYER'S GULL (w. N. America in winter). Hybrids are larger and bulkier overall than Thayer's Gulls with broader wings, shorter wing projection, and a larger and stouter bill. Only the smallest female hybrids are likely to cause difficulties, and even these have stouter bills than Thayer's (noticeable in direct comparison). Wingtip patterns of hybrids can resemble Thayer's so closely as to be indistinguishable under field conditions. But hybrids are often slightly darker above (Kodak 6–8, versus Kodak 5–6 on Thayer's); often show some yellowish in their orbital ring; and can have winter bill patterns varying from bright (like Western) to pale with extensive dark marks (like Glaucous-winged)—unlike the pattern of adult winter Thayer's Gulls, which typically have a greenish bill with an orange-red gonydeal spot and a brighter yellow "saddle spot" on the maxilla above the gonys.

SLATY-BACKED GULL (N. Pacific). Hybrids average bulkier and broader winged with a more bulbous-tipped bill, paler upperparts (Kodak 6–8 versus 9.5–11.5), and their dorsal wingtips tend to be slaty blackish (or paler) rather than black. Wingtip pattern can be similar to Slaty-backed (Glaucous-winged pattern combined with Western Gull darkness) although hybrids with the darkest wingtips generally have narrow whitish tongue-tips and often lack a mirror on P9; and the white trailing edge to the secondaries averages wider on Slaty-backed. Also note Slaty-backed's reddish orbital ring, more parallel-edged bill, and rich pink legs.

AMERICAN HERRING GULL (widespread). Some pale backed, blackish winged hybrids can suggest American Herring Gull but their upperparts are slightly darker (Kodak 6 versus 4–5), wingtips tend to be more extensively blackish, eyes usually dusky (but can be staringly pale), and bill often relatively bulbous-tipped. Also note the thickset and broad-winged structure of hybrids, and check orbital ring for pinkish.

VEGA GULL (w. Alaska). Hybrid features such as upperpart tone, dusky eyes, and extensive white tongue-tips and mirrors in wingtip can all suggest Vega Gull—but note thickset and broad-winged structure of hybrids. Also, hybrid wingtips tend to be blackish, not contrasting sharply with gray primary bases; bill often relatively bulbous tipped; and orbital ring pinkish to yellow (reddish on Vega).

HYBRID GLAUCOUS-WINGED GULL × AMERICAN HERRING GULL. Can appear similar to hybrid Glaucous-winged × Western, but features indicative of American Herring Gull parentage may be discerned: structure often slighter overall with relatively longer and especially narrower wings and more slender, parallel-edged bill; upperparts average paler (Kodak 5–6, versus 6–8) with more-contrasting and often more-restricted blackish wingtips; and basic head streaking often finer.

HYBRID SLATY-BACKED GULL × VEGA GULL (N. Pacific) not well known. Presumed hybrids[14] have slaty gray upperparts (Kodak 9) with wingtip pattern similar to Vega Gull: fairly well-demarcated black wingtips both above and below, narrow white tongue-tips on P5–P7 (but not on P8), and no white mirror on P9.

HYBRID GLAUCOUS-WINGED GULL × SLATY-BACKED GULL (N. Pacific) not well known. Could be expected to resemble hybrid Glaucous-winged Gull × Western Gull; critical study needed.

First Cycle. THAYER'S GULL. Besides structural differences (with bill size and shape the most helpful), the following characters help separate hybrids from Thayer's—but a hybrid may resemble Thayer's Gull in each feature. Hybrids more often have the tertials, tail, and wingtips similar in tone; hybrids have more-diffuse contrast between outer and inner webs on the outer primaries; hybrids often have more solidly dark tails; hybrids often have more-advanced molt timing, with extensive scapular molt under way by midwinter; and hybrids often have duller, dusky pinkish legs.

SLATY-BACKED GULL. Hybrids average bulkier and broader winged with a more bulbous-tipped bill. Slaty-backed upperwing has contrastingly pale inner primaries and more-distinct inner web/outer web contrast on the outer primaries; also note more-extensive white tail base barring and relatively pale greater coverts on Slaty-backed.

AMERICAN HERRING GULL. Structure less thickset overall with relatively longer and especially narrower wings and more slender, parallel-edged bill; primaries and tail black or blackish, darker than hybrids, and with stronger contrast on upperwing between pale inner and blackish outer primaries; bill often has more pinkish at base.

VEGA GULL differs in same respects as American Herring Gull, but tail averages more extensively whitish basally with a broad blackish distal band, and underparts paler overall with whitish ground color and dusky brown streaking and mottling.

HYBRID GLAUCOUS-WINGED GULL × AMERICAN HERRING GULL. Besides structural differences, hybrids can show Herring characters, such as a broad dark distal tail band (with more-extensive white markings on outer web of R6 visible at rest) and more-extensive pinkish at bill base.

HYBRID SLATY-BACKED GULL × VEGA GULL not well known. Suspected hybrids look intermediate between parent species in structure and plumage characters such as tail pattern and primary pattern, so wingtips blacker than hybrid Glaucous-winged × Western gulls and tails with more-distinct white barring at base; critical study needed.

HYBRID GLAUCOUS-WINGED GULL × SLATY-BACKED GULL not well known; characters relative to hybrid Glaucous-winged Gull × Western Gull need study.

Second Cycle. Plumage highly variable; best identified by structural characters (see adult and first cycle).

Third Cycle. Differences from other species and hybrids much as adult cycle, which see.

HABITAT AND BEHAVIOR

Much as parent species. In cen. California in winter, hybrids resembling Glaucous-winged Gulls feed mostly with Glaucous-winged Gulls (for example, in rocky intertidal areas), whereas Western-like hybrids feed mostly with Western Gulls (for example, on sandy mudflats in tidal lagoons and harbors).[15]

DESCRIPTION AND MOLT

Descriptions focus on differences relative to parent species and are not comprehensive. Thus, leg color (pink) and adult tail color (white) are like both parent species and are not noted below.

Adult Cycle. Complete PB molt (mainly June–Dec.) produces adult basic plumage: variably intermediate between Glaucous-winged Gull and Western Gull. Mantle and primary melanism are good indicators of hybrid origin.[16] Some birds are almost as pale above as Glaucous-winged Gull but have blackish wingtips, but birds with dark upperparts and pale gray wingtips do not occur (wingtips mainly Kodak 9–16). Back and upperwings gray to pale slaty gray (mostly Kodak 6–8), often with more-extensive white mirrors and tongue-tips in outer primaries than Western Gull; darkest and most Western-like hybrids tend to have reduced white tongue-tips and mirrors and

paler, less-contrasting underside to wingtips. Eyes pale lemon (can be more staringly pale than typical of either parent) to dusky. Orbital ring pinkish to chrome yellow; can show patches of both colors or can be an intermediate color such as a fleshy ocher. Bill pale greenish yellow to orange-yellow with orange-red to red gonydeal spot, and often a dark distal mark. Partial PA molt (Oct.–Feb.) produces adult alternate plumage: head and neck clean white. Orbital ring, bill, and legs brighter, bill lacks dark distal marks.

First Cycle. Juvenile (Aug.–Jan.): resembles a dark Glaucous-winged Gull or a slightly washed-out Western Gull. Intermediate birds often have two-tone outer primaries combining outer web darkness from Western with contrast break at shaft from Glaucous-winged (and thus resemble Thayer's). Wingtips, tertial centers, and tail often similar in tone, medium brown to blackish brown, or with wingtips or tail blacker; dark secondary bar varies from distinct to muted. Inner primaries often show as relatively contrasting pale inner panel, suggesting Herring Gull. Tail usually looks solidly dark, although outer web of R6 can have some white spots and notches, at least basally. Upperparts range from finely patterned and relatively muted like Glaucous-winged to boldly checkered like Western. Eyes dark, bill blackish and can show dull pinkish basally by midwinter, legs dusky flesh to flesh pink. PA1 molt (starting between Oct. and Feb.) produces first alternate plumage: A1 scapulars vary from grayish with diffuse darker markings, to sooty gray-brown with dark centers. Eyes dark, bill blackish and often with some dull pinkish basally, legs dusky flesh to flesh pink.

Second and Third Cycles. Molt timing and age-related plumage variation parallel parent species (for example, complete PB molts mainly May–Nov., partial PA molts mainly Sept.–Mar.). Plumage and bare parts variably intermediate between parent species; see Adult Cycle (above).

NOTES

1. Bell 1996; 2. Ibid.; 3. Bell 1997; 4. Bell 1996; 5. Bell 1997; 6. Howell pers. obs.; 7. Ibid.; 8. Marshall et al. 2003; 9. Floyd 2002; 10. Bell 1996; 11. Bell 1997; 12. Hoffman et al. 1978; 13. Howell pers. obs.; 14. BM #1908.1.8.457 (NE China); 15. Howell pers. obs.; 16. Bell 1996

H2. GLAUCOUS-WINGED GULL × AMERICAN HERRING GULL
Larus glaucescens × *Larus [argentatus] smithsonianus*

LENGTH 22–26.3 IN. (56–67 CM)
PHOTOS H2.1–H2.23 (PP. 280–284); I.8

IDENTIFICATION SUMMARY

These two species interbreed mainly in s. Alaska, and the hybrids occur as migrants along the N. American Pacific Coast south to California. Hybrids show almost all combinations of parental plumage and structure[1,2,3] (see Glaucous-winged Gull and American Herring Gull accounts), and can also resemble other species, particularly Thayer's Gull. Because hybrids span the range of characters between parental types, it is difficult to establish where a pure Glaucous-winged Gull or American Herring Gull ends and a hybrid begins; our comments should be interpreted with this in mind. It can also be difficult to distinguish hybrid Glaucous-winged × American Herring gulls from hybrid Glaucous-winged × Western gulls.

Many birds are clearly intermediate between the parent species, but other hybrids are more subtle. Some adults look like American Herring Gulls, but their backs are a shade too dark, their wingtips blackish (versus black) with more-extensive white mirrors and tongues, their eyes flecked dusky, and their orbital rings mixed with pink. Others look like Glaucous-winged Gulls but have narrower wings and more slender bills, their wingtips are a little too dark, and their orbital rings are mixed with yellow. First-cycle presumed hybrids are also variably intermediate between the parent species, and their wingtips tend to be some shade of medium brown or dark brown. Second-cycle and third-cycle plumages are equally variable.

STATUS AND DISTRIBUTION

Common breeder from Cook Inlet east and south to vicinity of Juneau, se. Alaska and south locally to interior B.C.[4,5,6,7] Fairly common but local migrant and winter visitor (mainly Oct.–Apr.) south to cen. coastal Calif. (around 36° south): up to 12 percent of northbound migrant Glaucous-winged and American Herring Gulls at sites in cen. Calif. during late Jan. and Feb. show hybrid characters.[8] Hybrids less common south along Calif. coast and rare in n. Baja Calif. and n. Sonora.[9] Probably occurs in small numbers (but largely overlooked) in interior w. N. America, at least west of the Rockies.

FIELD IDENTIFICATION

SIMILAR SPECIES

Here we deal only with the commonest identification pitfalls caused by birds intermediate between the parent species. For hybrids that closely resemble the parent species, see differences from other species listed in Glaucous-winged Gull and American Herring Gull accounts.

Adult Cycle. THAYER'S GULL (w. N. America in winter) smaller overall and slimmer billed, although judging these features on a lone bird can be problematic. Possible plumage difference from Thayer's include more-extensive and relatively diffuse dark wingtip markings, especially on P9–P10, but critical examination of series of known hybrids is needed. Other hybrid indicators are yellow in the orbital ring and obvious dark bill markings in winter.

KUMLIEN'S GULL (ne. N. America in winter) markedly smaller overall with smaller and slimmer bill. Wingtip pattern can be similar to hybrids, and best identified by size and structure; adults rarely attain distinct dark distal bill marks in winter.

HYBRID GLAUCOUS-WINGED GULL × WESTERN GULL (w. N. America). This hybrid combination can appear similar to Glaucous-winged × Herring, but features indicative of Western Gull parentage may be discerned: structure heavier overall with relatively shorter and broader wings and heavier, bulbous-tipped bill; upperparts average darker (Kodak 6–8 and higher, versus 5–6) with less-contrastingly demarcated dark wingtips.

HYBRID SLATY-BACKED GULL × VEGA GULL (N. Pacific) not well known. Presumed hybrids[10] have darker upperparts (Kodak 9) with wingtip pattern similar to Vega Gull: fairly well demarcated black wingtips both above and below, narrow white tongue-tips on P5–P7 (but not on P8), and no white mirror on P9.

HYBRID GLAUCOUS-WINGED GULL × SLATY-BACKED GULL (N. Pacific) may be bulkier and broader winged, more like hybrid Glaucous-winged Gull × Western Gull in structure, with darker upperparts; study needed.

First Cycle. THAYER'S GULL smaller overall with more slender bill; upperparts typically more frosty and boldly patterned overall. Some presumed hybrids resemble Thayer's closely and may be difficult to identify without known species for comparison.

KUMLIEN'S GULL smaller overall with smaller and more slender bill. Wingtip pattern can be similar to hybrids; best identified by size and structure.

HYBRID GLAUCOUS-WINGED GULL × WESTERN GULL. Note structural differences (under adult). Also, a broad dark distal tail band (like some Herring Gulls) may not occur in Western Gull hybrids, which also generally show little or no white spotting and ribbing on outer web of R6.

SLATY-BACKED GULL (N. Pacific). Slaty-backed upperwing typically has relatively pale and plain greater coverts, contrastingly pale inner primaries, and more-distinct inner web/outer web contrast on the outer primaries; but all of these features may be matched on hybrids. Deep pink legs of some Slaty-backeds may be outside range of hybrids; study needed.

HYBRID GLAUCOUS-WINGED GULL × SLATY-BACKED GULL may be bulkier and broader winged, more like hybrid Glaucous-winged Gull × Western Gull, but study needed.

Second and Third Cycles. THAYER'S GULL and KUMLIEN'S GULL are again the main problems, and identification criteria for these age classes (other than size and structure, especially of the bill) need study.

HYBRID GLAUCOUS-WINGED GULL × WESTERN GULL. See structural characters (under adult) and also note tone of upperparts.

SLATY-BACKED GULL distinguished by dark slaty feathers on upperparts; legs often brighter pink.

HYBRID SLATY-BACKED GULL × VEGA GULL presumably shows darker gray on upperparts; needs study.

HYBRID GLAUCOUS-WINGED GULL × SLATY-BACKED GULL may be bulkier and broader winged with darker upperparts, more like hybrid Glaucous-winged Gull × Western Gull; needs study.

HABITAT AND BEHAVIOR

Much as the parent species but, in California, hybrids winter mainly in areas where American Herring Gulls are common rather than along the immediate coast where Western and Glaucous-winged Gulls, and their hybrids, dominate.[11]

DESCRIPTION AND MOLT

Descriptions focus on differences relative to parent species and are not comprehensive. Thus, leg color (pink) and adult tail color (white) are like both parent species and not noted below.

Adult Cycle. Complete PB molt (mainly late May/June–Dec.) produces adult basic plumage: variably intermediate between Glaucous-winged Gull and Herring Gull. Upperparts mainly Kodak 5–6 with slaty gray to blackish wingtips (Kodak 11.5–16),[12] typically with white mirrors on P9–P10, white tongue-tips on P6–P8/P9, and often a dark subterminal mark on P5; dark on the outer webs of P9–P10 usually extends to primary coverts. Eyes pale lemon with dusky flecking to mostly dark. Orbital ring pinkish to yellowish, can show patches of both colors or be an intermediate color. Bill pale greenish yellow to fleshy yellow with orange-red to red gonydeal spot and often a dark distal mark. Partial PA molt (Oct.–Feb.) produces adult alternate plumage: head and neck clean white. Orbital ring, bill, and legs brighter; yellow bill lacks dark distal marks.

First Cycle. Juvenile (Aug.–Jan.): resembles a dark Glaucous-winged Gull or slightly washed-out Herring Gull. Intermediate birds often have two-tone outer primaries combining outer web darkness from Herring with contrast break at shaft from Glaucous-winged (and thus resemble Thayer's). Wingtips, tertial centers, and tail often similar in tone, medium brown to blackish brown, or with wingtips or tail blacker; dark secondary bar varies from distinct to muted. Tail varies from almost solidly plain (like Glaucous-winged) to having a broad dark distal band (like Herring and Thayer's); outer web of R6 often with relatively extensive white notches and ribbing. Eyes dark, bill blackish and often with some dull pinkish basally, legs dusky flesh to flesh pink. PA1 molt (probably starting between Oct. and Feb.) in combination with bleaching and wear produces first alternate plumage: A1 scapulars grayish with diffuse darker markings, possibly not showing distinct blackish bars of Herring Gull.

Second and Third Cycles. Molt timing and age-related plumage variation presumably parallel the parent species (for example, complete PB molts May–Nov., partial PA molts Sept.–Mar.), but details of appearance poorly known.

NOTES

1. Howell pers. obs.; 2. Patten 1980; 3. Williamson and Peyton 1963; 4. R. J. Cannings pers. comm.; 5. Merilees 1974; 6. Patten 1980; 7. Williamson and Peyton 1963; 8. Howell pers. obs.; 9. Ibid.; 10. BM #1908.1.8.457 (NE China), BM #1910.5.2.21 (S China); 11. Howell pers. obs.; 12. MVZ specimens

H3. GLAUCOUS GULL × AMERICAN HERRING GULL

Larus hyperboreus × *Larus [argentatus] smithsonianus*

LENGTH 22–28.5 IN. (56–72.5 CM)
PHOTOS H3.1–H3.17 (PP. 285–288)

IDENTIFICATION SUMMARY

These two species interbreed in nw. Canada (involving intergrade *barrovianus/hyperboreus* Glaucous Gulls) and ne. Canada (involving *hyperboreus* Glaucous Gulls); migrants occur in winter south to nw. Mexico and e. U.S. The name Nelson's Gull (originally described as a species from the Bering Sea coast of Alaska)[1] is sometimes used for this hybrid. Hybrids apparently show almost all combinations of parental plumage and structure and can resemble other species. Can also be difficult to distinguish from hybrid Glaucous-winged × American Herring gulls, and see hybrid Glaucous Gull × Vega Gull and hybrid Glaucous Gull × European Herring Gull.

Many birds are intermediate between the parent species, but other hybrids are more subtle. Some adults resemble American Herring Gulls, but their backs are a shade too pale, their wingtips blackish to slaty with more-extensive white than typical. Others resemble Glaucous Gulls but show a ghosting of dusky, Herring-like pattern on the outer primaries. First-cycle presumed hybrids are also variably intermediate between the parent species, and their wingtips tend to be some shade of medium brown or dark brown; many resemble Herring Gulls but with slightly browner wingtips, more-extensive pale on inner webs of outer primaries, and bill often Glaucous-like. Second-cycle and third-cycle plumages not well known but presumably show intermediate characters paralleling other ages.

STATUS AND DISTRIBUTION

Confirmed interbreeding occurs in the Mackenzie Delta, N.T., where up to 5 percent of adults show hybrid characters;[2] presumed hybrids are uncommon to locally fairly common at Inuvik, N.T., in summer and early fall, comprising up to 10 percent of adults.[3] Hybrids are rare in winter (mainly Nov./Dec.–Mar./Apr.) along Pacific Coast of N. America south to Calif. and nw. Mex.,[4,5] rare to casual inland in the West, and rare in ne. Canada and on Great Lakes, becoming rare to casual south along Atlantic Coast to at least Mid-Atlantic states.

FIELD IDENTIFICATION

SIMILAR SPECIES

Here we deal only with the commonest identification pitfalls caused by birds intermediate between the parent species. For hybrids that closely resemble the parent species, see differences from other species listed in the Glaucous Gull and American Herring Gull accounts.

Adult Cycle. THAYER'S GULL (w. N. America in winter) smaller overall and slimmer billed, although judging these features on a lone bird can be problematic. Thayer's slightly darker above (Kodak 5–6) and generally has bolder and more cleanly cut pattern of white mirrors and tongue-tips on outer primaries; eyes are often dusky (rarely staring pale lemon) with a pinkish orbital ring, and adults rarely attain distinct dark distal bill marks in winter.

KUMLIEN'S GULL (ne. N. America in winter) markedly smaller overall with smaller and slimmer bill. Wingtip pattern can be similar to hybrids and best identified by size and structure; eyes are rarely staring pale lemon, and adults rarely attain distinct dark distal bill marks in winter.

HYBRID GLAUCOUS GULL × GLAUCOUS-WINGED GULL (N. Pacific) averages darker upperparts (Kodak 4–5) and has white wingtips with faint gray subterminal bands on outer primaries. Other Glaucous-winged features that may be shown are duskier eyes, a pinkish orbital ring, broader wings, and a more bulbous-tipped bill.

First Cycle. THAYER'S GULL smaller overall with more slender, dark bill. Its wingtip pattern can be similar to hybrids (study needed) and best identified by size and structure.

KUMLIEN'S GULL markedly smaller overall with smaller, slimmer bill. Wingtip pattern can be similar to hybrids (study needed); best identified by size and structure.

SLATY-BACKED GULL (N. Pacific) has blackish bill in first winter; upperwing typically has relatively pale and plain greater coverts, contrastingly pale inner primaries, and more-distinct inner web/outer web contrast on the outer primaries (at least in fresh plumage); but all of these features may be matched on hybrids. Deep pink legs of some Slaty-backeds may be outside range of hybrids. Until individual variation in both Slaty-backeds and hybrids is established, identification of problem birds may not be possible.

HYBRID GLAUCOUS-WINGED GULL × WESTERN GULL (w. N. America) bulkier and broader winged with bulbous-tipped bill that is mostly black in first winter.

HYBRID GLAUCOUS GULL × GLAUCOUS-WINGED GULL not well known, and some may not be safely distinguishable. Possible differences include broader wings and more bulbous-tipped bill, paler wingtips (creamy brown to whitish).

Second and Third Cycles. THAYER'S GULL and KUMLIEN'S GULL are again the main problems, and identification criteria for these age classes (other than size and structure, especially of the bill) need study.

HYBRID GLAUCOUS GULL × GLAUCOUS-WINGED GULL not well known, and some may not be safely distinguishable. Possible differences include broader wings and more bulbous-tipped bill, paler wingtips.

HABITAT AND BEHAVIOR

Much as the parent species and usually found in areas where American Herring Gulls or both parent species are common.

DESCRIPTION AND MOLT

Descriptions focus on differences relative to parent species and are not comprehensive. Thus, bare-part colors (pale lemon eyes, yellow-orange orbital rings, pink legs), and adult tail color (white) are like both parent species and are not noted below.

Adult Cycle. Complete PB molt (mainly late May/June–Dec.) produces adult basic plumage: upperparts pale gray (mainly around Kodak 4). Details of variation in wingtip pattern need study but often consist of bold blackish gray to inconspicuous smoky gray wingtip markings that vary in extent from similar to an American Herring Gull pattern to only faint marks on P7–P10. Partial PA molt (Oct.–Mar.) produces adult alternate plumage: head and neck clean white. Orbital ring, bill, and legs brighter.

First Cycle. Juvenile (Aug.–Jan.): some birds resemble variably washed-out Herring Gulls, typically with medium brown to blackish brown wingtips. Outer primaries typically dark on outer webs and pale on inners, creating variably distinct two-tone pattern and reducing contrast with pale inner primary panel. Tail solidly dark brown to medium brown with diffuse whitish markings. Other birds whitish overall, and might be passed off as Glaucous Gulls, but outer primaries, secondaries, and tail are washed brown in a pattern reflecting Herring Gull. Eyes dark, bill flesh pink with clean-cut black tip (like Glaucous) to blackish with variable dull flesh basally (like Herring). PA1 molt (probably starting between Oct. and Feb.) produces first alternate plumage: new scapulars grayish with diffuse darker markings, possibly not showing distinct blackish bars of Herring Gull.

Second and Third Cycles. Molt timing and age-related plumage variation presumably parallel the parent species (complete PB molts mainly May–Nov., partial PA molts Sept.–Mar.), but details of appearance poorly known.

NOTES

1. Henshaw 1884; 2. Spear 1987; 3. B. Mactavish pers. comm.; 4. Howell pers. obs.; 5. Jehl 1971

H4. GLAUCOUS GULL × GLAUCOUS-WINGED GULL
Larus hyperboreus × *Larus glaucescens*

LENGTH 22–26.3 IN. (56–67 CM)
PHOTOS H4.1–H4.7 (PP. 289–290)

IDENTIFICATION SUMMARY

These two species interbreed in w. Alaska (involving *barrovianus* Glaucous Gulls), with migrants probably occurring south in winter to California. Hybrids apparently show almost all combinations of parental plumage and structure, and adults can be passed off easily as pure Glaucous Gulls unless details of wingtip pattern are studied. Immature plumages not well known.

STATUS AND DISTRIBUTION

Not well known. Presumably fairly common breeder in w. Alaska on Nunivak Is. and along adjacent mainland coasts from Cape Romanzof south to Kuskokwim Bay;[1,2,3] hybridization might also be expected on St. Matthew Is., Bering Sea, where Glaucous-winged is a relatively recent colonist.[4] In winter, ranges in Bering Sea to waters around Pribilof Is.,[5] and some apparently occur south to cen. Calif.[6]

FIELD IDENTIFICATION

SIMILAR SPECIES

Adult Cycle. GLAUCOUS GULL (n. latitudes). Hybrids average slightly darker above (Kodak 4–5) with reduced white on outer primaries, which have variable pale gray subterminal marks or bands (often difficult to see, even in the hand, and can be absent in worn plumage); white trailing edge to remiges contrasts more sharply with gray upperwing. Hybrid eyes often speckled dark to overall dusky, orbital ring often purplish pink or mixed pinkish, bill sometimes bulbous tipped, and dusky mottling and streaking average heavier on head and neck in basic plumage.

KUMLIEN'S GULL (ne. N. America in winter) markedly smaller overall with smaller and slimmer bill. Wingtip pattern can be similar to hybrids (needs study); best identified by size and structure. Kumlien's eyes rarely "staring" pale lemon, and adults rarely attain distinct dark distal bill marks in winter.

HYBRID GLAUCOUS GULL × AMERICAN HERRING GULL averages slightly paler upperparts (Kodak 3–4) and stronger dark marks on outer primaries; eyes pale lemon and orbital ring yellow-orange (can be flesh pink in winter).

First Cycle. KUMLIEN'S GULL markedly smaller overall with smaller, slimmer bill. Wingtip pattern can be similar to hybrids (needs study); best identified by size and structure.

HYBRID GLAUCOUS GULL × AMERICAN HERRING GULL usually has darker wingtips (medium brown to blackish brown); study needed of variation in both hybrids.

Second and Third Cycles. KUMLIEN'S GULL and HYBRID GLAUCOUS GULL × AMERICAN HERRING GULL are again the main problems, and identification criteria need study; note size and structure of former (especially bill), darker wingtips of latter.

HABITAT AND BEHAVIOR

Much as the parent species and usually found in areas where one or both parent species are common, such as rubbish dumps and scavenging around fishing boats at sea.

DESCRIPTION AND MOLT

Descriptions focus on differences relative to parent species and are not comprehensive. Thus, leg color (pink) and adult tail color (white) are like both parent species and are not noted below.

Adult Cycle. Complete PB molt (mainly late May/June–Nov.) produces adult basic plumage: upperparts pale gray (mainly Kodak 4–5); white trailing edge to secondaries and inner primaries varies from sharply demarcated to diffuse. Outer primaries tipped white, white tips vary from fairly clean-cut to diffuse and clouded with pale gray; gray often extends well out along leading edge of outer web, and outer 4–5 primaries often with solid to speckled, pale gray subterminal bands. Eyes pale lemon, typically with variable dark speckling (some looking dark overall); orbital ring purplish pink or mixed pinkish and yellow.[7,8] Partial PA molt (Oct.–Mar.) produces adult alternate plumage: head and neck clean white. Orbital ring, bill, and legs brighter.

First Cycle. (Aug.–May): not well known. Presumably intermediate between parent species; thus, resembles a Glaucous Gull with variably brown-washed primaries; bill may vary from Glaucous-like (pink with a black tip) to Glaucous-winged-like (blackish overall).

Second and Third Cycles. Molt timing and age-related plumage variation presumably parallel the parent species, but details of appearance poorly known. Two presumed hybrids[9] molting into second basic resemble slightly pale Glaucous-winged Gulls with strongly bicolored, Glaucous-like bills.

NOTES

1. McCaffery et al. 1997; 2. Strang 1977; 3. Swarth 1934; 4. Winker et al. 2002; 5. Larry B. Spear photos; 6. Howell pers. obs.; 7. CAS specimens; 8. Strang 1977; 9. CAS specimens

H5. THAYER'S GULL × KUMLIEN'S GULL/ICELAND GULL

Larus thayeri × *Larus [glaucoides] kumlieni/Larus [g.] glaucoides*

LENGTH 19–25.2 IN. (48–64 CM)
PHOTOS H5.1–H5.8 (PP. 291–292)

IDENTIFICATION SUMMARY

The taxonomy of Thayer's Gull and Kumlien's Gull/Iceland Gull remains unresolved (see introduction to the Iceland Gull complex, p. 462) and, similarly, the extent of possible hybridization among these taxa is unclear. Distinguishing between putative Thayer's × Kumlien's Gull hybrids and Thayer's × Iceland Gull hybrids is not possible given present knowledge, so we lump them here as Thayer's × Kumlien's/Iceland hybrids. Presumed hybrids (discussed below) show structural and plumage characters intermediate between the parent species; small numbers can be found in the winter range of both Thayer's and Kumlien's Gulls.

STATUS AND DISTRIBUTION

Not well known. Hybridization between Thayer's Gull and Kumlien's Gull has been reported in low Arctic Canada from e. Baffin Is.[1,2] and from e. Southampton Is.[3] At a colony on Southampton Is., 41 of 43 adults were identified as either pure Thayer's or Kumlien's (95 percent pure); and of 12 mated pairs, 6 were deemed pure Thayer's, 1 pure Kumlien's, and 5 comprised pure Thayer's mated with pure Kumlien's (58 percent pure and 42 percent mixed pairs).[4] However, characters of wingtip pattern and plumage tone used to identify the parent taxa at both Baffin and Southampton is. were not critically defined, so the true extent of interbreeding is difficult to assess.[5] Pale-winged putative Thayer's Gulls from Ellesmere Is. in high Arctic Canada[6,7,8] may reflect hybridization between Thayer's and Iceland Gulls,[9,10] but this is conjectural. In winter, small numbers of possible hybrids have been reported (<5 percent of Thayer's types in se. Alaska[11] and cen. Calif.[12] and <5 percent of Kumlien's types in Nfld.[13]). Such birds can be expected elsewhere; they might even be commoner relative to pure parental types in geographically intermediate regions such as the Great Lakes.

FIELD IDENTIFICATION

SIMILAR SPECIES

Because the characters and variation within Thayer's, Kumlien's, and Iceland Gulls have yet to be determined, our discussion of putative hybrids is necessarily tentative. But we offer it here to stimulate thought about this problem. The only truly similar species to consider are Thayer's and Kumlien's Gulls; see Similar Species sections in those species' accounts for separation from other species and hybrid combinations.

Adult Cycle. THAYER'S GULL (w. N. America in winter) averages larger and bigger billed than hybrids. Pointers for possible Thayer's × Kumlien's hybrids are birds that have slightly paler upperparts and paler wingtips than typical Thayer's, and which may be slightly smaller and shorter billed. Possible Thayer's × Iceland Gull hybrids might not be distinguishable from Kumlien's Gulls, although some may have darker upperparts and different wingtip patterns: for example, white wingtips with subterminal slaty gray bands on the outer primaries, as shown in figure 63a of Godfrey.[14]

KUMLIEN'S GULL (ne. N. America in winter) averages smaller and shorter billed than hybrids. Pointers for possible Thayer's × Kumlien's hybrids are birds that have slightly darker upperparts and darker wingtips than typical Kumlien's, and which may be slightly larger and longer billed.

First Cycle. THAYER'S GULL averages larger and longer billed with darker, dark brown to blackish brown wingtips on typical birds. In fresh plumage, birds structurally similar to Thayer's but with solidly medium brown to pale brown wingtips and a secondary bar poorly defined or lacking may be hybrids. Birds resembling Kumlien's in overall frosty, pale tones and medium to pale brown wingtips, but with relatively coarse patterning on their upperparts, may be Thayer's × Iceland hybrids.

KUMLIEN'S GULL averages smaller and shorter billed with medium brown to pale brown wingtips on typical birds. In fresh plumage, birds structurally similar to Kumlien's but with dark brown wingtips and a well-defined secondary bar may be hybrids.

Second and Third Cycles. THAYER'S GULL and KUM-

LIEN'S GULL. Birds with intermediate structural or plumage characters (especially wingtip tone and pattern) may be hybrids.

HABITAT AND BEHAVIOR

Much as the parent species, with which hybrids are likely to occur.

DESCRIPTION AND MOLT

Molt timings probably correspond to the parent species, for example, complete adult prebasic molts mainly during June/July–Nov./Jan. and partial adult prealternate molts ending in Mar./Apr. Insufficient information is available to provide detailed descriptions; see the Similar Species section (above) and photos for possible field characters.

NOTES

1. Godfrey 1986; 2. Snell 1989; 3. Gaston and Decker 1985; 4. Ibid.; 5. Howell and Elliott 2001; 6. Godfrey 1986; 7. Parmelee and MacDonald 1960; 8. Snell 2002; 9. Howell and Elliott 2001; 10. Howell and Mactavish 2003; 11. S. Heinl pers. comm.; 12. Howell and Elliott 2001 13. Howell and Mactavish 2003; 14. Godfrey 1986

RARER ATLANTIC COAST HYBRIDS

H6. AMERICAN HERRING GULL × GREAT BLACK-BACKED GULL
Larus [argentatus] smithsonianus × *Larus marinus*

PHOTOS H6.1–H6.2 (P. 293)

Interbreeding of these two species presumably occurs in ne. N. America, although hybrids have only been found in winter, on the e. Great Lakes and from Newfoundland south to the Mid-Atlantic Coast (Jehl 1960, Andrle 1972, Foxall 1979, E. S. Brinkley, pers. comm.). Such hybrids could be misidentified as Western Gull, which differs in head and bill structure, or as black-backed gulls.

Adults are intermediate in size and struc-ture between the parent species (larger than Lesser Black-backed Gull and Yellow-legged Gull) with pale slaty gray upperparts (estimated Kodak 7–8), pale flesh to flesh pink legs, and yellow to red orbital rings. Head streaking in winter varies from moderate to light, P10 has a large white mirror or white tip, P9 typically has a small white mirror, and there are white tongue-tips out to P7 or P8. Immatures appear to be undescribed.

H7. AMERICAN HERRING GULL × LESSER BLACK-BACKED GULL
Larus [argentatus] smithsonianus × *Larus fuscus graellsii*

PHOTOS H7.1–H7.4 (P. 294)

Hybridization between these two taxa is presumed to occur in N. America (McWilliams and Brauning 2000) and seems highly likely given the recent rapid increase in numbers of Lesser Black-backed Gulls. Presumed hybrids are seen occasionally from Newfoundland south to the Mid-Atlantic Coast. This hybrid should be ruled out when considering a vagrant Yellow-legged Gull in e. N. America.

Relative to Lesser Black-backed Gull, characters of adult and near-adult presumed hybrids include paler slaty gray upperparts (estimated Kodak 7–8), slightly stockier build, shorter wing projection, stouter bill, and flesh to yellowish flesh legs. Relative to Yellow-legged Gull, adult hybrids may average slightly darker above and typically have extensive dusky head streaking in winter, but identification criteria need elucidation.

H8. AMERICAN HERRING GULL × KELP GULL
Larus [argentatus] smithsonianus × *Larus dominicanus*

Interbreeding of these two species has been reported from Louisiana since the 1990s (Purrington 1998, 1999, Dittman and Cardiff 2005), and hybrids probably range throughout the Gulf of Mexico and perhaps the Caribbean. These hybrids (especially as immatures) could be mistaken for Kelp Gull, Lesser Black-backed Gull, Yellow-legged Gull, and Yellow-footed Gull.

The presumed F1 hybrid adults resemble Lesser Black-backed Gull (*graellsii* subspecies) or Yellow-footed Gull in their slaty gray upperparts (estimated Kodak 7–11). They tend to be similar in size and structure to Kelp Gulls, with swollen-tipped bills, yellow to greenish yellow legs, and orange orbital rings. Their underwings show a black wingtip similar to or more extensive than that of Herring

Gull, and more cleanly demarcated from the smoky gray inner primaries and secondaries than on Lesser Black-backed and Yellow-footed Gulls. Wingtip pattern and upperpart tone (which can look darker in overcast conditions) separate F1 hybrids from Kelp Gull. Presumed F2 hybrid adults have mantle tones variably intermediate between Kelp and Her-ring, and legs ranging from pale yellow to greenish gray. Immatures have not been described satisfactorily, but some presumed second-cycle hybrids closely resemble Lesser Black-backed Gull but are bulkier, with bigger and bulbous-tipped bills and more-extensive black on the tails.

H9. EUROPEAN HERRING GULL × LESSER BLACK-BACKED GULL
Larus argentatus argenteus × *Larus fuscus graellsii*

Interbreeding of these two species occurs in Britain (Harris et al. 1978, M. T. Elliott pers. comm.) but is generally rare, and this hybrid combination seems like an unlikely candidate to occur in N. America. It could be confused with Yellow-legged Gull.

Known or presumed F1 hybrid adults are intermediate in upperpart tone between the parent species (around Kodak 7), have yellowish flesh to pale yellow legs, and orange to orange-yellow orbital rings. Details of wingtip pattern have not been described. Relative to hybrids, Yellow-legged Gull adults have reddish orbital rings, yellow legs, and, in winter, lack heavy dusky streaking on the head and neck.

H10. GLAUCOUS GULL × GREAT BLACK-BACKED GULL
Larus hyperboreus × *Larus marinus*

PHOTOS H10.1–H10.4 (P. 295)
Interbreeding of these two species presumably occurs in ne. N. America, although hybrids have only been found in winter, at least in Newfoundland (B. Mactavish pers. comm.). Hybrids generally look like Great Black-backed Gulls variably diluted by Glaucous Gull characters. Adults are usually slightly paler above than Great Black-backed but have all-white wingtips like Glaucous Gull; immatures have overall paler and frostier upperparts and diluted wingtip pigmentation. First-cycle birds usually have mostly dark bills, but some have the basal two-thirds of the bill dull flesh pink (photo in *Birders Journal* 75:21, 2004).

H11. GLAUCOUS GULL × EUROPEAN HERRING GULL
Larus hyperboreus × *Larus argentatus*

Interbreeding of these two species occurs in Iceland (Ingolfsson 1987) and presumably elsewhere in n. Europe, and hybrids might occur in ne. N. America in winter. No consistent differences are known relative to hybrid Glaucous Gull × American Herring Gull (see that account).

RARER NORTH PACIFIC HYBRIDS

H12. GLAUCOUS GULL × VEGA GULL
Larus hyperboreus pallidissimus × *Larus [argentatus] vegae*

PHOTOS H12.1–H12.5 (P. 296)

Interbreeding of these two species has been reported once in w. Alaska (Kessel 1989) and presumably occurs in e. Siberia and perhaps on islands in the n. Bering Sea; hybrids probably occur rarely in w. Alaska. Details of appearance apparently overall similar to hybrid Glaucous Gull × American Herring Gull; that is, resembling Glaucous Gull overall but with darker, at times blackish, wingtips. Adults and older immatures may average darker gray on upperparts than hybrid Glaucous Gull × American Herring Gull (Kodak 4–6 versus Kodak 4–5), and eyes may be speckled dusky. Field characters need study.

H13. SLATY-BACKED GULL × VEGA GULL
Larus schistisagus × *Larus [argentatus] vegae*

PHOTOS H13.1–H13.3 (P. 297)

Interbreeding of these two species has been reported from e. Siberia (Vaurie 1965:735), and hybrids could occur in w. Alaska, although details of appearance are not well known. Relative to Vega Gull, presumed adult hybrids (BM #1908.1.8.457, BM #1910.5.2.21) have darker upperparts (Kodak 9) and seem more likely to be confused with Slaty-backed Gull. Relative to Slaty-backed Gull, these two birds have slightly paler upperparts, a less stout bill, and a wingtip pattern more like Vega, with more sharply demarcated black wingtips both above and below, narrow white tongue-tips on P5–P7 (but not on P8), and no white mirror on P9. First-cycle suspected hybrids look intermediate between the parent species in structure and in plumage characters such as tail pattern and primary pattern. Field characters need study.

H14. GLAUCOUS-WINGED GULL × SLATY-BACKED GULL
Larus glaucescens × *Larus schistisagus*

PHOTOS H14.1–H14.3 (P. 298)

Interbreeding of these two species has been reported from the Kamchatka Peninsula and Commander Is. (Firsova and Leveda 1982, King and Carey 1999, Grabovsky et al. unpubl. data). Hybrids could occur in w. Alaska but details of appearance not well known. Grabovsky et al. noted that at least 3 percent of putative hybrid adults on the Commander Is. had upperparts intermediate in tone between the parent species or closer to Slaty-backed Gull (estimated Kodak 8–9). Intermediate wingtip darkness might also be expected, as with hybrid Glaucous-winged × Western Gulls, and this character might help distinguish all ages of Glaucous-winged × Slaty-backed hybrids from Vega × Slaty-backed hybrids. Field characters need study.

ACKNOWLEDGMENTS

The vast resource of museum specimens is often overlooked by birders but has been largely responsible for the text and illustrations of the field guides we use and take for granted. For their assistance and permission to examine specimens we thank personnel at the California Academy of Sciences (John P. Dumbacher, Maureen Flannery, Douglas J. Long), the Museum of Vertebrate Zoology, University of California, Berkeley (Carla Cicero), the American Museum of Natural History, New York (George F. Barrowclough, Paul Sweet), the British Museum, Tring (Mark Adams, Robert Prys-Jones), the University of Alaska, Fairbanks (Daniel D. Gibson, Kevin J. Winker), the Museum of Wildlife and Fisheries Biology, University of California, Davis (Andy Engilis, Jr.), the Natural History Museum of Los Angeles County (Kimball L. Garrett), the San Diego Natural History Museum (Philip Unitt), and the National Museum of Natural History (Smithsonian Institution), Washington, D.C. (James Dean, Gary R. Graves).

For their company in the field, thoughtful discussions, and hospitality while visiting far-flung sites and museums we thank Jonathan K. Alderfer, Doug Bell, Anthony Collerton, Lyann Comrack, Elaine Cook, Chris Corben, Judy Davis, Martin T. Elliott, Richard A. Erickson, Annika Forsten, Kimball L. Garrett, Jennifer Green, Robb Hamilton, Ted Hoogendoorn, Dan Lane, Paul Lehman, Tony Leukering, Ian Lewington, Antero Lindholm, Bruce Mactavish, John P. Martin, Mario Mosqueira, Michael O'Brien, Peter Pyle, Will Russell, Debra L. Shearwater, David A. Sibley, Diana Stralberg, Sophie Webb, and Christopher L. Wood. Will Russell, Greer Warren, Parker Backstrom, and Shawneen Finnegan of WINGS helped both of us directly and indirectly in numerous ways. Logistical support was provided to Howell by Point Reyes Bird Observatory (PRBO).

Information on status and distribution was gathered primarily from regional, national, state, provincial, and more local published works on distribution (see Geographic References, pp. 509–512); reports in *Birders Journal* and *North American Birds* (and its predecessors *Field Notes* and *American Birds*); and summaries in the *Birds of North America* series. Dunn's primary responsibility was compiling status and distribution text for North America (north of Mexico), and Howell had primary responsibility for Latin America. We attempted to include information published (which does not include Internet websites) through 2004, but it is inevitable that we overlooked some records; nonetheless, patterns of distribution and seasonal occurrence are at least broadly outlined. We particularly thank Daniel D. Gibson (Alaska), Bruce Mactavish (Newfoundland), and Mark Pearman (Argentina) for answering numerous queries and sharing unpublished information. The following reviewed introductory material and species accounts: Sue Abbott, Jessie Barry, Edward S. Brinkley, Cameron Cox, Martin T. Elliott, Ted Floyd, Steve Ganley, Kimball L. Garrett, Steve Heinl, Alvaro Jaramillo, Paul Lehman, Tony Leukering, Ron LeValley, Bruce Mactavish, Bert McKee, Martin Meyers, Killian Mullarney, José Fernando Pacheco, Peter Pyle, Robert L. Pyle, David E. Quady, Thomas S. Schulenberg, Bret Whitney, Rik Winters, and Christopher L. Wood.

And lastly, but obviously not least, a photographic guide would be nothing without photographs. We are indebted to numerous photographers who provided photos for review and, in some cases, took it upon themselves to target "missing" images: Göran Altstedt/Windrush Photos, George L. Armistead, Theo Bakker, Chris Batty, Robert A. Behrstock/Naturewide Images, Louis R. Bevier, Brian Boldt, Brad Bolduan, Edward S. Brinkley, Peter Burke, Geoff Carey, Igor I. Chupin, Enrique Couve/Fantastico Sur, Willie D'Anna, Mike Danzenbaker, Judy Davis, Paul Doherty, Michael Donohue, Philippe J. Dubois, Cameron Eckert, Carol E. Edwards, Martin T. Elliott,

Shawneen E. Finnegan, Guy Flohart, Annika Forsten, Phyllis and Tony Frank, J. Fuhrman/ VIREO, Steve Ganley, Kimball L. Garrett, John P. Gee, Gonzalo González C., Ed Greaves, Roberto M. Guller, Martin Hale, Bruce Hallett, W. Ed Harper, Steve Heinl, George Higgins, Rich Hoyer, Marshall J. Iliff, Alvaro Jaramillo, Kevin T. Karlson, Yasuhiro Kawasaki, Barbara Knapton, Kenneth Z. Kurland, S. LaFrance/VIREO, Dan Lane, Greg W. Lasley, Peter La Tourrette, Paul Lehman, Harry J. Lehto, Henry Lehto, Tony Leukering, Derek Lovitch, Bruce Mactavish, Manuel Marín, Martin Meyers, Arthur Morris/VIREO, Killian Mullarney, Michael O'Brien, Rudy Offereins, Mark Pearman, Pablo F. Petracci, Robert L. Pitman, Peter W. Post, Eric Preston, Martin Reid, George Reszeter, Michael M. Rogers, Gary H. Rosenberg, Ron Saldino, Larry Sansone, Debra L. Shearwater, Brian E. Small, John Sorensen, Larry B. Spear, Michael D. Stubblefield, David Tipling/Windrush Photos, Antero Topp, Osao and Michiaki Ujihara, Arnoud B. van den Berg, Jorge Veiga, Tom Vezo/VIREO, Yoshiaki Watanabe, Rik Winters, Christopher L. Wood, Alan Wormington, Pierre Yésou, Steve Young, and numerous respondents to requests for photos posted on the ID Frontiers website.

This is PRBO contribution number 1054.

GLOSSARY

A1, A2, etc. (alternate plumage). Immature alternate plumages, that is, first alternate, second alternate, etc.

adult. A bird in adult plumage, in other words, a plumage whose appearance does not change appreciably with age, other than seasonally. The Humphrey-Parkes (1959) system uses the term "definitive" for this plumage stage. Does not necessarily reflect sexual maturity.

albino. Completely lacking in pigmentation; i.e., with completely white plumage and pink eyes, bill, and legs. Patches of white plumage, or even all-white birds with normal bare-part coloration, are better termed leucistic.

alternate plumage. Any plumage in addition to—and which alternates with—basic plumage (see introductory section on molts and plumages); attained by a prealternate molt, which is usually partial (not involving flight feathers).

AMNH. American Museum of Natural History.

aspect. The overall appearance of a bird, which can be a composite of basic and alternate plumages; for example, large white-headed gulls with clean white heads manifest a "breeding aspect," even though they may not be breeding or may have started prebasic molt.

auriculars. Feathers covering the ear region on the side of the head, also known as ear-coverts.

B1, B2, etc. (basic plumage). Immature basic plumages, that is, first basic, second basic, etc.

basal. Toward the base, used in reference to pale areas on the bill, or on the outer primaries. See medial and distal.

basic plumage. The plumage attained by the prebasic molt (which is complete or nearly so) and presumed to be homologous (see introductory section on molts and plumages).

bleaching. Whitening, fading, or becoming colorless as a result of exposure primarily to sunlight.

BM. British Museum.

breeding. Overall aspect of a gull as typically seen in the breeding season: for example, a masked gull with a full hood or a large white-headed gull with a clean white head.

CAS. California Academy of Sciences.

culmen. The dorsal ridge of the maxilla, which curves down distally and may project over the tip of the mandible as a hook.

cycle. A regularly repeated phenomenon, such as a molt cycle; a basic molt cycle extends from the start of one prebasic molt to the start of the next prebasic molt.

distal. Toward the tip. Refers here to dark areas on the bill, or on feathers such as rectrices or primaries where the pale feather tipping is so slight that in the field the dark area looks like a terminal band (although, technically, it is subterminal); see basal, medial, and subterminal.

ear-spot. A contrasting dark spot or mark on the auriculars, such as on a nonbreeding Bonaparte's Gull.

eye-crescents. Contrasting white crescents (at times almost joined posteriorly) above and below the eye, such as on Franklin's Gull.

F1 (formative plumage). Any first-year plumage (attained by a preformative molt) that lacks a counterpart in the adult plumage cycle (see introductory section on molts and plumages). Most conventional "first basic" plumages are formative plumages, for example, of small gulls.

flight feathers. The remiges and rectrices collectively, in other words, the main feathers of the wings and tail; elsewhere (such as in Britain) used only for the remiges.

four-cycle gull. A gull in which most individuals attain adult plumage aspect in their fourth plumage cycle, following the fourth prebasic molt; also known as a four-year gull.

gonydeal expansion. The point at which the two lateral plates of the mandible meet near the tip and fuse into the gonys. The ventral edges of the plates often expand slightly at this point and accentuate the gonydeal expansion (see introductory section on bill structure).

gonydeal spot. The typically reddish spot around the gonydeal expansion on the mandible of large white-headed gulls.

gonys. The ventral ridge of the mandible tip (see introductory section on bill structure).

half-hood. A partial dark hood extending over the crown but not including the forehead or throat, as on nonbreeding Franklin's Gulls.

hindcollar. A dark half-collar on the lower hindneck, as on juvenile kittiwakes.

homologous. Sharing common ancestry.

hood. A contrasting (usually dark) head, as on breeding Laughing Gulls.

hybrid. The product of interbreeding between two full species; see intergrade. Includes subsequent generations of interbreeding among hybrids, such as with Glaucous-winged Gulls and Western Gulls.

immature. A general term for any non-adult plumage, including juvenal.

intergrade. The product of interbreeding between two subspecies; see hybrid.

juvenal. The plumage in which a bird fledges — its first coat of "true" or vaned feathers; used here as an adjective and considered synonymous with first-basic plumage.

juvenile. A bird in juvenal plumage, used here as a noun.

LACM. Natural History Museum of Los Angeles County.

leading wedge. A contrasting white or black wedge along the leading edge of the outer wing formed by the outer primaries, outer primary coverts, and sometimes the alula; for example, the white leading wedge of adult Bonaparte's and Black-headed Gulls.

leucistic. Milky colored or white plumaged due to deficiency of pigmentation; see albino.

M pattern. A contrasting dark pattern on the upperwings formed by dark outer primaries and primary coverts joined to a dark ulnar bar, sometimes connected across the rump.

mandible. The lower half of the bill (also called the lower mandible).

maxilla. The upper half of the bill (also called the upper mandible).

medial. Refers to the central portion of a feather, especially the primaries, for example, black medial stripes on the outer primaries of an adult Andean Gull; see basal, subterminal, and distal.

mirror. A white spot or patch within the dark (often black) subterminal band or tip of the outer primaries (see tongue-tip)

mirror-band. A band or patch in the wingtip formed by adjacent mirrors, usually on the outer 2–3 primaries, such as on adult Gray-hooded Gull.

mirror-tongue. A pattern on the outer primaries whereby the white mirror area (or white primary tip) is continuous along the inner web with a white-tipped tongue; in other words, the medial dark band is incomplete; some adult Thayer's Gulls show this pattern.

molt. A period of normal and regular growth of feathers (molting), by which plumages are attained; feather loss is a passive byproduct of molting.

monotypic. Literally, of one type. A monotypic species is one for which no subspecies are recognized, usually indicating that geographic variation is absent or poorly defined. A monotypic genus is one containing only a single species.

MVZ. Museum of Vertebrate Zoology, University of California, Berkeley.

NAB. North American Birds (journal).

nominate. Refers to a subspecies bearing the same scientific name as the species name: for example, *Larus occidentalis occidentalis* is the nominate subspecies of Western Gull, usually written *Larus o. occidentalis*.

nonbreeding. Overall aspect of a gull as typically seen in the nonbreeding season, for example, a masked gull with a dusky ear-spot, or a large white-headed gull with dusky head and neck streaking.

orbital ring. A ring of naked skin around the eye, often brightly colored on adult gulls in the breeding season.

P (primary). The wing feathers attached to the hand bone, or manus, and whose bases are protected by the primary coverts. Gulls (like most birds) have ten visible primaries, numbered from P1 (innermost) to P10 (outermost). P9–P10 indicates P9 and P10 inclusive; P7/P8 indicates P7 or P7–P8.

PA (prealternate) molt. The molt by which alternate plumage is attained (see introductory section on molts and plumages).

PB (prebasic) molt. The molt by which basic plumage is attained (see introductory section on molts and plumages).

PF (preformative) molt. The molt by which formative plumage is attained (see introductory section on molts and plumages).

postocular crescent. Contrasting white crescent (at times slightly broken) behind the eye, such as on a breeding adult Bonaparte's Gull.

primary projection. The projection of the closed primaries beyond the tertials (see wing projection).

R (rectrices; singular: rectrix). The main tail feathers, numbering 12 in gulls (six pairs each side of the central point; R1 is the central rectrix, R6 the outer rectrix). Their bases are protected by tail coverts.

remiges (singular: remex). The main flight feathers of the wing, collectively referring to the primaries and secondaries.

ribbing. A pattern of white notches on the outer web of outer rectrices of immature gulls.

scapular crescent. A contrasting, usually crescent-shaped white area on the back of adult and near-adult gulls, formed by white tips to the subscapulars (see tertial crescent).

scapulars. A group of feathers that originate from a point at the base of the humerus and fan out to protect the base of the wings at rest; they form a seamless join between the wings and body in flight.

secondaries. The secondary wing feathers attached to the forearm bone (numbering 16–23 in gulls) and whose bases are protected by secondary coverts (often simply called wing coverts).

secondary bar. A contrasting dark bar formed when darker secondary bases contrast with their paler coverts on either the upperwing or underwing.

skirt. Tips of the secondaries visible along the bottom of the closed wing and typical of broad-winged species such as Western Gull, adults of which often show a narrow white skirt.

subscapulars. The longest underlying scapulars (numbering 4 in large white-headed gulls, 3 in most ternlike gulls), often tipped white on adult gulls and thereby forming a scapular crescent.

subspecies. A taxonomic category below the level of species, referring to populations that can be distinguished by differences in plumage, measurements, etc., but which are not considered distinct enough to be treated as species.

subterminal. Immediately behind the tip (terminus) of a feather, such as the subterminal blackish tail band of a first-winter Franklin's Gull; see medial and distal.

superspecies. A taxonomic term for two or more (presumed) closely related taxa that replace each other geographically, with the superspecies (or "mother species") name indicated in brackets, e.g., Vega [Herring] Gull and American Herring [Herring] Gull are members of the so-called Herring Gull superspecies.

taxon (plural: taxa). A general taxonomic category, helpful when referring to populations whose taxonomic status is unresolved—for example, taxa can be subspecies or species.

tertial crescent. A contrasting, generally crescent-shaped white area on the upperparts of adult and near-adult gulls formed by white tips to the tertials (see scapular crescent); on broad-winged species, often contiguous with the white skirt.

tertials. Used here for the inner secondaries, which act as coverts on the closed wing.

three-cycle gull. A species in which most individuals attain adult plumage aspect in their third plumage cycle, following the third prebasic molt; also known as a three-year gull.

tibia. The shorter, upper part of the visible leg.

tongue. On the middle and outer primaries, a paler basal or medial area projecting into the dark distal portion of a feather; see tongue-tip.

tongue-streak. A contrasting pale streak visible on fully spread primaries (formed by a pale tongue on the inner web) but concealed on the closed wing, as on an adult Sabine's Gull.

tongue-tip. A white area between the dark subterminal band or tip and the paler basal portion (or tongue) of the middle and outer primaries, such as on adult Mew Gulls.

two-cycle gull. A species in which most individuals attain adult plumage aspect in their second plumage cycle, following the second prebasic molt; also known as a two-year gull.

ulnar bar. A diagonal bar (dark in gulls) across the secondary upperwing coverts, roughly tracing the path of the underlying ulna bone; sometimes termed a carpal bar.

wear (or plumage wear). The abrasion of feather tips and edgings by contact with water, blowing sand, vegetation, etc.; compounded by weakening due to bleaching.

wing projection. The projection of the wingtip beyond the tail on resting birds (see primary projection).

wingtip. At rest, the exposed tips of the outer primaries. In flight, the outer portion of the wing (largely formed by the tips of the outer primaries).

GEOGRAPHIC TERMS

Atlantic Canada. Newfoundland, the Gulf of St. Lawrence, and the Maritime Provinces.

East (eastern North America). Generally the continent east of the Great Plains (roughly, east of the 100° west meridian).

Great Basin. The interior basin east of the Cascades and Sierra Nevada, west of the Rockies.

Great Lakes region. The Great Lakes and adjacent land areas. The northern Great Lakes region refers to Lake Superior, northern Lake Michigan, and northern Lake Huron; the southern Great Lakes region to southern Lake Michigan, southern Lake Huron, Lake Erie, and Lake Ontario; the eastern Great Lakes to Lake Huron, Lake Erie, and Lake Ontario; and the western Great Lakes to Lake Superior and Lake Michigan.

Great Plains. East from the Rockies roughly to the 100° west meridian, north into the Prairie Provinces, south to northern Texas.

Gulf states. States that border the Gulf of Mexico, from eastern Texas to western Florida.

Holarctic. The temperate northern regions of the Earth, comprising the Palearctic (northern Eurasia) and the Nearctic (North America).

Maritime Provinces. Nova Scotia, Prince Edward Island, and New Brunswick.

Mid-Atlantic coast. From Long Island, New York, south to the Outer Banks, North Carolina.

Midwest. Roughly east of the 100° west meridian, north of the Ohio River, west of the Appalachian Mountains, and south of the northern Great Lakes region.

New England. The six northeastern states of the U.S., from Maine southwest to Connecticut.

Northeast. From the Maritime Provinces south to New York, and east of the St. Lawrence River and Appalachian Mountains.

Northwest. Western British Columbia, Washington, Oregon, and northern Idaho.

Pacific states. Washington, Oregon, California.

Palearctic. The temperate northern regions of Eurasia; see Holarctic.

Prairie Provinces. Alberta, Saskatchewan, and Manitoba.

Southeast. Roughly, south of the Ohio and Potomac rivers and east of the 100° west meridian.

Southwest. The interior region including southeast California, southern Nevada, southern Utah, Arizona, New Mexico, and west Texas.

West (western North America). Generally, the continent west of the 100° west meridian.

U.S. State Abbreviations

Alabama	Ala.
Alaska	Alaska
Arizona	Ariz.
Arkansas	Ark.
California	Calif.
Colorado	Colo.
Connecticut	Conn.
Delaware	Del.
Florida	Fla.
Georgia	Ga.
Hawaii	Hawaiian Is.
Idaho	Idaho
Illinois	Ill.
Indiana	Ind.
Iowa	Iowa
Kansas	Kans.
Kentucky	Ky.
Louisiana	La.
Maine	Me.
Maryland	Md.
Massachusetts	Mass.
Michigan	Mich.
Minnesota	Minn.
Mississippi	Miss.
Missouri	Mo.
Montana	Mont.
Nebraska	Neb.
Nevada	Nev.
New Hampshire	N.H.
New Jersey	N.J.
New Mexico	N.M.
New York	N.Y.
North Carolina	N.C.
North Dakota	N.D.
Ohio	Ohio
Oklahoma	Okla.
Oregon	Ore.
Pennsylvania	Pa.
Rhode Island	R.I.
South Carolina	S.C.
South Dakota	S.D.
Tennessee	Tenn.
Texas	Tex.
Utah	Utah
Vermont	Vt.
Virginia	Va.
Washington	Wash.
West Virginia	W. Va.
Wisconsin	Wisc.
Wyoming	Wyo.

Canada

Alberta	Alta.
British Columbia	B.C.
District of Mackenzie	Dist. of Mack.
Labrador	Lab.
Manitoba	Man.
New Brunswick	N.B.
Newfoundland	Nfld.
Northwest Territories	N.T.
Nova Scotia	N.S.
Ontario	Ont.
Prince Edward Island	P.E.I.
Quebec	Que.
Saskatchewan	Sask.
Yukon	Yukon

BIBLIOGRAPHY

ABBREVIATIONS:

ABA: American Birding Association
AMNH: American Museum of Natural History
AOU: American Ornithologists' Union
BOC: British Ornithologists' Club
BOU: British Ornithologists' Union
ICBP: International Council for Bird Preservation

ABA. 2002. *ABA Checklist: Birds of the Continental United States and Canada.* Colorado Springs: ABA.

Adriaens, P., and B. Mactavish. 2004. "American Herring Gull." *Dutch Birding* 26:151–79.

Allaine, D., and J.-D. Lebreton. 1990. "The Influence of Age and Sex on Wing-tip Pattern in Adult Black-headed Gulls." *Ibis* 132:560–67.

Almeida, A.N.F. 2003. "First Documented Record of Franklin's Gull *(Larus pipixcan)* in Brazil." *Ararajuba* 11:268–69.

Amos, J. R. 1991. *The Birds of Bermuda.* Published by author.

Andrle, R. F. 1972. "Another Probable Hybrid of *Larus marinus* and *L. argentatus.*" *Auk* 89:669–71.

Anon. 2003. "Rare Birds in Canada, 2002." *Birders Journal* 12:211–15.

AOU. 1931. *Check-list of North American Birds,* 4th ed. Lancaster, PA: AOU.

AOU. 1957. *Check-list of North American Birds,* 5th ed. Washington, D.C.: AOU.

AOU. 1973. "Thirty-second Supplement to the AOU Check-list of North American Birds." *Auk* 90:411–19.

AOU. 1998. *Check-list of North American Birds,* 7th ed. Washington, D.C.: AOU.

Babarskas, M., and J. C. Chebez. (1999). "Notas breves sobre aves de la Argentina y paises vecinos." *Nuestras Aves* 39:12–14.

Bailey, A. M., C. D. Brewer, and L. B. Bishop. 1933. *Birds of the Region of Point Barrow,* *Alaska.* Chicago: Program of Activities of the Chicago Academy of Sciences 4:15–40.

Baird, P. H. 1994. "Black-legged Kittiwake *(Rissa tridactyla).*" No. 92 in *The Birds of North America,* A. Poole and F. Gill, eds. Philadelphia: Birds of North America Inc.

Bakker, T., K. van Dijken, and E. B. Ebels. 2001. "Glaucous-winged Gull at Essaouira, Morocco, in January 1995." *Dutch Birding* 23:271–74.

Balten, B., E. B. Ebels, and W. Hoogendoorn. 1993. "Mystery Photographs." *Dutch Birding* 15:267.

Banks, R. C. 1986. "Subspecies of the Glaucous Gull *Larus hyperboreus* (Aves: Charadriiformes)." *Proceedings of the Biological Society of Washington* 99:149–59.

Barth, E. K. 1974. "Moult and Taxonomy of the Herring Gull *Larus argentatus* and the Lesser Black-backed Gull *L. fuscus* in Northwestern Europe." *Ibis* 117:384–87.

Bayer, R. D. 1989. "Records of Bird Skins Collected along the Oregon Coast." *Studies in Oregon Ornithology* No. 7. Newport, Ore.: Gahmken Press.

Belant, J. L., and R. A. Dolbeer. 1996. "Age Classification of Laughing Gulls Based on Summer Plumage." *Journal of Field Ornithology* 67:565–74.

Bell, D. A. 1996. "Genetic Differentiation, Geographic Variation, and Hybridization in Gulls of the *Larus glaucescens-occidentalis* Complex." *Condor* 98:527–46.

Bell, D. A. 1997. "Hybridization and Reproductive Performance in Gulls of the *Larus glaucescens-occidentalis* Complex." *Condor* 99:585–94.

Belton, W. H. 1984. "Birds of Rio Grande do Sul, Brazil, Part 1." *Bulletin of the AMNH* 178(4):369–636.

Bergman, G. 1982. "Why Are the Wings of *Larus f. fuscus* So Dark?" *Ornis Fennica* 59:77–83.

Blake, E. R. 1977. *Manual of Neotropical Birds,* vol. 1. Chicago: University of Chicago Press.

Blokpoel, H., L.-G. Naranjo, and G. D. Tessier.

1984. "Immature Little Gull in South America." *American Birds* 38:372–73.

Blokpoel, H., P. J. Blancher, and P. M. Fetterolf. 1985. "On the Plumages of Nesting Ring-billed Gulls of Different Ages." *Journal of Field Ornithology* 56:113–24.

Boertmann, D. 1994. "Meddelelser om Gromland. An Annotated Checklist to the Birds of Greenland." *Bioscience* 38:1–63.

Boertmann, D. 2001. "The Iceland Gull Complex in Greenland." *British Birds* 94:547–48.

Boss, W. R. 1943. "Hormonal Determination of Adult Characters and Sex Behavior in Herring Gulls (*Larus argentatus*)." *Journal of Experimental Zoology* 94:181–209.

BOU. 1991. "Records Committee: Fifteenth Report (April 1991)." *Ibis* 133:438–41.

Braune, B. M. 1987. "Body Morphometrics and Molt of Bonaparte's Gulls in the Quoddy Region, New Brunswick, Canada." *Condor* 89:150–57.

Braune, B. M. 1989. "Autumn Migration and Comments on the Breeding Range of Bonaparte's Gull, *Larus philadelphia*, in Eastern North America." *Canadian Field Naturalist* 103:524–30.

Brazil, M. A. 1991. *The Birds of Japan*. Washington, D.C.: Smithsonian Institution Press.

Brewster, W. 1883. "On an Apparently New Gull from Eastern North America." *Bulletin of the Nuttall Ornithological Club* 8:214–19.

Brock, K. J. 1997. *Birds of the Indiana Dunes*, rev. ed. Published by author.

Brooke, R. K., and J. Cooper. 1979. "The Distinctiveness of Southern African *Larus dominicanus* (Aves: Laridae)." *Durban Museum Novitates* 12:27–37.

Brooks, W. S. 1915. "Notes on Some Birds from East Siberia and Arctic Alaska." *Bulletin of the Museum of Comparative Zoology* 59:261–413.

Brousseau, P. 1996. "Black-legged Kittiwake." In *The Breeding Birds of Québec: Atlas of the Breeding Birds of Southern Québec*, J. Gauthier and Y. Aubry, eds. Montreal, Quebec: Association québécoise des groupes d'ornithologues, Province of Quebec Society for the Protection of Birds, Canadian Wildlife Service, Environment Canada, Québec Region, Montréal.

Browning, M. R. 2002. "Taxonomic Comments on Selected Species of Birds from the Pacific Northwest." *Oregon Birds* 28:69–82.

Burger, J. 1996. "Laughing Gull (*Larus atricilla*)." No. 225 in *The Birds of North America*, A. Poole and F. Gill, eds. Philadelphia: Birds of North America Inc.

Burger, J., and M. Gochfeld. 1996. "Family Laridae (Gulls)." In del Hoyo, J., A. Elliott, and J. Sargatal, eds. *Handbook of the Birds of the World*, vol. 3. Barcelona: Lynx Edicions.

Burger, J., and M. Gochfeld. 2002. "Bonaparte's Gull (*Larus philadelphia*)." No. 634 in *The Birds of North America*, A. Poole and F. Gill, eds. Philadelphia: Birds of North America Inc.

Byrd, G. V., and J. C. Williams. 1993. "Red-legged Kittiwake (*Rissa brevirsotris*)." No. 92 in *The Birds of North America*, A. Poole and F. Gill, eds. Philadelphia: Birds of North America Inc.

Byrd, G. V., et al. 1997. "Trends in Populations of Red-legged Kittiwake *Rissa brevirostris*, a Bering Sea Endemic." *Bird Conservation International* 7:167–80.

Campbell, R. W., et al. 1990. *The Birds of British Columbia*, vol. 2. Victoria: Royal British Columbia Museum.

Carey, G. J., and P. R. Kennerley. 1996. "'Mew' Gull: The First Record for Hong Kong and the Identification and Systematics of Common Gull Forms in East Asia." *Hong Kong Bird Report* 1995:134–49.

Cawkwell, E. M., and J. E. Hamilton. 1961. "The Birds of the Falkland Islands." *Ibis* 103a:1–27.

Chapman, S. L. 1969. "The Pacific Winter Quarters of the Sabine's Gull." *Ibis* 111:615–17.

Chardine, J. W. 2002. "Geographic Variation in the Wingtip Patterns of Black-legged Kittiwakes." *Condor* 104:687–93.

Chartier, B., and F. Cooke. 1980. "Ross's Gulls (*Rhodostethia rosea*) Nesting at Churchill, Manitoba, Canada." *American Birds* 34:839–41.

Chase, C. A., III. 1984. "Gull Hybridization: California × Herring." *Colorado Field Ornithologists' Journal* 18:62.

Chisholm, G., and L. A. Neel. 2003. *Birds of the Lahontan Valley*. Reno: University of Nevada Press.

Chu, P. C. 1998. "A Phylogeny of the Gulls (Aves: Larinae) Inferred from Osteological and Integumentary Characters." *Cladistics* 14:1–43.

Clements, J. F., and N. Shany. 2001. *A Field Guide to the Birds of Peru*. Temecula, Calif.: Ibis Publishing Company.

Collar, N. J., et al. 1992. *Threatened Birds of the Americas*. Cambridge, U.K.: ICBP.

Contreras, A. L. 2003. "Black-legged Kittiwake." In *Birds of Oregon: A General Reference*, D. B. Marshall, M. G. Hunter, and A. L. Contreras, eds. Corvallis: Oregon State University Press.

Cottaar, F. 2004. "Yellow-legged Gulls and Hybrids Breeding at Ijmuiden" [in Dutch with English summary]. *Dutch Birding* 26:36–42.

Couch, F. G. 1977. "Changes in the Avifauna of the West Foxe Islands, Northwest Territories, 1956–1976." *Canadian Field Naturalist* 91:314–17.

Coulson, J. C. 1959. "The Plumage and Leg Color of the Kittiwake and Comments on the Non-breeding Population." *British Birds* 52:189–96.

Coulson, J. C., et al. 1982. "Variation in the Wing-tip Pattern of the Herring Gull in Britain." *Bird Study* 29:111–20.

Cramp, S., and K.E.L. Simmons, eds. 1983. *Handbook of the Birds of Europe, the Middle East, and North Africa,* vol. 3. New York: Oxford University Press.

Crochet, P.-A., F. Bonhomme, and J.-D. Lebreton. 2000. "Molecular Phylogeny and Plumage Evolution in Gulls (Larini)." *Journal of Evolutionary Biology* 13:47–57.

Crochet, P.-A., J.-D. Lebreton, and F. Bonhomme. 2002. "Systematics of Large White-headed Gulls: Patterns of Mitochondrial DNA Variation in Western European Taxa." *Auk* 119:603–20.

Crochet, P.-A., et al. 2003. "Genetic Differentiation at Nuclear and Mitochondrial Loci among Large White-headed Gulls: Sex-biased Interspecific Gene Flow?" *Evolution* 57:2865–78.

Curtis, W. F. 1994. "Further South Atlantic Records." *Sea Swallow* 43:19–28.

Degtyaryev, A. G., Y. V. Labutin, and Y. Y. Blohin. 1987. "Ross's Gull (*Rhodostethia rosea*): Migration and Breeding Cycle Near the Borders of Its Range[in Russian with English summary]." *Zoologicheskii Zhurnal* 12:1873–85.

De Knijff, P., et al. 2001. "Genetic Affinities within the Herring Gull *Larus argentatus* Assemblage Revealed by AFLP Genotyping." *Journal of Molecular Evolution* 52:85–93.

Delhey, J.K.V., P. F. Petracci, and C. M. Grassini. 2001. "Hallazgo de una nueva colonia de Gaviota de Olrog (*Larus atlanticus*) en la ría de Bahía Blanca, Argentina." *Hornero* 16:39–42.

del Hoyo, J., A. Elliott, and J. Sargatal, eds. 1996. *Handbook of the Birds of the World,* vol. 3. Barcelona: Lynx Edicions.

Dement'ev, G. P., and N. A. Gladkov, eds. 1969. *Birds of the Soviet Union,* vol. 3. Jerusalem: Israel Program for Scientific Translations.

Devillers, P. 1977. "Observations at a Breeding Colony of *Larus (belcheri) atlanticus.*" *Gerfaut* 67:22–43.

Devillers, P., and J. A. Terschuren. 1977. "Some Distributional Records of Migrant North American Charadriiformes in Coastal South America (Continental Argentina, Falkland, Tierra del Fuego, Chile, and Ecuador)." *Gerfaut* 67:107–25.

Dittman, D. L., and S. W. Cardiff. 2005. "Origins and Identification of Kelp × Herring Gull Hybrids." *Birding* 37:266–76.

Divoky, G. J., et al. 1988. "Fall Migration of Ross's Gull (*Rhodostethia rosea*) in Alaskan Chukchi and Beaufort Seas." Anchorage, Alaska: Final Report (unpubl.) to U.S. Minerals Management Service.

Drennan, M. P., D. C. Folger, and C. Treyball. 1987. "Common Black-headed Gulls on Petit Manan Island, Maine." *American Birds* 41:195–96.

Dubois, P. 2001. "Atlantic Islands Yellow-legged Gulls: An Identification Gallery." *Birding World* 14:293–304.

Dubois, P. J., and P. Yesou. 1984. "Identification of Juvenile Yellow-legged Herring Gulls." *British Birds* 77:344–48.

Duffy, D. C., C. Hays, and M. A. Plenge. 1984. "The Conservation of Peruvian Seabirds." In *Status and Conservation of the World's Seabirds,* J. P. Croxall, P.G.H. Evans, and R. W. Schreiber, eds., 245–59. Cambridge, U.K.: ICBP.

Duncan, C. D. 1982. "Western Gull in Alabama and Northwestern Florida." *American Birds* 36:899–902.

Dwight, J. 1917. "The Status of '*Larus thayeri*, Thayer's Gull.'" *Auk* 34:413–14.

Dwight, J. 1925. "The Gulls (Laridae) of the World: Their Plumages, Moults, Variations, Relationships, and Distribution." *Bulletin of the AMNH* 52:63–402.

Erard, C., J. J. Guillou, and N. Mayaud. 1984. "Sur l'identité spécifique de certains laridés nicheurs au Sénégal." *Alauda* 52:184–188.

Erickson, R. A., and R. A. Hamilton. 2001. "Report of the California Bird Records Committee: 1998 Records." *Western Birds* 32:13–49.

Escalante, R. 1966. "Notes on the Uruguayan Population of *Larus belcheri.*" *Condor* 68:507–10.

Espinosa, L., and A. von Meyer. 1999. "Nidificacion de Gaviota Austral (*Larus scoresbii*) en Isla Doña Sebastiana, Provincia de Llanquihue, Chile." *Boletín Chileno de Ornitología* 6:28–29.

Everett, W. T., M. L. Ward, and J. J. Brueggeman. 1989. "Birds Observed in the Central Bering Sea Pack Ice in February and March 1983." *Gerfaut* 79:159–66.

Ewins, P. J., H. Blokpoel, and J. P. Ludwig. 1992. "Recent Extensions of the Breeding

Range of Great Black-backed Gulls (*Larus marinus*) in the Great Lakes of North America." *Ontario Birds* 10:64–71.

Faber, M., et al. 2001. "Mixed Colonies of Large White-headed Gulls in Southern Poland." *British Birds* 94:529–34.

Fairbank, R. J. 2002. "Ring-billed *Larus delawarensis* and Lesser Black-backed Gulls *L. fuscus* in Venezuela." *Cotinga* 17:78.

Farmer, M. 1990. "A Herring Gull Nest in Texas." *The Bulletin of the Texas Ornithological Society* 23:27–28.

ffrench, R., and G. White. 1999. "Verification of Rare Bird Records from Trinidad and Tobago." *Cotinga* 12:80–82.

Finch, D. W. 1978. "Black-headed Gull (*Larus ridibundus*) in Newfoundland." *American Birds* 32:312.

Firsova, L. V., and A. V. Levada. 1982. "Ornithological Finds at the South of Koriak Plateau" [in Russian]. *Ornithologia* 17:112–18.

Fjeldsa, J., and N. Krabbe. 1986. "Some Range Extensions and Other Unusual Records of Andean Birds." *Bulletin of the BOC* 106:115–24.

Fjeldsa, J., and N. Krabbe. 1990. *Birds of the High Andes*. Copenhagen: Zoological Museum, University of Copenhagen.

Floyd, T. 2002. "Great Basin Regional Reports." *North American Birds* 56:200–203.

Foxall, R. A. 1979. "Presumed Hybrids of the Herring Gull and the Great Black-backed Gull—A New Problem in Identification." *American Birds* 33:838.

Garner, M. 1997. "Identification of Yellow-legged Gulls in Britain." *British Birds* 90:25–62.

Garrett, K. L., and K. C. Molina. 1998. "First Record of the Black-tailed Gull for Mexico." *Western Birds* 29:49–54.

Gaston, A. J., and R. Decker. 1985. "Interbreeding of Thayer's Gull, *Larus thayeri*, and Kumlien's Gull, *Larus glaucoides kumlieni*, on Southampton Island, Northwest Territories." *Canadian Field Naturalist* 9:257–59.

Gee, J. P., and C. E. Edwards. 2000. "Interesting Gull Records from Northeast Tamaulipas, Mexico." *Cotinga* 13:65, 68.

Gibson, D. D., and G. V. Byrd. *Birds of the Aleutian Islands*. Unpubl. ms.

Gibson, D. D., and B. Kessel. 1997. "Inventory of the Species and Subspecies of Alaska Birds." *Western Birds* 28:45–95.

Gochfeld, M., and J. Burger. 1996. "Family Sternidae (Terns)." In *Handbook of the Birds of the World*, vol. 3, J. del Hoyo, A. Elliott, and J. Sargatal, eds. Barcelona: Lynx Edicions.

Godfrey, W. E. 1986. *The Birds of Canada*, rev. ed. Ottawa: National Museums of Canada.

Goetz, R. E., W. M. Rudden, and P. B. Snetsinger. 1986. "Slaty-backed Gull Winters on the Mississippi River." *American Birds* 40:207–16.

González-Bernal, M. A., X. Vega, and E. Mellink. 2003. "Nesting of Western Gulls in Bahía de Santa María-La Reforma, Sinaloa, Mexico." *Western Birds* 34:175–77.

Gosselin, M., and R. Pittaway. 2002. "European Herring Gull in Ontario." *Ontario Birds* 20:3–6.

Grabovsky, V. I., A. Degen, and B. Rupprecht. "Hybridization of Slaty-backed Gull (*Larus schistisagus*) and Glaucous-winged Gull (*L. glaucescens*) in the Commander Islands: Background and Effects. Unpubl. ms.

Grant, P. J. 1982. *Gulls: A Guide to Identification*. Vermillion, SD: Buteo Books.

Grant, P. J. 1986. *Gulls: A Guide to Identification*, 2nd ed. San Diego: Academic Press.

Guerra, C. G., et al. 1988. "Reproductive Consequences of El Niño-Southern Oscillation in Gray Gulls (*Larus modestus*)." *Colonial Waterbirds* 11:170–75.

Gustafson, M. E., and B. G. Peterjohn. 1994. "Adult Slaty-backed Gulls: Variability in Mantle Color and Comments on Identification." *Birding* 26:243–49.

Haase, B.J.M. 1993. "Sight Record of Black-legged Kittiwake in Peru." *American Birds* 47:382–83.

Haase, B. 1996. "Kelp Gull *Larus dominicanus*: A New Breeding Species for Ecuador." *Cotinga* 5:73–74.

Hailman, J. P. 1964. "Breeding Synchrony in the Equatorial Swallow-tailed Gull." *American Naturalist* 98:79–83.

Haney, J. C. 1993. "A Closer Look: Ivory Gull." *Birding* 25:331–38.

Hardy, L. 2003. "The Peculiar Puzzle of the Pink Ring-billed Gulls." *Birding* 35:498–504.

Harris, M. 1982. *A Field Guide to the Birds of Galápagos*, rev. ed. London: Collins.

Harris, M. P., C. Morley, and G. H. Green. 1978. "Hybridization of Herring and Lesser Black-backed Gulls in Britain." *Bird Study* 25:161–66.

Hayes, F. E., et al. 2002. "First Records of Kelp Gull *Larus dominicanus* for Trinidad and Barbados." *Cotinga* 18:85–88.

Hein, K., and S. Martens. 2002. "Biometry, Colouring, and Movements of Common Gulls (*Larus canus canus* and *L. c. heinei* = *L. c. major*) Captured and Ringed in Schleswig-Holstein and Hamburg" [in German]. *Corax* 19:49–65.

Heinl, S. C. 1997. "New Information on Gulls in Southeastern Alaska." *Western Birds* 28:19–29.

Hellmayr, C. E. 1932. "The Birds of Chile." *Field Museum of Natural History Publication, Zoological Series* 19:1–472.

Henshaw, B. 1992. "Ontario Round-up." *Birders Journal* 1:167–75.

Henshaw, H. W. 1884. "On a New Gull from Alaska." *Auk* 1:250–52.

Hoffman, W., J. A. Wiens, and J. M. Scott. 1978. "Hybridization Between Gulls (*Larus glaucescens* and *L. occidentalis*) in the Pacific Northwest." *Auk* 95:441–58.

Holt, D. W., et al. 1986. "First Record of Common Black-headed Gulls Breeding in the United States." *American Birds* 40:204–6.

Hoogendoorn, W. 1993. "First Record of Laughing Gull in Chile." *American Birds* 47:156–58.

Howell, S.N.G. 1996. "Review: The Essential Guide to Birding in Chile." *Cotinga* 5:81–82.

Howell, S.N.G. 1998. "Shades of Gray: The Catch 22 of Thayer's Gull?" *Birders Journal* 7:305–9.

Howell, S.N.G. 2001a. "A New Look at Moult in Gulls." *Alula* 7:2–11.

Howell, S.N.G. 2001b. "Feather Bleaching in Gulls." *Birders Journal* 10:198–208.

Howell, S.N.G. 2001c. "Molt of the Ivory Gull." *Water birds* 24:438–42.

Howell, S.N.G. 2002. "Individual Variation in First-Winter California Gulls." *Birding* 34:540–44.

Howell, S.N.G. 2003a. "Shades of Gray: A Point of Reference for Gull Identification." *Birding* 35:32–37.

Howell, S.N.G. 2003b. "All You Ever Wanted to Know about Molt but Were Afraid to Ask. Part 2: Finding Order in the Chaos." *Birding* 35:640–50.

Howell, S.N.G. 2003c. "The Occurrence of Vega [Herring] Gull in Canada." *Birders Journal* 12:246.

Howell, S.N.G., and C. Corben. 2000a. "Molt Cycles and Sequences in the Western Gull." *Western Birds* 31:38–49.

Howell, S.N.G., and C. Corben. 2000b. "A Commentary on Molt and Plumage Terminology: Implications from the Western Gull." *Western Birds* 31:50–56.

Howell, S.N.G., and C. Corben. 2000c. "Identification of Thayer's-like Gulls. The Herring × Glaucous-winged Gull Problem." *Birders Journal* 9:25–33.

Howell, S.N.G., and C. Corben. 2000d. "Retarded Wing Molt in Black-legged Kittiwakes." *Western Birds* 31:123–25.

Howell, S.N.G., and M. T. Elliott. 2001. "Identification and Variation of Winter Adult Thayer's Gulls, with Comments on Taxonomy." *Alula* 7:130–44.

Howell, S.N.G., and S. J. Engel. 1993. "Seabird Observations off Western Mexico." *Western Birds* 24:167–81.

Howell, S.N.G., and B. Mactavish. 2003. "Identification and Variation of Winter Adult Kumlien's Gulls." *Alula* 9:2–15.

Howell, S.N.G., and B. McKee. 1998. "Variation in Second-Year Mew Gulls." *Birders Journal* 7:210–13.

Howell, S.N.G., and C. Wood. 2004. "First-Cycle Primary Moult in Heermann's Gulls." *Birders Journal* 75:40–43.

Howell, S.N.G., J. Correa S., and J. Garcia B. 1993. "First Records of the Kelp Gull in Mexico." *Euphonia* 2:71–80.

Howell, S.N.G., J. R. King, and C. Corben. 1999. "First Prebasic Molt in Herring, Thayer's, and Glaucous-winged Gulls." *Journal of Field Ornithology* 70:543–54.

Howell, S.N.G., et al. 2003. "The First Basic Problem: A Review of Molt and Plumage Homologies." *Condor* 105:635–53.

Howell, S.N.G., et al. 2004. "The First Basic Problem Revisited: Reply to Commentaries on Howell et al. (2003)." *Condor* 106:206–10.

Howell, S.N.G., et al. 1992. "New and Noteworthy Bird Records from Belize." *Bulletin of the BOC* 112:235–44.

Howell, S.N.G., et al. 2001. "Recent New Gull Records from Mexico." *Cotinga* 16:63–65.

Hughes, R. A. 1970. "Notes on the Birds of the Mollendo District, Southwest Peru." *Ibis* 112:229–41.

Humphrey, P. S., and Parkes, K. C. 1959. "An Approach to the Study of Molts and Plumages." *Auk* 76:1–31.

Humphrey, P. S., and Parkes, K. C. 1963. "Comments on the Study of Plumage Succession." *Auk* 80:496–503.

Ingolfsson, A. 1987. "Hybridization of Glaucous and Herring Gulls in Iceland." *Studies in Avian Biology* 10:131–40.

Isleib, M. E., and B. Kessel. 1973. "Birds of the North Gulf Coast–Prince William Sound Region." *Alaska Biological Papers of the University of Alaska* no. 14.

Jehl, J. R., Jr. 1960. "A Probable Hybrid of *Larus argentatus* and *L. marinus*." *Auk* 77:343–45.

Jehl, J. R., Jr. 1971. "A Hybrid Glaucous × Herring Gull from San Diego." *California Birds* 2:27–32.

Jehl, J. R., Jr. 1987. "Geographic Variation and Evolution in the California Gull (*Larus californicus*)." *Auk* 104:421–28.

Jiguet, F. 2002. "Taxonomy of the Kelp Gull *Larus dominicanus* Lichtenstein Inferred from Biometrics and Wing Plumage Pattern, Including Two Previously Undescribed Subspecies." *Bulletin of the BOC* 122:50–71.

Jiguet, F., A. Jaramillo, and I. Sinclair. 2001. "Identification of Kelp Gull." *Birding World* 14:112–25.

Johnson, A. W. 1967. *The Birds of Chile and Adjacent Regions of Argentina, Bolivia, and Peru*, vol. 2. Buenos Aires: Platt.

Johnson, A. W. 1972. "Supplement to *The Birds of Chile and Adjacent Regions of Argentina, Bolivia, and Peru*." Buenos Aires: Platt.

Johnson, D. B., et al. 1995. "First Confirmed Record of the Glaucous-winged Gull." *Meadowlark* 4:47–50.

Johnson, S. R., and D. R. Herter. 1989. *The Birds of the Beaufort Sea*. Anchorage, Alaska: BP Exploration Inc.

Jones, H. L. 2000. "First Record in the Galapagos Islands of Grey-headed Gull *Larus cirrocephalus*." *Cotinga* 14:103.

Jones, H. L. 2002. "Erroneous and Unconfirmed Bird Records from Belize: Setting the Record Straight." *Bulletin of the BOC* 122:201–16.

Jones, H. L. 2003a. "Central America Regional Report." *North American Birds* 57:270–71.

Jones, H. L. 2003b. "Central America Regional Report." *North American Birds* 57:414–16.

Jonsson, L. 1998. "Baltic Lesser Black-backed Gull *Larus fuscus fuscus* — Moult, Ageing, and Identification." *Birding World* 11:295–317.

Jonsson, L., and B. Mactavish. 2001. "American Herring Gulls at Niagara Falls and Newfoundland." *Birders Journal* 10:90–107.

Kehoe, C. 1992. "A Possible Hybrid Ring-billed Gull × Common Gull." *Birding World* 5:312–13.

Kessel, B. 1989. *Birds of the Seward Peninsula, Alaska*. Fairbanks: University of Alaska Press.

Kessel, B., and D. D. Gibson. 1978. "Status and Distribution of Alaska Birds." *Studies in Avian Biology No. 1*.

King, J. R. 2000. "Field Identification of Adult *californicus* and *albertaensis* California Gulls." *Birders Journal* 9:245–60.

King, J. R. 2001. "First Record of California Gull *Larus californicus* from the East Coast of Mexico." *Cotinga* 15:37.

King, J. R., and G. J. Carey. 1999. "Slaty-backed Gull Hybridization and Variation in Upperpart Colour." *Birders Journal* 8:88–93.

Klein, R., and A. Buchheim. 1997. "The Western Black Sea Coast as a Contact Zone of Two Distinct Forms of the *Larus cachinnans* Group" [in German with English summary]. *Vogelwelt* 118:61–70.

Knudsen, B. 1976. "Colony Turnover and Hybridization in Some Canadian Arctic Gulls." *Pacific Seabird Group Bulletin* 3:27.

Koerkamp, G. G. 1987. "Common Gull with Pale Iris." *British Birds* 80:628–29.

Komar, O. 2001. "Contribuciones a la avifauna de El Salvador." *Cotinga* 16:40–45.

Krabbe, N., S. James, and B. Walker. 2001. "An Observation of Herring Gull *Larus argentatus* on the Peruvian Coast." *Cotinga* 15:66–67.

Lambert, K. 1973. "The Migration of Sabine's Gulls, *Xema sabini*, in the Northwest Atlantic." *Canadian Field Naturalist* 87:57–60.

Langman, M. 2000. "Hybrid Mediterranean × Black-headed Gulls." *Birding Scotland* 3:56–65.

Larkin, P. 1999. "Black-headed Gull with Black Bill." *British Birds* 92:612.

Lethaby, N., and J. Bangma. 1998. "Identifying Black-tailed Gull in North America." *Birding* 30:470–83.

Levine, E., ed. 1998. *Bull's Birds of New York State*. Ithaca, N.Y.: Cornell University Press.

Liebers, D., and A. J. Helbig. 2002. "Phylogeography and Colonization History of Lesser Black-backed Gulls (*Larus fuscus*) as revealed by mtDNA sequences." *Journal of Evolutionary Biology* 15:1021–33.

Liebers, D., A. J. Helbig, and P. de Knijff. 2001. "Genetic Differentiation and Phylogeography of Gulls in the *Larus cachinnans-fuscus* Group (Aves: Charadriiformes)." *Molecular Ecology* 10:2447–62.

Liebers, D., P. de Knijff, and A. J. Helbig. 2004. "The Herring Gull Complex Is Not a Ring Species." *Proceedings of the Royal Society of London: Biological Sciences* 271:893–901.

Lock, T. 1981. "A New Breeding Gull for Nova Scotia." *Nova Scotia Birds* 33:48.

Lockwood, M. W. 2001. *Birds of the Texas Hill Country*. Austin: Texas University Press.

Lonergan, P., and K. Mullarney. 2004. "Identification of American Herring Gull in a Western European Context." *Dutch Birding* 26:1–35.

Ludwig, J. P. 1974. "Recent Changes in the Ring-billed Gull Population and Biology in the Laurentian Great Lakes." *Auk* 91:575–94.

Mackiernan, G., et al. 2001. "Observations of Seabirds in Peruvian and Chilean Waters during the 1998 El Niño." *Cotinga* 15:88–94.

Macpherson, A. H. 1961. "Observations on Canadian Arctic *Larus* Gulls and on the Taxonomy of *L. thayeri* Brooks." *Arctic Institute of North America Technical Papers* 7:1–40.

Malling Olsen, K., and H. Larsson. 2003. *Gulls of North America, Europe and Asia*. Princeton, N.J.: Princeton University Press.

Mallory, M. L., et al. 2003. "Local Ecological Knowledge of Ivory Gull Declines in Arctic Canada." *Arctic* 56:293–98.

Marín, M. A., and E. Couve. 2001. "La gaviota de Franklin, *Larus pipixcan* Wagler (Laridae), al sur de latitud 41° S, con nuevos registros de distribución." *Anales del Instituto de la Patagonia* 29:161–63.

Marín, M. A., L. F. Kiff, and G. L. Peña. 1989. "Notes on Chilean Birds, with Descriptions of Two New Subspecies." *Bulletin of the BOC* 109:66–82.

Marshall, D. B., M. G. Hunter, and A. L. Contreras, eds. 2003. *Birds of Oregon, a General Reference*. Corvallis: Oregon State University Press.

Mazar B. J., and M. Pearman. 2001. *Annotated Checklist of the Birds of Argentina*. Barcelona: Lynx Edicions.

McCaffery, B. J., C. M. Harwood, and J. R. Morgart. 1997. "First Breeding Records of Slaty-backed Gull *(Larus schistisagus)* for North America." *Pacific Seabirds* 24:70.

McNair, D. B. 1999. "The Gray-hooded Gull in North America: First Documented Record." *North American Birds* 53:337–39.

McPeek, G. A., and R. J. Adams, eds. 1994. *The Birds of Michigan*. Bloomington: Indiana University Press.

McWilliams, G. M., and D. W. Brauning. 2000. *Birds of Pennsylvania*. Ithaca, N.Y.: Cornell University Press.

Mellink, E. 2001. "History and Status of Colonies of Heermann's Gull in Mexico." *Water birds* 24:188–94.

Merilees, W. J. 1974. "A Glaucous-winged Gull Mated to a Herring Gull on Okanagan Lake, British Columbia." *Canadian Field Naturalist* 88:485–86.

Monaghan, P., and N. Duncan. 1979. "Plumage Variation of Known-age Herring Gulls." *British Birds* 72:100–103.

Montevecchi, W. A., et al. 1987. "The Status of the Common Black-headed Gull in Newfoundland and Labrador." *American Birds* 41:197–203.

Moskoff, W., and L. R. Bevier. 2002. "Mew Gull *(Larus canus)*." No. 687 in *The Birds of North America*, A. Poole and F. Gill, eds. Philadelphia: Birds of North America Inc.

Moynihan, M. 1959. "A Revision of the Family Laridae (Aves)." *Novitates* 1928:1–42.

Murphy, R. C. 1936. *Oceanic Birds of South America*. 2 vols. New York: AMNH.

Muth, D. P. 1988. "Central Southern Region." *American Birds* 42:274–79.

Noble, G. K. 1916. "The Resident Birds of Gua-deloupe." *Bulletin of the Museum of Comparative Zoology* 60:359–96.

O'Donnell, P., and O. González. 2003. "First Documented Record of Laughing Gull in Departmento Madre de Dios, Peru." *Cotinga* 20:104.

Osborne, T. O., and L. Y. Osborne. 1986. "A Ross's Gull Incursion into Interior Alaska." *Murrelet* 67:63–64.

Parker, T. A., III, S. A. Parker, and M. A. Plenge. 1982. *An Annotated Checklist of Peruvian Birds*. Vermillion, S.D.: Buteo Books.

Parkes, K. C. 1952. "Taxonomic Notes on the Laughing Gull." *Proceedings of the Biological Society of Washington* 65:193–96.

Parmelee, D. F., and S. D. MacDonald. 1960. "The Birds of West-Central Ellesmere Island and Adjacent Areas." *National Museum of Canada Bulletin* 169, biol. ser. no. 63.

Parmelee, D. F., W. R. Fraser, and D. R. Neilson. 1977. "Birds of the Palmer Station Area." *Antarctic Journal* 12:14–21.

Patten, M. A., P. Unitt, and G. McCaskie. 2003. *Birds of the Salton Sea: Status, Biogeography, and Ecology*. Berkeley: University of California Press.

Patten, S. M. 1980. "Interbreeding and Evolution in the *Larus glaucescens–Larus argentatus* Complex on the South Coast of Alaska." Unpubl. Ph.D. thesis.

Pearman, M. 1995. *The Essential Guide to Birding in Chile*. Belper, U.K.: Worldwide Publications.

Pearson, D. L., and M. A. Plenge. 1974. "Puna Bird Species on the Coast of Peru." *Auk* 91:626–31.

Peredo, R., and N. Amado. 1995. "Primer registro de *Larus cirrocephalus* para Chile." *Boletín Chileno de Ornitología* 2:36.

Peterjohn, B. G. 2001. *The Birds of Ohio*. Wooster, Ohio: Wooster Book Company.

Peters, H. S., and T. D. Burleigh. 1951. *The Birds of Newfoundland*. Province of Newfoundland: Department of Natural Resources, Province of Newfoundland, St. John's.

Peters, J. L. 1934. *Check-list of Birds of the World*, vol. 2. Cambridge, Mass.: Harvard University Press.

Pineau, O., et al. 2001. "The Kelp Gull at Banc d'Arguin—A New Western Palearctic Bird." *Birding World* 14:110–111.

Pitman, R. L. 1986. "Atlas of Seabird Distribution and Relative Abundance in the Eastern Tropical Pacific." National Marine Fisheries Service Administrative Report LJ-86-02C.

Pitman, R. L., L. B. Spear, and M. P. Force. 1995. "The Marine Birds of Malpelo Island, Colombia." *Colonial Waterbirds* 18:113–19.

Pittaway, R. 1992. "Recognizable Forms: Sub-species of the Iceland Gull." *Ontario Birds* 10:24–26.

Pittaway, R. 1999. "Taxonomic History of Thayer's Gull." *Ontario Birds* 17:2–13.

Poole, A., and F. Gill, eds. 1992–2002. *The Birds of North America*, nos. 1–716. Philadelphia: The Birds of North America Inc.

Poor, H. H. 1946. "Plumage and Soft-part Variations in the Herring Gull." *Auk* 63:135–51.

Portenko, L. 1939. "On Some New Forms of Arctic Gulls." *Ibis* ser. 14, 3:264–69.

Post, P. W. 1971. "Additional Observations of Sabine's Gull from Coastal Peru and Chile." *Ibis* 113:517.

Post, P. W., and R. H. Lewis. 1995a. "The Lesser Black-backed Gull in the Americas, Occurrence and Subspecific Identity. Part 1: Taxonomy, Distribution, and Migration." *Birding* 27:282–90.

Post, P. W., and R. H. Lewis. 1995b. "The Lesser Black-backed Gull in the Americas, Occurrence and Subspecific Identity. Part 2: Field Identification." *Birding* 27:371–81.

Prince, P. A., and J. P. Croxall. 1996. "The Birds of South Georgia." *Bulletin of the BOC* 1996: 81–104.

Pugesek, B. H., K. L. Diem, and C. L. Cordes. 1999. "Seasonal Movements, Migration, and Range Sizes of Subadult and Adult Bamforth Lake California Gulls." *Water birds* 22:29–36.

Pulich, W. M. 1988. *The Birds of North Central Texas*. College Station: Texas A&M University Press.

Pullan, G., and J. P. Martin. 2004. "Presumed Hybrid Gull Resembling Adult Franklin's Gull." *British Birds* 97:264–69.

Purrington, R. D. 1994. "Central Southern Region." *Audubon Field Notes* 48:950–53.

Purrington, R. D. 1998. "Central Southern Region." *Audubon Field Notes* 52:464–67.

Purrington, R. D. 1999. "Central Southern Region." *North American Birds* 53:395–98.

Raffaele, H., et al. 1998. *Birds of the West Indies*. Princeton, N.J.: Princeton University Press.

Reid, K. 1998. "Franklin's Gull *Larus pipixcan* at South Georgia." *Bulletin of the BOC* 118:55–56.

Ridgely, R. S., and P. J. Greenfield. 2001. *The Birds of Ecuador*, vol. 1, *Status, Distribution, and Taxonomy*. Ithaca, N.Y.: Cornell University Press.

Roberson, D. 2002. *Monterey Birds*, 2nd ed. Carmel, Calif.: Monterey Peninsula Audubon Society.

Roberson, D., S. F. Bailey, and R. Caratello. 2001. "First Successful United States Nest-ing of Heermann's Gull: Challenges of an Urban Colonist." *North American Birds* 55:375–78.

Rosche, L. O., and R. L. Hannikman. 1989. "A Wintering Sabine's Gull in Ohio." *Birding* 21:241–46.

Rottenborn, S. C., and J. Morlan. 2000. "Report of the California Bird Records Committee: 1997 Records." *Western Birds* 31:1–37.

Sanger, G. A. 1970. "The Seasonal Distribution of Some Seabirds off Washington and Oregon, with Notes on Their Biology and Behavior." *Condor* 72:339–57.

Schulenberg, T. S., and T. A. Parker III. 1981. "Status and Distribution of Some Northwestern Peruvian Birds." *Condor* 83:209–16.

Scott, J. M. 1971. "Interbreeding of the Glaucous-winged Gull and Western Gull in the Pacific Northwest." *California Birds* 2:129–33.

Shuford, W. D., and T. P. Ryan. 2000. "Nesting Populations of California and Ring-billed Gulls in California: Recent Surveys and Historical Status." *Western Birds* 31:133–64.

Sibley, C. G., and B. L. Monroe, Jr. 1990. *Distribution and Taxonomy of Birds of the World*. New Haven, Conn.: Yale University Press.

Sibley, D. A. 1994. "A Guide to Finding and Identifying Hybrid Birds." *Birding* 26:163–77.

Sick, H. 1979. "Notes on Some Brazilian Birds." *Bulletin of the BOC* 99:115–20.

Siegel-Causey, D., and T. E. Meehan. 1981. "Red-legged Kittiwakes Forage in Mixed-Species Flocks in Southeastern Alaska." *Wilson Bulletin* 93:111–12.

Smith, M. R., P. W. Mattocks, Jr., and K. M. Cassidy. 1997. *Breeding Birds of Washington State*, vol. 4. Seattle: Seattle Audubon Society.

Smith, N. G. 1966. "Evolution of Some Arctic Gulls (*Larus*): An Experimental Study of Isolating Mechanisms." *Ornithological Monographs* no. 4.

Snell, R. R. 1989. "Status of *Larus* Gulls at Home Bay, Baffin Island." *Colonial Water birds* 12:12–23.

Snell, R. R. 1991. "Conflation of the Observed and Hypothesized: Smith's 1961 Research in Home Bay, Baffin Island." *Water birds* 14:196–202.

Snell, R. R. 2002. "Iceland Gull (*Larus kumlieni*) and Thayer's Gull (*Larus thayeri*)." No. 699 in *The Birds of North America*, A. Poole and F. Gill, eds. Philadelphia: Birds of North America Inc.

Snow, B. K., and D. W. Snow. 1969. "Observations on the Lava Gull *Larus fuliginosus.*" *Ibis* 111:30–35.

Snow, D. W., and B. K. Snow. 1967. "The Breeding Cycle of the Swallow-tailed Gull *Creagrus furcatus.*" *Ibis* 109:14–24.

Spear, L. B. 1987. "Hybridization of Glaucous and Herring Gulls at the Mackenzie Delta, Canada." *Auk* 104:123–25.

Spear, L. B., and D. W. Anderson. 1989. "Nest-site Selection by Yellow-footed Gulls." *Condor* 91:91–99.

Spear, L. B., W. J. Sydeman, and P. Pyle. 1995. "Factors Affecting Age and Recruitment Probability in the Western Gull *Larus occidentalis.*" *Ibis* 137:352–59.

Steullet, A. B., and E. A. Deautier. 1939. "Sobre la prescencia de *Larus fuscus* y *Speotyto cunicularia juninensis* en la Argentina." *Notas del Museo de la Plata 4, Zoología* 21:245–249.

Stevenson, H. M., and B. H. Anderson. 1994. *The Birdlife of Florida.* Gainesville: University Press of Florida.

Strang, C. A. 1977. "Variation and Distribution of Glaucous Gulls in Western Alaska." *Condor* 79:170–75.

Strewe, R. 2000. "New Distributional Sightings of 28 Species of Birds from Departamento Nariño, SW Colombia." *Bulletin of the BOC.* 120:189–95.

Swarth, H. S. 1934. "Birds of Nunivak Island, Alaska." *Pacific Coast Avifauna* no. 22.

Taverner, P. A. 1937. *The Birds of Canada.* Ottawa, Ontario: National Museum of Canada.

Threlfall, W., and D. D. Jewer. 1978. "Notes on the Standard Body Measurements of Two Populations of Herring Gull (*Larus argentatus*)." *Auk* 95:749–53.

Tinbergen, N. 1929. "A Breeding Pair of Herring Gull (*Larus a. argentatus* Pont.) × Lesser Black-backed Gull (*Larus fuscus* subspec.)." *Ardea* 18:1.

Tobish, T. G., Jr. 1996. "Alaska Region." *National Audubon Society Field Notes* 50:318–321.

Tozer, R. G., and J. M. Richards. 1974. *Birds of the Oshawa–Lake Scugog Region Ontario.* Oshawa, Ontario: Alger Press Ltd.

Tufts, R. W. 1986. *The Birds of Nova Scotia,* 3rd ed. Halifax, Nova Scotia: Nimbus Publishing Limited and the Nova Scotia Museum.

Vaurie, C. 1965. *The Birds of the Palearctic Fauna. Non-Passeriformes.* London: H. F. and G. Witherby.

Verbeek, N.A.M. 1993. "Glaucous-winged Gull (*Larus glaucescens*)." No. 59 in *The Birds of North America,* A. Poole and F. Gill, eds. Philadelphia: Birds of North America Inc.

Vermeer, K., et al. 1963. "Aberrant Glaucous-winged Gulls." *Condor* 65:332–33.

Vinicombe, K., and D. L. Cottridge. 1996. *Rare Birds in Britain and Ireland: A Photographic Record.* London: HarperCollins.

Voous, K. H. 1959. "Geographical Variation of the Herring Gull, *Larus argentatus,* in Europe and North America." *Ardea* 47:176–87.

Wahl, T. R., B. Tweit, and S. G. Mlodinow, eds. 2005. *Birds of Washington: Status and Distribution.* Corvallis: Oregon State University Press.

Walters, J. 1978. "The Primary Moult in Four Gull Species near Amsterdam." *Ardea* 66:32–47.

Weber, J. W. 1981. "The *Larus* Gulls of the Pacific Northwest's Interior, with Taxonomic Comments on Several Forms (Part II—Conclusion)." *Continental Birdlife* 2:74–91.

Weeks, R., and M. A. Patten. 2000. "First Texas Record of Yellow-footed Gull." *Texas Birds* 2:25–33.

Weir, D. N., A. C. Kitchener, and R. Y. McGowan. 1996. "Biometrics of Kittiwakes *Rissa tridactyla* Wrecked in Shetland." *Seabird* 18:5–9.

Weseloh, D. V. 1981. "A Probable Franklin's × Ring-billed Gull Nesting in Alberta." *Canadian Field Naturalist* 95:474–76.

Weseloh, D. V. 1987. "Little Gull." In *Atlas of the Breeding Birds of Ontario,* M. D. Cadman, P.F.J. Eagles, and F. M. Helleiner, eds., 178–79. Waterloo, Ontario: University of Waterloo Press.

Weseloh, D. V. 1994. "A History of the Little Gull in Ontario, 1930–1991." In *Ornithology in Ontario,* M. K. McNicholl and J. L. Cramer-Byng, eds., 240–259. Witherby, Ontario: Hawk Owl Publishing.

Weseloh, D. V., and P. Mineau. 1986. "Apparent Hybrid Common Black-headed Gull Pair Nesting in Lake Ontario." *American Birds* 40:18–20.

White, M. 1999. "An Unusual Plumage of Bonaparte's Gull." *Birders Journal* 8:38–39.

Wilds, C., and D. Czaplak. 1994. "Yellow-legged Gulls (*Larus cachinnans*) in North America." *Wilson Bulletin* 106:344–56.

Williams, A. J. 1989. "Courtship Feeding and Copulation by Hartlaub's Gulls *Larus hartlaubii* and Probable Hartlaub's × Grey-headed Gull *L. cirrrocephalus* Hybrids." *Cormorant* 17:73–76.

Williams, R. 1995. "Neotropical Notebook." *Cotinga* 4:65–69.

Williamson, F.S.L., and L. J. Peyton. 1963. "Interbreeding of Glaucous-winged and Herring

Gulls in the Cook Inlet region, Alaska." *Condor* 65:24–28.

Wilson, N. H. 1951. "Hybrid Glaucous × Great Black-backed Gull at Limerick." *British Birds* 44:286–87.

Winker, K., et al. 2002. "The Birds of St. Matthew Island, Bering Sea." *Wilson Bulletin* 114:491–509.

Woods, R. W. 1988. *Guide to the Birds of the Falkland Islands*. Oswestry, U.K.: Nelson.

Woods, R. W., and A. Woods. 1997. *Atlas of Breeding Birds of the Falkland Islands*. Oswestry, U.K.: Nelson.

Wormington, A. 2003. "Early Fall Migration of Bonaparte's Gull at Point Pelee." *Ohio Cardinal* 27:38–44.

Wright, E. G., and E. Komarek. 1928. "The Western Gull (*Larus occidentalis wymani*) in the Chicago Area." *Auk* 45:200.

Yésou, P. 1991. "The Sympatric Breeding of *Larus fuscus, L. cachinnans*, and *L. argentatus* in Western France." *Ibis* 133:256–63.

Yésou, P. 2002. "Systematics of *Larus argentatus-cachinnans-fuscus* Complex Revisited." *Dutch Birding* 24:271–98.

Yésou, P. 2003. "Les goélands du complexe *Larus argentatus-cachinnans-fuscus*: où en est la systématique?" *Ornithos* 10:144–81.

Yorio, P., et al. 1997. "Newly Discovered Breeding Sites of Olrog's Gull *Larus atlanticus* in Argentina." *Bird Conservation International* 7:161–65.

Yzurieta, D. 1995. *Manual de reconocimiento y evaluación ecológia de las aves de Córdoba*. Córdoba, Argentina: Gobierno de Cordoba, Ministerio de Agricultura, Ganadería y Recursos Renovables.

Geographic References

Canada and Greenland

Boertmann, D. 1994. "Meddelelser om Gromland. An Annotated Checklist to the Birds of Greenland." *Bioscience* 38:1–63.

Cadman, M. D., P.F.J. Eagles, and F. M. Helleiner, eds. 1987. *Atlas of the Breeding Birds of Ontario*. Waterloo, Ontario: University of Waterloo Press.

Campbell, R. W., et al. 1990. *The Birds of British Columbia*, vol. 2. Victoria: Royal British Columbia Museum.

Carey, B., et al. 2003. *The Birds of Manitoba*. Winnipeg: Manitoba Naturalists Society.

Gauthier, J., and Y. Aubry, eds. 1996. *The Breeding Birds of Québec: Atlas of the Breeding Birds of Southern Québec*. Montreal, Quebec: Association québécoise des groupes d'ornithologues, Province of Quebec Society for the Protection of Birds, Canadian Wildlife Service, Environment Canada, Québec Region, Montréal.

Godfrey, W. E. 1986. *The Birds of Canada*, rev. ed. Ottawa, Ontario: National Museums of Canada.

James, R. D. 1991. *Annotated Checklist of the Birds of Ontario*, 2nd ed. Toronto: The Royal Ontario Museum.

Peters, H. S., and T. D. Burleigh. 1951. *The Birds of Newfoundland*. Province of Newfoundland: Department of Natural Resources, Province of Newfoundland, St. John's.

Salomonsen, F. 1951. *The Birds of Greenland*, vol. 2. Copenhagen: Munksgaard.

Salt, W. R., and J. R. Salt. 1976. *The Birds of Alberta*. Edmonton, Alberta: Hurtig Publishers.

Semenchuk, G. P. 1992. *The Atlas of Breeding Birds of Alberta*. Edmonton, Alberta: Federation of Alberta Naturalists.

Smith, A. R. 1996. *Atlas of Saskatchewan Birds*. Regina, Saskatchewan: Nature Saskatchewan and Environment Canada.

Squires, W. A. 1976. *The Birds of New Brunswick*, 2nd ed. Saint John, New Brunswick: The New Brunswick Museum, Monographic Series no. 7.

Tozer, R. G., and J. M. Richards. 1974. *Birds of the Oshawa–Lake Scugog Region, Ontario*. Oshawa, Ontario: Alger Press Ltd.

Tufts, R. W. 1986. *The Birds of Nova Scotia*, 3rd ed. Halifax, Nova Scotia: Nimbus Publishing and Nova Scotia Museum.

United States

Alcorn, J. R. 1988. *The Birds of Nevada*. Fallon, Nev.: Fairview West Publishing.

Andrews, R., and R. Righter. 1992. *Colorado Birds*. Denver, Colo.: Denver Museum of Natural History.

Baumgartner, F. M., and A. M. Baumgartner. 1992. *Oklahoma Bird Life*. Norman: University of Oklahoma Press.

Beardslee, C. S., and H. D. Mitchell. 1965. *Birds of the Niagara Frontier Region*, vol. 22. Buffalo, N.Y.: Buffalo Society of Natural Sciences.

Beaton, G., P. W. Sykes, Jr., and J. W. Parrish, Jr. 2003. *Annotated Checklist of Georgia Birds*. Atlanta, Ga.: Georgia Ornithological Society, Occasional Publication no. 14.

Behle, W. H., E. D. Sorensen, and C. M. White. 1985. *Utah Birds: A Revised Checklist*. Salt Lake City, Utah: Utah Museum of Natural History, Occasional Publication no. 4.

Bohlen, H. D. 1989. *The Birds of Illinois*. Bloomington: Indiana University Press.

Brock, K. J. 1997. *Birds of the Indiana Dunes,* rev. ed. Published by author.

Burleigh, T. D. *Birds of Idaho.* 1972. Caldwell, Idaho: Caxton Printers, Ltd.

Duncan, R. A., and L. R. Duncan. 2000. *The Birds of Excambia, Santa Rosa, and Okaloosa Counties, Florida,* 2nd ed. Published by authors.

Foss, C. R., ed. 1994. *Atlas of Breeding Birds in New Hampshire.* Concord: Audubon Society of New Hampshire.

Fussell, J. O., III. 1994. *A Birder's Guide to Coastal North Carolina.* Chapel Hill: University of North Carolina Press.

Gabrielson, I. N., and F. C. Lincoln. 1959. *Birds of Alaska.* Washington, D.C.: Stackpole Company, Harrisburg, PA, & Wildlife Management Institute.

Gaines, D. 1992. *Birds of Yosemite and the East Slope,* 2nd ed. Lee Vining, Calif.: Artemisa Press.

Garrett, K., and J. Dunn. 1981. *Birds of Southern California, Status and Distribution.* Los Angeles: Los Angeles Audubon Society.

Gibson, D. D., and G. V. Byrd. *Birds of the Aleutian Islands.* Unpublished manuscript.

Gibson, D. D., and B. Kessel. 1997. "Inventory of the Species and Subspecies of Alaska Birds." *Western Birds* 28:45–95.

Grinnell, J., and A. H. Miller. 1944. *The Distribution of the Birds of California.* Berkeley, Calif.: Cooper Ornithological Club, Pacific Coast Avifauna no. 27.

Hall, G. A. 1983. *West Virginia Birds.* Pittsburgh, Pa.: Carnegie Museum of Natural History, Special Publication no. 7.

Hamilton, R. A., and D. R. Willick. 1996. *The Birds of Orange County, California: Status and Distribution.* Irvine, Calif.: Sea and Sage Audubon Society.

Harris, S. W. 1991. *Northwestern California Birds.* Arcata, Calif.: Humboldt University Press.

Heinl, S. C. 1997. "New Information on Gulls in Southeastern Alaska." *Western Birds* 28:19–29.

Hess, G. K., et al. 2000. *Birds of Delaware.* Pittsburgh, Pa.: University of Pittsburgh Press.

Iliff, M. J., R. F. Ringler, and J. L. Stasz. 1996. *Field List of the Birds of Maryland,* 3rd ed. Baltimore: Maryland Ornithological Society, Maryland Avifauna no. 2.

Imhoff, T. A. 1976. *Alabama Birds,* 2nd ed. Tuscaloosa: University of Alabama Press.

Isleib, M. E., and B. Kessel. 1973. *Birds of the North Gulf Coast—Prince William Sound Region, Alaska.* Fairbanks: University of Alaska Press.

James, D. A., and J. C. Neal. 1986. *Arkansas Birds, Their Distribution and Abundance.* Fayetteville: University of Arkansas Press.

Janssen, R. B. 1987. *Birds in Minnesota.* Minneapolis: University of Minnesota Press.

Jewett, S. G., et al. 1953. *Birds of Washington State.* Seattle: University of Washington Press.

Johnson, S. R., and D. R. Herter. 1989. *The Birds of the Beaufort Sea.* Anchorage, Alaska: BP Exploration Inc.

Kain, T. 1987. *Virginia's Birdlife, an Annotated Checklist,* 2nd ed. Lynchburg: Virginia Society of Ornithology, Virginia Avifauna no. 3.

Kent, T. H., and J. J. Dinsmore. 1996. *Birds in Iowa.* Published by authors.

Kessel, B. 1989. *Birds of the Seward Peninsula, Alaska.* Fairbanks: University of Alaska Press.

Kessel, B., and D. D. Gibson. 1978. "Status and Distribution of Alaska Birds." *Studies in Avian Biology No. 1.*

Laughlin, S. B., and D. P. Kibbe, eds. 1985. *The Atlas of Breeding Birds of Vermont.* Lebanon, NH: University Press of New England.

Lehman, P. E. 1994. *The Birds of Santa Barbara County, California.* Santa Barbara: Vertebrate Museum, University of California.

Levine, E., ed. 1998. *Bull's Birds of New York State.* Ithaca, N.Y.: Cornell University Press.

Lockwood, M. W. 2001. *Birds of the Texas Hill Country.* Austin: University of Texas Press.

Lockwood, M. W., and B. Freeman. 2004. *The TOS Handbook of Texas Birds.* Texas A&M Press.

Lowery, G. H., Jr. 1974. *Louisiana Birds,* 3rd ed. Baton Rouge: Louisiana State University Press.

Marshall, D. B., M. G. Hunter, and A. L. Contreras, eds. 2003. *Birds of Oregon, a General Reference.* Corvallis: Oregon State University Press.

McNair, D. B. and W. Post. 1993. *Supplement to Status and Distribution of South Carolina Birds.* Charleston, S.C.: Charleston Museum, Ornithological Contribution no. 8.

McPeek, G. A., and R. J. Adams, eds. 1994. *The Birds of Michigan.* Bloomington: Indiana University Press.

McWilliams, G. M., and D. W. Brauning. 2000. *Birds of Pennsylvania.* Ithaca, N.Y.: Cornell University Press.

Mitchell, H. D., and R. F. Andrle. 1970. "Birds of the Niagara Frontier Region Supplement." *Bulletin of the Buffalo Society of Natural Sciences,* vol. 22, Supplement 1970.

Monson, G., and A. R. Phillips. 1981. *Annotated Checklist of the Birds of Arizona,* 2nd ed. Tucson: University of Arizona Press.

Mumford, R. E., and C. E. Keller. 1984. *The*

Birds of Indiana. Bloomington: Indiana University Press.

Murie, O. J. 1959. *Fauna of the Aleutian Islands and Alaska Peninsula.* Washington, D.C.: Department of the Interior, U.S. Fish and Wildlife Service.

Oberholser, H. C. 1974. *The Bird Life of Texas.* Austin: University of Texas Press.

Opperman, H. 2003. *A Birder's Guide to Washington.* Colorado Springs, Colo.: ABA.

Palmer, R. S. 1940. "Maine Birds." *Bulletin of the Museum of Comparative Zoology,* vol. 102.

Palmer-Ball, B., Jr. 2003. *Annotated Checklist of the Birds of Kentucky.* Lexington: Kentucky Ornithological Society.

Patten, M. A., P. Unitt, and G. McCaskie. 2003. *Birds of the Salton Sea: Status, Biogeography, and Ecology.* Berkeley: University of California Press.

Peterson, J., and B. R. Zimmer. 1998. *Birds of the Trans Pecos.* Austin: University of Texas Press.

Peterson, R. A. 1995. *The South Dakota Breeding Bird Atlas.* Aberdeen: South Dakota Ornithologists' Union.

Peterjohn, B. G. 2001. *The Birds of Ohio.* Wooster, Ohio: Wooster Book Co.

Phillips, A., J. Marshall, and G. Monson. 1964. *The Birds of Arizona.* Tucson: University of Arizona Press.

Post , W., and S. A. Gauthreaux, Jr. 1989. *Status and Distribution of South Carolina Birds.* Charleston, S.C.: Charleston Museum, no. 18.

Potter, E. F., J. E. Parnell, and R. P. Teulings. 1980. *Birds of the Carolinas.* Chapel Hill: University of North Carolina Press.

Pulich, W. M. 1988. *The Birds of North Central Texas.* College Station: Texas A&M University Press.

Robbins, M. B., and D. A. Easterla. 1992. *Birds of Missouri.* Columbia: University of Missouri Press.

Robbins, S. D., Jr. 1991. *Wisconsin Birdlife.* Madison: University of Wisconsin Press.

Roberson, D. 2002. *Monterey Birds,* 2nd ed. Carmel, Calif.: Monterey Peninsula Audubon Society.

Robertson, W. B., Jr., and G. E. Woofenden. 1992. *Florida Bird Species, An Annotated List.* Maitland: Florida Ornithological Society, Special Publication no. 6.

Robinson, J. C. 1990. *An Annotated Checklist of the Birds of Tennessee.* Knoxville: University of Tennessee Press.

Sharpe, R. S., W. R. Silcock, and J. G. Jorgensen. 2001. *Birds of Nebraska.* Lincoln: University of Nebraska Press.

Skaar, P. D. 1996. *Montana Bird Distribution,* 5th ed. Helena: Montana Natural Heritage Program, Special Publication no. 3.

Smith, M. R., P. W. Mattocks, Jr., and K. M. Cassidy. 1997. *Breeding Birds of Washington State,* vol. 4. Seattle, Wash.: Seattle Audubon Society.

Stephens, D. A., and S. H. Sturts. 1991. *Idaho Bird Distribution.* Pocatello: Idaho Museum of Natural History, Special Publications no. 11.

Stevenson, H. M., and B. H. Anderson. 1994. *The Birdlife of Florida.* Gainesville: University Press of Florida.

Stewart, R. E. 1975. *Breeding Birds of North Dakota.* Fargo, N.D.: Tri-College Center for Environmental Studies.

Stewart, R. E., and C. S. Robbins. 1958. *Birds of Maryland and The District of Columbia.* Washington, D.C.: U.S. Department of the Interior, Fish and Wildlife Service.

Sutton, G. M. 1967. *Oklahoma Birds.* Norman: University of Oklahoma Press.

Tallman, D. A., D. L. Swanson, and J. S. Palmer. 2002. *Birds of South Dakota.* Aberdeen: South Dakota Ornithologists' Union.

Thompson, M. C., and C. Ely. 1989. *Birds in Kansas,* vol. 1. Lawrence: University of Kansas Museum of Natural History, Public Education Series no. 11.

Turcotte, W. H., and D. L. Watts. 1999. *Birds of Mississippi.* Jackson: University Press of Mississippi.

Unitt, P. 1984. *The Birds of San Diego County.* San Diego, Calif.: San Diego Society of Natural History, Memoir no. 13.

Veit, R. R., and W. R. Peterson. 1993. *Birds of Massachusetts.* Lincoln, Mass.: Massachusetts Audubon Society.

Wahl, T. R., B. Tweit, and S. G. Mlodinow, eds. 2005. *Birds of Washington: Status and Distribution.* Corvallis: Oregon State University Press.

Walsh, J., et al. 1999. *Birds of New Jersey.* Bernardsville: New Jersey Audubon Society.

Zeranski, J. D., and T. R. Baptist. 1990. *Connecticut Birds.* Lebanon, N.H.: University Press of New England.

WEST INDIES, MEXICO, AND CENTRAL AMERICA

Amos, J. R. 1991. *The Bird of Bermuda.* Published by author.

Bradley, P. E. 2000. *The Birds of the Cayman Islands.* BOU Checklist no. 19.

Brudenell-Bruce, P.G.C. 1975. *The Birds of the Bahamas.* New York: Taplinger Publishing Company.

Buden, D. W. 1987. *The Birds of the Southern Bahamas.* BOU Checklist no. 8.

Chardine, J. W., et al. 2000. "Status and Conservation Priorities for Laughing Gulls, Gull-billed Terns, Royal Terns, and Bridled Terns in the West Indies." In *Status and Conservation of West Indian Seabirds,* E. A. Schreiber and D. S. Lee, eds. Ruston, La.: Society of Caribbean Ornithology, Special Publication no. 1, 65–79.

Erickson, R. A., and S.N.G. Howell, eds. 2001. *Birds of the Baja California Peninsula: Status, Distribution, and Biogeography.* Colorado Springs, Colo.: ABA, Monographs in Field Ornithology 3.

Evans, P. 1990. *Birds of the Eastern Caribbean.* London and Basingstoke: MacMillan Press Ltd.

Garrido, O. H., and A. Kirkconnell. 2000. *A Field Guide to the Birds of Cuba.* Ithaca, N.Y.: Cornell University Press.

Howell, S.N.G., and S. Webb. 1995. *A Guide to the Birds of Mexico and Northern Central America.* New York: Oxford University Press.

Howell, S.N.G., et al. 1993. "North American Migrant Birds on Clipperton Atoll." *Western Birds* 24:73–80.

Jones, H. L. 2003. *Birds of Belize.* Austin: Texas University Press.

Keith, A. R. 1997. *The Birds of St. Lucia.* BOU Checklist no. 15.

Keith, A. R., et al. 2003. *The Birds of Hispaniola.* BOU Checklist no. 21.

Pitman, R. L. 1986. *Atlas of Seabird Distribution and Relative Abundance in the Eastern Tropical Pacific.* National Marine Fisheries Service Administration Report LJ-86-02C.

Raffaele, H. A. 1989. *A Guide to the Birds of Puerto Rico and the Virgin Islands,* rev. ed. Princeton, N.J.: Princeton University Press.

Raffaele, H., et al. 1998. *Birds of the West Indies.* Princeton, N.J.: Princeton University Press.

Ridgely, R. S., and J. A. Gwynne, Jr. 1989. *A Guide to the Birds of Panama,* 2nd ed. Princeton, N.J.: Princeton University Press.

Stiles, F. G., and A. F. Skutch. 1989. *A Guide to the Birds of Costa Rica.* Ithaca, N.Y.: Cornell University Press.

van Halewyn, R., and R. L. Norton. 1984. "The Status and Conservation of Seabirds in the Caribbean." In *Status and Conservation of the World's Seabirds,* J. P. Croxall, P.G.H. Evans, and R. W. Schreiber, eds. Cambridge, U.K.: ICBP, Technical Publication no. 2, 169–222.

White, A. W. 1998. *A Birder's Guide to the Bahama Islands (including Turks and Caicos).* Colorado Springs, Colo.: ABA.

SOUTH AMERICA AND ANTARCTIC REGION

Antas, P.T.Z. 1991. "Status and Conservation of Seabirds Breeding in Brazilian Waters." In *Seabird Status and Conservation: A Supplement,* J. P. Croxall, ed. Cambridge, U.K.: ICBP Technical Publication no. 11, 140–58.

Belton, W. H. 1984. "Birds of Rio Grande do Sul, Brazil, Part 1." *Bulletin of the AMNH* 178(4):369–636.

Duffy, D. C., C. Hays, and M. A. Plenge. 1984. "The Conservation of Peruvian Seabirds." In *Status and Conservation of the World's Seabirds,* J. P. Croxall, P.G.H. Evans, and R. W. Schreiber, eds. Cambridge, U.K.: ICBP Technical Publication no. 2, 245–59.

Escalante, R. 1991. "Status and Conservation of Seabirds Breeding in Uruguay." In *Seabird Status and Conservation: A Supplement,* J. P. Croxall, ed. Cambridge, U.K.: ICBP Technical Publication no. 11, 159–64.

Fjeldsa, J., and N. Krabbe. 1990. *Birds of the High Andes.* Copenhagen: Zoological Museum, University of Copenhagen.

Harris, M. 1982. *A Field Guide to the Birds of Galapagos,* rev. ed. London: Collins.

Hayes, F. E. 1995. *Status, Distribution, and Biogeography of the Birds of Paraguay.* Colorado Springs, Colo.: ABA, Monographs in Field Ornithology 1.

Hilty, S. L. 2003. *Birds of Venezuela,* 2nd ed. Princeton, N.J.: Princeton University Press.

Hilty, S. L., and W. L. Brown. 1986. *A Guide to the Birds of Columbia.* Princeton, N.J.: Princeton University Press.

Humphrey, P. S., et al. 1970. *Birds of Isla Grande (Tierra del Fuego).* Washington, D.C.: Smithsonian Institution Press.

Johnson, A. W. 1967. *The Birds of Chile and Adjacent Regions of Argentina, Bolivia, and Peru,* II. Buenos Aires: Platt.

Johnson, A. W. 1972. *Supplement to The Birds of Chile and Adjacent Regions of Argentina, Bolivia, and Peru.* Buenos Aires: Platt.

Murphy, R. C. 1936. *Oceanic Birds of South America.* 2 vols. New York: AMNH.

Pitman, R. L. 1986. "Atlas of Seabird Distribution and Relative Abundance in the Eastern Tropical Pacific." National Marine Fisheries Service Administration Report LJ-86-02C.

Prince, P. A., and J. P. Croxall. 1996. "The Birds of South Georgia." *Bulletin of the BOC* 1996:81–104.

Ridgely, R. S., and P. J. Greenfield. 2001. *The Birds of Ecuador: Status, Distribution, and Taxonomy,* vol. 1, Ithaca, N.Y.: Cornell University Press.

Sick, H. 1993. *Birds in Brazil: A Natural History.* Princeton, N.J.: Princeton University Press.

Venegas, C. 1994. *Aves de Magellanes.* Punta Arenas, Chile: University de Magellanes.

Woods, R. W. 1988. *Guide to the Birds of the Falkland Islands.* Oswestry, U.K.: Nelson.

Woods, R. W., and A. Woods. 1997. *Atlas of Breeding Birds of the Falkland Islands.* Oswestry, U.K.: Nelson.

LIST OF PHOTOGRAPHERS

Göran Altstedt/Windrush Photos www. davidtipling.com
George L. Armistead/VIREO www.ansp.org/vireo
Theo Bakker
Chris Batty
R. A. Behrstock/Naturewide Images http://naturewideimages.com
Louis R. Bevier
Brad Bolduan
Geoff Carey
Igor Chupin
Enrique Couve www.fantasticosur.com
Willie D'Anna
Mike Danzenbaker www.avesphoto.com
Judy Davis
Philippe J. Dubois
Cameron D. Eckert
Martin T. Elliott
Annika Forsten
J. Fuhrman/VIREO www.ansp.org/vireo
Kimball L. Garrett
Gonzalo González Cifuentes
Roberto Guller
Martin Hale tmmh@netvigator.com
Bruce Hallett
W. Edward Harper
Steve Heinl
George Higgins
Marshall J. Iliff
Alvaro Jaramillo www.fieldguides.com
Kevin T. Karlson www.kevinkarlsonphotography.com
Yasuhiro Kawasaki

KOCI Inc. (Brian Boldt)
Kenneth Z. Kurland
S. LaFrance/VIREO www.ansp.org/vireo
Dan Lane
Greg W. Lasley www.greglasley.net
Peter LaTourette www.birdphotography.com
Harry J. Lehto http://users.utu.fi/hlehto/photo
Henry Lehto
Tony Leukering
Bruce Mactavish
A. Morris/VIREO www.ansp.org/vireo
Killian Mullarney
Michael O'Brien
Rudy Offereins www.xs4all.nl/~calidris/gullindex.htm
Pablo F. Petracci
R. L. Pitman
Eric Preston www.ericpreston.com
Martin Reid www.martinreid.com
Gary H. Rosenberg
Larry Sansone
Debra L. Shearwater www.shearwaterjourneys.com
Brian E. Small briansmallphoto.com
John Sorensen www.johnsorensen.com
Larry B. Spear
Michael D. Stubblefield
Antero Topp www.alula.fi
Arnoud B. van den Berg www.dutchbirding.nl
Jorge Veiga
Yoshiaki Watanbe
Rik Winters
Chris Wood
Steve Young www.birdsonfilm.com

INDEX

Larus (cont.)

  hyperboreus × *Larus argentatus argentatus*, *491*

  hyperboreus × *Larus argentatus smithsonianus*, **285–88**, *484–85*

  hyperboreus × *Larus argentatus vegae*, **296**, *492*

  hyperboreus × *Larus glaucescens*, **289–90**, *486–87*

  hyperboreus × *Larus marinus*, **295**, *491*

  livens, **148**, **226–34**, **393**, *448–52*

  maculipennis, **48**, **59–63**, **301**, *312–15*

  marinus, **15**, **17**, **21**, **147**, **205–12**, **393**, *434–37*

  marinus × *Larus argentatus smithsonianus*, **293**, *490*

  marinus × *Larus hyperboreus*, **295**, *491*

  michahellis, **147**, **180–86**, **393**, *417–21*

  minutus, **67**, **68–70**, **319**, *320–22*

  modestus, **95**, **96**, **100**, **107–9**, **356**, *360–62*

  occidentalis, **16**, **29**, **34–43**, **148**, **221–25**, **242**, **264**, **276**, **393**, *442–47*

  occidentalis × *Larus glaucescens*, **14**, **15**, **29**, **274–79**, *479–81*

  philadelphia, **20**, **48**, **49–52**, **53**, **69**, **70**, **301**, *302–5*

  pipixcan, **48**, **90**, **95–97**, **301**, **345**, *350–53*

  ridibundus, **48**, **53–55**, **72**, **301**, *306–8*

  schistisagus, **19**, **28**, **148**, **175**, **213–20**, **296**, **393**, *438–41*

  schistisagus × *Larus argentatus vegae*, **297**, *492*

  schistisagus × *Larus glaucescens*, **298**, *492*

  scoresbii, **100**, **110–13**, **356**, *363–65*

  serranus, **48**, **64–66**, **301**, *316–18*

  thayeri, **15**, **16**, **19**, **20**, **27**, **149**, **167**, **252**, **263–73**, **393**, *471–77*

  thayeri × *Larus glaucoides kumlieni*/*Larus glaucoides glaucoides*, **252**, **291–92**, *488–89*

Pagophila eburnea, **88–89**, **342**, *343–44*

Rhodostethia rosea, **67**, **71–73**, **319**, *323–25*

Rissa

  brevirostris, **74**, **79–81**, **326**, *331–33*

  tridactyla, **20**, **74**, **75–78**, **79**, **80**, **81**, **326**, *327–30*

Xema sabini, **82**, **83–85**, **334**, *335–38*